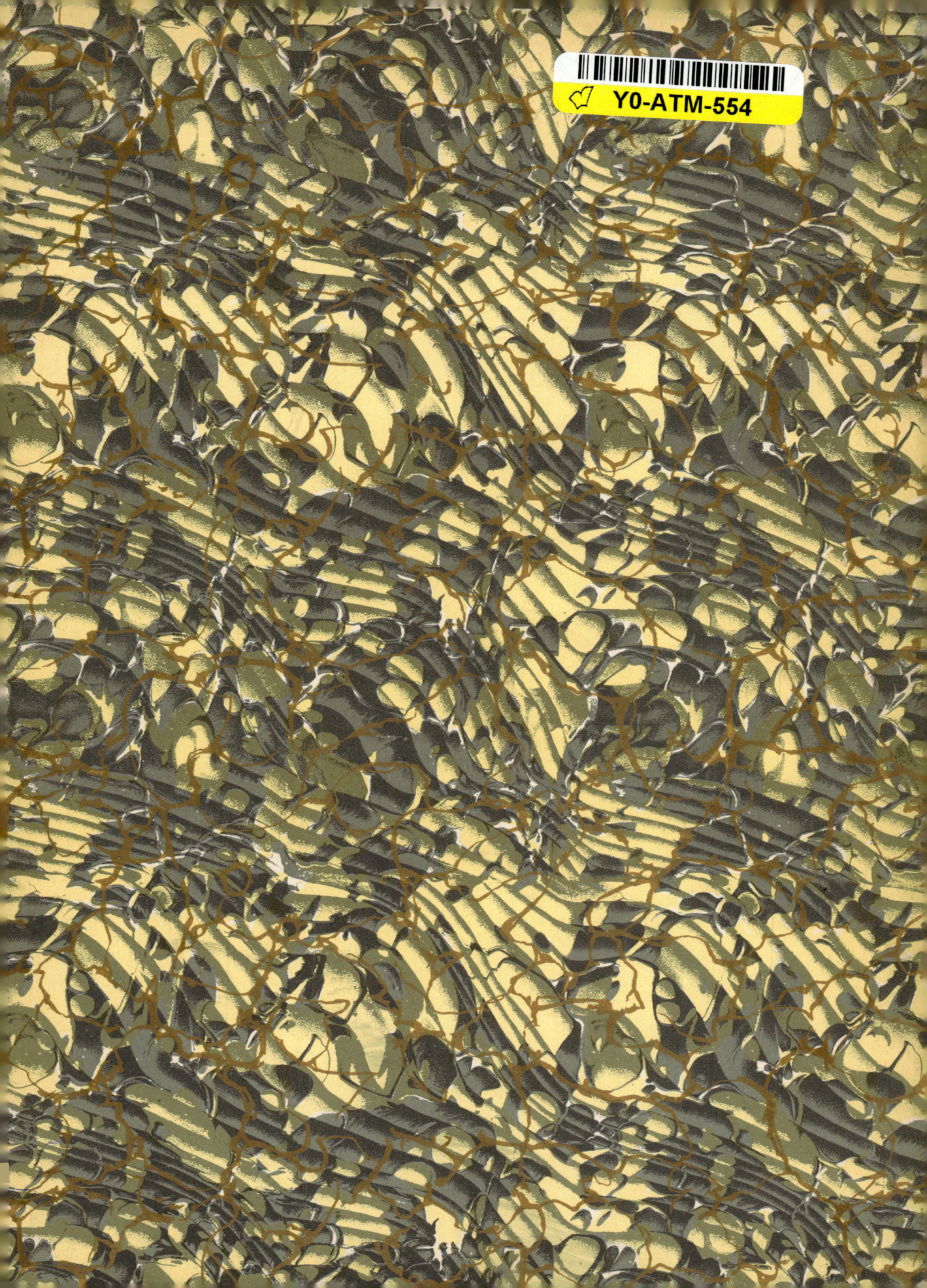

STATE CAPITOL, SPRINGFIELD

HISTORY

OF

ILLINOIS

AND

HER PEOPLE

BY

PROFESSOR GEORGE W. SMITH, M. A.

Head, Department of History, State Teachers College, Carbondale, Illinois;
Author of a Student's History of Illinois; Member Board
of Directors, State Historical Society

Assisted by an Advisory Board

IN SIX VOLUMES

ILLUSTRATED

VOLUME II

PUBLISHERS
THE AMERICAN HISTORICAL SOCIETY, Inc.
CHICAGO AND NEW YORK
1927

Copyright 1927
The American Historical Society, Inc.

From Statehood to the Civil War

History of Illinois

CHAPTER I

ILLINOIS AND NATIONAL EXPANSION

Self-Government—Expansion Westward—Political Expansion — Court Decisions — Economic Expansion — Population Expansion—Approaching Danger

Illinois was admitted to the Union December 3, 1818. The English speaking people of this state had been held more or less in subjection to an external political authority since the days of Col. John Todd. Following the departure of John Todd, the first civil governor, in 1782, there was a period of anarchy lasting from the end of Todd's control till the coming of Governor St. Clair in 1790. St. Clair was a non-resident ruler so far as Illinois was concerned. He was in the Illinois Country but a few short months. And from the summer of 1790 to the creation of the Indiana Territory, of which Illinois was a part, the control of Illinois was of the most trifling sort. Governmental control came a little closer to Illinois upon the passing of the Northwest Territory from a territory of the first class to that of a second class.

SELF-GOVERNMENT

Governor St. Clair issued his proclamation directing the election of representatives to a second grade Territorial Legislature in October, 1798. Elections were held on December 3, 1798, Illinois as a subdivision of the Northwest Territory was entitled to one representative. The people chose as their representative Shadrach Bond. Mr. Bond attended the meeting of the Territorial Legislature which was held at Cincinnati, beginning January 22, 1799. This Legislature confirmed the laws which the governor and three judges had enacted while the territory was of the first class and in addition passed thirty-eight new ones.

In 1800 the Congress created the Indiana Territory, which included Illinois. This was of the first class. Illinois was therefore without any voice in self-government till the separation of Illinois from the Indiana Territory in 1809. And even here the governor, Ninian Edwards, was a non-residenter. He ruled the territory from 1809 till 1812 as a first class territory. In 1812 the territory passed to the second class and the people had the chance to elect the members of the Upper and the Lower House of the Legislature. The people really enjoyed this participation in their government. But by the generosity of Congress in the summer of 1818, the territory was allowed to make a Constitution and take its place in the Union on an equal footing with the original states.

Up to the admission of Illinois into the Union, the people had not been conscious of a very close relation between themselves and the government and the people east of the Alleghanies. In many ways they had been a self-sufficing community. In the matter of government, the relation, as has been shown, was not a very strong tie. Economically and socially there was little dependence upon the East. It would not be strange then if we should find that when the people do come into statehood that they should consider themselves as an independent community which had little to do with other groups.

It has been pointed out that the government was in a measure aristocratic. The only officers the people were allowed to elect were the governor, lieutenant-governor, sheriffs, coroners, and members of the Upper and Lower Houses of the Legislature. All other officers were appointed by the governor or the Legislature.

The people of the new state gave considerable attention to military matters. This gave those who had had some experience in war a chance to take command of units of the militia and assume the high sounding titles that go along with military organization. Muster days were marked events in the calendar of the year.

The new state had started well under Governor Bond. The first session of the Legislature had been diligent in enacting such laws as their needs seemed to require. Courts had been organized, county officers appointed, and the machinery of civil government was fairly well adjusted. The governor was able to report a healthy financial condition of the state's new treasury department. At the meeting of the second Legislature, which convened in December, 1820, and held over into the year 1821, there were quite a few laws passed and some subjects considered which were taken up at later sessions.

Expansion Westward

Illinois approached statehood and was initiated into the family of states at a very important period of the nation's life. The War of 1812 brought on a critical period for the Territory of

Illinois. The country was sparsely settled and the means of realizing the full strength of its man power was a great handicap. It was so far away from the seat of authority that little was done for it by the Federal Government. But when the war was over, and the forces that were destined to produce such a wonderful economic development in the United States began to move, Illinois began to feel the new blood tingle in her veins. There was a great increase in her population, in her trade relations, and in her ambitions. The population grew from 12,282 in 1810 to 55,162 in 1820. Great waves of people came from the older states into Ohio, Indiana, Illinois, and Missouri; and Illinois received her share of this great westward expansion in

VIEW OF THE MISSISSIPPI FROM THE WATER TOWER AT CHESTER

population. If we would correctly interpret the history of Illinois in the first decade of her statehood, we must discover her relation to the older portions of the Union and seek to find the common ground between her and the older portions of our great country.

"The keynote of the period of American history from the close of the second war with England to the presidency of Andrew Jackson in expansion—the amplification of the power of the central government in acts of Congress, in decisions of the Supreme Court, in the development of industry, in manufactures, in agriculture, and in the extension of our frontier beyond the Mississippi. This triple process of political, economic, and geographical adjustment brought new forces into play in our American life and raised the problems of states' rights, protectionism, the status of territories, internal improvements, sectional rivalries and slavery, which characterized the years 1815-1860—the middle period of our history."

"The American people ceased to be provincial and began to appreciate its oneness, it began to feel and act as a nation. Before this time American politics had been dominated by European politics,—there had been British parties and parties favoring France. The War of 1812, and the economic changes consequent on the restoration of peace in Europe completely changed these conditions."

POLITICAL EXPANSION

These three forms of our national expansion, political, economic, and geographic or territorial, are vitally related to each other and it is very difficult to trace the development of any one without at the same time encroaching upon the subject matter of one of the others. But let us take up the expansion of the powers of the national Congress and see wherein this affected the growth and development of the country as a whole. President Madison's annual message to Congress, December 5, 1815, resulted in a bill to incorporate a United States bank. This bill speedily became a law and the second United States bank was authorized by Madison April 10, 1816. The capital was $35,000,000 and the government was entitled to one-fifth of the capital and to a fifth of the membership of the Board of Directors. The bank was to pay the sum of $1,500,000 for its charter which sum was to go into the national treasury.

The first United States bank was the creation of Alexander Hamilton. It was chartered in 1791 with a capital stock of $10,000,000, the national government holding one-fifth of the stock. The Anti-Federalist greatly opposed this bank. In 1811 when the charter expired the same party prevented its recharter. The War of 1812 was fought on a hodge podge system of paper money. There was little gold and silver in circulation and the paper issue was virtually irredeemable. By 1816 the party in power, the successor to the Anti-Federalist party, lost no time in chartering a bank to be linked up in management with the national government. The right of Congress to create a national banking system was not questioned by any one though many of the statesmen who declared that the first or Hamilton bank was unconstitutional were still living and active in political life. It is said that Madison, "surmounting the prejudices of a lifetime," signed the bill. Henry Clay who had been largely instrumental in defeating the recharter of the Hamilton bank in 1811, now in 1816, descended from the speaker's chair to urge the passage of the bill to create the new bank, "willing to sacrifice the pride of consistency rather than the welfare of the country."

State banks had increased from 100 in 1811 to 300 in 1816. Prior to the passage of the United States Bank bill, in 1816, there were very few of the three hundred state banks that were on a specie paying basis. But after the charter of the United States Bank the State Bank must resume specie payment or surrender the government deposits which they held. But it cannot be said that the new national banking system greatly helped the northwest at least not for several years. The Illinois Territorial banking system of 1816-17 as well as the creation of a state banking system in 1821, brought little or no relief to Illinois. And the hard times of 1821-2 were said to be the result of keeping slavery out of Illinois. This will be taken up later.

Court Decisions

The second way in which the expansion of the national power in government was shown was through Supreme Court decisions. The law, creating the second United States bank, provided that the stock of the bank should be non-taxable. The State of Maryland took the position that this law was unconstitutional and that a state could tax this stock. A case was carried into the Supreme Court and Chief Justice John Marshall rendered a decision that in substance said: "A national bank is an appropriate means to carry out some of the implied powers conferred on the national government by the Constitution. If the end is within the scope of the Constitution, all means which are plainly adapted to that end, and which are consistent with the spirit of the organic law, are constitutional." The second case was the celebrated Dartmouth College case. This decision denied the right of a state to annul a contract between the King of England and certain trustees in perpetuity of a college in America. A third very noted case was one in which the State of Georgia attempted to annul grants of land supposed to have been fraudulently obtained. The Supreme Court decided the grants could not be annulled though fraudulently obtained. In all these decisions the conclusions were that the Supreme Court was the highest power in the adjudication of a case. The state must bow to the authority of the national government.

Economic Expansion

The policy of nationalization received no more powerful support than was found in the tariff laws of the first and second decade of the nineteenth century.

England had furnished America her manufactured products from the earliest days to the days of the Jefferson Embargo. The Embargo, the Non-Intercourse Policy, the Decrees and Orders, and the War of 1812 itself all operated to change the economic life of the American people. Prior to these commercial restrictions we shipped to western Europe—to England chiefly—raw materials—lumber, naval stores, cotton, tobacco, fish, wool, hides, pig iron, cereal grains, and a number of other American products. In return we received manufactured goods, furniture, tools and machinery, leather and leather goods, iron and steel, woolens, cottons, clothing, wines, jewelry, silks, coffee, tea, carpets and a long list of less important articles.

The above named commercial restrictions forced America into the manufacture of the necessities, and in some measure to forego the luxuries, of life.

American capital driven from the world's commercial transactions sought new fields of investment. The new fields of enterprise which were opening for the profitable investment of American capital and for the assistance of American genius were found along the rugged coasts and the thickly populated areas of the middle and north Atlantic states. Here the famed "infant industries" had their beginning. The spindles and looms were the first to beckon the waiting laborers. Then the tanneries, the iron furnaces and forges, the shoe factories, the furniture and implement shops, and a score or more of centers of skilled labor.

Then England began to unload her manufactured goods in the American ports. These manufactured goods had accumulated during the years preceding the treaty of Ghent. They could be sold more cheaply than the goods of the American manufacturer and the "infant industries" appealed to the national government for protection from destruction. Thus was introduced the great American system—protection to American industry by a protective tariff. Here then we find the party in power, the successors of Anti-Federalists of an earlier date, enacting laws which killed two birds with one stone—prohibited the English goods from underselling American products and added at the same time to the United States treasury.

How can it be shown that an expansion in agriculture came from the conditions following the War of 1812. The American industrial revolution began in 1816 when the protective tariff of that year was enacted. The English cotton mills in competition with the American spindles were clamoring for raw cotton. There was an immediate increase in the cotton acreage. The alluvial lands of Mississippi and Louisiana were planted to cotton. In 1816 and 17, the government sold more than a million acres of land in the Mississippi Territory.

The farmers of the West—Kentucky, Tennessee, Ohio, Indiana, Illinois, and Missouri were raising grains, hogs, horses, cattle, sheep and other forms of provisions. Steam boats were coming into general use, but the good markets were in the manufacturing centers of Pennsylvania, New York, New Jersey, and New England, and what was badly needed was roads over the Alleghanies, connecting the Ohio Valley with the Atlantic Coast cities. As factories increased on the Atlantic slope, the demand for western food products grew proportionately. As the raising of grains, and meats became profitable in the west the demand for good farms increased. "As the Western farmers and Southern planters enlarged their production of grain, livestock, and cotton, they increased their purchases from the eastern merchants. Immigration into the west greatly increased. Twelve thousand freight wagons went from Philadelphia and Baltimore to Pittsburg in 1817, earning 300,000 English pounds as freighters."

DR. GEORGE CADWELL, FIRST ILLINOIS PHYSICIAN

The opening of the Cumberland Road in 1818 gave Wheeling an opportunity to share the eastern wagon trade with Pittsburg. From these cities flatboat stores floated down the Ohio and the Mississippi, the owners peddling boots and shoes, clothing, furniture, household utensils, hardware, all kinds of agricultural implements, tobacco, liquor and groceries from village to village and plantation to plantation.

Nothing gave more impetus to the nationalization of the country than the different forms of internal improvements. These forms may be enumerated under canals, railroads, wagon roads, bridges, and rivers. The first great step toward connecting the agricultural West with manufacturing East was the building of the Erie Canal. This was begun July 4, 1817, and was built to connect the City of New York with the growing West. "The building of the Erie Canal was one of the shrewdest things the merchants of New York ever did to advance their interests. A ton of flour which formerly required several weeks for conveyance from Albany to Buffalo at a cost of $100 or more now went through (after the completion of the canal) in as many days for $10." Philadelphia, seeing the advantages which New York was enjoying, both as an import and an export city, determined to construct a canal from the Delaware to the Ohio. This was completed about ten years later than the Erie Canal. It connected Philadelphia with Pittsburg. These two canals were of very great value in the settlement of Illinois in the first few decades of statehood.

Shortly after steamboats came into general use, the general government began the improvement of river navigation by the removal of obstructions in the form of snags, sand bars, and rocks. Some help was also given the local authority in the improvement of harbors. It would be difficult to understand how this western country could have been so quickly developed without the aid of steamboats and river navigation. We have already spoken of the influence of the Cumberland Road in the development of the West. In addition the several states of Ohio, Indiana, and Illinois were doing what they could in the opening of wagon roads, building bridges, establishing ferries, and encouraging the erection and maintenance of inns or taverns along the public roads. Within the first two decades of statehood, the railroads had been of little service in building up the West. But they had their beginning in this period and later were powerful agents in national expansion.

Population Expansion

There were fewer than 50,000 people northwest of the Ohio River in 1800. But south of the Ohio, Kentucky and Tennessee had been admitted to the Union as states, and in 1803 President Jefferson bought Louisiana with a population of 50,000. The westward extension of settled areas was inextricably bound up with the slavery question. This can be shown to the eye by the following scheme.

The Original Thirteen

Slave States	Free States
Georgia	New Hampshire
South Carolina	Massachusetts
North Carolina	Rhode Island

Virginia	Connecticut
Maryland	New York
Delaware	New Jersey
	Pennsylvania

New States

1792	Kentucky		1791	Vermont
1796	Tennessee		1803	Ohio
1812	Louisiana		1816	Indiana
1817	Mississippi		1818	Illinois
1819	Alabama		1820	Maine
1821	Missouri			

Twenty-four United States Senators who will vote for the interests of the slave-holder.   Twenty-four United States Senators all of whom can not be depended on to vote against the spread of slavery.

While we talk of national expansion we at the same time must talk of sectional interests. No one of the six states south of the Mason and Dixon line and the Ohio River, could by any sort of political legerdemain have been admitted as a free state, while Ohio, Indiana and Illinois out of the five north and west of the Ohio and the Mason and Dixon line, might have done so.

It was in the midst of this wonderful period of expansion and nationalization, that Illinois grew from a scattering population of 12,000 in 1812 to a population of 55,000 in 1820 and to 157,000 in 1830. Just what effect this move in nationalization in political, economic, and territorial interests had it may be difficult to trace, but that Illinois was profoundly affected by this national expansion is very certain. The presence of slaves in Illinois, the remnant of the old French slaves, was an entering wedge for the making of Illinois a slave state. The existence of an indentured system made it much easier for the friends of slavery to hope for the admission of Illinois as a slave state.

The doctrine grew up that the Ordinance of 1787 was a "dead letter." When the question of accepting the constitution of Illinois was before Congress in November, 1818, William Henry Harrison a member from Ohio in response to some remarks by Mr. Tallmadge of New York said: "In regard to the supposed compact, however, and its efficacy, I have always considered it a dead letter." Mr. Harrison said he could not put his hand on the page, but he believed it would be found in one of the numbers of the Federalist, that Alexander Hamilton had expressly declared the same opinion. The doctrine was put forth that there could be no compact where both parties had not freely assented thereto. When Virginia made her cession to the general government, and when Congress enacted the Ordinance of 1787, prohibiting slavery in the Northwest Territory, there were no people in the territory to assent to the compact, so there really was no compact.

APPROACHING DANGER

Many people in Illinois were thoroughly converted to the doctrine that the Ordinance was not binding and would have ignored that document in the making of the Illinois Constitution had it not been for fear Congress would not accept a constitution permitting slavery. The next best thing the friends of slavery could do was to word the Constitution so that the French slaves would not be disturbed, and at the same time save as much as they could out of the indenture system, biding their time when the state could rewrite its constitution and admit slavery. The state was admitted into the Union with a constitution which said "Neither slavery (n) or involuntory servitude shall hereafter be introduced into this state, otherwise than for the punishment of crimes, whereof the party shall have been duly convicted; etc." Nothing was to be done about Illinois becoming a slave state till after the territory was admitted and then the constitution would be rewritten.

The slave interests easily saw that if the Mason and Dixie line and the Ohio River separating slavery from freedom, should extend westward through the Louisiana purchase and eventually to the Pacific coast, that the great Northwest—five states east of the Mississippi, and a half dozen or more west—would overwhelm the slavery interests in the Senate and the House of Representatives, and slavery itself in the home of its birth would be in great danger of legal extinction.

The slavery interest had failed with Ohio and Indiana and it looked as if there were little hope for their cause in Illinois until after the admission of that territory as a state. But now comes Missouri ready for admission into the Union. It had grown in population from 20,000 in 1810 to 66,000 in 1820. Missouri, a part of the Louisiana Purchase, held slaves through rights granted in treaties of transfer and purchase back to the days of the earliest French occupation.

Illinois' application for admission was presented in Congress the 16th of January, 1818, by the delegate, Mr. Nathaniel Pope. An enabling act was signed on April 18, 1818. On Dec. 3, 1818, the constitution which Illinois presented was accepted and Illinois was a sovereign state.

In March, 1818, Missouri applied for admission. The application was not taken up in Congress till February, 1819, and the state was not admitted till March 3, 1820. During this period of two years from March, 1818, to March 1820, there was a discussion in Congress of the extension of slavery. The part taken by the representatives of Illinois and the two senators will throw some light on the slavery struggle soon to take place in Illinois. It is said that the two senators from Illinois, Ninian W. Edwards and Jesse B. Thomas both, at all times, voted on propositions which would favor Missouri's coming into the Union as a slave state. John McLean, the state's representative favored the admission of Missouri as a slave state. But McLean's term expired March 4, 1819, and a special congressional election was held to fill his place. The leading candidates were David P. Cook and John McLean. McLean had defeated Cook for Congress in the fall of 1818 by only fourteen votes. Cook and his friends assailed McLean for the stand he took in favoring the admission of Missouri as a slave state. McLean was defeated by 633 votes. It must not be thought that Cook was elected because he was anti-slavery, for without doubt most of the people in Illinois at this time were favorable to slavery.

CHAPTER II

FOR OR AGAINST SLAVERY

FOUR CANDIDATES—COLES A VIRGINIAN—AMBASSADOR—SLAVES FREED—GOVERNOR-ELECT—THE MESSAGE—CRITICAL SUBJECT—REPORT OF COMMITTEE—CONTESTED ELECTION—A REVERSAL—PUBLIC APPEALS—PUBLIC MEN—OUTSIDE HELP—A BITTER CAMPAIGN—PUBLIC SPEAKINGS—SECRET SOCIETIES—THE CHURCHES—THE PAPERS—THE ELECTION—REFLECTIONS.

The makers of the Constitution of 1818 were opposed to the monopoly of official positions. Article III, Section 3, says: "The governor shall hold his office for the term of four years and until another governor shall be elected and qualified; but he shall not be eligible for more than four years in any term of eight years." The governor could not succeed himself, but might later be elected a second time. Governor Bond's term would expire the first Monday in December, 1822. The election to choose his successor would come in August preceding. Governor Bond had no opposition when he was a candidate in 1818, but in 1822 there were several ambitious statesmen who would like to be governor of Illinois.

FOUR CANDIDATES

The candidates for the governorship began their canvasses rather early—the election was to be held the first Monday in August, 1822. Edward Coles announced his candidacy October 30, 1821—nine months before the day set for the election. Joseph B. Phillips, chief justice of the State Supreme Court, came out February, 1822. A third candidate, Justice Thomas C. Browne, of Shawneetown, was urged to announce his candidacy by the friends of Phillips, hoping that he would draw votes from Coles on the east side of the state where the latter was said to be very popular. Late in the campaign Gen. James B. Moore of St. Clair County offered as a candidate for governor.

There can be little doubt that the question of making a slave state of Illinois was a prominent subject of discussion. It was generally well known that Coles was a strong anti-slavery man. General Moore also was known as an opponent of slavery. Both Chief Justice Phillips and Associate Justice Brown were pronounced pro-slavery men and that they favored making Illinois a slave state. Moses History says, "The slavery question was by no means a new one in Illinois. It had been the subject of frequent and always exciting discussion in and out of the Legislature from the time of the territorial organization." Again: "Senator Thomas, who was a candidate for reelection and known as a pro-slavery champion naturally interested himself to secure the election to the Legislature of those who were in sympathy with him on this subject, and whenever it could be done safely, the issue of slavery was made." Pease, in Volume 2 of the Centennial History of Illinois, says: "The canvass for governor in 1822 turned frankly on the question of slavery."

The election was held on the first Monday in August and resulted in the election of Edward Coles as governor, but of a Senate of eighteen members, twelve of whom were pro-slavery and six anti-slavery. The House consisted of thirty-six members, twenty-three of whom were pro-slavery and thirteen of whom were opposed to slavery—at least in Illinois.

Coles a Virginian

Edward Coles, the successful candidate for governor in the election of 1822, was a native of Virginia. He was born December 15, 1786. His father was a colonel in the Revolutionary war. Young Coles was college bred, but not a graduate. He had for college classmates, Gen. Winfield Scott, President John Tyler, Senator Wm. S. Archer, and Justice Baldwin of the Supreme Court. The Coles family was in close social and political relations with the families of Thomas Jefferson, Patrick Henry, James Madison, James Monroe, John Randolph, and other prominent Virginians.

In 1809, Edward Coles found himself the owner of a large Virginia estate and a score or more slaves, the bequest of his father, deceased. He had spent his time, after leaving college, on his father's estate and in his father's library. His whole life had been passed in the society of educated and cultured people. He was not only well bred and well read, but he had begun in his early young manhood to study a social and economic problem to which many of the wisest men in America have given their earnest thought. That was the subject of human slavery.

James Madison was inaugurated President March 4, 1809. In casting about for a suitable person for his private secretary he was attracted to the young Virginian, Edward Coles. In those days the position of private secretary was of course, not so important as it is today—at least not of the same kind of importance. However, the years from 1809 to the close of the War of 1812 were stormy times not only politically within the United States but internationally. Our relations with France and England may be judged when we know that "Public sentiment in America was setting strongly toward war. It was felt that we should have done with protests and expedients, with shifting policies that waited on Napoleon's whims or Wellesley's pride, and manfully assert our rights as a free people." And it is asserted that there were statesmen who felt that the causes of war with France were as justifiable as those stated in the declaration of war against England. We may therefore conclude that the private secretary to the President, through these troublous times must have been a man with a broad grasp of international relations.

Young Coles acted as private secretary to President Madison from the summer of 1809 to the summer of 1815. He was unmarried and was a member of the household of the President. In these years he became personally acquainted with all the public men who had to do with the prosecution of the war. It was in the midsummer of 1814 that a lasting friendship began between Edward Coles and Thomas Jefferson. The basis of this friendship was the identical views which they held as to the political, economic, and social iniquity of human slavery. In July, 1814, Mr. Coles addressed a very lengthy letter to Mr. Jefferson in which he appealed to the ex-president to exercise his great powers to bring about the emancipation of the slaves in the United States. In his reply, which too was of considerable length, Mr. Jefferson said: "Your solitary but welcome voice is the first which has brought this sound to my ear, and I have considered the general silence which prevails on this subject as indicating an apathy unfavorable to every hope, yet the hour of emancipation is advancing in the march of time. It will come. —This Enterprise (the work of emancipation) shall have all my prayers, and these are the only weapons of an old man."

It was while serving Mr. Madison that Mr. Coles became acquainted with Nicholas Biddle, for thirteen years president of the second United States bank. The acquaintance ripened into interest and friendship and out of it all came the moral and financial help of Robert Vaux, a rich Quaker of Philadelphia in the great fight on slavery in Illinois in 1823-4.

Ambassador

In 1815 Mr. Coles resigned his position as private secretary to the President and traveled extensively in the west seeking a place where he might take his slaves, free them, and give them a start in the world. He visited Ohio, Indiana, Illinois and Missouri and returned to Virginia by way of New Orleans and the Atlantic coast.

In July, 1816, President Madison offered him the appointment as special ambassador to Russia. The business was of a delicate and intricate nature. The appointment was accepted and the duties satisfactorily performed. On his return to the United States Mr. Coles spent some time in France where he was kindly

EDWARD COLES

received by La Fayette, who entertained him royally and presented him to the King, Louis XVIII. Mr. Albert Gallatin was the American Minister at Paris and he took a very great interest in the young diplomat. The fact of Coles' personal acquaintance with Jefferson, Madison, Henry, Monroe, and that his father was a Revolutionary officer, gave him and General La Fayette common ground for many a social and reminiscent hour.

From France Mr. Coles visited London and various parts of the British Isles. While investigating the agricultural processes in England he made the acquaintance of Morris Birkbeck, a successful tenant farmer of Wanborough, Wiltshire, twenty-two miles southwest of Oxford. Mr. Birkbeck was cultivating a large estate and had accumulated a large amount of property, but was desirous of coming to the United States to secure an estate of his own. Mr. Coles told Mr. Birkbeck about the great prairies and the rich soil of Illinois. From this description Mr. Birkbeck visited Illinois and eventually settled near the present town of Albion, Edwards County.

When Mr. Coles returned from his diplomatic mission, he made known his plans of selling his Virginia estate and removing to Illinois with his slaves. These plans coming to the ears of President James Monroe, he offered Mr. Coles the position of registrar of the land office at Edwardsville. This was a good position as far as salary was concerned and an excellent one in which to become acquainted with people.

Mr. Coles made a visit to Illinois in the summer of 1818, and was in Kaskaskia while the Constitutional Convention was in session. While in Illinois at this time he selected Edwardsville as his future home and secured a good body of land for his future farm. In the early spring of 1819 he finished all arrangements as to the care of his estate in Virginia and with wagons and teams he started for the new home in the far West. There were three or four wagons loaded with movables from his estate together with some twenty slaves. The wagons were in charge of one of his mulattoes by the name of Ralph Crawford. He was a slave of intelligence and experience. The other slaves seemed to realize they had a long journey before them, but they had implicit confidence in Mr. Coles as well as in Crawford who had accompanied Mr. Coles into the West on an earlier journey. Mr. Coles followed after a day or so on horseback. At Brownsville, Pennsylvania, they embarked on two large flatboats and proceeded to Pittsburg and thence down the Ohio.

Slaves Freed

Mr. Coles gave an extended account of a scene which transpired on the Ohio a short distance below Pittsburg. He had planned to free his slaves in Illinois but they knew nothing of the plan. On a bright morning in April, he pulled the boats to shore and called his slaves all before him. He told them where he was going, something of the rich fields, and the opportunities to make a living in this new land. When he had their imaginations wrought up, he suddenly told them he had decided to set them all free. Mr. Coles seemed to take pleasure in thus breaking the news to them for he says he wished to see what effect the news would have upon their simple minds. He then offered to release them and allow them to go back to Virginia or elsewhere, or they could go with him to Illinois. If they went with him to Illinois he would provide each head of a family with 160 acres of land that he should own, and in addition he would help them get started to farming. The unmarried members of his flock, he said, could go to St. Louis and find work or settle near Edwardsville. They all agreed to go with him to Illinois.

Before Mr. Coles left the boats he gave the ex-slaves a certificate of freedom which they were to keep as evidence of their manumission. They eventually reached Edwardsville where they were distributed on their several holdings. Mr. Coles took up the work of the registrar in the land office. Here he rapidly made friends with those who had business in the land office. He was attentive, agreeable in manners, well dressed, and withal a conscientious, honest, accommodating public official. His acquaintances and friends were found wherever there was a citizen who had done business with the registrar of the land office.

As has been stated Mr. Coles announced his candidacy for the governorship as early as October, 1821. There does not appear to have been any prominent Illinois politician who championed Mr. Cole's candidacy. His attitude toward slavery was well known. But outwardly, at least, slavery was not an issue in the campaign. However Chief Justice Phillips of the Supreme Court was an open champion of slavery. Ninian Edwards who was in the United States Senate and who was constantly writing to politicians in Illinois at this time, never mentions the name of Coles either before or after the election. When the election was over it was found that Mr. Coles was the high man of the four candidates. Coles, 2,810 votes; Phillips, 2,760; Brown, 2,543; Moore, 522. Brown was brought out to take votes away from Coles on the Wabash. But he developed unlooked for strength and fell behind Phillips by only 217 votes.

Governor Elect

The question which came before the people of the state in the Legislature and in the heated campaign which followed the session of the General Assembly, was so vital to the welfare and happiness of the people of the state that it is thought best to give the names of those who precipitated the conflict and the names of those who did their duty in trying to check the spread of this social and economic malady—human slavery.

Senators

* Those marked with a star voted against the convention resolution.

Adolphus F. Hubbard, lieutenant-governor.
Sangamon—Stephen Stillman.*
Madison—Theophilus W. Smith.
Washington—Andrew Bankson.*
Union and Alexander—John Grammar.
Crawford, Clark and Edgar—Daniel Parker.*
Hamilton, Jefferson and Marion—Thomas Sloo, Jr.
Bond, Fayette, and Montgomery—Martin Jones.
Jackson—William Boon.
Randolph—Samuel Crozier.
Wayne and Lawrence—William Kinkade.*
Greene, Morgan, etc.—George Cadwell.*
White—Leonard White.
Edward Frazier.*
Johnson and Franklin—Milton Todd.
St. Clair—William Kinney.
Monroe—Joseph A. Beard.
Gallatin—Michael Jones.
Pope—Lewis Barker.

Members of the House

Monroe—William Alexander.
Pope—Samuel Alexander, James A. Whiteside.
Union—Alexander P. Field, John McIntosh.
Madison—Curtis Blakeman,* George Churchill,* Emanuel J. West.
Fayette and Montgomery—William Berry.
Lawrence—Abraham Cairns.*
Hamilton, Jefferson, and Marion—Zadock Casey.
Franklin—Thomas Dorris.
Gallatin—J. G. Daimwood, James S. Davenport.
White—John Emmitt, Alexander Philips, G. R. Logan.
Crawford—David McGahey,* R. C. Ford.
Johnson—Wm. McFatridge.
Pike and Fulton—Nicholas Hansen,* John Shaw.
Clark and Edgar—Wm. Lowery.*
St. Clair—Risdon Moore,* Jacob Ogle,* James Trotier.
Randolph—Thomas Mather,* Raphael Widen,* John McFerron.
Bond—Jonathan H. Pugh.*
Edwards—Gilbert T. Pell.*

Greene and Morgan, etc.—Thos. Rattan.
Washington—James Turney.
Jackson—Conrad Will.
Sangamon—James Sims.*
Wayne—James Campbell.

The Legislature met on the first Monday in December, 1822. The credentials were passed upon and the vote for state officers canvassed. On the 5th of the month Governor Coles delivered his inaugural address.

THE MESSAGE

The governor called attention to four matters of public interest—finances, agriculture, canal, and slavery.

The financial situation has been fully discussed elsewhere and we shall give but a brief resume. The old banks chartered by the Illinois Territorial Legislature were either defunct or had been merged into the State Bank. The second General Assembly had chartered a bank known as the State Bank of Illinois. Its capital was put at $500,000; but only $300,000 in bills had been issued. These were all in circulation, but were passing at a discount—in some cases as low as 25 cents on the dollar. There was little gold and silver and a scarcity of the bills of the United States Bank. There were bills from banks in the adjoining states, but their value was not always known. Governor Coles said: "A currency changeable in value can form no standard for the value of other things; and of course fails in its object, inasmuch as it is always operating injuriously and unjustly in the discharge of debts, by a greater or less amount, intrinsically, than was contracted for."

He then called attention to the Agricultural Society. This had been formed on the 10th of November, 1819. It was the result of a call published in the Edwardsville Spectator. The writer signed himself "A Farmer of Madison." Everyone thought the author was Edward Coles. At that time Edward Coles and Morris Birkbeck most nearly approached scientific farming of any one in the state. At the meeting, Morris Birkbeck was elected president and Edward Coles vice-president. This society sought to improve the quality of wheat, corn, fine live stock, hemp, flax, cotton, homespun cloth, etc. In fact it was the modern county or state fair in miniature. The plan was that societies might be organized in the several counties where the interest was great enough and that these county societies should be affiliated with the State Society. Premiums were offered for the best samples shown at the regular meetings.

The State Society had been in existence a part of three years but already articles had been written and printed and pamphlets had been distributed which discussed matters of vital interest to the farmer. One article urged the people to turn their attention to grazing, dairying, and the production of a finer grade of wool. Mr. Birkbeck who had farmed land in England that had been in cultivation for many centuries urged the people to look to the preservation of the strength of the soil by fertilization and rotation of crops. In these articles in the local newspapers there were many very valuable articles if they had been read and pondered by unprejudiced farmers. The governor in his message asked the Legislature to take such action as would materially help the society and spread a favorable impression of what the society was hoping to accomplish.

The third subject to which the governor called the attention of the Legislature was the importance of taking steps to further the work of the canal which would connect the head waters of the Illinois River with Lake Michigan—generally called the Illinois and Michigan Canal. This indeed was a big subject, but not at all a visionary one. The Erie Canal from Albany on the Hudson River to Buffalo, at the east end of Lake Erie, was then under construction. De Witt Clinton, the father of the Erie Canal, was much interested in the Illinois and Michigan Canal and took the trouble to write to Governor Coles about several features of the Illinois canal.

The Critical Subject

The last matter which Governor Coles discussed in his inaugural message was the straw that broke the camel's back. This was the emancipation of the slaves then held in Illinois. The slavery question was no new one to the public men, at least, of the state. It had been prominently before the public in the days when Illinois was a part of the Indiana Territory. Again when the Territory of Illinois became a separate political unit, and when it was in the first and second stages of territorial organization, slavery was always a troublesome matter. When the Constitutional Convention was in session, no other subject required so many compromises as the slavery subject. The constitution would have been written providing for slavery, if the leading men had believed that Illinois would be admitted by Congress. But Ohio and Indiana had been admitted with prohibition of slavery in their constitutions. Ohio had not in any way bound herself never to revise her constitution so as to admit slavery, but Indiana had inserted a clause in her first constitution prohibiting any amendment of the constitution so that slavery should be legal in that state. Mr. Tallmadge of New York in the House of Representatives in opposing the acceptance of the constitution of Illinois, said that the State of Indiana already admitted from the same territory (the Northwest Territory), had been very careful in the framing of their first constitutional enactment. Not only so, but had inserted a clause which would in all future time prohibit any change in the constitution which would permit slavery in that state.

It seems then that the three constitutions which had been made for the three states that had been carved out of the Northwest Territory presented three distinct types of constitution. Indiana's constitution not only prohibited slavery, but bound the people for all time to come never to revise their constitution

HENRY EDDY
Editor of *The Shawnee Chief* and of *The Illinois Emigrant* in 1818, and of *The Illinois Gazette* in 1819

in such a way as to legalize slavery in that state. The second type of constitution was found in Ohio's fundamental law which prohibited slavery, but did not bind the people never to legalize slavery by constitutional enactment in the future. The third kind of constitution was seen in that of Illinois which impliedly recognized slavery in Illinois, but prohibited its future introduction. The constitution also recognized and worked out somewhat in detail the indenture system which was virtually a system of slavery. Mr. Harrison of Ohio on the floor of the House resented the allusion of Mr. Tallmadge of New York that Ohio was not willing to insert a clause in her constitution forbidding the future change of her constitution so as to admit slavery.

It was in Mr. Harrison's reply that the slavery supporters in Illinois took their cue. Mr. Harrison argued that after a state was in the union it was a sovereign state and was under no obligations to ask any one what she should do. The expression in the Enabling Act which said "shall be admitted into the Union upon the same footing with the original states, in all respects whatever," was taken to mean that Illinois had a perfect right to rewrite her constitution at any time after admission into the Union.

The fight between slavery and freedom, which was precipitated by the application of Missouri for admission into the Union encouraged the slavery interests in Illinois to take hope since the two United States Senators from Illinois were voting with the slavery party on all questions which came before the Senate as to the admission of Missouri as a slave state. In 1819, as previously stated, Cook beat McLean for the seat in Congress. In the campaign Cook assumed that the majority of the people in Illinois were opposed to slavery and charged McLean with betraying his constituency by voting to admit Missouri as a slave state. McLean defended his vote by saying that to dictate to Missouri what she should do about slavery was a violation of a state's sovereignty.

It has heretofore been suggested by some writers that the change in the constitution permitting slavery was not a subject of discussion in the campaign of 1822, but there can be no doubt on that question. There may have been men who were candidates and for the sake of getting elected kept the slavery subject in the background, but the men in the state who hoped for a change in the constitution knew what was wanted and what was needed. Mr. Pease in Volume 2 of the Centennial History of Illinois says the files of the papers of 1820 show that Henry Eddy as early as that date announced himself for the Legislature with the statement that he was in favor of amending the constitution—not to introduce slavery but to secure a better situation as to the indenture laws. In his announcement to the voters of Gallatin County he says: "With regard to the Saline, then, I am clear for extending to it, for another term of years, the privilege which it now enjoys of hiring and indenturing servants for the purpose of working the same. And being of this opinion, I am, of course, in favor of a convention, for that object can only be effected through the means of another convention, our present constitution having limited the time during which the privilege may be claimed to the year 1825." The position of Mr. Eddy must have been purely a local one since when the real fight came on, he allied himself with Coles and Birkbeck.

The preceding discussion in looking forward to the securing of the correct status of public sentiment at the time that Governor Coles delivered his inaugural address.

It could not certainly be maintained that the governor's request for action looking to the emancipation of the slaves, then held in Illinois, was a great surprise to the slavery people, for without doubt, they were ready for action whether the governor should introduce the subject or not. It probably could be maintained that the anti-convention people were not ready for a test of strength. It is doubtful whether Governor Coles himself expected such hasty and radical action as the slavery people did take. Mr. Pease thinks that Coles probably thought a bold course was the best one and that the sooner the matter was settled the better it would be.

There were three things that the governor suggested under the fourth head as appears in the earlier part of this chapter. First, the abolition of slavery which then existed in Illinois. Second, the repeal of the disgraceful black code. Third, the passage of laws which would effectually put a stop to the kidnapping of free blacks.

Report of Committees

The governor's address was delivered before the joint assembly, and it appears a joint committee was appointed to consider that part of the address which dealt with slavery. Five Senators—Beard, Boon, Ladd, Kinney, and White; and three representatives, Moore, Emmitt, and Will, constituted the committee. The Senate committee was hand-picked as everyone of them voted for the convention, while Risdon Moore was the only one of the eight who voted against the convention.

The report which was made by the five Senators in part said: "Your committee are clearly of opinion that the people of Illinois have now the same right to alter their constitution as the people of Virginia or any other of the original states and may make any disposition of negro slaves they choose without any breach of faith, or violation of compact, ordinance or act of Congress." No one had ever denied the legal right of the State of Illinois to change its constitution the same as Virginia or any other state. This was not germane to the subject matter in the governor's address. The governor had suggested the abolition of slavery in Illinois, the repeal of the black laws, and more effective laws to prevent kidnapping. Governor Coles was not opposed to a revision of the constitution provided it should result in the abolition of slavery. But it was now known far and near that a convention called to rewrite the state's constitution would put into that document a clause legalizing slavery.

The committee from the Senate recommended the adoption of the following resolution:

"Resolved, that the General Assembly of the State of Illinois (two-thirds thereof concurring therein), do recommend to the electors, at the next election for members to the General Assembly, to vote for or against a convention, agreeably to the seventh article of the Constitution."

It should be said that Risdon Moore and John Emmitt reported adversely and recommended the abolition of slavery. Conrad Will made a report which was neutral.

Contested Election

These reports being in and acted on by acceptance of the resolution in the Senate, the General Assembly turned its attention to other matters. Among the things that must be attended to at once was the settling of a contested election case before the House. It appeared that upon the face of the returns, that Nicholas Hansen, a young lawyer, was elected from Pike County to the lower branch of the Legislature. He presented the certificate of election, but John Shaw, his opponent in the campaign, was present on the opening of the session and on the 4th of December presented his contest papers. On the 9th of December Hansen was seated, upon the recommendation of the Committee on Elections, which was made up of those who favored a convention and those who opposed a convention. The Senate, to which the Committee on the Governor's Address had been referred, was not willing to take up the matter of ordering the vote at the next election (which would come August, 1824) till some organization work had been attended to. Besides, John Grammar, of Union County, was not present, and his vote was needed to carry the measure in the Senate.

Again, one of the matters to be attended to was the election of a United States senator to succeed Jesse B. Thomas. The joint assembly proceeded to the election on January 9th, 1823. Jesse B. Thomas received twenty-nine votes, John Reynolds received sixteen votes. Leonard White received six votes, and Samuel D. Lockwood received two votes. Mr. Thomas was declared elected. Other matters occupied the attention of the Legislature till the 10th of February. Mr. Harris, in "Negro Servitude in Illinois," says the reason the Senate did not act sooner on the calling for a vote on a convention was because of the absence of John Grammar, and his vote was needed to give the two-thirds majority. Grammar arrived at Vandalia on February 7, which was on Friday. On Monday, the 10th, the call for a vote on a convention was passed by a vote of twelve to six (see the table of members on previous page). On the same day the secretary of the Senate transmitted the bill to the House.

After the holiday recess and up to the arrival of John Grammar, the House was trying to determine how the vote stood in that body. It was believed the slavery party lacked but a vote or so. But the longer they delayed, the more intense became the demand for a convention.

It is said by E. B. Washburne, in the sketch of Governor Coles, that everything was done to force doubtful members to vote for the convention. "Legislative despotism ruled supreme. The action of the convention party in the Legislature was to the last degree unfair, tyrannical, and insulting. In the House, so far

PETER WHITE

In 1844 this man was ten years old. He and three smaller children were kidnapped in Equality and taken to Arkansas, where they were sold for $800. They were rescued by Walter White, a nephew of Gen. Leonard White.

as I am able to gather, no general discussion was allowed." And Harris says the war cry became "The Convention or Death." "Promises, alluring inducements, and even threats were freely indulged in. Numbers of lobby members from Kentucky, Tennessee, Missouri and our own state hung about the corridors and anterooms stimulating sentiment in favor of the introduction of slavery." During the earlier days of the excitement it was understood that Rattan, of Greene County, and McFatridge, of Johnson County, were anti-convention. This was discovered by introducing into the House a resolution identical with the Senate resolution (which was pending in the Senate). The vote stood twenty-two to fourteen, Hansen voting for it, and McFatridge and Rattan voting against it. McFatridge supposedly voted his convictions, while Rattan voted against it so he could move a reconsideration. And McFatridge announced his change of heart when the proslavery group promised they would move the county seat of Johnson County from Vienna to Bloomfield (which they never did).

These two changes gave the proslavery men twenty-four votes, while the anti-convention men could muster only twelve. The convention men were happy beyond all estimate. The Senate resolution was passed on the 10th of February and presented in the House the same day. Haste was now the order.

On February 11th the Senate resolution, which had been held in abeyance till it was known what the House could do, and also awaiting one affirmative vote, Mr. Grammar, from Union County, was taken up in the House. There were thirty-six members in the House, they were all present, a test vote had been taken and the slavery party needed two votes. These had been won over in the persons of Rattan of Greene and McFatridge of Johnson. The twenty-four votes were all at their posts. The roll was called upon the passage of the resolution and lo! and behold! The affirmative had only twenty-three and the opponents had thirteen and the measure was lost. Who is the traitor? Who has betrayed his pledge? When the smoke of the battle had cleared away it was found that Mr. Hansen, from Pike, had without a moment's warning voted with the anti-convention group. Mr. Daimwood, of Gallatin, who had voted in the affirmative, moved a reconsideration, but the speaker of the House, Mr. William Alexander, of Alexander County, ruled against Mr. Daimwood, who appealed from the chair, and upon the vote's being taken, the House sustained the speaker. The House then adjourned.

A Reversal

That night a noisy meeting was held at the statehouse. Speeches were made by some of the lobbyists and members of the Legislature. When the meeting was over crowds with tin pans and horns and lusty voices visited the homes of some of the anti-convention men, and among other things an effigy of Hansen was burned in the streets. A move was started that night to turn Hansen out of the Legislature and put Shaw in his place. On the 12th of February the House voted to reconsider the resolution which seated Hansen at the time of the contest, and Shaw was seated in his place. When Shaw arrived and took his seat, a motion to reconsider the vote on the Senate resolution was made. This had to be done by some member who voted in the affirmative. The speaker reversed his decision and a reconsideration was carried. The motion was then upon the passage of the Senate resolution that a vote be taken for and against a convention at the next regular election, August, 1824. It resulted in twenty-four votes for and twelve against. The resolution was therefore adopted and the real contest was still ahead.

It would be natural that the anti-convention people would be very much discouraged, and cast down. One thing, they can look every one in the face and say we have done nothing of which we are ashamed. The facts are that the unfair methods of the convention party, the illegal procedures, the ungentlemanly conduct toward those opposed to slavery, all worked powerfully to weaken their cause. The anti-slavery people seemed to renew their determination and their strength.

Before we get too far from Mr. Hansen, it should be stated that he gave to the public an "address" in which he attempted to explain his action of voting in the affirmative on the test vote and afterwards voting against the convention when the Senate resolution was before the House. Some have thought his explanations were weak and that he was not justified in changing, but he seems very straightforward and earnest to others. In the first place he stated he was always opposed to slavery and that he had not tried to make any one believe otherwise. He voted with the slavery party on the test votes, as he knew it was not intended to be a bona fide attempt to pass the measure, but just a feeler. He affirms that he was intimidated, and on two occasions was threatened with expulsion from the House if he did not vote with the slavery party. He said he discovered the convention party was bound to carry their point and that he reserved his vote till the real question was the issue. Mr. Washburne shows that Mr. Hansen lived in Pike County following this trying time and held several offices of minor importance. He was a man of education.

Governor Ford, who has written very fully and accurately of those days, says: "The night after this resolution passed, the convention party assembled to triumph in a great carousal. They formed themselves into a noisy, disorderly and tumultuous procession, headed by Judge Phillips, Judge Smith, Judge Thomas Reynolds, later governor of Missouri, and Lieutenant-Governor Kinney, followed by the majority of the Legislature and the hangers-on and the rabble about the seat of government; and they marched with the blowing of tin horns and the beating of drums and tin pans, to the residence of Governor Coles, and to the boarding houses of their principal opponents, towards whom they manifested their contempt and displeasure by a confused medley of groans, wailings, and lamentations. Their object was to intimidate and crush all opposition at once."

Another historian, Governor John Reynolds, has written very frankly about the passage of the convention resolution and of the action of the friends of slavery at that time. In speaking of unseating Hansen, he says: "This proceeding in the General Assembly looked revolutionary and was condemned by all honest reflecting men. This outrage was the death blow to the convention. The night after the passage of the resolution, there was in the seat of government a wild and indecorous procession of torchlight and liquor, that was also unpopular." This is the procession that Ford says was headed by Judge Phillips.

Public Appeals

It was indeed a time of deep gloom for the anti-slavery party. They were amazed and for a while unnerved at the action of the convention majority. "There were, however, courageous hearts who determined to accept the gauntlet which had been thrown down.

The resolution was passed by the House on the 18th of February and the Legislature adjourned. The conventionists had, however, held a meeting on the 15th and appointed a committee to draft an appeal to the people of the state to support a call for a convention on the ground that there was a number of points in the Constitution that needed amending. No reference was made to slavery in this appeal. The public speakers and the press that was favorable to the convention persistently denied that the call for a convention was in any way connected with the subject of slavery. The appeal ordered by the conventionists in their caucus on the night of the 15th of February was published and scattered broadcast. The slavery party called their publication "An Appeal to the Citizens of Illinois." It was published in the Spectator on March 1, 1823.

As soon as the Legislature adjourned on the 18th, Governor Coles invited the principal anti-convention men to meet with him for the purpose of laying out a campaign against the proposal to vote on holding a convention to amend or rewrite the Constitution, which was really only a little more than four years old. At this meeting the whole subject was gone over and it was decided to lose no time in laying the purposes of the conventionists before the people of the state. The members of the Legislature who had opposed the convention were asked to put forth an address which would give openly and above board the conspiracy to make Illinois a slave state. "It was an impassioned appeal to the people to rise up in their might and save the state from the greatest shame and disaster that could ever be visited upon any people." The readers were asked to consider the "spectacle that would be presented to the civilized world of the people of Illinois innocent of this great national sin, and in the full enjoyment of all the blessings of free government, sitting down in solemn convention to deliberate and determine whether they should introduce among them a portion of their fellow beings, to be cut off from those blessings, to be loaded with chains of bondage, and rendered unable to leave any other legacy to their posterity than the inheritance of their own servitude. The wise and the good of all nations would blush at our political depravity." Fifteen out of the eighteen men who voted against a convention in the two houses of the Legislature signed this anti-convention appeal. Ten of the eighteen men were from slave states. These anti-conventionists called their address "An Appeal to the People of Illinois."

Public Men

At first glance it appeared that the convention forces included the most prominent men in the state. But the race is not always to the swift nor the battle to the strong. But David's supporters must have faith in the justness of their cause. The public men who favored a convention, and therefore wished incidently to introduce slavery into Illinois, included the following:

Elias Kent Kane was a graduate of Yale, a lawyer, member of the constitutional convention, secretary of state under Governor Bond, member of the General Assembly, United States senator, and a member of a very noted family. He also acted as a U. S. district judge a short time before Illinois was admitted to the Union. During the campaign for and against a convention, Mr. Kane managed the Republican Advocate, at Kaskaskia, a newspaper which was strong for the convention.

Thomas Reynolds was a lawyer of considerable standing at the bar. He was chief justice for a period and assisted Mr. Kane in managing the Republican Advocate. He later moved to Missouri, where he was elected governor of that state.

Theophilus W. Smith studied law under Aaron Burr. He was a citizen of Madison County, served in the Legislature and was a judge of the Supreme bench. He was one of the strong advocates of the convention. He is said to have learned politics from Tammany Hall. He had the credit of being the author of every move that was rash, reckless, and unprecedented. He was a very prominent politician.

Samuel McRoberts was a native of Monroe County. He was well educated. He served in minor offices and became a lawyer and a judge. He served in the Legislature, was United States district judge. He was a solicitor of the general land office, and served as United States senator.

Emanuel J. West was a citizen of Madison County. He was at one time a very energetic friend of Ninian Edwards, but later deserted Edwards' cause. He was a member of the Lower House in the Legislature when the convention question was before that body. He was resourceful and a constant fighter for the cause of slavery.

Alexander P. Field was from Union County. He was one of the leaders of the convention party in the Lower House. He was a Kentuckian. He was regarded as a very powerful lawyer. He served as secretary of state in Illinois for many years. He was secretary of Wisconsin Territory. He was hot and cold as a Union man in time of the Civil war. He lived at New Orleans at that time. He claimed a seat in the Thirty-eighth Congress and was supported by Judge Gillispie. He was seated and afterward refused the seat by the Congress.

Richard M. Young was a Kentuckian who settled in Jonesboro about 1817. He was a lawyer and was a member of the second General Assembly. He was a judge for many years. He was also a United States senator and held other offices of national importance.

John McLean was a lawyer at the age of twenty-three. He settled at Shawneetown in 1815. He was an orator of great power. He was Illinois' first representative in Congress. He was a member of the General Assembly. In 1824 he was elected United States senator to succeed Ninian Edwards, resigned. McLean County was named in his honor.

Jesse B. Thomas, a descendant of Lord Baltimore, came into Illinois through residence in Indiana, where he was an official in the Territorial Legislature. He favored the division of Indiana Territory and was one of the three judges of Illinois while it was a Territory. He was the president of the constitutional convention and was one of the first United States senators from Illinois. He was an avowed advocate of slavery, and was the author of the Missouri Compromise.

Shadrach Bond was a Maryland farm boy; came to Illinois in 1794. He lived with an uncle by the same name in the American Bottom. He served in the Indiana Territorial Legislature, and also as a delegate in Congress from the Illinois Territory. He was a receiver of public moneys in the Kaskaskia Land Office. He was the first governor of Illinois. He tried for other public offices, but was never successful in his campaigns. Reynolds thinks Bond was a blameless man.

Joseph Phillips was a Tennesseean who as a young man was a captain in the United States Rangers in the War of 1812. He became a lawyer. Was secretary of the Illinois Territory when it was admitted as a state. He was the first chief justice of the state. He was a candidate for governor in 1822 and was a strong pro-slavery man. In the campaign on the convention he was a pro-slavery champion.

John Reynolds was the fourth governor of Illinois. He came to Illinois as a young boy of eleven in 1800. He was very well educated. Was a member of the first Supreme Court. He was for slavery, but probably not rabid. He says that he was not elected on the Supreme Court for the second term because he was in favor of the convention. He was a member of Congress and served in the State Legislature.

William Kinney was a Baptist preacher and a politician. He was a good public speaker and a prominent worker in the campaign for the convention. He was influential in St. Clair County.

He served in the Legislature and was a prominent candidate for governor in 1834, but was defeated by Joseph Duncan.

Nearly all the writers who have spoken of a comparison between the advocates and opponents of the convention have regarded the pro-slavery group as the more prominent, and including the more influential public men. It will therefore be interesting to place over against the foregoing public men those who gave of their time, their means, and their prayers that the curse of slavery should not blacken the fair name of Illinois.

The following list includes some of the most prominent and influential anti-convention workers:

Edward Coles, a Virginian of education and culture, came into Illinois in 1819. He was conscientiously opposed to slavery. He freed some twenty slaves on his way from Virginia to Illinois. He was registrar of the Land Office at Edwardsville, was elected governor in 1822 against Judge Phillips, Judge Browne, and General James B. Moore. It was known that Coles was opposed to slavery, but not much emphasis was put upon the slavery question in the election of August, 1822. Mr. Coles gave his entire salary as governor, $4,000, to help carry on the convention fight.

Morris Birkbeck was an English immigrant who settled in Edwards County in 1818. He was very earnestly opposed to slavery and came into Illinois to settle because he thought the Ordinance of 1787 would forever prohibit slavery in this state. Mr. Birkbeck was a fluent writer and a fine conversationalist, but he seems not to have been a public speaker. His writings were published in the Illinois Gazette, edited by Henry Eddy, at Shawneetown.

John M. Peck was a Baptist preacher. He had come into Illinois about 1817 and had been very active in religious matters. He worked mostly along missionary lines. For nine years he rode up and down in Illinois and Missouri. In 1820 Mr. Peck settled at Rock Springs, eight and a half miles north of Belleville, St. Clair County. Here he founded the Rock Springs Seminary in 1826. This school was the beginning of Shurtliff College. Mr. Peck organized a sort of anti-convention society in St. Clair County immediately after the passage of the convention resolution by the Legislature. This St. Clair County society came to be known as the parent society, and fourteen other societies were organzied in as many other counties. Perhaps Mr. Peck's chief value to the cause of freedom in this great struggle was along the line of organization of the anti-convention forces.

Samuel D. Lockwood was from New York. He was admitted to the bar at the age of twenty-two in 1811. He held minor offices in New York State and in 1818 came down the Ohio River in company with William H. Brown. They landed at Shawneetown and walked to Kaskaskia. He was attorney-general in 1821 and when the convention fight came on he was one of the staunchest supporters of Governor Coles. He held many positions of honor in the state. He was elected a member of the Supreme Court in 1824-5. He lived in later life in Jacksonville, where he was a warm friend of Illinois College. Judge Lockwood's contribution toward the defeat of slavery in Illinois has been universally acknowledged. He was a vigorous contributor to the press.

Thomas Lippincott was a minister. He lived a while above Alton probably in Pike County and later worked in the land office in Edwardsville. His writings show that he was a man of considerable education and of deep convictions. For a short while he edited The Edwardsville Spectator. Later he took up the active work of the ministry in the Presbyterian church.

George Churchill was from the State of Vermont where as a young man he learned the art of journalism. He was a sort of rover and visited many of the larger eastern cities before arriving in St. Louis, Missouri in 1817. Later he took up land near Edwardsville and became a confirmed farmer. He was a warm friend of Hooper Warren and was a frequent contributor to The Spectator while the convention fight was on. He served long and faithfully in the State Legislature. He was held in high esteem by the leading men of his day.

David Blackwell belonged to a prominent family of the early years of statehood. He was a lawyer who resided at Belleville. In 1820 he was elected a member of the State Legislature. He was secretary of state in 1823. He was connected with the intelligencer which opposed the convention. The paper was first pro-convention but was bought by Blackwell and put to work against slavery.

Daniel P. Cook was a friend to Edward Coles. He was a Kaskaskia lawyer at the age of twenty in 1815. He was part owner of The Illinois Intelligencer, and at the same time was auditor of the Illinois Territory. He was a special messenger from President Monroe to John Quincy Adams, our minister at the court of St. James. He was the state's first attorney-general. He labored to prevent Illinois from becoming a slave state. He was a son-in-law of Ninian Edwards. He was a great campaigner. He used all his bright talents to prevent the curse of slavery from spreading over Illinois.

Thomas Mather was a merchant, but that did not prevent him from taking an active interest against making Illinois a slave state. He carried on a big trade between Kaskaskia and New Orleans. He was a United States commissioner to locate a road from Independence, Missouri, to Santa Fe, New Mexico. He vigorously opposed the passage of the convention resolution.

Hooper Warren was a newspaper man. He came from Vermont to St. Louis, working on the big papers along his way. He is said to have been bitterly opposed to slavery. He established The Spectator in Vandalia and it entered heartily into the work of saving Illinois. He afterwards established the first paper in Springfield and still later one in Galena. After some local office holding he published a paper in Chicago. He made his final residence at Henry, Marshall County.

Jonathan H. Pugh was an emigrant from Kentucky. He was a member of the Legislature when the convention question was raised. He represented Bond County. He took an active part in the cause of freedom though not a leading part. He moved to Springfield and was the second lawyer to establish himself there.

George Forquer was a prominent official in early Illinois history. He was a half brother of Governor Ford. He settled at New Design in 1804, and later was interested in the town of Waterloo. He was secretary of state, attorney-general, representative in the General Assembly, register of the land office in Springfield. He was a good friend to Governor Coles.

Henry Eddy was in his early years a printer, but he was also a lawyer of prominence in the southeastern part of the state in the first two decades of statehood. He brought his printing press with him from Pittsburg. He located in Shawneetown and put out the first issue on September 5, 1818. The paper was first called the Shawnee Chief, but the name was later changed to Illinois Emigrant, and in 1819 the paper was named the Illinois Gazette. Henry Eddy was probably not radical, but is said to have favored the anti-convention doctrines. He was at least willing to print both sides of the case. However, it has been observed that the convention people did not rush into print as did the "antis." Mr. Birkbeck wrote many articles which were printed in Mr. Eddy's paper.

William H. Brown was a native of New York where he studied law. He came to Illinois about the time Illinois was admitted to the Union. He served as clerk of the United States District Court, Judge Pope, presiding. While residing at Vandalia, he became part owner of the Illinois Intelligencer with Mr. Wm. Berry. The latter was a member of the Legislature and was favorable to the convention. The work of unseating of Hansen and seating of Shaw was given in full in the first issue of the Intelligencer, which was printed after these events occurred. The printing of these details caused Mr. Brown to be compelled to sell his share of the paper to Mr. Robert Blackwell. Another change in ownership in the winter of 1823-4, made the paper anti-convention, and it was a powerful organ for freedom to the close of the campaign. Mr. Brown moved to Chicago where he became engaged in many public enterprises. He was a personal friend of Mr. Lincoln.

From these short sketches of the men who were the chief actors in the drama of 1823-4, we can easily see that the important men of the state were concerned either for or against the proposition to make Illinois a slave state.

Outside Help

It should be said that there were strong forces at work beyond the borders of the state both for and against the convention. "The press of the South as well as the papers of St. Louis, which had a considerable circulation in Illinois at that time, ably supported the convention." The cause of freedom had the help of Henry Biddle of Philadelphia, and of Roberts Vaux and other rich Quakers of that city. "At first the weight of influence and power seemed to be on the side of the conventionists"—"The chief strength of the opponents of the convention lay in the number of gifted writers and thinkers who enlisted in their cause. Many of the articles written by them were so exceedingly well conceived and so cleverly put, that the conventionist writers were never able to controvert them.—It is a notable fact, moreover, that a large number of ministers took part in the contest, and always on the side of the anti-conventionists." The Rev. John M. Peck, who organized the St. Clair Anti-Convention Society, stated that there were thirty ministers present when the organization was formed.

There is no doubt that the purpose of rewriting the Constitution of 1818 and so modifying it as to establish slavery as an institution on the same footing as it then had in the Carolinas, or Virginia—there is no doubt that this purpose was in the minds of many people in the years immediately following the admission of the state in 1818. Nor can we easily conceive that such a question could be hidden under a bushel. The anti-slavery people knew that the matter was considered and would likely soon come up as an embarrassing question to be dealt with. Now while it is true that the friends and the foes of slavery knew that the battle would soon need to be fought out, there seems to have been only the broad outlines of plans of procedure worked out by the conventionists, and few or no plans of defense agreed upon by the anti-convention forces. And while this appears to be the facts in the case, a careful analysis of the various means made use of by both sides would tend to lead us to believe that they had long been in contemplation.

A Bitter Campaign

And now began one of the most important campaigns, because so far reaching in its consequences, that was ever waged in any state of this Union. The slavery party had become intoxicated with its success and was not in a frame of mind to take a dispassionate view of the problem before it. So far the supporters of slavery had succeeded by mere brute force and unscrupulous scheming, but now the final victory can not be so won. The supporters of slavery must go before the people and show the advantages of slavery, if it have any. It is now a question to be solved by the Christian conscience of the people.

But the struggle before the people and among the people, was destined to be a very bitter and violent one. When selfish personal interests are at stake, and when great and fundamental principles are involved, the contest is sure to be accompanied by demonstrations of violent passions. "Never was such canvass made in the state before. The young and old, without regard to sex, entered the arena of party strife; families and neighborhoods became divided, and surrendered themselves up to a bitter warfare. Detraction and personal abuse reigned supreme, while conflicts were not infrequent.

PAMPHLETS, APPEALS, POSTERS, ETC.

Among the means made use of by both sides was a form of publicity which appears modern. The convention people seem to have realized first, the need of getting their case before the people. The conduct of public servants the night of February 11th, following the losing vote in the House by reason of Hansen's failure to vote for the convention, and the hasty procedure in the halls of legislation on the 12th when Hansen was unseated and Shaw was voted a seat, were acts that must be counteracted by an appeal to ignorance and prejudice.

The conventionists held a meeting on the night of the 15th of February as has been mentioned, and issued "An Appeal to the Citizens of Illinois." This appeal was first put out in a broadsheet but later published in the newspapers. It was the policy of the pro-slavery people to keep the subject of slavery in the background. No mention was made of slavery in this first appeal. The appeal was made on the ground that there were several features of the Constitution that ought to be amended. These were minor matters. Governor Reynolds wrote in 1855: "If the deranged state of the currency had not existed, and the country had been in a happy and prosperous condition, a convention to introduce slavery would never have been dreamed of." At first as has been said the conventionists kept the slavery question in the background, but long before the campaign was over the real purpose of the convention was admitted by all.

On the 18th of February as has been stated, the anti-conventionists put forth an "Appeal to the People of Illinois." This appeal boldly denounced the action of the Legislature in forcing upon the people this question of making Illinois a slave state.

The purpose to force slavery upon the state was affirmed in this appeal.

In addition to these two appeals there were hundreds of pamphlets, tracts, hand bills, and posters scattered broadcast over the country. It is said some of these pamphlets, bills, etc., were very inflammatory. The authors of much of this literature as well as those who distributed it were not known to the general public. But it must not be thought that everything of this kind was done in the dark, for many on both sides were very bold in their work.

There was no one who with either tongue or pen, did more to bring about the triumphant defeat of the slavery party than Morris Birkbeck of Wanborough, Edwards County. Mr. Birkbeck was a polished and fluent speaker and writer. He wrote with ease and great force, and being thoroughly sympathetic with the anti-convention cause he gave of his time and energy unreservedly. He wrote pamphlets which were scattered throughout the state. On January 29, 1824, Governor Coles wrote to Mr. Birkbeck saying: "I had the pleasure to receive—six of your pamphlets, which you were so good as to send me.—I could not but wish that every conventionist in the state had it and was compelled to read it with attention. Our society at Edwardsville intends to have another and larger edition of it reprinted for the purpose of having it extensively circulated."

No one person did more to distribute these pamphlets, hand bills, and circulars than the Rev. John M. Peck. Mr. Peck was a Baptist preacher, and acted as agent for the American Bible Society. His duties as agent for this organization were to travel over the state and distribute bibles where there seemed little religious interest. Mr. Peck had no conscientious scruples against distributing pamphlets and loose literature in favor of freedom, at the same time that he distributed bibles. And thus he performed a great service to humanity—a double service. He brought spiritual light to benighted souls and moral and political insight for all into the duties of American citizenship. The old fashioned saddle bags which every traveler carried in those days were found well adapted for this kind of campaigning.

PUBLIC SPEAKING

In the early days that we are now studying, oratory was one of the essential qualifications of a successful lawyer. Public speaking was an art that was cultivated by every one who expected to hold public office or engage in most of the professions. The personal appeal is often effective in stirring up sluggish minds where other forms of persuasion are not effective. The human voice is attractive, and when accompaning a chain of logic is convincing. It will be noticed that among twenty-seven prominent men who took part in the convention fight that fourteen of them were lawyers, three of them preachers.

The man who expected to address the assembled people provided himself with a firstly, a secondly, a thirdly, and sometimes a fourthly. And so it fell out that men, good speakers, went about over the state explaining, persuading, and begging the voters to come to the polls and do their duty as good citizens. The county seats, the sittings of the courts, and other public places and gatherings, furnished the occasions for the flow of persuasive oratory. At public dinners toasts were given which revealed the spirit in which the contest was carried on. Some of the toasts ran—"The Convention, the means of introducing and spreading the African family." "The Enemies of the Convention—may they ride a porcupine saddle on a hard trotting horse a long way without money and without friends." "The state of Illinois—the ground is good, prairies in abundance, give us plenty of negroes, a little industry and she will distribute her treasures." One need hardly be told that these toasts are the expressions of an intemperate, untenable, and losing cause. There are no signs in these toasts of seriousness, on indication of high and lofty ideal of social and political institutions. They breathe the spirit of revenge and an ungenerous heart.

In contrast with these we need only to quote a few toasts given by the fearless public speakers who were at all times conscious of the justness of their cause—the men who were fighting a winning battle. "The crisis—it is big with the fate of Illinois, and requires every friend of freedom to rally under the banners of the constitution." "The Freedom of the Late Northwest—may it be like the little stone that was cut out without hands and became a great mountain and filled the earth." "The convention or no convention—the world listens to hear the decision of our moral and political character pronounced by ourselves." "We have confidence in the people of Illinois to support a free constitution and prohibit slavery; if we should be disappointed in the people we still have confidence in the general government."

There can be little doubt that the ministers of the various churches were almost to a man on the side of the anti-conventionists. William H. Brown, who went through the campaign as an opponent of slavery, in an address before the Chicago Historical Society in 1864, said: "The Protestant Church in all its denominations, though divided in forms and doctrines, was united upon this vital question. Its members, active and diligent, labored to convince their convention neighbors of the error of their views, and to bring them over to the right side, and its ministers were heard not only in the pulpit, but upon the stump; and their influence was felt and acknowledged."

It is said of Daniel P. Cook that he was an invincible speaker for the anti-slavery side. The conventionists had no man who could meet him in public discussion. When he returned from Washington, D. C., in the early summer of 1824 and began his campaign for reelection to Congress, he coupled with his personal fortunes the fortune of the anti-convention cause and boldly went forth a champion whom no conventionist cared to meet. Mr. Cook's opponent was Ex-Governor Bond, who was not in a sense a public speaker but a man who was regarded very highly.

Secret Societies

It may be that this sub-title is not happily chosen, but if not the matter will be understood as we proceed. As soon as the convention resolution was passed and the Legislature was adjourned, the Rev. John M. Peck called a meeting of opponents in St. Clair County. This gathering organized as the "St. Clair Society for the prevention of Slavery in the State of Illinois." One of its purposes was the "disseminating light and knowledge on the subject of slavery by cool and dispassionate reasoning, by circulating pamphlets, hand bills, and other publications. The general plan was similar to that of our county central committee. There was a central organization of probably twenty men. Then in each part of the county—township or voting precinct there was a group of say five secret workers. These local workers in the various parts of the county would gather information as to the changes in sentiment in their vicinity and report these things to the central committee which had headquarters at the county seat. There were similar organizations in fourteen other counties beside the parent society in St. Clair.

The idea of secrecy was an essential thing and it was this that made it possible to carry on the work without hindrance by the opposing workers. The local workers were not known to the public and so their observations could be freely made without the enemy's knowing that they were being observed. The Rev. Mr. Peck was a sort of self-appointed generalissimo of all the societies that were thus organized. His county took the initiative in organizing the first one and naturally St. Clair County became the headquarters of all the anti-slavery societies.

The convention people also were organized very much as the anti-slavery people were, and their purposes were of course the dissemination of the convention argument, in the form of pamphlets, and other printed forms of campaigning.

The Churches

It is difficult for one born and bred in Illinois to imagine the churches, as organizations, taking sides with the cause of which, if it wins, will bring slavery into Illinois. Surely we will not find that any did. On the contrary we find that "The conventionists complained of the influence of the clergy which was generally thrown on the anti-slavery side. The Christian Church conference located on the Wabash and a Baptist sect, the Friends of Humanity, both denounced slavery as a sin. The Methodist circuit riders and preachers assailed slavery and slaveholders to the point of provoking bitter retorts." It has been stated that all the preachers of all denominations were zealously opposed to the convention.

The Newspapers

During the campaign there were published in Illinois five weekly newspapers. These papers were—

The Spectator. This paper was established at Edwardsville by Hooper Warren in the spring of 1819. When the slavery struggle opened up in 1822-3, The Spectator was against the convention. It has been authoritatively stated that Warren and Coles were not on good terms. But Coles seems to have supported Warren at least in the campaign of 1823-4.

When the anti-slavery people met on the 18th of February and drew up an appeal they made a contribution of nearly $200 to pay for extra copies of Mr. Warren's paper and to pay toward the cost of maintaining a loyal paper. The paper was probably the most powerful newspaper in the state.

The Illinois Intelligencer. This paper was formerly a Kaskaskia paper, but was moved to Vandalia when the capital was moved to the latter place. The paper was owned and edited by William Berry and W. H. Brown. Mr. Berry was a member of the Legislature and was pro-convention. Mr. Brown wrote an editorial which was published in the issue of February 15, 1823. In this editorial Mr. Brown asserted that the object of a convention was the introduction of slavery into the state. For this editorial, Mr. Brown was forced to sell his interest in the paper. The Intelligencer then became an outspoken champion of the convention. Toward the end of the campaign Mr. Berry failed in business and the paper fell into the hands of Mr. Coles's friends who reversed its policy. It was an anti-convention sheet till the close of the campaign.

The Illinois Gazette. This paper was founded in Shawneetown in 1818, by Mr. Henry Eddy, a lawyer of considerable ability. It was first called the Shawnee Chief, then the Illinois Immigrant, and again the name was changed to the Illinois Gazette. Henry Eddy is classed as an anti-conventionist. His paper was open to argument offered by both sides. Morris Birkbeck contributed many articles to the Illinois Gazette. Governor Reynolds, who was in official life during the convention struggle, says: "Hooper Warren, in his paper, the Edwardsville Spectator, and the paper at Shawneetown, edited by Henry

Eddy, together with the Intelligencer, waged a fiery efficient warfare during the whole canvass."

The Illinois Republican. The campaign work of the Illinois Republican was not of a very high order. It was vigorous, outspoken, and bitter. It was established to carry on the campaign for the conventionists. There was no responsible editor at times, but the paper was managed by a group of radical proslavery men among whom was Theophilus W. Smith. Pease says in Vol. 2, Illinois Centennial History: "Conventionist accused them (Methodist circuit riders) of denouncing slavery in Illinois and stopping at the houses of slaveholders in Missouri, and pronounced their real dislike of a convention due to the fear that it might exclude them from the Legislature."

Note: The point was that a new constitution might prohibit ministers of the Gospel from serving as members of the General Assembly. This matter was discussed in the Contitutional Convention of 1818.

Mr. Pease says further: "The Illinois Republican was so prolific in abuse of this sort that Warren took occasion to brand it as hostile to the Methodists as a body. He believed further, he said, that the clergy of all denominations were zealous in opposition to the convention."

Theophilus W. Smith, the manager of the Illinois Republican, as has been stated previously, had his early training under Aaron Burr, and this fact may account for the spirit of the paper.

Just what influence the five papers had in determining the final result is not easy to estimate. All the evidence points to the fact that the papers were all vigorously, if not always conscientiously, edited, and they were always open to contributions from the best writers of those days. One thing we know, the papers were eagerly read, and we may conclude that in their respective fields of circulation they exerted an influence which was not less important than that of any other agency made use of in the campaign.

The Election

The constitution provided for a general election in August of each even numbered year. At this election only state and county officials were elected—a governor, lieutenant-governor, state senators, representatives in the General Assembly of the state, sheriffs, and coroners. All other state and county officials provided for in the constitution were to be selected either by appointment of the governor and confirmation by the Senate or by election in joint session of the Legislature. The election of Congressmen was held in November, the first Tuesday after the first Monday.

The resolution providing for a vote by the people on the

question of a convention for amending or rewriting the constitution of 1818, named the next general election, namely, August, 1824, as the date when the election should take place. At this general election the people should vote for or against a convention. The fateful day arrived. The election was orderly but full of interest. There were at that time thirty counties in the state. The total vote was 11,612; 4,972 for the convention, and 6,640 against the convention. The anti-slavery party had won by 1,668 votes.

Vote By Counties
General Election, 1824

Abstract of vote for and against convention August 2, A. D. 1824:

Counties	For Convention	Against Convention
Alexander	75	51
Bond	63	240
Clark	31	116
Crawford	134	262
Edgar	3	234
Edwards	189	391
Fayette	125	121
Franklin	170	113
Fulton	5	60
Gallatin	597	133
Greene	164	379
Hamilton	173	85
Jackson	180	93
Jefferson	99	43
Johnson	74	74
Lawrence	158	261
Madison	351	563
Marion	45	52
Monroe	141	196
Montgomery	74	90
Morgan	42	432
Pike	19	165
Pope	263	124
Randolph	357	284
Sangamon	153	722
St. Clair	408	506
Union	213	240
Washington	112	173
Wayne	180	111
White	355	326
	4,972	6,640

Majority against the convention, 1,668

Some notion may be had of the interest in the convention question by noting the votes for presidential electors in the following November compared with the vote on the convention question. Pope cast 397 votes on the convention proposition, while her total vote for electors was 84. Gallatin cast on convention question 730 votes, on electors 315. St. Clair on convention question 914, on electors 399.

The total vote cast on the convention question was 11,612, while the total vote for presidential electors at election in November of the same year in the thirty counties was but 4,671.

After any election in which there is considerable interest, there are always wise-acres who can tell just how it happened. It is said that the anti-convention people were full of hope that the election would be favorable to freedom. It is also stated that the convention people were somewhat discouraged as to the outcome. But at this date we may make a few observations as to the general attitude of the people toward the question to be settled. It appears that there were four distinct elements in the population that were determining factors in the election.

1. The remnant of the old French settlers who held slaves, together with those Americans who had settled along the Mississippi River and either owned slaves or would if they were able. This group would of course vote for the convention.

2. There was a strong pro-slavery leaning among those immigrants who had come into Illinois from the old slave states. They had always been used to the "peculiar institution" and would like to see it established in Illinois. This group voted for the convention.

3. A third group who favored the introduction of slavery was made up of those men who were either directly or indirectly connected with the manufacture of salt in Illinois. In the early days of statehood the salt industry in Illinois was not only a source of revenue to the state, but as an economic activity it produced large returns to the people directly and indirectly connected with it. These voted for slavery.

4. The anti-slavery views of those people who had come into Illinois from the free states were difficult to change. Many of them were conscientiously opposed to slavery and to the indenture system. It mattered not to them that slavery would relieve the economic stress of the farmers, timber men, and manufacturers. They were champions of free labor and voted against the convention.

5. The intense disfavor with which all English immigrants looked upon slavery was a barrier against which arguments, sophistry, personal gain or threats made little or no headway. Morris Birkbeck and George Flower set the standards for the English settlers.

6. Lastly we may call attention to the large sprinkle of German and Swiss immigrants which had settled in the western and northern counties. It was indeed an absurd proposition for any European laborer to come to the United States to better his life and then to sit down and deliberately vote to introduce slavery into the state.

REFLECTIONS

In the congressional election which occurred in November, 1824, the candidates were Daniel P. Cook, candidate for reelection, and Ex-Governor Bond. In the convention campaign Cook was opposed to the convention and Bond was for it. Cook was elected by a good majority—out of only 4,707 votes cast in comparison with the 11,612 cast in August.

The Legislature, which was elected in August, at the time the convention was defeated, was anti-slavery. But on joint ballot John McLean, a brilliant convention orator from Shawneetown, was elected United States senator over Ninian Edwards, who was neutral in the convention struggle. A week later than the election of McLean, Elias Kent Kane, another convention champion, defeated Governor Coles and Samuel D. Lockwood for United States senator.

The two men who did most to keep slavery out of Illinois, Governor Coles and Morris Birkbeck, profited nothing from all their unselfish work. We have just seen that Coles was defeated by a Legislature that was largely against slavery. Coles' nominees to office were rejected by the Senate, and his recommendations to the Legislature were ignored Suit was brought against him to recover $200 for each slave which he brought to Illinois and freed. The state won the suit and the penalty hung over his head for some time before the whole matter was dropped. Nearly all the buildings on his farm at Edwardsville, together with 200 fruit trees, were consumed in an incendiary fire.

Morris Birkbeck's nomination as secretary of state was rejected by the Senate. He was disappointed in the returns from his farming enterprises, estranged from his friends, criticised for his lack of religion, hanged in effigy in the state's capital, hunted with pistols, and forced to make his escape to save his life. He lost his life while crossing a swollen river and thus ended the life of the most talented man connected with the early history of Illinois.

On the 9th of December, the old frame statehouse which had been erected as the first capitol at Vandalia burned to the ground, consuming many of the state's records. The anti-slavery party accused the conventionists of setting fire to this building. Harris, in "Negro Servitude in Illinois," says a mob paraded the streets, set fire to the statehouse and hanged Governor Coles in effigy, amid mournful groans. The supposition was that the conventionists set the statehouse on fire in order to burn up the records of the session of 1822-3. This it would appear was a serious charge, but Mr. Harris says that the convention people never successfully denied the charge.

Between December 9, 1823, when the wooden capitol burned, and November 15, 1824, a substantial brick capitol had been erected at Vandalia, at a cost of $12,381.50, of which amount the citizens of Vandalia paid $3,000.

CHAPTER III

POLITICS, NATIONAL AND STATE

PARTIES—COMPROMISE—CAMPAIGN 1826—GOVERNOR EDWARDS—THE COURTS—PENITENTIARY—PUBLIC LANDS—PUBLIC MEN

From the adoption of the Constitution, and election of Washington, to 1800, when Jefferson was chosen President, there were no well organized political parties. There were well defined differences in the policies of statesmen concerning the organization and administration of government. This difference came out of the question of the interpretation of the Constitution. The group of statesmen into whose hands the Government fell believed in a liberal interpretation of the Constitution, that there were implied powers; while their opponents believed in a strict interpretation and rejected the implied powers theory.

PARTIES

From the coming of Jefferson as President to the close of the War of 1812, the strict constructionists held sway. This group was known as anti-federalists or republicans. The party, if it may be so called, championed these principles—equal and exact justice to all, peace and friendship with all nations, alliances with none, respect for the rights of the state governments, the preservation of the rights of the National Government, free elections, free speech, free press, reliance in a disciplined militia, public economy, encouragement to agriculture and commerce, trial by jury, persuasion in preference to force. Alexander Hamilton believed the new party more revolutionary in theory than in practice. The old federalist party, which had laid the foundations of the Government in a strong centralization of power, and in the doctrine of implied powers, was an onlooker from 1800 to 1815.

At the close of the War of 1812, the statemen who had championed the rights of Americans upon the seas, and had pushed the war to a successful conclusion, reversed the Jeffersonian policies, at least to the extent that practically the old federalist doctrines of protection, a national banking system, and internal improvements were adopted. These measures and others were supported so generally by the representatives from all sections of the Union that they became national measures, and sectionalism disappeared at least until the Territory of Missouri applied for admission into the Union.

Illinois came into the Union just at a time when sectionalism was revived and the foundations of future political parties were being laid. The two United States senators from Illinois who took their seats in the early winter of 1818 were soon tempted to enter into the national political game then beginning. Ninian Edwards and Jesse B. Thomas were chosen to the upper branch of the National Congress. But when these two statesmen were put into the Senate classes they fell into short term classes. Mr. Edwards' time expired March 4, 1819, while Thomas' term ended March 4, 1823. Mr. Edwards, who had served as territorial governor from 1809 to 1818, wished very much to succeed himself, and so announced himself. He was opposed by Col. Michael Jones, of Shawneetown. Here there was developed an anti-Edwards party. But when the test came Mr. Edwards was elected by a vote of twenty-three to nineteen. Thomas and Edwards were therefore in the United States Senate all through the Missouri struggle and both are said to have "consistently supported the cause of Missouri." In the meantime John McLean, in the House of Representatives, voted also in favor of the slavery party on the Missouri question. The Congress which received our senators and our representative expired by limitation on March 4, 1819. Since there was no Federal election in Illinois in November, 1818, it was necessary to hold an election in the summer of 1819 so the state would have a representative in Congress at the opening of the session in December, 1819. In the contest for this place there appeared Daniel Pope Cook and John McLean. The latter was taken to task for voting for slavery in the preliminary skirmish in the effort to admit Missouri as a slave state. "Mr. McLean defended his vote on the ground that the attempted dictation to Missouri of an anti-slavery proviso was a violation of state sovereignty." Cook was elected.

Compromise

Although Edwards' friends claimed that he was not a pro-slavery man, he voted with the pro-slavery party in the admission of Missouri. Thomas made no effort to conceal the fact that he was for slavery and won considerable notoriety by introducing the compromise resolution in the United States Senate as follows: "That in all that territory ceded by France to the United States under the name of Louisiana, which lies north of 36° 30' north latitude, not included within the limits of the state contemplated by this act, slavery—shall be and is hereby forever prohibited." In the Lower House of the National Legislature Cook voted against the admission of Missouri as a slave state.

Many thoughtful people in Illinois both for and against slavery studied very carefully the conflict waged by the opposing forces in the Missouri struggle. Those who favored slavery felt encouraged when the slavery interests won in the Missouri battle.

The friends of freedom foresaw that the same struggle was to be fought out in Illinois, and so there was unrest and uncertainty from 1822 to 1824.

Edwards and Thomas were not as well united on the support of a presidential candidate in 1824 as they were on the admission of Missouri. Thomas seemed to favor Crawford for President, while Edwards was for Calhoun. They were not harmonious about the distribution of patronage. As early as May, 1823, Calhoun had suggested to President Monroe the appointment of Edwards as minister to Mexico. In January, 1823, Thomas was elected to succeed himself as senator, though there was a strong effort made to defeat him.

Trouble of a business nature was brewing between Crawford, the secretary of the treasury and Senator Edwards, who was a stockholder in the Bank of Edwardsville. The Edwardsville Bank was made a bank of deposit of the funds derived from the sale of public lands. The bank was very lax in its dealings with the United States Treasury, and in 1821 the bank failed and the Government lost something like $50,000 in the crash. The gap widened between Crawford and Edwards. A bitter personal controversy ensued between the secretary of the treasury and the senator from Illinois. Both had appeared before a committee of investigation and both had been unwise in accusations against the other.

The President sent the name of Senator Edwards to the Senate as minister to Mexico. The politics in this seemed to be that Calhoun wished to secure Illinois in the presidential contest of 1824, and to that end he was willing to recommend Edwards to President Monroe, while Cook, a strong man in the House of Representatives, had allied himself with Adams, secretary of state to the President. It was in this way that influence was brought to bear upon President Monroe to make the appointment.

Edwards had not been an influential member of the Senate in the years 1822-23. He was disturbed by financial troubles at home, and somewhat handicapped by ill health. He was no doubt conscious of his loss of standing before the public through his unfortunate contention with Mr. Crawford, the secretary of the treasury. The Senate hesitated to confirm the appointment, but was finally led to do so. Mr. Edwards made preparations to take up his work at Mexico City, but before his departure a fresh cause of outbreak between Crawford and Edwards developed. The House of Representatives had appointed a committee to investigate the conduct of the treasury and Edwards was called to Washington to testify before this committee. It turned out that Edwards could not make good on all the charges he had previously made against Crawford, and Edwards was discredited. In this investigation Crawford's friends took especial pains to make it appear that much of the criticism of Crawford's management of the treasury, especially in its relation to the banks of the country, was without any basis in fact. The committee exonerated Crawford, which of course left Edwards in an embarrassing situation.

Mr. Edwards was forced to resign his appointment as minister to Mexico, having previously resigned the senatorship. He was now left at the bottom of the ladder and it was a question whether he could ever "come back." In the meantime his son-in-law, Daniel Pope Cook, was holding up the sinking fortunes of the Edwards family. In 1819 he defeated John McLean for a seat in Congress, in 1820 he defeated Elias Kent Kane, in 1822 he beat McLean, and in 1824 he defeated Bond. These three defeated candidates, McLean, Kane and Bond, were strong and popular fellows, but Cook was able in spite of combinations and bitter opposition to win in these congressional campaigns.

In 1824 the presidential campaign was on. There were four prominent men before the country for this high office. John Quincy Adams, of Massachusetts, secretary of state under Monroe; William Crawford, of Georgia, secretary of the treasury in the Cabinet; Henry Clay, of Kentucky, speaker of the House of Representatives; John C. Calhoun, secretary of war in the Cabinet; and Andrew Jackson, of Tennessee, senator from that state. In the preliminary skirmish, as has been said, Edwards was favorable to Calhoun, while Cook supported Secretary of State Adams. There were no political organizations and the contest among these five men resolved itself into a personal and sectional campaign. As the campaign opened in 1824 for the November elections, the situation was somewhat relieved by the fact that Calhoun withdrew from the presidential race and entered for the vice presidency.

Illinois was entitled to three votes in the electoral college and the three electors were to be chosen in three electoral districts, the Southwestern the third, the Southeastern the second and the Northern the first. In the first after playing much local politics, there were four candidates—one each for Jackson, Clay, Crawford, and Adams. The Adams elector was chosen. In the third district there was little trouble in selecting a Jackson elector, and in the second district after a good deal of scheming to beat the Jackson elector he was elected. The elector from the first electoral district, the Northern, was William Harrison; from the second district, the Southeastern, Henry Eddy; from the third district, the Southwestern, Alexander Field.

It was generally believed that with four strong candidates running for the presidency, that the election would be thrown into the House of Representatives. It was therefore desirable to know how the representative, Mr. Cook, would vote since he was a candidate for reelection. He probably did not wish to tie his hands, but let it be understood that he would vote for the one who received the highest vote in Illinois. The vote stood, Adams, 1,542; Jackson, 1,272; Clay, 1,047; Crawford, 219. This vote does not include 629 cast for a candidate who was not definite about for whom he would vote. When it was found that there was no choice by the electoral college, and that the election would go to the House of Representatives, the battle was begun anew. Cook, being the only representative from Illinois, cast the vote of this state for John Quincy Adams, who was elected.

Campaign of 1826

The presidential election of 1824 being over, the people and politicians began early to consider men and measures for the Illinois campaign of 1826. At the election there were to be elected a governor to succeed Coles, lieutenant governor, and members of the general assembly, and other officials. A member of the Lower House of Congress to succeed Mr. Cook was to be elected.

When Mr. Edwards had time to recover from the humiliation which came from his contest with Crawford, he was anxious to get back into public life again. He was a candidate to fill the vacancy made by his own resignation from the United States Senate. But he was beaten by John McLean, who had suffered defeat at the hands of Cook for the lower house. Mr. Edwards was now in the summer of 1825 out of public office. He had been in office in Illinois since 1809. He was territorial governor till 1818 and then elected United States Senator. He is said to have lost $50,000 since he had given his time to the public service. Surely, if any one ever had cause for discouragement, Mr. Edwards had at this time. But he could not believe that the action of the General Assembly in electing McLain United States senator over himself was a correct index of the attitude of the people of the state toward one who had served them so faithfully. He therefore, as early as June, 1825, decided to appeal directly to the people for an expression of their confidence and interest in himself. He announced himself as a candidate for governor of Illinois. The election would be held in August, 1826. His judgment of the people's interest in himself was good as shown by the election, but it is more than likely that he did not think that the old feud once so bitter could be so easily revived.

Mr. Edwards' opponents were Thomas Sloo, Jr., and Lieutenant Governor Hubbard. These were strong Jackson men. Edwards had favored Calhoun until he withdrew and offered himself for the vice presidency. He then supported Jackson but not strong enough to offend the Adams men in the state. Mr. Sloo had come into prominence as a successful business man in McLeansboro and as a state senator in the convention fight. He was a quiet gentleman of fair ability only. He was not well known over the state. Mr. Hubbard was a lawyer of Shawneetown and was a well known character. He also desired to test his popularity in the race for governor.

Mr. Edwards met with much encouragement in the early days of the canvass. The Jackson men in Illinois were anxious to show Mr. Crawford that he had misjudged the people in the presidential election in 1824. They thought the best way to humiliate Crawford would be to elect his enemy, Mr. Edwards, governor. Mr. Edwards decided upon a thorough canvass, but he could not withstand the temptation to expose the tottering condition of the State Bank and to condemn the action of the general assembly in paying the officials of the state three times as much in the State Bank bills as they were entitled to in good money. The issuing of auditor's warrants on the same plan was vigorously assailed. Very naturally enough, the men who sat in the Legislature at the time these questionable things were done were all against Mr. Edwards. He was attacked by writers in the papers as a broken down autocrat of a former regime. He was told that the men over whom he used to hector in territorial days were no longer subject to his orders or if they were, they were no longer of any political influence. John Marshall warned him: "You must be aware now that the freedom with which you commented on the management of the finances, State Bank, etc., however just, was nevertheless very unpolitick."

At the same time that Edwards was running for the governorship, his son-in-law, Daniel Pope Cook, was asking for reelection as congressman from Illinois. Mr. Cook had for his opponent a quiet man who was not yet so well known, Joseph Duncan. Mr. Duncan had won well deserved honors in the War of 1812. He might carry if he wished a sword presented to him by Congress as a token of the nation's gratitude for faithful services rendered at a critical time. He had served a term in the state Senate and was now ambitious to represent Illinois in the halls of Congress: The opponents of Mr. Cook could muster only two objections to him as a candidate. One was that he had voted for Adams in the election which had been thrown into the House in the winter of 1825. The other was that he belonged to the Edwards dynasty. In his favor it could be said that Cook was a faithful public servant, he was now recognized as one of the strong men in the Lower House. It should be stated that Cook had defeated McLean, Kane and Bond for Congress and their friends would naturally be lined up for Mr. Duncan. When the smoke of the battle had cleared away it was found that Edwards was elected by a small margin, while Duncan had defeated Cook by a safe majority.

Daniel P. Cook was a man who did much for Illinois. He is credited with securing the passage of the law which granted to Illinois the alternate five sections upon each side of Illinois and Michigan Canal route from Chicago to Ottawa. It was with the proceeds of the sale of this grant of land that the state was assisted in the building of the canal. In honor of the unflagging interest which Cook showed in this enterprise the state named the county of Cook after this distinguished Congressman.

Governor Edwards

The Legislature elected in August, 1824, was made up largely of new men. There were, however, some familiar faces in both houses. Field, McLean, Will, Reynolds, Hall, Casey, Gard and others. The governor was inducted into office in December, 1826. He was known as a very dignified, formal gentleman. He appeared before the joint assembly in costume of the Revolutionary days—gold lace, ruffles, knee breeches, silk stockings and powdered hair. He presented for the consideration of the General Assembly a number of subjects among which were taxation, expenditures, and mismanagement of the state bank. The Legislature was very largely Jackson men and there was no sympathy with the governor's plans for working out state problems.

As Edwards' troubles in Congress came out of his accusations against Mr. Crawford, Secretary of the Treasury, for bad financial policies, so, as a candidate for governor, he drew upon himself the wrath of the large number of local politicians who had had to do with the management of the State Bank. He showed in his public addresses that the state was in debt $150,000; and that the annual expenses were $25,000 a year while the income was about $40,000 yearly. He showed that most of the state's revenue came from the taxing of non-resident land owners. The taxes were required to be paid every two years, while resident property owners were forced to pay their taxes annually.

The whole campaign in the latter part of 1825 and the first part of 1826 was given over, on the part of Mr. Edwards, to an enumeration of the shortcomings of those who had carried on government for the past three or four years. In the inaugural he spoke of the delinquencies of the State Bank and said "its concerns had been loosely and irregularly conducted." He said money had been loaned without security and in amounts contrary to law. The law provided that no person could borrow more than $100 on personal security and not more than $1,000 on real estate security. In subsequent messages he showed that a loan of $2,050 had been made on real estate and when the mortgage was foreclosed, the real estate was valued at $737.75, and when sold brought only $491.83. In another case a loan was made upon realty of $6,625, and when the land was revalued its value was placed at only $3,140.71. He also called attention to the fact that a loan was made to a certain number of proslavery men, and that this money was used to purchase and establish a proslavery press at Edwardsville. In the early part of the year 1827, he submitted a series of charges to the House of Representatives as follows: 1. Loans had been made for more than $1,000. 2. Loans of more than $100 had been made upon personal security. 3. The president of the bank had borrowed at two separate times loans of $1,000 on personal security. 4. The bank had loaned on real estate that was not free from incumbrances. He also showed that there were many promissory notes in the bank that were over due by three years time, and that there were eleven forgeries detected in the notes of the bank as early as 1822 and no steps had been taken to punish the offenders. There were several other serious charges made in this exhibit which the governor laid before the House of Representatives. The House could no longer ignore these specific charges and they were obliged to go through the forms of an investigation. A committee was appointed with power to summon persons and papers and requested to investigate these charges and report the same to the house. The committee consisted of Henry J. Mills, George Churchill, Thomas Reynolds, William Sim, W. Cavarly, and Conrad Will. This committee is supposed to have made a very thorough investigation of the management of the bank. While this investigation was going on, other charges were being investigated, and the excitement and anger were rising to a dangerous pitch. These later charges were against J. M. Duncan and Theophilus W. Smith while acting as cashiers. They were both exonerated. It now came time for the committee to report on the general charges. Governor Ford in his History of Illinois says of the report of this committee: "The evidence before the committee undoubtedly showed great mismanagement of the bank. But a committee of investigation had been "packed for the purpose, and such was the influence of a combination of the officers of even an insolvent bank, that a report was made without hesitation against the governor's charges."

THE COURTS

When the Constitution of 1818 was written a Supreme Court of four members was created. The judges were appointed early the first session of the Legislature. The terms of office expired at the end of 1824. Another set of judges was appointed and at the same time five circuit judges were provided for. These five circuit judges held court in five districts. The cases heard in the circuit courts might be appealed, under certain rules, to the Supreme Court which thus became a sort of appellate court. In 1827, this law creating the circuit courts was repealed and the supreme judges were required to do the circuit court work. The state was still divided into five districts. One of the five circuit judges, R. M. Young, was retained to act as a circuit judge in one of the five districts, known as the military tract district. This law caused more or less confusion as all the nine judges were opposed to the change, and it could easily be seen that the whole move was a political scheme.

In 1824-5 the members of the Supreme Court were made a committee to codify the laws of Illinois. They reported in 1827 and their work was greatly commended. The laws were grouped under property, contracts, civil actions, rights of persons, and modes of redress. Committees from the two house added several revised groups, and the laws began to assume the character of the statute laws of the older states.

Penitentiary

There were some important local laws enacted during Edward's term as governor. One was the first step taken to establish a penitentiary. John Reynolds who had been defeated for reelection to the Supreme Court in 1824, was elected to the Legislature in 1826. In the session of the Legislature in 1826-7, Mr. Reynolds introduced a bill for the building of a state prison. He says that he was led to do this because the laws provided for forms of punishment that were barbarous and had no element of reform in them. Whipping, pillory, and hanging were the three chief forms of punishment for offenses. The older states had adapted the system of punishment by imprisonment at hard labor, and Reynolds favored such a system in Illinois. Mr. Reynolds found that there were many public men who agreed with him as to the need of a reform in the matter of punishments for crimes. They however could not see how the state in its depressed financial condition could or should undertake such an enterprise. Mr. Reynolds was equal to the emergency. He suggested that the state should petition Congress to donate to the state the saline lands that were no longer of value in the manufacture of salt because the timber had all been used in the salt-making process.

A petition was addressed to the Congress asking for the gift of these lands. The petition was granted. Something like 80,000 acres were now the possession of the state. It was sold and the money placed in the state treasury subject to an appropriation for the building of a state prison.

However, it had been agreed that half of the money for which the salt lands should be sold, should be expended in the improvement of the roads and navigable streams in the eastern part of the state, and that the other half should be used for the penitentiary. Several sites were considered for the location of the prison, but finally Alton, then a growing town, was selected as the site. Gersham Jayne, Governor Bond, and William P. McKee were to locate the site in Alton.

When Reynolds became governor, he pushed actively the work

of constructing buildings and preparing the same for the reception of the convicts. The buildings and grounds were very small compared with what is needed today, but they were sufficient till after the Civil war, when larger quarters were constructed at Joliet. In Civil war times the penitentiary at Alton was used as a prison for the safe-keeping of Confederate prisoners, for a while at least, until they could be forwarded to other points.

During the administration of Governor Edwards, the Supreme Court, a sort of committee appointed to revise the laws, made its report. This court was made up of strong men for the early days, and their report was received by the General Assembly and, with slight changes, adopted. To show the value of their work we only need to call attention to the fact that much of the statute law which was reported by this committee, the Supreme Court, has remained up till the present time.

Public Lands

It was a provision in the cessions of the several states of their claims to western lands that the lands should be disposed of for the common good of all the states. It was therefore implied that the lands should be sold. When the ordinance was drawn up, the idea still obtained that the lands in the Northwest Territory should be sold. At the time the ordinance was written the Rev. Mr. Cutler arranged with Congress to purchase a large tract consisting of thousands of acres. When the survey of the territory was in progress there were different plans for selling the lands in large quantities. At one time not less than 4,000 acres could be bought and then the amount was reduced still further. When Wm. H. Harrison was a delegate in Congress in 1799-1800, he secured the enactment of laws reducing the amount of land which an individual could buy. The minimum amount was fixed at 320 acres, half of a section. He got the price fixed at $2.00 per acre, one-fourth of the price must be paid in cash and three-fourths might be paid in the near future.

By 1820, the people owed the government $20,000,000 for lands bought on credit. "Senator Richard M. Johnson, of Kentucky, introduced a bill which was enacted into law providing that those who were indebted to the government for lands might relinquish enough land to pay their debts to the government and thus receive a clear title to the remainder of their claims. The law also provided that the price of land should be reduced to $1.25 per acre—cash."

In 1820 when the bill to abolish the credit system and to reduce the price per acre of land, Edwards in the Senate and Cook in the House voted against the measure. The people were greatly pleased with the action of Congress in reducing the

From Illinois Blue Book

BEAUTY SPOTS IN ILLINOIS
(1) Entrance to Fort Massac. (2) Castle Rock, Dixon. (3) Ohio River near Elizabethtown. (4) Apple River Canyon.

price of land, and were displeased with the action of Edwards and Cook. Senator Edwards argued that they were justified in voting against the bill since it would, if enacted into law, abolish the credit system in the west and poor people would be deprived of a sort of preemption right in the lands they wished as their future homes. The personal and political enemies of Edwards and Cook said that the "Edwards dynasty" was selfish in their actions, that they wished to keep the price of land high since they were large holders of speculative lands. At any rate, their enemies kept repeating these statements and no doubt they both suffered from these charges.

In the session of the Legislature of 1826-7 there was a memorial addressed to Congress, praying for the reduction of the price of the public lands. Along with this memorial went another which asked for a grant to the state of all public lands within the limits thereof. In the discussions of these requests there seemed to be some sign of a lack of earnestness. Mr. Blackwell suggested as an amendment to the general proposition that Congress should make the grant "on condition that the state at all times grant to actual settlers each not less than a quarter section, to be occupied and improved." Governor Edwards also made a proposition that the public lands should be granted to the state, that the state should sell the lands at 25 cents per acre and turn the proceeds over to the general government.

These schemes may appear very foolish but similar plans for the disposal of the public lands were brought forward in Congress by men who stood high in public esteem. The idea that it would be wise policy to cede the public lands to the several states wherein they lay, was a practical interpretation of the states' right idea. This doctrine was very plausibly set forth by Governor Ninian Edwards in his second annual message to the General Assembly in 1828.

In this message, the product of a strong and mature mind, filled with stores of legal wisdom, and ambitious to place himself before the public in the light of a champion of the people, Governor Edwards carried states right to its logical conclusion. "He showed that the Articles of Confederation not only affirmed the right of every state to all the lands within its limits, but expressly declared that no state shall be deprived of territory for the benefit of the United States, by the terms of the constitution the Federal Government could not acquire or hold any land in any original state, even with its own consent, except what may be necessary for the erection of forts, magazines, arsenals, dock yards, and other needful buildings; that as this state (Illinois) had been admitted on an equal footing with the original states, the United States could hold no more land than for these purposes within its limits, and for anything more the general government had to obtain the consent of the

Legislature of the state; that till the admission of the state into the Union, it had no rights as a state under the constitution, and consequently no competency to act in that character; it was like a minor not within the age of consent; that the state could not therefore be bound by the acts of the territory, in consenting for the United States to hold lands within her limits; that if the Federal Government enjoyed this privilege of dominion over the public lands during its political minority, it ceased on the admission of the state into the Union, having thence forward the same rights of sovereignty, freedom, and independence as the other states; that the sovereignty of a state includes the right to exercise supreme and exclusive control over all lands within it; that the freedom of a state is the right to do whatever may be done by any nation, and includes the right to dispose of all the public lands within its limits, according to its own will and pleasure; that the independence of a state includes an exemption from all control by any other state or nation over its will or action, within its own territory."

At this date we may well question whether Edwards was in dead earnest. The coming of Jackson into power in 1829 may have directed the public mind toward other matters so that the question of the disposal of public lands gives way nationally to the tariff, and locally to the Indian disturbances.

Public Men

The most prominent man in Illinois during the first twelve years of Illinois as a state, was Ninian Edwards. He was a Kentucky-bred gentleman, a man of wide acquaintance, of striking address, cultured, resourceful, and tenacious. He was governor of Illinois Territory from 1809 to 1818. Almost immediately after giving up the governorship of Illinois, he was elected to the United States Senate. Here he served six years, following which he served four years as governor of the state. This makes a period of nineteen years of public service. His controversy with William Crawford, the Secretary of the United States Treasury, and his persistent efforts for four long years to bring about an honest management of the State Bank, brought him into very great prominence. So prominent was he in the political activities of the state and nation that people talked about the Edwards faction.

Among the members of this faction we may mention Natianiel Pope. He was a friend of Edwards, but after he became a United States judge he could not participate actively in state politics. He was a cousin of Edwards and was helpful to him in many ways.

Another strong supporter of Edwards was Daniel Pope Cook, a nephew of Judge Pope and a son-in-law of Ninian Edwards. Cook had beaten McLean for a seat in Congress which McLean had held for a short time. He later defeated Bond and Elias Kent Kane for the same position. Cook championed the cause of John Quincy Adams in the election in the House of Representatives in 1825. This made a deadly enemy of Andrew Jackson.

Thomas C. Browne, of Shawneetown, was a friend of Edwards and was active in his support. He was elected to the Supreme Court in 1824-5.

Opposed to Edwards was Jesse B. Thomas, a prominent man in early Illinois history. He was territorial judge, president of the Constitutional Convention, and one of the two United States senators from 1818 to 1829. He headed an anti-Edwards party.

John McLean belonged to this anti-Edwards party. He was defeated by Cook for a seat in Congress and Cook belonged to the Edwards faction. McLean was elected to the United States Senate to succeed Edwards, resigned, 1824-5. He died in 1830.

Shadrach Bond was a member of the anti-Edwards faction. He ran against Cook for Congress in 1824, but was defeated. He was the first governor of Illinois.

James Hall, who was one of the most scholarly men in Illinois was bitterly opposed to Cook and of course opposed Edwards. He was not an active and influential politician, but his influence was not unfelt by the Edwards faction.

Joseph Duncan had taken little part in state and national politics till the summer of 1828. He was probably not a strong anti-Edwards man, but was put forward by the anti-Edwards people as the only man that they thought could defeat Cook. His friends in the anti-Edwards faction made much capital in the campaign out of the fact that Duncan was a farmer and had a brilliant military record, while Cook had always been an office holder. Duncan won partly because Cook had voted for Adams and also from the fact that Illinois was becoming a strong Jackson state.

John Reynolds had served in the War of 1812 and was called the "old ranger." He liked the title. He was one of the supreme judges from 1818 to 1824. John Reynolds was not the equal of Ninian Edwards and Jesse B. Thomas and he was busy in his own class of minor statesmen. He was, in the earlier years, opposed to Edwards but toward the close of Edward's term as governor he and Edwards entered into a coalition. Edwards supported Reynolds for governor in 1830. Thomas Reynolds was an uncle of John Reynolds. He was a lawyer and in 1822 when Justice Phillips resigned from the Supreme Court Thomas Reynolds was elected to fill the vacancy. Thus uncle and nephew were on the Supreme Court at the same time. Thomas also served in the Legislature and was a strong Jackson man.

William Kinney was a prominent politician, but was handicapped in his usefulness and power by his lack of an education.

He held quite a few offices. In 1826 he was elected lieutenant-governor over Rev. Samuel M. Thomason who was Edwards' running mate. Mr. Kinney was a Baptist preacher.

Thomas Sloo was in no sense a politician but an influential citizen. He was a successful business man. He was put forward as the candidate of the anti-Edwards faction in the gubernatorial contest of 1826. He was beaten by Edwards by a vote of 6,280 to 5,834.

A man who was very prominent in local politics in the first years of statehood was George Forquer. He was a half brother of Governor Ford. He began life as a business man, but turned his attention to law. He served as secretary of state and in the General Assembly. Probably no other man held more different offices in Illinois than did George Forquer. Forquer was a strong anti-slavery man. He became an opponent of Edwards and was an active Jackson supporter.

Elias Kent Kane took an active part in the work of securing the admission of Illinois into the Union. He probably had more to do in writing the Constitution of 1818 than any other man. It has been said of him that he was "the chief of the faction when ever he chose to exert his influence." He served two terms in the United States Senate. He was a friend to William Crawford and that would put him in the faction opposed to Edwards. He was in 1831 under certain arrangements willing to support Edwards for Congress. He was at times a warm friend of Jackson.

Joseph M. Street was a prominent politician of Shawneetown. In the race in 1824 he claimed to be a Jackson man but it was suggested that at heart he was for Crawford. He encouraged Edwards and prophesied the weakening of the Jackson forces, but he was a poor prophet. Street was a perrennial officer seeker.

Theophilus W. Smith was a man to be considered in any factional skirmish in Illinois between 1818 and 1830. In the earlier days he was an Edwards man, a Crawford supporter, later he went over to Jackson. He was elected a member of the Supreme Court in the spring of 1824. He was active in politics and was not always sure just where he belonged in political contests. In the slavery struggle he was for slavery, yet in 1836 a member of the Supreme Court he rendered a decision which greatly reduced the legal basis for slavery in Illinois.

Edward Coles following his term of office as governor tried to "come back" into politics in Illinois, but it seemed his proposed candidacy created little interest. He left Illinois in 1833 and resided in Philadelphia.

Nathaniel Pope if a politician at all was of the better sort. He was appointed a United States judge when Illinois was admitted into the Union, which place he held till 1850. He was a friend to Edwards and an uncle of Cook and was interested in their political fortunes. He tried a time or two to break into the United States Senate, but was never successful.

Samuel D. Lockwood was one of Governor Coles' supporters in the convention fight. He was elected to the Supreme Court in the Legislature of 1824-5. He too would have been glad to be selected as a United States senator, but he was never chosen. He did not take a very active part in party politics.

Emanuel J. West was a radical pro-slavery member of the Legislature of 1822-3 from Madison County. Judge Gillespie says of West: "If he had lived he could have figured in public life."

Alexander P. Field was a prominent politician from Union County. He and West were the head and shoulders in the Legislature of 1822-3 of the party that favored a convention. Later he favored the Edwards faction. He worked for Jackson. He and Breese were opponents on most topics. He went to New Orleans shortly before the Civil war and there he championed the cause of the union.

Zadoc Casey was an active office holder. He favored slavery. He was elected lieutenant-governor with Reynolds in 1830. He was elected to Congress and secured the gift of land to construct the Illinois and Michigan canal and also helped to secure the grant to build the Illinois Central railroad. He was not a very active partisan.

These are the names of men who had to do with determining the policies for Illinois from 1818 to 1830. There were other men who played their parts, but those named above were the prominent men in the political life of Illinois in the days of early statehood.

CHAPTER IV

A DISTINGUISHED VISITOR

IMMIGRATION—AN INVITATION—IN ST. LOUIS—AT KASKASKIA—AT SHAWNEETOWN.

In the election held in August, 1824, a new General Assembly was chosen. There were some new men in this body when it met in special session in November 15, 1824. Joseph Duncan and Thomas Varlin were two new senators. In the House Elias Kent Kane and George Forquer were new men. The election of two United States senators was attended to with the result as stated in the preceding chapter. The governor's message was a dignified document asking that the Legislature might take steps to abolish slavery in Illinois, repeal the Black laws, and to put a stop to the scandalous business of kidnapping. He called attention to the desirability of taking action which would further the interests of the Illinois and Michigan Canal, and to the need of a state system of free public schools. The last subject was the only one of his recommendations that engaged their attention. Senator Duncan from Jackson County secured the passage of a school law which organized a free school for the state. This law has been considered in a preceding chapter.

IMMIGRATION

Immigration poured into Illinois following the close of the War of 1812, for reasons which have been pointed out. This flow was checked in 1817 and the first part of 1818 as it was not known what action the constitutional convention would take with regard to slavery. When it was known that "neither slavery nor in voluntary servitude shall hereafter be introduced into this state," the movement of population set in again. It was at this time that the capital was moved to Vandalia and the whole front line of pioneer life moved northward. When the fight to make Illinois a slave state began, there was naturally a hesitation on the part of the people from the older states about coming into Illinois. When the convention fight closed in August, 1824, and it was known that slavery would not be introduced, then the movement began again.

"In the summer of 1825 immigration revived considerably. A great tide set in toward the central part of the state. Through Vandalia alone 250 wagons were counted in three weeks' time, all going northward. Destined for Sangamon County alone, eighty wagons and 400 people were counted in two weeks' time. Sangamon County was, at that time, without doubt the most populous county in the state. All the northern counties were most disproportionately represented in the General Assembly. While such counties as Randolph and White had each a senator and three representatives, Sangamon had one representative and one senator only." At the election in August, 1824, Randolph cast 641 votes, indicating a population of 3,205; while Sangamon cast a vote of 873, showing a population of 4,365. The constitution of 1818 provided that the census should be taken every five years beginning with 1820. In that year the population by the Federal census was 55,162. In 1825 the state enumeration showed 72,817. This increase, while not so great as one might expect, was largely in the Sangamon region and along the eastern side of the state as far north as Danville.

An Invitation

A writer has said this about LaFayette: "In the dark days of the Revolution, when in the bloom of his young manhood, this doughty Frenchman had left his youthful wife and his luxurious home to offer his life and his fortune in the holy cause of liberty; and now at the end of half a century he returned to visit the land he had never ceased to love. And never in the history of the United States has any other foreigner received the glad welcome, the universal homage of the people, that he did. LaFayette had greatly changed. His love of liberty was still warm and young; but the blithe step was gone, his hair was silvered, and his brow was furrowing with age. But greater was the change in the land that his eyes now looked upon—then a few distracted colonies struggling toward the light, now a nation that commanded the world's respect, with its rising cities, its opening industries, its continental domain."

The Congress of the United States had invited General LaFayette to visit this country as the guest of the nation, and he was now in the year 1824 complying with that kind invitation. General LaFayette and his party arrived in New York August 15, 1824. He was accompanied by his son, George Washington LaFayette, and his private secretary, M. Levasseur. The arrangements were made that he should land on Staten Island where he was received by his fellow countryman, Joseph Bonapart, who was then a resident of Bordentown, New Jersey. He was later received in New York City by a double line of old Revolutionary soldiers amid the roar of canon and the strains of martial music. Everywhere the same profound respect and triumphant welcome awaited the nation's guest.

The year 1825 was a notable one for the young State of Illinois. For it was in the spring of this year that Illinois had the honor of entertaining this noble friend of humanity, soldier, statesman, and patriot, General LaFayette. When it was known in Illinois that the Congress of the United States had invited LaFayette to visit the scenes of his military achievement and to mingle once more with the thinning ranks of Revolutionary heroes, it was conceived by the good people of Illinois that it would be an exceedingly happy and appropriate thing for LaFayette to visit the old seat of French empire in the great Mississippi Valley. Here was Old Kaskaskia, on the banks of the mighty river familiar ground to Father Marquette, Joliet LaSalle, Tonti, Father Membre, D'Iberville, Fathers Mermet and Charlevoix. Here were the remains of old Fort Chartres, the greatest military defense ever erected on the continent of North America by the king's forces. Here the Lilies of France waved over the pride and beauty of France. It was to this historic region where there were still signs of the Old Regime that Illinois with much justification presumed to invite this hero of two great revolutions.

When the General Assembly met in the early fall of 1824, that body extended a cordial invitation to General LaFayette to visit Illinois if he should come west of the Alleghanies. This invitation from the General Assembly was supplemented by a very affectionate letter from Governor Coles. It will now be remembered that when Edward Coles was returning from St. Petersburg as special embassador from President Madison to the Emperor Alexander, that he spent some time in Paris where he was presented to the King of France, Louis XVIII, by Mr. Gallatin, the United States Minister to the French government. It was while in Paris at this time that he also met General LaFayette who was kind enough to invite Mr. Coles into his home where the host was glad to hear of all his friends of Revolutionary days who were still living—Jefferson, Adams, Madison, Monroe, and the Pinkneys. Not a single officer of high rank in Washington's army was living. Mr. Coles could tell LaFayette of all the living and the dead.

Upon receipt of the invitation from the General Assembly and the letter from Governor Coles, General LaFayette answered by saying: "It has ever been my eager desire and it is now my earnest intention to visit the western states and particularly the State of Illinois. I shall, after the celebration of the 22d of February anniversary day, leave this place for a journey to the southern, and from New Orleans to the western states so as to return to Boston on the 14th of June, when the corner stone of the Bunker's Hill monument is to be laid; a ceremony sacred to the whole Union, and in which I have been engaged to act a peculiar and honorable part."

On the 12th of April, 1825, General LaFayette wrote to Governor Coles from New Orleans, saying he would reach Illinois about the end of the month of April. He suggests to Governor Coles that his time was very limited and that he was obliged to be in Boston the 15th of June, as he owes it to the Revolutionary army to be present at the laying of the corner stone of the Bunker Hill monument. He proposed that Governor Coles should meet him at either Kaskaskia or Shawneetown. He calls attention to the fact that he has promised General Andrew Jackson to spend a day with him at the "Hermitage." He points out that he will be ready to leave St. Louis on the 29th of April and will leave the future plans to Governor Coles.

The following manuscript copy is in possession of the descendants of Governor Coles:

Edwardsville, April 28, 1825.

Dear Sir: This will be handed to you by my friend and Aide de Camp, Col. William Schuyler (Stephen) Hamilton, who I take particular pleasure in introducing to you, as the son of your old and particular friend, Gen. Alexander Hamilton. As it is not known when you will arrive at St. Louis or what will be your intended route from thence, Colonel Hamilton is posted there for the purpose of waiting on you as soon as you shall arrive, and ascertaining from you, and making known to me, by what route you propose to return to the eastward, and when and where it will be most agreeable for you to afford me the happiness of seeing you and welcoming you to Illinois.

I am, with great respect and esteem, your devoted friend,

EDWARD COLES.

General LaFayette.

On April 28th, the steamboat Natchez, with General LaFayette and party on board, consisting of his son, George Washington LaFayette, his secretary, Colonel Levasseur, and a committee of honor from the states of Louisiana, Mississippi, and Tennessee, landed at old Carondelet, a French village a few miles south of St. Louis. On the 29th the governor of Missouri, Mr. William Clark, Governor Coles of Illinois, Colonel Benton of Missouri and others repaired to Carondelet where they boarded the Natchez and received and welcomed the nation's guest to the two states of Missouri and Illinois.

In St. Louis

The party then steamed up the river to the water front where another demonstration of welcome was accorded the visitors. The entire party then proceeded to the residence of Pierre Chouteau where a formal reception was held. The day was ended by a general reception and a ball given in the Massie Hotel which was attended by the entire party.

At Kaskaskia

On the morning of April 30, Saturday, the Natchez conveyed LaFayette and a distinguished party to Kaskaskia, the old seat of French empire in the West. A vast throng of patriotic citizens bade LaFayette welcome. A reception was held at the home of Gen. John Edgar. Governor Coles delivered a glowing address of welcome to which LaFayette responded with considerable feeling.

Just here in the proceedings a very touching scene occurred. A few old Revolutionary soldiers who had fought with LaFayette at Brandywine and at Yorktown, were presented. Although

THE RAWLINGS HOTEL IN SHAWNEETOWN, WHERE GENERAL LAFAYETTE WAS ENTERTAINED

General LaFayette did not remember them personally the meeting revived youthful memories and carried them back to the camps, the marches, and battle scenes of the Revolutionary war.

The entire party repaired to the hotel kept by Colonel Sweet where a bountiful dinner had been prepared. The ladies of the town had decorated the dining room and parlors of the hotel with a profusion of wild flowers. These had been gathered from the fields and woods about the town. Following the meal there was a number of toasts given. One by Governor Coles: "The inmates of La Granges (LaFayette's home)—let them not be anxious; for though their father is 1,000 miles in the interior of America he is yet in the midst of his affectionate children."

Following the dinner the party repaired to the commodious home of William Morrison where another American ball was given to entertain the European guests. General LaFayette, though lame from wounds received at Brandywine, led the grand march. His partner was Miss Alzire Menard, a daughter of Pierre Menard. (Miss Menard is remembered by the older people in and about Chester.)

An interesting story is told of an incident that occurred while the people were being entertained at the home of Mr. Morrison. Levasseur, the secretary to General LaFayette, was disappointed in the general appearance and surroundings in the town of Kaskaskia and found it difficult to interest himself in the functions of the day. He therefore spent his time in studying the Indians who were camped near the town. In his conversations he made the acquaintance of an Indian woman, the daughter of a New York chief named Panisciowa. She had been brought up in the home of Pierre Menard, but married a man by the name of Skiakape. She showed Levasseur a letter which she said General LaFayette had given her father while the former was in command in New York State at the close of the Revolutionary war. The Indian woman was introduced to General LaFayette who vouched for the letter and the story.

AT SHAWNEETOWN

At midnight LaFayette continued his journey, accompanied by Governor Coles. They sailed down the Mississippi, up the Ohio and the Tennessee to Nashville. From here they made the short pilgrimage to the Hermitage to visit General Jackson, the hero of the Battle of New Orleans. On their return to the Ohio and as they proceeded up the Ohio to Pittsburg, they stopped for a brief stay in Shawneetown, then the largest town in the southeast part of the state. Here LaFayette was feasted in the large brick house called the Rawling's Hotel. When the boat landed the guests were led to the hotel which stood on the bank of the river over a walk made of wild flowers which the people had gathered from the woods and fields. Judge James Hall, one of the most brilliant public men in Illinois in that day, gave a beautiful welcome which was replied to by General LaFayette with a warmth of feeling which he could scarcely control. From Shawneetown General LaFayette proceeded on his way to fulfill his appointment at the laying of the corner stone of the Bunker Hill monument.

CHAPTER V

A SHORT RETROSPECT—1830

COMPARISON — SOME IMMIGRANTS — TRADE AND COMMERCE — ROADS—NEWSPAPERS—NEW COUNTIES—DISTRIBUTION OF POPULATION—INDUSTRIES—RELIGION—SOME LEGISLATION—SOCIAL PROGRESS—THE PENITENTIARY.

The growth of the state in population is shown by the census reports: for 1810—12,282; for 1820—55,162; for 1830—157,445. Wherever we have population we have homes—homes mean cultivation of the soil, the opening of roads, the presence of villages, stores, the operation of grist mills, and saw mills, the building of bridges, the manufacturing of many of the necessities of life.

COMPARISON

In 1810 Missouri had a population of 20,845; in 1820 of 66,557; in 1830 of 140,455. In this it will be noticed that whereas Missouri had nearly twice as many people in 1810 as Illinois had; by 1830 Illinois has 17,000 more people than Missouri. Indiana had in 1810—24,520; in 1820—147,178; in 1830—343,031. If the anti-slavery people had known these figures in 1823-4, the argument would have been advanced that slavery was a detriment to the growth of population. This is probably the fact in this case—population increased more rapidly in free states than in slave states. Now the increase in the population of any state at any time is dependent on two factors: one the increase from births, and the other the increase of immigration. Now since Missouri had twice as many people (nearly) in 1810 as Illinois had, we may easily affirm that the increase from births in Missouri was greater between 1810 and 1830 than in Illinois for the same time. And since Illinois has several thousand more people in 1830 than Missouri, the conclusion is easily drawn that more people came into Illinois from the other states and other counties between 1810 and 1830 than came into Missouri for the same time.

SOME IMMIGRANTS

Reynolds says the first colony of foreign immigrants who settled in Illinois was a group of Irish people who came out of Kentucky about 1805 and settled on the Ohio River fifteen miles above Golconda in Pope County. They were led by Samuel

O'Melveny. Mr. O'Melveny was a river man—made flat boats and made trips to New Orleans. This Irish colony was made up of ten or more families—some sixty people in all. Samuel O'Melveny was a member of the constitutional convention in 1818 from Pope County. There were enough in this colony, and they were so well organized as a sort of social unit, that they were able to defend themselves against the Indians. They grew rapidly and by 1830 there were probably as many as seventy-five families who had come into that neighborhood. They were mostly Irish.

A group of Irish also settled on Plumb Creek in Randolph County some six miles northeast of Kaskaskia at an early date. They were there before 1810.

The English settlement in Edwards County led by Morris Birkbeck and George Flower was the most noted foreign settlers in Illinois prior to 1830. The number of people as well as the character of these settlers gave prominence to the settlement. There were perhaps as many as 300 or 400 families in this locality prior to 1830 probably not all English. In 1824 when the vote was taken on the slavery question there were 580 votes polled in Edwards County. Three hundred and ninety-one of these were against slavery and that might be interpreted to mean that these 391 voters were English people, as the English immigrants were uniformly against slavery. These people were educated and strong minded people. The settlements are sometimes called the Marine Settlement from the fact that many of the people had formerly been sailors.

Another group of English colonists came into what is now Monroe County as early as 1817. There were perhaps as many as twenty or more families. Thomas Winstanley was the leader of this colony from Lancashire in England. They settled in Prairie du Long Creek, and erected there a Catholic Church.

Germans came in large numbers. On account of their language they were able to hold their community together and were therefore easily marked off from other neighborhoods. A group of German families came into St. Clair County and settled near the Mississippi Bluffs somewhere near a direct line from St. Louis to Belleville. The leaders were named Germain and Markee. This was about 1815. This settlement was the beginning of large migrations of the Germans to this county. Another settlement of Germans was in the southeast part of St. Clair County near the Kaskaskia River. It was called Dutch Hill. About the time Illinois was admitted into the Union, a German settlement was begun on Clear Creek some four or five miles southwest of Jonesboro. The colony flourished. They raised grapes, carried on certain forms of manufacturing, and sustained schools and a church. Several of them were German-Austrians. The settlement was called Kornthal.

Ferdinand Ernest who has been mentioned in connection with the first buildings in Vandalia led a colony of Germans from Hanover to the vicinity of Vandalia about the time the capital was moved from Kaskaskia to Vandalia. Mr. Ernest was a man of wealth and was influential among his friends. These colonists became a model community for order and industry.

There were in Illinois by 1830, considerable numbers of foreign people probably in this order as to number, the Germans leading. The others in this order—English, Irish, Scotch, French, Swiss, Welsh and Spanish. The rate being about one foreigner to every seven native Americans.

Trade and Commerce

By 1830 trade and commerce had assumed large proportions. The means of traffic with the outside world were still lacking. The rivers were being used more and more, and the wagon roads, bridges, and ferries were improving. The State Legislature declared many of the smaller rivers navigable and expectations ran high as to their use in trade and commerce. While not a foot of earth had yet been moved from the Illinois and Michigan canal, the constant reference to it in legislation and messages kept expectation at a high pitch. We have already spoken about the prevalence of flat boats on the Wabash, the Ohio, and on the Mississippi. The boats as has been shown were built in the smaller streams and loaded with the products of the farms, the timber, or from the crude factories which were springing up in the more thickly settled parts of the country. Steamboats were on the upper Mississippi in 1817 and by 1830 they were plentiful on all the larger navigable rivers. Sawmills were furnishing lumber, the mines were just beginning to furnish a considerable amount of coal and lead. By 1830 barges of coal were to be seen on the Mississippi.

The country and village stores of the early days lingered till the days of the Civil war and many people now living can describe the character of the stocks and give the characteristics of the proprietors and their patrons. Who of us can not remember the bouquet of odors which assailed him upon his entrance into the enclosure. The distance from the markets and the lack of suitable transportation facilities were prohibitions upon the acceptance by the proprietor of the farmers' eggs, butter, lard and other perishable farm products. Along the streams there were many people engaged in hunting and trapping. One would not suspect that a variety of fur-bearing animals would have their habitat as far south as the settled parts of Illinois prior to 1830. But there were a great many of the smaller fur-bearing animals along the streams. Barter was not practiced between the storekeeper and the farmers and the woodsmen.

When the pioneer merchant had considerable capital or when his credit was good in Pittsburg, Louisville, Cincinnati, or New Orleans, he sold freely on credit. When the farmer's account had reached rather alarming proportions, he would be asked to settle his account by a promissory note often secured by a mortgage on a portion of the farmer's real estate. The mortgage was often foreclosed, and the pioneer storekeeper became a land holder. In this way he became so well off that he no longer need to keep store and gave his time to collecting his rents from those who occupied his land.

We have previously called attention to the fact that in the mouths of all the creeks of considerable size, flatboats were constructed which when loaded with the produce of the neighborhood would journey to New Orleans where there was a good market. Ford, in his History of Illinois, says, it was no uncommon practice for farmers to combine in the construction of the flatboat and then to accept the non-perishable products of the farms for transit to New Orleans. The cargo consisted of bacon, eggs, lard, hides, certain vegetable, beeswax, tallow, lumber, furs, products of the loom, flour, wheat, corn, oats, and often livestock. The men who accepted the responsibility of marketing the produce of their neighbors were careful to keep accurate accounts of the goods sold, and of the receipts for the same.

ROADS

Intimately connected with the subject of Trade and Commerce was the question of roads and other means of transportation. The first roads were of course nothing more than the Indian trails somewhat improved, but they usually went in direct lines from one center to another. These trails would be used awhile and then an act of the law-making branch of government would transform them into public roads. The national government helped some by declaring certain roads mail routes. There were mail routes laid out in Illinois as early as 1805. In that year a mail route was declared between Vincennes and Cahokia. In 1806, a road was established between Vincennes and Shawneetown. In 1810, a route was declared between Vincennes and St. Louis via Prairie du Rocher and Cahokia. About the same time a route was declared between Vincennes and Cape Girardeau via St. Genevieve. In 1822 Edwardsville, Springfield and Peoria were connected by a mail route. In 1824 a route was fixed between Vandalia and Springfield. The mails were ordered carried between Chicago and Galena, and between Chicago and Danville in 1826. There were eight state roads from Kaskaskia to as many points in the central and eastern part of the state, prior to 1830. There were scores of well-traveled roads that were not established by law. The people

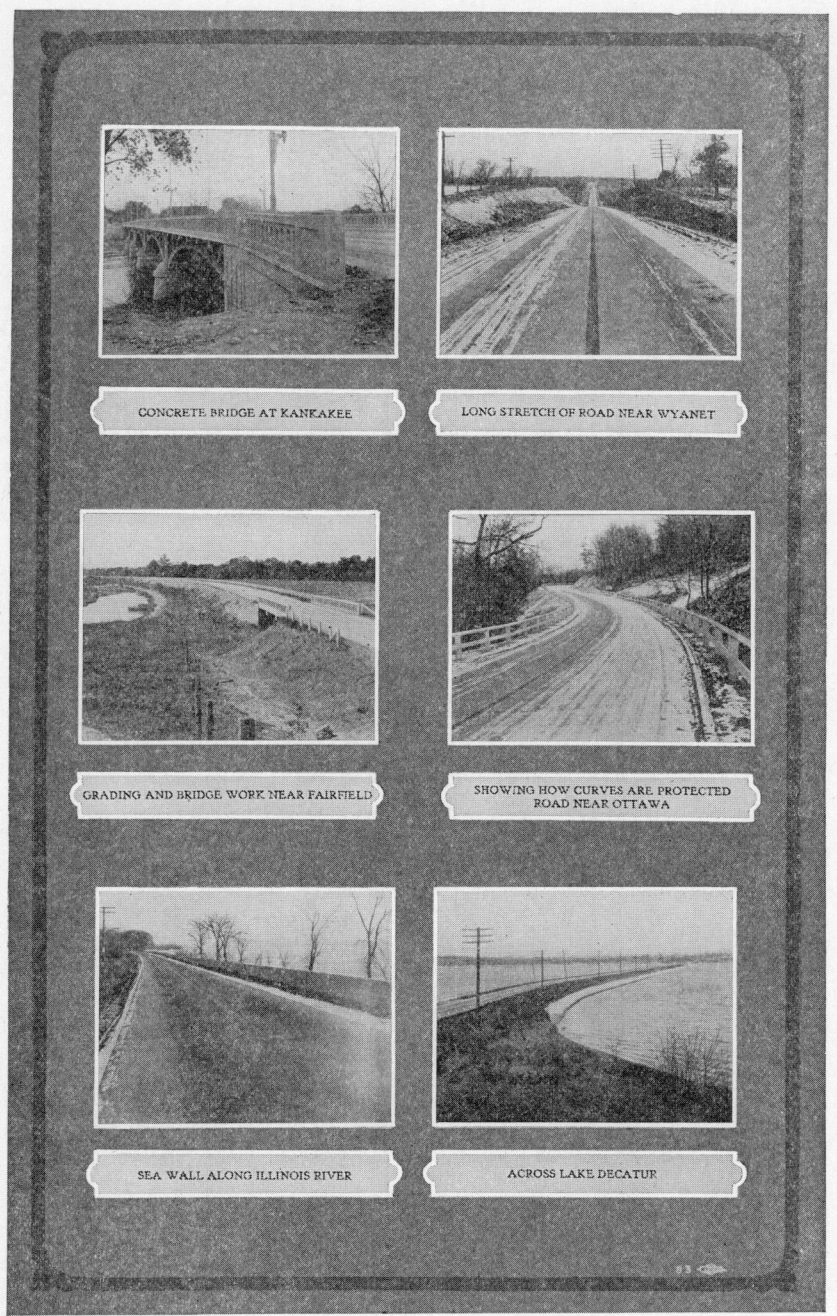

From Illinois Blue Book
TYPICAL HIGHWAY SCENES IN ILLINOIS

used them much and worked them a little. Governor Duncan probably did more than any other early governor to call attention to the need of good public roads.

Newspapers

The crude beginnings of what afterwards comes to be a great and flourishing institution are always very interesting. Certainly no other institution in this state had humbler beginnings, and as surely we can truthfully say that no other enterprise has reached such perfection as that of turning out the "World's Greatest Newspaper."

The early newspapers were named in the chapter giving the slavery fight. The first established was the Illinois Herald. This paper was located in Kaskaskia and had for its purpose the printing of the laws, both territorial and national. Its name was changed in 1816 to the Western Intelligencer and in 1818 to the Illinois Intelligencer. It was a four-column paper. The oldest number which has been preserved was issued on Wednesday, December 13, 1814. When the capital of the state was moved from Kaskaskia to Vandalia in 1820, this paper was moved to the new seat of government.

The second paper in age was the Illinois Emigrant which was established in Shawneetown in 1818. In 1819 the name was changed to the Illinois Gazette. The paper was started, and continued for some years by Henry Eddy and Singleton H. Kimmel. The Gazette took quite an active part in the convention fight in 1824.

The Spectator was established in Edwardsville in 1819. The editor was Hooper Warren, assisted by George Churchill. It was strongly opposed to the convention in 1824. It was started largely to oppose the convention.

The Star of the West was first published in Edwardsville in 1822-23. It was sold in a short time and the name was changed to the Illinois Republican. This paper under both names was strongly pro-slavery. The paper ceased when the convention fight was over. The Illinois Corrector was published a short time by R. K. Fleming in Edwardsville. It, too, was pro-slavery, and supported Jackson's candidacy. It was published in 1827-8.

The Republican-Advocate was published in 1823. It was renamed the Kaskaskia Republican in 1824. It did not live long. It changed its name to the Illinois Reporter but died in 1827.

Very closely connected with the publishing of these newspapers was the question of roads—mail routes. In 1814 there were nine postoffices in Illinois, and 388 miles of established post roads. Some of these established post roads were the simplest sort of trails or paths from one post office to another, though there were some good roads. The number of postoffices

THE OLDEST KNOWN COPY OF ANY ILLINOIS PUBLICATION

grew as the population increased. The postoffices were often established at the home of some farmer.

Mr. Scott who edited Volume VI of the Illinois Historical Collections, says: "The general character of the newspapers of the period was political, the tone frequently controversial, but highly moral and religious." The papers gave attention to the publishing of laws, both state and national. There was a dearth named above, the Spectator was the most ably edited of the whole group. But later James Hall entered editorial work, and of local news. Only the unusual received notice. Of the papers he is regarded as the greatest literary character in Illinois for the first third of the nineteenth century. It is probably true that few of these early papers could have lived without the support which they received from the publication of state and national laws, and advertisements.

New Counties

When Illinois came into the Union in 1818, there were fifteen counties. Beginning at the south they were as follows: Pope, Johnson, Union, Gallatin, Franklin, Jackson, White, Randolph, Edwards, Washington, Monroe, St. Clair, Crawford, Bond, and Madison. The census of 1820 gave the counties comprising the territory north of an east and west line through the mouth of the Illinois River, a population less than 20,000, while the population of the entire state was slightly more than 55,000. There were only three counties, Clark, Bond, and Madison to the north of the above mentioned line, while there were sixteen to the south of the line. The three counties to the north contained 6,650 people to each county, while the sixteen counties to the south of the line contained only 22,220 people.

In the first session of the Legislature after the state was admitted into the Union, there were four counties created. Alexander was made to include the territory south of Union and west of Johnson. Crawford was reduced to include parts of several present counties beside itself and Clark County was constituted of all the territory north of Crawford. Jefferson and Wayne were made from the west part of Edwards as it was in 1818.

In 1821 Lawrence County was made of the north part of Edwards and the south side of Crawford. Fayette was taken from the west part of Clark. Montgomery was made of the south part of Bond. Hamilton was created from the west part of White. Pike included everything west of the Illinois River and north of the Kankakee. Sangamon was the territory west of Fayette, east of the Illinois and north of the present Macoupin and Montgomery. Greene lay east of the Illinois River and included the present Jersey with Scott, Morgan, and Macoupin attached for governmental purposes.

Courtesy of Miss Emma Rebman

WINTER SCENE, REBMAN PARK, FERNE CLYFFE, JOHNSON COUNTY

In 1823, Clark was reduced to include beside itself only Cumberland, while Edgar was created just north of Clark with the territory north attached. Marion was made of the north end of Jefferson. Fulton constituted all territory north of the Illinois River and east of the fourth principal meridian. Morgan was detached from Greene, and included Scott and Cass.

In 1824 Clay was made from Wayne and Fayette. Clinton was made from the north side of Washington. Wabash was taken from the east side of Edwards.

In 1825 the Legislature created ten new counties. Calhoun from the south end of Pike. Adams from the west side of Pike. Hancock from the west side of Pike, just north of Adams. Henry was all territory north of Knox which lay just north of Fulton. Mercer and Warren were placed west of Henry and Knox. Peoria from the territory attached to Fulton and the east of the latter county, adjoining the Illinois River. Putnam was all territory north of the Illinois River and east of Henry. Schuyler from territory attached to Pike. In 1826 two new counties were created. The first was Vermilion which was constituted of territory attached to Edgar. McDonough was made of territory attached to Schuyler. It lies just south of Warren.

In 1827 four new counties were created. Shelby out of Fayette. Perry from the east end of Randolph and north side of Jackson. Tazewell from territory north of Sangamon. Jo Daviess was made from the north part of Henry and the west part of Putnam.

In 1829-31, nine new counties came upon the map. Macoupin from the attached territory of Greene. It lies just east of Greene. Macon was made from Fayette. Coles was taken from the north side of Clark and from territory attached to Edgar. McLean was made from Tazewell and from territory attached to Shelby. Cook from Putnam and included all present counties that touch the lake. LaSalle was made from Putnam and territory attached to Tazewell. Putnam was reduced greatly, but still included Bureau, Marshall and the east part of Stark. Rock Island was created out of Mercer and Jo Daviess. Effingham was taken from the east side of Fayette. Jasper was made from the west side of Crawford.

The Legislature of 1833 created two new counties and the session of 1836 laid out six new counties. In 1837 six new counties were created and 1839 fifteen new ones were laid out, making the 102 of today.

Distribution of Population

It is difficult to get a very definite idea of the changes in the density of population from time to time because of the fact that the counties are being divided up and new counties organized, but we can get a very good idea of the distribution by means of

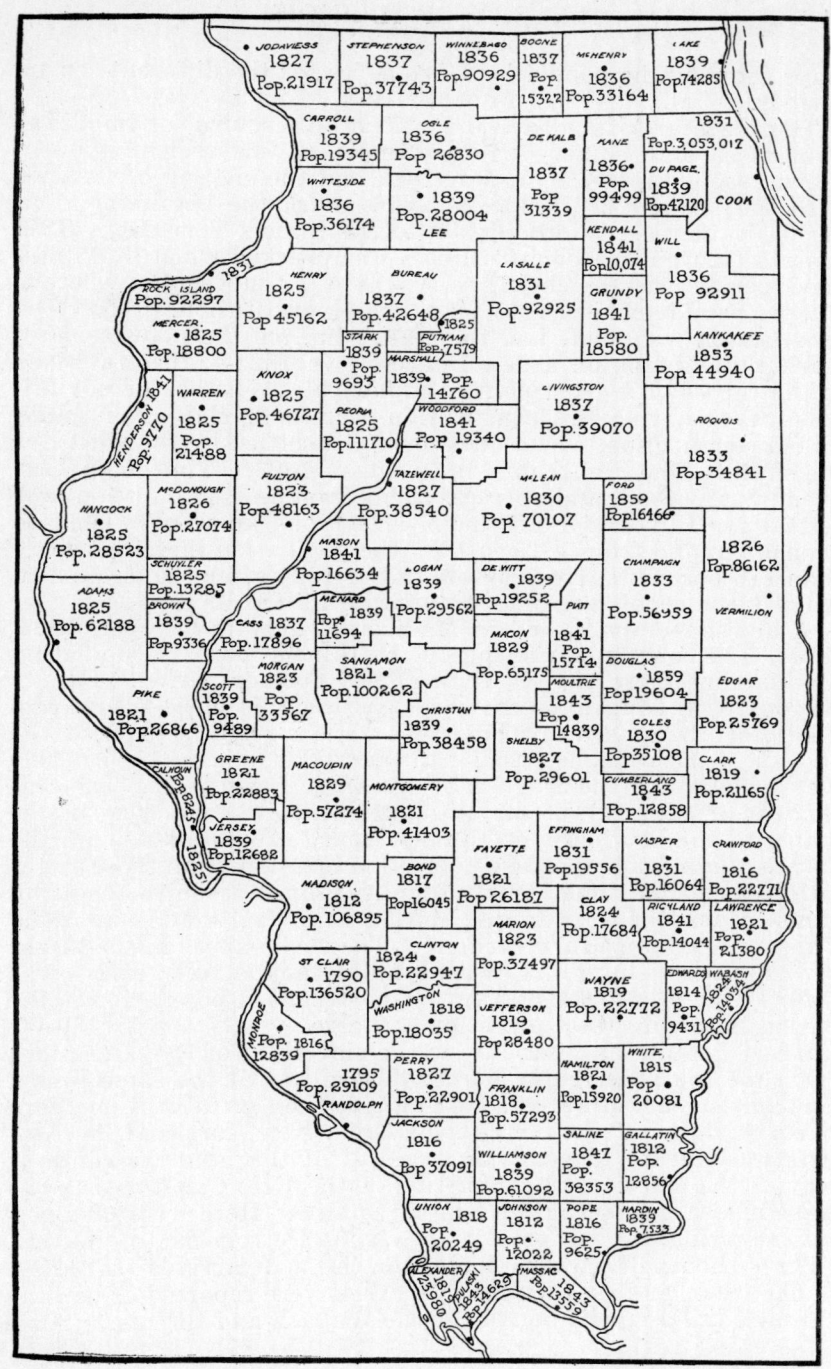

MAP OF ILLINOIS
Showing date of organization and population of counties

From Illinois Blue Book

maps showing the population of counties for the different census periods.

There are always good explanations of a revival of immigration into a new country. For example, as has been previously shown, the close of the War of 1812 and the signing of treaties with the Indians of Illinois in 1816, mark the beginning of a period of increased immigration to the Illinois Territory. This renewed movement toward Illinois was checked when the Statehood period was reached for it was a bit uncertain whether Illinois would make a free or a slave constitution. After the constitution was made and the state admitted the movement toward Illinois took on a new interest. In 1823-4, the state was in the throes of a great political upheaval. Whether or not Illinois was to have a new constitution permitting slavery or retain its old constitution, was a question to be settled by the voters of the state. The test came in August, 1823. The reply was prompt, vigorous, and correct. This troublesome question was settled for Illinois for all time. Every one knew now what to depend on, and from 1825 to 1830 the population increased more than 116 per cent. Even by the fall of 1824 after the election in August, the people began to stream into Illinois.

A newspaper published in Madison County in October, 1824, said: "The country bordering on the Illinois River is populating at this time more rapidly than at any former period. Family wagons with emigrants are daily passing this place (Edwardsville), on their way thither." We have already spoken of the stream of 250 wagons passing through Vandalia in 1825 in five weeks bound for the Sangamon country. Boggess, in "The Settlement of Illinois," points out that economic conditions in the states to the southeast of Illinois from 1825 to 1830 were the causes of a marked increase in the immigration from those states to Illinois at that time. Forty families from Yorkshire, England, came by way of Canada and settled near Jacksonville in 1829. They came equipped for farming. The local papers in the larger towns in the vicinity of Edwardsville, Vandalia, and other towns refer frequently to the northward movement of population in the period following the convention struggle.

These quotations refer only to the movement of the migrations from the southeast going north. There was at the same time a constant stream of settlers coming into the central and northern parts of Illinois from the Pennsylvania, New York and the New England states. The tide from north of the Potomac came by way of the lakes. The completion of the Erie Canal assisted in some measure to reach the lake at Buffalo. Here were lake vessels to bring the people to Cleveland, Detroit or to Chicago. "Three thousand persons bound for the west arrived in Buffalo in one week, and six thousand per week were reported as passing through Indianapolis bound for the Wabash and Illinois." Some general notion of the growth of population by the statement that the gain in population for each ten years from 1810-1820 and so on was as follows: 1810-1820, 348 per cent; 1820-1830, 185; 1830-1840, 202; 1840-1850, 83; 1850-1860, 101; 1860-1870, 48; 1870-1880, 21 per cent.

INDUSTRIES

The conclusion is easily reached that prior to 1830 the chief economic activity in Illinois was farming. True, one might think that with easy access to the greatest river system, and likewise to the greatest inland lake system in the world, that the people of Illinois could easily have become a great commercial people. Before a people can become commercial in their activities they must become a producing people—producing agricultural products, a mining people, a lumbering people or a manufacturing people. The people of Illinois prior to 1830 were not a mining people. The mining of coal was not thought of in Illinois, prior to 1830. Lumbering in various forms was practiced in Illinois from the earliest period, but only for local use. Saw mills were found in nearly every community, but no lumber was offered for markets outside of the state. Manufacturing was carried on in a very large way, but the articles manufactured were only for the local trade.

Manufacturing was an important industry. The lumber from the crude mills was used for building purposes—houses, barns, bridges, wagons, farm implements, and furniture. There were several motive powers used in sawing lumber. One of the first was the water wheel. If a sufficient fall could be secured, and a sufficient quantity of water was available a water wheel could be used. Many mills of this kind sawed lumber and ground the grain into flour. An interesting method of producing power was with horses. A master wheel—a wheel some seven or eight feet in diameter—lay horizontally. On the outer rim of the wheel were cogs which worked on small pinions which produced a rapid rotation of a horizontal shaft, which was transformed into a vertically rotating motion in the saw. As many as eight or ten horses were used in sawing large logs. The use of steam for running saw mills was common by 1830.

Quarries were worked in Illinois prior to 1830 only for local purposes. Limestone was burned into lime which was used in mortar for brick and stone buildings, and for plastering. Old lime kilns were to be seen about Alton prior to the Civil war, and these had been in general use for many years. The fact is that the French who lived in the American bottom prior to the coming of the English were accustomed to burn lime from the limestone bluffs which skirted that alluvial plain.

Coal was used for fuel in Illinois as early as 1818 or 1819. Travelers are quoted who speak of the substitution of coal for wood where the home is located in the prairies. Coal was mined near the present city of Murphysboro in Jackson County in 1825. It was mined and shipped in barges down the Big Muddy. In 1835 a charter was obtained from the Legislature creating The Mount Carbon Coal Company. In 1836, the property of this company was offered for sale, and the advertisement gives such an account of the mines, mills, boats, timber, land and machinery as to lead one to believe that coal had been mined at this place for several years.

The manufacturing processes were carried on in a very simple way. There were few companies with charters engaged in the manufacturing business. The saline in Gallatin County was the largest plant, but it was under the management of the state though private capital was invested in the enterprise. Salt was produced at Brownsville, Jackson County, near Waterloo in Monroe and on Silver Creek in Madison. There was also a "works" on Shoal Creek in Bond County. The "works" at Brownsville were owned by Conrad Will, and they were very productive, though it is said that Mr. Will did not profit from his salines.

There were wagon-makers to be found about the larger villages and towns. That does not mean that we are to understand that new wagons were made, but wagons were repaired. It would often occur that the same man was a wagon maker and a blacksmith. In other words he could if necessary not only make a wagon, that is build the wood-work, but that he could "iron" the wagon as well. Probably the most generally distributed form of manufacturing was that of making barrels and casks. The cooper was not a differentiated occupation, but it was found that any person who was handy with tools could make barrels. There was an abundance of choice oak timber which was very suitable for staves and heads.

Brick making and bricklaying were among the skilled occupations. Stone masons and plasterers were in general demand. Professional bridge builders were scarce, though two bridges were built across the Kaskaskia about the time Illinois was admitted into the Union. One spanned the river at Kaskaskia and the other at Covington. The one at Kaskaskia fell into the stream shortly after 1832 as stated by Mr. Gustavus Pape, who as a boy of eight or nine years came to Kaskaskia in 1832. He lives in Chester and has a clear and full memory of the "old town" reaching back to 1832. Tanneries and rope-walks were to be found in every community. Carding wool was carried on by machinery and by hand. We have spoken of a carding mill operated by Jesse B. Thomas in the town of Cahokia. Spinning and weaving were carried on in nearly every home.

RELIGION

It is no exaggeration to say that religion was the concern of the great mass of the people from the earliest times. In many localities in the early day where there was no ordained minister, the people met together and had a sort of informal service. Songs were sung, scriptures read, and sermons were repeated by one of their number. When some ordained minister would appear in a neighborhood, all the people regardless of creeds would meet to hear the preaching of the Word, and to enjoy religious intercourse. No houses of worship were built in the Territorial period and very few churches prior to 1820. Buildings which had been used as school houses were frequently used for preaching service. But more frequently the homes of the settlers were the places for religious gatherings.

There were four "denominations" in Illinois prior to 1820—Methodist, Baptist, Presbyterian, and Catholic. There were missionaries from other churches but these four were the only ones that had organized congregations prior to 1820. The work of the Methodist Church was carried on largely by the Reverend Jesse Walker. The Methodists had come into Illinois as early as 1793. Circuit riders were sent here, and they were very active. The Rev. Jesse Walker arrived in 1806. He had preached in North Carolina, and from there came by way of Tennessee into Illinois. Walker was a tireless worker and was a co-worker with Bishop McKendree. About the time Illinois was admitted he transferred his labors to St. Louis. In 1824 the Rev. Mr. Walker was preaching in the north part of Illinois to whites and savages alike. He eventually located in Chicago about 1826 where he preached for several years. He had a small building, at the forks of the river, in which he lived and in which he held preaching services. He was also engaged in missionary work at the same time. He died in 1835.

The Methodist Church also had the support of a powerful pioneer preacher, the Rev. Peter Cartwright. He came into the Sangamon country in 1823. He was a prominent character in Illinois till his death in 1872. We shall speak further of him in a future chapter.

The Presbyterians had sent a few missionaries into Illinois before 1817. In that year the Rev. Mr. Samuel Wylie appeared in the vicinity of Kaskaskia and organized a settlement east of the Kaskaskia River. These people were known as "covenanters" and there are still large numbers of them in Randolph County. Other congregations were formed in the settled parts prior to 1830. A Mr. Kent established a congregation at the lead mines as early as 1829. A young Presbyterian minister by the name of Elbridge Gerry Young reached Vandalia in the fall of 1824. He had ridden on horseback from Worcester, Massachusetts, to Vandalia, a distance of 1,342 miles. This Mr. Young went north and preached at Carrollton, and at Apple Creek, which evidently was White Hall. He preached at Diamond Grove where he selected a place to live which was afterwards selected as the site for Illinois College. Mr. Young afterwards moved to Springfield, where in 1827 he took steps to build a Presbyterian Church. Greenville and vicinity became the center of Presbyterian activity. Shawneetown was visited by nearly all the missionaries as they journeyed down the Ohio and out into the interior of Illinois. A Mr. Low in 1816 visited the town and says: "Among its two or three hundred inhabitants there was not a single soul that made any pretensions to religion. Their shocking profaneness was enough to make one afraid to walk the street; and those who on the Sabbath were not fighting and drinking at the taverns and grog-shops, were either hunting in the woods or trading behind their counters." A Mrs. Tillson was there in November, 1822. She says: "One hotel, the only brick house in the place, made quite a commanding appearance from the river." She then tells how desolate and disgusting the interior of this commanding brick hotel was. (This hotel was called the Rawlins House and stood a few doors up the bank of the river from the large hotel which now faces the river.) "The finish was of the cheapest kind, the plastering hanging loose from the walls, the floors carpetless. The landlord was a whiskey keg in the morning and a keg of whiskey at night. Her description of the conduct of the son-in-law and his wife shows how crude the people and how low the social standards. The Presbyterian Church at Shawneetown was organized by the Rev. B. F. Spillman in December, 1823. The first church was a one-story frame house erected about where the Riverside Hotel now stands. This was about 1832. Prior to that date the congregation met in private houses, halls or warehouses.

Presbyterianism was planted in Jacksonville, Illinois, June 30, 1827. At that time a group of people who belonged to that faith met in the barn of Judge Leeper, one mile south of the village. All who attended were already church members. They had been thoughtful to bring into this new country certificates of their membership in the old churches back east. They entered into a sort of compact with one another and with God and thus established the basis of the first Presbyterian Church in Jacksonville. The membership was as follows: "John Leeper and Fidelia, his wife; Edwin A. Mears and Sarah, his wife; James Mears and Polly, his wife; Marvey McClung; James Kerr and Janet, his wife; Wm. C. Posey and Sarah, his wife; and Hector G. Taylor." It was to this congregation which the Rev. John M. Ellis came about 1828. The Rev. Mr. Ellis laid the foundations for the Jacksonville Female Academy and for Illinois College. A Presbyterian Church was organized in Carmi in November, 1827, by the Rev. B. F. Spillman.

The Synod of Indiana, in 1828, created The Center Presbytery of Illinois. The first presbytery met at Kaskaskia in January, 1829. At this Presbytery report showed eight ministers and twenty-one churches in Illinois. One year later the membership was reported at 432.

The Baptist faith was planted in Illinois as early as 1787. New Design, which was located four miles south of Waterloo, the present county seat of Monroe County, was the center of this planting. Although no church of the Baptist faith was organized until 1796, there was probably more activity among the Baptists than among the Methodists. A missionary by the name of James Smith came to New Design from Kentucky in 1787. There were several early settlers about New Design. Some of them were soldiers with General Clark in 1778. The Reverend Smith preached and there were many conversions. In 1794 the Rev. Josiah Dodge, also from Kentucky, came to New Design and preached effectively. Among those converted under his preaching was James Lemen, who later became a preacher in the Baptist Church. The first Baptist Church was organized by the Rev. Joseph Chance and Elder David Badgley. This was in 1796. Among the noted Baptist preachers who gave of their time and talents to the spreading of the Gospel in Illinois were: Father Clark, who was a teacher as well as a preacher. He was held in high esteem and performed invaluable services in spreading the Baptist faith in this state. The Reverend James Lemen was also held in great respect and even reverence by those who came to know him. A Rev. Mr. Lindley preached in the open in the Sangamon country. He was probably not a scholarly preacher, but he ministered acceptably to the early pioneers. Other of the Lemen family beside James became preachers. But without doubt the most noted preacher in the Baptist Church was the Rev. John M. Peck, who came into the state as early as 1817 or 18. Dr. John Peck had two special missions—one to oppose the introduction of slavery into Illinois and the other to get people to do more reading of the Bible. Doctor Peck was not only a real missionary preacher, but he was a writer of no mean ability. He was self made in an educational way but his learning and the facility of his pen enabled him to make a real contribution to the literature of the day. The Baptist churches grew in number and in membership.

The Catholic Church came into Illinois with the first whites, the first church, of course, being the mission of the Immaculate Conception. Churches or missions were established at various points in the early days. Kaskaskia was the most important church, but the one at Cahokia was also an important station. A mission was established at Fort Massac and also one at Peoria. It does not appear that there was any church or mission at or near Starved Rock in the days of the territorial period, or in the early days of statehood. Governor Reynolds, who knew Illinois well from 1800 till the Civil war, says there were missions or churches established on Prairie du Long Creek in Monroe County as early as 1816; this location was in what is now Prairie du Long Township in the extreme eastern end of Monroe County. Another station was located some miles south of Prairie du Rocher, probably at what is now the Station of Madoc on the railroad from Chester to Prairie du Rocher. Prior to 1830 a small colony of Kentuckians who were of the Catholic faith settled in Sangamon County. But the most noted church after the church at Kaskaskia was the church at the village near the great Fort Chartres. This church was the Church at St. Anne. At the village of Prairie du Rocher there was located the Church of St. Joseph. This was a weak church and was called a "succursal" of the St. Anne Church, or a "chapel of ease" to the St. Anne Church.

The Church of St. Anne was, so long as the fort was occupied, one of the most important Catholic churches in Illinois. From the earliest date it was the representative of the church as a whole while the military commander and the officers and soldiers were representatives of the government of France. Thus the church and the state worked side by side.

The records of the St. Anne Church are or were, recently, in the keeping of the priest in charge of the St. Joseph Church in Prairie du Rocher. Among the articles saved from the St. Anne Church are the following: The Register from 1716 to the date when the village was deserted, some time about the end of the 18th century; the mission chalice and patten, the pyxis, the sacred vessel in which holy communion was brought to the sick; baptismal requisites; oil stocks; the ostensorium. These sacred relics are well preserved and are kept as reminders of the days of great prosperity in both church and state.

When the French government outlawed the Jesuit order in France in 1763, and when the Superior Council of Louisiana suppressed the order in the Province of Louisiana, there was a decline in the activities of the Catholic Church. Three Jesuit fathers were deported, everything belonging to the order confiscated except books and clothing belonging to the priests. The suppression of the Jesuit order was a great blow to the cause of the Catholic Church. While Illinois was passing through the territorial stages the Catholic Church was barely holding its own. There were no churches outside of the French settlements, but before 1830 there were other churches than those in the French villages. Governor Reynolds locates three English speaking Catholic congregations in Illinois prior to 1830. He says: "These colonies of Americans, together with the French, embraced all the Catholic congregations in early days. (Prior to 1825.)

Some Legislation

In the period from 1809 to 1830, there were some important laws enacted. The laws, provided for the Territory of Illinois from 1809 to 1818, were enacted by the Legislative arm of the government. This was the governor and the three judges from 1809 to 1812. The territory passed into the second class in 1812 to 1818. In this second period there was a Legislature of a Lower and Upper House. The Ordinance provided that the laws and the first grade of territory should be selected from the laws of the older states. These were to be reported to Congress, which should endorse or reject them. While this was the theory a good many laws were put into operation and enforced that Congress did not have an opportunity to endorse. In 1818 when Illinois was admitted into the Union the laws which had been in operation in the territorial period were carried over into the period of statehood and were valid until they were set aside by the General Assembly.

The most noted law applicable to the people of the Illinois Territory was what was known as the Preemption Law. This was a Federal law, but its enactment was secured by the delegate from Illinois in the National Congress. The law provided that a settler who built a home on a piece of Government land and improved it could not be dispossessed by another person until the first one had had a fair opportunity to enter the land himself.

Another important law which was enacted by the Legislature in 1816 was the chartering of banks. It was a common thing for the territorial legislatures to grant charters for the organization of banks within the territory. In 1816 the General Assembly chartered three territorial banks. One at Kaskaskia, one at Shawneetown, and one at Edwardsville. In the next session of the Legislature a bank, called the Bank of Cairo, was chartered. There was only a prospective Cairo, and the bank opened in Kaskaskia and began to issue bank bills and do other things which banks usually do.

When the state came into the Union, it was necessary to enlarge on the laws used during the territorial period. One law which was considered necessary consisted of twenty-five sections, and was called the Black Code. It dealt with nearly every imaginable relation which the black people might have with the whites and with the state. It was not repealed till the Civil war.

Another law passed by the first General Assembly under the constitution provided for a request of Congress for the granting of four square miles of land upon which the state might erect a capitol building—the part not used for the building and necessary grounds would be sold and the money used as a public fund. The grant was made by the General Government and commissioners located the new city where Vandalia now stands—the capital was removed thither in 1820.

Probably the most important law enacted by the Illinois General Assembly was a law passed in 1821 creating the State Bank of Illinois. This bank had a parent bank at Vandalia and branches at Shawneetown, Edwardsville, and at Brownsville. The capital was fixed at $500,000. The state was behind the bank and held itself responsible for all its obligations. The bank was so badly managed that the end of the charter period in 1831, the state was obliged to borrow $100,000 to pay up the losses of the bank.

The act of the general assembly in 1823 providing for a vote for or against the calling of a convention to revise the Constitution of Illinois, precipitated one of the hardest political contests ever known in the history of Illinois. The campaign for and against the calling of the convention lasted from the early spring of 1823 to August, 1824, a period of one and a half years. This contest developed the management of newspapers in a marked degree. It also gave occasion for the development of skill in debate and argument. While men's passions were stirred to the highest pitch, there was a sudden cooling off after the August election. The proof of this is the fact that the anti-slavery people won in the convention fight and elected a Senate and House which was anti-slavery, yet in the election of the two United States senators in the following winter, two pro-slavery men were elected.

There is no reference to schools or education in the Constitution of 1818. And there seemed to be little interest in education among the mass of the people except on the part of the ministers of the several churches. Although Governor Bond had in his first message called the attention of the Legislature to the value of education and the obligation of the Legislature to provide for its dissemination, nothing was done till 1825. At the session of the Legislature which met December, 1824, Senator Joseph Duncan from Jackson County introduced a bill which was enacted into the first free school law in Illinois. The majority of the people in Illinois at that time were from states where free schools supported by general taxation were unknown. They were therefore much opposed to the law which the Legislature had enacted establishing free education at public expense. The law was very much like the law of 1855 which in its main features is similar to the school law in Illinois today. The law in its essential features was repealed in 1829.

Social Progress

The great body of people in Illinois, prior to 1830, came from a simple folk in the older states. There were of course no classes in America. There were wealthy people and there were poor people, but there was no impassable gulf between them. In Virginia and the Carolinas there was a rich planter class. None of these came to Illinois. Immigrants to Illinois from the southern colonies came from the small land owner or from those who belonged to the landless class. In New England there were many educated people. There were many families which had wide connections and a long noted ancestry. The Livingstons, the Adamses, and the Lees were noted families. None of this class came into Illinois prior to 1830.

The people who did come into Illinois, with exceptions, were of the laboring class. They had been used to hard work prior to coming to Illinois, and their lot was no easier here. They worked in the soil, in the timber, or in shops—blacksmiths, wagon-makers, coopers, weavers, tanners, or woodsmen. They were, before coming to Illinois, busy providing the essentials of life—food, clothing and shelter. They were an uncultured

THE ONLY REMAINING HOUSE IN OLD BROWNSVILLE, THE FIRST COUNTY SEAT OF JACKSON COUNTY. BUILT ABOUT 1830.

people because they lacked leisure. Men and women who work from the sun's rising to its setting will not take time to expose themselves to the refining influences that people of wealth can have access to. Travelers have given us true pictures of the social life in which the early settlers lived, and from these descriptions we are compelled to admit that the pioneers were crude, honest, hardworking people with few of the agencies which bring refinement and culture into their lives.

We must not conclude that there were no agencies of culture accessible, and no leisure for some. Many of the people who came into Illinois and engaged in public life in various ways were college men, many were graduates of reputable colleges of the middle and northern states. Along with this mental training they brought wealth, books, paintings, and a taste for the good things they found about them. Such persons would be a cultured class in the wilderness. But these people were found among the doctors, lawyers, judges, editors, merchants, and preachers. And the number of men in each class was not large.

Schools and churches, the agencies of culture and knowledge for the common people, were woefully lacking till after 1830. If there were schools they were held in places where the outlook upon the world counteracted the tendency to discipline of mind and the culture of the soul. Abandoned houses, store rooms, residences and sometimes especially constructed log schoolhouses furnished the meeting place for a dozen children from the humble homes of the neighborhood. There were not many church buildings except in the larger towns. The nature of the sermons, the songs, and the prayers were not conducive to light hearts and happy minds.

The purely social gatherings were often crude and not cultural in their influences. There was the pioneer custom of visiting. Families would often go on visits to neighboring families and stay for one or two meals. In such cases the men would spend their time about the stables, pig pens, horse lots, and other places where the farmers' interests centered. The women folk would center their interest in the preparation of the meals and perchance in the loom which was just ready to discharge a piece of cloth for the winter clothing. The children grouped themselves according to age about games, or crude toys which the older boys were often able to produce. The simple, though bountiful, meal of pork or fowl, or game from the woods and streams, was reenforced by the products of the garden and the farm. Turnips in season, cabbage, sweet potatoes, corn bread, milk, butter and cottage cheese, sorghum molasses, wild honey, and on rare occasions coffee sweetened with the sugar from the maple tree, pumpkin pies, with now and then preserves prepared by the good housewife—these were the substantial delicacies which were placed before the visitors. But the climax was reached when the "pound cake" was "passed" at the close of the meal.

There was more or less of the real social life of the country people shown at the church services. People came to the place of worship before the hour set for the sermon. If it were a hall, school house, or church building in which the services were to be held, the women usually entered and took seats on one side of the room. The men would gather about the yard in knots of three or four, where the crops were discussed or the latest bit of news was related. After the sermon and the benediction the good people often lingered about the place of worship and exchanged greetings and compliments.

Funerals and burials were the occasions for the exchange of

S. NO. 1.

A BILL

Providing for the establishment of Free Schools.

To enjoy our rights and liberties, we must understand them: their security and protection ought to be
2 the first object of a free people: and it is a well established fact, that no nation has ever continued long
3 in the enjoyment of civil and political freedom, which was not both virtuous and enlightened: and believ-
4 ing that the advancement of literature always has been, and ever will be, the means of developing more
5 fully the rights of man; that the mind of every citizen in a republic is the common property of society,
6 and constitutes the basis of its strength and happiness: it is therefore considered the peculiar duty of a
7 free government like ours, to encourage and extend the improvement and cultivation of the intellectual
8 energies of the whole: Therefore,

SEC. 1. *Be it enacted by the People of the State of Illinois represented in the General Assembly,* That
2 there shall be established a common school or schools in each of the counties of this state, which shall
3 be open and free to every class of white citizens between the ages of five and eighteen years.

SEC. 2. *Be it further enacted,* That the county commissioners' courts shall, from time to time, form
2 school districts in their respective counties, whenever a petition may be presented for that purpose, by
3 a majority of the qualified voters resident within such contemplated district: *Provided,* That all such
4 districts, when laid off, shall, respectively, contain not less than thirty families.

SEC. 3. *Be it further enacted,* That the legal voters in each district to be established as aforesaid,
2 may have a meeting at any time thereafter, by giving ten days previous notice of the time and place of
3 holding the same; at which meeting they may proceed by ballot to elect three trustees, one clerk, one
4 treasurer, one assessor, and one collector, who shall respectively take an oath of office faithfully to dis-
5 charge their respective duties.

SEC. 4. *Be it further enacted,* That it shall be the duty of the trustees to superintend the schools
2 within their respective districts, to examine and employ teachers, to lease all land belonging to the dis-
3 trict, to call meetings of the voters whenever they shall deem it expedient, or at any time when reques-
4 ted so to do by five legal voters, by giving to each one at least five days notice of the time and place of
5 holding the same, appointing one or more persons living within the district to serve the necessary
6 notice, to make an annual report to the county commissioners' court of the proper county of the num-
7 ber of children living within the bounds of such district, between the ages of five and eighteen years,
8 and what number of them are actually sent to school, with a certificate of the time a school is actually
9 kept up in the district, with the probable expense of the same.

SEC. 5. *Be it further enacted,* That each and every school district, when established and organized as
2 aforesaid, shall be, and they are hereby, constituted a body politic and corporate, so far as to commence
3 and maintain actions on any agreement made with any person or persons for the non-performance

From Illinois Blue Book

FACSIMILE OF FIRST PAGE OF ORIGINAL BILL CREATING FREE
SCHOOLS IN ILLINOIS, 1825

the social amenities. There were no undertakers in those days, and all those trying kindnesses of neighbors in pioneer times were bravely assumed by the good neighbors of the deceased. When a death occurred in the rural community the body of the neighbor was "laid out" by strong men with tender hearts. Coffins were made in the shop of some neighbor. It was no uncommon thing to find laid away in the sheds or overhead in the home, the lumber which the good man had saved for an emergency of this kind. The grave was dug by neighbors and the body was conveyed from the home of the deceased to the place of interment by friends who wished to be of service in this sad bereavement. It was not customary for any one to leave the grave until it had been filled and the mound "patted" into shape with spades and shovels of friends. It was on such occasions that the real spirit of the pioneer life revealed itself.

There were gatherings of a less serious and sober kind. There were quilting, log-rollings, house raisings, singing-schools, corn huskings, dances, and other phases of social life which were participated in by young and old. Horse-racing and foot-racing were diversions enjoyed by all the people. A combination of the social and the religious life of the people was found in the early camp meetings. These social and religious functions did not develop to their full stature till later than 1830. They will therefore be described in a later chapter.

It was said by Mr. Fred Gerhard, who wrote a few years after the period we are considering that there were marked changes in the social life between 1820 and 1830. He says: "The coonskin cap, the hunting shirt, and leather breeches, the moccasins, and the belt around the waist, to which the hunting-knife and tomahawk were appended, had entirely disappeared before the coming of modern forms of apparel." The women had begun to exchange their home made cloth for dresses, for calico, cosmetics, and woolens, and now and then for a silk garment—much of the home made cloth was dyed by the housewife by the use of berries, barks, and nuts from the forest. In the early days the housewife wore upon her head a handkerchief usually of bright colors, which was later changed for the split bonnet. It has been said that along with the desire for better dress among women, at least, there comes a desire for more refined society. It may be that the desire for better dress is not a cause but an accompaniment of the desire for better cultural conditions.

A writer, Mr. Nathan Dillon, was a settler in Sangamon County as early as 1821. He describes the election of August, 1822, and says that they had three candidates and that all had whiskey with which they treated their supporters. While there was plenty to drink there was no fighting. The use of intoxicating liquor was common and no public gathering was held without the liquor vender. The farmer kept a good supply on hand and at threshing time, or at a house raising, or log rolling intoxicating liquors were freely drunk.

Early settlers who lived through the first ten or fifteen years of the state's history and left any record at all, all come to the same conclusion as to the social progress up to 1830. There were many encouraging improvements in nearly all phases of the social life of the people. People lived better in their homes, they had better food, at least a greater variety, they wore better clothes, roads were improving, there were more church houses, the towns were growing, there was more leisure, and there were more books, newspapers, and magazines.

The Penitentiary

We have already spoken of the move on the part of Governor Reynolds when he was in the General Assembly in 1826 to build a penitentiary in order that there might be introduced into Illinois a more humane method of punishment for the commission of crimes. The money with which to build this prison was obtained from the sale of the salt lands which Congress had donated to Illinois. In 1830 when Governor Reynolds was inaugurated as governor, he reported in his message to the Legislature that Alton had been selected as the place where the prison should be located. Commissioners had been selected and they had begun the erection of the necessary buildings. The governor reported that twenty-six cells had been begun and would be completed in the summer of 1831. There remains to this day the ruins of the old cell house as a grim reminder of the first penitentiary in Illinois.

CHAPTER VI

EARLY HISTORY OF CHICAGO

THE NAME—THE WINTER OF 1674-5—THE TREATY—THE FIRST CITIZEN—THE FIRST WEDDING—CHICAGO IN 1812—NEW FORT DEARBORN—FUR TRADING—TREATY—CHICAGO GROWS —COOK COUNTY.

Rufus Blanchard, in his history "Discovery and Conquest of the Northwest with the History of Chicago," is authority for the statement that the word Chicago means, in the Illinois Indian tongue, "onion"; and in the Pottawattomie language "polecat." And La Moth Cadillac, writing in 1695, says: "The post of Chicago comes next. This word means the river of Garlic."

THE NAME

These statements of Mr. Blanchard are endorsed by Mr. Gurdon S. Hubbard who was at that time eighty years old. He had all his life been associated with the Indians, being a fur trader.

Father St. Cosme and party sent out by the Bishop of Canada, left Michilimackinac, September 14, 1669, and reached the Chicago portage October 21, 1669. Going farther south, they found a Jesuit Mission house on the banks of Calumet Lake in charge of Father Pinet.

Charlevoix, in his "History of New France," says that Nicholas Perrot who was sent into the West to invite the several Indian tribes to send delegates to the Indian Congress to be held at the Falls of St. Mary, was escorted by Pottawattomies from Green Bay to the Chicago portage. Here Perrot found the Miamis camped to whom he delivered the invitation to attend the congress in the summer of 1672.

Joliet and Marquette, on their return from the lower Mississippi in the summer of 1763, ascended the Illinois River as a nearer route to Lake Michigan than the one by the Fox-Wisconsin portage. Father Marquette preached to the Indians at Peoria and at the Kaskaskia village near Starved Rock. At the latter place he found what he thought was a superior group of chiefs and warriors. They were deeply interested in his story of the cross and secured from him a promise that he would return and further instruct them in the Christian religion. When he was ready to proceed a number of chiefs and warriors accompanied Marquette's party to the Chicago portage. This was in September, 1673. On a map made by Father Marquette, of

Lakes Superior and Michigan, together with the Fox-Wisconsin portage, the Mississippi and Illinois rivers, there is no sign or name or anything to indicate the portage which would seem to show that at that time not much importance was attracted to this point.

The Winter 1674-5

In the fall of 1674, Marquette accompanied by two Frenchmen, Perre and Jacques, and some Indians made his way from Green Bay to Chicago on his way back to the village of Kaskaskia to fulfill his promise that he would return and tell them more of the story of the cross. The party reached the Chicago River on the 12th of December. They proceeded up the Chicago River turning into the south branch and after arriving at the portage, about six miles from the mouth of the river, they built a cabin to shelter themselves from the severe weather. They killed buffaloes, deer and turkeys. These were plentiful. They from lack of food were very poor, and some deer they killed they could not use and left on the ground where killed.

The severe weather not abating, they decided to winter in the cabin they had built. Marquette says his malady, dysentery, had so weakened him that he was unable to proceed. Marquette says on the 14th of December that Illinois Indians passed his cabin with a large stock of furs. His party traded French tobacco for three large buffalo robes which did them good service in the winter.

Eighteen leagues away was stationed some fur traders among whom was a doctor who, hearing of Marquette's illness, came to him, bringing "berries and bread." The doctor ministered to Marquette and returned to his station. On the 26th of January Marquette's cabin was visited by a number of Illinois Indians who brought food and asked for powder. Marquette told them this his mission to the Indians would not permit him to give them powder to carry on war with the Miamis. Marquette describes their stay in the cabin until the spring thaws opened the streams. On the 28th of January there was a flood of the south branch of the Chicago River. Their cabin was endangered and the people housed there were forced to move their goods to the nearby trees.

On the 30th of January they started on their way to Kaskaskia but the weather was changeable and they suffered from exposure. On the 18th of April Marquette arrived at Kaskaskia where he established a mission which was known as the "Immaculate Conception of our Lady."

Marquette remained in Kaskaskia till after Easter when he returned to the Chicago portage accompanied by many friends. From here he passed around the southerly curve of Lake Michigan thence along the eastern side of the lake to the present city of Ludington, Michigan, where he died and was buried.

Green Bay was very early known by the French missionaries, and following the winter of 1674-5 which Marquette spent at the portage of the Chicago, occasional visits were made to Chicago by the traders and missionaries from that station.

La Salle's party explored the entire length of the lower Mississippi and discovered its mouth in the summer of 1682, April 9. On the 10th they began their return journey. They stopped at Starved Rock where they built Fort St. Louis. The Chicago portage now became a prominent place as all traffic between Fort St. Louis and Canada would naturally pass through the Chicago portage.

THE TREATY

In 1795, Anthony Wayne, representing the United States, made a treaty with the Indians of the Northwest, including the Wyandottes, the Delawares, the Shawnees, the Ottawas, the Pottawattomies, the Miamis, the Chippewas, the Eel River tribe, the Weas, Piankashaws, the Kickapoos and the Kaskaskias. It is known as the Treaty of Greenville. In this treaty, Article III, there are sixteen distinct cessions of land to the United States. Cession No. 14 enumerates—"One piece of land six miles square, at the mouth of Chicago River, emptying into the southwest end of Lake Michigan, where a fort formerly stood." In the intercourse between the military commanders and the Indians of the Northwest, from the close of the French and Indian war to the end of the century, there was a very general use of the word Chicago as a sort of center of Indian life.

THE FIRST CITIZEN

In 1794 a San Domingo negro named Jean Baptiste Pont Au Sable settled on the north side of the river. Here he built a hut and traded extensively with the Indians. He is reported to have been "well educated and handsome." In 1796 he is said to have sold out his business to one Le Mai, a Frenchman. At that time the Pottawattomies were making the Chicago River and the region thereabouts their headquarters. Le Mai sold his business to John Kinzie a business man from Canada. John Kinzie was a fur trader. He came to Chicago July 4, 1804. The contract with Le Mai had probably been made the year previous. Major John Whistler with some companies of infantry arrived at the same time for the construction of Fort Dearborn. The hut into which John Kinzie moved on July 4, 1804, was the hut which was built in 1794 by Pont Au Sable or in 1796 by Le Mai. At the coming of Kinzie there were two or three other huts to the north of the river.

Following the purchase of Louisiana in 1803, the general government felt that a fort in the region of the south end of Lake Michigan was a pressing necessity. Commissioners were immediately sent into the West to select a suitable site. The mouth of the St. Joseph River had some features which seemed to commend it to the commissioners. This place was selected, but the Indians made objection and refused to cede the land for the fort. The commissioners then turned their attention to the Chicago portage. Here by the Greenville treaty the United States had been ceded a plat six miles square. There had been a fort at this place prior to 1795 since the last clause in Section 14 of Article 3 of the treaty says this grant was to be located "at or near the Chicago River—where a fort formerly stood."

Capt. John Whistler (brevet Major) was, in the summer of 1803, stationed at Detroit with a small detachment of United States troops. Late in the fall the troops were marched overland to Chicago. Captain Whistler and family came in the spring or summer of 1804. The fort was erected after the fashion of block houses of those early days. A couple of heavily built log houses with two blockhouses and smaller warehouses all enclosed by a strong picket fence made of large timbers set on end in a trench, filled in to hold them in place. It was on the south side of the river opposite or nearly so the residence of John Kinzie. Beside John Kinzie's house there were three other cabins occupied by Frenchmen. They were the homes of Le Mai, Ouilmette (Wilmette), and Pettell.

First Wedding

Major John Whistler had a son John who was married about the time his father came to Chicago. He also had a daughter Sarah who had been courted while she lived in Detroit by a merchant, James Abbott. At any rate in the fall of 1804 a wedding was celebrated in the unfinished fort. The commandant, Major Whistler posted on the bulletin board at the fort this notice: "The commandant and Mrs. John Whistler request the pleasure of your presence at the marriage of their daughter, Sarah, to James Abbott of Detroit, at the fort on November 1, 1804." The notice was read by the passer-by and upon the evening of the first of November, a select company assembled in a suitable room in the fort where John Kinzie performed the marriage ceremony. On the morrow the bride and groom started on their honeymoon through the wilderness to Detroit.

Chicago in 1812.

The point which we call Chicago did not grow very much from 1804 to 1812. There were in 1812, according to a map which is found in Blanchard's Northwest and Chicago, the fort on the south side of the river, an old house between the fort and the mouth of the river on the south side, the agency house close to the fort on the same side but up the river, Kinzie's residence

CHICAGO IN 1831, SHOWING FORT DEARBORN

just opposite the fort on the north side of the river, and near it the house of Ouilmette. Farther up the river on the north side was Burn's house, and opposite this home on the south side of the river an Indian encampment. Several miles up the south branch of the river was Lee's place. This man was engaged in farming and had some hired help.

The incidents connected with the Fort Dearborn Massacre have been given in a preceding chapter and need not be given here. Following the massacre the troops and the wounded were scattered among the Indians who were glad to hold them as a sign of personal bravery. The Lee family, excepting one, were butchered. The Burns family were carried away. The French family was not disturbed and the Kinzies remained in their home after the Indians had departed with their prisoners.

News of peace of Ghent reached America in the early part of the year 1815. In 1816 the Government began to plan for the defense of the Northwest. Old Fort Dearborn had been burned by the Indians following the massacre. The place was practically deserted. There was no one even to bury the dead after the massacre was over. Nothing was done till the coming of Captain Hezekiah Bradley whom the Government sent with a small army of two companies to reconstruct Fort Dearborn.

New Fort Dearborn

The new buildings were placed very nearly on the old spot. A single block house was built. To the east of this were barracks, and storage buildings. The whole was enclosed with a high palisade. At the same time Major Long was sent by the Government to make a survey between the lake and the head waters of the Illinois with the idea in mind that eventually a canal would be constructed.

Ninian Edwards, William Clark, and Auguste Chouteau were authorized to enter into a treaty with the Ottawas, Chippewas, and Pottawattomies. This treaty was made at St. Louis in August, 1816. The purpose was to secure a new cession of all lands south of the parallel of the southern end of Lake Michigan, and to secure a cession of a strip of land some twenty miles wide from Chicago to Ottawa, the mouth of Fox River, which should serve as a right of way upon which to build the canal of which we have just spoken.

During the summer of 1816, Mr. John Kinzie returned to his home in Chicago. His house had not been disturbed by the Indians when they burned Fort Dearborn. The house had been occupied by a Frenchman who was on good terms with the Indians. Captain Bradley was still busy in the early spring of 1817 completing the details of the fort and surroundings. The bricks from the old ware house just outside the first fort were used to build a magazine in the new structure.

In 1818 when Nathaniel Pope was securing the passage of the Enabling Act for the admission of Illinois into the Union he plead before the House of Representatives for the boundary line to be placed as far north as 42° 30′; he argued that Chicago would some day be a large port and that it would be the end of a canal which would connect Lake Michigan with the Illinois River. Mr. Blanchard says at that very moment there were but two white families in Chicago, that of John Kinzie and that of Ouilmette.

FORT DEARBORN MARKER

Fur Trading

About this time, 1818, a fur trading station had been established at the Lee farm on the south branch of the Chicago River. Shortly after this date the American Fur Company bought out the company which had a post at the Lee farm and for many years the American Fur Company was a prominent business institution in the village. Mr. John Baptist Beaubien who was the agent of the American Fur Company was displaced by Mr. John Crafts, who had managed the first trading post. Mr. Beaubien moved over on the Des Plaines. His descendants have been about Chicago for one hundred years. Gordon S. Hubbard, a young man of sixteen, came from Montreal by way of Mackinaw to Chicago in company with 100 clerks and traders on their way into Illinois to buy furs for the American Fur Company. Young Hubbard was the guest of John Kinzie and is authority for the statement that Kinzie and Ouilmette were the only persons permanently residing in Chicago—excepting of course the garrison at the fort. Connected with the garrison was an Indian agency with two officials. These men were useful in keeping down misunderstandings, and contentions. They also had large quantities of goods furnished by the Government which they were required to sell to the Indians at ten per cent less than to the whites. The American Fur Company was so well organized that it could undersell the Government factory and the latter lost its importance.

TREATY

In August, 1821, a great treaty congress was held in Chicago. To this congress 3,000 warriors came. They came from Michigan, and Governor Cass of that territory represented the Government. Henry R. Schoolcraft, the writer of Indian life, passed through Chicago at this time and he says there were but two families outside of the garrison.

A Mr. James Galloway of Pennsylvania came to Chicago to hunt out a good location for a house. He arrived in 1824. He got acquainted with Billy Caldwell and Alexander Robinson, two Indian chiefs. In addition there were Doctor Woolcott, Ouilmette, and John Kinzie. Chicago then had five residents. Mr. Galloway returned to Ohio for his family. After many adventures he reached Chicago and wintered 1825-6 in a house near Lee's Farm. At the place called Lee's Farm there were four men and now Chicago is growing. In 1829 Mary Galloway and Archibald Claybourn were married and settled in Chicago.

Chicago was laid out in town lots in 1829. The town was platted on the grounds granted in the Canal Bill of 1827. In the latter part of 1827 the Winnebago war broke out, but there were at that time no troops at Fort Dearborn and the war had to be fought with regulars from Fort St. Louis and militiamen from southern Illinois. This flurry called the Winnebago war will be discussed in connection with the Blackhawk war.

CHICAGO GROWS

The talk of the Illinois and Michigan Canal and the laying out of Chicago into town lots were the cause of a rush to Chicago of many adventurers. John Wentworth in a lecture before the Chicago Historical Society in 1876 gives the names of sixteen taxpayers in Chicago in 1825. This list includes people who lived far away from what was then Chicago, however there are some familiar names,—Beaubien, Clybourne, Kinzie, LaFramboise, Robinson, Ouilmette. In 1826 there were thirty-five people who could vote--three-fourths of them were French and half-breed Indians who probably had no settled home in or about Chicago. In 1830 only three paid taxes, John B. Beaubien, Joseph LaFramboise, and David McKee. Old settlers like Crafts, Clybourne, Kinzie, Robinson, Woolcott, and Ouilmette did not vote. Only six of those who voted in 1826 voted in 1830. Mr. Wentworth suggested that the French and half-breeds may have been away on hunting and trading expeditions. We conclude from a remark he makes about the people voting with the fort, that some or all of the soldiers in the fort voted when soldiers were stationed there. If the soldiers voted, the number of votes misleads as to the number of settlers. Mr. Wentworth says there was nothing south of the river except the fort, the factory-warehouse, light house, a log hut near the lake where one of the Beau-

SANGANASH HOTEL, CHICAGO
Built about 1832 and managed by a Mr. Beaubien. The small log house is Philo Carpenter's drug store

biens lived and a log house near the forks of the river where the other Beaubien resided. A comparison of names in the list of voters in 1826 with the list of 1830 shows a marked change from French to Anglo-Saxon. In the tax list of 1825, the voting list of 1826, and the voting list of 1830 there are sixty-five different names and Mr. Wentworth thinks these are the people from whom the old people in Chicago were descended. In 1876 when Mr. Wentworth delivered his second lecture on Chicago he said there were just three of the sixty-five men living—Mark Beaubien in 1876 was seventy-six years old. He was the father of twenty-three children, fifty-three grandchildren, and quite a few great-grandchildren. The second person lived at that time near Peoria. He was a Government blacksmith to the Indians by the terms of the treaty made by General Cass with the Michigan

Indians in 1821. The third man was Medard Beaubien. This man was in 1876 living with the Pottawattomie Indians in Kansas.

Cook County

1. Cook County, as it is today, was from June 20, 1790, to February 3, 1801, at part of Knox County, Northwest Territory.

2. From February 3, 1801, to September 14, 1812, it was a part of St. Clair County, Indiana and Illinois Territories.

3. From September 14, 1812, to November 28, 1814, Cook County was a part of Madison County, Illinois Territory.

4. From November 28, 1814, to December 31, 1816, it was a part of Edwards County, Illinois Territory.

5. From December 31, 1816, to March 22, 1819, Cook County was a part of Crawford County, Illinois Territory and State of Illinois.

From March 22, 1819, to January 31, 1821, Cook County was a part of Clark County, Illinois.

From January 31, 1821, to January 28, 1823, Cook County was a part of Pike County, Illinois.

From January 28, 1823, to January 13, 1825, Cook County was attached to Fulton County, Illinois.

From January 13, 1825, to January 15, 1831, Cook County was a part of Putnam County, Illinois.

Cook County was created by the Legislature January 15, 1831. At that time it included the north part of Will, all of Du Page, all of Lake, a strip off the east part of McHenry, and a small rectangle from the northeast corner of Kane, as well as the present area of the county.

At the first election in Cook County, in 1832, there were 114 votes cast. But as there was but one voting place in the county there evidently were many who did not vote. The population of Putnam County in 1830 by the Federal census was 1,310, including the territory of Peoria. One hundred fourteen votes would indicate a population of 570.

CHAPTER VII

THE LAST INDIAN WAR

TREATIES—THE LEAD MINES—BLACK HAWK—THE WINNEBAGO WAR—RAISING TROOPS—THE MILITARY TRACT—SAUKENUK BOUGHT—VOLUNTEERS—THE ARMY—THE INTERIM—MILITIA CALLED—ORGANIZATION—THE MARCH—STILLMAN'S DEFEAT—BURYING THE DEAD.

From the earliest coming of the English speaking people into the Illinois country till the close of the Black Hawk war, there was never a time when there was not a "red" peril. It is within the limits of truth to say that as a class of people there was no dependence to be placed in the red man. There were of course some good Indians, but it has been said that "a good Indian is a dead Indian." It has remained as a problem to understand how so small a number of Indians could seriously interfere with the settlement and development of the state. By the census of 1810 there were twelve thousand people in Illinois. Of this number, by the rule that one-fifth of the population constitutes the fighting strength, the territory of Illinois had 2,458 men who could bear arms. In 1830 there were 157,445 people in Illinois and by the above rule there were 31,500 men able to bear arms. At this time there were no more than a few thousand Indian warriors all told within the limits of Illinois. When we make the comparison, and remember that in the presence of such a strong army as Illinois could raise, the Indians were but a drop in the bucket, we are at a loss to know just why so small an affair as the Black Hawk war should have occupied the attention of the state and of the United States for so long a period as to cost $2,000,000.

TREATIES

In 1804, June 27, William Henry Harrison, Governor of Indiana Territory and of the District of Louisiana, Superintendent of Indian affairs, being appointed a commissioner plenipotentiary to conclude treaties with Indians in the Northwestern Territory, did on the above date, conclude a treaty at St. Louis, Missouri, with five of the chiefs of the Sac and Fox Indians. In this treaty the chiefs released all claims to all lands west of Fox River and the Illinois River, and east of the Mississippi, and south of the Wisconsin River. For this cession the United States was to pay certain sums of money annually and goods of certain values so long as the United States should hold the ceded territory. But it was agreed in Article 7—"As long as the lands which are now ceded to the United States remain their property, the Indians belonging to said tribes shall enjoy the privilege of living and hunting upon them." This article was afterwards interpreted to mean that whenever the United States should survey and sell this land to actual settlers, that then the Indians should vacate the territory thus ceded.

It should be stated here that Black Hawk, an Indian belonging to the Sac and Fox tribes, was born on Rock River in 1767; he was therefore at the time this treaty was made a warrior of twenty-seven years. He claimed the pretended treaty, made by Mr. Harrison with five chiefs of the Sac and Fox tribes, was a fraud and a deception. That the chiefs were made drunk and were loaded down with presents and their signatures secured while they were drunk.

One article provided that the United States should have the privilege of building a fort on or near the Mississippi River in the vicinity of the mouth of the Wisconsin River, and a tract of land not exceeding two miles square was ceded by the chiefs for that purpose.

Provisions were made whereby Indian agents who should be licensed by the commissioner of Indian affairs, might live in the territory ceded and carry on trade with the Indian tribes.

The War of 1812 came in due course of time. The Indians northwest of the Ohio River entered into this war on the side of the British. It was thought best at the close of the war, to conclude treaties with the several tribes of the northwest following the treaty of Ghent. General Harrison and Lewis Cass on behalf of the United States made treaties with the Delawares, Shawness, Senecas, and Miamis at Greenville, Ohio. William Clark, governor of Missouri, Ninian Edwards, governor of Illinois, and Hon. Auguste Chouteau of St. Louis were appointed commissioners to conclude treaties with the Indians farther west. These three commissioners met the Pottawattomies on the east bank of the Mississippi opposite the mouth of the Missouri River where they, July, 1815, made treaties in which the above tribe ceded a strip of land reaching from Lake Michigan to Ottawa. This strip of land was granted by the Indians with the understanding that a canal would be dug from the lake to the Illinois River at Ottawa. The grant is said to have contained 9,911,411 acres of land. In another treaty made at the same time with the same Indians, all lands within the limits of the present State of Illinois west of the meridian running through the southerly bend of Lake Michigan and reaching as far west as the Mississippi was ceded to the United States. The Sac Indians did not take part in this treaty but later they entered into a treaty renewing the treaty at St. Louis in 1804.

Following the War of 1812 and the treaties of Greenville, and of St. Louis in 1815, there was for a decade perfect quiet so far as the Indians were concerned. The public mind was concerned about the admission of Illinois into the Union, the election of officers, the struggle against slavery, and the political activities over state and national questions. In this decade there was an extension of settlements toward the north, the building of roads, towns, and homes far north along the east line of the state and along the Mississippi and Illinois rivers. There was also a goodly number of people who had come into Illinois by way of the northern routes through Ohio and Indiana. These had settled along the eastern side of the state, a few venturing along the water courses which make up the Illinois River.

The Lead Mines

The French early dug lead about the present city of Galena, but there was little interest by Americans prior to 1823. In that year the Government leased the mines on the Fevre River to Colonel James Johnson, a brother to Hon. Richard M. Johnson of Kentucky. Colonel Johnson brought into the district a complete outfit of tools, machinery, and overseers to carry on an extensive operation. For a while there was much interest in the digging of lead, but by 1826 the interest had abated and it is said there were fewer than a hundred people about the mines; but "in 1828 the country was almost literally filled with miners, smelters, merchants, speculators, gamblers, and every description of character."

An appeal was made to the Home Missionary Society for workers and Bibles. It was said that when the rush began that there were 1,500 people and that two-thirds were Americans, and one-third were Irish Catholics. The appeal said there were no preachers, Protestant or Catholic, but that an effort was being made to erect a house of worship and to secure a preacher. "Every steamboat brings workers and by July it is thought there will be 10,000 people here." More than five million pounds of lead were taken from the mines. There were also some settlements scattered along the Illinois River and along other streams. The white settlers were often very scattered. One missionary passing over the county said of a village on the Illinois, that a hundred miles of wilderness separated it from the capital at Springfield.

Black Hawk

Black Hawk was a Sac Indian born in 1767 on the Rock River near its mouth where his tribe lived. He was a keen, shrewd, unprincipled Indian who had all the advantages of living among white people. He was morose, resentful, and secretive. He had the effrontery to contend about things and deny their existence

VIEW ALONG BLACK HAWK TRAIL NEAR DIXON

From Illinois Blue Book

when documentary evidence proved him a falsifier. He has been pointed to as a defender of his people and one who could put self-interest behind him and serve for others. Early in his life he became envious of Keokuk, who has been characterized as a great chieftain. Black Hawk was not a chief in his tribe although he is often so designated. He held a deadly hatred of the Osages. When the five chiefs of the Sac tribe were making the treaty of 1804 with the United States Commissioners Edwards, Chouteau, and Clark, Black Hawk was hidden in the bushes near the council table and afterwards claimed his tribe knew nothing of the treaty till it was made and accepted by the United States.

When the War of 1812 came on, Black Hawk joined the British band in the northwest. The pioneers of the northwest had had prior to this war a hard struggle. The Indians under the influence of British agents, who operated from Canada, were a constant menace to the frontiersmen in northern Ohio, Indiana, and Illinois. The loss of Detroit, Mackinaw, and the Fort Dearborn Massacre, all in the summer of 1812, opened the flood gates of Indian barbarity in northern, central, and even in southern Illinois. Black Hawk, with 200 braves, joined the British at Detroit and was with them till the end of the war. Instead of submitting to the results of the War of 1812 and the treaty of peace signed at Ghent in January, 1815, Black Hawk put in most of his time working up dissatisfaction among his followers and now and then killing and scalping a few whites.

In 1822 another treaty was made with the Sac and Fox Indians. These Indians confirmed and acknowledged the binding force of the treaty of St. Louis made in 1804 in which the tribe ceded all lands east of the Mississippi to the United States. Black Hawk signed the treaty of 1822 and thus gave sanction to the treaty of 1804. In 1825 another treaty was made chiefly for the purpose of bringing about peace among the Indians themselves. In this treaty the one of 1804 was confirmed.

The Winnebago War

This war, so called, was not at all different from what had been transpiring on the northwest frontier of Illinois for the past two decades. Its story has become a part of the history of Illinois though occurring partly beyond the limits of the state. Mr. Frank Stevens, who has written an authentic account of the Black Hawk war, gives a simple account of the cause of the Winnebago scare. The Dakotas, a western tribe, wantonly murdered two Chippewa Indians near Fort Snelling in the early summer of 1827. As the crime was committed within the territory under the control of the commandant at Fort Snelling, that official caused the arrest of the four Dakotas guilty of the murder of the two Chippewas. The murderers were given the chance to run for their lives, but were shot down by the bullets of the Chippewas. The Winnebagoes, who lived in the northwest corner of Illinois, were friendly to the Dakotas, who lived west of the Mississippi. It happened that the Winnebagoes had a matter to settle with the Chippewas and after a short conflict the Winnebagoes were worsted and returned crestfallen. While they were thus grieving over their defeat, they were approached by agents of the Dakotas who succeeded in making the Winnebagoes believe that the four Indians killed by the Chippewas were not Dakotas, but were Winnebagoes. It was further established in the mind of Red Bird that the whites—particularly the commandant at Fort Snelling—were responsible for the death of the four Winnebagoes. Thus was laid the foundation for acts of vengeance upon the whites. Red Bird, a chief of the Winnebagoes, together with two of his warriors, visited the trading post at Prairie du Chien, in June, 1827. The garrison and the Government goods had been removed to Fort Snelling and there were only a few people left about the station. Red Bird succeeded in getting a quantity of powder from a trader and a limited supply of whiskey. With these the three Indians prepared for a diabolical scene which almost beggars description.

These Indians visited the home of a young French citizen, Registre Gagnier, who lived not far from the post of Prairie du Chien, and found in the home the man, his wife, two children and an old American soldier. The Indians were fed. And at a moment when the white men were off their guard, the Indians fell upon them and killed them. The wife obtaining the gun of her dead husband, drove the three Indians into the yard, then making her escape to the post, made report of what had happened. A few whites returned with her to her home to find her baby scalped but not dead. The Indians had made their escape.

On the same afternoon, June 26, 1827, two boats returning from Fort Snelling, which was situated near the present City of Minneapolis, were attacked above the mouth of the Wisconsin by a large number of Indians. Two of the crew of one boat were killed and four wounded. Several Indians were killed. Red Bird, chief of the Winnebagoes, was not in this attack on the keel boats, but Black Hawk was, as he afterwards admitted.

The news of this attack upon the boats soon reached the region in the northwest corner of the state and several thousand people in the vicinity of Galena fled to that town for protection. Reports spread to the settlements about Ottawa and shortly reached Chicago. No doubt many of the reports were greatly exaggerated, and among these was one which purported to be an order issued by the Winnebago chiefs ordering a general massacre of the whites in the northwestern corner of Illinois and in the southwestern corner of Wisconsin.

5V2

RAISING TROOPS

Governor Cass, who at this time was holding a conference at Green Bay with the Winnebagoes and the Menominee Indians, hearing of the battle on the Mississippi and hearing also of the reported uprising of the Winnebagoes, made haste to reach St. Louis by way of Green Bay, Fox River, the Wisconsin, and the Mississippi. At St. Louis he conferred with General Atkinson, who immediately started up the Mississippi with 600 infantry and 130 mounted riflemen. Governor Cass accompanied the expedition as far as the Illinois River. Here he began his return trip to Chicago and Green Bay.

On passing through Chicago, Governor Cass conferred with the leading people in and about the villages. At this time there were no troops at Fort Dearborn, the fort being occupied by traders, voyageurs and citizens. Among those in the village who had a great deal of experience in dealing with the Indians, was Gurdon S. Hubbard. Mr. Hubbard has told in detail of his wild ride from Chicago to Danville to spread the alarm and to raise a company to protect Chicago against the coming horrors of the red men. He rode through storm and rain, night and day, swam streams, and reached the vicinity of Danville in less than twenty-four hours. The news of Chicago's danger spread rapidly and volunteers began to arrive in Danville for enlistment. One hundred men offered their services. They elected a Mr. Morgan as their captain. These hundred militiamen reached Chicago on the seventh day from the time that Hubbard had left with his message of alarm.

A few hundred men were enlisted in Sangamon and Morgan counties and placed under the command of T. M. Neale, who marched his little army to Galena. The people of this thriving town had organized a committee of safety, raised several companies of militia, and erected defenses.

General Atkinson reached Prairie du Chien and with the help of some volunteers went in pursuit of the troublesome redmen. They were found in central Wisconsin. They immediately sued for peace, and General Atkinson returned with seven of the principal offenders. Among these were Red Bird and Black Hawk. They were all cast into prison at Prairie du Chien, where Red Bird died. The others were tried after much delay and those found guilty were executed. Black Hawk was not convicted and was released to continue his intrigues.

Governor Cass was authorized to negotiate with the Indians concerned in the recent disturbances. Red Bird, though a cold blooded murderer, was considered a very good friend of the whites and was well liked by his people. He gave himself up to the Government in order to save his people from having to undergo the horrors of war.

ILLINOIS RIVER FROM PROSPECT HEIGHTS, PEORIA

From Illinois Blue Book

The whole affair collapsed when the Government troops penetrated the central part of Wisconsin.

THE MILITARY TRACT

At the close of the War of 1812, the general government set aside a large tract of land in western Illinois for the benefit of the soldiers who had fought in the second war with England. Land warrants were issued to the soldiers, who might come and settle on a piece of land or they might dispose of their land warrant for other things of value and then the one to whom the warrant was assigned could come and locate and take possession of the land.

This body of land lay between the Illinois River and the Mississippi and extended north to the parallel of some twelve miles south of the mouth of Rock River. Many of the soldiers came into this military tract and made their homes. In other cases many who had come into possession of these warrants by trade or otherwise had come to make their home in the military tract. The settlements moved north very rapidly in this tract from 1820 to 1830. The territory north and west of Rock River was pretty well occupied with people who had come by reason of the lead fever. Over on the Illinois the settlements were dotting the country. The Winnebagoes were occupying the region of Rock River. The Sac and Fox tribe occupied the peninsula formed by the Rock River and the Mississippi. The Sacs occupied the right bank of the Rock River near its mouth while the Foxes were located on the left bank of the Mississippi some miles above the mouth of the Rock River. It has been said that the Sac and Foxes were more difficult to manage than any of the Indians in the northwest. The Winnebagoes occupied the territory along the Rock River and over toward the Wisconsin River. The Pottawattomies were located to the east of the Winnebagoes. They were kept in a friendly attitude toward the whites, because they received annually nearly $6,000 to be distributed among their 3,000 people.

SAUKENUK

The Sacs and Foxes were two tribes that had federated. They came from the region of Green Bay into the northwest part of what is now Illinois. They must have come into this part of Illinois shortly after the French and Indian war, for Black Hawk says he was born in Saukenuk in the year 1767. He says rival tribes drove his people from Quebec to Montreal, thence to Mackinaw and thence to Green Bay. Here the two tribes, the Sacs and Foxes federated and later moved to the northwestern part of Illinois and built the village of Saukenuk at the mouth of Rock River. This village eventually came to be one of the best Indian villages in the West. The huts were in the early part of the nineteenth century very comfortable homes. The village was situated on a marked elevation of ground on the peninsula formed by the junction of the Mississippi and the Rock rivers. The site was a place of beauty and the surrounding country was fertile and attractive in many ways. And it is no mystery that the whites desired to occupy this beautiful region. It has been said that the cabins in the village of Saukenuk would shelter a population of 6,000 or 7,000. The lodges or houses were about 700 in number and were constructed after the style of the "long houses" of the Mohawks. Rows of long poles were let into the earth while their tops were brought together making a broad rounded roof which was covered with bark or thatched in such a way as to make a weather proof wall and roof. Some of these lodges were as many as 100 feet long and often from 20 to 30 or more feet wide. If these 700 lodges would shelter as many as ten persons then 7,000 people could easily find protection therein.

The site of Saukenuk as an Indian village was occupied many years before the coming of the Sacs and Foxes. The grave yard of the tribes was the center of much interest. It had been the burial place of the tribes for nearly three-quarters of a century. This cemetery was a sort of shrine for the mothers, wives and sisters who made annual pilgrimages to the sacred precincts. The dead had been buried and it was the custom to keep the mound which marked the resting place of departed kin well rounded and free from weeds and other unattractive objects. These mothers and sisters and wives brought food and drink which were left for the spirits of the departed.

Hundreds of acres were indifferently cultivated by the Indian women. Their agricultural implements were of the crudest sort, yet they raised and reaped plentiful, if not abundant, harvests. The products of this cultivation were corn, beans, pumpkins, and potatoes. These rich lands which the Indian squaws were cultivating were coveted by the whites who were now, 1829-30, gradually encroaching upon the territory which the Indians were still occupying. The treaty of St. Louis, Missouri, in 1804, made by William Henry Harrison and five representatives of the Sacs and Foxes—Article 7—said that so long as the lands, ceded by these tribes was occupied or held by the United States, that the Indians should continue to use and hold it. The inference was that whenever the United States should put this land on the market and individual ownership began, then the Indians would have to yield and go to such lands as might be provided for them by the general government. And although Black Hawk claimed that this treaty was a cheat and a swindle and that his people did not authorize it, yet on at least three occasions the tribe ratified the treaty of 1804.

SAUKENUK BOUGHT

The settlers were coming closer and closer all the time, and the hunting grounds were rapidly disappearing. The lands in the vicinity of the mouth of the Rock River were not yet on the market, and no one could legally own land, but there was a plan by which they could secure possession to land which proved just as annoying to the Indians as if the lands were on the market. This was the privilege of preemption. Citizens could squat on the lands of their choice and take out preemption papers, and thus to all intents and purposes become private possessors of the lands which were still owned by the general government, but presumably in possession of the Indians. That is, the squatters, who heretofore had been trespassers, had now become preemptioners with legal property rights. These preemptioners made demands upon the Indians to remove from the east side to the west side of the Mississippi River. Black Hawk in the meantime had secured the advice of a number of persons as to what he and his people should do relative to the encroachment of the whites upon the lands of his people.

During the fall of 1829 Colonel Davenport, the Indian agent at Rock Island, bought the lands or at least a part of them, where the village of Saukenuk was situated. During the winter of 1829-30, the Indians, while on the annual hunt, had held several conferences relative to their action in resisting the encroachment of the whites. They made up their minds that if they were removed by force to the west side of the river that the blame should be laid on certain men in authority. A quotation from Black Hawk's autobiography will explain the situation:

"We concluded that if we were removed by force, the trader, agent and others must be the cause, and that if they were found guilty of having driven us from our village they should be killed. The trader stood foremost on this list. He (Colonel Davenport) had purchased the land on which my lodge stood, and that of our graveyard also. We therefore proposed to kill him and the agent, the interpreter, the great chief at St. Louis, the war chiefs at Forts Armstrong, Rock Island and Keokuk, these being the principal persons to blame for endeavoring to remove us."

In the summer and fall of 1830, Black Hawk had sought information and advice of a number of prominent Indians and whites. He visited Malden Canada, to confer with the British commander who advised him that he should go to his American father who would see that justice was done him. A Great Chief on the Wabash was visited who told him if his people had not sold their village and its grounds that the Government would not dispossess them. He also visited Detroit where he got the same information as at other places visited. He then returned to Saukenuk late in the fall of 1830, but found his people gone on

From Illinois Blue Book

BEAUTY SPOTS IN ILLINOIS

(1) Glen Fern, Johnson County. (2) Lotus pond near Chillicothe. (3) Piasa Chautauqua. (4) Rock River from Castle Rock, Grand Detour.

their annual winter hunt. Straggling members of his tribe were about and he learned that the women of his tribe had failed to raise sufficient crops for the needs over the winter and for the next spring planting. Here also he learned that a treaty had been made at Prairie du Chien the past summer which he thought was greatly favorable to the Pottawattomies. Keokuk of the Fox tribe was at this meeting and took notes as to the terms of the treaty.

Black Hawk laments the fact that for two years his people had laid aside their pastimes and sports to attend to the more serious matter of protecting their homes and their land. He states himself that he had tried to interest Keokuk in some of his efforts in the summer of 1830, but for some reason Keokuk was indifferent. He says his tribe and the Foxes were divided and that Keokuk, in order to gain favor from the whites, was willing to barter away their villages and their lands. He says: "I considered, as my people and I had no agency in selling our country, and that, as provision had been made in the treaty of 1804 for us to remain on the land so long as it belonged to the United States, I thought we could not be forced away."

The winter of 1830-1 passed with no serious incidents. However, Keokuk was creating dissensions among Black Hawk's band. In the spring of 1831 Black Hawk made efforts to secure help from the various men who he thought would help him, but no one would lend him any aid, or advise him the way he wanted to be advised. The whites who had settled upon lands near the village of Saukenuk reported to the governor that the Indians about this village had persistently trespassed upon their lands, allowing their horses to trample down the grain and in many ways endangering the peace and happiness of more than fifty white families. A petition signed by about forty heads of families was sent to Governor Reynolds, bearing date April 30, 1831, in which they enumerate the many complaints which they had against the Sac Indians. The governor not replying to this petition at once, a second petition was sent May 10, 1831. These two petitions were reenforced by depositions taken before justices of the peace relative to the unbearable conduct of Black Hawk and his band.

Many letters passed between Governor Edwards, General Gaines, commander of the Military District of St. Louis, Felix St. Vrain, Indian Agent at Rock Island and Gen. William Clark, Superintendent of Indian Affairs.

Out of all this correspondence, the general government ordered six companies of United States troops, stationed at Jefferson Barracks, St. Louis, to repair to Rock Island for the purpose of restoring order and securing safety for the white settlers in the Rock River region. In a letter to Governor Reynolds of the date of May 29, 1831, General Gaines informs the governor of Illinois that he does not think it at all necessary or advisable for the governor to send militia troops to the Rock River region. But the governor of Illinois had on the 26th of May called for 700 volunteers, and the troops were to assemble at Beardstown on the Illinois River not later than June 10, 1831. On June 5, 1831, General Gaines wrote Governor Reynolds that since arriving at Rock Island and learning of the formidable array of warriors which Black Hawk could muster, he had changed his mind about the use of the State Militia, and hoped Governor Reynolds could forward to his support the battalion of mounted men which was assembling on the Illinois.

Volunteers

When General Gaines reached the mouth of Rock River, he made a hasty survey of the situation. He called a conference of Black Hawk and his leaders with General Gaines at Fort Armstrong. In this conference Black Hawk plainly told General Gaines that he would not leave his village and remove to the west side of the Mississippi. There appeared bad blood in this conference, and an observer thought that General Gaines was in personal danger, since Black Hawk's band attended the conference heavily armed, while the United States troops were a quarter of a mile away.

The Army

Governor Reynolds came into great prominence as the commander-in-chief of the volunteer troops. The plan of organization of the 700 troops was as elaborate as would have been needed for an army of several thousand. The governor had two field aids, James D. Henry and Milton K. Alexander. Many politicians clamored for positions in the military organization. While the call was for 700, many more troops appeared than were needed. Joseph Duncan, a young veteran of the War of 1812, and one who was to play an important part in Illinois politics, was made brigadier general. He was to command the troops in the field. There was a paymaster general, a brigade quartermaster, an inspector general, adjutants, aids, and assistants ad infinitum. The whole brigade was divided into two regiments, an odd battalion, and a spy battalion. The First Regiment was officered by Col. James D. Henry, Lt.-Col. Jacob Fry, Major John T. Stuart, Adj. Thomas Collins, Quartermaster Edward Jones, Paymaster Thomas M. Neale. The Second Regiment had for officers Col. Daniel Lieb, Major Nathaniel Butler, Quartermaster W. Jordan. The odd battalion had three companies in command of Major Nathaniel Buckmaster, Adj. James Semple, Quartermaster David Wright, Paymaster Joseph Gillespie, Charles Higbee, Surgeon. The spy battalion had four companies. The officers were Major Samuel Whiteside, Adj.

Samuel F. Kendle, Quartermaster John S. Greathouse, Paymaster P. H. Winchester, Armorer John F. Gilman.

The troops assembled at Beardstown. Many came without any kind of firearms, some on horseback and many on foot. There were 1,600 officers and men. The state's supply of guns which the general government had provided for Illinois was at Bearstown, but there was not a sufficient supply though hundreds brought their own arms. A merchant in the town, a Mr. Earnst, had in stock several hundred stands of arms which he sold to the governor. These were small brass barreled guns made to meet the trade in South America.

The army left the vicinity of Rushville northwest of Beardstown, on June 15, 1831, for Rock River. After a four days' march they reached the Mississippi eight miles below the mouth of Rock River where they met General Gaines with a boat load of supplies. The Illinois militia was sworn into the United States service. These troops were legally no longer under the orders of the governor, though Governor Reynolds accompanied the army and was in close touch with the commanding officers. The combined army reached the island opposite the mouth of Rock River and proceeded to drive out any red men who might be lurking there. They then crossed over to the village of Saukenuk which they found deserted greatly to their chagrin.

Black Hawk says he and his people had determined to stay in the village and hold out by "passive resistance," but when his spies had returned and reported the number and character of the army under General Gaines, they changed their plans and immediately crossed over the river to the west side.

When the troops saw the village was deserted and that they had been cheated out of the glory of a victory, they wreaked vengeance on the Sacs by burning most of the lodges. The troops were then moved to the present site of the City of Rock Island opposite the island of the same name.

On the last day of June General Gaines and Governor Reynolds representing the United States entered into a treaty with Black Hawk's band and the Foxes. The treaty was signed by the above named officials and twenty-eight chiefs, warriors, and braves, and witnessed by thirteen officials and citizens. The treaty consisted of two preliminary paragraphs and seven articles, a synopsis of which follows:

Paragraph 1 names the parties to the agreement.

Paragraph 2 enumerates the several violations of the treaties of 1804, 1816, and 1825 by the Indians, and confesses by the terms of this paragraph that these Indians had been guilty of actually plotting war against the United States and the State of Illinois, and now in the presence of a superior force do sue for peace and voluntarily abandon their hostile attitude toward the aforesaid United States and the State of Illinois, according to the following several provisions:

First—The undersigned Chiefs, Warriors, and Allies bind themselves, their tribes, and heirs to keep the peace.

Second—The Black Hawk band submits to the oversight and control of the chiefs and braves of the united Sac and Fox tribe, and to live and hunt on the lands west of the Mississippi River, and that no member of this tribe shall cross to the east side of the Mississippi without the expressed permission of the President of the United States or the governor of the State of Illinois.

Third—All lands claimed by the Sac and Fox tribes west of the Mississippi River is confirmed to them by the United States.

Fourth—The Indians agree to cease communication with the British posts and garrisons and not to admit their agents into the tribe under any pretense.

Fifth—The United States reserves the right to build forts and roads in the territory, claimed by the said Indians, west of the Mississippi River.

Sixth—The chiefs and headmen of the Sac and Fox tribe bind themselves to exert their power to cause the treaty to be kept. They further agree to report any tendency toward disobedience of this treaty by their allies, the Pottawattomies, Kickapoos, or the Winnebagoes.

Seventh—The contracting parties are proclaimed permanent friends, and peace is hereby established between the United States and Illinois and the tribes represented by the following signatures.

Here follows the signatures.

Following the signing of the treaty General Gaines and Governor Reynolds learned of the sad plight of the women and children who were camped a few miles below the mouth of Rock River. They were without food and many women were without clothing. The above officials were moved to generous treatment by giving to these distressed creatures large quantities of food —enough to last them a year. The goods to be delivered at intervals to meet their needs.

The United States troops returned to Jefferson Barracks while the Illinois troops returned by various routes to their homes in Illinois. It is strange but true that the volunteers were greatly disappointed in not being permitted to engage in a pitched battle with the red men. They were really out of humor with the governor and General Gaines for entering into a treaty with Black Hawk. The returned soldiers called the treaty a corn treaty. They said we gave them food when it ought to have been lead.

The Interim

The treaty between General Gaines and Governor Reynolds on the part of the United States and Black Hawk and other Indians was signed June 30, 1831. In 1825 a general treaty had been signed at Prairie du Chien to secure peace among the several tribes as follows: Chippewas, Sacs, Foxes, Sioux, Menominees, Winnebagoes, Iowas, Ottawas, and Pottawattomies. Gen. William Clark, Superintendent of Indian Affairs, and Lewis Cass, Secretary of War, negotiated this treaty among the several Indian tribes enumerated above. It was the purpose of this treaty to put a stop to the destructive incursions of one tribe into the territory of another tribe. Boundaries were located and a pledge of obedience to the rules laid down in this treaty was exacted of every tribe. Article 10 acknowledged the controlling power of the United States.

Unmindful of these solemn promises, the Sac and Fox Indians made an incursion into the territory of the Sioux in July, 1831, and murdered two Sioux, avenged the death of their two warriors by ambushing the Foxes and killing Kettle, the Fox Chief.

Black Hawk began fomenting trouble as soon as the soldiers had returned to their homes, and kept at it throughout the summer and fall of 1831. He sent agents to Canada and to other points where he was encouraged to try to regain his village on the east side of the Mississippi. His people wasted the provision which General Gaines gave them and before the early winter of 1831-2, the women and children were in dire distress. Black Hawk was charged with making raids upon the store houses of the whites, stealing grain and vegetables therefrom All through the winter of 1831-2 this stealing from the whites was continued. Black Hawk also accused of keeping emissaries in the village of the Foxes on the Iowa River where dissatisfaction was fed with supposed injuries. At a critical time Black Hawk marched with his band to the Fox village where he succeeded in winning the Fox warriors to his side. "The rifle was loaded and the knife and hatchet strapped about the warrior's loins. They had importuned Keokuk to lead them to battle, and so subtle had been the work of Black Hawk's men that those importunities could not be ignored. The torrent of mighty and heedless anger raged and carried conservatism, treaties, sentiment and every motive before it. Menaced now by Black Hawk, who had so recently solemnly promised to behave himself for all time, every frontier family stood in danger of the tomahawk."

This was indeed a critical time, for had Black Hawk succeeded in uniting the Sacs and Foxes in a war against the whites, the whites in northern Illinois would have been massacred before help could have come from the general government or the State of Illinois. But fortunately Keokuk took the orator's stump and made such a telling speech to his own people that to a man they refused to join Black Hawk who was compelled to depart without the help of the Fox warriors.

On July 30, 1831, the Sacs and Foxes had fallen upon a band of Menominee Indians who were under the influence of liquor and killed twenty-five of them. The general government determined to punish the guilty Sacs and Foxes and to that end gave an order to the officer in command at St. Louis, General Henry Atkinson, to proceed to the vicinity of Rock Island and demand the surrender of the ten Indians who had been guilty of killing the Menominees the previous summer. This order was issued by the war department March 17, 1832, and was received by General Atkinson April 1, 1832. On April 8th, General Atkinson started with six companies of United States troops (220 men) for the country of the Sacs and Foxes.

When Black Hawk was repulsed by Keokuk as related above, he returned to the camp of his people which was located where old Fort Madison had stood (just opposite Hancock County). The emissaries which he had sent to Canada, Detroit, the Wabash, and elsewhere, returned and brought him words of encouragement in his purpose to return and recover the site of the village of Saukenuk. In the early part of April, 1832, Black Hawk and his warriors 500 strong, together with 1,500 women and children moved along the west side of the Mississippi from old Ft. Madison to the mouth of Rock River. His braves were all on horse back while the women and children ascended the river in canoes and boats. Black Hawk says that as they proceeded up the river, General Atkinson and his little army, in two steamboats, Enterprise and Chieftain, passed his people, but it was in the night and probably General Atkinson did not discover the Indians as they were encamped on the west side of the river. General Atkinson proceeded to Fort Armstrong where he called Keokuk into a council and demanded the men who had killed the Menominee Indians the summer previous. Keokuk said he could not deliver the men, as they were partly with Black Hawk and some were with the Prophet (the chief of the Winnebagoes). Keokuk knew that Black Hawk had crossed the Mississippi and was marching up the Rock River.

Black Hawk says he received an order to return to the west side of the river. He returned word to General Atkinson that he was acting peaceably and did not recognize the general's right to order him to return. He also told General Atkinson that he was going to join the Winnebagoes in the raising of a crop of corn.

Just after the conference between General Atkinson and Keokuk on the 13th of April, General Atkinson called on Governor Reynolds to aid him in expelling Black Hawk from the country east of the Mississippi River.

MILITIA CALLED

On the 16th of April Governor Reynolds issued an appeal to the militia to assemble for service in driving the hostile Indians from the state. Beardstown was named as the place of rendezvous. For the protection of certain exposed localities he later called for 200 men to assemble from Fulton County under Major Isaiah Stillman; also 200 under Major David Bailey of Tazewell County. The governor had kept exceedingly well informed through the winter of 1831-2 as to the movements of Black Hawk. He had also, it seems, taken certain people into his councils and when the critical time came in the spring of 1832, there was prompt response to his calls for help. The following is his call for volunteers:

"To the Militia of the Northwestern Section of the State.

Fellow Citizens: Your country requires your services. The Indians have assumed a hostile attitude, and have invaded the State in violation of the treaty of last summer.

The British band of Sacs and other hostile Indians, headed by Black Hawk, are in possession of the Rock River country to the great terror of the frontier inhabitants. I consider the settlers on the frontiers to be in imminent danger.

I am in possession of the above information from gentlemen of respectable standing, and also from General Atkinson, whose character stands high with all classes.

In possession of the above facts and information I have hesitated not as to the course I should pursue. No citizen ought to remain inactive when his country is invaded, and the helpless part of the community are in danger. I have called out a strong detachment of militia to rendezvous at Beardstown on the 22d instant.

Provision for men, and food for the horses will be furnished in abundance.

I hope my countrymen will realize my expectations, and offer their services, as heretofore, with promptitude and cheerfulness in defense of their country."

Governor Reynolds himself left home in Belleville for Beardstown. He held conferences and made plans as he proceeded. At Jacksonville he found sympathetic workers and so it was everywhere. At Beardstown the troops were gathering. They came on horse back with gun, powder horn, 100 bullets, food for five days and with such extra clothing as forethought provided. On the day the call went out to assemble at Beardstown, the governor sent an explanatory letter to the Secretary of War. In this letter the governor desired that the general government should understand that he wished to cooperate with the United States forces for the safety of life and property in the state. A second letter was sent to the Hon. Joseph Duncan, the representative in Congress from Illinois. In this letter the governor made it clear to Mr. Duncan that the Illinois volunteers would assemble at the request of General Atkinson and that the troops would be taken into the United States service and would therefore properly be entitled to pay from the United States treasury. This shows the governor was not only thoughtful, but sound in his philosophy as to the relation that properly should exist between a state and the Federal Government.

The army remained at Beardstown till the 27th of April. The governor was a good judge of human nature and he saw that the sooner the men were occupied with the serious business of war, the better for all concerned. The general plan was to unite the volunteers with the regulars as soon as possible and to federalize the militia at the earliest moment. The governor had dispatched Col. Enoch C. March to St. Louis to procure supplies for the army with orders to meet the army at Yellow Banks on the Mississippi River (the present site of Oquawka, Henderson County). Accordingly, early on the morning of the 27th of April, the army broke camp and began a long and trying march to Yellow Banks. There were constant rains and the weather continued cold. The roads were in bad condition and the streams were swollen. It was fortunate that many of the soldiers were woodsmen as the problem of building crude bridges and boats was ever present. Not all were on horse back and the foot soldiers had to undergo great trials. At Henderson River the entire army of nearly 2,000 halted as there were no bridges and the fords were many feet deep as the stream was greatly swollen. Trees were felled from opposite banks, and their tops interlocked so as to form a sort of foot bridge.

The army reached Henderson River about 12 o'clock on May 3d. Here they remained till the 7th. They were waiting for the provisions which were coming from St. Louis. These arrived on the 6th and the army was supplied with rations. Word came to Governor Reynolds that his force was needed at the mouth of the Rock River and to this point he marched arriving late on the 7th of May. Two days later the trip up Rock River in search of Black Hawk was begun. The two days the army lay at the mouth of Rock River were used in organizing the army and in the induction of the volunteers into the service of the United States. The organization of the state troops was as follows:

(From the Black Hawk War, by Frank E. Stevens.)

ORGANIZATION
Governor John Reynolds, Commander-in-Chief.

GENERAL STAFF
James Turney, Paymaster General. Cyrus Edwards, Quartermaster General. Vital Jarrot, Adjutant General. Joseph M. Chadwick, Aide de Camp, with rank as Colonel. James T. B.

Stapp, Aide-de-Camp, with rank as Colonel. Reddick Horn, Chaplain.

BRIGADE OFFICERS

Samuel Whiteside, Brigade General. Nathaniel Buckmaster, Brigade Major. William Ross, First Aid. James Semple, Second Aid. David Prickett, Third Aid. William E. Starr, Brigade Paymaster. William Thomas, Brigade Quartermaster.

FIRST REGIMENT

John Thomas, Jr., colonel. Solomon Preuitt, lieutenant-colonel. John Starky, major. A. W. Snyder, adjutant. J. A. Blackwell, quartermaster. William G. Brown, paymaster. Richard Roman, surgeon. J. M. McTyre Cornelius, surgeon's mate. Samuel Sybold, quartermaster's sergeant. Alexander Shields, sergeant-major.

SECOND REGIMENT

Jacob Fry, colonel. William Weatherford, lieutenant-colonel. Alexander Beall, major. Murray McConnell, adjutant. Hiram C. Bennett, quartermaster. James Durley, quartermaster's sergeant. E. L. R. Wheelock, paymaster. William H. Dulaney, surgeon. John F. Foster, surgeon's mate. Calvin Roberts, sergeant-major.

THIRD REGIMENT

Abraham B. DeWitt, colonel. William Weatherford, lieutenant-colonel. Alexander Beall, major. Murray McConnell, adjutant. George Orear, quartermaster. Andrew Mackitee, paymaster. Samuel M. Prosper, surgeon. James Morrison, surgeon's mate. Levin N. English, quartermaster's sergeant. Robert Davis, sergeant-major.

FOURTH REGIMENT

Samuel Thompson, colonel. Achilles Morris, lieutenant-colonel. Moses G. Wilson, major. John B. Watson, adjutant. Samuel Horney, quartermaster. William Carpenter, paymaster. Jacob M. Eddy, surgeon. Adams Dunlap, first surgeon's mate. William Constant, second surgeon's mate. Edward Doyle, sergeant-major. A. McHatton, sergeant-major (successor). William Fitzpatrick, quartermaster's sergeant. William Sprouce, gunsmith. Richard Jones, color bearer. James Baker, wagon master.

SPY BATTALION

James D. Henry, major. William L. E. Morrison, adjutant. Montgomery Warrick, quartermaster. Robert Blackwell, paymaster. Joseph C. Woodson, surgeon. Peter Randall, first surgeon's mate. Benjamin Birch, second surgeon's mate. M. E. Rattan, sergeant-major. John F. Posey, quartermaster's ser-

HISTORY OF ILLINOIS

geant. Jesse M. Harrison, paymaster's sergeant. William Cook, color bearer.

Second Spy Battalion

Thomas James, major. James Moore, adjutant. James Whitlock, quartermaster. Scipio Baird, quartermaster (successor). Michael Horine, paymaster. William Headen, surgeon. George Gordon, surgeon's mate. N. C. Johnston, sergeant-major (resigned). John James, sergeant-major. James W. Vaughan, armorer. Moses Haskins, bugleman. J. Milton Moore, color bearer.

Foot Battalion

Thomas Long, major. John Summers, adjutant. Vawter Henderson, quartermaster. J. L. Thompson, paymaster. Mathew Duncan, surgeon. Jonathan Leighton, surgeon's mate. Sion R. Green, sergeant-major. Thomas J. Marshall, quartermaster's sergeant. Benjamin Howard, fife major. Thomas Burton, drum major.

The First Regiment contained six companies, and therefore six captains, besides lieutenants and non-commissioned officers. The Second Regiment had nine companies, with nine captains and nine lieutenants and minor officers. The Third Regiment had six companies, the Fourth Regiment had four companies, the First Spy Battalion had four companies, the Second Spy Battalion had three companies and the Foot Battalion had three companies.

The March

On the 9th of May General Atkinson issued the following order:

"Headquarters Right Wing, West. Dept.,
"Mouth of Rock River., 9th May, 1832.
"Order No. 12.

"The mounted volunteers will move in the morning under Brigadier-General Whiteside, by the route of Winnebago Prophet's Village, with a view of reaching the hostile band of Indians assembled on Rock River, near or above Dixon's Ferry. The regular troops will move by water and meet the mounted troops at Prophet's Village. Should General Whiteside, however, on reaching Prophet's Village, be of opinion that it would be prudent to come up with the enemy with as little delay as possible, he will move upon him, and either make him surrender at discretion, or coerce him into submission."

The army was now ready to march up Rock River in quest of Black Hawk. The mounted men under General Whiteside marched along the river and reached the Prophet's town by the middle of the afternoon of the tenth. From spies returned from scouting service, it was learned that Black Hawk was supposed to be many miles above Dixon's Ferry. The volunteers were greatly disappointed not to find Black Hawk at a nearer point on the river and in their anger they set fire to the Prophet's village. About three or four hours march up the river the army camped for the night. On the morning of the eleventh when ready to break camp, for some cause or other, the commanding officer allowed the army to abandon all baggage not in actual use, and all provisions except a few days' rations, expecting to receive an abundant supply when the infantry and the boats should reach them —probably at Dixon's Ferry. It has been suggested that this abandonment of luggage and provisions was the result of a demand on the part of the Illinois soldiers who thought they knew as much about military tactics as the officers in command. After piling up their luggage and provision, they began the march and reached Dixon's Ferry the forenoon of the twelfth.

The regulars and the infantry of the Illinois troops made the trip up the Rock River in boats. The boats were propelled by oars, the wind, and by ropes. The trip was a trying ordeal. The lands on each side of the river were swampy and the men were obliged often to wade the swamps in their progress up the river. The regulars and the Illinois infantry reached Dixon's Ferry on the seventeenth. The mounted volunteers had been at this point since the eleventh. Already there was great disappointment and dissatisfaction among the Illinois volunteers and the greatest confusion and disorder prevailed. This disorder increased upon the arrival of the soldiers who came by boat. So alarming had the disorder become that Col. Zachary Taylor issued an order that no more firing of guns or pistols should be indulged in without the permission of the superior officers.

Stillman's Defeat

When Governor Reynolds, who marched with the mounted soldiers, reached Dixon, he found two battalions from the central part of the state. These battalions were in command of Major Stillman and Major Bailey. From Mr. John Dixon, after whom the town of Dixon was named, the governor received reliable information to the effect that Black Hawk's band was several miles up the Rock River, and that the warriors were scattered over the country in search of food and at the same time gathering into their ranks as many warriors from other tribes as they could. Spies had been sent out to try to locate the main army of the Indians. These had returned to Dixon with wild stories as to the presence of Indians all over the country.

The next day after arriving in Dixon, Governor Reynolds issued an order to Major Stillman as follows:

"Dixon's Ferry, May 12, 1832.

"To Major Stillman: You will cause the troops under your immediate command, and the battalion under Major Bailey, to proceed without delay, with four days' provision, to the head of 'Old Man's Creek,' where it is supposed there are some hostile Indians, and coerce them into submission.

"John Reynolds,
"Com. in Chief of the Illinois Militia."

On the morning of the 13th of May, Major Stillman with much military display marched out from the Dixon camp with 275 men with provisions and necessary equipment for a four days' campaign to locate and punish Black Hawk's band. The little army was accompanied by a supply train of six wagons drawn by oxen. They only made about ten miles the first day on account of a heavy rain. On the fourteenth they proceeded toward Old Man's Creek, which they reached about sundown on that day. They crossed the small stream and prepared to make camp for the night. These men were farmer-soldiers and were evidently not under very strict military discipline. Some were starting fires, gathering fuel, caring for the horses and doing other acts preparatory to the evening meal. They suddenly discovered three unarmed Indians bearing a flag. They were told to come into the camp, where they were guarded, as no one was able to determine certainly the purpose of their visit. Very shortly five other Indians appeared on a nearby hill. The excitement in the camp grew and without orders, many individuals mounted their horses and with their rifles made a dash for the five Indians who wheeled their horses and retreated in haste. In this pursuit the soldiers killed two of the five Indians and followed the others to within a dangerous proximity of Black Hawk's camp.

Black Hawk says in his autobiography that he was camped at the mouth of Kishwaukee Creek. He had previously held conferences with the Pottawattomies in whose territory he was now camped. He says that while holding another conference with the Pottawattomies, at which time they were all having a dog feast, word came to his council that White Beaver (General Atkinson) was only eight miles away. He affirms he sent three young men with a white flag to offer to hold a council with White Beaver and that he was willing to descend the Rock River and to cross the Mississippi and live in peace. He also says he sent five other men to see how the three got along. This story corresponds with the facts as stated by the soldiers.

When the men in camp saw what was taking place out on the prairie, they fell upon the three Indians they were guarding in the camp and killed one, but the other two made their escape and returned to Black Hawk's camp. When the chief received word of the near approach of the whites he sounded the alarm and about forty of his braves responded, the others were miles away in search of food. Then began a hasty forming of a line of ambush. The white men had halted when they saw signs of the Indian camp. Presently the Indians, with a whoop which some of the farmer-soldiers had never heard before, came from their ambush and charged the soldiers, who retreated toward the camp on Old Man's Creek, distant six or more miles. Black Hawk says his warriors could not keep up with the soldiers in their retreat, and he and a half of his warriors returned to his own camp. About twenty-five of his warriors pursued the retreating soldiers. When not far from the soldiers' camp the Indians overtook one soldier whose horse was mired in the swamp. This was James Doty. He was killed and scalped. Further on another, Gideon Munson, of the regulars, a scout, was slain.

It was now getting dark, and it was difficult at a short distance to distinguish friend from foe. Many of the soldiers had mounted their horses and were miles on their way back to Dixon. But others were not so fortunate and were unable to keep far in advance of the pursuing redmen. Captain Adams with a small band of self-sacrificing soldiers attempted to stand their ground to give those who were late in getting started a chance to reach the open country toward Dixon. "Captain Adams and his little band fell one by one, until the last man bit the dust.—The names of the men who fell in this stand are Captain Adams, David Kreeps, Zadock Mendinall, Isaac Perkins, James Milton, Tyrus M. Childs, Joseph B. Farris, Bird W. Ellis, John Walters." Bird W. Ellis was a young man who when struck down by the Indians crawled through the grass a distance of two miles where he was found dead beside the dead body of a large Indian. The body of Joseph Draper was found five miles from the camp on Old Man's Creek.

When the darkness brought an end to the butchery, the braves returned to the soldiers' camp and feasted on the unserved supper of the soldiers. They found two or three kegs of liquor in the wagons. This they made use of to their appetite's content. They broke up the wagons by knocking out the spokes and thus rendered them useless. Some of the provisions were appropriated and the rest was destroyed. Black Hawk states, however, that his warriors after burying their dead on the morning of the fifteenth visited the camp of the soldiers and appropriated whatever they could use. He says they found guns, powder, saddles, saddle bags, whiskey and food, all of which they were glad to get. Black Hawk was greatly surprised, so he says, to find his unarmed emissaries attacked in the soldiers' camp, especially as he was making overtures to return to the west side of the Mississippi. He says he was making this request because he had been deceived as to the help which he thought he could get from both the Winnebagoes and the Pottawattomies.

About 2 o'clock on the morning of the 15th of May the camp at Dixon was aroused by the return of the first straggling soldiers from the battlefield at Old Man's Creek. This stream was a continuing one, the last ones coming in as late as the morning of the above day. The camp was in great confusion. The stories were conflicting as to details, but about one fact they all agreed —that the task before them of "killing injuns" was a job that it would take an army of real soldiers to accomplish.

Governor Reynolds says that his impression from the first arrivals was that the whole battalion was wiped out, but as time wore on he saw this was not the case. In the early morning the battalion was paraded and fifty-two were absent from roll call and very naturally it was thought this number was killed, but it has been stated that about forty of those engaged in the battle and lived through it decided to march in a body to their homes in the vicinity of Ottawa. This is plausible as they were not in the United States service.

There immediately arose a very great dissatisfaction among the Illinois soldiers. They demanded an immediate discharge from the service and it was only after strong influences were brought to bear that they were for the time quieted. The governor was in Dixon with his Illinois mounted men. General Atkinson and the regulars were slowly ascending the Rock River, and did not reach Dixon until the 17th of May. Governor Reynolds quickly took in the situation, at least as he saw it, and issued a call for 2,000 additional troops to assemble at Hennepin on the Illinois River on the 10th of June. The order was written by candle light and was forwarded to central and southern Illinois by three trusty friends, John Ewing, Robert Blackwell, and John A. Wakefield. They departed at once on their mission. The governor also wrote to General Atkinson and told him of the disaster of the night before. A letter was dispatched to Colonel March at St. Louis to provide provision for 2,000 soldiers and to deliver them at Hennepin by the 10th of June. Colonel Strode of Jo Daviess County, in whom the governor seems to have had great confidence, was ordered to recruit 200 men about Galena for the defense of that region. Governor Reynolds says these orders were all written by candle light and that the several messengers were on their way by sunrise.

Burying the Dead

On the morning of the 15th, beef cattle were slaughtered and provision made for the march of the entire army to Old Man's Creek. It was a tramp of twenty-five miles. The battle field was reached in the afternoon. The sight was heart rending for the soldier-farmers. Many horses had been killed, the dead bodies of their comrades lay scattered here and there, their scalps taken and the bodies otherwise mutilated. The camp was in confusion. The bodies of the dead were buried, and the army went into camp on the old camp site which Major Stillman occupied. On the sixteenth the army returned to Dixon.

On the seventeenth General Atkinson with his regulars and the foot soldiers of the volunteers arrived at Dixon with a large quantity of provision. He ordered a fort constructed on the north side of the river for the storing of the provisions and ammunition. Up to the time of the arrival of General Atkinson there was great dissatisfaction among the volunteers. They said there was no definite time of service stated at the time they volunteered. They had left their homes in haste and in many instances their families had not been provided with food, and their crops, which had just been started, would fail if they could not be allowed to return home. The governor saw that these men were stating the facts in the case and he readily recognized the justness of their demands. He at once set about to convince the men of their duty to stay in the service a few days longer, and stated that he had already ordered 2,000 recruits to take their places. After a good deal of very effective work on the part of the governor, the troops found themselves in a better frame of mind. The troops of Major Stillman and Major Bailey were organized into a regiment, and Colonel Johnson, of McLean County, was put in command. They were taken into the United States service and a part was sent to Ottawa to guard the settlers in that locality. The troops were now ready for an aggressive campaign against the Indians.

CHAPTER VIII

THE LAST INDIAN WAR
(Continued)

Up Rock River—In Captivity—The New Army—Disobeys Orders—Battle of Wisconsin—General Scott—Noted Men

The first phase of the war lasted from the call of troops on the 16th of April, 1832, to the end of the Stillman disaster, on May 20th. The Illinois troops had been under orders about a month, and, as stated above, this was really as long as they thought they would be needed. But the governor had prevailed on them to forget the things that were behind and to press forward to the mark which was the capture or the dispersion of Black Hawk's band. It had now dawned upon officers and men how foolish it was to have abandoned supplies as they ascended Rock River. On the morning the governor's mounted troops started to Old Man's Creek to bury the dead, there was a scant amount of food for the twelve or thirteen hundred men at Dixon's Ferry. On this morning Mr. Dixon allowed the army to have his cattle, which were butchered and cooked, and eaten without salt. But the coming of Atkinson on the 17th brought a temporary relief, and by the 18th the army was ready for the second attack upon the Indians.

Up Rock River

Order 17 disposed of the troops for the next movement. General Whiteside was to have charge of the main army, which was to move up Rock River in search of Black Hawk. Colonel Dodge had been directed to secure order and safety in the lead region. He left at once with a considerable contingent for the southwest corner of Wisconsin. Colonel Dodge and Col. Henry Gratiot, agent of the Winnebagoes, proceeded to the Four Lakes, where on the 25th of May the two gentlemen succeeded in getting the Winnegaboes to declare neutrality in the existing conflict. One detachment was sent back to guard the region about Fort Armstrong, and a small body was left at Dixon to guard that section.

On the 19th the army was set in motion and the march up Rock River was begun. Elijah Iles and four other picked men had been sent out to ascertain the whereabouts of Black Hawk. They found that he had marched around the Kishwaukee River and then turned north to the Rock River. The soldiers marched twelve miles the first day, and on the second afternoon reached the Stillman battlefield. At this point word was received of the massacre of fifteen white people on Indian Creek, some ten miles up the Fox River from Ottawa. This massacre was instigated by three of Black Hawk's braves who had left his troops on the head waters of the Kishwaukee River. These three Sacs were assisted by more than fifty disaffected Pottawattomies. This settlement on Indian Creek was begun in the spring of 1830 by one William Davis, who owned a blacksmith shop and had erected a mill for the grinding of grains. The Pottawattomies claimed that Davis had built a dam across Indian Creek which prevented the fish from going up that stream, and the Pottawattomies were prohibited from catching fish. At any rate, the Indians fell upon the settlement, which had gathered about Davis' blacksmith shop, and massacred fifteen persons. The story of the Indian Creek massacre has been told by two of the survivors, Mrs. Rachel Hall Munson and her sister, Mrs. Sylvia Hall Horn. These two Misses Hall were aged respectively fifteen and seventeen.

The story in brief is that the people in the vicinity of Mr. Davis' blacksmith shop had been warned by Shabbona, a friendly Indian, to be on the watch for savage red men. Some men in the immediate vicinity had taken Shabbona's warning to heart and had sent their women and children to Ottawa for safety. But in one or two cases the people had become careless and allowed the women and children to return. The people of the neighborhood had been accustomed to pass their time in groups—sometimes they passed the day with one family, then with another. On May 20, 1832, the settlers were at the home of Mr. Davis. Six men were in the field and were cut off from getting to the house and had to take shelter in the blacksmith shop, some distance from the house. The Indians forced their way into the Davis home and killed all the women and children except the two Hall girls. A part of the attacking band surrounded the blacksmith shop and eventually drove out the six men, most of whom saved their lives.

In Captivity

The two girls were rescued by the help of Winnebago Indians and returned to their original homes, where they were later married. This massacre when told in the army and in the settlements aroused great resentment and there ought to have been a more determined prosecution of the war. The two Indians who carried the two girls into captivity were afterwards indicted and tried, but the court failed to convict them. They afterwards admitted their part in the sad affair.

When the news of the Indian Creek massacre reached the army which was marching up the Rock River, General Atkinson returned to Dixon with the regulars in order that he might give protection to the frontier settlements. The army of volunteers was ordered to continue the search for Black Hawk. After several days' marching the expedition reached the Kishwaukee River, where the abandoned camp of Black Hawk was found. Here in caches were found many articles taken from the Stillman camp and scalps and articles from the Indian Creek massacre. But Black Hawk was gone. He says, "I directed my course toward sunset." He took a sort of circuitous route and found himself in the region of Galena. He speaks of seeing a fort which the white people had built. This was known as Apple River Fort. After supplying himself and his followers—some 200 of them—with flour, meat, horses, and cattle, he turned east again. On the way east he and his braves came in contact with the soldiers who had been sent to Kellogg's Grove under command of Major Dement. This battle between Major Dement and Black Hawk occurred on the road from Dixon to Galena, about fifteen or twenty miles east of Apple River Fort. (This and the Kellogg Grove battle will be described later.) While Black Hawk was traveling east by Kellogg's Grove, there was brought to his camp two young white squaws—the two Hall girls that had been carried off from Mr. Davis' home when the Indian Creek massacre occurred. These two girls were finally ransomed through the friendly offices of the Winnebago Indians —the price was $2,000.

From the vicinity of Kellogg's Grove Black Hawk and his people moved up Rock River to the Four Lakes. Here they felt they were secure from attack on account of the swampy nature of the land and the absence of white settlements. He says his people suffered from hunger. They subsisted on roots, bark, and what animals and fish they could procure. Several of the older and feeble men of the band died from lack of nourishment.

We left the Illinois volunteers at Black Hawk's camp on the Kishwaukee not far from the mouth of that stream. It was soon learned that Black Hawk had left that region and it was generally believed that he had gone north into Wisconsin. The question was that of pursuing him into the wilds of Wisconsin or of going south to the Illinois at Ottawa and there being discharged. General Atkinson had given Governor Reynolds the privilege of mustering out the volunteers at any time. A council of officers was held and there was a tie between those who wished to pursue Black Hawk and those who wished to be mustered out. It was finally decided to proceed to Ottawa, where the troops were to be mustered out. On the 27th and 28th of May the troops were all mustered out at Ottawa. General Atkinson arrived at Ottawa and confirmed what the governor had done.

THE NEW ARMY

General Atkinson asked the governor if he could raise another thousand in addition to the 2,000 who were assembling on the Illinois. The governor issued a call for a thousand volunteers.

KELLOGG GROVE MONUMENT, BLACK HAWK WAR

When the work of mustering out was over, at the request of General Atkinson, the governor called upon those just released from military duty to again volunteer for a short period of service. Enough volunteered to form a regiment. Jacob Fry, of Greene County, was elected colonel, James D. Henry was made lieutenant-colonel, and John Thomas major. There were six companies of sixty or seventy men each. Adam Snyder, of Belleville, was captain of one company. He was ordered to proceed with a part of his company to Kellogg's Grove for the protection of the people in the vicinity. The camp was located in the grove and before morning there were signs of a bitter feeling between the soldiers and the stragglers from Black Hawk's band. On the second day at the Grove expeditions were sent out about the fort to determine the strength of the Indians. Four were discovered, who eluded the soldiers at first, but later a conflict ensued, when one soldier was mortally wounded and the four Indians were slain. The soldier mortally wounded was being carried to the fort and the soldiers were set on by nearly a hundred of Black Hawk's band and two of the soldiers were killed. The little band stood their ground till relief came from the fort at Kellogg's Grove. The three dead were buried at the Grove and Captain Snyder and his volunteers were relieved and mustered out at Dixon. The regiment that volunteered for twenty days was also discharged by Colonel Taylor.

The new levy which was called for from Dixon on the 15th of May had begun to arrive. The country was in great danger apparently. The Indians seemed to be everywhere. White people were being killed in their homes and about the farms or on the public roads. It was about this time, the middle of June, that Black Hawk had attacked the Apple River Fort. Colonel Dodge, hearing of the attack on Apple River Fort, hastened from the lead region to the defense of the fort, but the Indians were gone. Colonel Dodge gave pursuit and overtook them at Pecatonica Creek, where an important engagement was fought. Colonel Dodge, with twenty-one soldiers, hemmed in seventeen Indians in the Horse Shoe Bend of the Pecatonica and killed or wounded every one of the seventeen.

There was great activity among the officials in receiving the new recruits and mustering out those whose time had expired. The new soldiers were received at Fort Deposit, afterwards to be called Fort Willbourn. About the middle of June, Billy Caldwell, Shabbona and Waubausee came to General Atkinson and revealed the whereabouts of Black Hawk. They said he was at the four lakes at the head waters of Rock River, that he had from 1,000 to 2,000 warriors, and that he was well intrenched. They offered to furnish an additional company of soldiers. The new troops were organized into brigades, with Gen. Alexander Posey in command of the first, Gen. Milton K. Alexander in command of the second, and Gen. James D. Henry in command of the third. They were received into the service of the United States by General Atkinson. The first brigade contained 1,001 men; the second, 959; the third, 1,232. Governor Reynolds caused other independent commands to be organized to defend the frontier from the Mississippi to Chicago. Forts were constructed and large quantities of food and other supplies were provided. The general Government had informed Governor Reynolds that the United States would pay all bills and that there should be no lack of supplies of any kind.

Major Dement received orders on the 18th of June as follows:

"Order No. 37.

Major Dement's Battalion of Volunteers will be prepared for detached service as early tomorrow morning as practicable, supplied with provisions for ten days. Major Dement will make a requisition on the ordnance officer for ammunition for his command, and report to the commanding general for instructions relative to the service to be performed." He was ordered to find the murderers of a Mr. Phillips, on Bureau Creek, in Bureau County. Thence he was to proceed to Dixon to receive orders from Colonel Taylor. He reached Dixon on the night of the 22d. His troops were tired and not in the best of humor. But after a rest of part of the day the troops were ordered to proceed to Kellogg's Grove to protect that vicinity. On the night of June 24, a Mr. Funk on his way from Galena to Dixon stopped at Kellogg's Grove and reported to Major Dement that large bands of Indians were seen in that vicinity. A council was held and it was decided that on the 25th a detachment of twenty-five volunteers should be sent out to reconnoiter. These men were not careful in their investigations and were decoyed by Black Hawk, who was in personal charge of his troops. The front line of scouts were fired on and two men were killed and one wounded. On the retreat Dement's force was pressed backward very rapidly, but the firing from both side was continuous and several Indians were known to have been killed. Three soldiers returning from hunting their horses were caught by the Indians in their wild advance and slaughtered. Major Dement and his men finally reached the log house and barns, where they took shelter. The buildings were soon surrounded by Indians. The soldiers were stationed where they could do the most execution. The Indians remained most of the day, and when they saw they could do little harm to the men, they began the slaughter of the horses which were in the open lot. About forty of the horses were shot down. Reinforcements reached the besieged men late that afternoon. The Indians finally retired, leaving nearly a dozen dead on the field.

Black Hawk in his Autobiography, page 104, gives an account

Courtesy of Illinois State Historical Library

SHABBONA

of this battle. He was on his way from the attack on the Apple River Fort to his future camp at Four Lakes.

The three brigades of volunteers that were received into the service at Fort Willbourn, on the Illinois, were under Generals Alexander, Posey, and Henry. General Alexander was ordered to guard the territory along the Mississippi near Galena. General Posey was at Kellogg's Grove, but was ordered to Fort Hamilton. General Henry's brigade and the 700 regulars were marched from Fort Willbourn to Dixon preparatory to the pursuit of Black Hawk, who was now known to be moving along the Rock River into the present state of Wisconsin. After a short rest the brigade commanded by General Henry was ready for a march to find Black Hawk.

General Atkinson ordered General Posey to march east and meet the other divisions of the army on the Rock River. General Alexander was to move along the northwest side of the Rock River, while General Atkinson, General Henry and Governor Reynolds, with the regulars, cannon, and General Henry's brigade, marched along the east side of the Rock River. They were all to center at Koshkonong Lake, an enlargement of Rock River in Southern Wisconsin. By July 4th the main army had arrived at the lake. There were no signs of Black Hawk. Governor Reynolds says: "The provisions were wasting away, almost gone, and the enemy had not been chastised. Two or three thousand fine soldiers under arms, and nothing done, caused reflections in the breasts of the officers, and to many of the privates the situation was extremely mortifying and painful." The commands of General Posey and General Alexander joined General Henry's brigade and the regulars on the 7th of July. Indians were seen in different parts of the country, but there were not enough in one group to make it advisable to pursue them.

An old Winnebago chief, Decari, who claimed to be a friend to the whites, told Atkinson that Black Hawk was down the Rock River. This caused some hesitation and some time was lost. Governor Reynolds said if at this time they had marched forward with some speed they could have found Black Hawk and captured him. He says the regulars and the cannon moved so slowly that they would never overtake the Indians. The governor and many prominent men who were not in the service, but accompanying the army, left the main army above Lake Koshkonong and returned to the frontiers. He visited Galena and the several points from the Mississippi to Chicago. He speaks of the excellent work that was being done by small bodies of troops along this frontier line. After inspecting these positions the governor returned to Belleville, his home.

General Atkinson remained in the vicinity of Lake Koshkonong till the 10th, when General Alexander and General Henry and Colonel Dodge were dispatched to Fort Winnebago, some sixty or seventy miles northwest of the camps above Lake Koshkonong. On the 13th of July word reached the camps that supplies were on the way to the army from Blue Mounds, a station some fifty miles northwest of Lake Koshkonong and some forty miles east of the Mississippi. On the 16th the supplies from Blue Mound reached Atkinson's army. The three officers with their commands reached Fort Winnebago in due season and portions returned with the supplies sent for. But General Henry and Colonel Dodge remained in that region hoping to have some news of Black Hawk. They were rewarded by information obtained through some Winnebago Indians, who said Black Hawk was at the falls of Rock River.

Disobeys Orders

General Henry called a conference of officers to ask what they should do when they were so close to the wily Indian chief. General Alexander said he and his men could not disobey orders, and must return to the camp at Koshkonong. Colonel Dodge said his men and horses were too exhausted to go in pursuit of the Indians. This left Henry to speak. He said he and his men would pursue Black Hawk. He therefore made preparation to make a real effort to find Black Hawk and punish him. But just as General Henry was ready to march a serious matter arose. The officers of General Fry's regiment presented to General Henry a protest against the pursuit of Black Hawk. General Fry did not sign the protest and was not in sympathy with it. General Henry studied the situation carefully and then ordered the signers under arrest, to be delivered to General Atkinson for punishment. General Fry begged for a few minutes for a conference with his officers, when he returned to General Henry with a plea that they had signed the petition not knowing what was in it, and begging his pardon, and upon being received back into his favor promised faithful obedience to all orders. It is said that General Henry granted their request and from that day on he had no more loyal men than those in General Fry's regiment.

Colonel Dodge's battalion having been recruited to 120 strong, and fresh horses having been provided, he was ready to join with General Henry in the pursuit of Black Hawk. General Henry's force had been considerably reduced, as he wished to take only the best fitted men. The combined force now numbered not many more than 600 effectives. From Fort Winnebago the little army moved east to Rock River and thence down that stream a distance, and thence southwest to the present site of Madison, Wisconsin. Here were the first positive signs of the retreating foe. It was now the 21st of July and the horses and men were greatly fatigued. The men had had, for at least one meal, only raw meat and flour mixed with water and eaten without baking. The soldiers had abandoned much of their equipment and were carrying only the absolutely essential things. The men slept on the bare ground with no blankets, while the rain poured in torrents.

BATTLE OF THE WISCONSIN

The army was following the trail of the Indians, which bore in a northwesterly direction. A few Indians were seen as the army advanced, but as they neared the Wisconsin River, thirty odd miles northwest of Madison, they overtook the main body of the retreating Indians. Here occurred the "Battle of the Wisconsin River." This battle was fought within a mile of the Wisconsin River. General Adams received word that the Indians were taking a position on the bluffs, or in the hills, which skirted the Wisconsin River. General Henry moved northwesterly in this order: Colonel Dodge was on the extreme right; to Dodge's left was Colonel Jones' regiment; to Jones' left was Colonel Collins' regiment. These three regiments were in a sort of bow, with the rounding part facing the Indians. The soldiers occupied rather elevated places, while the braves also were on elevated ground. There was some low ground between them. Colonel Dodge and Colonel Fry, with a regiment of reserves, charged the warriors and drove them to a position nearer the river, where they made a more determined stand. But from this second position they were routed by the bayonets of the left wing, General Collins and General Jones. From this stand they were driven into the marshes next to the river, when night put an end to further pursuit. The army lay upon the battlefield, but the Indians crossed to an island, and from there to the north bank of the river. The loss of the Indians in this battle is stated to have been sixty-eight killed and many more wounded. The Americans lost but one killed and eight wounded. Black Hawk says he would not have fought this battle if it had not been that he desired time to get his women and children across the Wisconsin. Black Hawk was already on his way to the Mississippi. A large part of his women and children descended the Wisconsin, hoping to be able to cross over the Mississippi to their own lands. General Henry's provisions were low and he was obliged for the time being to move south some twelve miles to Blue Mounds, where supplies had been provided. This prevented an immediate pursuit of Black Hawk.

At Blue Mounds General Atkinson had gathered the regulars and one or more regiments of volunteers which had been doing guard duty. These were all moved to Helena, on the Wisconsin, where they crossed and were soon on the trail of Black Hawk, who was rapidly approaching the Mississippi. It was while following this trail that the soldiers began to learn something of the desperate straits to which Black Hawk's band had been reduced. It was discovered that the Indians were living on buds and bark of the trees along the way. They had also devoured the flesh of their ponies as they died on the march.

Battle of Bad Axe

The march northwestward was over a very rough country and the signs of great distress in Black Hawk's ranks were abundant. When the warriors reached the bluffs of the Mississippi, Black Hawk himself moved up the river along the foot of the bluffs, accompanied by about twenty of his select braves. The warriors continued their march to the river. The army came over the bluffs and marched across the bottom and drove the Indians from the bank of the river over a slough to a small island, where they thought they were fairly safe. The soldiers plunged across this slough and were soon in control of the island. Then began the slaughter. Indians were shot down, many attempted to swim to the west shore of the Mississippi, but the soldiers had no mercy on them and they were killed while swimming to safety. It has been estimated that at least 150 Indians were killed in the battle of Bad Axe. Reynolds reports that some squaws were killed in this battle, since they were dressed like the men and therefore could not be easily distinguished.

A story is told of a boat called the "Warrior" carrying fifteen regulars and six volunteers that had been holding a conference with the Sioux, which came along just as Black Hawk and his warriors reached the Mississippi, and were in the act of transferring the women and children and old men to the west shore. When Black Hawk saw it was a United States boat he raised the white flag and offered to surrender, but the captain of the Warrior told Black Hawk he must come aboard the boat, but Black Hawk said this was impossible, for he had no boat or canoe. The Warrior then opened fire with a six pounder loaded with canister. Three times this little cannon belched forth its message of destruction. There were men, women, and children on the bank, the regulars and volunteers behind them, and the Warrior and the broad Mississippi in front of them. Fortunately for the poor Indians, the fuel of the Warrior gave out and the boat had to drop downstream for wood for the furnaces. On the morrow when the boat returned the soldiers were pouring a deadly fire in to the Indians. The boat took up the work of the day before and before long there were no Indians to resist.

Black Hawk, in the night following the attack by the Warrior, seeing the utter uselessness of further resistance, stole away from his camp and fled to the east, where he hoped to find refuge among the Winnebagoes. He took refuge in the hills and woods to the east of the scene of his defeat. He was followed by two Winnebago Indians, who had been engaged to overtake and capture him and return him to General Street, the Indian agent

BEAUTY SPOTS IN ILLINOIS
(1 & 2) Pines near Polo. (3) Starved Rock Park. (4) Park scene, Quincy.

at Prairie du Chien. This the two Indians did, and on the 27th of August he was delivered up to General Street.

There were probably 150 Indians taken prisoners, a very few crossed the Mississippi, the rest were killed or fled from Black Hawk's band on some of his long marches. The tribe was completely broken up. Black Hawk was taken from Prairie du Chien to St. Louis and remained for some time at Jefferson Barracks. Here he remained over the winter of 1832-3. From here he was taken to Washington by order of President Jackson. He went by boat to Wheeling from which place he reached Washington by stage. He had a brief conference with President Jackson, after which he was taken to Fortress Monroe, where he stayed a short time. From that point he was returned to the remnant of his people after having passed through many eastern cities. Black Hawk died in Davis County, Iowa, October 3, 1838.

General Scott

President Andrew Jackson was greatly interested in the Black Hawk war. The President was something of an Indian fighter himself, and it appears that he was often impatient at the lack of vigor which the officers frequently showed. And when we look over the whole situation we certainly feel that with the proper amount of energy and military skill the whole affair should have been nothing but a "before breakfast" job.

The interest which the President had in the war may be surmised when we remember that he sent Gen. Winfield Scott, one of the most noted generals of the War of 1812, with a detachment of nine companies of regulars to Chicago in 1832. General Scott left Fortress Monroe the 20th of June and reached Chicago July 10. A score or more of the cadets from West Point accompanied the regulars at least a portion of the way. When General Scott reached Detroit he decided to make a brief stop and while here two of his soldiers sickened and died within two hours with what proved to be Asiatic cholera. General Scott hastened to depart from Detroit. Several cases appeared on the ship as they were on their way to Chicago. They halted at Fort Gratiot near the outlet of Lake Huron, where five companies and the cadets were landed. The story of these 300 soldiers left at this point is heartrending. Many died in the hospitals, many made their escape into the woods and were found about the cabins of the settlers who shut the doors in their faces, refused them food and drink, and turned them into the woods to die of starvation. Out of nearly 300 of these unfortunate souls only nine survived. The cadets were returned to the East. From Fort Gratiot the ship made its way to Mackinaw. It was not thought the ravages were over, but from Mackinaw to Chicago the scourge broke out again and several deaths, about thirty, occurred, the bodies being buried overboard. "War has means of destruction more formidable than the sword. Of the thousands and tens of thousands that perish, a small part ever feel the stroke of the enemy—the rest languish in tents and ships amid damps and putrefaction—pale, torpid, spiritless and helpless; gasping and groaning, unpitied by men made obdurate by misery, and are at last whelmed in pits, or heaved into the ocean, without notice and without remembrance."

On the arrival of the remnant of General Scott's army at Chicago, Fort Dearborn was turned into a hospital, the few troops that were stationed there bivouacked on the open prairies. Ninety of General Scott's soldiers died within the first thirty days of his stay in Chicago. Graves were dug and awaited their occupants. Several bodies were buried in the same grave. No coffins, no ceremony, no tears. General Scott was tireless in his efforts to relieve those attacked by this dreadful disease. And he never gave up or thought of deserting his soldiers until the disease was entirely stamped out. All who lived through these dreadful days testified to the wonderful amount of energy which General Scott displayed on shipboard and at Fort Dearborn.

On July 29th finding no signs of the disease, General Scott began his journey to the scenes of conflict with Black Hawk. He traveled the main route from Chicago to Galena which place he reached on August 3d. From Galena he took the boat for Prairie du Chien, which he reached on August 7th. Here he assumed command of all the troops. The work of dispersing Black Hawk's band had been accomplished by the few regulars under General Atkinson and by the state volunteers under Governor Reynolds. The few regulars who had escaped the deadly enemy, the cholera, followed General Scott under command of Colonel Eustis. The Colonel was ordered to proceed from Dixon to the mouth of Rock River and establish camp on Rock Island, at Fort Armstrong. To this point General Scott came after having ordered the muster-out of all volunteers.

General Scott was authorized by President Jackson to associate with himself Gov. John Reynolds for the purpose of making a treaty with the Sacs and Foxes. All prisoners were ordered to Fort Armstrong that General Scott might obtain information as to the war with the end in view of making a just and binding treaty. But just at this juncture the cholera broke out among the troops at Fort Armstrong. The disease was, if anything, more virulent than it was at Fort Dearborn. It therefore became necessary to dismiss the prisoners with instructions to reassemble upon due notice. The soldiers were poorly sheltered, and the cold rains added to the embarrassment of the authorities and the misery and suffering of the sick. There were 300 cases of the dread disease, but only fifty deaths.

General Scott, as at Fort Dearborn, was ceaseless in his attentions to the needs of his soldiers. As soon as the disease was checked the Indians were summoned to return and the treaty was considered.

The treaty bears date of September 21, 1832, the United States commissioners were Gen. Winfield Scott of the United States Army and Gov. John Reynolds, governor of the State of Illinois. The Indians were represented by nine members of the Sacs, including Keokuk, and the Foxes by twenty-four members of the Fox tribe. There were twelve articles in the treaty as follows:

Art. 1. The Sac and Fox nations cede all lands they claim except a reservation which is definitely bounded.

Art. 2. The reservation shall contain 400 square miles and shall be laid off under the direction of the President of the United States.

Art. 3. In consideration of the great extent of the grant made by the Sac and Fox tribes, the United States agreed to pay to the tribes the sum of $20,000 in specie, annually for a period of thirty years.

Art. 4. The United States agreed to maintain a blacksmith shop and a gunsmith shop. Also to deliver to the two tribes forty kegs of tobacco and forty barrels of salt annually for thirty years.

Art. 5. The United States promised to pay debts owed by the two tribes to Farnham and Davenport, Indian traders, at Rock Island, the sum of $40,000.

Art. 6. The United States agreed to grant Antoine Le Claire, interpreter, two sections of land for services rendered.

Art. 7. The United States surrendered all prisoners of these two tribes, except certain named Indians held as hostages.

Art. 8. The two tribes shall never allow any other tribes to become a part of themselves, and the lands reserved for them shall be used by them alone.

Art. 9. Peace between the United States and the Confederated Tribes of Sacs and Foxes is declared and a solemn promise to maintain the same.

Art. 10. In consideration of the straitened circumstances in which the two tribes were at the time of the treaty, definite amounts of provisions were donated to the tribes.

Art. 11. Suitable rewards shall be made to members of the tribes for the discovery of any mines of metal more valuable than lead.

Art. 12. The treaty shall be binding as soon as it is ratified by the President and by the Senate of the United States.

Dated September 21, 1832.

Now that the famous Black Hawk war was over, the volunteers who had left their offices, their farms, their work benches, and their several occupations, have returned to the quiet pursuits of civil life. Many reputations were made in this war and for many it would have been well if they had not participated in it. The cost of the war was over $2,000,000 besides the loss of life and property.

NOTED MEN

The Black Hawk war has been considered a sort of historical joke. Few people have gotten into the merits of the conflict and hence it has little meaning in it for them. The war was, however, one of the most serious of the many Indian wars in which the United States has ever engaged. The war stands alone in the annals of the country when we consider the large number of the prominent soldiers and civilians who gave time, money and service to make Illinois safe for democracy. Following are a few of the noted people who participated in the war:

Ford, Thomas. Private in Whiteside's battalion. Prosecuted two Indians for carrying off the two Hall girls. Was circuit judge and associate judge of the Supreme Court, and governor of Illinois, 1842-1846.

Cartwright, Peter. Private in Captain Brown's company, Colonel Collin's regiment. Served in Illinois Legislature, preached over a large part of Central Illinois, the most noted camp-meeting preacher in Illinois.

Carlin, Thomas. Captain of a company in the Spy Battalion, commanded by Maj. James D. Henry. Receiver of public moneys, served in Legislature, governor from 1838 to 1842.

Keokuk, chief of the Sacs and Foxes. Said to be friend to the whites. Dissuaded Black Hawk from his invasion of Illinois. Signed treaty with United States in 1832.

Whiteside, Samuel. One of a famous family of Indian fighters. Captain of a company of Rangers in War of 1812. Brigadier-general in the Black Hawk war. Served in the General Assembly. Lived in Madison County.

Iles, Elijah. Early settler in Sangamon County. First postmaster at Springfield, state Senator. Major in Winnebago war. Private in Black Hawk war. Advanced to captain. Abraham Lincoln was private under Elijah Iles.

Atkinson, Henry. Was general in command of the regulars and the Illinois volunteers. He treated Governor Reynolds with great deference. After the war he returned to Jefferson Barracks. Black Hawk spent the winter of 1832-3 at the Barracks and speaks in great praise of White Beaver, General Atkinson.

Wood, John. Founded Quincy. Served in Legislature. Was private in Captain Flood's company which was made up in Quincy. Was elected lieutenant-governor in 1856, and filled out Governor Bissell's term.

Raum, John. Served in War of 1812 as first lieutenant. Was

brigade major in Black Hawk war. Served in General Assembly. His two sons, Green B. and John M., were brigade general and major respectively, in the Civil war.

Buckmaster, Nathaniel. Major of the old battalion of three companies. He also served as brigade major under General Whiteside. He reenlisted at the end of his first period of enlistment. Served in the General Assembly.

Hardin, John. A lawyer of Jacksonville. Was inspector-general on the staff of Gen. Joseph Duncan. Later colonel and inspector-general. Member of Legislature, member of Congress. Colonel in Mexican war. Killed at battle of Buena Vista, February 27, 1847.

Davis, Jefferson. Was a graduate of West Point, class of 1828. Was second lieutenant in regular army at Jefferson Barracks in 1832. Served under Col. Zachary Taylor at Dixon as aid. Conveyed Black Hawk a prisoner from Prairie du Chien to Jefferson Barracks. He was elected to Congress. Was made President of the Southern Confederacy.

Eddy, Henry, was editor of the Shawneetown Gazette. He was quartermaster-general with the rank of colonel in the Black Hawk war. After the war he served in the General Assembly and was elected circuit judge, but resigned after a short period of service. He was a brilliant lawyer.

Wilson, Harrison. The father of Harrison Wilson came to Shawneetown in 1800. The son, Harrison, was an ensign in the War of 1812. He was also a captain in the Black Hawk war. His brother, Beuford Wilson, was adjutant-general in the Civil war. His son, Maj.-Gen. James H. Wilson, was in command of the expedition that captured Jefferson Davis. He was the military representative of the United States Army at the crowning of King Edward VII. Capt. Harrison Wilson fought by the side of Lieutenant Jefferson Davis in the battle of Bad Axe.

Lincoln, Abraham. Lincoln was a clerk in a store at Salem when the call came for troops. He was a private in Captain Iles's company. When his time expired, he reenlisted and was made a captain of a company. He studied law, served in the Legislature, secured the removal of the capital to Springfield, served in Congress, championed the right of Congress to limit the spread of slavery, served as President from 1861 to 1865.

Logan, John A. Lived among the Shawnee and Delaware Indians in Missouri near Grand Tower. Volunteered in the Ninth Regiment in 1831. In 1832 volunteered again and was a surgeon's mate in Col. Jacob Fry's regiment. Later was colonel of the Forty-fourth Regiment, State Militia. Graduated in medicine. Colonel of the Thirty-second Regiment, Illinois Volunteers, in the Civil war. Was breveted brigadier general. Was United States marshal for the Southern District of Illinois, 1866-70.

McClernand, John A. Was an editor in Shawneetown at the outbreak of Black Hawk war. He was assistant quartermaster-general in Posey's brigade. He was acquainted with Lieutenant Jefferson Davis and remembered with great pleasure his days about Dixon's Ferry. Served in the Legislature and in Congress. Was a presidential elector. Was made a brigadier-general in the Civil war, and soon rose to major-general of volunteers. He held high civil positions till late in life.

Scott, Winfield. Gen. Winfield Scott served with great distinction in the War of 1812. Was breveted major-general for his services. Brought a regiment of United States troops from Fortress Monroe to Chicago in the summer of 1832. Took charge of the closing matters of the Black Hawk war. Was a conspicuous figure in the Mexican war, marching to Mexico City, where he conquered a peace with the Mexicans. He was lieutenant-general of United States Army at the outbreak of the Civil war, but soon resigned on account of age.

Semple, James. Was a lawyer in Edwardsville. Volunteered and was adjutant of the Old Battalion commanded by Maj. Nathaniel Buckmaster. Later was aide to General Whiteside. He volunteered as a private under Captain Snyder for the campaign to Kellogg's Grove. He later was appointed brigadier-general. Served in the Legislature, was attorney-general of Illinois, was minister to Granada, United States Senator. Had a long and honorable public life.

McConnell, Murray. Was a truly Western pioneer. Located in Jacksonville, where he became a great lawyer. He was adjutant under Col. Abraham B. DeWitt. Later was brigade inspector under General Henry. Was major in march from Fort Winnebago to Bad Axe. Performed distinguished service in the Bad Axe battle. He took great interest in the internal improvement of Illinois. Served in Legislature, and was an active politician.

Snyder, Adam W. Was an early comer to Illinois. He was a protege of Jesse B. Thomas, and through Mr. Thomas he became a lawyer. Earlier he was a wool curler, or roll-maker, in a fulling mill in Cahokia, as early as 1817. Was a member of the Legislature, and enlisted in the Black Hawk war. He was adjutant of the First Regiment commanded by Col. John Thomas. Following the Stillman defeat, new regiments were formed, and Mr. Snyder was made a captain in Colonel Fry's regiment. Captain Snyder fought a battle in the vicinity of Kellogg's Grove. After the war he was elected to Congress. Was the democratic candidate for governor but died before the election and Judge Ford was put upon the ticket and was elected.

Shabbona. A good Indian. Fought with Tecumseh in the War of 1812. After the defeat of Tecumseh at the battle of the Thames, Shabbona and Billy Caldwell both deserted the

British cause and were held by General Lewis Cass at Detroit. He opposed the Black Hawk war. Shabbona was holding a conference with Black Hawk the night of the Stillman defeat. He worked to prevent ill feeling among the Pottawattomies toward Mr. Davis, who built a dam across the Indian Creek. He signed the bond which released from confinement the two Indians who carried the Hall girls into captivity. He lived in Shabbona's Grove in the southwest part of DeKalb County. Later he lived near Morris, Illinois.

Anderson, Robert. The first we hear of Mr. Anderson was in Order No. 14, which said: "Lieut. Robert Anderson, Third Regiment Artillery, will, till further orders, perform the duties of assistant quartermaster-general of the troops now in the field." Lieut. Robert Anderson mustered out troops at Fort Willbourn following the twenty-day enlistment. He was assistant inspector-general on the staff of General Atkinson. At the breaking out of the Civil war, Gen. Robert Anderson was in charge of Fort Sumter, which he was forced to surrender to the Confederate troops April 14, 1861. He resided in New York City after the close of the Civil war.

Breese, Sidney. Was assistant secretary of state in 1820, and had charge of the removal of the archives of the state from Kaskaskia to the new capital, Vandalia. He volunteered in the Black Hawk war and was elected major in the Third Regiment, commanded by Col. Gabriel Jones. Later he was promoted to lieutenant-colonel. He returned to Southern Illinois with Governor Reynolds in the latter part of July, 1832. Served on the Supreme Court; was United States Senator. Was instrumental in securing the grant of land for the Illinois Central Railroad. Later served on the Supreme Court. He lived at Carlyle.

Gillespie, Joseph. Worked in the lead mines from 1827 to 1829. Served in two campaigns in the Black Hawk war. He was paymaster in the Old Battalion. Maj. Nathaniel Buckmaster. When his first enlistment was up, he volunteered as a private in Col. Jacob Fry's regiment for twenty days. He marched to Kellogg's Grove with Captain Snyder to protect that part of the country till the new levies could arrive. He was a warm personal friend of Mr. Lincoln. He presided over the Republican State Convention in Decatur in the summer of 1860. He served long on the circuit bench.

Fry, Jacob. Built the first house in Carrollton, Greene County. He served as a sheriff, enlisted and was lieutenant-colonel and then colonel of the Second Regiment. Reenlisted to serve till the arrival of the new volunteers. Performed valuable service in the campaign about the Four Lakes. Took an active part in the battle of the Wisconsin River. Also rendered good work at Bad Axe. He and General Henry should be given the credit for the final capture of Black Hawk. Held many civil positions of responsibility. Although sixty-two years old he commanded the Sixty-first Illinois Volunteers in the Civil war.

Duncan, Joseph. Won honors in the War of 1812. Was awarded a sword. Was major-general of Illinois militia in 1823. State senator, and was made brigadier-general in the campaign of 1831. He was serving in Congress from 1827 to 1834 and seems not to have enlisted in the campaign of 1832. He was elected governor of Illinois in 1834 to 1838. Is said to have erected the first frame house in Jacksonville in 1834. He was a great friend of Illinois College.

Hubbard, Gurdon. Spent his early years as an agent of the American Fur Company. Knew Indian life. Was in Chicago in 1818. Was an independent trader with Chicago as his headquarters. He learned of the breaking out of the Winnebago war from Gen. Lewis Cass who came to Chicago on his way from Jefferson Barracks to notify the United States of the need of troops. Mr. Hubbard carried the news from Chicago to Danville between 4 P. M. of one day and the forenoon of the third day and gathered 100 men to march to the relief of Chicago. Hubbard was lieutenant in Captain Bailey's company of Col. Isaac R. Moore's regiment. The regiment was for the defense of the west of Chicago. He was a public-spirited citizen and Chicago owes him a debt of gratitude. He served as captain in the Civil war.

Browning, O. H. Lived in Quincy when the Black Hawk war broke out. He was but twenty-one years of age, but had been admitted to the bar. He was a private in the Quincy company. He found fault with the management of the campaign, but Mr. Frank Stephens in his admirable history of the war has told us that Mr. Browning was too critical and that it was from such critics came much of the lack of cooperation and lack of success. Mr. Browning was a staunch friend of Mr. Lincoln and helped to secure his nomination for the Presidency. He succeeded Stephen A. Douglas as United States Senator, and in 1866 was secretary of the interior under President Johnson. Died in Quincy at the age of seventy years.

Ewing, Wm. L. D. Was an official in the land office in Shawneetown, and brigadier-general of the state militia. Was major of the "Spy Battalion" in the Black Hawk war. Took part in the battle of Wisconsin River. Major Ewing followed Black Hawk closely from Wisconsin River to the battle of Bad Axe. Served for fifteen days as governor, 1834, Governor Reynolds and Lieut.-Gov. Zadoc Casey having both been elected to Congress. Was elected a United States Senator in 1835 to succeed Elias Kent Kane. He defeated Abraham Lincoln for speaker of the House of Representatives of the Illinois Legislature in 1840. He held a number of civil offices.

Johnston, Albert Sidney. Lieut. Albert Sidney Johnston was

stationed at Jefferson Barracks when General Atkinson was sent to restore order at the mouth of the Rock River in 1832. He acted as adjutant-general to General Atkinson in the summer of 1832. He praises General Henry for the service he rendered in the capture of Black Hawk. He was a West Point graduate. Resigned from the army in 1834. Fought as a private for Texan independence. Was colonel in the war with Mexico. Was in command of Confederate forces in Kentucky in 1861. Attacked Grant at Shiloh in 1862 and was killed in that battle.

Johnston, Joseph E. Was graduated from West Point Military Academy in 1829, and was a lieutenant till 1846. He was stationed at Fortress Monroe when his company was selected to come to Chicago in the summer of 1832 to assist in capturing Black Hawk and destroying his band. He escaped the cholera and went from Chicago to Rock Island and was one of the witnesses to the treaty made by General Scott and Governor Reynolds with the remnant of the Sacs and Foxes. When Lieutenant Johnston returned to Norfolk, Virginia, in November, 1832, there was 180 men left out of about 500 who left that point in June of the same year. Served in the Mexican war as captain. When the Civil war broke out he was made a brigadier-general in Confederate army. He unsuccessfully opposed Sherman's march to the sea.

Casey, Zadoc. Son of a Revolutionary soldier. Came to Illinois in 1817. Served in the Legislature. Elected lieutenant-governor with John Reynolds as governor in 1830. Volunteered in the Black Hawk war and was elected paymaster of the "Spy Battalion," commanded by Maj. John Dement. Took an active part in the battle of Kellogg's Grove. His horse was wounded and he only saved his life by putting up a strong fight with the Indians. Was elected to Congress. Served also in the General Assembly. He was wealthy and public spirited.

Hamilton, Wm. S. A son of Alexander Hamilton. He was a cadet at the West Point Military Academy, but resigned in 1817. He settled in Sangamon County in this state and was engaged in surveying the public lands. Served in the Legislature in 1824-5. Was military aid to Governor Coles with the rank of Colonel. Took part in the reception to La Fayette in 1825. Went to the lead mines in 1827; was there when the Black Hawk troubles occurred. When Governor Reynolds reached Dixon's Ferry he found among other prominent people Colonel Hamilton, who offered his services. Fort Hamilton was erected at the "Hamilton Diggins" on Pecatonica River just in the edge of Wisconsin. Colonel Hamilton was associated with Colonel Dodge, who was a sort of whirlwind in Indian fighting. Colonel Hamilton commanded a company of Indians. He rendered most acceptable service to the cause of the Government.

When gold was discovered in California he went to that El Dorado where he died in 1850.

Cass, Lewis. General in the War of 1812. Governor of Michigan Territory. Secretary of war, 1831-36. Minister to France, United States Senator, democratic candidate for the presidency in 1848, secretary of state under President Buchanan. In 1825 General Cass, as governor of Michigan Territory, made treaty of Prairie du Chien. During the year 1827 he gave much attention as governor of Michigan to the Indian troubles in Illinois. He made a trip from Green Bay to St. Louis to notify the army of the Winnebago war. In 1831 as secretary of war he was still deeply interested in the Indian troubles.

Chouteau, Auguste. Was a noted Frenchman of St. Louis. Was present when Gen. William Henry Harrison made the treaty in St. Louis in 1804 in which the Sacs and Foxes ceded all their lands east of the Mississippi River to the United States. Was commissioner of the United States in the treaty of friendship made at Portage des Sioux with the Sacs, 1815. Was also commissioner in the treaty of St. Louis in 1816 with Sacs. Mr. Chouteau was a friend to Ninian Edwards and was greatly interested in the people in Illinois.

Reynolds, John. An early pioneer in Illinois. Was a ranger in War of 1812. Member of Supreme Court, 1818-24. Governor, 1830-4. Took the field with his troops in both phases of the Black Hawk war. Some have thought the Black Hawk war would have been finished earlier if Reynolds could have had entire control. Served in Congress and later in the Legislature. Acted as agent for Illinois in the period of international improvement. Wrote several books in such a style as to portray admirably the life of the times. Died in Belleville, 1865.

Stuart, John T. A prominent lawyer in Springfield, the friend and law partner of Abraham Lincoln. Was major in Col. James D. Henry's regiment. After he was mustered out at end of first enlistment period, he volunteered as a private in Colonel Fry's regiment for service for twenty days. As a private he marched and camped and hungered with other privates—General Henry, Abraham Lincoln, Joseph Gillespie, Frances Jarrott, Pierre Menard, John Dement, James Semple, John J. Hardin, Samuel Whiteside and Richard Roman. In 1883, Captain Iles, in writing about his company, said that of all the men in his company in the war, Maj. John T. Stuart was the only one living. He died in 1885.

Taylor, Zachary. Was a lieutenant in the regular army in 1808 at age of twenty-four. Was a major in War of 1812. Was lieutenant-colonel the early part of the Black Hawk war in charge of the command at Fort Crawford. Promoted to colonel. He was active in all the campaigns to the battle of Bad Axe, and was next in command to General Atkinson. Was brevet brigadier-general in charge of troops in Texas at outbreak of Mexican war. Fought battles of Palo Alto, Resaca de la Palma, Monterey, and Buena Vista, and won each battle. Was promoted to major-general. Elected President of the United States in 1844, died July 9th, 1850.

Dodge, Henry. Belonged to a noted family of Indian fighters. He lived in what is now Wisconsin, but then Michigan Territory. He organized a band of about sixty men and guarded the lead region till troops could arrive. His numbers grew and were called Dodge's Squadron. He was a sub-agent of the Winnebagoes and thus influenced them not to join Black Hawk. He was active in affording protection from Chicago to the Northwest. Dodge's most pretentious engagement was the battle of Pecatonica River in which he killed seventeen Indians. He engaged in the last campaign by way of the Four Lakes and the battle of Wisconsin to Bad Axe where he rendered important services. Colonel Dodge was governor of Wisconsin and United States Senator.

Waubunsee. A good Indian. He belonged to the Pottawattomies. He and Shabbona withstood the pleadings of Black Hawk to enter into the war with the Sacs. He in conjunction with Billy Caldwell and Shabbona offered General Atkinson a hundred Indians to fight Black Hawk.

CHAPTER IX

MARTYRDOM OF LOVEJOY

POLITICS—RADICALS AND CONSERVATIVES—A MORAL HERO—
BIOGRAPHY — OUT WEST — CONVERTED — PREACHING —
THE OBSERVER—SLAVERY EDITORIAL—NEW CODE—REPLY—
JUDGE LAWLESS—MOVED TO ALTON—SECOND PRESS—AMALGAMATION — ANTI-SLAVERY SOCIETY — ANTI-ABOLITION —
ADDING FUEL—LAST APPEAL—THE GUARD—THE MOB.

A very large share of the early history of Illinois is inseparably connected with the subject of slavery. It has been shown that slavery existed in what is now the Territory of Illinois since the coming of Phillip Francois Renault in 1719. "The French slaves" were the negroes and mulattoes whose ancestors were those Guinea negroes brought from the West Indies, by Renault in the above mentioned year. In the latter part of the eighteenth century and the first part of the nineteenth century, another form of forced labor existed in Illinois, by what was known as the indentured system.

POLITICS

In 1818, in the Constitutional Convention, slavery was a subject which engaged the most earnest and thoughtful attention of the delegates. In 1820-23 the Missouri Compromise, although a national matter, came very close to the political life of Illinois. The Senators in Congress from Illinois did their little bit to further the interests of the Southern statesmen in fastening slavery upon one of the sovereign states. From 1820 to 1824 the state was a seething cauldron of bitterness and strife over the question of introducing slavery into Illinois by rewriting the constitution. The friends of slavery were defeated, however, and Illinois in theory, at least, remained a free state. Locally the question of slavery was not prominent in Illinois for several years after the great convention struggle in 1824. But from 1830 to 1840 the subject was constantly before the national Congress and the public mind was greatly agitated by the discussions in and out of the halls of national legislation.

It has been said that the public mind was greatly pacified by the Missouri Compromise. It was fondly hoped that the subject would rest for many a decade. It may have been that this legislation known as the Missouri Compromise did for a short time allay the public mind on the slavery question, but the pacification was in no sense a permanent one. In fact public sentiment in neither North nor South was crystallized as early as 1830. In the year 1826, it is said, more than a hundred anti-slavery societies existed in the slave states, and this number is said to have been three times as many as existed in the Northern or free states.

The agitation of the slavery question by such publications as those edited by Lundy, Birney, and Garrison, resulted in the formation of the National Anti-Slavery Society in Philadelphia in 1833. This society began an active campaign for the abolition of slavery. They sent pamphlets, hand bills, and newspapers broadcast into slave territory. This greatly incensed the slave holders and their friends. In New York City, the postmaster took from the mails anti-slavery matter and destroyed it. So also did the postmaster at Charleston, South Carolina. This conduct was reported to the postmaster-general, Mr. Amos Kendall, and he virtually approved of this open violation of the law. Andrew Jackson, in his message to Congress, asked that Congress might pass a law which would prevent the passage "through the mails of incendiary publications intended to instigate the slaves to insurrection." Anti-slavery meetings were broken up in many Northern cities by those who bitterly opposed any agitation of the abolition question.

Earnest appeals from the South came to the North to suppress the abolitionists. But those in authority could do no more than to stand by the first amendment of the constitution which says, "Congress shall make no law respecting an establishment of religion, or prohibiting the free exercise thereof: or abridging the freedom of speech, or of the press; or the right of the people peaceably to assemble, and to petition the Government for a redress of grievances." This is the first and most sacred right which is guaranteed in the Bill of Rights found in the first ten amendments to the Constitution of the United States. Public assemblies and free speech are thus guaranteed, and no legislation can in any way abridge them. From these anti-slavery societies and from other organizations there poured into Congress hundreds of petitions praying for some legislation looking to the relief of the slave. All means which the friends of slavery in the North had tried, in the early days of the conflict, to check the growing anti-slavery sentiment, had failed. They thought there was at least one means which would annihilate the abolitionists, this was the violence of mob force. "Violence was the essential element in slavery—violence was the law of its being." This violence was directed against individuals, assemblies, and the press.

Radicals and Conservatives

There was a lack of unity among the anti-slavery people of the North as to the best means of furthering their cause, and men upon whose souls lay the burden which the nation itself ought to have cheerfully lifted, were in no sense fully agreed upon the final end and aim of their struggle. "It was fashionable to stigmatize them (the anti-slavery people) as ultra progmatic and angular, and to hold up their differences and divisions as a foil and a shield against the arguments and appeals. Thousands consoled and defended themselves in their inaction because anti-slavery men were not agreed among themselves." But while there was a lack of unity in method, there was at least a line of cleavage which separated the anti-slavery party into two great classes. In one class were those who believed that the end, whatever it might be, was to be reached through constitutional means—through legislation. These men might be called conservatives. They were fully persuaded that their friends in the other class were not safe in their counsel. These men were found in the two political parties then recognized or soon to be recognized—the whig party and the democratic party.

In the other class were those men who were not willing to wait for the long deferred day when the curse of slavery should be destroyed by the slow process of legislation. For they knew that any legislation not the outgrowth of public sentiment would be a dead letter upon the statute books. Legislation must follow public sentiment, it cannot create it. And to the men of the Garrison cast there was no sign of any growth of a sentiment in favor of the freedom of the slave in the South. These men saw not the least ray of hope as to the final extinction of slavery. The fact was that by 1835 the public men of the South who had formerly favored some form of emancipation were now bitterly opposed to any effort looking toward the abolition of slavery. The fact was that by 1835 the public men of the South who had formerly favored some form of gradual abolition were now bitterly opposed to any efforts being made along that line.

This restless, radical class which had no faith in a soft pedal style of agitation were known as "Garrison Abolitionists." Their fundamental doctrines were "No union with slave holders," and "the United States Constitution is a covenant with death and an agreement with hell!" There never was any doubt of the sincerity of purpose of these "Garrison Abolitionists." Nor must we imagine that they were fanatics. They were men of great power and consecration. They belonged to that class to whom the world pays homage. They are the men for whom we erect monuments. They are the men and women whose birthplaces we search out and whose homes though humble we mark with bronze tablets and marble. They are they whose lives are a benediction and whose death is a national calamity. True these men were iconoclasts, they were revolutionists, they would not be limited by any law, constitutional or legislative,

Sec 1 Be it enacted by the people of the State of Illinois represented in the General Assembly— That Reuben Harrison, John Clary and Sandy James be and they are hereby appointed commissioners to view, mark and permanently locate so much of the State road, leading from Springfield in Sangamon county to Lewiston in Fulton county, as lies between Springfield and George G. Miller's ferry on the Sangamo river

Sec 2. Said commissioners or a majority of them shall meet at the town of Springfield on the second Monday in March next or as soon thereafter as practicable and after being duly sworn by some officer authorized to administer oaths, shall proceed to perform the duties required of them by this act; avoiding as much as possible the injury of private property—

Sec 3 The said commissioners shall as soon thereafter as convenient, cause to be filed with the clerk of the county commissioner's court of the county of Sangamo a report and complete map of said road which report and map shall be preserved and shall form a part of the record of said court— Said road when so established shall be kept in repair as other State roads are—

Sec 4 The county commissioners court of Sangamon county shall allow to said commissioners out of the county treasury; such compensation, as, to them shall seem just and reasonable—

Passed H. R. Feb 5. 1835
H. Shickitt Clk H R

FACSIMILE OF BILL IN HANDWRITING OF ABRAHAM LINCOLN

antagonistic to the law of conscience and God. They openly preached disunion. They did not hesitate to state their "unalterable purpose and determination to live and labor for the dissolution of the present union by all lawful and just though bloodless and pacific means and for the formation of a new republic, that shall be such not in name only, but in full living reality and truth."

Believing in free speech and in free press, they made use of both to spread their ideas and win many to their cause. True, in those days, the newspaper was an infant compared with the great newspapers of today. Not only were papers small in size, but their influence was very much limited by the very small numbers reached by their circulation. All the papers which plead the cause of the "Garrison Abolitionists" were poorly supported financially.

Among these newspapers the reading public is quite familiar with Lundy's Genius of Universal Emancipation, Garrison's Liberator, The Philanthropist, The Emancipator, and the Alton Observer.

The spirit of violence above referred to which Mr. Henry Wilson in his "Rise and Fall of the Slave Power in America," calls the fundamental idea in slavery, began now to spend its fury on these newspapers, presses, and their editors. We are now in a position to understand the life-work and the martyrdom of the editor of the Alton Observer.

A Moral Hero

Few names will live longer in the history of the state than that of Rev. Elijah Parish Lovejoy. Many honorable names may be found in the several fields of activity from the earliest days to the present time. Our military annals of Illinois present some of the greatest names of modern times; the names associated with the great inventions and improvements in social and economic progress may be read upon the pages of Illinois history; the never-to-be-forgotten pioneers of Illinois who conquered the forces of streams, and forests, and prairies deserve, and will hold, a sacred place in the hearts and minds of generations yet unborn; the praises of her great orators shall continue to be sounded; the wisdom of her world renowned jurists will be revered so long as civil liberty is cherished by an intelligent citizenship; but the name of Elijah Parish Lovejoy, poet, minister, editor, publicist, friend of the slave—defender of his home, his wife, and his unborn—martyr to the cause of free speech, free press, and free religion, shall never be forgotten, so long as the citizens of a great state shall believe in the declaration that "all men are born equal, that they are endowed by their Creator with certain inalienable rights, that among these are life, liberty, and the pursuit of happiness."

Biography

Elijah Parish Lovejoy was a son of Massachusetts, one of the states where the first legal steps were taken to condemn the practice of slavery "as an institution, politically incompatible with a free constitution, and religiously incompatible with the laws of God." Massachusetts had lived under a "provincial charter" from 1691 to the close of the Revolutionary war. The constitution she made in 1780 was the work of delegates elected from among the people for the especial purpose of framing a fundamental law. The constitution contained three distinct political phases—a frame of government, a bill of rights, and a declaration of independence. In the Bill of Rights John Adams wrote a clause which declared that "all men are born free and equal." Three years later the Supreme Court of Massachusetts interpreted this to mean that no person could legally be held as a slave in the commonwealth of Massachusetts. And immediately the shackles fell from the hands and feet of all men and women held in bondage in that state.

It was in the atmosphere of such political principles as this one laid down by John Adams that the son of a devout minister of the Gospel was born. He breathed the free air not only of the state but of the church. The father, the Rev. Daniel Lovejoy, received his theological training at Byfield, Massachusetts, under the loving care of the Rev. Elijah Parish. He began his ministerial labors in 1805 and served the church faithfully till his death which occurred in 1833. The ancestors of the subject of this sketch were of Scotch descent.

Elijah Parish Lovejoy was born in 1802 and was thirty-five years of age the day before his burial in Alton. His was a mature mind from the earliest years. He read with remarkable ease the Bible at the age of four years. While still a youth he had read all the books in his father's library and had access to a well stocked small library of the village where his father was preaching. He committed with ease the 119th Psalm and twenty church hymns between two Sundays. "Poetry he drank in like water." Later he recited 150 of Watt's hymns at a single sitting. His mother who was a cultured lady had given him great attention in all the branches then thought necessary as a preparation for college. Our young friend had had but a few weeks of instruction in Latin yet in one quarter of college study he read all of Virgil, and gave much time to Cicero and Sallust. He graduated first in his class from Waterville College, September, 1826, and was engaged in teaching for one year. He was in no sense a dreamer, yet he gave much time to the study and composition of poetry. One poem entitled "Europe" is a portrayal of the strife in which Europe had been for ages engaged. For his graduation exercise he produced a poem, "Inspirations of the Muse," which was read before the class and the assembled friends.

OUT WEST

In May, 1827, he left home, friends and native state with his eyes fixed on the growing West. He had eagerly read much of the broad expanse of fields and forests. In his earliest years he had taken great delight in the athletic sports common to the interior of New England. He was a good swimmer and was much given to other physical exercises. It would seem that he wished to measure his physical strength with the forces of nature in a new country. Likewise he wished to give his mind the opportunity to expand with the expanding social and religious forces of a new state. Before his departure he spent much time in contemplation. He found it no small task to leave his old associates, friends, and parents. All his correspondence with his home folks while a resident of St. Louis and Alton breathes the spirit of devotion to his parents and to his brothers and sisters. His attachment to the land of his youth was strong and manly. He was no sickly sentimentalist, but he loved with a strong and courageous heart. In a poem which he wrote just prior to his departure, with the title "The Farewell," he paid his soul's tribute to his native land and prophesied his own death. A few lines will reveal the mood in which he bade adieu to his home and its surroundings.

"Land of my birth! my natal soil farewell:
The winds and the waves are bearing me away
Fast from thy shores; and I would offer thee
This sincere tribute of a swelling heart.
I love thee: witness that I do, my tears
Which gushingly do flow, and will not be restrained
At thought of seeing thee, perchance no more.

Thy sons are noble, in whose veins there runs
A richer tide than Europe's Kings can boast,
The blood of free men: Blood which oft has flowed
In freedom's holiest cause; and ready yet to flow,
If need should be; ere it would curdle down
To the slow sluggish stream of slavery.

But time is speeding; and the billowy waves
Are hurrying me away. The misty shores
Grow dim in distance; while yon setting sun
Seems lingering fondly on them, as 'twould take
Like me, a last adieu. I go to tread
The western vales, whose gloomy cypress tree
Shall happily soon be wreathed upon my bier:
Land of my birth, my natal soil, Farewell.

On his way West, somewhere on the shore of Lake Erie, he wrote "The Wanderer." It is a sad, gloomy dissertation upon the world about him, which may be somewhat explained by the fact that he was just recovering from a season of sickness.

He must have lingered on his way from Maine to St. Louis, as he did not reach the latter place till the fall of 1827. He left the East in the early summer. On arrival in St. Louis he writes an affectionate letter to his parents—he was very homesick. But the world was a busy one and there was no time for homesickness. He taught school, wrote for the newspapers, and gave some attention to the reading and writing of poetry. The two papers of St. Louis at that time, the Missouri Republican and the St. Louis Times, were both pleased to have articles from his pen.

Converted

In the winter of 1831-2 there was a great revival in the Protestant churches of St. Louis. Mr. Lovejoy was attracted to these revivals and was converted, and united with the Presbyterian organization, the pastor at that time being Rev. Dr. W. S. Potts. Being naturally seriously minded, he felt he ought to give his life to the ministry, and he was therefore the more easily prevailed upon by his pastor to enter the theological seminary at Princeton, New Jersey, in the spring of 1832. Here he remained one year, after which he was licensed to preach by the Second Presbyterian Church of Philadelphia. He spent the summer of 1833 in New York and in other Eastern cities, and in the fall of that year he returned to St. Louis.

The summer of 1832, which he spent in the theological seminary at Princeton, was a happy year for Mr. Lovejoy. He was near enough his parents to visit them and he was extremely happy in the choice of his life work. The several letters which he wrote to his parents and brothers and sisters are full of intense devotion. He dwells upon his own conversion as the snatching of a brand from the burning. Time and again he confesses his belief in the fact that the prayers of his father and mother were the sources not only of his conversion, but also of his strength to undertake the work of preaching the unsearchable riches of the Christian religion.

The Observer

Even before he returned to St. Louis, in the fall of 1833, he had received urgent requests from St. Louis friends to come to that city and begin the publication of a religious paper. Such an undertaking we find Mr. Lovejoy engaged in. His friends, whose names will appear later, entered into a sort of joint stock company, investing $1,200 for the purchase of a press, type, etc. They selected Mr. Elijah Parish Lovejoy as editor and made a contract with him which provided that he should have full and absolute control of the business, with the right to mortgage the presses, etc., for more money for an enlargement of the capacity of the enterprise. If the net income should exceed $500, the editor was to pay said excess to the proprietors, otherwise they were to receive no returns on their investment.

The first issue was put out on the 22d of November, 1833. The leading editorial was an article of more than a thousand words. "But while the Observer will thus seek to win its way to the hearts and consciences of men, by the kindness of the sentiments it breathes, it will not temporize as it goes." Some of the editorials were a sort of treatment of abstract subjects. One on "Truth" was a warning against allowing the doctrines of the philosophers to crowd out the preaching of Paul. In these non-religious editorials the editor shows himself quite at home quoting from the philosophers and writers of the ages. He wrote in an analytic style, making use of his firstly, secondly, and thirdly.

Preaching

Mr. Lovejoy was a frequent visitor to the Presbyterian churches within a reasonable distance of St. Louis. He made these visits on horseback, which was the usual mode of travel in those days. On one occasion he visited Apple Creek Presbyterian Church, which was located in the Village of White Hall, in Greene County. He was much impressed with this visit, made May 22d, 1835. Mr. Lovejoy describes at length the assembling of the members of the congregation. "To see the congregation assemble reminded me of the descriptions I have often read of the gathering of the Highland clans at the muster call of their leaders." Other towns were visited and their small congregations ministered to by the Rev. Mr. Lovejoy. He must have preached often in St. Charles, Missouri, for he afterwards married his wife in that town.

It can not be affirmed that Mr. Lovejoy's editorials were always wisely chosen; he touched some discords when he left the subject for which the paper was founded. There was no objection to the discussion of subjects purely religious, but there was much debatable ground which Mr. Lovejoy wished to traverse which some of his friends much desired he should refrain from entering. One of those digressions led to the discussion of slavery. There were occasional references to slavery from the very beginning, but they were not "leading editorials" and they did not greatly disturb his general readers. Lovejoy's mental vigor and his religious zeal and the tendency to an unreserved criticism, led him more and more to give his attention to the consideration of the slavery subject.

Slavery Editorial

In June, 1834, Mr. Lovejoy wrote an editorial on slavery. In this editorial he discussed two phases of the question that was at that time greatly disturbing the public mind. In the Eastern states two movements had supporters. One movement looked to the colonization of the African slave, and the other's goal was the abolition of African slavery in the United States. The proponents of each had reached such fervor in their public meetings and discussions as to greatly weaken their causes before the great mass of people who had not entered into the consideration of either method as a remedy for a very great evil. Mr. Lovejoy argued in his editorial that the recent movements in Great Britain and the West Indies in the matter of abolishing human slavery could not pass us by without also greatly affecting us. That "Slavery is a curse, politically and morally, to every state where it exists, is a sentiment to which the South and the West respond. And this response is given by the slaveholder, with a deeper and more experimental conviction in the South than in the East. The great disideratum with the reflecting (minds) in both sections of the country, is to get rid of the evil." Mr. Lovejoy feared the slow process of abolition which was supported in the East. It was the slow process of "the dissemination of light, thereby creating a correct public opinion."

At this time Mr. Lovejoy was plainly in favor of colonization. His arguments were in favor of that method of dealing with the slavery problem. But he closes the editorial by saying, "We are not sensible that we possess any prejudices upon the subject. We do not promise, by any means, that we shall not become an abolitionist, strictly, at some future day—and forsake the colonization enterprise, but arguments of sufficient weight must be laid before us in order to this consummation."

On April 16, 1835, another article appeared in the Observer on slavery. In this article Mr. Lovejoy discussed the obligations of Christians to ally themselves with those who look upon slavery as a great wrong. In this he protests that he is not in favor of immediate and unconditional emancipation, as he thought it would be a great misfortune for the slaves to be set free without some help in the care of themselves before they were turned loose upon the world. "While Christians have been slumbering over it (slavery), the eye of God has not slumbered, nor has His Justice been an indifferent spectator of the scene. The groans, and sighs, and tears, and blood of the poor slave have gone up as a memorial before the throne of heaven. Look at the manner in which our sister state, Louisiana, is treating her slaves. Why, as surely as there is a thunderbolt in heaven and strength in God's right arm to launch it, so surely will it strike the authors of such cruel oppression. Look, too, at the slave drivers, who go up and down our own streets, lifting their heads and moving among us as if they had not forfeited all claim to the name of man. If the laws protect the miscreant who coins his wealth out of the heart's blood of his fellow creatures, he can at least be crushed beneath the odium of public opinion."

Mr. Lovejoy quotes a short extract from the St. Louis Republican. The short article refers to the convention soon to meet in Missouri to rewrite that state's Constitution: "We look to the convention as a happy means of relieving the state, at some future day, of an evil which is destroying all our wholesome energies, and leaving us, in morals, in enterprise, and in wealth, behind the neighboring states. We mean, of course, the curse of slavery. We only propose that measures shall now be taken for the abolition of slavery, at such distant period of time as may be thought expedient, and eventually for ridding the country altogether of a colored population. Let us to the work then firmly and heartily." On April 30th, 1835, another article appeared. This was of the nature of a comparison between Illinois, a free state, and Missouri, a slave state.

On the 4th of March, 1835, he was married to Miss Celia Ann French, of St. Charles, Mo. On the 10th of that month he wrote his mother, apprising her of his marriage. Through the summer of 1835 there was no one incident which disturbed the early days of his married life. During these passing years Mr. Lovejoy was an active minister and gave much of his time to attendance upon the meeting of Presbyteries and Synods. It appears that he did not withdraw his memberships from the church in St. Louis, yet he is recorded as in attendance at the Presbyteries and Synods in Illinois. In the issue of 1835, October 8th, a short notice said "The Editor will be absent two or three weeks in attendance on Presbytery and Synod." While Mr. Lovejoy was away the publishers of the Observer received a communication from the patrons of the paper relative to the articles which had been published on slavery and requesting that no more articles on slavery should be published. It appeared that an article on that subject was printed while Mr. Lovejoy was gone.

New Code

While the editor was still absent the proprietors inserted in the paper a public notice in which they state that they had previously agreed that henceforward no more articles on slavery should be printed in the Observer. They state also that evil disposed persons had threatened to destroy the office of the Observer. Such persons were warned that the owners of the paper, though one and all are opposed to the "mad schemes of the abolitionists," will not stand idly by and see their property destroyed. The owners of the paper further state that they believe the present excitement will subside, that it came out of the fact that some white men had been accused of decoying St.

Louis slaves into Illinois, and that these white men had "been dealt with according to the new code by serval of our most respectable citizens, and that they will see that no evil arises out of that excitement."

The new code that the owners of the paper referred to was the whipping of these two white men by sixty "respectable citizens." The two men had been taken about two miles out of St. Louis and whipped between 100 and 200 lashes. The "respectable citizens" had taken turns in applying the lash. Before whipping the two men, a vote was taken whether they should be hanged or whipped. Twenty out of the sixty were for hanging. The crime that these two men were guilty of was that of decoying two Negroes belonging to Major Daugherty, of St. Louis, into Illinois, probably with the intention of giving them a chance to escape to Canada.

Prior to this application of the "New Code" to the regulation of society in St. Louis, nine prominent friends of Mr. Lovejoy, one of whom was the Rev. W. S. Potts, under whose pastorate of the Presbyterian Church Mr. Lovejoy united with that body, addressed a letter to Mr. Lovejoy, bearing date October 5, 1835. It was a bit of friendly advice, which was not heeded by Mr. Lovejoy. A few extracts will reveal the import of the letter. "The undersigned, friends and supporters of the Observer, beg leave to suggest, that the present temper of the times require a change in the manner of conducting that print in relation to the subject of domestic slavery. The public mind is greatly exercised, and owing to the unjustifiable interference of our Northern brethren with our social relations, the community are, perhaps, not in a situation to endure sound doctrine in relation to this subject. Indeed, we have reason to believe that violence is even now meditated against the Observer office, and we do believe that true policy and the interest of religion require that the discussion of this exciting question should be at least postponed in this state." These friends further say to Mr. Lovejoy that they hope the concurring opinions and the interests of religion will induce him to "so far change the character of the Observer, as to pass over in silence everything connected with the subject of slavery." The names signed to this appeal were:

Archibald Gamble   G. W. Call
Nathan Ranney   H. R. Gamble
Wm. S. Potts   Hezekiah King
John Kerr   Beverly Allen
         J. B. Bryant

Mr. Lovejoy seems not to have made an immediate reply directly to these friends, but some two years later he made a memorandum indorsement on the back of this letter as follows: "I did not yield to the wishes here expressed, and in consequence have been persecuted ever since. But I have kept a good conscience in the matter and that more than repays me for all I have suffered, or can suffer. I have sworn eternal opposition to slavery, and, by the blessing of God, I will never go back. Amen. E. P. L.

October 24, 1837.

At a public meeting of the citizens of St. Louis, a general discussion of the attitude of Lovejoy toward his right to a free discussion of the slavery question was engaged in. Out of this general discussion there was a set of resolutions adopted which contained the notion of the supporters of slavery with regard to Mr. Lovejoy's rights as editor of a public newspaper. The resolution contained the following "principles":

1. The meeting deprecates the interference of foreign emissaries on the subject of slavery. (Mr. Lovejoy, having come to St. Louis from New England, is considered a foreign emissary.)

2. The right of free press and free speech guaranteed in the Constitution does not imply a moral right on the part of the abolitionists to freely discuss the question of slavery, for the works of the abolitionists are seditious and calculated to incite insurrection and anarchy.

3. That the doctrine of amalgamation is peculiarly baneful to the interests and happiness of society. The union of black and white, in a moral point of view, we consider as the most preposterous and impudent doctrine advanced by the infatuated abolitionists.

4. The sacred writings furnish abundant evidence of slavery from the earliest periods. Our Savior recognized the relation between master and slave, and deprecated it not. His followers in all countries have recognized the relation of master and slave. "Therefore, resolved, That we consider slavery as it now exists in the United States, as sanctioned by the sacred Scriptures.

5. Resolved, That a vigilance committee shall be appointed to administer the new code on suspected abolitionists.

REPLY

In the same issue of the Observer in which was printed the resolutions passed by the citizens' meeting, Mr. Lovejoy also printed his reply to the resolutions. He also called attention to the danger of mob law as described in the whipping of two white men by sixty "respectable citizens." He further says that it was his opinion that if he had been in St. Louis when the excitement was at its highest, he too would have been subject to the "new code." With regard to the resolutions passed by the citizens' meeting, he takes them up one at a time, as follows:

1. With regard to the first resolution, he says he perfectly agrees that the citizen has no right to interfere with the domestic relations between master and slave.

2. Mr. Lovejoy says that his fellow citizens are discussing

the moral right of a person to print and speak freely. Whereas he, Lovejoy, is contending for the civil and political right to do these things, which he understands the Constitution of the United States guarantees to him as an American citizen. "If I abuse that right, I freely acknowledge myself amenable to the laws. But it is said that the right to hold slaves is a constitutional one, and therefore not to be called in question. I admit the premise, but deny the conclusion. * * * We have slaves, it is true, but I am not one. I am a citizen of the United States, a citizen of Missouri, free born; * * * I am ready not to fight but to suffer, and if need be, to die for them! Kindred blood to that which flows in my veins flowed freely to water the tree of Christian liberty, planted by the Puritans on the rugged soil of New England. It flowed as freely on the plains of Lexington, the heights of Bunker Hill, and the fields of Saratoga. And freely, too, shall mine flow, yea, as freely as if it were so much water, ere I surrender my right to plead the cause of truth and righteousness, before my fellow citizens, and in the face of all their opposers."

3. Mr. Lovejoy points out that with all their errors of theory, he has never seen the least evidence of a desire to affect amalgamation of the races. He challenges the respectable citizens who formulated the resolutions to tell him where they have ever seen any evidence that the abolitionists have ever supported in theory or practice any such a doctrine or any such practice. But Mr. Lovejoy says there are lots of practical amalgamationists to prove which, walk the streets or visit the plantations of the states where slavery is defended. Mr. Lovejoy thinks that if an abolitionist were to be stoned in St. Louis for preaching amalgamation and the same rule should hold that our Savior established in the case of the women taken in adultery, that there would be some who would not cast the first stone.

4. The fourth resolution resolved that the Bible teaches that slavery such as we have in the United States is right and is therefore sanctioned by holy writ. "What is this system of slavery which the holy scriptures sanctions? A system which buys and sells human being for gain; a system which separates husband and wife; a system which provides for a class of slave catchers; a system which provides for a market where men and women and even children may be sold to the highest bidder; a system which allows nameless pollutions and unspeakable abominations. And this is the system which the Prince of Mercy and Love, and the God of Holiness and Purity sanctions!

5. This resolution recommends the appointment of a committee of eighty-three who shall report all persons suspected of preaching abolition doctrines, and if the civil authorities fail to punish such persons, they shall be turned over to an executive committee, which shall subject them to the "new code." Mr.

Lovejoy asks if the principles of the Lettres de Cachet have been driven from France and have taken refuge in America. The French Kings sent men to the bastile on suspicion; we, more humane, establish a "new code" and whip men to death or near to that point. The inventor of the guillotine was indeed not the last man to suffer on that instrument, and there will be a reaction to this dreadful attitude in which respectable citizens find themselves.

After an appeal to his Protestant brethren to consider the position they have taken as to the treatment of those who claim the right to print and speak freely on the subject of slavery, he finishes his address with the following declaration:

"I do, therefore, as an American citizen, and Christian patriot, and in the name of Liberty, and Law, and Religion, solemnly protest against all these attempts, howsoever or by whomsoever made, to frown down the liberty of the press, and forbid the free expression of opinion. Under a deep sense of my obligation to my country, the church, and my God, I declare it to be my fixed purpose to submit to no such dictation. And I am prepared to abide the consequences. I have appealed to the Constitution and the laws of my country; if they fail to protect me, I appeal to God, and with Him I cheerfully rest my cause."

The reason Mr. Lovejoy says he is prepared to abide the consequences, he is referring to the frequent threats upon his person and the office of the Observer. He explains to his supposed friends that the press and other material things are not his property, but belong to their neighbors, and that the young men who work in the office and produce the paper from week to week have property interests in the office, but are in no way responsible for the subject matter of the editorials. He hopes for the sake of the owners of the press and the young men who work in the office that no harm may be done to the property interest of these people. Mr. Lovejoy simply says to the mob, let these go their way and wreak your vengeance on me.

JUDGE LAWLESS

In the fall of 1835 Mr. Lovejoy wrote many letters to his mother and to his brothers and sisters. To them he explained somewhat in detail the matters considered in the preceding pages. He told his brother that he was in daily peril of his life, that he was accused of being an abolitionist, and that he was threatened with violence. He says, "I am sure it (his work) is doing good, or the Devil would not be so mad about it." Later in the fall of 1835 he says to his mother that the people who have been so very bitter against him are beginning to act a little more reasonably. He reports in a letter written January, 1836, that he is the only Protestant minister in the city and is treading the wine press alone. However, as just stated, there was a kindlier feeling toward him, and there might have been a truce had it not been for the happenings in connection with two horrible crimes.

Two boatmen on the levee were in an altercation, and when the sheriff and a deputy tried to arrest them, the officers were pounced upon by a big mulatto and the two boatmen escaped. The Negro was arrested, and on the way to the jail he drew a dirk knife and killed the deputy and seriously wounded the sheriff. The murderer was finally lodged in the jail. A mob was hastily organized which proceeded to the jail, where with much deliberation the Negro was taken out and hurried to the outskirts of the town, where he was chained to a tree and burned to a crisp. A rabble of small boys gathered and threw rocks at the charred remains with much glee. The body was left where it burned till the next day.

In the course of time the grand jury met and was instructed by Judge Lawless as to their duty in reference to the burning of the Negro. The judge said: "If, on the other hand, the destruction of the murderer of Hammond (the deputy) was the act, as I have said, of the many—of the multitude, in the ordinary sense of the word, not the act of numerable and ascertainable malefactors; but of congregated thousands, seized upon and impelled by that mysterious, metaphysical and almost electric frenzy, which, in all ages and nations, has hurried on the infuriated multitude of deeds of death and destruction—then, I say, act not at all in the matter; the case then transcends your jurisdiction—it is beyond the reach of human law."

This instruction to the jury resulted, of course, in no indictment. When the instruction to the jury became known, Mr. Lovejoy attacked it in the most vigorous manner. He attributes the judge's philosophy to the fact of his being a foreigner and to his schooling. Quite a bit of discussion arose over the instruction of the judge, and the judge in defending himself intimated that since he had stood between the office of the Observer and an angry citizenry, it was poor taste for the Observer to be criticising the judge. This greatly angered the editor of the Observer, and he still continued his condemnation of the whole judicial farce.

Shortly following this battle of words, a mob broke into the office of the Observer and destroyed much of the type and other material, but fortunately did not seriously damage the press. Prior to this, however, Mr. Lovejoy had held conferences with friends in Alton looking toward the moving the press and offices to that city. In these conferences with the Alton people, they were very anxious to know something of what Mr. Lovejoy would do about discussing the subject of slavery in case he should remove to Alton. He said slavery was a subject that ought to be faithfully discussed in our religious and political journals, and as editor he should never relinquish his right to discuss that or any other subject. He pointed out to his Alton friends that his paper was a religious publication and that its mission was that of religious instruction.

MOVED TO ALTON

While absent from St. Louis on this visit to Alton, his friends in the former city got together in a conference and agreed that the paper ought not be moved to Alton, and Mr. Lovejoy was urged to again assume editorial charge of the paper in St. Louis. But he had made up his mind that it would be best to remove the paper, though it remained a short while in St. Louis. The original owners of the stock had virtually given over their stock, since a mortgage for a sum was paid by a Mr. Moore, and the paper transferred to Mr. Lovejoy by Mr. Moore. The press and type were boxed and consigned to Alton. They reached the wharf at Alton on the morning of the 21st of July, 1836. Mr. Lovejoy did not receive the press on the 21st, as that day was Sunday. The press lay on the wharf till 2 or 3 o'clock Monday morning, the 22d. At this time the press was broken to pieces and the type thrown into the river.

On the 22d of July a meeting was held in the Presbyterian Church to express their disapproval of the dastardly deed of the mob that destroyed the press. But this meeting also condemned the abolition movement, which was then just beginning to draw to this party many of the people who had longed for some method of ending the institution of slavery. This meeting at the Presbyterian Church became a contention in after years as to the part played by Mr. Lovejoy. His enemies said he promised that if the citizens would replace the press destroyed, he would say no more about slavery. Mr. Lovejoy says in his issue of September 8th that "on the same day of the outrage, at a very full meeting of the citizens, they voluntarily and unanimously pledged themselves to make good the loss occasioned by the destruction of the press, they surely must be acquitted of all participation, in thought or deed, in the disgraceful act."

SECOND PRESS

At the meeting at the Presbyterian Church money was pledged to purchase a new press. Just how many people made pledges is not known. Mr. Lovejoy said in a letter to his mother, "A few of the brethren here immediately convened after this event, and it was determined that a new print-press should be procured without delay from Cincinnati. Mr. Lovejoy proceeded to Cincinnati, where he purchased his second press and shipped the same to Alton. It arrived and was duly installed, and the first issue came out on Thursday, September 8, 1836. It was volume

3, No. 36, whole No. 140. From this date it was issued regularly till August 21, 1837.

Amalgamation

Through the winter of 1836-7 there were no open hostilities toward Mr. Lovejoy, although some of his articles in the paper were very outspoken. The Baptist Banner, published in Louisville, Kentucky, printed a short article in which the editor said the abolitionists were throwing off their masks and were advocating the intermarriage of the whites and blacks. Mr. Lovejoy, after challenging the Banner to produce the proof of the statement, said: "But secondly, if God has put the black and white races so far asunder, how does it happen that they come together so readily in the state where you live? Is not the Vice President of these United States, and one of your own citizens, an amalgamator, as you phrase it? Are not his amalgamated daughters among you, respectably married to men of pure Saxon blood— the sons of Chivalrous Kentucky?" Such attacks as this were calculated to stir the friends of slavery to vigorous opposition to Mr. Lovejoy. A careful reading of his extended articles in the winter of 1836-7 will reveal bitter attacks against slavery.

In the issue of June 29, Mr. Lovejoy published an article which explained that he had been solicited to assist in forwarding petitions to Congress asking for the abolition of slavery in the District of Columbia. The request came from the secretary of the American Anti-Slavery Society. Mr. Lovejoy asked the people of the state who favored such a move to send their names to him, and urged an earnest interest in the effort to rid the District of Columbia of slavery.

Anti-Slavery Society

On July 6, 1837, Mr. Lovejoy proposed a state anti-slavery society, and asked all who were favorable to such an organization to write him, naming the place and the time where and when such meeting should be held. In this suggestion he says there are already quite a number of local societies in Illinois and their efforts should be strengthened by an organization of state-wide importance. "With many we are already a 'fanatic' and an 'incendiary,' as it regards this matter, and we feel that we must become more and more vile in their eyes. We have never felt enough, nor prayed enough, nor done enough in behalf of the perishing slave." Mr. Lovejoy wrote this article on the 4th of July, and he says in the article, which was published on the 6th, that even as he writes people are rushing along the street to the place appointed for public speaking, where they will listen to the reading of the declaration that "all men are born free and equal," while the orator denounces the attempt of England to lay yoke upon the shoulders of our fathers. What mockery is this! "We thank God for our freedom and eat and drink and make merry while our feet are on the necks of three millions of our fellow men. Brethren and friends, this must not be—it can not be—for God will not endure it much longer. Come then to the rescue, 'unloose the heavy burden, and let the oppressed go free.'"

Owen Lovejoy, who kept in pretty close touch with his brother's activities, says this appeal to organize an anti-slavery society was a very obnoxious thing in the minds of those who sympathized with slavery. On Monday morning, July 8th, an anonymous hand bill appeared on the streets of Alton, requesting the friends of the Observer who were dissatisfied with the course the paper was taking to meet in the Market House on Thursday evening, July 11th, to take some action relative to the policy of said paper.

ANTI-ABOLITION

The meeting was well attended and the speeches and action very decidedly against Mr. Lovejoy. Doctor Halderman was made chairman, and J. P. Jordan secretary. After short speeches, a committee was appointed, consisting of J. A. Townsend, Dr. H. Beall, and S. L. Miller, to present resolutions. The committee reported shortly with whereases and resolutions. The first whereas stated that Mr. Lovejoy was, contrary to a solemn and voluntary promise that he would not discuss slavery in his paper, doing so, greatly to the disapprobation of the citizens of Alton. And again that contrary to his promise as a clergyman, he had wantonly violated his pledge. The resolutions cover pretty much the same matter:

1. That the Rev. E. P. Lovejoy has advocated abolitionism, contrary to the will of a majority of the people of Alton, and contrary to his sacred pledge not to do so.

2. That we, the citizens of Alton, censure Mr. Lovejoy for thus violating his pledge.

3. That a committee of five be appointed to wait on Mr. Lovejoy and ascertain from him whether he intends in the future to continue to disseminate the doctrines of abolitionism in the Observer.

The report was warmly approved, and the president of the meeting appointed the following committee to wait on Mr. Lovejoy: B. K. Hart, L. J. Clawson, Col. N. Buckmaster, B. I. Gilman, Col. A. Olney, and Dr. J. A Halderman's name was added by request.

Col. A. Botkin arose and offered another set of resolutions which said that all good citizens deprecated mobs, but intimating incendiary doctrines invite mob violence. The chairman of the meeting, Doctor Halderman, also offered four resolutions, the first of which was a protest against the possibility of a division of churches on the basis of slavery and anti-slavery sentiment. The second one defined modern abolitionism to be the "admittance to all the privileges, suffrages, offices, immunities, and preferments, civil, political, and religious, in common with ourselves." The third declared the sense of the meeting as decidedly opposing abolitionism and slavery, but favorable to any system of gradual emancipation or to a system of colonization. The fourth asked the papers of the South and West to copy the account of the meeting and the resolutions.

Inasmuch as the resolutions of the Market House meeting emphasize a supposed pledge which Mr. Lovejoy was said to have made at a meeting in the Presbyterian Church immediately after the destruction of his press on the wharf, it seemed necessary that the truth should be made known as to what Mr. Lovejoy did say. A paper was signed by ten men, four being abolitionists, five being hostile to any discussion of slavery. This document gave at some length a review of the meeting in the Presbyterian Church. They then testify as to Mr. Lovejoy's concluding words at that meeting, which were as follows: "But gentlemen, as long as I am an American citizen, and as long as American blood runs in my veins, I shall hold myself at liberty to speak, to write, and to publish whatever I please on any subject, being amenable to the laws of my country for the same."

George H. Walworth	James Moss, Jr.
A. B. Roff	F. W. Graves
Solomon E. Moore	W. L. Chappell
Effingham Cock	A. Alexander
John W. Chickering	Charles W. Hunter"

The Market House meeting was called for the "friends of the Observer" who were dissatisfied with the policy of the paper. There were a few such persons present, but not a single person appointed on a committee was a subscriber to the Observer.

Alton, July 24th, 1837.

To the Rev. E. P. Lovejoy:

Dear Sir:—In the proceedings of a public meeting of the citizens of Alton, a copy of which is herewith transmitted to you, you will find the following resolution:

(Here follows the resolution providing for appointment of a committee to wait on Mr. Lovejoy.)

The views and feelings by which the citizens were actuated and their wishes and expectations are set forth in the reported proceedings to which we respectfully invite your attention. We respectfully request that you will at your earliest convenience, answer the inquiries embodied in the above resolution, so that we may report the same to the public, in the discharge of our duty. Nothing but the importance of the question which the meeting was called to consider, and the dangers which its unwise agitation threatens, not only to the community, but to the whole country, could have induced us to take the steps we have. * * * etc.

Your obedient servants,
B. K. Hart,
L. J. Clawson,
N. Buckmaster,
A. Olney.
Alton, July 26, 1837.

Messrs. B. K. Hart, L. J. Clawson, N. Buckmaster, A. Olney, John A. Haldeman.

Gentlemen:—(Here follows a very courteous preliminary to the real matter in hand.)

I cannot consent, in this answer, to recognize you as the official organ of a public meeting convened to discuss the question, whether certain sentiments should, or should not be discussed in the public newspaper of which I am the editor. By so doing, I should virtually admit that the liberty of the press and freedom of speech, were rightfully subject to other supervision and control, than those of the land. But this I can not admit. On the contrary, in the language of one of the speakers at the meeting, I (also) believe that 'the liberty of our forefathers has given us the liberty of speech, (and that) it is our duty and high privilege, to act and speak on all questions touching this great commonwealth.

Believing, therefore, that everything having a tendency to bring this right into jeopardy, is eminently dangerous as a precedent, I cannot admit that it can be called in question by any man or body of men, or that they can with any propriety, question by any man or body of men, or that they can with any propriety question me as to my exercise of it. * * * All virulence and intemperance of language, I should conceive to be "unwise agitation." I hope to discuss the overwhelmingly important subject of slavery with the freedom of a republican and the meekness of a Christian.

With much respect.
Your friend and fellow citizen,
ELIJAH P. LOVEJOY.

Adding Fuel

From this time, the latter part of July, 1836, threats of violence were openly and frequently heard. The Missouri Republican, printed in St. Louis, contained editorials and correspondence which did not tend to the allaying of the mob violence spirit. It gave very full and detailed accounts of the meetings in Alton whose purpose was the expression of the public indignation toward Mr. Lovejoy. "The Editor of the Observer has merited the full measure of the community's indignation; if he will not learn from experience, they are likely to teach him by practice. He has * * * forfeited all claims to the protection of that or any other community." On the 17th of August the Republican said: "We had hoped that our neighbors would have ejected from amongst them that minister of mischief, the Observer, or at least corrected its course. Something must be done in this, and that speedily. The good people of Illinois must either put a stop to the efforts of these fanatics, or expel them from their community."

On the early evening of the 21st of August a band of men gathered with the intention of visiting the home of Mr. Lovejoy and apply the New Code. They met Mr. Lovejoy going to his home with medicine for his wife who was ill. He told his mission and offered to go with them if they would take the medicine to his wife. This one of their number did; then their hearts failed them and they released him. They returned to the city and told the story to Col. George T. M. Davis. Later in the same evening a band of men gathered in front of the pressroom of the Observer and rocked the house and drove out some workmen who were employed within. The mob then went in and destroyed everything connected with the paper. The work of the mob attracted a large assemblage of men about the office, but no efforts were made to stop the destruction of property. The next morning the expressions—"good enough for him," "served him just right" and "glad of it" were common.

Within a few hours after the second press had been destroyed on August 21, 1837, an order was sent for the third press. This press arrived in September, and in the absence of Mr. Lovejoy, who was attending Presbytery, the press was stored in a warehouse. This press was demolished and thrown into the Mississippi River. A fourth press was sent for. It arrived the night of November 6, 1837, and was stored in the warehouse of Godfrey, Gilman & Co.

ANTI-SLAVERY SOCIETY

Let us return a few weeks to the call for a meeting to consider the formation of a State Anti-Slavery Society. We have called attention to the article in the Observer of July 6th. At this time there were several local anti-slavery societies in Illinois, and the desire for a state society was becoming general. His request for the names met with a hearty response. Mr. Lovejoy was in close touch with Dr. Edward Beecher, president of Illinois College. He and Dr. Beecher had some difference of opinion as to what should be discussed and who should be invited to the meeting. The Madison County Anti-Slavery Society invited the proposed convention to meet at Upper Alton October 26, 1837.

The suggestion of a state organization was noised abroad, and it was generally understood that there would be a meeting at Upper Alton at the time suggested by Mr. Lovejoy. The call as issued by Mr. Lovejoy called for those persons who were opposed to slavery and thought it a sin. Doctor Beecher thought this was too narrow a basis for a profitable discussion. The call was modified on October 18, 1837, only a week before the meeting. Doctor Beecher had visited Alton and had conferences with Mr. Lovejoy and many leading citizens of Alton. By the latter part of September as many as 242 persons had signed a call for this anti-slavery convention. The convention met on Thursday, the 25th of October, 1837. The broadening of the invitation was unfortunate. The friends of "Free Discussion" came in large numbers and took charge of the meeting. Uriah H. Linder, the attorney-general of the state, ably assisted by the Rev. John Hogan, a Methodist minister, was able to organize the meeting by the help of those present who came as "inquirers." The meeting adjourned in confusion but on Saturday, the 28th of October, about sixty people met in the home of Rev. T. B. Hurlbut in Upper Alton and organized the State Anti-Slavery Society of Illinois. The following Sunday, the 29th, the Rev. Edward Beecher preached a sermon in Upper Alton. On Monday, October 30th, several from the convention together with friends from Alton met in the store of Alexander & Co., where they discussed the propriety of continuing the Observer and the question of defending it against mob violence. Both of these questions were decided in the affirmative—that they would reestablish the Observer in Alton and that they would defend it to the last.

Last Appeal

A counter meeting was held in the Riley Building on the same day as the one in Alexander store. This meeting was dominated by Mr. Linder and Mr. Hogan. Mr. Hogan spoke first. He was followed by Mr. Linder, who bitterly denounced Mr. Lovejoy and all abolitionists, and in fact all men engaged in what we generally know as the moral and religious work of the community. Mr. Lovejoy then took the floor and in a very deliberate and dignified manner made what was his last appeal. He said it was not true that he held in contempt the feelings and sentiments of the community. But though he valued the good opinion of his fellow-citizens as highly as any man could, yet he was governed by higher considerations than either the favor or the fear of man. He told the meeting that he had not asked or desired any compromise; he had asked for nothing but to be protected in his rights which God had given him and which were guaranteed to him in the constitution. He said: "What infraction of the laws have I been guilty of? Whose good name have I injured? When and where have I published anything injurious to the reputation of Alton? Have I not in common with the rest of my fellow-citizens striven to promote the reputation and the interest of Alton? What has been my offense? Put your finger upon it, define it, and I stand ready to answer for it. If I have been guilty, you can easily convict me. You have public sentiment in your favor. You have your juries, and you have your attorney (referring to Mr. Linder), and I have no doubt you can convict me, but if I have been guilty of no violation of the laws, why am I hunted up and down continually as a partridge upon the mountains? Why am I threatened with the tar barrel? Why am I waylaid from day to day and from night to night, and my life in jeopardy every hour?" * * * "This is the question: Whether my property shall be protected; whether I shall be suffered to go home to my family at night without being assailed and threatened with tar and feathers and assassination; whether my afflicted wife, whose life has been in jeopardy from continued alarms and excitement, shall night after night be driven from a sick bed into the garret to save her life from the brickbats and violence of the mob. That, sir, is the question." The house was in tears, and Mr. Lovejoy wept as he alluded to his wife. He assured them that his tears were not from fear. He had no fears for himself. Not that he was able to cope with the community physically, but where should he go? If it be not safe in Alton, neither in St. Charles. Violence might overtake him on his way to a retreat. He had finally come to the determination, after consulting friends, and earnestly seeking counsel of God, to remain in Alton, and here to insist upon protection in the exercise of his rights. If the civil authorities refuse to protect him, he must look to God for protection. And if he very soon found a grave in Alton, he was sure he should die in the exercise of his duty.

When he had finished he walked from the room, but Mr. Linder was on the floor at once and denounced Mr. Lovejoy as a hypocrite, a fanatic, and a dangerous man in the community. Mr. Cyrus Edwards, the presiding officer, tried to undo some of the mischief that Mr. Linder had set afoot, but the meeting sided with Mr. Linder and adjourned determined to lay violent hands on Mr. Lovejoy. This meeting in which Mr. Lovejoy made his final appeal was on Monday, October 30, and that night the Rev. Edward Beecher, president of Illinois College, was to deliver an address in the Presbyterian Church on The Times. The friends of Mr. Lovejoy asked the mayor, Mr. J. M. Krum, if they might take their guns with them to the meeting, but the mayor treated the matter lightly and told them they might take their guns to a nearby house and leave them and if any serious trouble arose he would command them to keep the peace. They did not trust the mayor, but elected one of their own number as captain. When Mr. Beecher was about half way through with his address, a brickbat crashed through the window and barely missed the speaker.

THE GUARD

The friends of Mr. Lovejoy expected the fourth press nearly any day as it came only from St. Louis. The mayor had consented to the organization of a militia company under the provisions of the state law, and about sixty had enlisted. The captain of the boat had instruction to land the press in the night of the 6th of November. On that night the militia company, sixty strong, drilled in Godfrey and Gilman's warehouse, a double-gabled stone building with the rear ends next the river and the fronts facing a street parallel to the river. Next to the street the building was two stories high but next the river four stories high.

When the press was landed the mayor was sent for and the boxes were brought inside the building. There was no demonstrations by the slavery party. This was about 2 o'clock Tuesday morning, the 7th of November. The militia lingered till day when they dispersed. All through the day the talk of the town was the arrival of the fourth press. It was also noised about that the building would be entered that night and the press destroyed. Because there was no demonstration when the boat was landed, it was not thought that there would be an attack now that the press was securely stored in the Gilman warehouses. Later in the day "the friends of good order" became uneasy as to the safety of the press and about twenty of them were stationed in the warehouse to guard the press through the night.

THE MOB

About 7 o'clock on Tuesday evening, November 7th, word was received that a mob was gathering. The sixty men in the volunteer company gathered at the warehouse early in the evening. The press was stored on one side of the double warehouse, while the other side was being used by the militia. These volunteers remained till 9 o'clock when it was decided that there would be no demonstration that night. All but about twenty of the militia retired to their homes and the others were told by Mr. Gilman to make themselves comfortable, as he also expected to remain in the building to protect his property against damage.

Nothing occurred for some time to indicate that there would be any trouble. Later there were signs of the gathering mob. Edward Keating, a lawyer, and Henry W. West, a merchant, came to the warehouse and asked to see Mr. Gilman. They were admitted into the building. This was thought later to have been a serious blunder as it was believed they were merely spies for the mob. Their admission to the building revealed to them the small number of defenders there were present. They informed Mr. Gilman that they had come to request that he, as owner of the building, should deliver the press to the gentlemen outside, and to inform him that in case of his refusal the building would be burned. A consultation of Mr. Gilman and the men in the building resulted in a refusal to comply with the demands of the mob. Some of those inside were in favor of keeping the lawyer and the merchant as hostages till morning. This might have prevented a clash that night, but it would only have deferred the final test of strength between those who believed in law and order and those who were willing to make mob law a means of accomplishing their ends.

When the two emissaries had returned to the gathering crowds and reported, the people within the warehouse could tell by their shouts that the warehouse would soon be attacked. It has been stated by responsible men who were familiar with the incidents of that fateful evening, that the attacking party had freely patronized the saloons and grogshops earlier in the night. Presently the mob drew near the building; stones were hurled against the doors and through the windows, while shots began to pierce the doors and windows. The militiamen had selected as captain, Deacon Enoch Long, who at this juncture began to temporize. He was promptly told that the mob should receive what they sent. The militiamen from that time on each followed his own judgment as to the policy of defense. They scattered to different parts of the building and chose their own manner of warfare.

The mob now attacked the doors to the front part of the building. The men in the building began throwing jugs and jars, of which there was a large quantity in the upper rooms, down on the men working at the front doors. These missiles were dangerous objects falling from the upper stories, and the work at the doors was therefore not prosecuted vigorously. The men in the upper stories came below where a conference was going on. While the men were in this conference one of the militiamen had deliberately taken aim and fired into the mob. A man fell dead. He was taken into a doctor's office near, but he was beyond the doctor's aid.

The mayor of the town had come into the building, and the men inside asked to be led out into the streets under his orders where they wished to act under the law and repel the mob. He would not do that as he said it would be nothing but a slaughter. Just here the mob returned to the attack and with ladders and fire began to ascend to the roof with the aim of setting the house on fire. There was a dead wall on one side and this protected the men who were climbing the ladders. A call was made inside for volunteers to go out and prevent the men from setting the roof on fire. The volunteers were Mr. Lovejoy, Amos B. Roff, and Royal Weller. As they emerged from the back door and stepped around where they could see the men on the roof, a man behind a pile of lumber near, fired at Lovejoy. The aim was good and Mr. Lovejoy received five bullets in his body. Both of the other men were seriously wounded. Mr. Lovejoy walked into the building and up the inside stairs where some men were grouped and there exclaimed, "I am shot! I am shot! I am dead!" He was immediately helped to lie down where he immediately expired.

The men within were now greatly depressed in spirits. The man whose life and property they had volunteered to defend was dead and the mob outside was greatly augmented. Presently the church bells began to ring, the men outside were shouting and cursing, and the situation was enough to appal the stoutest hearts.

Two men, Keating and West, came to the doors next to the river carrying a white handkerchief attached to a stick as a flag of truce. They made a second demand on Mr. Gilman for the press. Mr. Gilman though warmly in sympathy with Mr. Lovejoy, taking everything into consideration—the large amount of goods belonging to merchants in different parts of the state, and the probability of a great loss of life, agreed to surrender the press on condition that the property in the warehouse should not be disturbed, and that the men should be permitted to leave the building without molestation. The two agents of the mob departed to report to their friends. The militia secreted their guns and left the building by the doors next the river and made their way through the open space by the side of the warehouse. Here they were fired on by the mob but fortunately no one was injured.

The press was taken out to the bank of the river, broken to pieces and the parts thrown into the Father of Waters where there now lie four printing presses, the property of Lovejoy and his friends, mute witnesses of a land of free speech and free press.

The body of Mr. Lovejoy lay on a cot in the Gilman warehouse till the morning of the 8th, when it was quietly removed to his home. As the hearse passed through the streets it was met by the hisses and scoffs of the men who were loafing about the streets. There was no inquest and no funeral. The body was buried on the 9th of November on a bluff overlooking the Mississippi River.

In the home of Elijah P. Lovejoy as the body lay ready for burial, Owen Lovejoy, standing by the silent form of his brother, vowed that from thenceforward he would fight the cursed institution of slavery which had been the cause of the death of his

OWEN LOVEJOY

brother. Eleven years after this sad event, the Rev. Thomas Dimnock, then a young man living in Alton, in company with an older citizen, found the grave of Mr. Lovejoy which was marked by a board on which were the initials E. P. L. carved in the face of the board. The grave was between two large oak trees. When the ground was fenced and laid off as a cemetery, a street ran directly over the grave. The two trees were cut down and the board disappeared. The superintendent of the cemetery knew where Mr. Lovejoy was buried. Seeing the roadway or street would soon efface all signs of the grave he planted two stones, one at the foot and one at the head of the grave, letting the stones down level with the top of the ground. Thus the grave remained in the middle of the street for several years.

Eventually Mayor Charles W. Hunter had the remains disinterred and buried on his own lot. The work of removal was done by a colored man who had dug the first grave and had helped in the burial of Lovejoy; he was therefore able to identify the place of the grave in the cemetery road. When the remains were removed by Mayor Hunter a crude sort of stone was placed at the head of the grave and marked Lovejoy. In later years the Rev. Mr. Dimnock purchased a simple marble scroll resting on a block of granite and upon the scroll he had inscribed:

"Hic Jacet Lovejoy. Jam Parce Sepulto."
"Here lies Lovejoy. Spare him now that he is dead."

The lot was transferred from Mayor Hunter to the Rev. Mr. Dimnock, and in August, 1885, he transferred all right, title, and interest in the lot to the colored people of Alton. The City of Alton set aside a suitable lot upon which to erect a monument and an association was formed and considerable interest was manifested in the erection of a suitable monument. But nothing of any importance was accomplished till June 17, 1895. In that year the General Assembly appropriated the sum of $25,000 for the purpose of erecting a monument to the memory of this martyr to the cause of free speech, free press, and free men. The citizens of Alton supplemented this sum with a smaller amount and thus there stands in the cemetery at Alton a beautiful shaft to perpetuate the memory of one of America's martyrs.

CHAPTER X

A PIONEER INDUSTRY

EVIDENCES—MR. SELLERS—SOURCES—SPRINGS LEASED—RESERVATIONS—GIFT TO ILLINOIS—INDENTURED SLAVES—THE ELLIOTTS—CONRAD WILL—OTHER WORKS—FUEL—THORN HOUSE—COLONEL SELLERS

The evidence that salt was made within the limits of the present State of Illinois by other people than Indians and Europeans is regarded as very trustworthy. To one not accustomed to view things from a rather scientific point of view, the evidence might not appear very convincing. But to the man who is accustomed to look into things about him in a scientific way, there is abundant evidence that salt was manufactured at least in one place many decades if not centuries before the coming of white men to this portion of the Mississippi Valley.

EVIDENCES

Evidence of prehistoric salt-making, in the southern part of the state, rests very largely upon the character of pottery which has been found in abundance along the streams in Gallatin County. The presence of this pottery near the more modern centers of salt production is another fact which helps to confirm the belief in the manufacture prior to the coming of the Indian as he was known to the white people of the sixteenth and seventeenth centuries.

On the Saline River, which flows toward the east and southeast through the counties of Williamson, Saline, and Gallatin, there are two very noted localities. They are about four miles apart. One locality is noted for a very strong salt spring, a strong sulphur spring, and a fresh water spring. This locality has several names, but is usually called the "Nigger Spring," the "Nigger Well" and the "Nigger Furnace." It is four miles down the river from the present town of Equality. The other locality is marked by what in early times was called the "Half Moon Lick," and also by very strong deep wells. This point is about one mile from the town of Equality and very near the Saline River.

The earliest known English people to settle in this locality came about 1800, or possibly in 1802. In the region of the "Nigger Spring" and in that of the "Half Moon Lick," the earliest English settlers found large quantities of all sorts of pottery, tomahawks, arrowheads, vases and other similar articles. In addition to these familiar articles, there was found a species of pottery unlike that found in other localities. These pieces of pottery seemed to be parts of large vessels.

A sketch of Illinois published in Philadelphia in 1837 contains a short account of Gallatin County. The "Nigger Spring" is called the "Great Salt Spring." This sketch says: "The principal spring was formerly possessed by the Indians, who valued it very highly, and it appears probable that they had long been acquainted with the method of making salt. Large fragments of earthenware are continually found near the works, both on and under the surface of the earth; they have on them the impression of basket or wicker work."

Mr. George E. Sellers, a very noted man of Gallatin County, in an article in the September issue of the Popular Science Monthly for 1877, attempts to disprove the current belief that the markings on this pottery were made by a basket or frame work in which the vessel is supposed to have been molded. His theory is that the impressions were made by wrapping coarse cloth around the vessels as they were lifted off of the mold, which was within the vessel. Mr. Sellers quotes from a number of scientific writers who seem to have either visited the region around the "Great Salt Spring" or else had specimens of pottery from that locality. All the gentlemen who have examined this peculiar pottery are of the opinion that the vessels were used in the manufacture of salt.

Mr. Sellers

Mr. Sellers first visited the place as early as 1854, and he says at that time that all about the salt springs there was an abundance of this pottery. Just above the springs on a ridge which was in cultivation as early as 1854, Mr. Sellers found acres actually covered with the old salt pans. He thinks the people, whoever they were, were accustomed to take the water upon the hill and there in the pans let the water evaporate. Possibly the process was hastened by dropping to the pans large stones, previously heated in a fire. Again all around the "Half Moon Lick," which is near the Town of Equality, large quantities of the same kind of pottery have been found. In the report of the Illinois Board, World Fair Commissioners, 1893, page 283, Prof. William McAdams says these salt pans have been found in abundance both in and around the salt works in Illinois, and in Missouri near St. Genevieve. He describes them all as having those peculiar markings to which we have referred. Mr. McAdams found two of these pans entire near the salt works at St. Genevieve, Missouri. They were serving for a coffin. It seemed the corpse was put in one of these pans and another pan inverted over the first one, and then some earth thrown over the casket. Professor McAdams says these salt pans are from 3 to 5 feet in diameter.

There are traditions that the salt springs, wells and licks on the Saline River, in Gallatin County, were operated by the Indians and French for many years previous to the coming of the English about 1800. Certain it is that the French understood the salt-making process; the Indians without doubt knew where the springs and licks were. An English gentleman, writing to the Earl of Hillsboro in 1770, in speaking of the region around the mouth of the Wabash and the Saline Rivers, mentioned the abundance of salt springs in that region.

A SECTION OF WOODEN PIPE USED IN THE SALT WORKS AT EQUALITY

Capt. Thomas Hutchins, in a book called "Topographical Description of Virginia," in describing the region of the Wabash, says: "The Wabash abounds with salt springs and any quantity of salt may be made from them in a manner now done in the Illinois country." This was in 1778, twenty-two years before the coming of any English people.

Sources

Mr. Charles Carrol, of Shawneetown, told the author it had always been his understanding that the French operated the wells and springs several years previous to 1800. A history of Illinois said to have been written by Calvin Leonard and published by Ivison, Blakeman, Taylor & Company, about 1870, has an account of salt-making by the French and of a massacre of them by the Shawnee Indians. The Chicago Historical Society knows nothing of such a book, and I have doubts of its existence.

Count Volney, who made a tour of North America from 1795 to 1798, spent considerable time in Vincennes in 1798, and speaks of the "brine springs" at St. Genevieve, Missouri, but says not a word about the springs on the Saline River. Mr. William McAvoy, who lived in Equality, says that Gen. Leonard White knew Volney very well and says that General White told him (McAvoy) that Volney stayed a month in the neighborhood of the salt works. Mr. McAvoy was pressed very closely and he still insisted that Gen. Leonard White had often told him of Volney's visit to that locality. But not a single word about the salt works on the Saline is found in Volney's writings. So there is some error, probably in Mr. McAvoy's tradition.

The conclusion is that the earliest reference to salt making to be found is in the American State papers in the law of May 18th, 1796. In an act of this date it is made the duty of the surveyors working for the United States and making surveys in the territory northwest of the Ohio River "to observe closely for mines, salt springs and salt licks and mill seats." Evidently there were no wells or springs operated in Ohio this early, for in the life of Ephraim Cutler, son of Rev. Manasseh Cutler, he says that in 1796, when he came to the settlements below Marietta, that there was no salt to be had west of the mountains except at Marietta, and what was for sale here had been brought over the mountains on pack horses; he says further that this salt was sold for 16 cents per pound.

Mr. Cutler further says that in 1798 the Shawnee Indians told Lieut. George Irving that fifty miles inland from the Ohio River there was a salt spring. Search was made and the spring found near what is now the Town of Chandlersville, ten miles southeast of Zanesville. A salt company was organized by four settlements, and men sent to make salt—four men could make six bushels a week by hard work.

In the winter of 1799 and 1800, William Henry Harrison was the delegate in Congress from the Territory of the Northwest. In his report Mr. Harrison says: "Upon inquiry we find that salt springs and salt licks on the east of the Muskingum, and near the Great Miami, are operated by individuals, and timber is being wasted: Therefore we recommend that salt springs and salt licks, property of the United States in the territory northwest of the Ohio, ought to be leased for a term of years."

The report was referred to the committee of the whole, but no definite action was taken on the committee's recommendation. Harrison became governor of the Indiana Territory in the summer of 1800. In 1802 he visited Kaskaskia and was there importuned to call a convention to take steps looking toward the introduction of slavery into the Northwest Territory. The convention was called in the fall of 1802. Among other things, the convention asked Congress to annul the sixth article of the

Ordinance of 1787, and to grant the Saline below the mouth of the Wabash to the territory. Congress received the memorial, but granted neither of the two requests.

On March 3, 1803, Congress authorized the secretary of the treasury to lease the salt springs and licks for the benefit of the Government. On June 7th of the same year, Harrison negotiated a treaty at Fort Wayne between the Government and five Indian tribes. This treaty ceded to the United States 2,038,400 acres of lands in what is now Southern Indiana and Illinois.

Springs Leased

In the same summer of 1803, Governor Harrison leased the saline on the Saline River, in Illinois, to a Captain Bell, of Lexington, Kentucky. We are inclined to think that probably this Captain Bell was at that time working the salt springs on Saline River by permission of the Indians. Reynolds says the first white man to settle in Shawneetown was Michael Sprinkle, who came about 1802, and about the same time a Frenchman, La Boissiere, settled there and ran a ferry to accommodate people who were coming out of Kentucky to the salt works on the Saline River.

Captain Bell no doubt worked the salt springs till the end of 1806, for the records show that for the year 1807 the works were leased to John Bates, of Jefferson County, Kentucky.

By Act of Congress, March 26, 1804, there were established three land offices—one at Kaskaskia, one at Detroit, and one at Vincennes, and by the same act all salt springs, wells, and licks, with the necessary land adjacent thereto, were reserved from sale as the property of the United States. The territorial governor was authorized to lease these salt wells and springs to best advantage of the Government. On the 30th of April, 1805, Governor Harris appointed his friend, Isaac White, then of Vincennes, to be government agent to reside at the salt works and receive the rental due the United States. Mr. White assumed the duties of his position and was assisted by John Marshall who probably lived in Shawneetown. Just where White resided is not known, but presumably what was designated as the "Nigger well," some four miles below Equality. In 1806, September 8th, Governor Harrison appointed Mr. White a captain in the Knox County militia. From evidence of a private nature, White himself became lessee of the salt works in 1808 and perhaps retained control of them till 1810 or 1811. While Captain White was residing at the salt works he became involved in a difficulty with a Captain Butler and Butler challenged White to mortal combat. The challenge was accepted, and two days before the day set for the duel Captain White wrote his wife, who perhaps was at Vincennes, a very touching letter telling her he expected to be killed. On the same day that he wrote his wife, he made his will, signed, and sealed it. On the day set for the duel Butler and White both appeared on the appointed spot and they were informed by their seconds that horse pistols were the weapons—distance six feet. Butler backed down and refused to fight, saying that it would be murder and he could not engage in such affair.

In 1811 Captain White, now a colonel in the Illinois militia, sold out his interest in the salt works to three men, Jonathan Taylor of Randolph County, Illinois, Chas. Wilkins and James Morrison of Lexington, Ky. From the beginning of 1808 to 1811 Leonard White afterwards known as Gen. Leonard White, seems to have been the Government agent. He himself later on became interested in salt-making. In the summer of 1811 Col. Isaac White was in Vincennes and was initiated into the Masonic Lodge at that place; and on September 19, 1811, he was raised to the sublime degree of Master Mason. Col. Joe Daviess of Kentucky, who was in Vincennes at that time, acted as worshipful master. Colonel Daviess was in Vincennes in response to an invitation from Governor Harrison preparatory to an attack upon the Indians. On November 7, 1811, Colonel Daviess and Colonel White fell side by side in the battle of Tippecanoe.

RESERVATIONS

On February 12, 1812, Congress created the Shawneetown land district. Thos. Sloo was appointed registrar and John Caldwell was made receiver. In this same act a provision authorized the President to reserve not less than one township of the land around the salt works from sale. Leonard White, Willis Hargrave and Philip Trammell were made a commission to select the lands which should be reserved as the "Saline reservation." They performed their duty and set aside 96,766.79 acres. This was something over four townships. This was and is yet called, the "reservation." About the same time Mr. Sloo notified the general land office that there were saline indications in other localities in Southern Illinois and he was accordingly authorized to make reservations adjacent to such springs or licks. Mr. Sloo made a tour of inspection and as a result about 84,000 acres additional were reserved for saline purposes.

From 1807 to August 26, 1818, the entire rental accruing to the United States from the salines on the Saline River was 158,-398 bushels, and the total cash turned into the treasury for the same time was $28,160.25. Ohio turned in $240 in the same time, while Indiana, Kentucky and Missouri made no returns.

GIFT TO ILLINOIS

In 1818, April 18, an Enabling Act was passed by which Illinois was permitted to make a constitution and apply for admission into the Union. The act contains seven sections; the sixth section has four parts. Part two reads as follows: "All salt springs within such state, and the land reserved for the use of the same shall be granted to the said state, for the use of said state, and the same to be used under such terms, and conditions, and regulations, as the Legislature of the said state shall direct: Provided, the Legislature shall never sell, nor lease the same for a longer period than ten years, at any one time."

In pursuance of this act the Constitutional Convention met at Kaskaskia in the summer of 1818 and made a constitution. In that constitution are provisions that used to be a great mystery. Act 6 deals with the question of slavery. Section 2 of the 6th article reads as follows: "No person bound to labor in any state, shall be hired to labor in this state except within the tract reserved for the salt works near Shawneetown; nor even at that place for a longer period than one year at any one time; nor shall it be allowed there, after the year 1825. Any violation of this article shall effect the emancipation of such person from his obligation of service." The second section of the 6th article provides that all indentures entered into without fraud or collusion prior to the making of the constitution, according to the laws of Illinois Territory, shall be held as valid and the person so "indented" must be held to a fulfillment of the agreement in the contract. Section 1 provides that no person could be held to service under an indenture hereafter to be made, unless the person was in a state of freedom at the time of making his contract. And indentures made by negroes and mulattoes are not valid for a longer time than one year. This sixth article deals almost wholly with conditions at the salt works on the Saline River at the time the constitution was made.

Congress, as well as the Territorial Legislature of the Northwest Territory, was memorialized time and again for some relief from the 6th article of the ordinance of 1787. As soon as Indiana Territory passed into the second grade of political organization the Legislature passed a law permitting the bringing into the territory of negroes and mulattoes who were slaves in other states.

Indentured Slaves

The law which regulated the bringing in of the slaves while Illinois was a territory was passed by the Legislature of Indiana in 1805. It provided (1) that slaves over fifteen years of age might be brought in from slave states and within thirty days the owner might enter into an agreement with the said slave by which the slave agreed to work in Illinois for a stated time for a consideration. (2) If within the thirty days the slave refused to enter into such an agreement his master had thirty days in which to return him to a slave state. This law was applicable in any part of the Indiana Territory, but it was specially advantageous to the lessees of the salt works on Saline River. Mr. Sellers says, in the article in the Popular Science Monthly, that the "Nigger well or salt works was worked almost wholly by negro slaves."

The Rev. Samuel Westbrook, now deceased, told the author he came to Johnson County in 1812, and from there finally to Equality in 1826. At that time the wells about the "Half Moon Lick" were vigorously operated. The author was very particular to ask him about the use of slave labor, and he seemed to think there were a great many negroes and mulattoes at work in the various forms of industry, but he seemed to think that most of the colored people were free at that time.

The author, in his search for information relative to the use of slave labor in the manufacture of salt in the mines near Equality, was directed to the residence of a colored family living a few miles northwest from Equality. Here he found a colored man, Mr. George Elliott, a prosperous farmer who, together with two sisters, lived on the homestead of their parents. Mr. Elliott was a man of some fifty years while his sisters were several years his senior. The writer secured an easy entrance into the confidence of these people through a letter he carried from a mutual friend, a colored lawyer.

When the preliminaries were over and the writer's mission made plain, a large package of old deeds, records, etc., was brought from a place of safety and explained in great detail. From these papers and the testimony of the brother and sisters the following facts were learned: Their father, Cornelius Elliott, was born a slave in 1791. His master was John Elliott, of Maury County, Tennessee. Cornelius had evidently been a laborer in the salt works on the Saline River from the time he was old and large enough to be of service. In 1819 Timothy Guard, one of the lessees of the salt works, seems to have gone into Tennessee and bought this slave, Cornelius, of John Elliott. Cornelius was a cooper, and barrels were in great demand. In 1821 Timothy Guard had it in his heart to set Cornelius free. It appears that Cornelius had earned $1,000 in the three years. Either Mr. Guard had received directly the profit of the negro's labor and counted it worth $1,000, or else the slave had been permitted to "lay by" his earnings. At any rate the author read papers of freedom on parchment which was written in Timothy Guard's handwriting in which he says that in consideration of $1,000 cash in hand, he gives Cornelius his freedom. The document is signed by Timothy Guard and sworn to before John Marshall, a justice of the peace. Following which is a certificate by John M. Street, who was clerk of the court, to the effect that John Marshall was a justice of the peace.

Within a few years after Cornelius had purchased his own freedom he bought the freedom of his mother and three brothers. For one of his brothers he paid the sum of $550, and we read the manumission papers. In 1828 Cornelius married a free negress from Kentucky. He then bought eighty acres of land and commenced farming. He afterwards bought more land, and at the time of his death he owner 360 acres of good farming land six or seven miles northwest of Equality.

This story of Cornelius Elliott is probably only one of scores of similar stories which may be truthfully told of the period of "industrial service" in the salt works in Gallatin County.

In 1818, when Illinois became a state, the salt springs, wells and licks, with the lands adjacent, became the property of the State of Illinois. At this time there were in existence five distinct leases of salt wells and springs from the United States to individuals. The leases had been made by Ninian Edwards, representing the Government, and all bore date of 1817. One was with Willis Hargrave and Meredith Fisher, a second was with Jonathan Taylor, a third with George Robinson, a fourth was with James Ratcliff, a fifth with Timothy Guard.

Conrad Will

The benefit of the unexpired leases from December, 1818, to June 19, 1820, fell to the State of Illinois. The Legislature which met at Kaskaskia the winter of 1818-19 authorized the governor of the state to continue these leases with the above named gentlemen. The governor was also authorized to lease the Big Muddy Saline for a term of ten years. This saline was in Jackson County, three miles west of the present City of Murphysboro. This saline had been leased to Conrad Will, March 25, 1815, for three years. Brownsville was made the county seat of Jackson County in 1816. The salt wells were near the town; one, a half mile above, and one, a mile below or down the river from the town. Mr. Will came to Kaskaskia from Pennsylvania about 1811. He bought a drove of cattle and took them back to Pennsylvania. He must have returned shortly after this, for he seems to have been in Kaskaskia some time previous to his leasing the wells in 1815. It is more than probable that either Mr. Will or some one else was working the wells on Big Muddy prior to 1815. At least Mr. Wills returned to Pennsylvania the second time, it seems after kettles to make salt. These kettles Mr. Will probably brought down the Ohio, up the Mississippi, and then up the Big Muddy on keel boats. He brought his family to Brownsville about 1814 or 1815. They lived at first in a double log house which is said to have stood for many years. Help was scarce in Jackson County in 1815, so Mr. Will is said to have gone into Kentucky and brought slaves to his salt works. Conrad Will was a doctor, and his granddaughter, now living in Carbondale, has some of his books. He made salt and ran a tan-yard. He served in the constitutional convention of 1818 and in several of the early legislatures. He has one granddaughter who was born in 1828, several years before Mr. Will's death.

In 1824 the Legislature authorized the governor to lease the Big Muddy saline to James Pearce. In 1827, Mr. Pearce, not having accomplished much in his salt making, the Legislature relieved him of his obligation relative to the salt works. In 1834 the wells were leased to Conrad Will again till 1840, at this time, 1840, the lands should be sold. There is no record of any

A KETTLE USED BY CONRAD WILL IN MAKING SALT

income to the general government or to the state from the Big Muddy saline.

At this place, there were two wells scarcely a mile apart. The machinery consisted of a row or double row of kettles set over an open ditch; the sides of this ditch were lined with cut sandstone; at one end of the row of kettles the fires were kept going and at the other end of the row was a smokestack. The kettles were very large, holding about 100 gallons each. To within the past forty years the old furnaces were quite undisturbed, but of late the rocks have all been taken out to make foundations.

The old kettles are scattered over the neighborhood and are used chiefly for scalding the hogs at butchering time. One of the wells had a copper pipe running down into the earth through which the water flowed out at the top. A few years ago an enterprising citizen hitched his team to the pipe and twisted it off several feet below the surface. Water still flows out at that point.

OTHER WORKS

There was in the first part of the last century a saline in Monroe County, nine miles due west of the present City of Waterloo. It was owned and worked by General Edgar. The Hon. A. C. Bolinger, of Waterloo, took the pains to secure some facts about this saline, but he was unable to secure any information of special value. Col. William R. Morrison was unable to furnish anything definite, but suggested that Dr. Lewis James, of Old Mines, Missouri, might be able to give some valuable facts concerning this saline, but a letter addressed to the doctor failed to bring a response.

In 1826 the United States Senate asked the Secretary of the Treasury for a complete report of all incomes from the salines and also a description of all reservations. In this report from the Secretary of the Treasury no mention is made of salines in Monroe, Madison or Bond counties. However, from reliable sources we know that Judge Biggs made salt in Madison, on Silver Creek, and in Bond on Shoal Creek. And from an act of the Legislature in 1827, it appears that Stephen Galliard and Samuel Montgomery were lessees of a saline on Shoal Creek, in Bond County. By act of the Legislature, January 23, 1833, the governor was authorized to lease the salines in Bond County, or to appoint an agent to take charge of them.

The wells were on Section 32, in Township 6, Range 4. One section was reserved from sale. The first well was just at the edge of the water of Shoal Creek. The settlers dug a second well on higher ground and drew the water with ordinary water buckets. The boiling was done in kettles, and it is said there were as many as ninety of them. Many of the kettlers are to be found in the locality.

Besides Montgomery and Galliard above referred to, James Coyle, ———— Spencer, John Lee, and others made salt here. James Coyle settled near the wells in 1817, and on April 4, 1822, a son, Jeremiah Coyle, was born, and he still lives on the old homestead. The writer is indebted to the Rev. Thomas Hynes for the facts about the Shoal Creek saline.

FUEL

In the early days of salt making on the Saline River wood only was used for fuel. The water was boiled in large cast iron kettles, holding from 60 to 100 gallons. They were placed in rows, and one furnace would sometimes have from twenty to thirty kettles. At first the furnace was close to the well or spring. Timber was plentiful and it was not difficult to keep the furnace supplied with fuel. As time went on the process became more systematic and the work grew. More timber was needed to make more salt. The item of hauling wood three or four miles became a serious one. On those days there were "professional axe-men," "expert teamsters," and "skilled firemen." It was a busy scene; twenty or thirty axe-men in the timber, eight or ten four- or six-mule teams on the roads from the timber to the furnaces, six or eight regular firemen, kettle hands, coopers, salt packers, salesmen, time-keepers, boarding-house keepers, freighters, hoop-pole merchants, and hangers-on by the score.

The water was put in fresh at the fire end of the row and moved from kettle to kettle back toward the chimney where there was a large, flat stirring off pan. Attached to this pan was a large draining board; the salt was scraped up to one side of the pan and shoveled up on this board. The water drained back into the pan and the salt became dry. It was then taken to the salt shed, where it was packed in barrels, and was then ready for the market.

When the timber had been used up back three or four miles, then they moved the works to the fuel. The water must now be gotten to the furnaces. This to modern engineers would be a simple problem, but to our friends of 100 years ago, it was not so simple a task. The plan required a long, tedious preparation. Large, straight trees, from 16 to 20 feet long in body, were cut. They must be at least ten inches in diameter at the small end; this would make them 14 to 16 inches in diameter at the large end. With a four-inch augur, a hole was bored lengthwise through this log. The opening in the large end was reamed to about six inches in diameter, while the small end of another log was forced into the large end of the first log. The second log was driven into the first with a sort of battering ram such as we have used to bombard the large hickory trees to knock off nuts in the fall of the year. These wooden pipes were laid from the spring or well to the furnace, which was often three to five miles away. The pipe lines are said to have been always straight, and went over hills and across creeks. However, the country is comparatively level. When the pipes crossed the creeks they weighted the pipes to the bottom of the stream with large castings in the general form of a horseshoe. These are straddled over the logs and are said to have weighed 250 to 300 pounds. All the pipes made prior to 1850 were made by hand, but about 1850 or probably a little later they were bored by horse power. As said before, the pipe line took a straight line from the well to the furnace. At the well a pump, or rather an elevator was rigged up, a continuous belt with flat buckets riveted to it. This crude elevator raised the water 12, 20, or 30 feet as needed, and thence it flowed down an upright pipe which connected at the bottom with the regular pipe line. The author was not able to determine whether or not there were relay stations, but was inclined to think there were. The cisterns where these elevators were located were called "histing cisterns."

The fact that this piping system was in use in an early day has led to some errors with regard to wells. Some people living in those regions have thought there was a well wherever there was a furnace, and the old furnaces are thick all over the country. This is not the case; there were few wells, but the piping system carried the water in all directions. The two chief places where wells were sunk were at the "Nigger Spring" and at the "Half Moon Lick." It has been estimated that 100 miles of pipe were laid from 1800 to 1873.

The first wells were probably square and were 20 feet in diameter, and about 60 feet deep. They were walled up with logs. All the old wells as they appear today are circular and are about 20 or 25 feet in diameter and from 4 to 10 feet deep with sloping sides. The water rose in these wells to within a few feet of the top of the ground. In what may be called the middle period of salt making, pipes were sunk in the bottom of these wells and a stronger brine secured.

Timothy Guard, who was connected with salt making as early as 1816 and as late as 1830 or later, dug a deep well near the "Half Moon Lick" perhaps as late as 1825. The well was dug down some 60 feet and walled up and then a boring was made in the bottom of this well. A very fine quality of brine was thus secured, and Guard's well is a very noted place, though few could point out the exact spot. A large tree is growing on the inner margin of this well; its banks are grassy and water stands in it some 6 feet below the surface of the ground. This well was used till about 1854. About this time a company was formed consisting of Stephen A. Rowan, Andrew McAllen, Chalon Guard, Abner Flanders, Broughton Temple and Joseph J. Castle. They made preparation to manufacture salt on a more extensive scale than ever before. They sunk another deep well at great expense, and expended so much money that the company broke up and Castle and Temple eventually became the owners of the grounds and improvements. These two men proceeded to complete the preparations for the manufacture of salt. Large boilers, engines and pumps were installed. Large boiler-iron evaporating pans were placed over the furnaces instead of the kettles. These pans were from 12 to 20 feet wide and extended from the grates to the smoke stack, a distance of 60 or 70 feet. There were three such rows of pans all connected with the same smoke stack. The old pans are lying there now in the weeds and brush. The author calculated their area and found they covered about 3,000 square feet. The pans were from 10 to 12 inches deep. Coal had been discovered in a nearby hill and it was substituted for wood. A tramway was built from the coal mine to the furnaces.

Thorn House

The water or brine was pumped from the deep wells to the top of the 'thorn house." This thorn house was a frame structure resembling in general appearance the false work used in constructing a bridge across a small river. It was 20 or 30 feet wide at the bottom, and extended 60 feet high narrowing toward the top. This would be the end view. It extended some 150 or 175 feet in length. There was quite a number of cross beams, ties and braces and the whole inner space was filled with bundles of thorn bushes. These bundles of thorn bushes were carefully packed in the frame work in such a way that all space was completely filled with them. These thorn bushes were found in great quantities all about the works. On top of this thorn house running its entire length was a trough full of small holes. The brine was pumped into this trough and allowed to flow gently to the other end, and if it did not all trickle through the holes on the first trip it was guided into another trough and caused to flow down it till all had passed through the openings in the bottom of the trough. This brine now trickled through the thorn faggots to the bottom of the structure where it was caught in a large trench and conveyed to a large retaining basin. This "thorn house" was a great mystery to the infrequent visitors to the salt works. There are two explanations of its office in salt making. One that the brine, in passing from the top of the structure to the bottom, lost by evaporation 40 per cent of the water. This was a great saving of fuel and labor in the boiling process. Another explanation of its use was this: In evaporating the brine by boiling the water there were deposits of some substance like gypsum in the bottom of the pan which adhered to the bottoms of the pans and if not often removed would prevent the passage of the heat from the fire to the water and thus the pans would be burned. Now the thorn bushes were supposed to have the power to crystallize this foreign matter and thus purify the brine.

This plant was owned and operated by Temple and Castle from about 1854 to 1870. They are said to have made 500 bushels of salt every twenty-four hours.

In about 1873 Temple and Castle constructed a very complete plant a mile away at the coal mine, thinking it cheaper to move the water to the coal than the coal to the water. The plant was an expensive one and when everything was nearly ready for work, hard times came on, salt became cheap, and the new works were never put into operation. In course of time the machinery was removed, and little is left to mark the new plant.

On December 18, 1903, the author visited this region. He spent four days in gathering up the facts concerning this great industry of a former age. It was a pleasant task. Mr. A. D. Blankenship, a former student in the State Normal, was kind enough to furnish the author a conveyance and to aid him in his investigations. On reaching Equality he was fortunate to make the acquaintance of Messrs. Moore, druggists, who were very much interested in preserving the story of early days about their town. Mr. Harry Moore accompanied the author to the old works. The ground was quite level and subject to overflow. The day was an ideal spring day, and as we stood on the spot where for three-fourths of a century a great industry flourished we had a strange feeling. It was deathly still, there were no noises, no bird songs, no cattle, no life. A mile away we could hear the noise of the village, a passing train, and the noise about the coal mine and coke ovens. We soon came to the cinder roads and then we knew we were near the furnaces. Now and then we passed an old well. We had a camera and we took views of wells, pans, thorn bushes, etc. We found the old furnaces. The outlines of the old pans are still to be seen. One old pan is quite well preserved, but it will soon be molded back to earth whence it came. We found the old retaining cistern and found the location of the old residence of Temple and Castle. About a quarter of a mile away we visited the noted "Half Moon Lick." This is about one-half quarter long and half quarter wide at the widest part. It is about 20 or 25 feet deep and is destitute of any growth except some willows and tufts of grass. This lick is supposed to have been the resort of wild animals for centuries past. The teeth and bones of mastodons have been found here. We got a fairly good view of this lick.

The afternoon was spent with Mr. McAvoy, a very intelligent and courteous old gentleman who came to Equality about 1855. Mr. McAvoy was a friend of Mr. Temple and was in possession of much valuable information which he had gathered in the last half century. The second day we visited the "Nigger Well," four miles below Equality and across the river from the town. There was a downpour of rain, which prevented us from making a close study of this region. However we were able to find the exact spot, the "Nigger Spring" which was salt and is the one evidently formerly used. The sulphur spring which was found very strong and was evidently formerly in use for the old timbers were still to be seen imbedded in the mud, and the fresh water spring not far away. These were all described by Colonel Sellers as early as 1854. Just to the right as one goes down the river toward the southeast is a high range of hills and at the "Nigger Well" the bluffs come close to the river and it is just up on these bluffs where Colonel Sellers used to find the Indian graves and evidence of a village. A few yards below the springs we found a native to the manor born. He had lived in that immediate vicinity for fifty years, and seemed a little surprised to think any one would attach any importance to these old salt springs. He told us that in a little bottom field just in front of his house and lying just below the springs that he had plowed up bushels of broken pottery and that the whole field seemed to be one big furnace. We asked him if any salt had been made there within the last fifty years, and he said that everything looked just as it did fifty years ago. We examined carefully the trees and we were sure there were many of them three feet in diameter and yet Colonel Sellers affirms that in any early day every stick of timber was cut off for fuel. We learned from the native above referred to that there was an old pipe line running from the springs near to an old furnace down the creek, but across from his house, and he said that he was sure the old kettles were there yet, but said they were covered up in the dirt but he was sure they could be found. He said further that another line of pipe led to a furnace further down the river. This line may have led to Weed's works which were one-half mile below the island ripple.

Colonel Sellers

We visited Shawneetown and spent considerable time with Mr. Charles Carroll whom we found to be a very pleasant gentleman. He was probably the best informed man in Shawneetown on early Gallatin County history. We spent some time in the recorder's office verifying some facts which we had gathered elsewhere. Incidentally we took occasion to visit the old flag said to have been carried in the Revolutionary war by General Posey. We also viewed for a few moments the old brick house in which General LaFayette was entertained. This was called the Rawlins house.

The third day, in company with Mr. McAvoy, Mr. McIntyre, Mr. Bunker, and Mr. Smith, we visited again the old salt works on the outskirts of Equality. This second visit was very profitable, for Mr. McIntyre was, from a boy, an employe about the works, most of the time in the capacity of cooper. Mr. McIntyre knew every foot of the ground and with his help we drew a map locating every important place of interest about the grounds. On this day, in company with Dr. Gordon and Mr. McAvoy, we called to see Uncle Peter White (colored) then seventy years old. Uncle Peter was brought up in the immediate vicinity of the salt works. When he was ten years old he and three other children were kidnapped and taken into Arkansas and sold. He was afterwards rescued by Watt White.

Uncle Peter's memory was good and we gathered some valuable information from him.

On the fourth day we visited the Elliott family previously referred to and also the Rev. Samuel Westbrook then living in El Dorado.

Mr. Westbrook was born in 1809. He came to Johnson County in 1812, and in 1826 he came to Equality and began laboring in various capacities in the salt making business. He was, among other things, a teamster. He had lived in the immediate vicinity of the salt works for the past seventy-eight years and had a very vivid picture of most of the incidents which occurred within that period.

The men and women who have lived in this region from a very early day are very few and their ranks are thinning every day. In a few years there will be none living whose lives cover the period of salt making. And so far as the author has been able to find out little, if anything, has ever been written and printed of this great industry of southern Illinois.

CHAPTER XI

INTERNAL IMPROVEMENTS

The Canvass—Local Interests—Canals—Indian Cessions—Canal or Railroad—Railroads—In Illinois—Roads, Bridges, etc.—Lotteries—Banks—Inaugural Message—Boosting Alton—More Legislation—Governor's Message—Noted Men—The Convention—The Law—Log Rolling—Long Nine—Fund Commissioners.

In a previous chapter we have given brief sketches of a score or more of public men who were connected with the Black Hawk war. Some of these men were prominent in Illinois politics or business before the war broke out. These men dropped their work and proceeded to the front and served, many of them, in very humble positions. When the war was ended and peace and quiet were restored many men came into prominence in public life. The lieutenant-governor, Mr. Zadock Casey, resigned his office and was elected to Congress in the fall of 1832, and served in the Twenty-third, Twenty-fourth, Twenty-fifth, Twenty-sixth and Twenty-seventh Congresses. In the summer of 1834, Charles Slade, representing the Belleville District, the first, died and Governor John Reynolds was a candidate to fill the vacancy and was elected. He resigned the governorship and Gen. William L. D. Ewing, president pro tem of the State Senate, finished the term of fifteen days.

The Canvass

In the regular election in the summer of 1834, Joseph Duncan of Jacksonville, at that time the representative in Congress from the First District, was the successful candidate for governor against Mr. William Kinney, who had been lieutenant-governor under Governor Edwards, 1826-30. The canvass was a tame affair. Mr. Duncan remained in Washington and carried on his canvass by correspondence. It is explained that Mr. Duncan had been out of favor with President Jackson and it was not thought wise to come into Illinois and make a personal canvass, for it would certainly be noised abroad that he was not supporting heartily General Jackson and that would lose him votes since Illinois was strong for Jackson. It appears that Mr. Duncan was interested in securing some appropriations for internal improvements. He introduced a bill for the improvement of the Chicago harbor and another one for an appropriation for the improvement of the Wabash River. In addition there was very great interest among western congressmen in continued appropriations for the National Road, which started at Cumberland, Maryland, and ran thence over the mountains and thence by way of Wheeling, Columbus, Indianapolis, Terre Haute, Vandalia and thence to St. Louis and a branch to Alton. At this time Mr. Duncan was deeply interested, not only in his two local bills, but also in the appropriation for the National Road. He was a candidate for the governorship. If he could secure the two local appropriations it would greatly aid his canvass for the coveted position. President Jackson was not greatly interested in assisting anyone into office and he therefore vetoed all these appropriation bills. This was the occasion of the breach between Duncan and Jackson.

Joseph Duncan was a man admirably suited to serve in the office of governor of the State of Illinois. He was a native of Kentucky, had served in the War of 1812 with Colonel Croghan in the defense of Fort Stephenson, had been granted a sword by Congress for his services and had come to Illinois about 1817 or 18 with all these honors upon him. He had served in the Legislature and had introduced the free school law of 1825. He had served in Congress and now was elected governor over Mr. Kinney by a majority of some seven thousand votes. Some writers have lamented the break between Duncan and Jackson. If Duncan had remained with Jackson he might have received the help which Jackson was abundantly able to give. At least he would have continued a regular democrat. But as it was he gradually moved away from democratic principles and eventually took up the whig doctrines and was later a whig candidate for governor. The cause of the break does appear to have been trivial and not of sufficient importance to have parted two prominent men in the same party.

Mr. Duncan came to the governorship at a time when the public mind was unsettled both nationally and locally. The friends of sound finance as they were frequently called had just lost in a struggle with Jackson over the rechartering of the second United States Bank. The proposed moving of the surplus of the national treasury from the United States Bank to the pet banks scattered through the New West and the South was greatly exciting both friends and foes of Jackson. The compromise of 1833 over the nullification scarecrow had not found favor everywhere. In spite of the fact that the United States Bank was doomed to close up its business in 1836, the president, Mr. Biddle, was still a strong man in financial matters in 1834. The friends of the people who would eventually become the nation's bankers after 1836, were elated that the moneyed power of the East was broken. But to strike a parting blow at the South and West, President Biddle has refused loans to the cotton dealers and there was a halt in the movement of the cotton crop of 1833.

The state banks could not step in to save the cotton merchants as their capital was very limited and they had not yet received the promised surplus from the United States treasury. Money became scarce and rates of interest rose. "Petitions were pouring into Washington by the thousand, and delegations of business men appeared almost daily at the White House, asking Jackson to restore the deposits and surrender to the great corporations, thus acknowledging the subordination of the country to one of its interests." "For weeks and even months the Senate was the scene of the most extraordinary denunciations and the press of the country was burdened with the attacks and counter-attacks of the parties to this fierce and unrelenting struggle. In the East business failures, the closing of the doors of manufacturing establishments, and the discharge of small armies of employees furnished all the proof necessary that the distress was real. From all sections of the country cries of distress, memorials and petitions came up to Washington."

LOCAL INTERESTS

While the above described distress was largely financial and economic, yet the influence reached every other department of the public's life. But within the state there were problems of no less far-reaching importance. Or maybe best to say that the local interests were parts of a nation-wide interest in the same things. Internal improvement had been a national issue from the earliest days of the Government. "To promote the general welfare" was one of the explicit purposes of the Government. The friends of internal improvement had, as early as 1806, secured appropriations from the national treasury for the construction of the National Road. In the chartering of the second United States Bank in 1816, the Government had exacted from the corporation one and a half millions as the price of the charter. This money was of course turned into the treasury, but it was the purpose of those who favored internal improvements to secure the appropriation of this million and a half for the construction of the National Road. This road came into Illinois eight or ten miles east of Marshall, Clark County, and thence through the towns on a line from Marshall to Vandalia. From Vandalia the road was surveyed to St. Louis and also to Alton, but no funds from the United States treasury were spent on the road west of Vandalia.

CANALS

Canal building was begun at an early date, but only three short ones had been completed in the United States prior to the War of 1812. One of these was in the northeast corner of Virginia, one known as the Santee Canal in South Carolina, and a third one in Massachusetts known as the Middlesex Canal. In

CAIRO-VANDALIA HIGHWAY NEAR COBDEN

From Illinois Blue Book

1817 DeWitt Clinton, governor of New York, began the digging of the Erie Canal, reaching from the upper courses of the Hudson to Lake Erie at Buffalo. This canal had been called "a bond of union between the Atlantic and the western states." This canal was the first bid by the metropolis city, New York, for the trade of the Northwest. This would interest Illinois, for by 1825 there was considerable commerce from Northern Illinois which found its way to the markets of the East through the Great Lakes; and so rapidly had Chicago grown that it was chartered as a city in 1837. This rapid growth was partly caused by the ease with which transportation was carried on between Chicago and New York City.

The first white people who visited Chicago were the French. These early visitors were perfectly familiar with the canal systems of France and other European countries. These French travelers, traders, and missionaries were impressed with the great value of a canal which would connect the Illinois River with the Great Lakes. The portage between the upper waters of the Chicago River and the Des Plaines was short and in the early day was thought to lend itself to easy excavation. Louis Joliet on his return from the voyage down the Mississippi River in 1673 was impressed with the value of a canal at this place in case the country should be settled by civilized people. La Salle, a very practical Frenchman, saw the value of a canal from Lake Michigan to the Illinois River. Other travelers and missionaries were quick to see the need of a canal between Lake Michigan and the head waters of the Illinois River. In 1818 Albert Gallatin, then secretary of the treasury under Jackson, made a report to the President in which he pointed out the great value of a canal from the lakes to the Illinois River. In 1811 a bill was introduced into Congress which provided for the construction of this canal. In 1812 the value to the United States of a canal was seen as a means of national defense. In 1814, President Madison, in his message to Congress, called attention to the importance of this canal, and a committee was appointed to make an investigation of the subject. The committee reported that it was "the great work of the age" both for military and commercial purposes.

An editorial is quoted from Niles Register, volume 6, page 394, as follows:

'By the Illinois River, it is possible that Buffalo in New York may be united with New Orleans, by inland navigation through the Lakes Erie, Huron, and Michigan, and down through that river to the Mississippi. What a route! How stupendous the idea! How dwindles the importance of the artificial canals of Europe compared with this water communication! If it should ever take place (and it is said the opening may be easily made) the territory (of Illinois) will become the seat of an immense commerce and a market for the commodities of all regions."

INDIAN CESSION

In 1816 in the treaty which Governor Edwards, William Clark, and Auguste Chouteau made with the Pottawattomies, Chippewas, and Ottawas, there was ceded to the United States a tract of land including Chicago and a strip of land joining the lake with the Illinois River. Governor Edwards says that at that time the Indians were made to believe that the Government wanted the land in order to build thereon a canal, and he further states that the Indians were made to believe that this canal would be of great advantage to the Indians as well as to the whites, and further that the cession was made by the Indians with that understanding.

In 1817 Major Long made a report to Congress that "a canal uniting the waters of the Illinois River with those of Lake Michigan, may be considered the first in importance of any in this quarter of the country, and the construction would be attended with very little expense compared with the magnitude of the object." In 1819 Mr. Calhoun, secretary of war, directed the attention of Congress to the canal on account of its importance for military purposes. In 1822 Congress made a grant of land to the state for the purpose of constructing a canal from the lake to the Illinois River, the grant being ninety feet wide on each side of the proposed canal. The lands adjacent were taken from the market until further notice. There was a proviso in the grant—that the canal must be begun within three years and completed within twelve years.

The first governor of the state, Shadrach Bond, in his first message to the General Assembly, recommended the building of the canal. In fact each governor following, either directly or otherwise, called attention to the importance of this particular public improvement.

In 1822-3 the General Assembly passed an act providing for the appointment of a board of canal commissioners who should cause to be made estimates, etc., on the construction of the canal. Emanuel J. West, Erastus Brown, Theophilus W. Smith, Thomas Sloo and Samuel Alexander were appointed upon this commission. Two engineers, Justine Post and Rene Paul, were employed as engineers. These men made a preliminary survey and estimated that the building of the canal would cost not to exceed $700,000. This very favorable report was received by the Legislature at its cession, 1824-5. It seemed at this early date that it was the general belief that corporations were more efficient agents for the construction of large enterprises than states or nation. In consequence a corporation was created which was called the "Illinois and Michigan Canal Association." The capital stock was $1,000,000. The charter provided that "all cessions, grants, and transfers, made, or that may be hereafter made, by the Government of the United States for the purpose of promoting the completion of the canal, shall pass and vest in said corporation."

Congressman Daniel P. Cook saw that unless this charter were quickly revoked it would be impossible to get Congress interested in any grants or concessions. The Congress would readily grant lands or other things of value when the general public was to profit, but when there appeared the likelihood that private individuals were to profit there would be some hesitancy in making the grants. The charter of 1825 was therefore revoked or annulled, and in 1827 Mr. Cook with the help of Elias Kent Kane and Jesse B. Thomas, United States senators from Illinois, secured a grant of land "for the purpose of aiding her in opening a canal to connect the waters of the Illinois River with those of Lake Michigan." The grant was to run from Chicago to Ottawa, to be ten miles wide, and the state was to have every alternate section on either side of the canal, together with large grants at Chicago and Ottawa. The number of acres included in this grant is said to have been 224,322. This land was to be sold and the money applied to the construction of the canal.

In 1826 the Legislature created another board of canal commissioners to carry on the work of surveys, etc. The names of the commissioners were Dr. Gershom Jayne, Edward Roberts, and Charles Dunn. A new survey was made by Engineer James M. Bucklin, but the report was not encouraging. Every report put the cost of construction higher than previous reports. In 1829 a supplementary act was passed which enabled the commissioners to exercise a closer supervision over the sale of the lands along the proposed canal route. In the exercise of their new powers, the commissioners laid out the towns of Chicago and Ottawa at the ends of the proposed canal.

Canal or Railroad

There was much interest in the two towns and when the lots were put on sale there was a rush for choice locations. The sale of land and lots brought an income of $18,924.83. The estimate made by Mr. Bucklin as to the cost of construction was $4,043,386.50. At the same time or a little later at the suggestion of interested parties, he submitted an estimate of the cost of a railroad connecting the towns of Ottawa and Chicago. He placed the cost of the railroad at $1,052,488.19. The matter of a railroad also attracted attention of public men and a move was set on foot to substitute a railroad for the canal. Congress was requested to permit the state to substitute a railroad for the canal and by an act passed March 2d, 1833, such a grant was made by

Congress. The whole scheme dragged along until it was not till 1835 that further steps were taken to further the improvement. In 1835 the governor was authorized to borrow $5,000,000 on the credit of the canal lands, but the moneyed men were slow to buy these bonds. Ex-Governor Coles, then living in Philadelphia, notified the authorities in Illinois that he could not market the bonds in that city, because the act authorizing the loan did not provide that the State of Illinois was back of the bonds.

On the 9th of January, 1836, the credit of the state was pledged for the security of the bonds and it was not difficult to dispose of them. New life was now instilled into the project and on the 4th of July, 1836, the construction was formally begun with much ceremony in the young and growing City of Chicago. A new board of canal commissioners was created and the business side of the project was placed in their hands. These commissioners were to make reports to the state every three months. The board worked under the general direction of the governor. The board was to be elected by the people after January, 1837. Steps were taken to begin actual construction of the canal. The sale of lots was set for June 20, 1836. Much interest was taken by speculators and lots are said to have sold for large sums. Town lots were also sold in Ottawa.

On the 4th of July, 1836, a public celebration was held in Chicago with two ends in view. It was the nation's birthday; and the citizens wished to celebrate the beginning of actual work on the Illinois and Michigan Canal. The Honorable Theophilus W. Smith, a former canal commissioner, read the Declaration of Independence and Dr. William B. Egan delivered an able address.

RAILROADS

Railroads made their advent in England in 1822. George Stephenson was the son of a fireman of a colliery in Wylam, England. In 1814 he successfully put in operation a "traveling engine" which hauled coal from Wylam to the seaport, a few miles distant. The traveling engine was improved and was eventually used to transport passengers over what in England was called the train ways. Passengers were carried over these crude railroads as early as 1825. In 1825 also a wooden-rail track was first used in America. This road was used to haul excavated earth in the construction of the Delaware-Chesapeake Canal. In 1826 Stephen Van Rensselaer of New York procured a charter for a railroad which should be constructed between Albany and Schenectady. This road was known as the Mohawk and Hudson River Railroad. It began operations in 1831. In 1827 the Mauch-Chunk Railroad in the Lehigh Valley was constructed for the transportation of anthracite coal in that valley. In most if not all of these roads spoken of as in operation in the United States the motive power was horses and mules. But the first railroad in which the motive power was steam was put in operation in 1829 in South Carolina—from Charleston to the interior, eventually reaching Columbia. The Tom Thumb was the first steam engine built in the United States. It was constructed by Peter Cooper of New York. A railroad was built from Boston to Albany, from Albany to Saratoga, one from Richmond, Virginia, to Chesterfield in the same state. These were built prior to 1835. In that year Pennsylvania had 200 miles in operation, South Carolina 137 miles, Virginia 130 miles and Massachusetts, New York and New Jersey a hundred each—a total of 675 miles east of the Alleghanies.

In Illinois

In 1831 a railroad was chartered in St. Clair County, and in the same year the Legislature provided that a railroad running from Chicago to the head waters of the Illinois River might be substituted for the canal, with the permission of the United States Government. The canal gradually gained favor in the minds of the people and no steps were taken to build the railroad. These two proposed railroads were the objects of the first legislation along that line in Illinois. But from this time forward the Legislature was very liberal in granting charters for the construction of railroads. The first railroad actually put into operation in Illinois was a short line in St. Clair County. Governor John Reynolds who, it will be remembered, was elected to Congress in November, 1834, was not reelected in 1836, and when his term closed, March 4, 1837, he returned to his home in Belleville. Having nothing else to occupy his busy mind he conceived the project of building a railroad from the coal mines near Belleville to the river at St. Louis. The purpose of this road was the transportation of coal to the barges on the Mississippi. Governor Reynolds says he owned most of the land over which the road ran across the American bottom. He interested some of his friends in the enterprise and an engineer was secured who made all the surveys and planned the construction. This engineer made serious blunders in estimating the cost of construction and the road required an outlay about twice as large as was estimated. The stockholders worked on the job the same as the hired men and finally succeeded in completing the road. In one place piling was driven for more than 2,000 feet. The governor says that as many as three pilings were driven, one on top of the other to the depth of eighty feet. The battering ram was home-made and weighed 1,400 pounds. There were camps for the workmen, and the stockholders saw to the cooking, the care of horses, the procuring of food, and actually shoveled earth as did any hired hand. They had no iron for rails and therefore made use of wooden rails. They had no engine and must use horses or mules. They moved many thousands of tons of coal and the road was operated successfully for many years till the coming of steam.

ROADS, BRIDGES, ETC.

The first forms of Internal Improvement in Illinois were very simple. It was necessary for the pioneers to have roads, and to find some means of crossing the streams. Bridges could not be built very early and the only way to cross streams was to make use of the fordable places. The pioneers knew where the fords might be located. Our forefathers built an interesting sort of bridge across the streams called a "mud bridge." These bridges were constructed as follows: A place in the stream was found where the banks were firm and not too steep. Very tall, well proportioned trees were found of which to make mud sills. These sills were sometimes fifty to seventy-five feet long. The opposite ends of these sills, usually three or four, would be let into the banks, down to a level of the water at ordinary stages. Up on these mud sills heavy oak planks would be laid and securely fastened. The banks were then graded down so a team could easily ascend and descend. The side of the bridge toward the up-stream was usually six or eight inches lower than the side next to the down-stream. When the water began to rise the weight of the water in passing over the bridge had a tendency to hold the bridge down instead of to float it. Stakes were securely placed on the sides of the bridge to show the location of the bridge and also to give the depth when the bridge was covered with water. If the water covered the stakes the traveler was warned not to venture to cross. Many of these bridges, the remnants of a very early pioneer life, were to be found in the timbered districts of Illinois as late as the Civil war or later.

Bridges were built even across the larger streams as early as 1830. The pioneers who came to Illinois through Tennessee and Kentucky were often skilled workmen in framing large buildings—dwellings, barns, bridges, and warehouses. The early ferry boats were home made, and many devices about these first ferries showed constructive genius which would rank well along in the science of civil engineering. The earliest internal improvements were made without the consent or assistance of the Legislature or the public treasury. When the public improvements met the common needs, the people gladly gave of their time and energy in their construction. All that were needed to construct a bridge across a stream were axmen, scorers, hewers, and whip-saw men. The augur and the white oak pin served the purpose of the modern spikes.

Roads followed the Indian trails, and these followed the buffalo paths. They were seldom strait but usually followed the most feasible route. The earliest laws provided that roads might be laid out by the county commissioners. The law provided only

FORESTRY IN ILLINOIS

From Illinois Blue Book

(1) Fully stocked growth of pin oak, Hamilton County. (2) White pine plantation, fifty years old, Grundy County. (3) Pastured and unpastured woodland. (4) Fifteen-year-old catalpa plantation. (5) Catalpa posts from thirteen-year-old stand.

that the road should run from a certain town to another designated place, as from Fort Massac to Cahokia. It also provided that the road as laid out by the local authority should be along a practicable route. These roads were often called state roads.

Long before Illinois was a state, roads were established by authority of the territorial government as follows: From Lusk's Ferry, Golconda, to Shawneetown. From Kaskaskia to Cahokia. From Kaskaskia to Vandalia; this road was opened up after the capital was located at Vandalia, however there was travel over this road before it was marked out by Judge Breese. A road ran from Kaskaskia to Belleville and thence to French village near to the station on the Illinois Central called Church. From Kaskaskia to Covington on the Kaskaskia River at the northwest part of Washington County. One from Kaskaskia to Waterloo; this road was in use and was much used prior to its being laid out. In fact it was a part of the road from Kaskaskia to Cahokia. One from Kaskaskia to the Big Muddy in the neighborhood of the present City of Murphysboro.

The United States Government very early opened mail routes to the new territory west of the Alleghanies. A mail route was established from Philadelphia to Pittsburg in 1788. From Pittsburg it was extended by stages to Louisville and thence to Vincennes in 1800. From Vincennes it was laid out to Cahokia in 1805. In 1806 a road running from Shawneetown to Vincennes was made a mail route. A route from Vincennes to St. Louis was established. This road evidently was identical, at least a large part of the way, with the Vincennes and Cahokia route. A route was established from Louisville, Kentucky, to Shawneetown, and thence by way of Elvira, Johnson County, and thence to Belleville in 1818. In 1822 Edwardsville, Springfield and Peoria were connected by a United States mail route. In 1824 a mail route was located from Vandalia to Springfield. A road running along the eastern side of the state from Vincennes to Chicago was early in use. Roads were laid out from Chicago, Ottawa, and Rock Island to Galena and the lead mines.

In subjects so organically connected with the whole life of the people as roads, bridges, railroads, canals, and banks, it is extremely difficult to find the origin of any one of them. The fact is there is no formal beginning. Roads and trails were the earliest care of the permanent settlers. Fords, ferries and bridges were provided at a very early date. But it is probably due to Governor Reynolds to say that he is to be given credit for first calling the attention of the Legislature to the need of internal improvement. Governor Reynolds, in his inaugural address before the Legislature in December, 1830, had this to say on the general subject of internal improvement:

"The internal improvement of the country demands, and will receive your particular attention. There can not be an appropriation of money within the exercise of your legislative power, that will be more richly paid to the citizen, than that for the improvement of the country."

Governor Reynolds was clearly of opinion that the general government ought to carry on a system of national improvements, but he was as clearly of opinion that there were certain local improvements that ought to be fostered by the state. He urged attention to the report of the canal commissioners and hoped that the attention of Congress might be directed to the national importance of the enterprise. "The improvement of the navigation of the rivers adjoining and within this state, will be the subject of your serious consideration. Those improvements which are local to our state will receive your fostering care, so

GOVERNOR JOHN REYNOLDS

far as our means will justify without embarrassment to our people. The general good of the present and future population seems to require the permanent establishment of three public roads (wagon roads) in this state extending north; (1) on the western side of the state, by the principal towns on the most direct route to Galena. (2) Another to commence at Shawneetown passing north, through the center of the state to accommodate the present and future population, to the lead mines. (3) And one other, to commence on the Wabash River, near its confluence with the Ohio, passing through the principal towns on the eastern side of the state by Danville to Chicago, and thence to the lead mines."

Governor Reynolds believed the state government might be induced to construct these roads and that the counties might be required to keep them in repair. His idea was that a good road passing through an undeveloped region would be a very potent factor in the development of such a section. He specially called attention to the road leading from Vincennes through the state to St. Louis, saying it was much traveled.

LOTTERIES

The question of finance was an important one in the consideration of any form of public improvement. Most of the early settlers who came into Illinois were unaccustomed to the modern systems of taxation, and all sorts of schemes and devices were brought forward to provide funds for any suggested public work. It was in keeping with this aversion to direct taxation that a law was passed in Governor Bond's term to raise money for internal improvements by means of a system of lotteries. The improvement of the navigation of the Wabash River was urged by public spirited men, and plans were laid to secure the funds by a lottery. Stuve says: "Perhaps a superfluous provision in the law was, that the overplus of any moneys arising from the scheme should, at the discretion of the managers, be 'laid out' in further improvements." In the same way the American Bottom was to be drained and levees built. Little was accomplished by the lottery system.

BANKS

At first glance it might not appear that banks had anything to do with internal improvement, but the whole matter of public improvement is vitally dependent upon banks and banking. No public works such as canals and railroads could be constructed in the United States by such systems as similar public works have been carried on the old world. The Corvee system of the Feudal age was in operation in France when her wonderful roads were built and when her formidable castles were constructed. The walls of the great cities of the old world, the canals, the roads, the fortifications, and even the great monuments of the three eastern continents were all produced by systems of forced labor. Labor was never considered an equivalent of the coin of the land. If it had an exchangeable value at all it was estimated in terms of food and some forms of clothing. But in the new world, at least within the limits of the United States, there has been no such system of commanding the labor of human beings. However, the Anglo-Saxon system of government has recognized a form of taxation which had its equivalent in labor. This is what we know as a poll-tax system. In the first half of the nineteenth century it was the law in Illinois that each able-bodied man with few exemptions must work three days of each year upon the public highway. Later in the century the law provided that the citizen might choose between giving the three days' labor or paying a certain sum of money. While at present all charges against the citizen and his property appear as a part of his annually recurring taxes.

As early as the beginning of state-hood the need of money was clearly recognized. Banks were established in Illinois as early as 1816, and even before that we have at least one instance of a private individual who occupied the place of a public banker. In 1821, the general assembly was so impressed with the need of a stable circulating medium, that a bank was chartered which should have a capital of $500,000. The money of course was a paper currency and for its redemption the credit of the state was pledged. The bank was to continue for ten years. At the end of the ten years the state was required to pay all indebtedness of the bank which amounted to $100,000. After 1831, the end of the State Bank, there was no currency in circulation in Illinois except what came in from the adjoining states, together with a certain limited amount from the issue of the United States Bank and small quantities of gold and silver coin.

It will often happen with the individual that just when he thinks the conditions opportune for a profitable investment, it is then found that the means of making the investment, that is the money which he must have to carry out his plans, is not to be had. Money is scarce, interest is high, and the opportunity will not wait. In a similar way corporations and even states find themselves working against similar unfavorable conditions.

The opportunity for internal improvements on a large scale appears to be passing in the administration of Governor Joseph Duncan, 1834-1838. We had for more than a decade been building roads, establishing ferries, locating fords, creating new counties, discovering our hidden sources of wealth, and driving from our borders the last lingering menace to the expansion of our population into the rich prairies of the central and northern parts of our state. The agencies which were destined to play so important a part in the development and distribution of the wealth of our forests, our soil, and our mines were beckoning us to come to their support.

There were therefore two great problems before the people of Illinois in the second decade of statehood. One was the question of money the other the question of transportation. There were many phases of both of these larger problems.

INAUGURAL MESSAGE

In December, 1834, Governor Duncan was inaugurated as governor of Illinois. Following the custom set by the inauguration of presidents and other executives the incoming governor delivered his inaugural in which he outlined his ideas as to public questions. Touching the question of internal improvement he said the state should lay out public roads now, while the land was unsettled, for there was no hindrance to the opening of roads from one point to another on the most direct and practicable line. The Legislature responded to his request by giving authority to county commissioners to open forty-two roads in the state, and at a latter session forty more such roads were authorized.

As to the subject of banks he said: "Banks may be made exceedingly useful in society, not only by affording an opportunity to the widow, the orphan and the aged, who possess capital without the capacity of employing it in ordinary business, to invest it in such stocks; but by its use the young and the enterprising mechanic, merchant, and tradesman may be enabled more successfully to carry on his business and improve the country."

The Legislature to which the governor was directing this information was not directed by their constituency to legislate upon the subject of banks. If the question of banks had been a matter of consideration in the canvass of 1834, there would have been registered a very positive veto against any legislation looking toward foisting another banking system upon the people. It had only been four short years since the people witnessed the collapse of a state banking system in whose wreck there was left a state debt of $100,000. But it is very doubtful whether "history is philosophy teaching by example." It would at least appear that the experience of a people in the banking business with a bank for ten years, which left them in debt $100,000, would be such a lesson as they would not soon forget.

But since the collapse of the State Bank in 1831, the President, Andrew Jackson, had vetoed a bill which rechartered the United States Bank whose charter would expire in 1836. The Congress was not able to pass the bill over his veto, and it was known that this bank with a capital of thirty-five million dollars, whose management was in the hands of the shrewdest financiers in the United States, whose bills always passed at par value, and whose existence since 1816 had stabilized the financial world— at least that part of it in the United States—it was known that this bank would by 1836, redeem all its outstanding issue, close its doors, and leave the business of the United States in the chaos of state banking systems. And if, as to say, since all the other states are going into the business of issuing irredeemable paper money, why not the State of Illinois?

It must not, however, be thought that all the individual members of the Legislature who listened to the persuasive speech of the governor were convinced that Illinois should go into the banking business. But enough were in favor of it to make a working basis and the task of converting the indifferent ones began. One of the strings that was pulled was the proposal to tax the non-resident land owners so heavily that the owner would be forced to offer his lands at a reasonable price. There was a very bitter feeling in some quarters against those non-resident land owners. It was now proposed by those favoring the creation of a state bank, that a bill should be brought in which would greatly increase the taxes of the land owned by non-residents. Some votes were won for the bank bill by other plans of log rolling. Votes were obtained for the bank bill by taxing the non-resident's lands in the military tract higher than resident's lands and with the money thus raised to improve the public roads. Governor Ford in his history of Illinois gives an interesting method of securing votes for the bank bill. One senator bitterly opposed to the bank bill, voted for it when the bank friends elected him to the office of state's attorney. There were other questionable transactions in connection with the passage of the bank bill. The vote stood 27 yeas to 26 nays in the House; it had previously passed the Senate. Mr. Ford says this was in no sense a party vote.

The bank bill created a corporation with a capital of $1,500,000 with the privilege of increasing the capital by another million. The state reserved $100,000 of the stock for its own investment. The act required a deposit of ten per cent. in cash before the stock would be issued. The stock was two or three times oversubscribed, and there seems to have been a number of schemes by which advantages could be taken to locate the stock in the bonds of business or political friends. Much stock was subscribed for in the name of individuals in Illinois but in reality for eastern capitalists. The commissions who were to organize the bank, after a good deal of "jockeying and maneuvering for position," and after striking out non-resident applicants, assigned the stock in such a way that thirty-nine shares more than half of the stock fell to five holders while a little less than half fell to eleven persons. There was a head bank at Springfield and branches were established at Chicago, Vandalia, Galena, Jacksonville, and Alton. Later branches were organized at Danville, Quincy, Belleville, and Mt. Carmel

The bank was to be managed by a board of directors of nine men, one of whom should be president. If the bank should fail to redeem its issue, such failure would endanger its charter. The stock rose at one time to a premium of 13%. The bank stock was owned principally by whigs and in electing directors the board of control was favorable to the whigs. A few democrats were elected for the sake of appearance. Thomas Mather of Kaskaskia was made president of the bank.

Boosting Alton

In the years before and after the coming of Joseph Duncan as governor, there was great rivalry between Alton and St. Louis as commercial centers. The people who lived in Illinois were of course partial to Alton other things being equal, but St. Louis had gotten the start of Alton in business growth. The men who had set their hearts on boosting Alton were aided by the fact that they controlled a majority of the stock in the bank. The bank therefore was ready to lend its aid to the development of any enterprise which would help to build up Alton. Godfrey, Gilman, and Co., wholesale merchants of Alton, were accommodated with a loan of $800,000. This was not drawn from the bank but was subject to the drafts of this firm. At that time the most important product coming down the Mississippi River was lead from the Fever River region. Within the ten years prior to 1836, no less than 70,000,000 pounds of lead had been mined in the Galena and other districts in the northwest part of the state. Most of this lead had come down the Mississippi and found a market in either Alton or St. Louis. To monopolize this lead trade was the purpose of Godfrey, Gilman, and Co. When Alton came into the lead market as a rival of St. Louis, the price of lead advanced from 50 to 75%. Several hundred thousand dollars were invested in mines and mining equipment, and at the same time many thousands of dollars were invested in real estate in Galena. The product of the mines was cornered and held for increased prices. Two extensive wholesale companies were organized in Alton and were provided with capital by the bank. The lead which Godfrey, Gilman, and Co. had cornered failed to advance in price and became a drug on the market, the wholesale establishments failed and when the smoke cleared away it was found that a million dollars had been lost by the bank in its efforts to boost Alton.

More Legislation

The Legislature was called in special session in the fall of 1835 for the purpose of redistricting the state following the state census of 1835. The governor advised the purchase by the State of the one hundred thousand dollars of the reserved capital of the bank. The governor's plan was to resell the stock at 30% premium and thus realize $300,000, with which to replenish the treasury of the state. The Legislature did not fully agree with the governor but did authorize the sale of the $100,000 worth of stock reserved for the state, and the period allowed in which redemption could be deferred was increased from ten days to sixty days.

By an act passed March 4, 1837, the capital stock of the State Bank was increased by $2,000,000, the whole to be subscribed for by the state. In the act creating the State Bank in 1834-5, the Shawneetown bank which had been defunct for several years was revived by a charter permitting a capital of $300,000. In 1837 this capital was increased by $1,400,000, the state to subscribe for the million while the four hundred thousand was to be open to private subscription.

It was expected that the state's profits from the bank stock would be at least ten per cent, and this sum of $200,000 was to be applied to the payment of interest on the state's loans. It was also expected that the premium which would be received upon the sale of the improvement bonds would also make a large sinking fund. When the Improvement bonds were offered for sale, instead of receiving a premium for them they could not be negotiated even at par. Rather than allow the state's bonds to sell at below par the banks—the State Bank and the Shawneetown Bank—bought more than two and a half million of them at par. The state now owned more than three millions of the banks' stock while the banks held nearly three millions of the state's bonds. The two banks had an authorized capital of $5,200,000.

We have now studied somewhat in detail the efforts of the state to provide one of the factors in the development of the resources of the state. This factor was money—some sort of medium of exchange called barter, but there cannot, from the nature of the system, be any accumulation of capital, and without capital there cannot be a very complete development of resources. But when we think of it, $5,200,000 of currency for a state with a population of 300,000 only gives a circulation of less than $20 per individual. There was more money than this in circulation no doubt, as there was money from the bank of issue in the adjacent states. Then there was some money of the United States Banks' issue. But at best there was a dearth of money and then when we remember that much if not most of this money was below par, we can see what the business world had to contend with.

Governor's Message

When the Legislature convened in special session, December 7, 1835, Governor Duncan delivered his special message which touched upon the banking question and on internal improvement. His message in 1834 had produced the financial legislation we have just considered. His suggestions as to roads had provided over eighty roads in Illinois. Now in his special message he suggests the entrance of Illinois into the project of building railroads which shall supplement the rivers and canals as means of transportation. The public mind was acquainted with the general movement known as internal improvement. The states of New York, Pennsylvania, Ohio, and Indiana had given much attention to the subject of transportation. They had given attention to their rivers, had opened canals and were by 1835 constructing railroads. It was understood that railroads in the United States had grown from 23 miles in 1830 to eleven hundred in 1836. Pennsylvania had 218 miles of railroads, and 914 miles of canal in operation. The spirit of internal improvement had reached Illinois.

In the summer of 1835 there were a number of public meetings at which the matter of internal improvements was discussed. These meetings were not on a very large scale, but were made up of the most progressive people in each section. At these meetings the "march of progress" in other states was freely discussed. Many of the people knew of the good macadamized roads in Kentucky and of the steps that were being taken in Ohio and Indiana to further the cause of internal improvement. In these meetings there were two points that were stressed—first the ease with which railroads and canals could be built in Illinois and the other the crying need of the means of transportation.

It would appear that the people had built up a very good body of sentiment as to the proposed internal improvement schemes, and without doubt the governor shared the general enthusiasm for the "march of progress." In his message delivered to the Legislature in December, 1835, after suggestions as to the matter of banks, the governor approached the subject of internal improvement. He said:

"When we look abroad and see the extensive lines of intercommunication penetrating almost every section of our sister states—when we see the canal boat and the locomotive bearing, with seeming triumph, the rich productions of the interior to the rivers, lakes and ocean, almost annihilation time, burthen, and space—what patriotic bosom does not beat high with the laudable ambition to give to Illinois her full share of those advantages which are adorning her sister states, and which a magnificent Providence seems to invite by the adaptation of our whole country to such improvement."

The governor was not sure just how far this flight of oratory would carry the farmers, lawyers, doctors, merchants, and professional politicians who composed the Legislature, toward a complete indorsement of state supported internal improvement. But for fear he had overdone the matter he added: "While I would urge the most liberal support of all such measures as tending with perfect certainty to increase the wealth and prosperity of the state, I would at the same time most respectfully suggest the propriety of leaving the construction of all such works wherein it can be done consistently with the general interest, to individual enterprise." This was indeed wholesome advise and had the succeeding legislature taken his advise, the state would have greatly profited thereby.

The members of the Legislature were not converted to the idea of state participation in internal improvements, at least so far as railroads were concerned, for at this session nothing more was done than to charter a number of railroads for corporate construction, to increase the capital stock of the banks, and to appropriate a half million dollars for the furtherance of the work in the Illinois and Michigan Canal. But the governor's message, while not successful in creating enough interest among the members of the Legislature then in session, to champion a system of internal improvement, it seems to have awakened renewed interest throughout the state.

In the summer of 1836 a new Legislature was to be elected and one of the matters of general discussion was that of internal improvement. Local meetings were held in the summer as had been held in the preceding summer. The interest was increasing. The canal was actually begun on July 4, 1836, and Chicago was booming. The election of the members of the Legislature occurred in the early days in August, 1836. The Legislature would convene December 5, 1836. By reason of the increase in population as revealed in the state's census of 1835, and according to the provisions of the constitution, the state had been redistricted and several additional members had been added to the Legislature.

Noted Men

Moses' History of Illinois, in commenting upon the character of the men who sat in this tenth General Assembly, says: Among its members were included a future President of the United States, a defeated candidate for the same high office, six future United States senators, eight members of the national House of Representatives, a secretary of the interior, three judges of the State Supreme Court, and seven state officers. Here sat side by side Abraham Lincoln (aged twenty-seven), and Stephen A. Douglas (aged twenty-three); the gallant Edward Dickinson Baker, who represented at different times the states of Illinois and Oregon in the national councils; O. H. Browning, a prospective senator and future cabinet officer, and William L. D. Ewing, who had just served a brief period in the United States Senate; John Logan, father of the late senator, Gen. John A. Logan; Richard Cullom, father of Senator Shelby M. Cullom, John A. McClernand, afterward member of Congress for many years, and a distinguished general in the late Civil war; Uncle Jesse K. Dubois, afterward state auditor for eight years; Gen. James K. Shields; Col. John J. Hardin; William H. Richardson; John Hogan, Robert Smith; and Gen. James Semple, speaker of the house, most of them future members of Congress, either in the Senate or House or both; Augustus C. French, a future governor, Usher F. Linder, Milton Carpenter, John Moore, John Dougherty, Newton Cloud, Archibald Williams, Cyrus and Ninian Edwards; W. A. Marshall, Edwin B. Webb, William Thomas, and John Dement.

Dr. John Snyder, who has written the life of Adam Snyder

who was an active participant in the political life of these times, says as soon as the elections to the Legislature were over (the election being held August 19, 1836) an incessant and universal discussion began. There grew up the cry that the people had the right to instruct their representatives in the Legislature. Meetings were very generally held at which resolutions were passed favoring state participation in internal improvement. In addition a movement was sent on foot to hold a convention, which came to be known as the Internal Improvement Convention in Vandalia a few days prior or at the time of the assembling of the Legislature. The local meeting in various counties appointed delegates to this improvement convention. In naming delegates to this convention the local meetings acted wisely in naming as the delegate the member of the Legislature from their county when he was known to favor the general plan of internal improvements. In those counties whose representatives and senators were opposed, or lukewarm, it was necessary to select some enthusiastic supporter of the scheme of internal improvements.

THE CONVENTION

"The Internal Improvement Convention met in Vandalia, simultaneously with the convening of the Legislature, December 5, 1836, and was largely attended. The delegates, some of whom were members of the General Assembly were wildly enthusiastic for railroads at any cost. For two days they deliberated upon the momentous question before them, and finally embodied their conclusions in a set of resolutions to be presented to the Legislature demanding the construction of a system of railroads, and improvement of rivers for navigation, the estimated cost of which would amount to $7,450,000, to be paid for by the sale of bonds of the state. The resolutions were accompanied by an elaborate memorial setting forth, in florid language, the incomputable benefits the state and people would derive from the perfect feasibility of the grand scheme."

The convention was in session but a couple or three days, but before adjournment the members put into motion some practical politics. A bill was drawn as the convention directed and its introduction into the Legislature was confided to a friend of the measure. Another thing the convention did was to appoint a sort of steering committee or perhaps better a lobbying committee. This committee was to remain in Vandalia and keep an eye on the weak-kneed members of the Legislature, and use such means to hold them in line as they might think best.

The governor's message to the Legislature was a very sensible document. He recommended internal improvement legislation, suggested the establishment of a free school system, renewed his indorsment of the banking system, and took occasion to criticize the Jackson administration just then retiring from office. The Lower House answered Mr. Duncan by passing resolutions of commendation of Jackson by a vote of 64 to 18. There were several minor things before the Legislature, but two things were of absorbing interest—the moving of the state capital and internal improvement.

The improvement convention, before it adjourned had selected Mr. Stephen A. Douglas to introduce its bill into the Legislature. Mr. Douglas was one of the six representatives from Morgan County. He introduced the bill which had been drawn by the convention. It detailed the improvements to be made and set forth the doctrine that the work should be done and the improvements owned by the state, and that the necessary funds with which the pay for the cost of construction should be borrowed by the state upon its faith. The bill as drawn by the convention provided for an estimated outlay of only $7,450,000. When the bill was presented by Mr. Douglas it was referred to the committee on Internal Improvements. This committee was headed by Edward Smith of Wabash County. The bill in committee underwent some modification and enlargement. There was a good deal of whipping the devil around the stump in getting this bill before the General Assembly. Before the bill was presented by Mr. Douglas the whereases, and resolves, and memorials which had been formulated by the convention were read and commented on; and now before the bill was returned by the committee on Internal Improvements, there were other resolutions and memorials read. All this seems to have had for its purpose to build up the expectation of the public. The memorial which the committee presented was a sort of complement to the governor's message, and especially that part in which he favored internal improvement. Quoting from Stuve and Davidson: "The committee argued that public expectation, both at home and abroad, would be greatly disappointed if some system of internal improvement was not adopted at the present session; that the internal trade of a country was the greatest lever of its prosperity; that it was the legislator's duty, by his example, to calm the apprehension of the timorous and meet the attacks of calculating opposers of measures which would multiply the population and wealth of the state; that the surface of the state was peculiarly adapted to the construction of railroads, and that the practicability of removing obstructions to the navigation of our rivers could not be doubted; that a general system of internal improvements was then within the policy and means of the state, demanded by the people as expressed by their highly talented delegates, lately assembled in convention, and also looked forward to by the people abroad who had purchased lands here with a view to settlement, and whose expectations ought not to be disappointed by over cautious legislation on which would divert immigration to other states; that the railroads as fast as completed both ways from the crossings of rivers and important towns would yield the interests on the costs." The committee further argued that the state ought to enter large quantities of government lands which could be sold at an advance, thus clearing handsome sums for the state's treasury.

THE LAW

The committee after much jockeying reported the bill. It was entitled, "An act to Establish and maintain a general system of internal improvements," approved February 27, 1837. The provisions of the bill set aside certain amounts to build railroads when not even a trip over the proposed route had been made by any one. Think of an intelligent group of men sitting down with a map and marking out a railroad from Cairo to Galena and then setting aside a certain sum for its construction. But that is the way they did it and probably that is why the whole thing collapsed. The scheme is as follows:

For the construction of a railroad from Galena to Cairo	$ 3,500,000
For the Northern Cross Railroad through Springfield	1,800,000
For the Alton and Mt. Carmel Railroad	1,600,000
For the Peoria and Warsaw Railroad	700,000
For branch of the Central road to Terre Haute	650,000
For branch of Central Railroad to Alton	600,000
For Bloomington and Mackinaw Railroad	350,000
For Belleville and Mt. Carmel Railroad	150,000
For improvement of navigation of Wabash, Illinois, and Rock Rivers, each $100,000	300,000
For improvement of Little Wabash and Kaskaskia, each $50,000	100,000
To placate those counties having no rivers to be improved, and not traversed by any of the contemplated railroads, for their roads and bridges	200,000
Grand total	$10,200,000

LOG ROLLING

Three important matters were now before the Legislature or would soon be presented. They were the internal improvement schemes, the renewal of the capital, and the support of the Illinois and Michigan Canal. The friends of the improvement bill were quite willing to say they were neutral about the removal of the capital, and about the canal. They might be easily persuaded to vote for Springfield if the nine votes from Sangamon County would support the improvement bill. People about Chicago wanted the canal work continued and to get the help of the improvement people, they were willing to support that measure. Then there were the counties which would not be benefited from either the railroads or the canal. These were to have $200,000 to be divided among them according to their population. The agreement being that this sum should be used to improve their dirt roads and to build bridges. Finally there were the "financiers" that must be placated. Out of all these complications, by the swapping of votes, and the free use of Uncle Ebenezer Capps' place of business, the bills all passed.

Vandalia, Ill., February 28, 1837.

Col. Dawson	To E. Capps	Dr.
To 81 bottles of Champaigne at $2.00 each		$162.00
To Drinks		6.00
To 32 lbs. Almonds		8.00
To 14 lbs. Raisins		10.00
To Cigars		10.00
To Oysters		10.00
To Apples		3.00
To Eatables		12.00
To Breakage		2.00
To Sundries		.50
		$223.50

Received pay of N. W. Edwards, March 4th.

E. CAPP.

LONG NINE

By the apportionment law which was passed at the special session in December, 1835, based upon the census of Illinois taken in the summer of that year, Sangamon County was entitled to two senators and seven representatives in the Legislature. And although the whigs and democrats were pretty evenly divided in Illinois the entire delegation from Sangamon was whigs. But none of the measures which we have discussed involved the question of politics. Questions were therefore settled on their merits as the legislators saw them. The members of the Legislature from Springfield were as follows:

Senator Job Fletcher	Senator Archer G. Herndon
Rep. Abraham Lincoln	Rep. W. F. Elkin
Rep. Ninian W. Edwords	Rep. Robert L. Wilson
Rep. John Dawson	Rep. Andrew McCormick

Representative Dan Stone

These men were known as the Long Nine because their combined heights were fifty-four feet, an average of six feet to a man. In weight they averaged over 200 pounds. "We were not only noted for our number and length, but for our combined influence. All the bad or objectional laws passed at that session of the Legislature and for many years afterwards were chargeable to the management and influence of the "Long Nine." (R. L. Wilson.)

The "Long Nine" had been instructed by a mass meeting of the citizens of Sangamon County to vote "for a general system of internal improvements," and in addition to bring home the capital of the state. It was therefore the main purpose of the Long Nine so to vote on other measures in such a way as to secure the most help when the time should arrive to select a location of the capital. Alton had at a previous time been favored as the location of the capital when the twenty years' time was up in Vandalia. But friends of Alton were now turning their attention toward making that city a great commercial center; they were therefore willing to exchange the chances of securing the capital for the opportunity to make Alton a great railroad center. So, if you will examine the scheme, you will find that Alton is the terminal of three of the proposed railroads.

When the smoke of the battle cleared away it was found that the improvement scheme had carried, increased expenditures for the canal were authorizd, the counties not touched by railroads and river improvement, were given a bit of sop, the capital was moved to Springfield, and the banks were authorized to increase their capital. The vote on moving the capital was as follows, the first, second, third, and fourth ballots are shown:

BALLOTS

Place	1st	2d	3d	4th
Springfield	35	43	53	73
Jacksonville	14	15	9	1
Vandalia	16	15	16	15
Peoria	16	12	11	6
Alton	15	16	14	6
Illiopolis	--	10	3	--
Scattering	25	7	15	7
Total vote	121	118	121	108

Springfield was therefore declared the capital of the state after the twenty-year period had expired which would occur in 1840.

It must not be thought that the bill as reported by the committee on Internal Improvement had no opposition in the two houses. There was no little effort made to cut down the sum total of appropriations, but the opposition was not organized and it appears that each time an effort was made to secure the adoption of a sane procedure it resulted in an increase in the appropriations. The bill providing for the improvements was passed. It came before the council for revision, consisting of the governor and the state supreme judges. They vetoed the measure and returned it to the House of Representatives where it originated. Here it was quickly passed over the council's veto.

Fund Commissioners

The most pressing need now that the improvement bill had become a law was the money with which to construct these public works. A board of fund commissioners was created consisting of three persons whose business it was to make all contracts, and negotiate all loans authorized by the Legislature on the faith and credit of the state for objects of internal improvements on the best and most favorable terms. It was provided in the law also that these fund commissioners should "be practical and experienced financiers." These men were to go out into the financial markets of the world and place $10,000,000 or $12,000,000 of bonds. They were almost a law unto themselves as to the issuing of bonds and stock and should receive, manage, and care for all moneys which should be received from said bonds, etc.

The fund commissioners selected by the joint session of the Legislature were Charles Oakley, M. M. Rawlings, and Thomas Mather. These "financial experts" were to receive a per diem of $5.00. To unify, in some measure, the vast enterprises of canal building, railroad construction, and river improvement another board was created to be known as the "Board of Commissioners of Public Works." This board was to be made up of seven members—one from each judicial district. The members were to be elected by the joint vote of the two houses of the General Assembly. They were authorized to locate and to construct the public works provided for in the improvement act. These fund commissioners and the engineers who should be employed in locating and constructing these public works were under oath not to reveal any secrets that would in any way be of advantage to speculators in lands, and all vacant lands lying within five miles of any route of a railroad or to other public improvement should be entered in the name of the state and held to be resold by the state at whatever advanced price the lands might bring.

CHAPTER XII

COLLAPSE OF THE INTERNAL IMPROVEMENT SYSTEM.

SOME DETAILS—THE NORTHERN CROSS—THE FUND COMMISSIONERS—THE LAST MESSAGE—GOVERNOR CARLIN—MORE APPROPRIATIONS—THE BALANCE SHEET—SPECIAL SESSION—THE LOST INTEREST—NORTHERN CROSS—ELECTION—THE DEBT—THE WAY OUT—THE BANKS—SUSPENSION OF SPECIE PAYMENT

There are two very important factors in the prosecution of the internal improvement plans. These were the board of fund commissioners and the commissioners of public works. In the log rolling which took place before the improvement bill could pass, there was a modification of the original bill, which provided that the Illinois and Michigan Canal should be placed under the control of the new commissioners of public works. The work on the canal had just begun and considerable money had been appropriated for its prosecution. The canal work was now taken out of the hands of the canal commissioners and was placed with other forms of internal improvements under the control of the commissioners of public works. This board of public works was made up of the following gentlemen: Murray McConnell, William Kinney, Elijah Willard, Milton K. Alexander, Joel Wright, James W. Stephenson, and Ebenezer Peck.

SOME DETAILS

These fund commissioners were elected by the joint vote of the two Houses in the Legislature. At that time there were seven judicial districts in the state and the law provided that one commissioner should be elected from each judicial circuit. Before the Legislature got through with the details for the prosecution of the work it provided that the work on the railroads should begin simultaneously at the termini of each road, and at the crossing of all the navigable rivers and proceed from these points. There were nine roads and that would make eighteen starting places. Then there were five navigable rivers to cross that would make ten more centers of construction. Again work should start from each important town and proceed in opposite directions. There were at least eighteen important towns through which the proposed roads should run. This would make thirty-six additional centers of construction—total sixty-four.

The seven commissioners would have on an average nine construction centers to oversee.

Of course a good deal of this was on paper and never did have a counterpart in reality. But the public mind was wrought to a very high pitch and great expectations were fondly hoped to be realized. The dear people remembered the beautiful words of the governor in 1835 when he spoke of railroads and canals as "bearing with seeming triumph the rich production of the interior to the lakes, rivers, and ocean, almost annihilating time, burthen, and space." Governor Ford in his "History of Illinois" says that so great a number of public offices were created to carry on this improvement system that it was doubtful in the minds of many people if enough competent men could be found in Illinois to fill all these places. Two efforts were made by the Legislature to fill the seven places on the board of public works by electing the entire body of seven from the membership of the Legislature, though this was in direct opposition to the law creating the improvement system.

No surveys had ever been made for any one of the eight railroads. The distance from town to town along any proposed road was not known, nor the length of any road from one end to the other. No competent engineer had ever calculated the cost of any of these roads. The whole proposition was based on guess work. The commissioners of public works were very busy. Each one had over-sight of the work in his judicial circuit. They may have been good men, but what could they have known about the kind of work they were constructing?

THE NORTHERN CROSS

The law provided that the work might be let out by contract and much of it was done in this way. The Northern Cross Railroad—the one running from Quincy by way of Rushville, Meredosia, Jacksonville, Springfield, Decatur, Danville and to the Indiana line, was ordered to be constructed at once. The work began over the state in many different places, but that from Meredosia to Springfield—a part of the Great Northern Cross—was finally completed.

THE FUND COMMISSIONERS

The law putting this great system into operation also, as has been said, provided for a "fund commission." It was the business of this commission to provide the money with which the work was to be carried on—a sort of committee of ways and means. This board, as has been stated, was composed of Thomas Mathers, M. M. Rawlings, and Charles Oakley. These three men left for New York in July, 1837, to negotiate loans for the use of the commissioners of public works. It might be observed that

From Illinois Blue Book

FISH AND GAME PRESERVES

(1) Bass hatchery at Carlyle. (2) Spawning grounds at Carlyle. (3) State Hatchery, Yorkville. (4) Pheasant breeding pens, State Game Farm, Yorkville.

things were proceeding pretty rapidly for the law was passed February 27, 1837, and the fund commissioners were actively at work selling bonds by July of that year.

The commissioners proceeded to New York City, where they offered the state bonds. "They found the credit of Illinois to be rated as first class and notwithstanding recent bank suspensions and consequent depression of the money market, they succeeded before the final crash in selling $4,869,000 worth of bonds at par; a $100,000 worth at 5 per cent premium, and other amounts at other small rates above par.

But it turned out that much of the business of selling bonds had a very unbusiness-like phase to it. Large quantities of these bonds were sold on the instalment plan of payment, and out of many thousands of dollars' worth of bonds little or no money was ever received. But some money was gathered in by the fund commissioners and with it the work was begun and proceeded steadily and rapidly. In May, 1837, work on the Great Northern Cross road began. The work was later begun on other parts of the proposed roads. By the end of 1838, the commission of public works had expended nearly a million dollars on railroads, more than a hundred thousand on wagon roads, and about twenty-five thousand on rivers—a total of $1,079,793. When Governor Duncan came in as governor in December, 1834, the state debt was $100,000, which was the Wiggins loan and $117,276 which was the amount the state had borrowed from the school fund. At the close of Duncan's term in December, 1838, the state owed:

Bonds exchanged for bank stock	$2,665,000
Bonds issued for internal improvement	2,204,000
Bonds issued for construction of canal	1,000,000
Borrowed from school and seminary fund	719,784
Wiggins loan	100,000
Total debt	$6,688,784

The campaign for governor in the summer of 1838 was an interesting contest. The democrats as early as December, 1837, had nominated Col. James W. Stephenson for governor, while the whigs put forward Cyrus Edwards for that honor. In the early part of 1838 a disquieting rumor spread that Colonel Stephenson had been found to be very irregular in his accounts while receiver of public moneys for the sale of public lands. His friends prevailed upon Colonel Stephenson to withdraw from the race, and a convention was held at Vandalia in June, 1838, when Thomas Carlin was named as the head man on the state ticket for the election in August. Mr. Carlin had for several years been identified with the development of the west central part of the state—first in Greene County and then in Adams. He had been a receiver of public moneys in the land office and was well and favorably known. Cyrus Edwards, the whig candidate, was a brother of Ninian W. Edwards, a former governor and United States senator. He lived at Edwardsville and represented southern interests. He had served in the Legislature and in the Black Hawk war and was a lawyer of considerable prominence. Though Mr. Edwards failed of election the Legislature was whig in both branches.

When the Legislature met in December, 1838, the retiring governor delivered to that body his last message. Governor Duncan had done his best to prevent the Legislature from enacting the improvement measures. In his first message he suggested that such large enterprises as building railroads and digging canals should be left to the genius and capital of private persons or corporations. He appealed to the legislators who were now entering on their terms of office to call a halt in these vast enterprises. He prophesied all the evils that did result from the improvement schemes. He urged the Legislature to abandon the improvement schemes in such a way as not to do serious harm to the interests of the state. He said: "Experience has now sufficiently shown that all my objections to it must in time be fully realized. That there should have been many mistakes committed, and much waste of public money in conducting a system of internal improvements upon so large a scale, in a country almost entirely destitute of skill and experience in such works was to be expected. But I confess they have occurred to an extent never anticipated by myself—and whether by mistake or design it is very manifest that large sums have been squandered on objects of little or no general utility, and in some cases to be a detriment of the public interest. The want of economy and the deleterious effects of such a system owned, controlled, and carried on by the state, are great and insurmountable objections to it, but, in my opinion, not so great as the powers it confers on the state government, through its numerous officers and dependents to influence elections."

Governor Carlin

Three days after Governor Duncan had delivered this farewell message to the Legislature, Governor-elect Carlin appeared before the same joint session and delivered his inaugural message. His message was in marked contrast with the one delivered by Governor Duncan a few days before. His message was supposed to have been an effort to justify the action of his party in putting the scheme in operation. But many of Carlin's friends were greatly disappointed at finding their choice for governor heartily in sympathy with the chaos with which he was surrounded. He said: "The signal success which has attended our sister states in their extensive system of internal improvements can leave no doubt of the wise policy and utility of such works." He commented on the effort of the public spirited citizens to develop the natural and hidden resources of the country. He favored the plan of state construction and state ownership rather than the plan of private or cooperative control. "Under the present plan of proceeding near two million of dollars have been expended, and whatever diversity of opinion may now exist as to the expediency of the system as originally projected, all must admit that the character and credit of the state forbid its abandonment."

One thing that made it difficult to abandon the improvement system was the fact that many members in the present Legislature enthusiastically supported the plans originally, and they could not now muster the moral courage to turn their backs upon their own schemes at this time. Instead of abandoning any part of the scheme, the Legislature showed its faith by its works and appropriations were made for additional items to the previous plans. Among these were—$50,000 for the improvement of Rock River; $150,000 for the Little Wabash; $20,000 for the Big Muddy; $20,000 for the Embarrass; $10,000 for a road from Cahokia Creek to Kaskaskia; $100,000 to construct a railroad from Rushville, Schuyler County, to Erie on the Illinois River; and $20,000 to be expended on the Western Mail Route. Other small appropriations were made for other items, the whole amounting to nearly a million dollars. One lone member of the Legislature from the Wabash country introduced a bill for "An act to incorporate a company to build a railroad from Albion to Grayville." The bill was respectfully referred to the committee on internal improvements, whose chairman was one Edward Smith of Wabash County. After mature deliberations the committee through its chairman reported to the House that "In the judgment of the committee it is inexpedient for the Legislature to authorize corporations, or individuals, to construct railroads or canals calculated to come in competition with similar works now in course of construction under the state system of internal improvements."

One interesting proposition was brought forward, and when we know its author we hesitate to believe it was brought forward in dead earnest. Mr. Lincoln offered a resolution that the State of Illinois propose to the general government to purchase all the unsold land in Illinois, estimated at about 20,000,000 acres, at twenty-five cents an acre, "pledging the faith of the state to carry the proposal into effect if accepted by the general government."

More Appropriations

The Legislature, as has been said, was whig in each branch. It was difficult at all times to keep out of consideration national questions, and so we are not surprised to find that the Legislature resolved in favor of the rechartering of the United States Bank. Other questions of national importance received attention from the Legislature. But the law makers soon returned to their problems closer home. An act was passed directing the governor to negotiate a further loan of $4,000,000 for the prosecution of the Illinois and Michigan Canal.

The governor was not favorably impressed with the success of the fund commissioners in securing money for the work of railroad building and river improvement. In January, 1839, the Legislature directed the the fund commissioners to loan the canal commissioners $300,000 and also passed a law authorizing the four million loan mentioned above. To negotiate this loan the governor asked Ex-Gov. John Reynolds to accept the position of special commissioner. Mr. Reynolds was not willing to undertake so important a duty without aid, and at his suggestion, the governor appointed United States Senator Richard M. Young to cooperate with Ex-Governor Reynolds in the sale of these four million dollars worth of bonds.

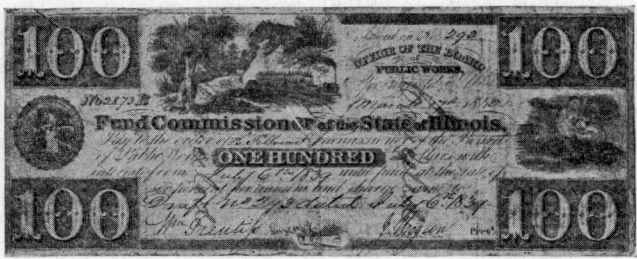

A ONE HUNDRED DOLLAR CANAL SCRIP BILL

Governor Reynolds went east in the early part of the summer of 1839. In Philadelphia he found General Rawlings and Colonel Oakley, fund commissioners, who were marketing the improvement bonds. The summer of 1839 was spent in Philadelphia and New York. Mr. Reynolds made such unbusinesslike contracts in the sale of the bonds that little good came from the returns of his sales. The eastern money market was at a low ebb and Governor Reynolds decided to proceed to Europe and try to interest the London and Paris money kings. Judge Young, who was serving in Congress and could not accompany Reynolds at that time, later joined him in London. The fund commissioners also visited the money centers of the old world. Reynolds put in quite a portion of the summer in "seeing Europe" and succeeded in selling a million dollars worth of bonds to Wright and Company of London, who advanced something like $150,000. The balance was never paid, as the firm went into bankruptcy and the state of Illinois got only a creditor's proportionate share of their resources.

The Balance Sheet

In December, 1839, the state's ledger showed the following indebtedness:

Bonds sold to the state bank for stock in the bank	$2,665,000
Bonds sold in United States	3,187,000
Bonds sold in London	1,500,000
Canal bonds sold	3,400,000
State house bonds	128,000
Borrowed from school fund	750,000
Due banks for auditors' warrants	142,550
Due to contractors	1,458,000
Total indebtedness	$13,230,550

The work of grading, cuts, and fills had proceeded since the summer of 1837. For many years the grades and cuts might be seen here and there. The work of railroad building in 1837-8-9 was not different from what it is today except in the use of steam power and complicated machinery. There were camps and all their accompaniments. The work lacked efficient oversight. There were no men in the West who had had any experience in such constructive enterprises.

By the beginning of 1840 it was seen that no more loans could be made as there was general financial distress everywhere. The second United States Bank had been refused another lease of life and had closed its doors in 1836. The financial panic of 1837 had swept the country. Irresponsible banks were springing up over the country whose issue was soon a drug on the market. Under these conditions a million dollar loan was made in London at a discount of 15 per cent. The proceeds of this sale were applied to the payment of contractors—in part. Contractors were unwilling to continue to work when pay was so uncertain. In the winter of 1839-40, the governor became alarmed at the growing debt and the rapidly depreciating value of the state's bonds. The people as a whole were not informed as to the real situation, but where the secrets of the real situation became known, discontent and severe criticism prevailed. The governor, who so easily counteracted the sober advice of Governor Duncan in his final message, and started the new Legislature of 1838-9 upon a road of reckless expenditures, had by the winter of 1839-40 a change of heart. Public meetings were held in several counties at which the real situation was revealed. The governor became more and more impressed with the critical situation in which public affairs were at that time and with the idea that the Legislature might see some way out of the financial bogs, he called the Legislature in special session to meet in Springfield, the new capital city. The new capital contained 1,400 people. There were no public buildings in

Springfield and the Senate met in the Methodist Church, the House met in the Second Presbyterian Church, and the Supreme Court occupied the Protestant Episcopal Church.

SPECIAL SESSION

When this special session convened September 9, 1839, it listened to the governor's message. He gave the Legislature his reasons for calling that body together. He frankly admitted that formerly he had been heartily in favor of internal improvements but that he was opposed to the far reaching extent to which the work had been carried. He said, "the ruinous policy of simultaneously commencing all the works and constructing them in detached parcels was alike a variance with the principles of sound economy, destructive to the interests of the state, and to the system in all its parts." He was in favor of turning the attention of the state to a few sections of the work and of finishing such portions as would be most likely to produce a revenue for the state.

The idea of abandoning the system was not pleasing to many individuals, but the contest for and against continuing the system did not produce party divisions. Those who wished to continue the system said if the construction work were abandoned the state would have nothing to show for the expenditure of millions of dollars. That was the real truth, and it came out of the foolish "simultaneous" policy of construction. If all the money which had been paid for labor and material on the several items of railroads, rivers, and wagon roads, had been expended on one or two particular items, they could have been completed and might have been earning an income.

It was urged by some that now was the time to call a halt and to gather all the resources and apply them to the completion of the Northern Cross Road and abandon the work on the other roads. But this moderate plan was not acceptable and after much discussion the whole system was virtually abandoned. An act provided for the payment of interest on bonds held by John Wright in London, and in order to pay the interest due in this country five thousand dollars were borrowed at home. Another act provided for the abolition of the board of fund commissioners and the board of public works. One fund commissioner was authorized to collect all moneys due the state, to withdraw all bonds from the market, and to take charge of all the material property belonging to the state. The unsold bonds were ordered collected and burned. A new board of public works was authorized to take charge of unfinished work and to settle with contractors. No employees were to be retained any longer than was really necessary to adjust all unfinished matters and to care properly for the property of the state.

THE LAST INTEREST

As early as 1839 it began to be talked that the state was not morally obliged to pay interest on only the actual cash received for the bonds. If bonds sold for $75 on the hundred then the state was obliged to pay interest on the $75 and not on the face of the bond. There were others who were intimating that the entire debt should be repudiated. In July, 1841, the state paid the interest due at that time. But this was the last interest the state paid in the closing years of the collapse. Ford says from this date forward the fair name of Illinois as well as that of other western states was a stench in the nostrils of the civilized world. The people in the eastern states who were looking for a place to buy land and settle permanently, shunned Illinois as they would a pestilence. He further says that this debacle had its effects upon the character of the people. They felt that if the state could treat its obligations as it was doing, that individuals might go and do likewise. There was such a dread of high taxes and of further burdens which might be imposed that there was a great desire to sell out and leave the state.

The Illinois and Michigan Canal, while an integral part of the improvement system, was not involved in the collapse of the system of railroad building and river improvement. The general plan usually provided for a separate fund commissioner for the canal from those who acted for the other forms of improvement.

CANAL COMMISSIONER

General Thornton was able to sell canal bonds in London at fifteen per cent below par. The proceeds, 85 cents on the dollar, was accepted by the canal contractors as full payment on the dollar. Bonds of the value of $1,000,000 were thus disposed of in 1840.

Following the final payment of interest in July, 1841, there was general despondency among the people. To add to their distress, the state bank ceased in 1842 to redeem its notes in gold and silver. The governor, the treasurer, and the auditor all sent out word that no more state bank bills would be received in payment of taxes. The treasury was empty and there was a general stagnation in business. Repudiation of the debts of the state was freely and pretty generally discussed.

NORTHERN CROSS

This road as first laid out had Quincy and the state line east of Danville as the termini. It passed through Meredosia, Jacksonville, Springfield, Decatur, and Danville. This seemed to be the road that was favored by nearly every one. Considerable work had been done on it before the system showed signs of collapse. When it came to the final test as to whether the system should be continued or dropped and it was decided to abandon the whole system there was a saving clause which provided that the Northern Cross should be finished from Meredosia, on the Illinois River, to Springfield via Jacksonville. The road was completed between Jacksonville and Springfield, but the treasury was empty and all sale of bonds was stopped. In this condition it appeared that the road could not be completed. In this case those in authority loaned $100,000 from the canal fund to the work of the Northern Cross. In this way the road was finished from Meredosia to Springfield, a distance of sixty miles or more.

The road was graded as we see it today. Cross ties were 5 by 8 inches laid flatwise. The rails were made of stringers of wood 5 by 6 inches. The rails were fastened to the cross ties by wooden pins filling bored holes one and a half inches in diameter. A flat strap of iron of the thickness of a wagon tire was laid on the longitudinal rails and fastened with iron rails. It is said that the New York Central was thus equipped as late af 1845.

An engine was bought and brought up the Mississippi and thence up the Illinois to the small Village of Meridosia. Several days were spent in the effort to get the engine from the boat to the railroad with no success. An incline was built from the end of the track to the boat and the engine headed up the incline. A sawmill man had been watching the futile efforts of the people to land the engine. He offered for a certain consideration to place the engine on the tracks. The contract was closed. He hitched eight or ten yoke of oxen to the engine and with "Buck and Bright" to lead the way these oxen walked up the incline with great ease.

The heavy weight of engine and cars on the straps of iron upon the wooden rails tended to work loose the nails that held the strips to the rails. The heavy weight also had a tendency to curl the rail up just behind the truck wheels. These snake heads would often push their way through the floor of the passenger coach and endangered life and limb—travelers thus lost their lives. It is told of this engine that it jumped the track at one time and the management having no means of replacing the engine, proceeded to equip the road with mules as motive power. It has been estimated that the road from Meredosia to Springfield cost a million dollars. The state sold the road later for $100,000 and accepted state bonds as pay, which were probably below par very considerably.

Election

Governor Carlin had a strenuous term. He came into office at a time when thoughtful people were halting between two opinions. Governor Carlin's experience in the world of big business had been limited. He had lived a while in Kentucky, and then in

Missouri, and later in Illinois. He had taken an active part in the War of 1812, and had commanded a spy battalion in the Black Hawk war. But he was probably unacquainted, through inexperience, with the problems which fell to his lot as governor to solve. The improvement system grew to such proportions that only the most skilled economists could have seen it from all its angles. Then there were the financial problems which would have baffled a Hamilton or a Gallatin. Mr. Carlin was rather unyielding in his opinions, but with the best of motives. He was by instincts and training suited to the quiet orderly life of the agriculturist. While not highly educated, he was a man of strong common sense, high moral standard, great firmness of character, and unfailing courage. Mr. Carlin had, early in his term, championed the improvement system, at a time when wise counsel advised its discontinuance, but as time went on he discovered the "impending ruin and dishonor" which was sure to come to the state if a radical change in policy were not adopted. Such a change was adopted, and the last half of Governor Carlin's term was devoted to the gathering up of odds and ends of abandoned enterprise of magnificent proportions.

The days of organized politics had appeared with the coming of Andrew Jackson. Political conventions, and party loyalty secured the nominations and elections of men to office, often without regard to fitness of the candidate and against the best judgment of the party followers.

The parties usually took kindly to long campaigns. There was only one well defined and well organized political party in Illinois until 1840. But men were for Jackson or against him. Those for Jackson regarded themselves as democrats while those opposed to Jackson were at least anti-Jackson if not always called whigs. Joseph Duncan had returned from Congress in 1834 to occupy the governor's chair as an anti-Jackson man though not as a whig.

The democrats in convention assembled, in December, 1841, nominated for governor Hon. Adam W. Snyder of St. Clair County. While in the early spring of 1842 the whigs put forward for governor Ex-Gov. Joseph Duncan. Mr. Snyder had had an honorable career from apprentice-boy to congressman. He had borne a responsible part in the Black Hawk war and had served his constituency to their entire satisfaction in the National Congress. As the canvass proceeded some vexing matters began to arise. Among these was the part Mr. Snyder had played, while a member of the Legislature, in the granting of a charter to the city of Nauvoo. But just as the canvass began to assume interesting stages, Mr. Snyder sickened and died. But the democrats were not cast down. The executive officers of the party, the state central committee, met in Springfield June 7th, 1842, and nominated Judge Thomas Ford of the Supreme Court.

HISTORY OF ILLINOIS

The canvass was continued and at the election in August, Ford was elected by a majority of more than 8,000.

THE DEBT

Mr. Ford was inaugurated in December, 1842. He faced the greatest task of any governor of Illinois, either before or since. He was equal to the task that was before him. Of course, the absorbing matter was the wreck of the improvement system. Governor Ford says in his history: "The domestic treasury of the state was indebted for the ordinary expenses of the government to the amount of about $313,000. Auditors' warrants on the treasury were selling at 50 per cent. discount, and there was no money in the treasury whatever; not even enough to pay postage on letters. The annual revenues applicable to the payment of ordinary expenses amounted to $130,000. The treasury was bankrupt; the revenues were insufficient; the people were unable and unwilling to pay high taxes; and the state had borrowed itself out of all credit; a debt of $10,000,000 (more correctly, $15,657,950) had been contracted for the canal, railroads, and other purposes. The currency of the state had been annihilated; there was not over $200,000 or $300,000 in good money in the pockets of the whole people, which occasioned a general inability to pay taxes. The whole people were indebted to the merchants, nearly all of whom were indebted to the banks or foreign merchants; and the banks owed everybody, and none were able to pay.

To many persons it seemed impossible to devise any system of policy, out of this jumble and chaos of confusion, which would relieve the state. Everyone had his plan, and the confusion of counsels among prominent men was equalled only by the confusion of public affairs."

Moses History of Illinois gives a summary of the state's indebtedness and it is inserted here to show just the nature of the indebtedness.

To banks for stock	$2,665,000
Internal Improvements (bonds)	6,014,749
Canal Debt (bonds)	4,504,160
Statehouse (at Springfield)	121,000
School, College, and Seminary fund, borrowed by the state	808,084
Due banks (borrowed)	664,188
Interest due Jan. 1, 1843	880,769
Total debt due Jan. 1, 1843	$15,657,950

In his message to the Legislature Governor Ford said there were two good reasons why there had been no increase in migrations to Illinois for the past few years. One was the fear the people of other states had of exhorbitant taxes to which they might be subject if they came to Illinois to settle. The other the contempt that people abroad had for the lack of ability to steer the ship of state found in the public men of Illinois, and the fear that the state would adopt repudiation. Governor Ford was very anxious that the state might be freed of these two loads. He said: "Let it be known in the first place that no oppressive and exterminating taxation is to be resorted to; in the second, we must convince our creditors and the world that the disgrace of repudiation is not countenanced among us—that we are honest and mean to pay as soon as we are able."

The members of the Legislature were opposed to taxation, at least to the amount that would be necessary to meet the state's interest even. They were just as much opposed to repudiation. There were but two or three candidates who offered for the Legislature in the summer of 1842 who publicly favored repudiation and they were defeated. There were, however, many outspoken repudiationists among the soap box orators. The governor was hostile to any plans looking toward repudiation. He recommended to the Legislature that in some appropriate way the creditors of the state should be assured that in due time the debt would be paid in full, and that there was no thought of those in charge of the government of giving any encouragement to the movement, if there were any, of repudiation. The Legislature was willing to comply with the governor's request. To assume further the creditors, an enumeration of the state's resources was made. The governor passing to the banks recommended that they should be required to resume specie payment or suffer the possibility of having their charters annulled. He further advised that the banks should surrender the amount of the state's bonds which the banks held while the state would surrender the same amount of the bank's stocks.

The state's financial situation has been shown on a preceding page. The current deficit in the states expense account was $30,000 annually and the accumulated deficit was $313,000. Auditor's warrants were 50 cents on the dollar and state bonds were 14 cents on the dollar. Resolutions were passed by the Legislature which were intended to acknowledge the states moral obligations to pay the debt in full, but at the same time to assure the creditors that there was not the possibility of paying in the immediate future.

The state's resources were enumerated as 42,000 acres of land purchased under the improvement system; 210,000 acres of land given the state by Congress in 1841; 230,467 acres of canal lands; 3,491 town lots; the canals value placed at several millions of dollars; a large amount of real value in the unfinished railroads; a large quantity of railroad iron; and stock in the banks. Some one suggested that this visible property be turned over to the creditors of the state for enough money with which to finish the canal. This was estimated as high as $4,000,000. The heavy capitalists who were holding most of the state's debt would not enter into such an unbusinesslike agreement, as it would set a precedent which would greatly embarrass them in many other states.

The Way Out

Mr. Ford says that in the summer of 1842, after all sorts of schemes had been suggested for meeting the embarrassing situation in which the state found itself, a Mr. Justin Butterfield, a lawyer of Chicago, in a conference with a Mr. Bronson, a wealthy capitalist of New York and a land holder in Northern Illinois, came to an understanding which eventually enabled Illinois to begin to see daylight through the darkness of a long night. The estimate was $4,000,000 as the amount necessary to complete the canal if the plan was to have what they called a deep cut or deep level, but if the plan was changed to a high level cut, it was estimated that less than half that amount only would be needed.

In this informal conference between Mr. Butterfield and Mr. Bronson, a proposition was suggested by Mr. Butterfield that was finally worked out in detail and passed by the Legislature. The plan in general was as follows: The capitalists who already were heavy holders of the state's canal bonds were to advance enough cash to finish the canal, estimated at $1,600,000. In return the state was to convey all the canal property in trust, to secure the new loan as well as for the payment of the whole canal debt. The state further obligated itself to raise by taxation a certain moderate sum which should be used in the discharge of the state's whole indebtedness. It was further provided that the capitalists who were already holding the state's bonds should all have the privilege of contributing to the new loan of $1,600,000, but if any should refuse to do so, they should not be regarded as preferred creditors, and those who would furnish the amount needed should have a lien on the canal, its lands, and its income until the $1,600,000 and the interest should be paid.

The bond holders thought well of the Butterfield plan, but there were questions which arose and there was delay in closing the deal. Two years later, a supplementary act was passed which cleared away the objections and the money was advanced for the completion of the canal. Another measure in the session of 1844-5 provided for one mill to be added to the 2 mill tax making a 3 mill tax which should constitute a permanent fund for the payment of the interest on the public debt.

The law of 1845 providing for this last loan was also slow of execution and the loan was not completed till June, 1845, and work did not begin in earnest till September, 1845. Promises were made that the canal would be in operation by July 4, 1847, but in this the people were disappointed. Finally in the spring of 1848 the canal was completed and turned over by the contractors. This was really a great project for a young state successfully to accomplish. It had engaged the public mind for nearly a half a century and had been twelve years in process of building.

The total cost up to the time the canal became an asset has been figured to have been $6,557,681. This waterway finished at so enormous a cost, has had a powerful effect upon the development of the middle and northern third of the state. This public enterprise occupied the attention of public men for many years and has been a large factor in the political affairs of the state. The importance of canals has been over shadowed by that of railroads and it is doubtful if ever canals and rivers will occupy so important a place in the country's development as they did in the last century.

The Banks

It will be recalled that the Illinois State Bank which was chartered in 1821 had a limited existence, the charter expiring in 1831. In 1824 the old Shawneetown bank, chartered in 1816, closed its doors. When the Illinois State Bank's charter expired in 1831 there was a low ebb in the money matters in Illinois. It was to relieve the local situation in Illinois that Governor Duncan recommended the chartering of a new state bank. The charter granted to the Shawneetown Bank in 1816 was to run for twenty years, but this bank ceased to function in 1824. It was therefore Governor Duncan's plan to renew the Shawneetown institution. There was quite a good deal of interest in the subject of banking between 1831 when the Illinois State Bank closed its doors and 1834 when Governor Duncan recommended a new bank for Illinois. But there was a decided objection to the creating of new banks if the state was to assume the responsibility for their management. It was known that Jackson was opposed to the United State Bank and in 1832 it failed to rechartering. The knowledge that the United States bank would close its doors in 1836, greatly encouraged many people in the belief that state banks or at least private banking corporations would do well in Illinois.

The Legislature which met in December, 1834, was apparently easily persuaded to comply with the governor's idea as to the value of banks. A State Bank was chartered with a capital of $1,500,000. It was a private corporation, and the state assumed no responsibility for the conduct of the bank. There was no trouble to secure subscribers for the stock. The bank was established at Springfield with branches at Danville, Quincy, Belleville, and Mt. Carmel. At the same time the old bank at Shawneetown which was originally chartered in 1816 or 1817 and whose charter was a run twenty years, was revived and a new charter granted with a capital of $300,000. This Shawneetown bank had not done any business for twelve years. The first of the two banks mentioned above was called the State Bank and its principal office was at Springfield. The second one was known as the Bank of Illinois with its office at Shawneetown. Both were private corporations.

In March, 1837, the capital of the State Bank was increased to $3,500,000, and the capital of the Bank of Illinois was increased to $1,700,000. The law provided that the State of Illinois might become a stockholder in either or both banks. At the time that the capitals of the two banks were increased a law provided that the banks should have sixty days in which to redeem their notes. Another law provided that the issue of these banks should be received in payment of all forms of taxes or debts due the state. Their charters provided that if the banks should refuse for a longer period than sixty days to redeem their issue, the charters would be forfeited and the banks should go into liquidation.

Suspension of Specie Payment

In May, 1837, the banks suspended specie payment. The banks in Illinois were not made depositories of the surplus funds received from the sale of public lands. And by reason of Jackson's specie circular no money was received for land but gold and silver. Land purchasers would gather up the notes of the banks and ask the banks to redeem them, and then with the gold and silver buy government lands. The gold and silver received by the land agents was shipped out of Illinois; and the banks were soon unable to meet the demands upon their gold and silver reserve and so suspension of specie payment resulted.

A special session of the Legislature was called for July 10, 1837. At this special session the Legislature legalized the suspension of specie payment. There now arose a very marked division between the democrats and what will soon be the whigs over the banks. The banks had been projected by the democrats as they were in a majority in both the Senate and House. But when it came to organize them the banks fell into the hands of the whigs. The whigs seemed to hav control of the money in the state. The suspension of specie payments was legalized for only a certain time.

The limitation of business by the banks annoyed the people and they began to discuss the banking system. But for nearly two years there was little attention given to the banks except an unorganized campaign of words. In the fall of 1839, the opposition to the banks was revived. The governor in his message to the Legislature took a strong stand against the banks.

Out of his stand against them a legislative investigation followed, and many irregularities were brought to light. Among these was the help of the bank in an effort to build up Alton as a rival of St. Louis. It appears that certain interests about Alton had borrowed nearly a million dollars to corner the product of the lead mines in the northwest corner of Illinois. A second suspension of specie payment was authorized in 1839. This was to last till the end of that General Assembly and a question arose as to just when that General Assembly ceased. By an adjournment of the special session called to meet ten days before the meeting of the Legislature in regular session in December, 1840, the banks were supposed to have lost their charters. The regular session began in December, 1840, and was apparently kindly disposed toward the State Bank. A new lease of life was granted the bank. The management was more and more questionable and the complaints against it more and more violent. In the early part of the summer of 1842 both whigs and democrats agreed to require the banks to resume specie payment or suffer their charters to be canceled. The stock of the State Bank was 37 cents on the dollar in the early part of 1842, and its bills were at a discount of 15 per cent., and eventually fell to 44 cents on the dollar.

The bank at Shawneetown was holding up fairly well and it was thought by some that even if the State Bank was obliged to surrender its charter, the Shawneetown Bank might be able to pull through, but they were tied up with the internal improvement scheme and if one must close so must the other. On the 24th of February, 1843, an act of the Legislature forced the State Bank into liquidation. On the 3d of March, 1843, the Bank of Illinois, the Shawneetown Bank, also went into liquidation. The act of January 24, 1843, which forced the State Bank into liquidation was "to diminish the state debt and put the State Bank into liquidation."

The act which forced the Bank of Illinois into liquidation provided for the state's taking forcible possession of the bank at Shawneetown by commissioners, and of all the assets of the bank or of any of its branches and of all belongings of whatever kind, for the benefit of the creditors of the said bank. The sheriff and all his people were authorized to assist the commissioners in the discharge of their assigned duties. If any official of the bank or any stockholder should interfere with the duties of the commissioners or with the sheriff or his deputies while they were assisting the commissioners, he should be held to be guilty of a felony and be sentenced to the penitentiary not to exceed ten years. On March 4, 1843, the Bank of Cairo was attacked in the Legislature and its charter canceled.

These acts of the Legislature seemed to be the result of a

species of madness. These banks had been of great service to the state. They were asked to purchase great quantities of the state's bonds and to loan money to the state, and in other ways serve the state. When the two banks went into liquidation in 1843 their bills were worth 50 cents on the dollar.

Both of these liquidating acts provided that the governor should exchange bank stock which the state held to the amount of more than three million dollars for bonds that the bank held or could obtain, and thus the state's debt was reduced more than three million dollars.

A statement of resources and liabilities of the Shawneetown Bank made November, 1841, was as follows:

Liabilities—
State capital stock	$1,000,000.00
Individual capital stock	349,240.00
Circulation notes	1,309,996.00
Due U. S. Treasurer	40.00
Unclaimed dividends	1,876.50
Individual deposits	70,708.28
Due other banks	7,497.78
Discounts, etc.	29,259.61
Surplus fund	115,463.35
Branch balance	2,317.59
Total	$2,886,398.51

Resources—
Bills discounted	$1,312,070.11
Bills of Exchange	295,795.47
Suspended debt	101,085.92
Illinois bonds	369,998.68
Illinois Scrip	819.55
Bank and Insurance Stock	11,900.00
Due from other banks	178,472.49
Real Estate	83,336.74
Expenses	7,428.34
Cash (Specie)	422,378.13
Notes of other banks	103,120.00
Total	$2,886,398.51

The Shawneetown Bank advanced to the Commission of Public Works the sum of $200,000. This was advanced at the solicitation of Governor Carlin who promised to deposit with the Shawneetown Bank as security, $500,000 in internal improvement bonds. The money was advanced to the Commissioners of Public Works, but the governor never did deposit the improvement bonds and the $200,000 was a loss to the bank. The Shawneetown Bank corporation erected in 1839-40 a very fine bank building on Main Street. The basement story is entirely above ground while the first floor is above the highest high water mark. It has living rooms above the first floor. It is a noble structure with a massive front whose projecting room is supported by five corrugated Doric columns. The building cost about $80,000. After the bank failed in 1843, the building was sold to Joel A. Matteson for $15,000, who in 1853 started a bank in the building under the "Free Banking" law of Illinois. Later when the National Banking laws were put into operation, the First National Bank was organized and has been doing business there since.

The Cairo Bank did business in Kaskaskia, but was never a very aggressive institution. It was chartered by the Territorial Legislature on the 9th of January, 1818. The title of the charter was "The City and Bank of Cairo." Most of the stockholders were from about Kaskaskia and the 10th section in the charter provided that the banking business should be carried on in Kaskaskia. The bank, as said above, was not very aggressive, at least it was not mixed up in politics and for that reason probably not much is recorded of this bank. But it shared the condemnation which the democratic party in Illinois heaped upon the State Bank and the Bank of Illinois. It has been stated that the charge against the Cairo Bank was that it was flooding the country with its bills, and it was classed with the other two banks named above. A bill was enacted into law March 4, 1843, repealing the act of January 9, 1818, which chartered the Cairo Bank. Thus the Cairo Bank was doomed.

The State Bank and the Bank of Illinois, as corporations, were controlled by the whigs. The democrats as a party were opposed to the banks. When the management of the banks made application to the secretary of the treasury of the United States praying that he would name the banks in Illinois as United States depositories, the secretary refused. He had been informed that the banks were in the hands of the whigs and that if they were selected as Government depositories, that would be a big load for the President's friends to carry in Illinois. The Secretary of the Treasury assigned as his reason for not patronizing the Illinois banks the unfair allotment of stock, the alleged unconstitutionality of the bank, and its refusal to redeem its issue at any one of its branches. The fight thus continued through the years. Every support of the state, in its struggle against the unwisdom of the improvement schemes, and the unpatriotic policy of repudiation, in the form of banks and banking facilities was withdrawn, and the business of the state must be carried on by means of the money of neighboring states' banks.

CHAPTER XIII

WHIGS AND DEMOCRATS

Party Politics—Election of 1824—Party Politics in Illinois—The Irish Vote—Secretary of State—Another Case—Whigs in Convention—Preliminaries—Friendly Debate — Monster Meetings — Log Cabin Campaign — State Central Committee—At Springfield.

When the United States Government, under the constitution, was set in motion in 1789, it fortunately fell into the hands of men whose vision was far reaching. The period of government under the articles of Confederation was a short one, but long enough to demonstrate the weakness of a system based on the idea of a loose federation of sovereign states. The phases of weakness of the articles may be inferred from the preamble to the constitution. "We, the people—a more perfect union—domestic tranquility—the common defense—general welfare—the blessings of liberty—do ordain and establish this constitution. If these desirable ends could have been secured through the articles, there would have been no occasion for the creation of a new Government. The statesmen who believed that the new Government had been brought into existence to compass the ends enumerated in the preamble to the constitution looked upon the constitution as a means to the ends enumerated. The constitution must therefore be interpreted in such a way as would promote and not hinder the accomplishment of the desired ends. Thus far there could be no difference of opinion; there could be no parties; there could be no factions; there could be no politics—at least no party politics.

Party Politics

Party politics arises when men group themselves around certain methods of procedure in the securing of certain ends. "Politics is the theory and practice of obtaining the ends of civil society as perfectly as possible." Politics then is the science and the art of government. The first divergence of opinion as to this science and art arose over whether the constitution should be interpreted literally or whether the principle of implication should hold. It was argued that if we do not follow the specific directions, and should admit the principle of implication, then the danger lies in the probability that each one in authority, for the time being, will hold to the application a different implication. There would thus be nothing permanent in our institutions. On the other hand it was argued that only an all-wise being could foresee the needs of a people and if a people should follow explicit provisions there would arise constantly the need of rewriting the constitution. Therefore constitutions should lay down only fundamental principles and not explicit directions. This argument, if sound, would necessitate a reliance upon implied powers. This was the argument and the practice of the Federalist party which controlled the policy of the Government for the first twelve years of our political life.

But it seemed that the interpretation of the powers of the constitution put forth by the party then called the federalists, was not the interpretation which the friends of a strict construction would have supported. The difference therefore between the federalist, lead by Alexander Hamilton and the republicans who followed Jefferson, was that the federalists were willing to enact such legislation as would in their estimation provide for the common defense and promote the general welfare. The republicans put stress upon the need of following strictly the provisions of the constitution, and thus giving the individual, more and more, the opportunity to participate in Government and secure the guaranties provided for in the bill of rights, the first ten amendments.

The Revolution of 1800 was not a revolt against the policy of government so much as it was a desire to punish individuals for arrogating to themselves the right of the few to administer government to the exclusion of those who did not fall in the class of the "well born." And here the party of opposition, during the reign of the federalists, was disappointed. Only a baker's dozen or so of the thousands of officials who had been installed in office by the federalists were removed by Jefferson. Almost immediately upon coming into office the great leader of the strict construction party, exercised such authority as would have been cautionsly used by the champions of implied powers. The Louisiana Purchase was thought by Mr. Jefferson to be beyond any interpretation of the constitution, and it remained for a federalist chief justice of the Supreme Court to legalize the President's acts by showing that the constitution clothes the chief executive with the treaty making power without at the same time limiting that official as to subject matter. Here was an act to be defended on the implied power theory—provide for the common defense, promote the general welfare.

In 1806, March 29, Jefferson approved "An Act to regulate the laying out and making a road from Cumberland, in the State of Maryland, to the State of Ohio." The act appropriated $30,000 for the preliminary survey. Between 1806, when the first appropriation from the public treasury was made, and 1844 when the last appropriation was made for the National Road, the sum of $6,824,919.33 was appropriated from the public treasury. This in spite of the fact that a strict interpretation of the constitution would not justify the expenditure. In 1816 a high protective duty was enacted and signed by James Madison who was following in the steps of his predecessor. Again in 1816 a United States bank was chartered with a capital stock of $35,000,000. The old Hamilton bank had been declared unconstitutional by the strict constructionists. Thus we see that along three lines of public policy the strict constructionists between the close of the War of 1812 and 1820 had adopted the policy of a protective tariff, internal improvements, and a United States bank.

James Monroe whose claim to the presidency had been championed by Madison and Jefferson became the greatest promulgator of nationalism. He announced the Monroe Doctrine in December, 1823. Between the close of the War of 1812 and the presidential campaign in 1824, there were no great questions upon which there could be a division into political parties. From 1824 to about the close of Jackson's second term of office, personal attachment was the basis of whatever divisions obtained in politics. All the early governors of Illinois were democrats. In the protracted contest over the admission of Missouri into the Union, Senators Edwards and Thomas favored the admission as a slave state while Daniel P. Cook, the Representative in the House, opposed the admission. Cook also opposed the making of Illinois into a slave state.

Election of 1824

The origin of the whigs in Illinois politics may be found in the presidential campaign of 1824. Jackson, Adams, Crawford, and Clay were presidential candidates. John Quincy Adams was not a democrat. His father, John Adams, had been next to Hamilton the most radical of the federalists. John Quincy Adams had served as President Monroe's Secretary of State and is said to have formulated the Monroe Doctrine. In the electoral vote for President in 1824 the four candidates stood—Jackson, 99; Adams, 84; Crawford, 41; Clay, 37. The choice must be made by the House of Representatives from the three highest on the list. Clay was Speaker of the House and could of course exert more or less influence in the choice of the President. Clay and Adams were destined to be identified with the whig party and by their combined interests, John Quincy Adams was chosen President. On the roll call of states, Daniel P. Cook recorded Illinois for John Quincy Adams. Cook did not think of himself as a whig at this time but here the whig party had its small beginning. Clay was made Secretary of State by Mr. Adams and they naturally had common interests.

Andrew Jackson forthwith began his canvass for the nomination and election in 1828. It eventually turned out that Adams was a candidate for reelection. Jackson was endorsed by two or three state Legislatures, but the caucus system was no longer in vogue. Its last function was the nomination of Crawford in 1824. The opposition to Jackson began to gather under the leadership of Clay and they called themselves national republicans, while Jackson's followers were called democrats.

The national republicans held a national party convention in Baltimore in December, 1831, where they nominated Henry Clay for the presidency. Jackson had been nominated by several Legislatures. Tennessee had nominated him as the democratic candidate for the campaign of 1828, as early as 1825. There was nothing for the Democratic Convention, which met in Baltimore in May, 1832, to do except to indorse what a half dozen Legislatures had already done. In addition the convention nominated Van Buren of New York for vice president. This was the first national convention for the democratic party and it was at this convention that the "two-thirds rule" was adopted which is still a marked feature of the national conventions of the democratic party.

Party Politics in Illinois

Party politics had its origin in Illinois during the administration of John Quincy Adams, 1825-1829. In the election of the President by the House of Representatives in the very early part of 1825, Daniel P. Cook, the representative from Illinois, voted for Adams against Jackson. He had publicly promised to support the candidate who had a majority of the votes in Illinois. One Adams elector and two Jackson electors were chosen. But the popular vote stood—Adams, 1,542; Jackson, 1,272; Clay, 1,047; Crawford, 219. Cook probably felt that the popular vote was sufficient authority to warrant his voting for Adams. This of course aroused a strong opposition to Cook, and his political enemies set about to secure his defeat in 1826. They put forward Joseph Duncan who had a brilliant military record in the War of 1812, and had made a good name for himself in the State Senate. Duncan himself took an active part in his own campaign. When the votes were counted Duncan had defeated Cook by a small majority.

Now when we remember that Cook voted for Adams in 1825, and when we also keep in mind that his defeat was attributed to this fact, it would be easy to draw the conclusion that Duncan was a Jackson man and that he would support the President when he took his seat as a congressman. But Duncan was not a very loyal Jackson man. He eventually broke with Jackson over the veto of some appropriations in which he, Duncan, was interested. At the close of the Black Hawk war there were new men before the public. The state was entitled to three congressmen by the census of 1830 and Charles Slade, Zadoc Casey, and Joseph Duncan were elected in the first, second, and third dis-

LAST STATE CAPITOL BUILDING AT VANDALIA

tricts, respectively. They were all put down as good Jackson men.

The division now became known as Jackson men and anti-Jackson men. But before 1840 the Jackson men came to be known as democrats and the anti-Jackson men as whigs. There were, of course, fundamental differences between these two parties, but the alignments were first made upon personal grounds.

The democrats believed in the policy of centering their support on one man as the surest way of securing the adoption and permanence of their political principles. This man, the candidate, embodied those principles since the convention was the central exchange of instructions formulated by the people in their local conferences. The need of party loyalty came from the danger that if two or more candidates were before the people the opposition who might center on one candidate would be successful and thus the opportunity of having principles incorporated in legislation and administration would be lost. The convention system was therefore adopted in Illinois at a very early date by the democrats. They argued that the wishes of the people were systematically carried along from the simplest form of mass meeting in the school district to the township, the county, to the judicial or congressional convention and thence to the state and to the national gathering. It was argued that the convention system was democratic in that it prevented wealth from determining choices in caucuses.

It was not an easy nor a speedy process—the adoption of the convention system in Illinois. It appeared inconvenient often to follow the process of the evolution of the national convention through the stages from the voting precinct through the several civil units to the natural gathering. And it not infrequently happened that measures were propagated in national gatherings and the people were asked to sanction them in the several larger units down to the county or voting precinct.

The whigs did not take kindly to the convention system. There was a general belief that the convention system was a scheme which deprived worthy people from offering themselves as candidates for office. The whig papers pointed out that a candidate for Congress was nominated by twelve delegates in a congressional convention, the district comprising twenty-three counties. The next year a convention was dominated by an over-representation from two of the twenty-three counties and the choice of these two counties was nominated. Thus it appeared that the convention was not always the concentrated wish of the voters determined before the day of election. But the convention system was destined to be a permanent institution not only with regard to national needs, but serving the interests of political parties in township, city, county and state.

The whigs eventually made use of conventions for the choice of candidates, but it was forced upon them and was not an evolution within the party. The whigs may be said to have been theoretically a conservative party. They reverted to the past and were not idealists. The whigs had the reputation of being men of wealth and experts in the business of the country. Although a minority party, the whigs bought most of the stock, and organized the State Bank and the Bank of Illinois in 1834, while the democrats looked helplessly on. They championed the three greatest factors in the development of the country—protection, internal improvements, and banks.

THE IRISH VOTE

The increase in population in the state is shown as follows: In 1830, 157,445; in 1840, 476,183. This was an increase of more than 200 per cent. This is the greatest gain in population for any decade in the history of Illinois. The explanation is not far to seek. After the close of the Black Hawk war the building of the Illinois and Michigan Canal was the most talked of enterprise in the state. The work actually began July 4, 1836. The Internal Improvement schemes were set in motion in the fall of 1837. Even by the summer of 1836 immigrants were coming into Illinois in great swarms. The Irish came in large numbers and found an opportunity for labor along the canal.

The constitution of Illinois, made in 1818, provided for the exercise of the right of franchise as follows:

"Article 2, Section 27. In all elections, all white male inhabitants above the age of twenty-one years, having resided in the state six months next preceding the election, shall enjoy the right of an elector; but no person shall be entitled to vote except in the county or district in which he shall actually reside at the time of election."

There were two interpretations to this clause. The democrats said this clause gave all men over twenty-one years of age who had resided in the district six months, the right to vote. This, the foreigners who had come to Illinois to secure work on the public improvements, had been accustomed to do. The whigs had opposed the claims of the foreigners and of the democrats. The whigs said that the voter must be a citizen of the United States and then an inhabitant of the district or county in which he resided for six months. This question took on an added interest when it was known that if they voted the state went democratic, but if the foreigners were prohibited from voting, then the state would go for the whigs. There were 10,000 of them and nine-tenths of the whole voted the democratic ticket.

Secretary of State

The situation was a very important one and had been earnestly discussed over the state. But just at this time another matter was bitterly fought out before the courts and before the public. In 1838 when Governor Carlin came into office he found Alexander P. Field, the Secretary of State, a whig in office. Mr. Field had held the office about ten years and the governor was very desirous of getting him out of office. Mr. John A. McClernand, a democrat of Shawneetown, was appointed by the governor, but the whigs in the Senate were joined by a few democrats and the nomination was rejected. After the Legislature adjourned, the governor appointed McClernand again, and the latter made a demand upon Field for possession of the office. Field refused to surrender the office and McClernand took the case before the Supreme Court. The court was made up of three whigs, Wilson, Brown, and Lockwood, and one democrat, Smith. Two of whig judges, Wilson and Lockwood, decided against McClernand. Smith decided in his favor and Brown gave no opinion on account of relationship to McClernand.

The democrats were wild in their condemnation of the Supreme Court, and immediately took steps to reorganize this honorable body.

Another Case

Another case came into the courts just at this time which greatly interested and perplexed the two political parties. It was agreed to have a friendly suit in the circuit court in the Galena district to decide upon the right of aliens to vote. The case was submitted to the judge without argument. The judge was a whig and when the case was decided the decision was that aliens could not vote. When the decision was made known, "it threw the leaders of the democratic party into perfect consternation." Preparations were made to carry the case before the Supreme Court. The ablest lawyers were obtained and the case argued at the December sitting of the court, 1839. The case was continued till June, 1840, and later till December, 1840. These continuances were the result of some skilful work on the part of the counsel for the democrats. At least it gave the aliens a chance to vote at the state and national elections in 1840.

A new way out of the danger of a whig Supreme Court was discovered by Adam W. Snyder, of St. Slair County. He introduced a bill to legislate all the circuit judges out of office and increase the Supreme Court by the addition of five new judges. The bill finally passed and the five new supreme judges, all democrats, were added to the Supreme Court. The court now stood, three whigs to seven democrats. The new court ruled that aliens could vote and that the governor could appoint a new Secretary of State at his pleasure. These ten supreme judges were required by the law creating this new court to hold circuit court through the several circuit districts of the state.

Whigs in Convention

The whigs had been slow to make use of the system of conventions which the democrats had so successfully used for the past decade. The whigs had formed a national organization out of the national-republican party of Jackson's first term. The whig party drew to itself all anti-Jackson men. At the close of Jackson's second term the democrats, under the influence of Jackson, nominated Van Buren for the presidency. The whigs were too timid and they held no national convention. There were four men, all whigs, who were candidates against Van Buren. They were Harrison of Indiana, White of Tennessee, Webster of Massachusetts, and Mangum of North Carolina. Van Buren received 170 electoral votes while the four whigs could muster but 124. But this compaign of 1836 taught tne whigs a lesson, and in 1840 the whigs centered on William Henry Harrison, the hero of Tippecanoe, as the standard bearer for the new party. The democrats nominated Van Buren and the campaign of 1840 was the most dramatic political contest the country had seen up to that period.

In Illinois the whigs had been growing in numbers and in political wisdom, and they had learned from their opponents the value of putting stress on policies instead of altogether upon men. In the rather peculiar relation of our state interest with those of the government at large, it is really necessary that there should be unity of action in political matters, at least in order to secure success in political policy. It was thought necessary, therefore, by the whigs of Illinois, to launch a state organization. The democrats were so well organized in both nation and state that nothing could separate them from the control of government except a similar or a more appealing presentation of principles. One fact made it difficult to connect Illinois politics with national politics. The state's civil life began in the fall of 1818. This was just half way between the presidential campaigns. There were no state officials to be elected by the people in 1840 except the members of the legislature. All other state officers were elected by the Legislature or appointed by the governor. The year 1840 was an off year for Illinois so far as interest in state politics was concerned. The members of the lower house of the General Assembly and one-half of the membership of the upper house were to be elected in August, 1840. But the candidates for these positions evoked nothing more than interest in the individual candidates or in some local question that might be up for consideration.

But the campaign for President was approaching and the whigs had cast aside their fear of the charge of imitation and under the spur of aggressive newspapers had called a convention for October 7, 1839. The convention was to be held in Springfield and the appeal to the several counties to send delegates was earnest and convincing. The purpose of this first whig convention was—1. To effect an organization of the whig party in Illinois. 2. To name delegates to the national whig convention which was called to meet at Harrisburg, Pennsylvania, in December 4, 1839. 3. To name presidential electors at large, and for each of the three congressional districts. Thirty out of the eighty-seven counties were represented. Wm. Moore was the permanent presiding officer. A state central committee was appointed, composed of A. G. Henry, Richard F. Barrett, Edward D. Baker, Abraham Lincoln, and J. F. Speed. It was given to this committee to organize the whigs of the state into a real positive, aggressive, political force. The delegates to the national convention were George W. Ralph, Ezra Baker, Wm. B. Warren, Wm. A. Marshall, and Walter L. Newberry. Candidates for presidential electors were named as follows: Cyrus Walker and Buckner A. Morris for electors at large; Samuel D. Marshall for the first congressional district including the Southwestern part of the state; Edwin B. Webb was the candidate in the second district which included the Southeast part of the state; and Abraham Lincoln was the candidate in the third district which included the Central and Northern part of the state. The convention was made up of a representative body of Illinois citizens and was earnest and even enthusiastic as to the outcome of the campaign just ahead of them. Mr. Lincoln wrote to John T. Stuart, his law partner, who was then in Congress, that "The nomination of Harrison takes first rate. You know I am never sanguine, but I believe we will carry the state. The chance of doing so appears to me twenty-five per cent better than it did for you to beat Douglas." Stuart had defeated Douglas in the election of 1838 by a majority of fourteen votes out of a total poll of thirty-six thousand.

The national democratic convention met also in Baltimore on May 5, 1840. It was inevitable that Van Buren should receive the nomination. He had served in many places of distinction and honor in the United States Senate, as governor of his state, New York, as Secretary of State under Jackson, and as vice president from 1833 to 1837. As President he is said to have "inherited the office without the popularity of Jackson, he also inherited the evils of Jackson's administration." Two important events absorbed the attention of the country in his administration—the financial panic of 1837 and the establishment of the independent treasury.

Preliminaries

Springfield, the new capital city became the central heating plant for the whole state. Two men destined to hold the attention not only of the people of Illinois, but of the whole nation had recently appeared upon the scenes in Springfield. They were not strangers to each other. They sat in the now famous Legislature of 1836-7 and helped to start the ball of internal improvements rolling. They had many things in common. They were both aliens (not born in Illinois). They were both poor. They were both lawyers. They were both ambitious. They were both good debaters. They were each already the strong man of his party. They were destined to become participants in the greatest forensic contest that is recorded on the pages of American history. They each had characteristics which gave them a marked individuality. One was short, thickset, bright-faced, jovial, optimistic, impulsive, irresistibly eloquent, immediate. The other was tall, angular, homely, sad-faced, melancholy, far-seeing, remote, argumentative, convincing, humorous, self-conscious.

Lincoln served in the ninth General Assembly, 1834-37, from Sangamon County. In this body also sat John T. Stuart, a brilliant lawyer also from Sangamon County. In the tenth assembly Lincoln sat with Stephen A. Douglas, from Morgan County. In this tenth General Assembly a law was enacted moving the capital to Springfield. At this time Lincoln lived at Salem and was studying law under John T. Stuart. He decided, when the law passed moving the capital to Springfield, that he would move from Salem to the new capital city. This he did in the summer of 1837. He roomed with Joshua Speed, over the latter's store. He thus became a citizen of Springfield.

Stephen A. Douglas was a native of the village of Brandon, Vermont, having been born April 23, 1813. He learned the cabinet trade, attended an academy for nearly three years, a part of the time studying law. He came west by way of Canandaigua, N. Y., Cleveland, Cincinnati, Louisville, and St. Louis. He arrived in Jacksonville, Illinois, then a small village, in late November, 1833. He walked to Winchester, Scott County, where he earned a few dollars clerking for a sale. He then taught a private school at forty dollars per month, read law, and practiced before the village justice. Was admitted to the bar in March, 1834. He opened an office in Jacksonville. He went from Springfield to Bloomington and tried a case for five dollars. He was elected a state's attorney in 1835 and a member of the tenth General Assembly in August, 1836. In 1837 was appointed registrar of the land office, and that fall ran against John T. Stuart for seat in Congress and was defeated by only fourteen votes. He returned to the practice of law. He was McClernand's attorney in quo warranto proceedings against Alexander Field for possession of the office of Secretary of State, but lost his case.

The whigs were represented in Springfield in 1839-40 by Abraham Lincoln, John J. Harding, John T. Stuart, Ninian W.

Edwards, Jesse K. Dubois, and O. H. Browning. The democrats by Stephen A. Douglas, William L. D. Ewing, Ebenezer Peck, William Thomas, James Shields, and John Calhoun. Of course, the two great leaders were Lincoln and Douglas. They often met in friendly contests in law cases, or in the less serious engagements of every day life. Local issues had almost wholly disappeared from public consideration. But the campaign of 1840 was approaching. Harrison, the embodiment of Western ideals, had been named as the whig candidate for the presidency. The blood had begun to circulate a little faster in the veins of the whig leaders. The democrats were not so enthusiastic for their candidate, but the danger of defeat had begotten a determination which nerved every Jackson democrat to do his best for "Little Van."

Friendly Debate

The winter evenings of 1839 in the new capital were occupied in friendly debates. The Legislature was in session, and while serious problems were before that body, they were the threadbare topics left over from the past two or three years. The compelling subject was the approaching presidential campaign. Out of all the private contests between whigs and democrats, there grew up a plan of having a series of public discussions upon the absorbing subject of the platforms of the opposing parties. The series was to occupy eight evenings and the "big guns" were to take part in the engagement. By some arrangement both advantageous and disadvantageous to Mr. Lincoln, he was the last speaker. The people tired of the speech making and when it came Mr. Lincoln's turn to speak he was much discouraged. The audience was small and there was an evident lack of interest. He spoke in his opening remarks in such a way as to lead all his hearers to feel that he was much cast down in his spirits. The discussions seemed to turn upon the expenditure of $40,000,000 by the Van Buren administration in the year 1838. Douglas had disposed of the complaints about the expenditure by Mr. Van Buren's administration in a way that seemed perfectly proper, and the audience was quite satisfied with Mr. Douglas' explanation. Mr. Douglas had shown that the $40,000,000 had been spent as follows:

1. A certain amount as payment to Indians to release certain lands.
2. A certain amount expended in moving Indians to the west.
3. Five millions paid to France for indemnity claims.
4. Five millions paid out for the postoffice department.
5. Ten millions were appropriated in anticipation of war with England over boundary disputes.

When Mr. Lincoln began to discuss this expenditure, he showed by quoting the records that "the majority of them are wholly untrue." This reply of Mr. Lincoln was so convincing that he was thanked and congratulated by nearly every one present.

Monster Meetings

The whigs put out what came to be called a platform. It dealt with three things. It favored internal improvement in the United States at the expense of the public treasury; favored a protective tariff; and supported a national bank. The democratic convention was satisfied to state that the party was not for these things. It was also very decidedly against any interference of the national government with any domestic institution in any state. It favored the sub-treasury scheme which the President had urged upon Congress and which was enacted into law in the summer of 1840.

Log Cabin Campaign

The national whig convention after nominating Harrison placed on the ticket as his running mate a Virginia democrat, an anti-Jackson man, John Tyler. There was method in this madness. Clay's friends had hoped that he would be placed at the head of the ticket and when Harrison was named, John Tyler wept as a child. He was then offered the vice presidential nomination to appease the southern democrats who had bolted from the Jackson regime. The alliteration of "Tippecanoe and Tyler too" soon became the war cry of the whigs and anti-Jackson democrats. The editor of a Baltimore paper who ought to have known better, suggested that Harrison (because he was a western man) would be more in his element sitting in his log cabin with his barrel of hard cider, than sitting in the White House. The whigs took up the challenge and adopted the visible sign of a "Log Cabin and Hard Cider." Songs were composed, glee clubs organized, log cabins built, and hard cider was forthcoming. Never before in America was there so much enthusiasm. True, the campaign, at least outwardly, was not pitched upon a very high plane. It became one of shouting, singing, marching, together with the exhibition of log cabins transported on wheels, live coons in trees planted on the platforms beside the log cabin. Coon skins were tacked about over the cabin. Pioneers were represented about and in the cabins smoking their cob pipes or chewing the "long green." Badges were worn some of which may be seen today. Banners were carried with inscriptions some of which were not calculated to raise the standards of political campaigns. The democrats affected to treat this pioneer, if not backwoods, enthusiasm with contempt. They argued that this outward display was not the counterpart of an abiding mental attitude toward the great political questions of the day. "They, too, held meetings, but these fell far short of those of the whigs in numbers and enthusiasm. They attempted to reason and argue; but the people preferred to sing and shout. And the result was a crushing defeat for Van Buren."

A careful writer has said that "no regular army was ever better organized, equipped, or drilled than the contending hosts on either side."

STATE CENTRAL COMMITTEE

This leads us to consider briefly the work of Mr. Lincoln as a member of the State Central Committee. The committee consisted of five men. Although such organization work was new to public men in Illinois, the whig committee seemed to rise to the occasion. Mr. Lincoln was probably the mainstay on this committee and the confidential circular sent out by the committee provided:

"The county shall be divided into small districts, and there shall be a sub-committee in each district. This sub-committee shall make a list of all the voters and ascertain how they will vote in the coming elections. The committee shall also make a separate list of doubtful voters. The committee shall keep in close touch with the doubtful voters and by many devices win them to the cause of the whigs. Papers must be mailed, pamphlets distributed, and personal conversations held.

The sub-committee shall make frequent reports to the county officials and they to the State Central Committee.

They shall report changes from supporting one party to another.

When these reports are received the State Central Committee will tabulate them and return a copy of the abstract to each sub-committeeman. Thus there would be obtained very reliable information of the way the people would probably vote."

AT SPRINGFIELD

A monster whig meeting was planned for Springfield in the summer of 1840. The meeting was advertised far and near. Public speakers were secured, their names emblazoned on posters and in papers. Mr. Lincoln being a candidate for elector, felt he must do well for the party and so he went about over the state speaking for his party. In this way he was very well known as a public speaker. On these tours he often came in contact with Stephen A. Douglas and frequently they would engage in an informal debate. While there were other good speakers, none was so well known as Mr. Lincoln.

It is affirmed that twenty thousand people assembled in Springfield to attend this great meeting. They came from all directions—far and near. A delegation came from Chicago. It took fourteen teams to haul the Chicago delegation to Springfield. They were seven days going and seven days returning, beside spending several days in Springfield. They carried four large tents. They captured in Chicago a government yawl which they rigged as a two-masted ship. This was placed on a strong wagon drawn by six fine gray horses. There were four sailors, a band of music, and a six pounder in position. The band played and the cannon boomed at the entrance to every village. Captain David Hunter, afterward a major general in the Civil war, was in command of the expedition. At Joliet, which they reached at the end of the second day, they encountered a mob of roughs who were working on the canal. The mob tried to hinder their progress but when the men drew their pistols the mob fled in all directions. The ship was a great sight to many inland people who had never seen anything like it. The ship attracted the attention of thousands in the line of march in Springfield. But another object stirred the blood of the pioneers. It was a log cabin 12 x 16 feet, borne on a wagon with wooden wheels made from a large tree by cutting cross sections several inches in thickness. The cabin had a yard; trees, a hard cider barrel, live coons and backwoodsmen. The latch string was hanging on the outside. The whole display was hauled through streets of Springfield by thirty yoke of oxen.

At the proper moment the ship was presented to the whigs of Sangamon County on behalf of the Chicago delegation by William Stuart, Editor of the Chicago American. In response the whigs of Sangamon presented, through Edward D. Baker, a live grey eagle. Baker said the eagle's broad flight was emblematical of far reaching victories of Harrison. At this point the eagle responded by rearing his head, expanding his wings, and giving a loud cry. This action of the bird, the knowing ones took to presage a great victory for Harrison.

Gen. Thomas J. Henderson, an honored citizen of Northern Illinois, before his death, wrote reminiscences of the day which he spent in Springfield when the above described monster meeting was held. He says:

"The first time I remember to have seen Abraham Lincoln was during the memorable campaign of 1840, when I was a boy 15 years old. It was at an immense whig mass meeting held in Springfield, Illinois, in the month of June of that year. The whigs attended this meeting from all parts of the state in large numbers, and it was estimated that from forty to fifty thousand people were present. They came in carriages and wagons, on horse back and on foot. They came with log cabins drawn on wheels by oxen, and with coons and coon-skins and hard cider. They came with music and banners; and thousands of them came long distances. It was the first political meeting I had ever attended, and it made a very strong impression upon my youthful mind.

"My father, William H. Henderson, then a resident of Stark County, Illinois, was an ardent whig; and having served under General William Henry Harrison, the then whig candidate for

President, in the War of 1812-1815 he felt a deep interest in his election. And although he lived about a hundred miles from Springfield, he went with a delegation from Stark County to this political meeting and took me along with him. I remember that at this great meeting of the supporters of Harrison and Tyler there were a number of able and distinguished speakers of the whig party of the state of Illinois present. Among them were Colonel Edward D. Baker, who was killed at Ball's Bluff, on the Potomac, in the late war, and who was one of the most eloquent speakers in the state; Colonel John J. Hardin, who was killed at the battle of Buena Vista in the Mexican war; Fletcher Webster, son of Daniel Webster, who was killed in the late (Civil) war; S. Leslie Smith a brilliant orator of Chicago; Rev. John Hogan, Ben Bond, and Abraham Lincoln. I heard all these men speak on that occasion. And while I was too young to be a judge of their speeches, yet I thought them all to be great men, and none of them greater than Abraham Lincoln."

Judge John M. Scott, Chief Justice of the Supreme Court in the latter part of the nineteenth century, was a young man of sixteen years at the time of the campaign of 1840. He was a bright student even that early of passing events and he gives the following account of the great meeting at Springfield.

"Mr. Lincoln stood in a wagon, from which he addressed the mass of people that surrounded it. The meeting was one of unusual interest because of him who was to make the principal address. It was at the time of his greatest physical strength. He was tall and perhaps a little more slender than in later life, and more homely than after he became stouter in person. He was then only thirty-one years of age, and yet he was regarded as one of the ablest of the whig speakers in this campaign. There was that in him that attracted and held public attention. Even then he was the subject of popular regard because of his candid and simple mode of discussing and illustrating political questions. At times he was intensely logical, and was always most convincing in his arguments. The questions involved in that canvass had relation to the tariff, internal improvements by the federal government, the distribution of the proceeds of the sales of the public lands among the several states, and other questions that divided the political parties of that day. They were not such questions as enlisted and engaged his best thought; they did not take hold of his great nature, and had no tendency to develop it. At times he discussed the questions of the hour in a logical way, but much time was devoted to telling stories to illustrate some phase of his argument, though more often the telling of these stories was resorted to for the purpose of rendering his opponents ridiculous. That was a style of speaking much appreciated at that early day. In that kind of oratory he excelled most of his contemporaries—indeed he had no equal in the state. One story he told on that occasion was full of salient points, and well illustrated the argument he was making. The story told on this occasion was much liked by the vast assembly that surrounded the temporary platform from which he spoke, and was received with bursts of laughter and applause. It served to place the opposing party and its speakers in a most ludicrous position in respect to the question being considered, and gave him a most favorable hearing for the arguments he later made in support of the measure he was sustaining."

The democrats held many meetings over the state at which enthusiastic speakers praised the virtues of Little Van. Stephen A Douglas and John T. Stuart were candidates for Congress from the third district which included the central and north portions of the state. Lincoln was at that time a candidate for the position of elector for the third district, and also a candidate for the Legislature.

The democrats carried the state by 1939 votes, but Stuart defeated Douglas by fourteen votes. It is generally agreed that the whigs lost out because the foreigners along the canal and those in St. Clair County voted the democratic ticket. The Legislature was also democratic in both houses. In the Senate the democrats had twenty-six votes, while the whigs had fourteen. In the House the democrats had fifty-one and the whigs forty. Lincoln was the whig candidate for speaker of the House but was defeated by Ewing by 46 to 36 votes. New names in the Legislature included Lyman Trumbull, Wm. H. Bissell, Thomas Drummond, Joseph Gillespie, and David M. Woodson, in the House. In the Senate the names of Thomas M. Kilpatrick, John Moore, and Richard M. Cullom.

CHAPTER XIV

THE MORMONS

Religious Freedom—Origin—A Bible Student—A Religious Romance — Witnesses — Church Organized — Smith a Banker—The Gap Widens—Nauvoo—Smith in Washington—Politics—A Charter—For the Democrats—Another Warrant — New Features — Old Citizen — Spiritual Wives—The Expositor—More Habeas Corpus —Governor Ford—Some Complaints—In Jail—The Crime—Apostles Reign—Immigrants—The Wolf Hunt —The Preparation—Real War.

The American people of the twentieth century have received from their forbears three most precious legacies. These are not of the nature of lands that may be occupied, or wealth that may be possessed, or accumulated wisdom which should be cherished. But they are of the nature of fundamental principles in civil government. They are the last grants of abolution in the conflicts originating in the middle ages between the divine right of kings and the divine right of the people. It was out of these conflicts that many of the old thirteen states were settled. The key to the situation is found in the attitude and the threat of the "wisest fool" who ever reigned over a people, when he said "If this be all they have to say, I shall make them conform themselves, or I will harry them out of the land, or else do worse." But the same spirit which flamed in the hearts of twenty thousand who were driven from mother England between 1630 and 1640 because of a desire for religious freedom, is found in the revolts against the efforts of the king to curb the freedom of speech and of the press. The doctrine once prevailed that "the king can do no wrong." His judgments are true and righteous altogether. There is no method known to the world by which human thought can be controlled, and it may be said with equal truth that all efforts to prevent the expression of human thought have been futile. The dungeons of the middle ages, the torch of later centuries, the wheel of the inquisition, and the bastiles of modern times have all had their day, but out of it all has come to American citizens a triumvirate of guarantees which few other peoples of the world possess.

Religious Freedom

The rights of the individual and of the community in the freedom of religion, freedom of the press, and the freedom of speech have been safeguarded in national and state constitutions and legislative enactments. It may be a question in the minds of many as to where the line is to be drawn between liberty and license in the exercise of one's right in religious worship, or public expression in press or speech. The line is to be drawn by an enlightened conscience, and any tendency to pass from the domain of liberty to the broad field of license will be controlled by the enlightened conscience of the people whose institutions might be endangered by the tendency, if unchecked.

There were certain beliefs and practices of the Mormons which were and are entitled to the same protection as may be justly claimed by any other religious organization. It should be remarked that constitutional and legislative guarantees do not reach to the beliefs of the individual or the community, but only to their forms of expression in speech and conduct. The disgraceful conditions which obtained in Illinois in the years 1843-5, were the outward acts of a people whose thoughts and feeling were far below the standards of the enlightened conscience of the people among whom the Mormons came. In their quest for an abiding place, these people might have found some place on the earth, a people whose ideals were of the grade of those held by themselves. If they had gone to live among such a people there would probably have been no friction.

Origin

Origins are always interesting and may be highly profitable as subjects of study. One's estimate of a movement in the life of any people will often be determined by a knowledge of the origin and early growth of the movement. The story of the early life of the man whose name is indissolubly linked with the origin and growth of the Mormon religion is colorless and uninviting, and it was not till he approached manhood that the incidents of his life are of general interest.

Joseph Smith was born in Sharon, Windsor County, Vermont, December 23, 1805. His parents were in humble circumstances, and the means of an education were very crude. The opportunities of an education, meager though they were, may not have been embraced by the boy, for we know that many young people create their own opportunities. "He read indifferently, wrote and spelled badly, and made but little progress in arithmetic. Other and higher branches of learning to him were a sealed book, of which he was totally, and is now (1844) exceedingly ignorant." At the age of ten he moved with his parents to a small farm near Palmyra, Wayne County, New York. Here he remained with his parents till he was twenty-one years old. In a sketch of his own life he says that at the age of fifteen or sixteen he began to think seriously about the after-life. He points out the difficulty he found in applying to the available sources of information about the course he should pursue to make certain of a future salvation. He complained that each church gave him different directions as to what he should do here and now to make sure of the hereafter. Out of all of this confusion of information he decided they were all wrong and that the only thing for him was to go directly to the Lord for information. He says this made him an earnest Bible student.

A Bible Student

Young Smith became in some ways a hermit. He went to quiet and secret places to read his Bible and to pray. On these occasions of intense thought and emotion, he claimed to have seen visions, and to have been in direct communication with the spirit world. One of his visions was much like the vision which Moses

JOSEPH SMITH, MORMON LEADER

had when he saw the burning bush. It was while contemplating a great fire which enveloped him and all the surrounding objects, that he had his first intercourse with God. He was assured, he said, that all his sins were forgiven, and was further informed that all denominations which he knew about were wrong and that he was warned to put no trust in them. He describes other visions which he had at his secret places of worship. On one occasion he claimed to have been told that he had been elected to prepare the world for the second coming of Christ.

He was informed that the American Indians were the remnant of the Jewish race. It was hinted to him that the story of God's dealings with this remnant race had been recorded and was hidden from wicked hands. In another vision he was directed to proceed to the place where the records of God's dealings with the world and of his directions for the salvation of the world, might be found. He visited the place and a wonderful discovery was made. On the road from Palmyra, some twenty miles east of Rochester on the Erie Canal, to Canandaigua, some eighteen or twenty miles south, one passes the Village of Manchester. Some three or four miles south of Manchester on the side of a hill on the east side of the road buried in the ground was found the book of Mormon. A large hole had been dug in the side of the hill, the bottom covered with a flat slab and sides of flat rock formed a square, all cemented to prevent the injurious effects of moisture. In this crypt was found a book whose leaves were of metal, bound or held together by three rings passing through openings in the edges of the leaves.

Joseph Smith visited this place and made this discovery the 22d of September, 1823. He was at that time only eighteen years old. As he stood beside the open crypt and before he had removed the book, he had another vision, and he was told that at this time he could not have this book, but its possession should come only after long periods of prayer and faithfulness in obedience to the Lord. But the Lord would give a sign when the book might be had. It was revealed to Smith that he should be the one to whom the book should be given, but that he should undergo great temptations and dangers and when the world should persecute him then the time had come for him to come into possession of the Book of Mormon.

A Religious Romance

From the time Joseph Smith was a lad on the farm near Palmyra till he was a young man grown, he was known by his neighbors as a young profligate. This character he probably came by honestly. His father was known as a water witch. He and the son Joseph would go about finding where the farmers and others should dig wells. They used "a green rod." This may have been a forked stick of hazel or peach. Sometime while he was still a young lad, he made the acquaintance of one Sidney Rigdon, a rather intellectual sort of fellow, who spent a good deal of his time thinking about starting a new religion. It appears that Rigdon had read a religious romance which suggested this to him.

After the two adventurers had read and reread the romance, they began to plan the details of the new religion. It was arranged that Smith should be the prophet of this new religion, and it is charged that a part of the plan was to find a book which it would be claimed gave the story of the ten lost tribes and of the visit of Christ to these people in America. The story provided that the Christians in America were annihilated by heathen people in a great battle called Cumorah which was fought near

Palmyra, New York. Among the survivors of the Christians were Mormon and his son, Moroni. These two survivors were directed by God to record the story of the Christians and their utter defeat upon the plates of gold and deposit them in the earth.

When the book was found and the visions and revelations made known, there grew up all sorts of false reports, misrepresentations, and slanders, so Smith's biographers say, as to the truthfulness of Smith's statements. Efforts were made to get the plates or the book away from him and it was necessary for him to make a journey into Pennsylvania in order to translate the subject matter of the plates.

WITNESSES

The troublesome thing about the story is that there were no witnesses to the finding of the book or of its delivery by the angel into the hands of Joseph Smith. One Oliver Cowdry testified that he visited the hillside where the book was found in 1830. He reports that about the place there were several trees standing, and that probably the land was used as pasture ground. But when Joseph Smith took his plates and went into Pennsylvania to translate the book, there began to appear men who claimed to know certain facts about the whole incident. It appeared afterwards necessary to have some of these people testify concerning the book, etc. Oliver Cowdry, Daniel Whitmore, and Martin Harris all affirmed: "We certify that we have seen the plates which contain the records; that they were translated by the gift and power of God, for his voice hath declared it to us, wherefore we know that the work is true, and declare with words of soberness that an angel of God came down from heaven and laid the plates before our eyes, and we saw the engravings on them." Another group of eight witnesses declared: "Joseph Smith, the translator of this work, hath shown us the plates herein spoken of, which have the appearance of gold, and, as many of the leaves as the said Smith hath translated we have handled with our hands, and we also saw the engravings thereon, all of which had the appearance of ancient and curious workmanship."

Another story is told of a very great desire on the part of his early followers to see the book. After much importuning and solicitation he told them that the book could not be looked upon by the carnal eye, but that only those who had been able by fasting and prayer to see the hidden things of God could behold the book. They began a season of fasting and prayer which was long continued. In the meantime they renewed their requests to see the mystery. Seeing he could not longer defer the matter, he brought forth the box and after more prayers, he opened the box when to their great disappointment they said, "Brother

HISTORY OF ILLINOIS

Joseph, we do not see the plates." The prophet with a display of impatience said, "Oh ye of little faith, how long will God bear with a wicked and perverse generation? Down on your knees, brethren, every one of you, and pray God for the forgiveness of your sins and for the living faith which comes down from heaven." They all fell upon their knees and with great earnestness during a period of two hours prayed for the forgiveness of their sins and for the heavenly vision with which to see the hidden mystery. They again looked and behold they saw the plates.

Church Organized

The plates were delivered to Joseph Smith about 1827 or '28. For the next two years Smith was busy translating the plates and making their contents known. On April 6, 1830, a church was organized at Manchester, New York, a village some three or four miles south of Palmyra. The name of the church was the Church of Jesus Christ of the Latter Day Saints. The membership was at first small, but it increased quite rapidly and in 1833 the prophet and his followers moved to Kirtland, Ohio.

Smith a Banker

At Kirtland a temple was started and several thousands of dollars were expended thereon. In 1836 a sort of conference was held at Kirtland where several hundred missionaries gathered from the remote parts of England and the two Americas. These returned missionaries reported that thousands had been gathered into the fold. Joseph Smith was at this time one of the most aggressive preachers. He attacked the denominations with fury and soon had every minister as well as the laymen up in arms against Mormonism.

In the meantime he had organized a bank and had entered into business relations with the people of the community. It was a bank of issue and it was not long until the bank bills were in circulation. With the bills of his own bank he purchased large tracts of real estate. The purchases were made in the name of "the saints," and in the course of time transferred to certain persons. This banking enterprise was only one of hundreds, perhaps thousands, entered into just following the closing days of the second United States Bank. The bank failed and the bank bills could not be redeemed. The saints had large quantities of land for their trouble.

Feeling grew strong against the Mormons and particularly against Joseph Smith and his brother, Hyrum. This feeling brought together a determined set of more than twenty-five citizens who surrounded the home of the Smiths, took therefrom the two brothers and tarred and feathered them. They were ridden on rails and told to leave the community. It seems the feeling against them was more bitter on account of their attitude toward the churches than for their shortcomings in business matters. Their residence in Kirtland became irksome, they had lost standing in that locality and they gladly took their departure for Caldwell County, Missouri. This was in 1837. Here they purchased a large tract of land and announced the building of Zion. Smith and his associates began a warfare on slavery that immediately made a bitter enemy of every slave holder.

Without doubt many Mormons had reached Missouri before Joseph and Hyrum Smith came into that state. Brown, in the "History of Illinois," says they founded Independence, Missouri, in 1833, and later moved, or some of them did, to Clay County, just north of the Missouri River. When Joseph Smith came into Missouri from Kirtland, Ohio, he appears to have gone into Caldwell County, where he planted a new center. The Mormons were found in the counties of Jackson, Clay, Caldwell, and Daviess. The "saints," as they wished to be called, bought large tracts of land in these several counties and settled down to a life very different from that of the average citizens of Missouri. Just as they had won the disfavor of the people about Kirtland, so here they began and carried on in such a manner that any one could see that there would sooner or later be a clash between the "saints" and the Gentiles.

The Gap Widens

There were several causes of a widening gap between the saints and the gentiles: First, the bitter attacks by the prophet and the elders against slavery; second, the estimate in which the saints held the people of the churches; third, the disregard they manifested toward the rights of the citizens to their private property; fourth, their utter contempt for the recognized authority of civil magistrates. Much of the trouble arose from the practice among the Mormons of appropriating horses, cattle, sheep, fowls, and other things of value which they found on the lands of the farmers about their place of residence. The courts had difficulty in punishing individuals for the violations of the law. In some cases officials were members of the Mormon Church or were bidding for the support of its members.

Joseph Smith organized a sort of militia for the defense of his people and their city "Far West." Reynolds says there were 1,300 people assembled in this new city in an incredibly short time. Soon 500 able-bodied and determined men were armed, and drilled, and organized, to withstand the authority of the State of Missouri. They were called the "Danite Band." This band went about pretending to preserve order, but usually violating the law. The gentiles also organized a sort of home guard for the safety of their homes and property. It often happened that detachments of these two organizations would meet each other in a contest of arms. Some lives were lost. The governor took a hand in the execution of the laws and called out the militia for that purpose. On one occasion a body of militia fell upon a group of unarmed men, women, and children at a place called Hawn's Mill and killed sixteen Mormons, including some women and children. Prof. John Russell of Bluffdale, Greene County, this state, tells a revolting story of the cold-blooded massacre of a man and his small boy in the presence of the mother.

Governor Boggs called upon the militia to surround the town of Far West and take into custody Joseph Smith and the leaders of the Mormon movement. Joseph Smith and six associates were tried before a court martial and condemned to be shot. This sentence would probably have been carried out if it had not been for the determined efforts of Col. A. W. Doniphan who insisted that the condemned men should have the right to a civil trial. They were consequently placed in jail to await their civil trial.

Smith and his six associates had been indicted by the grand jury upon several counts, the indictments including charges against them for murder, treason, robbery and other crimes. At an opportune time they made their escape from the jail and eluding their pursuers made their way into Illinois.

When the City of Far West was captured by the Missouri militia, large quantities of stolen goods were recovered. The authorities were satisfied to hold Smith and his chief supporters responsible, though indictment could have been found against scores of individuals. All except Smith and his six associates were told that they could go free provided they immediately left the State of Missouri. Agents were immediately dispatched to Illinois and Iowa to seek a new home. After considerable time given to the locating of a new place for Zion, they decided on a village called Commerce in Hancock County. It is said that a Dr. Garland who lived in Quincy took great interest in helping to find a location and is largely responsible for the selection of commerce, a boat landing ten miles above Keokuk, Iowa, but on the Illinois side of the Mississippi. In 1839 this village had a postoffice, two stores, one grocery, and twelve or fifteen families.

Nauvoo

In 1839 four leaders in the Mormon Church made their appearance in the village of Commerce. They were Joseph Smith, Hyrum Smith, Sidney Rigdon, and George W. Robinson. They proceeded to lay off the city of Nauvoo. Its dimensions indicating an expected population of many thousands. The village of Commerce had previously been laid off, on paper, as a great city. It was chiefly owned by Dr. Garland who was anxious to dispose of his holdings which he did. The saints began to arrive even before Joseph Smith came to survey the city. They proceeded immediately to the construction of houses. Two farms were eventually brought within the limits of the city. One on the south edge of the original village owned by Hugh White and one about the center of the future city, owned by Daniel H. Wells who became an earnest supporter of the Mormon cause. Nauvoo means "beautiful situation." The place is a beautiful site for a city. It grew rapidly and as if by magic. The saints came from far and near. Dwellings were erected, stores, warehouses, workshops, and among other things the foundations were laid for a beautiful temple.

Smith in Washington

Smith and his friends made their escape from the Missouri jail in the summer of 1839. They also laid off Nauvoo that summer. In December of that year Smith, accompanied by some friends, went to Washington to see if the National Government would not guarantee his saints protection from the gentiles. One thing Smith was anxious to secure was the passage of a bill making an appropriation to his church for damage done in Missouri. The three congressmen, John Reynolds, Zadoc Casey and John T. Stuart were urged to support the appeal. When Smith showed up in Washington he presented letters of introduction from the most prominent men in Illinois to the congressmen and senators from this state. Smith was very ambitious to be presented to the President, Martin Van Buren. It fell to the lot of Governor John Reynolds to accompany Smith as he called on the President. After reaching the White House, Smith asked Reynolds to present him to the President as Mr. Smith of Illinois, a Latter Day Saint. Governor Reynolds was in a very embarrassing position and tried to show Smith that it was uncalled for, but Smith insisted and Reynolds carried out Smith's programme. The President smiled at the title, but treated his guest with scant courtesy. Smith's claim for damage done to his people in Missouri was presented in the Senate by Hon. Richard M. Young, senator from Illinois. But the two Missouri senators, Messrs. Benton and Lynn, opposed the matter with such "violence that it could obtain scarcely a decent burial." Joseph Smith returned to Illinois a confirmed whig.

Politics

The summer of 1840 was occupied in building the city of Nauvoo, preaching in the surrounding country, and electioneering for the whig tickets.

The people of llinois presented to the Mormons as they came in from Missouri a really warm and hearty reception. Many people who knew only of what the saints called their persecution in Missouri were really sympathetic with them. Of course, the good people who welcomed the exiles did not know both sides of the story and so some people from all churches and all political parties were ready to champion the cause of the Mormons. In fact, it has been said that people in other parts of Illinois were a bit envious of their more fortunate brethren of Hancock County who had so fortunately secured the location of this thrifty but unfortunate people. As has been said Smith returned from Washington a whig. While the Mormons were in Missouri they voted the democratic ticket but when they came to Illinois they held themselves in readiness to help the party that seemed to

MORMON TEMPLE, NAUVOO

have the most favors for them. But the lack of interest in them on the part of the national democratic party at Washington had dampened their ardor for that party.

The summer of 1840 was the great contest between the whigs and democrats, the Tippecanoe and Tyler, too, campaign. The Mormons voted with the whigs in the summer of 1840, the Constitution of 1818 allowed all males over twenty-one years of age to vote who had resided in the voting unit for the preceding six months. The Legislature which was elected in the August election in 1840, met in December. One Dr. John C. Bennett, who Mr. Stuve says was one of the most profligate men in the state, appeared in Springfield as a lobbyist for the Mormons. He first won over Senator Sidney H. Little, who lived in McDonough

County, and Stephen A. Douglas, who was secretary of state. With the backing of these two men and with the desire of the whigs and democrats, the former to hold the Mormons in their party and the latter to win them, it was easy for the Mormons to get any legislation they desired. The Legislature proceeded to comply with the demands of these people by passing three acts that applied particularly to them. The first was a charter for their city of Nauvoo.

A Charter

The Legislature met on the 7th of December and on the 16th an act known as the Nauvoo City charter was passed. This charter is a very remarkable document. It provided for a boundary which would equal those of a European city. Another part provided that any adjoining territory which had been laid off into town lots might become a part of the City of Nauvoo. Another section provided that the city could hold real estate outside of the city limits. One section of the act authorized the city to make any ordinance it wished, not repugnant to the Constitution of the United States or that of Illinois. The conclusion being that ordinances of the city of Nauvoo might be in opposition to the laws of Illinois. The mayor of the city had judicial functions but cases might be appealed to a municipal court consisting of the mayor and aldermen, and from this municipal court to the circuit court of Hancock County. The municipal court had the power to grant writs of habeas corpus. Another section of the charter authorized the city to organize an independent military company, to be known as the Nauvoo Legion, the commissioned officers constituting a perpetual court-martial. Its commanding officer bore the title of lieutenant-general; he would outrank any other military officer in the state except the governor. The act further gave the Nauvoo Legion its proportion of public arms. This equipment eventually consisted of three pieces of cannon, 250 stand of small arms and probably other material. Joseph Smith was made lieutenant-general. A university was authorized.

Another act of the Legislature created the "Nauvoo House Association." Since Joseph Smith was to furnish the lot on which this hotel or tavern was to be built, he was to have a room in this house free of cost. The Nauvoo House Association was to be a corporation. A third charter created the "Nauvoo Agricultural and Manufacturing Association" with a capital of $150,000. This company was to manufacture and ship flour, lumber, and other materials. In a separate act of the Legislature authorized any citizen of Hancock County to enroll voluntarily in the Nauvoo Legion. All these laws were enacted between December 7th, 1840 and February 27, 1841. Whigs and democrats were afraid to oppose any of these laws and in fact there was a sort of race as to which party would win the Mormons to its side.

In the election of members of the Legislature in August, 1842, William Smith, a brother of Joseph Smith, was elected to the Lower House of the Legislature from Hancock County. Thomas H. Owen was also a member from Hancock County. In the winter of 1843-4 the city council of Nauvoo passed an ordinance providing: "That it shall be lawful for any officer of the city, with, or without process, to arrest any person who shall come to arrest Joseph Smith with process growing out of the Missouri difficulties; and the person so arrested shall be tried by the municipal court upon testimony, and if found guilty, sentenced to imprisonment in the city prison for life."

This action of the city council may be understood when it is recalled that Smith and six associates had been indicted in Missouri charged with murder, robbery, treason and other crimes, and that they had made their escape in 1839 and had been at large in Illinois till the fall of 1841. In the latter part of that year the governor of Missouri issued his requisition on Governor Carlin for the arrest of Smith. The officer into whose hands the writ was placed for execution returned it to the governor unexecuted. Governor Carlin put the writ into the hands of another officer who arrested Smith who was released by Judge Stephen A. Douglas, who at that time was a member of the Supreme Court. The release was by writ of habeas corpus on the ground that the writ was dead because it had been returned to the governor's office indorsed "not served."

For the Democrats

The Mormons were in great glee over the decision of Judge Douglas, and the Prophet immediately issued a manifesto that all Mormons should support the democratic ticket at the next election. Doctor Bennett had been appointed master in chancery by Judge Douglas; Governor Carlin had previously appointed him adjutant-general; and now he was a member of the city council in Nauvoo and major-general of the Legion. There thus seemed to be a rather formidable alliance between the saints and the democratic party.

Another Warrant

An attempt upon the life of Governor Boggs of Missouri by unknown persons was laid to the Mormons, and an indictment was found against Smith and Rockwell. This was on the 5th of June, 1843. On the 7th of June a messenger arrived at Springfield with the requisition papers for the arrest of Smith. Governor Ford placed the writ in the hands of a Hancock County constable. He and the Missouri agent found Smith in the north part of the state. He was arrested and turned over to the agent who started to Missouri with him. Smith was forcibly taken from the Missouri agent and conducted to Nauvoo in great triumph. A farcical trial was conducted in habeas corpus proceedings and Smith was released. The Missouri agent requested the governor to furnish troops to secure the arrest of Smith, but the governor was not willing to do so, and Smith was given a short period to make up his mind as to future policies.

An election for congressman was held in the district in which Hancock County was situated in August, 1843. Cyrus Walker was the whig candidate and Joseph P. Hoge was the democratic candidate. Both men were very anxious to secure the vote of the Mormons. The democratic managers told the Mormons that if they would vote for Hoge, the governor would not send the militia against Smith and the City of Nauvoo. When the votes were counted it was found that about 3,000 Mormons had voted for Mr. Hoge, who was elected by less than 1,000.

Now that it was known that the Mormons were supporting the democrats, the whig press renewed its former attacks on the Mormons. These whig papers now began to reveal the real situation within the City of Nauvoo. Doctor Bennett had been turned out of the church and forced to leave Nauvoo. He was going about telling of the horrible things which were common events in the city of the saints.

When the ordinance which was passed by the city council in the winter of 1843-4, above referred to, the good people of the state stood in amazement. It now looked as if the Legislature had created a state within a state, and that there would surely come a real test between the City of Nauvoo and the State of Illinois.

New Features

In the early spring of 1844, events of far reaching importance happened in rapid succession. The people in Hancock County and adjoining counties were constantly missing things of value. The owners of this stolen property in some cases were bold enough to go into Nauvoo to search for their missing goods. They would be arrested and fined and cast into prison by the city government. In some cases the governor interfered and pardoned the gentiles. About this time the Mormons asked Congress to establish a territorial government for the City of Nauvoo and the surrounding country—set up a state within a state. Ford says the crowning folly was the announcement that Joe Smith was candidate for President. It is said 3,000 missionaries were sent out to preach and to electioneer for the prophet for President. Then Hon. George Edmunds, a lawyer in Western Illinois, who came here about the time the Mormons came, was asked concerning the political ambitions of Hyrum and Joseph Smith, said: "No doubt Joseph was ambitious politically. He aspired to be President of the United States, and was a candidate, I think in 1844, the year he was killed." Volume VII of the "Illinois Historical Collection" says that late in 1843 Smith wrote to both Clay and Calhoun asking each to state what position he would take as to the Mormons in case he were elected President of the United States. Both statesmen wrote evasive answers. The Times and Seasons, a Mormon newspaper published in Nauvoo placed the name of Joseph Smith at the head of its columns as the paper's choice for President. Smith's name carried the title general. A state convention was called for Nauvoo from which it was proposed to send delegates to the Baltimore convention where Smith's name for President was to be presented. But the times were so out of joint that these ambitious plans were never realized.

Old Citizen

The Mormons had become so powerful in politics that the gentiles—both whigs and democrats decided to lay aside any and all differences which separated them and to unite on the danger from a common enemy. The Mormons were so strong that they no longer allied themselves with any other political factions but swept the whole county at least for their own brethren. There were probably 5,000 voters in Nauvoo. But it was not so much the actual voting strength which the gentiles feared as it was the ease with which the Mormons could make the majority any size they wished. The gentiles therefore organized a new party to be called the "old citizen." The general election was to be held in August, but Smith was killed on June 27, 1844, and there was no longer any need of gentile unity on political questions.

Spiritual Wives

It seemed the public was treated to a new sensation each day. In the early spring of 1844 the Danite Band was reorganized. It was a sort of body guard. Joseph Smith was not taking any chances on traveling about over the country because he never knew how soon he might need the privilege of a writ of habeas corpus. Nor was it certain that officials, either state or national, might not at any moment swoop down upon the quiet City of Nauvoo and carry away its most idolized citizen. The Danite Band was for that reason reconstituted with a goodly number of strong men.

The above news was followed by the announcement that another band had been rejuvenated. This was the band of "Spiritual Wives." The new band included those females, married or unmarried, who believed that there was no way to reach heaven except to become the "spiritual wife" of an elder in the church. As there were many times as many females as there were elders it naturally followed that each elder had a large number of spiritual wives, most of whom also became carnal wives. In working out this theory of spiritual-wifeism, Joseph Smith was greatly desirous of having a Mrs. Law as one of his spiritual wives. The husband, William Law, a most talented and respectable member of the community, seriously objected to Smith's proposals.

In the meantime there was a constant flow of immigration from Europe as well as from many of the states of the Union to Nauvoo. In many cases these recruits to the church were without worldly means, and upon their arrival became a burden upon the city. There were efforts made to carry forward public works and private enterprises. The various tradesmen of the city banded themselves together in an effort to attract the attention of men who had capital, and to render aid for themselves and their constantly increasing numbers. Because of the unsatisfactory conditions which the newcomers found in the city, many of them removed into the more flourishing villages and towns, and some even hired themselves to the gentile farmers. There was a standing appeal in the papers for rich converts of the East to bring their idle capital and create an industrial boom for the "Holy City."

There was a strong anti-Mormon party within the City of Nauvoo. That is a strong party opposed to the growing highhanded, one-man power which Joe Smith was exercising. The people generally believed that the spiritual marriages was the grossest kind of immorality. Without the sanction of law, Joseph Smith established offices in Nauvoo for the purpose of regulating marriages and the transfer of real estate. No marriages could be celebrated in Nauvoo without the consent of Joseph Smith and no one could acquire real estate contrary to the wish of the prophet. If the saints decided to acquire a tract of land outside of the city limits, they adopted certain annoying processes which usually forced the owner to sell at the price fixed by the saints. Joseph Smith was the only one in the city who had the right to sell intoxicating liquors.

The Expositor

William Law, whose wife Joseph Smith had tried hard to persuade to marry an elder and a number of strong men in the city, determined on some corrective measures. Conditions were becoming intolerable and the prospects were that they would get worse. When it became known that William Law contemplated drastic measures, there were large numbers of dissenters who flocked to his side. The plan when finally matured provided for the purchase of a newspaper press and material for the weekly issue of a newspaper to be called the "Expositor." There was at this time, the summer of 1844, two papers published in Nauvoo. The older one, The Times and Seasons, a Mormon paper was founded in 1839 by Ebenezer Robinson and D. C. Smith the latter a younger brother of Joseph Smith, the prophet. This paper was issued twice monthly. It was supported by the church officials and might be considered the official organ of the church. Another paper called the Neighbor had been founded in 1843. It was edited by John Taylor, one of the twelve apostles. This paper also enjoyed the favor of the church.

It was now, 1844, felt that the unsavory condition of things in the city ought to be known by all. A paper was chosen as the best means by which exposures of the rotten condition of things might be brought about. The men directly concerned in establishing the Expositor were William Law, Wilson Law, Charles Foster, Robert D. Foster, Francis M. Highbee, Chauncy L. Highbee, and Sylvester Emmans. These were all Mormons, but opposed to the policies of Joseph Smith. On the 7th of June, the first and only issue appeared. The paper was issued on Friday. On Saturday the city council deliberated upon what steps should be taken to prevent further issues of the Expositor. It appears that no definite action was taken on that day, but on Monday, June 10, 1844, the city council took effective measures to stop the publication of so dangerous an organ as the Expositor. The council decided the paper was a nuisance and ordered it abated. Joseph Smith, with a sufficient force, went to the office of the paper and within two hours from the decision of the city council, the inflammable parts were going up in smoke and the press was undergoing a transformation at the hands of strong men and sledge hammers.

More Habeas Corpus

Law and his friends proceeded without delay to the county seat and swore out warrants for the arrest of the mayor and councilors of Nauvoo. The next question was, who can serve the warrants? It will be recalled that there was an ordinance which provided for the arrest and life imprisonment of any one who should attempt to serve in Nauvoo any warrant which had been issued by any official outside of Nauvoo. However, officers went to the city and served the warrants. A writ of habeas corpus was immediately obtained and the prisoners released. This was on the 17th of June, 1844. Public sentiment was at a high pitch. The gentiles of Hancock County began to talk of drastic measures. Meetings were held, public addresses were delivered, and steps taken for the organization of the anti-Mormon forces of the county. One proposition was advanced that all Mormons outside of the city of Nauvoo should be driven within the city. People began to discuss the more serious phase of the situation. Was not any press in danger of destruction? Is not a free press guaranteed by the Constitution of Illinois as well as by the Constitution of the United States. It is only necessary to mention that all the churches of Hancock County would be arrayed against the Mormons. Stories, probably exaggerated, were told of the threats that were made by the Mormons living in the various parts of Hancock County. One Mormon threatened to poison all the wells of the Gentiles. One Mormon said his religion would justify the commission of crimes if it were necessary in order to defend the Mormon Church. It was currently reported that a Danite Band would at an unexpected moment pounce upon the Warsaw Signal and destroy it root and branch.

On the same day that the persons, accused of destroying the press, were released by habeas corpus proceedings, a strong appeal was made to the governor to furnish protection to the people and to provide for the arrest of Joseph Smith. He was specifically asked to call out the militia. About the same time the prophet issued a sort of appeal or perhaps better, a sort of defense of the action of the municipal court in condemning and destroying the press upon which the first issue of the Expositor was printed. A part of this public statement was as follows: "Our city is infested with a set of blacklegs, counterfeiters and debauchees, and that the proprietors of this press were of that class, the minutes of the municipal court fully testify, and in ridding our young and flourishing city of such characters we are abused by not only villainous demagogues, but by some who, from their station and influence in society, ought rather to raise than depress the standard of human excellence. We have no disturbance or excitement among us, save what is made by the thousand and one idle rumors afloat in the country. Every one is protected in his person and property and but few cities of a population of 20,000 people in the United States hath less of dissipation or vice of any kind than the City of Nauvoo.

Of the correctness of our conduct in this affair (destroying the press), we appeal to every high court in the state and to its ordeal we are ready to appear at any time that His Excellency Governor Ford, shall please to call us before it. I, therefore, in behalf of the municipal court of Nauvoo warn the lawless not to be precipitate in any interference in our affairs, for as sure as there is a God in Israel we shall ride triumphant over all opposition."

It was generally understood that the Mormons were preparing for a test of strength with the Gentiles who were also holding meetings and taking council as to the imminent conflict.

Governor Ford

The situation was growing worse each day, and when on the 17th of June the governor was waited on by a committee sent by a meeting of the citizens of Carthage asking that the militia be called into service to support the civil authority, he hesitated and gave out word that he would visit the disturbed localities and see for himself what was best to be done. He reached Carthage on the morning of the 21st of June. The governor found a considerable body of armed men assembled in Carthage. They had gathered in response to the call of the constables, as the posse comitatus to assist the officers in executing the civil laws. The brigade general for that district had also ordered the militia in McDonough and Schuyler to assemble. Another military official had called the Hancock militia to assemble at Warsaw. The governor immediately took command of the militia and placed them under the proper officers.

A messenger was dispatched to Nauvoo by the governor to inform the mayor and common council of the nature of the complaints which the Gentile citizens had lodged against the Mormons, more particularly the mayor and the council. The mayor and council sent a committee to Carthage to present, informally, their defense. The committee reporting to the governor made such admissions as convinced the governor of the justness of the complaints of the Gentiles. The chief matter of complaint by the citizens was the destruction of the press of the Expositor. The representatives of the mayor who appeared before the governor admitted the facts in the case as charged by the Gentiles.

Some Complaints

As has been said the complaint about the destruction of the press was a serious one and was recent and could not be denied. The complainants about the destruction of the press were those who had bought the press and who had attempted to publish a paper. These men had all been expelled from the church and were moving about over the country telling their tale of woe. But there were other serious charges, many of which have been alluded to, but we will here enumerate them again so we may get at the foundation of the ill feeling which the Gentiles held against the Mormons.

It was reported and generally believed that Smith had announced himself king that he had been annointed and crowned with much ceremony, that a line of succession had been established.

The Danite Band had been reorganized. The individuals were under oath of obedience to Joseph Smith even to the extent of committing murder and treason.

Another organization included those who were sealed to eternal life against all crimes, except that of shedding innocent blood. Innocent blood was the blood of the members of the church.

The church was bold in claiming "the earth and the fullness thereof." This claim was based on the theory that the Mormons were God's saints on earth. All thefts, robberies, and illegal seizure of personal property was justified on the theory that this property was eventually theirs, why not now?

It was common for Gentiles to characterize the Mormon church as a nest of thieves, robbers, murderers and common outlaws.

It was currently believed that Joseph Smith had installed a counterfeiter's outfit in Nauvoo, and that spurious coins were turned out in large numbers and that certain outlaws were authorized to see that these coins were put into circulation.

Another story was in circulation which said that Joseph Smith was in alliance with several tribes of western Indians who were ready at a few hours' notice to join the Mormons in an exterminating war against the Gentiles.

But the climax was reached when it was noised abroad that a system of plural marriages had been introduced into the church. This was one of the wrongs which the Expositor was founded to expose. Ford says "that he himself (Joseph Smith) and many of his followers, had practiced upon the precepts of this revelation by seducing a large number of women." Henry Brown, the author of Brown's "History of Illinois," written in 1844, was personally acquainted with Joseph Smith and was familiar with the several incidents of the "Mormon war," in the appendix to his history says: "It is known that Joe had established a Sisterhood of Saints, for the vilest purposes. A Miss Brotherton makes affidavit that Joe wished to have her marry one of his confederates (Brigham Young), already a married man, and locked her up with Young to talk over the proposition."

The governor protested to the people of Carthage that he had no choice in the matter of taking sides, but had only one purpose—to assist in enforcing the laws. He therefore exacted a pledge from the officers and men in the militia that they would protect the prisoners if Smith and his city council should surrender. The pledge was given. The governor had failed in getting Smith to come to Carthage to stand trial, so now the governor gave those Mormons against whom warrants were standing assurances that he could guarantee them safety if they would come into court and place themselves under the protection of the law. However, the governor had just come to the conclusion that the civil officers as well as the militia were not to be depended on and he was now in a great doubt as to what he could and should do. Ford says that he later had doubts as to the real desire of the Gentiles to have the Smiths and their friends surrender. What the Gentiles wanted, so Ford seemed afterwards to think, was an excuse to raid the city and shoot up the town and drive the Mormons west of the Mississippi.

The governor sent an officer with a requisition to the mayor and officials of Nauvoo for the surrender of their arms which the state had allotted to them. These were readily given up. The city surrendered three cannon and 220 stands of small arms. It turned out afterward that there were over 2,000 men well armed and well drilled in Nauvoo.

In Jail

On the 24th of June, Joseph Smith and his brother, Hyrum, having been assured that they would be protected by the soldiers, decided to go to Carthage and surrender and let the law take its course. They proceeded to Carthage, which they reached about midnight. On the morning of June 25th, the governor and the two Smiths had a conference. It was in this conference that the governor repeated to the two Smiths that they should be protected. The two Smiths were then turned over to custody of an officer. They then gave bonds for their appearance at court and were preparing to return to Nauvoo, when they were served with new warrants charging them with treason, and they were committed to the county jail. On the morning of the 26th the governor and the two brothers had another conference and both parties were satisfied with the situation. On this day also a request was made of the jailer to allow the two brothers to occupy a large room called the "debtors' cell" instead of the smaller cells, which gave no opportunity for exercise or for conferences with friends.

The governor now decided to order the militia to return to their homes, excepting three companies, two of which were to remain in Carthage and one should go to Nauvoo to guard that city. One of the companies to remain at Carthage was the Carthage Grays. The governor knew that the Carthage Grays were bitter enemies of the Smiths and he was severely criticised for disposing of the troops as he did. On the 27th Governor Ford, with one company, started for Nauvoo, leaving the Carthage Grays in the town of Carthage. He gave special orders to the commander of the troops in Carthage to guard the jail with great care.

The governor, in company with Colonel Buckmaster, of Alton, and a company of dragoons, proceeded to Nauvoo on the 27th. He assembled the officials of the city and a great concourse of the inhabitants and delivered an address which was not so well received by the Mormons. Having some misgivings as to the safety of the two Smiths in the jail at Carthage, he hastened to return. When a few miles from Nauvoo, the governor met two men, who told them the Smiths were murdered about 4 or 5 o'clock.

The governor required the two men to return with him to Carthage. The governor reached Carthage some time before midnight. He found Dr. Willard Richards, John Taylor, and Samuel H. Smith preparing an address to the Mormons in Nauvoo. It was as follows:

Twelve O'Clock at Night, June 27.
Carthage, Hamilton's Tavern.
To Mrs. Emma Smith and Major-General Dunham, etc.

The governor has just arrived and says that all things shall be inquired into and all right measures taken. I say to all the citizens of Nauvoo: My brethren, be still and know that God reigns—don't rush out of the city—don't rush to Carthage—stay at home and be prepared for an attack from Missouri mobbers. The governor will render every assistance possible. He has sent out orders for troops. Joseph and Hyrum are dead—but not by the Carthage people. The guards were there, as I believe. We will prepare to remove the bodies as soon as possible. The people of the county are greatly excited; and fear that the Mormons will come out and take vengeance. I have pledged my word that the Mormons will stay at home (as soon as they can be informed), and no violence will be done on their part. Say to my brethren in Nauvoo, in the name of the Lord, be still—be patient—only let such friends as choose come there to see the bodies. Mr. Taylor's wounds are dressed, and not serious—I am sound.

William Richards,
John Taylor,
Samuel H. Smith.

Defend yourselves until protection can be furnished.
June 27, 1844.

Thomas Ford,
Governor and Commander-in-Chief.

The Crime

Mr. Ford gives the following version of the murder of Joseph and Hyrum Smith. A contingent of Warsaw Militia was marching up the river toward Nauvoo when they received orders from the governor to disband. They were disappointed and about 200 blackened their faces and turned their steps toward Carthage. They camped near Carthage and learned that one company, left to guard the city, had disbanded and returned to their homes. The other company, the Carthage Grays, were camped in the square of the town. Eight soldiers were detailed to guard the jail. It would appear that the guards were in conspiracy to permit the prisoners to be killed. It was claimed that their guns were loaded with blank cartridges and this was known by the attacking party. The gathering mob rushed to the jail, broke open the doors and made short work of the two Smiths. Dr. Willard Richards and John Taylor were in the large debtors' room when it was attacked by the mob. The guards fired at the mob, but no harm was done. The mob fired through the door of the large room, when Hyrum Smith was killed instantly; Joseph Smith, who was armed, fired at the mob and wounded three of his assailants. When Joseph saw that Hyrum was dead and that the door was no defense to him, he jumped from the second story window and was greatly shocked by the fall. He was unable to arise and was fired upon and killed where he fell. Doctor Richards and John Taylor, friends of the Smiths, were in the room with them when the mob attacked the jail. Taylor was wounded, but not seriously. Samuel H. Smith, who signed the letter with Richards and Taylor, was a brother to the two Smiths who had been killed.

The Legion of Nauvoo was called out on the morning of the 28th and apprised of the death of the two brothers. Addresses were delivered by Judge Phelps and Colonel Buckmaster, who had remained in Nauvoo as the representatives of the governor. The bodies of the deceased arrived at Nauvoo at 3 o'clock in the afternoon of the 28th and were buried with military honors.

Apostles Reign

As soon as the burial of the dead was over, there arose a great problem for the church. What should be the manner of government? The church was in the earliest days under the presidency of Joseph Smith, Hyrum Smith, and Sidney Rigdon. The first two were dead and Rigdon claimed the right of control. In the very earliest stages of the growth of the church, Rigdon was the prime minister. He is said to have exercised control of Joseph Smith, but in the later life of Joseph he was not much given to taking dictation from Rigdon. After the death of Joseph and Hyrum, Rigdon proposed that the church abandon Nauvoo and remove to Pittsburg, Pennsylvania; particularly was he desirous of having all the wealthy Mormons to do so. This plan he said was a revelation to him and must be obeyed. The rich were displeased with the plan, as their wealth was to some extent in houses and lands which would have to be sacrificed. The poor objected, as they would be left helpless if they were abandoned by the rich.

In the meantime the apostles who were out on far away missionary journeys began to return and immediately set up the theory that government fell to the apostles as it did in the day of Christ. The more the people thought things over, the more they inclined to apostolic control. Brigham Young, a shrewd apostle, put forth the doctrine that he was the Peter of the Twelve. The apostolic plan of government prevailed, Rigdon was driven out of the church, and missionaries were dispatched to the four corners of the earth to tell of the martyred Joseph. The missionaries preached with a fiery zeal, they abated not for summer's heat nor winter's cold, and it has been estimated that at this time there were between a quarter and a half million adherents to this strange faith.

IMMIGRANTS

It was always urged upon the new converts that if possible they should journey to Nauvoo and live among the redeemed. As early as 1842, a Mr. Henry Caswell, an English gentleman of wide travel and observation, visited the Mormon settlement at Nauvoo. On his way from some point on the lower Mississippi on a river steamer he fell in with a group of 300 English immigrants, and upon inquiry found that they were from near Preston, Lancashire, England. He said they were decent looking people and by no means of the lower class. He accompanied them to the City of Nauvoo. On Sunday he mingled with the people as they engaged in their services. The city, he says, was beautifully located, and from the upper stories of the unfinished temple a view of surpassing beauty and grandeur spread before the observer. The morning services were held in a grove and were attended by about 2,000 worshippers. They were well dressed and had the appearance of an unusually healthy and vigorous people. He quotes the prayer of one of the elders. "We pray also for the temple that the nations of the earth may bring gold and incense, that sons of strangers may build its walls and fly to it as a cloud and as doves to their windows. We pray thee also to hasten the ingathering of thy people, every man to his heritage and every man to his hand. * * * Bring thy sons from afar and thy daughters from the ends of the earth, and let them bring their gold and silver with them."

After the services Mr. Caswell was accompanied by a prominent Mormon about the city. He gave considerable attention to the temple, which was in process of construction. It was a magnificent building 120 feet by 100 feet, and 50 to the eaves. Its estimated cost was $300,000. In the basement there was among other matters of interest the laver or baptismal fount. It was about twenty feet square and rested upon the backs of twelve oxen of excellent sculpture and as large as life. The whole was of wood, but the plan was to gild all the parts.

Mr. Caswell describes a visit he made to Joseph Smith, the prophet. "He is a coarse plebeian person in aspect, and his countenance exhibits a curious mixture of the knave and the clown. His hands are large and fat, and on one of his fingers he wears a massive gold ring with some inscription on it. His dress was of course country manufacture, and his white hat was enveloped in a piece of black crepe, being in mourning for a brother. I had no opportunity of observing the eyes of Smith, he appearing deficient in that open, staid-fixed look which characterizes an honest man."

The Wolf Hunt

The internal conflict between Rigdon and his friends on one side and the "Twelve" and a very large following on the other, occupied the fall of 1844 and the winter following. During this long struggle between the factions of the church, there was a constant tendency toward disintegration. Outspoken members were being expelled from the church, and naturally each one took with him a few friends. Rigdon's defeat was followed by a claim set up by the wife of Joseph Smith in behalf of her young son, Joseph. Her claim for the rights of her young son was strongly supported by William Smith, a younger brother of the Prophet. But the powerful hand of Brigham Young was felt throughout all these controversies. In the fall of 1845 William Smith was excluded from membership in the church. He was now a free lance and began to "reveal" a good many mysteries which the outside world had long wished to know.

In the meantime the question of seeking a new Zion was constantly agitated. Many places were suggested as suitable for the new location—Texas, Oregon, and the borders of Mexico. Able men were sent into these new places to consider the adaptability of their situation. But there was a revelation that they could not leave Nauvoo till the completion of the temple.

The Gentiles were impatient of the dilatory movements of the Mormons. They thought the death of the Smiths was a sufficient signal for the Mormons to move West. The absent elders and missionaries were called home and new determination instilled into the people to withstand the aggressions of the Gentiles. New causes for bitter feeling were constantly arising. New converts were arriving in Nauvoo and the city was now thought to contain as many as 18,000 to 20,000 inhabitants. The Mormons were appealing to the governor to bring the murderers of the Smiths to trial, while the Gentiles were clamoring for the expulsion of the Mormons.

The citizens of Nauvoo had, contrary to the advice of their best friends, taken an active part in the election of 1844 and had voted solidly for the democratic candidates. This had greatly angered the whigs in all that part of the Northwest. They therefore, in order to make a demonstration and possibly to take more drastic measures, sent out an invitation to the militia captains of Hancock and adjoining counties to summon their companies and report in the vicinity of Nauvoo for the purpose of going on a great "wolf hunt." Serious charges were flying thick and fast against the conduct of the Mormons in and out of Nauvoo. The whig newspapers in and out of Illinois were ceaseless in their denunciation of the action of the democrats in allying themselves with the Mormons in the state and congressional elections.

Meanwhile the wolf-hunters were assembling in Hancock County for the purpose of attacking the wolves in their den. The governor was in close touch with the situation, and he decided to call on the militia of the state in those counties somewhat remote from the storm center. Brig.-Gen. J. J. Hardin, Colonel Baker, Merriman, and Weatherford were ordered by the governor to raise about 500 troops and hold themselves in readiness to proceed to Hancock County. On the 25th of October, the governor proceeded with his army of 500 into Hancock County. Upon the approach of the governor, many of the wolf-hunters and other anti-Mormon discontents fled to Missouri. Ford says the Carthage Grays were among those who made their get-away from Hancock County. It was the governor's plan to cross over into Missouri and bring back the leaders of the wolf-hunters, but the "invasion" of Missouri was not carried out. In the meantime some of those charged with the murder of the Smiths agreed to return and stand trial. This they did, but were declared "not guilty." The trial was a farce; no Mormons were allowed in or about the court at the time of the trial. Armed bands to the number of several hundred filled the courtyard and the courtroom. The judge was powerless and the result was the release of the prisoners. Later a Mormon jury tried the persons who destroyed the press of the Expositor, and they too were adjudged "not guilty."

In the fall of 1845 many Mormon homes in Hancock County were burned and the occupants told to take their personal effects and go to Nauvoo. In this way scores of families residing in the country were forced from their homes, the homes being burned.

The governor saw that any effort to execute the law in the County of Hancock would be futile, and knowing that the Mormons were already seeking a new location, advised their leaders that the only solution he could see was their withdrawal from the state. Gen. J. J. Hardin was sent to Nauvoo as the representative of the governor, and through his skill in diplomacy, an agreement was reached which provided that the state would cease all prosecutions if the Mormons would take their leave in the spring of 1846. A small detachment of militiamen was kept in or about Nauvoo in the winter of 1845-6, under the command of Major Warren, who it appears was well equipped in temperament to preserve the status quo.

The Preparation

All during the winter of 1845-6 there was great activity along many lines of industry in the City of Nauvoo. Never before were so many people in Nauvoo engaged in productive industry. The principal objects of construction was wagons. Harness also was manufactured. The spinning wheels and looms were busy and thousands of yards of woolens were turned out. It is said that 12,000 wagons were put in readiness by the spring of 1846. The author as a small boy remembers one of these wagons, and his remembrance of it is that it was a substantial structure easily able to transport a ton and a half. The horses used in the exodus were of the best grade, and many of those who went in the earlier departures went with an abundance of this world's goods. By the middle of February, 1846, 2,000 or 3,000 began crossing to the Iowa side of the river. They crossed on the ice and made their way westward. Others left in the early part of the summer. In the course of the summer 16,000 had crossed into Iowa. All had departed except a thousand people who had come to Nauvoo late in the period of the stay of the Mormons. They were not able to dispose of their property and could not well leave it behind.

Real War

In the August election of 1846 enough votes were cast by those still remaining in Nauvoo to carry the election for the democrats. This might not have been the result, but it is said that the Mormons themselves admitted that their voters were allowed to vote three and four times in order to make sure of electing the democratic candidates. The whigs were again so incensed that they proposed to make one more final effort to drive out the remnant of these troublesome people. The Mormons prepared for their own defense. They had about 250 effective soldiers. They were well armed. In addition they constructed five small cannon from the shaft of a steamboat and the whole force took up its position a mile east of the temple. Defenses were erected, and defenders awaited the attack of the enemy. The town was approached by 800 well armed citizens under the guise of the posse comitatus. They also had several small cannon. The engagement began at long range. The artillery was especially active. This was kept up for a day or so, when a compromise was reached, but not before lives were lost and wounded were found on the field of battle.

The compromise provided that the Mormons should lay down their arms and immediately leave the city for the Iowa side of the river. Certain designated Mormons were allowed to stay to dispose of their property. Thus the Gentiles had at last driven beyond the borders of the state what had come to be a numerous, thrifty, and powerful people, controlling the destinies of one of the sovereign states of the Union in social relationships, in religion, in education, and in politics.

The temple was completed in the fall of 1846. There had gone out a sort of revelation that the saints could not leave Zion until the temple was completed. It thus was the lot of the Mormons to hold at bay the aggressive Gentiles and at the same time to put on the finishing touches, the gilding on the angel and trumpet, at the apex of a lofty spire 165 feet above the ground.

It has been recorded by Colonel Kane that for one day the temple, marked as follows,

The House of the Lord
Built by the Church of Jesus Christ
of Latter Day Saints
Holiness to the Lord

stood intact. It was dedicated, and the furnishings somewhat imitating the temples of the old world were all in place. That night the work of removing the sacred furnishings began. As if by magic the holy structure was dismantled. When the morning of the succeeding day dawned all the ornaments and furniture had been removed to places of safety. This day the last of the elders took their departure. For days the sad, weary procession passed over the hills adjacent to the river. From each hilltop they turned their faces toward the glittering spire which marked the place of their abandoned homes.

The deserted city was occupied in the spring by the Icarian Community—a body of earnest people with a strange philosophy of life. Their short life in Nauvoo will be considered in another place in this work.

CHAPTER XV

A TRANSITION PERIOD

Transformation—Basis of Progress—Farmers—Manufacturing—Commerce and Transportation—Population—Higher Education—Second Township—Four Colleges—Shurtleff College—McKendree College—Illinois College—The Yale Bond—Opening Day—Knox College—Some Drawbacks—Repudiation

Illinois had had but one serious problem to solve prior to its venture in internal improvements. This was the problem of whether Illinois should be a free or a slave state. Fortunately, this problem was correctly solved. Another problem was presented in 1836-7. The state was not so wise in its second decision as in the first. The period from 1836 to the Mexican war was a really critical period for the young state.

Transformation

Many people are said not to know when they are well off. This might truthfully be said of Illinois in 1836. At that time the state was on the road to prosperity. True, its institutions were not very well developed, but there was a steady growth along all lines. The lines of progress were a little uncertain, but a decade or so would have stabilized the life of the people of the state and their institutions. It is not difficult to see that the great anti-slavery fight which the good people had to make in 1823-4 was a powerful check upon the progress of the state at that time. The people were asked to give their time, their thought, their physical energy to the great contest. The industrial activities were neglected and especially were men wary about the investment of capital in new enterprises. Many enterprises particularly suited to a free state were held in check, even though they were already founded and were somewhat active and prosperous. Immigration, the one essential to the development of the state's resources, ceased because men did not know what the outcome of the convention fight would be. But the greatest blow was the lowering of moral standards. Men who desired to fasten slavery on the young state did so against their own ideals of social, industrial, and political efficiency. This blunting of the moral and religious sensibilities was a strong tide against real progress. Strong men whose power to carry on a constructive programme were obliged to defer such application of ability and were forced to enter the field in opposition to evil tendencies. Take it all in all, the convention fight of 1823-4 set the state back a decade.

A similar period of marking time lasted from 1836 to the Mexican war or later. There was derangement in nearly every line of the people's life. Men were discouraged over the outcome of even the ordinary occupations. What use to strive to be prosperous, when there was a constant menace of high taxes? It was in this period, however, that the state passed through all the vagaries in politics, economics, religion, and social upheavals. The state was able to keep the bow of the ship toward the port of permanently established institutions. But when we recall the trying times through which our people passed we are surprised that the whirlpool of disorder and mismanagement did not engulf the whole people.

Basis of Progress

Probably the explanation of the triumph of the better forces of society may be found in the elements of strength which nature placed about the young state. These are found, first, in the soil. The agricultural possibilities of the "prairie state" drew here the best types of farmers not only from the old thirteen states, but from the old world also. The variety of soil was not known in the early day, before the universities had established the scientific method of determining soil qualities, but the most superficial observer and the most unscientific farmer from the Atlantic coast knew that here the basic crops in agriculture flourished. Wheat, corn, hay, vegetables of all sorts, the fruits, and pasturage were found or could easily be produced.

Farmers

At the period we are considering it is estimated that 95 per cent of the people were farmers. This class may not be quite so idealistic, but far more practical than the people who built up our early cities. They were not so progressive as we may find today, but substantial progress was being made. This substantial growth in the field of agriculture was begun when Morris Birkbeck and Governor Coles organized the State Agricultural Society. This society was tabooed by the farmers who came from the hills and small valleys of Tennessee, Kentucky, and the Carolinas. The society received little help from the Legislature. At first the aims of this organization were made known through the limited space of the county newspapers. A few pamphlets were published, but this was an expensive means of publicity and this method was used cautiously. Out of the continued discussion of better methods of farming came the first agricultural newspaper, the Union Agriculturist and Western

Prairie Farmer. This paper was the result of the progressive spirit engendered in the Union Agricultural Society. Its first issue was in 1841. It was edited by the corresponding secretary of the society, John S. Wright. At the end of two years it passed out of the control of the society and became the property of Mr. Wright and the title was changed to the Prairie Farmer. "The scope of the paper was enlarged to include mechanics and education. John Gage was the first editor of the mechanics department." The first issue of the Prairie Farmer was January 1, 1843. Since these early days of beginnings there has grown up an army of scientifically educated farmers, editors, and teachers.

The work of the State Agricultural Society and similar larger organizations had their effect, as is shown by the organization of county agricultural societies. It was one aim of these societies to secure a greater variety of agricultural products. It seems easy for the farmer to produce corn and wheat and oats and hay, with a few vegetables and fruits for home use. But the leaders in agricultural thought desired the farmers to produce cotton, flax, hemp, tobacco, etc. Many such products were already raised by the farmers who came from the Atlantic slope.

The tools and implements found on the farms were still crude in this period of transition. Wagons were home-made, and they were heavy and clumsy, with little of the artistic about them. Plows were likewise made by the blacksmith and the wood workman. The wooden mold-board was in use, the share and the bar being of iron. Wheat was reaped with sickle or cradle and threshed by the flail on the floor of the log barn. Wool was "picked" and the rolls carded by hand. Spinning was an accomplishment which all young women must acquire. Weaving was the work usually of the mother in the home.

The raising of live stock was urged by the agricultural societies as well as by the farm papers. Cattle, hogs, sheep and fowls were raised for the markets. Meat curing establishments were found in the larger towns. The plan of curing was the salt and smoke method. In the southern part of the state, Belleville and Alton came into prominence as markets for hogs and cattle. St. Louis was from the earliest times a good market for all forms of farm products.

Manufacturing

Manufacturing was still in its infancy. The chief lines were the making of such things as were needed in the region of the factory. Few things comparatively were made for the general market. There were few iron industries in Illinois, for the raw material would need to be brought in to keep them going. The chief materials for manufacturing were wood, leather, flour hemp, flax, salt, lead, coal, furs, lumber and castor beans. There were two small foundries in the state prior to 1840; one at Springfield and one at Mt. Carmel. The chief materials produced in Illinois either as raw materials or in the early stages of manufacture were woods in great variety, hides and leather, flour, hemp and flax, salt, lead, coal, furs, castor beans. In the census of Illinois taken in 1835 there was reported:

    Manufactures _____ 339
    Mills _____ 916
    Machines _____ 87
    Distilleries _____ 142

This report was not, at the time it was made, considered very reliable. Just what was considered as manufactures was doubtful. It was thought that any sort of a shop, as a blacksmith shop, where the workman made simple tools or implements for the nearby farmers, was considered a factory. The mills included those where corn was ground, or wheat, where lumber was sawed, where there was a turning lathe, or any place where machinery was operated. The machines included brick-making machinery, machines for handling heavy weights, fan mills, cider presses, oil presses, etc. The distilleries included all forms of stills, little and big. There was no internal taxes on the manufacture of liquors and many farmers manufactured their own supply of intoxicating drinks.

The industrial life of the people in 1836 was therefore in a healthy condition. Agriculture was thriving. Manufacturing was making headway, and the resources of the state were being developed. Another decade without serious derangements would have found the state strong enough to withstand the ordinary reverses which come to a growing state.

COMMERCE AND TRANSPORTATION

Commerce had greatly increased since 1818. The increase in population had greatly stimulated the consumption of those things which must come into the state from other parts of the country. The people in 1836 had become, to some extent, the buyers of "store goods." Cotton cloth, boots and shoes, hats and caps, silks, and many kinds of imported wares, were found on the shelves of the retail stores. There were more things to send to the outside markets than ever before. Flour, hides, meats, lead, lumber, wool, coal and a score of the minor things were easily marketed even in the larger cities, as St. Louis, Cincinnati, Louisville and New Orleans.

The movement of the things we were buying and selling called for better means of transportation. The rivers were here as they had always been. They were receiving more attention from the Government than heretofore. Public roads had wonderfully improved, bridges built, and new highways opened. There were no canals or railroads in Illinois in 1836. It was to meet the needs of the people along this line that the improvement system was started in 1836. However, the rivers, small streams, and wagon roads would have served the needs for another decade, at least they did do so, as the improvement schemes did not produce any improvement in the decade following 1836.

POPULATION

The growth in population from the admission of the state into the Union to 1850 had been very rapid. The census of 1810 gives Illinois 12,282. In 1820 the census shows 55,162. This was a growth of 350 per cent increase. In 1830 the census showed 157,445, an increase over 1820 of about 200 per cent. In 1840 there were 476,183 people in Illinois. This was a gain of about 200 per cent over 1830. We thus see the increase was very regular.

THE BUILDINGS OF AN OLD LEAD MINE NEAR GALENA PRIOR TO THE CIVIL WAR

Many causes brought these goodly numbers into the limits of the State of Illinois. Social and political disturbances in the old world drove thousands to our shores. The rich prairies, fertile valleys, and abundant forests brought many to Illinois. They came to stay and took on as rapidly as they could the forms of social, political, and economic life they found here. 'Tis true, however, that there were localities where the European colonists brought with them many of the characteristics of their life in the old country, and for many years they were in America, but not of it. The population which came in the decade following 1836 located in the northern part of the state, where the public improvements were being carried on. The immigrants from the older American states went into either the northern parts of Illinois, where they began farming, merchandising, manufacturing, banking, or other forms of business. Those who went into the south end of the state took up lands and became general farmers.

The distribution of population followed the rule of moving from the south end of the state toward the north, and from the north end toward the south. This left the central part of the state the last to be occupied by permanent settlements. The density of population obtained by dividing the population of counties by the area of each gives a very good notion of the distribution. The southeast third of the state had a density of about ten people per square mile. A few counties like St. Clair, Madison, and a few others, had a density of nearly eighteen people per square mile. In the central and north central part the density would not exceed five people per square mile. Champaign County and some neighboring counties contained less than two people per square mile.

Higher Education

The Ordinance of 1787 contained a provision which may be said to have been the germ of education in Illinois. Article III reads: "Religion, morality, and knowledge, being necessary to good government and the happiness of mankind, schools and the means of education shall forever be encouraged." The Ordinance of 1785, known as the Land Ordinance of 1785, directs the public surveyors to retain section numbered 16 in each township for the use of the public schools of that township. In 1804 the Congress, by Act of March 26, directed the secretary of the treasury to locate a seminary township in each of the districts in the Northwest Territory in which a land office was located. At that time there were three land offices, one at Kaskaskia, one at Vincennes, one at Detroit. It just turned out that Illinois, Indiana, and Michigan profited by this gift of 1804. The first General Assembly of the Territory of Indiana met at Vincennes in the fall of 1806. Illinois had two representatives in that Legislature, Jesse B. Thomas, who was speaker of the House of Representatives, and Pierre Menard, who was pro tempore president of the legislative council. At this session steps were taken to organize the University of Indiana Territory. The act provided for a faculty of not more than five members, one of whom should be president. The several courses were named, and provision was made for the schooling of young Indians and also an arrangement for the education of females when the available funds would permit.

The seminary lands, one township, were made available, at least to the extent of 4,000 acres. Twenty thousand dollars was allowed to be raised by lottery. Gen. William Henry Harrison was appointed the first president.

SECOND TOWNSHIP

The enabling act for the admission of Illinois, passed in the spring of 1818, contained a provision for the gift to Illinois of a second township. In 1828-9 a bill was introduced into the General Assembly creating a state university and providing for its support by setting aside the income from the two townships. The bill failed for two reasons—the first was that the "Springfield bunch" took steps to capture the location of the university, and second, the friends to denominational colleges just then forming were not willing to compete with a school supported by the state. The bill failed and the state university was obliged to wait for several decades.

FOUR COLLEGES

All the four colleges founded in Illinois in the early days were the product of religious zeal. In fact, with the exception of the state university, all the colleges in Illinois (excepting business and technical schools) were founded by the churches. The support came largely from the East. Two were founded by the Presbyterian Church—Illinois College and Knox College, and the other two, McKendree and Shurtleff, were the result of two other churches in Illinois—the Methodist and the Baptist, respectively.

SHURTLEFF COLLEGE

To the Rev. John Peck, of St. Clair County, is usually given the honor of setting on foot the movement out of which sprang the first institution for higher education in Illinois. He was a college bred man. His chief power, however, came from his schooling in the busy university of the great outdoors. He taught and preached in St. Louis in 1818, and in 1819 he labored in St. Charles, Mo. In 1821 he came into Illinois and secured a location at Rock Springs, some eight miles northeast of Belleville. On New Year's days, 1827, he invited his friends to his house to talk over the founding of an institution of higher education. They there decided to found at Rock Springs "The Theological Seminary and High School." Doctor Peck had previous to this New Year's day solicited funds for such an institution. With his own hands, with the help of his hired men, he cut the logs with which he built the first college building in Illinois. The school was opened in the fall of 1827 with an attendance of twenty-five students, which was increased before the end of the year.

While the school had the name of a Theological Seminary and High School, the studies pursued were many of them of college rank. John Messenger was without doubt the greatest mathematician in the West, and no one was in the same class with Prof. John Russell, of Bluffdale, in the field of Latin. The school was moved to Alton in 1832. A charter was passed by the Legislature in 1833, but was declined by the trustees on two grounds. One was a clause which forbade the teaching of theology in the school; the other was a clause which prohibited the corporation from holding more land than could be used for the school. There are different explanations of the action of the Legislature. One says that the native preachers were very much set against an

THE ROCK SPRING SEMINARY BUILT BY THE REV. JOHN PECK IN 1826

educated clergy. Again there was objection to a school's holding large tracts of land, as it gave it a worldly tendency. Another explanation which might apply against Illinois and Knox was that colleges were the special favorites of the Yankees, and the people in the southern part of the state were very antagonistic to any scheme which the Yankees favored.

When the school was opened in Upper Alton in 1832, its name was changed to the Alton Seminary. The charter offered it in 1833 was to establish Alton College. In 1836 the name was changed to Shurtleff, in honor of Doctor Shurtleff, of Boston, who gave the sum of $10,000 to assist the school. In the first twenty years there were but twenty-four graduated from the school. It is said the character of the work was not lowered to allow more graduates. The school had a hard struggle for a quarter of a century.

McKendree College

Peter Cartwright came into Illinois in the spring of 1823. He bought an "improvement" in Sangamon County for $200, and moved there in the fall of the year 1824. He preached up and down the state and was a successful camp meeting preacher. In the fall of 1828 he began raising funds for a Methodist college in Illinois. He selected White Hall, in Greene County, as the location for his college and the buildings were begun. About the same time the Methodists began to raise funds and had taken steps to build a college at Lebanon, St. Clair County. In the conference of the fall of 1828 the matter came up as to whether the conference should favor the White Hall project or the one at Lebanon. It was agreed that the efforts at White Hall should be abandoned, and the conference gave its blessing to the project then under way at Lebanon.

The school was opened November 24, 1828. Mr. E. R. Ames, afterwards bishop in the Methodist Church, was principal, and a Miss McMurphy was assistant. They were to receive $25 each per month for their services. The enrollment during the first term was seventy-two, among which were five young women. This marks McKendree as coeducational from the very beginning.

In 1830 Bishop William McKendree visited the school, then known as Lebanon Seminary. The Bishop was pleased with the school and with the location, and to prove his interest in the school he made a generous offer of 480 acres of good land in the vicinity of the school. In recognition of this generous gift and of his interest in the school, the name was changed from Lebanon Seminary to McKendree College. The last name was incorporated in the school's charter of 1839. The Rev. Peter Akers was made the first president in 1835. The first class graduated in 1841. The commencement was held in a grove near the buildings. There were seven young men in the class. McKendree, as well as Shurtleff, was handicapped for want of funds. In those early days endowments were next to impossible, for it took all that could be gathered to erect buildings and provide a living wage for the teachers. Great credit is due to the early professors of our denominational colleges. But there were always those who with the missionary spirit found their field at their door and the call of the Lord of the harvest called not in vain.

Illinois College

The story of Illinois College is a companion story to those of Shurtleff and McKendree. In 1825 the American Home Missionary Society of New England sent the Rev. John M. Ellis into the West to preach the Gospel. He was provided with a hundred dollars and in six weeks he made the journey from

New England to Kaskaskia. There were then three Presbyterian ministers in Illinois—the Rev. John Birch, of Jacksonville; the Rev. Stephen Bliss, of the Wabash country; and the Rev. B. F. Spillman, of the south end of the state. The Rev. Mr. Ellis settled temporarily in Kaskaskia, from which point he visited neighborhoods as distant as fifty or sixty miles.

On one of his horseback journeys he was returning from the Sangamon country. His way led him by Rock Springs, the home of John Peck. As he was passing through the forest near Mr. Peck's home, he was attracted by the heavy sounds of an axeman at some distance from the road. His curiosity led him into the wood far enough to see a man busily at work upon some trees he had felled. Coming closer, he attracted the attention of the axeman, and after the greetings of strangers, Mr. Ellis ventured to ask what the axeman was doing. The woodsman replied, "I am building a theological seminary." "What, in these barrens?" said the traveler. "Yes, I am planting the seed." The wood chopper was no less a personage than the Rev. Dr. John Peck, the founder of Rock Springs Seminary, the forerunner of Shurtleff College.

Common ground was immediately discovered upon which the traveler and the wood chopper could stand, for the Rev. John M. Ellis had been charged by the Presbyterian Church which sent him into the West "to build up an institution of learning which should bless the West for all time." In January, 1828, Mr. Ellis and Mr. Lippincott went on a tour of inquiry and observation to the Sangamon country. At Jacksonville, so charming was the landscape, so rich the soil, and so enterprising the people who had settled there, that Mr. Ellis appears to have concluded at once that this was the place for a seminary in preference to other towns he visited. Within a few days, with characteristic promptitude, he purchased eighty acres of land and set the stakes for a building. Mr. Ellis appears to have determined to remove to Jacksonville, and in the summer (1828) he took up his residence there."

The Rev. Mr. Ellis had already made a preliminary canvass for funds to carry out his plan of founding a college. On September 15, 1828, he writes, "A seminary of learning is projected to go into operation next fall. The subscription now stands at $2,000 or $3,000. The site is in this county (Jacksonville, Morgan County). The half quarter section purchased for it is certainly the most delightful spot I have ever seen. It is about one mile north of the celebrated Diamond Grove, and overlooks the town and country for several miles around. The object of the seminary is popular, and it is my deliberate opinion that there never was in our country a more promising opportunity to bestow a few thousand dollars in the cause of education and of missions."

The Yale Band

The above letter, written to friends in the East, attracted the attention of the young men of Yale College, and they immediately consecrated themselves to the task of answering the Macedonian call of the Rev. Mr. Ellis. They immediately entered into correspondence with Mr. Ellis, who informed them that he would be in New England in the summer of 1829 to solicit funds for the proposed seminary. A compact was signed by seven young men in the theological department "to devote their lives to the cause of Christ in the distant State of Illinois." These seven young men were Mason Gosvenor, Theron Baldwin, John F. Brooks, Elisha Jenny, William Kirby, Asa Turner, and Julian H. Sturtevant. The faculty of Yale entered into the spirit of the young men. It was agreed by faculty and young men that they should not go till they had raised $10,000 with which to begin the work of founding a theological seminary. The news of the movement spread all over New England and a very deep interest was manifested everywhere. Jacksonville, Illinois, became better known in the East than any other place in the state.

In the fall of 1829 Mr. Theron Baldwin and Mr. Julian Sturtevant came to Illinois. When they reached Jacksonville they were highly pleased and wrote glowing descriptions of the wonderful West, and particularly of the environs of Jacksonville. They began immediately the erection of buildings. These they hoped to have ready by New Year's day, 1830. Mr. Baldwin proceeded to Vandalia to labor with the members of the Legislature in the securing of a charter, but as has been stated, it was difficult to secure charters that were satisfactory to the founders of higher institutions of learning.

Opening Day

The first Monday in January, 1830, was set for the opening day of the college. On that day the first thing was to put up a stove which occupied two hours. This task engaged the attention of the trustees, the faculty, and students, and the carpenters. This first battle being over, the "school was called to order" and the nine young men took their designated places. The first thing was an earnest prayer in which "we commended ourselves and the whole great enterprise to God." Upon examination as to the advancement of the students, Mr. Sturtevant found that no one of the nine had ever studied English grammar, few were well founded in the principal operations in arithmetic, and only two had had any instruction in the rudiments of Latin.

The first class was graduated in 1835. Among those receiving diplomas was Richard Yates, Illinois' great "war governor." The school had its ups and downs, mostly downs, for the first dozen years, but after 1840 the school had the advantage of more help from the East. Illinois college played an important part in the slavery conflict between its founding and 1860.

Knox College

Knox college owes its founding and its early life to George Washington Gale, a native of New York. He was a graduate of Union College and later studied Theology at Princeton, New Jersey. He founded the Oneida Institute at Whitesboro, New York in 1827. Here he remained till 1834. In 1835 he sent a committee into Illinois to hunt out a location for a similar school to the one at Whitesboro. The site of the present city of Galesburg was selected and to this place Dr. Gale came in 1836 or the next year. In the year 1836 Dr. Gale and his friends determined on the school and it was named Prairie College. In 1837 its name was changed to "The Knox Manuel Labor College." A building was erected and school was opened in the fall of 1838. A village was started on the half section which was purchased by the committee which picked the site for the college. It was a Yankee school and the people who had moved into that part of Illinois from the southern states did not take kindly to patronizing it. The school was founded by the Presbyterians, but became non-denominational.

Some Drawbacks

The substantial growth of the life of the people from the close of the Black Hawk war to the Mexican war has been shown in many ways, yet in spite of a rapid growth in population, a diversified industrial activity, improved transportation, a rich and inexhaustible soil, and a broadened outlook upon the world as indicated by the unselfish activities in religion and education, there were discouraging problems which called for the most unfaltering faith that the dark clouds would give place to better and brighter days.

Nothing was more discouraging in these passing days than the attitude of the political parties toward the most threatening danger to which the state was probably ever subjected. The people of the state prior to 1836 had taken little interest in party politics. By 1840 the opposition to the Jackson democrats had crystallized about the doctrines of the whig party. Before this time however party politics had been carried into the complicated measures of the improvement system. Nor was the banking system free from the curse of party politics. The banking system which was inaugurated in 1834 was the work of the democrats, but from some cause or other the organization and conduct of the banks fell into the hands of the anti-Jackson men—the whigs. And there was not a year from 1834 to the final downfall of the system that the value of the banks to the people was not counteracted in some measure by the attitude of the political parties toward each other relative to the bank.

The complications which arose from the relation of the Mormons to the two political parties were calculated to cause honest patriotic people to question the professions of the politicians. It is within the bounds of reason to say that if the Mormons had been told by the whigs and democrats in 1839 that as a religious sect they would be protected by the law, but that neither party would do anything to aid them in building up a state within a state, there need not have been five or six years of disgraceful pretensions on the part of the Mormons that they could set aside

OLD MANSION HOUSE, BELLEVILLE
Where Charles Dickens dined when he visited Belleville in 1842

the laws of the state and defy its executive and judicial departments. There never was any justification for the issuing of the Nauvoo city charter. The whole matter of complying with the wish of the Mormons was a race between the whigs and the democrats to see which party would get the Mormons to cast enough votes to carry their side to victory in the election.

Lawlessness is a political disease which spreads in the same manner as other contagions. There was little but lawlessness practiced by many in and out of Nauvoo during the stay of the Mormons. It must not be thought that this disease was not among our people prior to 1839. The mob spirit which grew into murder in the Lovejoy riots is evidence that there was fertile soil in that section as early as 1836.

In 1840, in the northern part of the state, there were organized bands of counterfeiters, horse thieves, and swindlers. It was impossible to bring the members of these bands to justice as there were so many avenues of escape, changes of venue, perjured evidence, and tampered juries. The good people, after their patience was exhausted took the law into their own hands and by as unlawful acts as the counterfeiters and thieves were guilty of, they drove these people out of the land. The action of the good people was justified by the theory that an act may be unlawful but if it mete out justice it is permissible.

The most complete setting aside of the recognized procedure for the trial and punishment of violations of the law was found in Massac and parts of adjoining counties toward the close of Governor Ford's term. The Hon. James A. Rose, now deceased, for many years Secretary of State, has given a very full account of this period and of the particular participants in the disgraceful events. The article may be found in the Publication of the State Historical Society, No. 9.

In brief the story may be stated that a criminal under arrest revealed the existence of a large number of people banded together for the purpose of committing crimes in the counties of what is now Hardin, Pope, and Massac. In the election of August, 1846, these outlaws elected the sheriff and county clerk of Massac County. The better element then determined to meet these outlaws with illegal means since the legal processes were in the hands of the outlaws. Then the war began. Those citizens who banded themselves together to secure safety of life and property were called Regulators and those who had defied the law were called Flatheads. The Regulators seized suspected persons, punished some and tortured others and in this way secured the leaders of the outlaws and some knowledge of their organization. The feud spread and many people at first not interested later became active partisans. Efforts were made to bring criminals to justice, but with poor success. In one instance the sheriff's posse was overpowered, the jail emptied and some of the sheriff's posse carried off and punished. The disordered state of society in the region of the Ohio River attracted the attention of the governor and the Legislature. Special laws were enacted and special courts instituted and in the course of time order was restored.

A problem arose about the time the canal was under construction by reason of the presence of hundreds of foreigners who had come because of the demand for laborers. This problem became a political one. The Constitution of 1818 allowed any male to vote who was 21 or over, was white, and had resided in the county or voting district for six months preceding the election. Most of these laborers on the canal voted the democratic ticket, and the whigs took the matter before the courts. Here politics played an important part and resulted in a complete reorganization of the circuit and Supreme Courts.

REPUDIATION

When Governor Ford came into office, there was a very widespread feeling that the internal improvement debt of about $15,000,000 should be repudiated. Many public men talked repudiation but not for publication. Governor Ford had very positive views on the matter. He believed that we could eventually pay the debt and that we were morally bound to do so. A few brave souls took a strong stand against repudiation and its proponents were afraid to defend it for fear of their political future.

"Notwithstanding the evidences of healthy growth, Illinois at this period was in a crude and undeveloped condition. She had not yet come under the magic influence of the electric telegraph, nor the steam railway, which she was soon to feel, and had received but little benefit from the inventive genius of the American mechanic.—There were but five daily and forty-five weekly newspapers published in the state.—But two of the state benevolent institutions had been established, and they were operated on small scale. The land was still plowed by the cast-iron plow with wooden mold boards, the corn planted by hand, the golden grain gathered by the sickle or cradle, threshed by flail or horse power and winnowed by hand."

CHAPTER XVI

ILLINOIS IN THE MEXICAN WAR

THE SLOGAN—CALL TO ARMS—THE ORGANIZATION—OFF FOR THE WAR—POLITICS—ILLINOIS TROOPS RETURN

The two great political parties, the whigs and the democrats, were very evenly matched in numbers in 1840, but by 1844, the whigs had lost in the race. By the election of 1840, when there were three congressmen from Illinois, one was a whig and two were democrats. In 1844, there were seven congressional district. The whigs carried one and the democrats were successful in six. Illinois was therefore a democratic state in 1844, and more democratic in 1846. The democratic party had received a great setback in 1840, and though the death of Harrison had thrown the presidency into the hands of the democrats, yet they were scarcely able to recover by 1844. The admission of Texas into the Union had been before the Congress in one form or another since Texas gained her independence in 1836. Texas wanted to be admitted as a state into the Union. The southern democrats were favorable to the admission. Tyler who wished to restore himself in the favor of the South, openly favored the annexation of Texas. In the early part of the year 1844, Tyler negotiated a treaty of annexation with Texas. This he sent to the Senate for ratification, but it failed for want of a two-thirds majority. The presidential campaign was approaching and Texas must be annexed by hook or crook.

THE SLOGAN

The whigs were fairly well united in 1844. Their presidential candidate was Henry Clay. The democrats felt that Van Buren who had been beaten by Harrison in 1840, should be their leader, but a letter in which he stated his objections to the annexation of Texas, was his undoing. The convention named James K. Polk of Tennessee. The campaign cry was "The Reannexation of Texas and Fifty-four forty or Fight." Clay was unable to stem the tide against a war cry that appealed to the slave holding interests of the South and at the same time to the anti-slavery forces of the North. Polk was elected. Tyler now decided to approach the annexation of Texas from a different angle. A joint resolution was introduced providing for the admission of Texas into the Union as a state. The resolution passed both houses of Congress, the President signed it and it was ratified by the Texas government and the deed was done.

Texas claimed the Rio Grande as the western boundary while Mexico claimed the Nueces River as the eastern boundary of that country, and at the same time denied the independence of Texas. The United States designated the disputed territory as a revenue district for the collection of tariff duties. General Scott also was ordered to occupy the disputed area as United States territory. This then was the occasion of war. Mexican troops crossed into this disputed strip and a skirmish with United States troops resulted in the death of a few soldiers. It was then that the Congress declared that a state of war exists by the act of Mexico herself.

CALL TO ARMS

Legislation was now hurriedly passed authorizing the President to call for 50,000 volunteers and appropriating $10,000,000 with which to carry on the war. Polk, in his inaugural address, had said that there were four great measures which he wished to carry through during his administration. They were—first, to reduce the tariff; second, to reestablish the independent treasury; third, to settle the Oregon boundary; and fourth, to acquire California. Just what was the explanation of the President's declaration that the acquisition of California was one of four great measures? It belonged to a friendly nation who had on several occasions refused to sell it or in any way to part with it. The term California included more territory then than the present state of California.

The only way that we can see how he might acquire California was to provoke Mexico to war and then by overwhelming numbers and by unlimited resources crush her and take from her the fairest portion of her territory. The occasion for war was at hand. It was a strip of territory lying between the Rio Grande and the Nueces rivers.

Diplomatic relations had been suspended between the United States and Mexico at the passage of the annexation bill in 1845. It was generally known that Mexico would not tamely submit to the loss of Texas including the disputed strip between the two rivers.

Gen. Zachary Taylor was sent into the disputed territory with an "Army of Occupation" and a fleet of warships was in the Gulf of Mexico. Every one expected war. Illinois people were not especially interested in the conquest of Mexico. The slave interests had already profited politically and economically by the acquisition of Texas. Just why people in Illinois should be interested in a further acquisition of slave territory is difficult at this time to understand.

The news went abroad that "American blood had been shed on American soil." The call for troops caused the red blood to flow a little faster, and the opportunity was at hand for the adventurer to say nothing derogatory of the patriotic minded citizen who is always ready to answer the call of his country. The 50,000 volunteers were by some plan apportioned chiefly to the south and west. Illinois was authorized to furnish three regiments—3,000 troops. Illinois people were familiar with many of the officers of high rank in the United States army. Gen. Zachary Taylor who was in command of the "Army of Occupation," was familiarly known by scores of the men who were in

Courtesy Chicago Historical Society

MEXICAN WAR SOLDIER

the Black Hawk war. He was a major and later lieutenant-colonel. Jefferson Davis, who led a Mississippi regiment, was second lieutenant with the regulars in the Indian war. Gen. W. S. Harney led a cavalry contingent from Vera Cruz to Mexico City under General Scott. Harney was a captain in the Black Hawk war. General Twiggs, who commanded a division under General Scott. Lieut. Edward D. Baker, who was an active young officer in the Black Hawk war, was colonel of the Fourth Regiment, Illinois troops, in the Mexican war. Lieut. Albert Sidney Johnston was a young officer in the regular army in the Black Hawk war. So also was Joseph E. Johnston in the Illinois war. They both had honorable parts in the Mexican war.

When it was known that war had been declared and that Illinois was to furnish approximately 3,000 troops, there was great activity in military circles. The pay for privates was $8.00 per month, but with commutations it amounted to $15.50. The enlistments were for one year as it was thought that a peace could be conquered within that time. Governor Ford issued his general order, as commander-in-chief of the militia, to the officers in the several districts to call for volunteers for the war. On account of the long period of the Mormon disturbances, the militia was badly disorganized and to meet the situation the sheriffs were asked to convene the old organizations and to enroll such additional individuals as desired to enter the United States service. It was announced that each company would contain about eighty privates, and the first full companies organized would be accepted, till the state's quota was filled. Military orders were scattered over the state and patriotic speeches were made by ambitious military leaders. The gallant John J. Hardin was the first volunteer. There were prompt responses by the people to the call for the nation's defenders. In ten days, more than the state's quota was reported to the governor. It is said that by the middle of June forty companies above the quota were offered. Each company was to elect its own officers who should serve under certificates of election until the Government should issue commissions. Alton was designated as the place of rendezvous and to this point the several companies were ordered by the governor. There was great disappointment over the state among the companies that were not selected to fill the quota.

The Organization

The three regiments were organized:

First Regiment

Colonel—John J. Hardin, Jacksonville.
Lieutenant-Colonel—William Weatherford.
Major—W. B. Warren.
Adjutant—B. M. Prentiss.
Commissary—John Scanlan.
Quartermaster—S. M. Parsons.
Sergeant-Major—Edward A. Giller.
Drum-Major—A. W. Fry.
Surgeon—Dr. White.
Assistant Surgeon—Dr. Zabreskie.

Captains

J. D. Morgan, Adams County.
Elisha Wells, Cook County.
Noah Fry, Greene County.

J. S. Roberts, Morgan County.
W. A. Richardson, Schuyler County.
Lyman Mowers, Cook County.
T. Lyle Dickey, LaSalle County.
A. W. Crow, Jo Daviess County.
Wm. Weatherford, Morgan County.
Samuel Montgomery, Scott County.

Second Regiment

Colonel—Wm. H. Bissell, Belleville.
Lieutenant-Colonel—J. L. D. Morrison.
Major—H. F. Trail.
Adjutant—A. Whitesides.
Sutler—Lewis J. Clawson.

Captains

Peter Goff, Madison County.
*J. L. D. Morrison, St. Clair County.
Erastus Wheeler, Madison.
A. Dodge, Kendall County.
W. H. Bissell, St. Clair County.
E. C. Coffee, Washington County.
*H. T. Trail, Monroe County.
John S. Hacker, Union County.
L. G. Jones, Perry County.
H. L. Webb, Pulaski County.

Julius Raith, Joseph Lemon, and Madison Miller were also captains.

Third Regiment

Colonel—Ferris Foreman, Vandalia.
Lieutenant-Colonel—W. W. Wiley.
Major—Samuel D. Marshall.
Adjutant—J. T. B. Stapp.

Captains

*Ferris Foreman, Fayette County.
J. C. McAdams, Bond County.
M. K. Lawler, Gallatin County.
Teo. McGinnis, Pope County.
*W. W. Wiley, Bond county.
J. A. Campbell, Wayne County.
W. W. Bishop, Coles County.
A. G. Hicks, Jefferson County.
James Freeman, Shelby County.
J. P. Hardy, Hamilton.

Philip Stout and B. S. Sellers were also captains in this regiment.

---

*Promoted.

Fourth Regiment

Colonel—Edward D. Baker.
Lieutenant-Colonel—John Moore.
Major—Thomas L. Harris.
Adjutant—Wm. B. Fondey.
Quartermaster—James A. Barrett and Joel S. Post.

Captains

Garret Elkin, McLean County.
John C. Hunt, Logan County.
Edward Jones, Tazewell County.
John S. McConkey, Edgar County.
Achilles Morris, Sangamon County.
Daniel Newcomb, DeWitt County.
Isaac C. Pugh, Macon County.
Horatio E. Roberts, Sangamon County.
Lewis W. Ross, Fulton County.
Asa D. Wright, ——————.

Fifth Regiment

Colonel—W. B. Newby.
Lieutenant-Colonel—Henderson P. Boyakin.
Major—Israel B. Donaldson,
Adjutant—Wm. H. Snyder.
Surgeons—Daniel, Turney, and James D. Robinson.
Quartermaster—Richard N. Hamilton.

Captains

John H. Adams, Shelby County.
John M. Cunningham, Williamson County.
James Hampton, Jackson County.
George W. Hook, St. Clair County.
Wm. Kinman, Pike County.
Thomas B. Kinney, Cook County.
John C. Moses, Brown County.
Franklin Niles.
Henry J. Reed, LaSalle County.
Vantrump Turner, Marion County.

Sixth Regiment

Colonel—John Collins.
Lieutenant-Colonel—Stephen G. Hicks.
Major—Thomas S. Livingston.
Adjutants—Henry S. Fitch and James H. Sampson.
Surgeon—John L. Miller.
Quartermasters—Elisha Lewis and Lewis A. Norton.

Captains

David C. Beery.
James Bowman.
John Brestow.
James Burns.
John Ewing.
Henry S. Fitch.
Edward E. Harvey.
Harvey Lee.
Thomas J. Mooneyham.
John M. Moore.
James R. Pierce.
Levin H. Powell.
Wm. Shepard.
Sewell W. Smith.
Calmes L. Wright.

Independent Companies

First—Captain, Adam S. Dunlap.
Second—Captain, Wyatt B. Stapp.
Third—Captain, Michael K. Lawler.
Fourth—Captain, Josiah Littell.

The original order from the War Department was for three regiments from Illinois. It turned out that another regiment was accepted by reason of the influence of Congressman Edward D. Baker. Baker was made colonel of the regiment and he had only to name the companies already enlisted and ready to go on a moment's warning. In the spring of 1847 Congress made a second call for volunteers, and two additional regiments were assigned to Illinois. These were organized as shown above. This made six regiments of nearly a thousand each. In addition there were four independent companies as listed above. To all of these enlistments there should be added 150 individuals who enlisted in the regular army.

War is after all a hideous thing but in spite of that fact there are always great numbers of people who are ready for the call to arms. The state had been in a disturbed condition since 1840, and there had been many appeals to arms in that period. In many towns in Illinois there were well organized militia companies. These were made up of young men of good families. They frequently went to the expense of procuring uniforms, guns, and other equipment. They met regularly for drill and discipline. Attention has already been called to the Carthage Grays which were active in the latter part of the Mormon war. These independent militia organizations became

---

*This list includes promotions and appointments by reason of deaths and promotions.

the nuclei of the companies which made up the army from Illinois. It has been explained that the times were out of joint in Illinois when the Mexican war began and that the hard times and poor prices for farm products made a restless people.

OFF FOR THE WAR.

The First and Second regiments left Alton on July 17, 18, 19, on board three Mississippi steamers, the Convoy, the Missouri, and the Hannibal. They transhipped at New Orleans for Matagorda Bay, where they landed August 7th. They were accompanied by General Wool. From Port Levacca on Matagorda Bay the First and Second regiments marched up the San Antonio River to the vicinity of the City of San Antonio. The distance was 120 miles and was traversed between the 7th and the 23d of August. Here they remained from the 23d of August to the 26th of September. General Wool was in command and there were about 3,000 troops. On September 26th the little army broke camp and marched a little south of west about 140 miles to the vicinity of Eagle Pass, Texas. Here they crossed the Rio Grande and turned southwest toward Monclova, Mexico, which they reached November 23. From Monclova south and west to Parras thence southeast to the great road from San Luis Potosi to Saltillo. Here General Wool with the First and Second regiments of Illinois troops was joined by General Taylor with 5,000 troops. Here, where the great road runs through the "narrows" was fought the battle of Buena Vista. This battle was begun on February 22, 1847, but night stopped the conflict. It was renewed on the 23d and raged nearly all day. The Illinois troops, the First and Second regiments under Colonels Hardin and Bissell won great glory on this day. The battle was fought over broken plateaus and intervening gorges. Infantry, cavalry and artillery participated. The total American troops numbered not over 5000, while General Santa Ana is said to have had as many as 20,000.

At the close of the second day's battle, after the Mexicans were in full retreat, three colonels, Hardin and Bissell of Illinois, and McKee of Kentucky, pursued the retreating foe. Their commands were attacked by a force five times as numerous and in seeking a sheltered place from the attacks of the Mexicans they were entrapped in a gorge and after a slaughter of twenty minutes were relieved by the arrival of a battery, but among the dead was the beloved Colonel John J. Hardin.

Night put an end to this battle in the gorges and on the spurs of the nearby mountains. On the morning of the 24th there were no Mexican troops within sight or hearing of the American outposts. It was now a sad task for the living to care for the dead and wounded. The total loss on the American side was: killed, 264; wounded, 482. The loss of the Mexicans was

2,500. The First Regiment lost in this battle, 29 killed, and 16 wounded; the Second Regiment lost in killed 62, wounded, 69.

The Third Regiment of Illinois troops, Colonel Foreman in command, left Alton July 22, in the river steamers, Glencoe and John Aull. The Fourth Regiment had been in camp at Jefferson Barracks. On July 23, two other river steamers, the Sultana and the Eclipse, received the Fourth Regiment. The two regiments then steamed for New Orleans thence to Camargo, a mobilization point some distance up the Rio Grande. It was the plan that the Third and Fourth Illinois should reach Camargo in time to accompany General Taylor on his march up the Rio Grande but they were too late. In fact General Taylor left a strong garrison at Camargo, though he took about 7,000 with him in his march on Monterey.

Politics

The magnificent victories which Taylor had won—Palo Alto, Resaca de la Palma, Matamoras, Monterey, Saltillo, and Buena Vista—had been broadcasted in every whig newspaper in the United States. Already his name had been mentioned in connection with the whig nomination for the presidency. He was thought to be a whig, although he had taken little part in politics, and it has been said had never voted. The campaign for the presidency would occur in the summer of 1848. If Taylor shall have the support of the administration if men and money and a free hand can be provided he will soon bring the proud Mexicans to their knees. But Polk was a partisan first and last, and the possibility of Taylor's successful finish of the war must be prevented.

Gen. Winfield Scott was commander-in-chief of the armies and a man of wonderfully wide experience in war. He was not put into the field at the time the war came on and he had been fretting to get into the conflict. He too, was a whig, and had been an aspirant for the presidency. This may account for the choice of Taylor as commander of the army of occupation, as he was probably not an aspirant for the presidency. The field was thoroughly gleaned and there was not a democrat who could be given the task of conquering Mexico. The only thing to do now was either to let Taylor go on with the task or allow another to share the honors that were surely to fall to some one.

A new plan of campaign was thought out. An army of conquest must march from Vera Cruz to the capital of the republic. And as the thought was elaborated it was discovered that the easiest way to dispose of General Taylor would be to withdraw all his troops from him and turn them over to Scott and thus leave Taylor to mark time along the Rio Grande. This was the order—General Scott was to sail to Vera Cruz, capture that city and march triumphantly to the City of Mexico. Taylor was notified that he must send a large part of his troops along the Rio Grande to be added to those brought by Scott himself. There was the element of a good soldier in Taylor—obedience. The plan of attacking Mexico by way of Vera Cruz and Mexico City was decided on before the final great victory of Buena Vista. It was the knowledge of this change of plan on the part of the Government of the United States which brought on the last and greatest victory of General Taylor. Santa Ana thought he could attack and crush General Taylor at or near Monterey and return to the defense of Vera Cruz and Mexico City before General Scott could reach the Mexican coast. In this he was sadly mistaken, as we have seen.

General Scott had very early in the war outlined a plan of campaign for the conquest of Mexico. It did not meet with the endorsement of the President and so Scott did not get a chance to carry out his plan—at least not at that time. Now that the President and his advisers had determined to send Scott to Mexico, they were willing that he should follow his own plans. It was believed by the administration that Scott would take such an attitude toward Taylor that the latter would be put out of the race for the presidency, and yet it was hoped that Scott would not make capital enough to enable him to secure the whig nomination.

Illinois now had four regiments in Mexico. The First and Second at or near Monterey, while the Third and Fourth were at Camargo on the lower Rio Grande. When Scott's expedition sailed into the Gulf of Mexico, he wished to disembark at the mouth of the Rio Grande in order to have a conference with General Taylor, but Taylor had gone to Tampico and Scott failed to have a chance to confer with him. He took from Taylor such troops as he chose and among those selected were the Third and Fourth Illinois regiments at Camargo. The First and Second were left with Taylor, who was ordered to fall back to the Rio Grande and hold that region of the country. The Third and Fourth Illinois regiments and a New York regiment were made into a brigade and placed under Gen. James Shields.

The invading army was landed a few miles south of the City of Vera Cruz. It contained about 12,000 troops. The debarkation was a difficult task as all men and materials had to be taken ashore in surf boats. When everything was ready the army moved to within a few miles of the City of Vera Cruz. This was a walled city with forts at intervals around the semi-circular walls. Artillery was pushed to within range of the walls and forts, and the bombardment began March 9th, and was continued till the 27th of March. The city and harbor fortifications were surrendered with about 5,000 prisoners and 400 pieces of artillery.

It was now necessary to get the American soldiers away from Vera Cruz in order to escape the yellow fever which was due in the early summer. It was also necessary to leave a considerable force in Vera Cruz and along the route to Mexico City to secure communication with the base at Vera Cruz. The army consisting of about 10,000 men was organized in three divisions under the command of Generals Twiggs, Patterson, and Worth, and they moved in that order away from Vera Cruz. There were two fairly good roads from Vera Cruz to Mexico City. One called the south road passed through Cordova and Orizaba and reached the eastern end of the plain of Mexico City. The other called the north road passed through Cerro Gordo, Jalapa, Perote, Pueblo and joined the south road at the eastern edge of the plain of Mexico City. General Scott, after a careful study of the two roads, selected the north one.

The three divisions moved out as follows: Twiggs, April 8; Patterson, 10; Worth, 13. General Twiggs and General Patterson reached Cerro Gordo and awaited the coming of General Worth who arrived the 18th of April. Here they encountered General Santa Ana with 15,000 seasoned troops just from his defeat at Buena Vista. General Scott pronounced the position of Santa Ana impregnable, and ordered a road cut in the rear of the Mexican position. This task was accomplished. Here as elsewhere the Illinois troops won great praise. The new road in the rear of Santa Ana crossed a chasm at right angles several hundred feet deep. If batteries could be gotten across this chasm and placed on the farther hills, the enemy could be dislodged. The task of transferring a 24-pound battery across the chasm was assigned to Gen. James Shields' brigade made up of the Third Illinois, Col. Ferris Foreman commanding, and the Fourth Illinois, Col. E. D. Baker commanding, and a regiment from New York. This brigade under the intrepid leadership of General Shields let the cannon down on the rear side of the gorge by strong ropes. They were then pulled up the farther side in the same manner and during the night the battery was placed in position to the rear of Santa Ana's intrenchments. On the morrow the work of driving the Mexicans from their entrenchments began and before the close of the day the battle was won. Santa Ana was able to retreat on the road to Jalapa leaving the road to Vera Cruz open for the use of the Americans.

In the attack upon the Mexicans the battle raged with varying success. The Shields brigade faced a well manned battery of Mexicans and in the midst of the conflict, General Shields fell with a grape-shot through his lungs. He was reported mortally wounded and his obituary was printed in the several newspapers. But he survived and returned a great hero of the war. The command of the brigade devolved upon Col. E. D. Baker. Colonel Baker was equal to the demand upon him, but he says he was ably assisted by Colonel Foreman, Colonel Burnett of the New York regiment, and Major Harris of the Fourth Illinois. There was a loss of 70 killed and wounded in this brigade; 417 for the American forces—64 killed and 353 wounded.

General Twiggs speaks in the highest terms of the two Illinois regiments in the battle of Cerro Gordo and also in the pursuit of the retreating Mexicans. "The gallant troops of Illinois shared to no inconsiderable extent in the dangers, toils, and hardships, as their large ratio of losses attest, and their heroic deeds have reflected imperishable honor and glory upon our state."

Illinois Troops Return

From the victory of Cerro Gordo the American army marched along the national road to Jalapa, a place not defended by Santa Ana. Here the invading army halted for a considerble time. General Scott had about 9,000 men and he was anxious to give them advantage of a rest on this upland plain. It was a point noted for its healthfulness, and there was an abundance of food of needed variety. General Scott knew that the time of the enlistment of nearly half of his men was about to expire. Upon inquiring he found that the Third and Fourth Illinois regiments did not care to reenlist. They had served the one year which was the period of enlistment, and the year had been a trying one. They were therefore ready to take their leave of the land of cactus and hot tamales. General Scott was also looking for reinforcements and he waited at Jalapa to exchange 4,000 seasoned troops for as many or more fresh but untried enlistments. The Third and Fourth returned from the interior and reached New Orleans and were mustered out May 25. The veteran First and Second regiments left Buena Vista and rested at Camargo a short time before being mustered out at that place June 17, 1847. The First brought the body of their beloved colonel, John J. Hardin, who had made the supreme sacrifice at Buena Vista. He was buried at Jacksonville.

The Fifth Regiment was mustered in at Alton June 8, 1847. The colonel was E. W. B. Newby. On the 14th of June the regiment left by boat for Fort Leavenworth. From Fort Leavenworth the regiment marched overland to Santa Fe. Here they remained at garrison duty though some of the companies went as far as El Paso. Stuve says that some of the members of this regiment organized a Masonic Lodge while in far-away Santa Fe.

The Sixth Regiment was organized and entered service at Alton. At New Orleans the regiment was divided into two battalions, the first was sent to Vera Cruz and the second to Tampico. Garrison duty was the lot of these two battalions, though the first did guard duty on the national road for a short time.

The records show that during the time the United States was at war with Mexico there were 73,776 volunteers entered the military service (all branches), while at the same time there were 42,545 regulars enrolled. Illinois furnished 6,123 volunteers, suffered a loss of 80 killed, 12 died of wounds, and 160 wounded.

The return of a nation's soldiery from the field of war is a great event in the life of that people. Creeds and political differences are forgotten, and all join in one affectionate welcome. It was so when the heroes of Monterey, Buena Vista, Vera Cruz, and Cerro Gordo returned to their friends and loved ones. "Public dinners, complimentary toasts, flattering addresses, and fulsome speeches were showered upon them; the newspaper press vied with the orators of the period in praises of the heroic deeds of our volunteer soldiery, while, as aspirants for office, all mere civilians had to stand aside and leave the track for the proud patrons of Mars, or be crushed in the results."

One of the most touching incidents upon the return of the troops from Mexico was a detachment of 300 men out of the First Regiment who bore the remains of their beloved commander to his last resting place in the beautiful young city of his young manhood. Richard Yates, who had studied law under Colonel Hardin, was selected to deliver the funeral oration.

CHAPTER XVII

THE CONSTITUTION OF 1848

CONSTITUTION NOT SUBMITTED—FIRST EFFORT—SOME CHANGES—MEN OF PROMINENCE—ECONOMY—OTHER CHANGES—RATIFICATION—GOVERNOR FRENCH

The Constitution of 1818 was the product of only about a dozen days of actual convention work. The convention met on August 3, and adjourned the 26th of the same month. A committee of fifteen was named on the 5th whose duty it should be "to frame and report to this convention a constitution for the people of the Territory of Illinois." The committee reported on the 12th. Thus the convention marked time for the first ten days of the session. When the committee reported, the convention took up the work of either accepting or rejecting the various details of the proposed draft. A very large part of the dozen days the convention worked on the proposed plan, a large part was put in on a discussion as to the question of slavery.

CONSTITUTION NOT SUBMITTED

When the constitution was completed, a common courtesy would have suggested that it be turned over to the people for whom this basic law was written. But the people were not consulted as to whether they would accept its provisions or not. On the contrary it was presented to the Congress for its acceptance.

The expression, "constitutional convention," has more meaning in it today than it had in the early history of our country. When the thirteen colonies threw off the English control in the days of '76, there was need of constitutions for the new sovereign states. Connecticut and Rhode Island by slight changes in their charters, which had been granted by Charles the Second, adapted those charters to the needs of their states for nearly three-quarters of a century. All the other eleven states wrote anew their old charters or adopted entirely new basic laws. Massachusetts was the only state of the eleven whose constitution was made by a convention of delegates especially elected for that purpose. In all other cases the fundamental law was the handiwork of the legislative bodies, and so far as we have been able to determine, these constitutions were never ratified by the people of the several states. The Articles of

Confederation were framed by what was understood to be a legislative body.

But the day has passed when men understood that "government was of the people, for the people, and by the select few."

Another evidence of the disregard in which the common people were held in the matter of making the Constitution of 1818, was the very limited number of elective offices which the people were allowed to fill by the exercise of their franchise.

First Effort

The first effort to revise the constitution was not an effort to correct any of the real weak places in the constitution, but it was an effort in plain language to turn Illinois from a free state to a slave state. There were a few intimations that there were certain phases of the constitution which ought to be remedied. The real secret may be drawn from a clause in the report of the committee appointed to consider the governor's message. "Your committee are clearly of the opinion that the people of Illinois have now the same right to alter their constitution as the people of the State of Virginia, or any of the original states, and may make any disposition of Negro slavery they choose, without any breach of faith or violation of compact, ordinances or acts of Congress."

In the earlier stages of the canvass for or against the convention, there was a bit of timidity about acknowledging the real purpose of the friends of the convention, but long before the close of the campaign every one admitted that the purpose of the convention people was to make Illinois a slave state. In all probability if the convention cause had carried, there would have been some changes in the constitution that were made in 1848.

Another joint resolution by the Legislature was passed in the session of 1840-1. It provided for a vote for or against a constitutional convention at the general election in August, 1842. This proposition also was voted down by a small majority. Another joint resolution to hold a convention was passed by the Legislature in 1844-5. The election was held at the regular election in 1846. The proposition carried. At a special election held on April 19, 1847, delegates to a constitutional convention to be held in Springfield June 7, 1847, were chosen. The convention was made up of 162 delegates.

Some Changes

The constitution made so hurriedly in Kaskaskia in 1818, had been in use thirty years and the experience of practical people will be a guide in the revision of that document. There was some see-sawing between the whigs and democrats but that aside we enumerate some of the changes which were suggested beforehand. These suggested changes are not enumerated in any logical order.

In the Constitution of 1818 the judges of the Supreme Court were elected by joint ballot of the Legislature. This was changed to an election by the legal voters of the state.

The right to vote under the Constitution of 1818 included three requisites. One must be a white man over twenty-one years of age, and must have lived in the county or district in which he proposed to vote six months prior to the day of election. In the new constitution the one who wishes to vote must be a white male citizen over twenty-one years of age, and shall have resided in the state one year.

A third defect of the old constitution was found in the very limited number of officers who should be elected by the voters of the state. The governor, lieutenant-governor, members of the General Assembly, sheriffs, and coroners were the only elective officers. In addition to these the list of elective officers included a secretary of state, auditor of public accounts, a state treasurer Supreme judges, circuit judges, county judges, clerks of the Supreme and Circuit courts, state's attorneys. The foregoing are known as constitutional offices. The Constitution of 1818 also made provision for a few legislative offices.

The Constitution of 1818 did not limit the term of years of some of the officers. Considerable objection was made to this oversight on the part of our statesmen of 1818. Offices filled by the governor and some others came under this head. It was demanded that there should be a definte term of years stated for each office. This defect was remedied in the Constitution of 1848.

Considerable objection was found especially to the plan of the Legislature's electing the judges of the Supreme Court.

There was a demand also that the constitution prohibit the Legislature from organizing any form of banking system without a vote of the people. And also a similar prohibition that the Legislature could not borrow money only in limited quantities and for specific purposes.

In the old constitution there was created a Council of Revision, consisting of the governor and the four members of the Supreme Court. When bills were sent to the governor he with the members of the Supreme Court sat as a sort of council, and passed upon the wisdom or unwisdom of the laws. If three out of the five favored a proposed law it was signed by those three and became a law. If three or more objected to a law they entered their objection and the bill was returned to the house in which it originated. If each house should pass the bill the second time by a majority of the whole number elected it shall become a law. Most public men were of the opinion that the governor should have the veto power, and it was so provided in the Constitution of 1848, but a majority of those elected in each house could over ride the veto.

The old constitution limited the number of senators and representatives until after the state's population should exceed 100,000 people; after that the Legislature could increase or decrease the number of members of the two houses provided a certain ratio between the Senate and the House be maintained. The new constitution provided that there should be twenty-five senators and seventy-five representatives until the population of the state should reach 1,000,000, after which a plan was devised for an increase in the House but not in the Senate.

Another fault found with the old constitution was the matter of age requirement for public officials. This weakness in the requirement for public officials was corrected.

The Constitution of 1818 made a quorum to do business two-thirds of the number elected in each house. Then a majority of this two-thirds could enact laws. In this way laws could be enacted by one vote more than one-third of the number elected. The new constitution says, "No bill shall become a law without the concurrence of a majority of all the numbers elected in each house."

In the old constitution provision was made which put the business of the county in the hands of commissioners. There was complaint that the business of the county was often poorly managed and there was a demand for a system which would put the care of the county government into the hands of the people. Section 6 of Article XII of the Constitution of 1848 provides for a system of "township government" which may be adopted at any time the majority of voters decide to inaugurate that plan of county government.

The Constitution of 1818 authorized the governor to convene the Legislature at any time he desired but did not require him to state the purpose of their assembling until after they were convened. This was changed to provide that the governor must state the purpose of the extra session, and the Legislature is forbidden to legislate on any subject not named in the call for the special session.

The proposition for and against a constitutional convention was voted on in 1846 and the vote would indicate a lack of interest as the result was 58,339 for a convention and 23,013 against a convention. Delegates were elected on the 19th of April, 1847. The whole number was 162 and was divided between the democrats and whigs, 92 to 70, respectively. The convention met at Springfield June 7, 1847. Newton Cloud of Morgan County was elected president of the convention. Mr. Cloud was a man of no unusual ability. He was a farmer-preacher, who took considerable interest in public affairs. He served in nine sessions of the General Assembly. He was a man in whom the public had great confidence. Henry W. Moore of Gallatin County was made secretary, and Herman G. Reynolds of Rock Island County was assistant secretary. The following is a complete list of those who sat in the convention.

Augustus Adams, Kane.
George W. Akin, Franklin.
Willis Allen, Franklin.
Samuel Anderson, Will.
Wm. R. Archer, Pike.
George W. Armstrong, Grundy.
Martin Atherton, Alexander.
Patrick Ballingall, Cook.
Montgomery Blair, Pike.
Wm. H. Blakely, Cumberland.
Ben. Bond, Clinton.
Wm. Bosbyshell, Calhoun.
James Brockman, Brown.
Geo. T. Brown, Madison.
George Bunsen, St. Clair.
Horace Butler, Lake.
Albert G. Caldwell, Gallatin.
James M. Campbell, McDonough.
Thompson Campbell, Jo Daviess.
John Canaday, Vermilion.
Thomas B. Carter Livingston.
Franklin S. Casey, Jefferson.
Zadoc Casey, Jefferson.
Charles Choate, Hancock.
Selden M. Church, Winnebago.
Alfred Churchill, Kane.
Eben F. Colby, Cook.
Chas. Henry Constable, Wabash.
John Crain, Clinton.
Robert J. Cross, Winnebago.
Samuel J. Cross, Woodford.
Michael G. Dale, Bond.
David Davis, McLean.
James M. Davis, Montgomery.
Thos. G. C. Davis, Massac.
John Dawson, Sangamon.
Peter W. Deitz, McHenry.
John Dement, Lee.
Henry E. Dummer, Cass.
James Dunlap, Morgan.
Harvey Dunn, Pike.
Daniel Dinsmore, Scott.

Joseph T. Eccles, Montgomery.
John Wm. F. Edmonson, Fayette.
Cyrus Edwards, Madison.
Ninian Wirt Edwards, Sangamon.
Edward Evey, Shelby.
Seth B. Farwell, Stephenson.
Frederick Frick, Mercer.
James Graham, Macoupin.
Thomas Geddes, Hancock.
Rev. Henry R. Green, Tazewell.
Peter Green, Clay.
William B. Green, Jo Daviess.
David L. Gregg, Cook.
Wm. A. Grimshaw, Pike.
Abner C. Harding, Knox.
Justin Harlan, Clark.
Joshua Harper, Henry.
Curtis K. Harvey, Knox.
Jeduthan Hatch, DuPage.
Nelson Hawley, Crawford.
Daniel Hay, White.
Samuel Snowdon Hayes, White.
Reuben E. Heacock, Cook.
Hugh Henderson, Will.
George W. Hill, DeKalb.
Abraham Hoes, LaSalle.
James M. Hogue, Wayne.
Wm. H. Holmes, Tazewell.
Samuel Hunsaker, Union.
Stephen A. Hurlburt, Boone.
John Huston, Warren.
Aaron C. Jackson Whiteside.
James A. James, Monroe.
Alex. M. Jenkins, Jackson.
Humphrey B. Jones, Perry.
Thomas Judd, Kane.
Alvin R. Kenner, Edwards.
Simon Kinney, Bureau.
William C. Kinney, St. Clair.
Alfred Kitchell, Richland.
Augustus R. Knapp, Jersey.
Nat. Morse Knapp, Scott.
Lincoln B. Knowlton, Peoria.
James Knox, Knox.
George Kreider, Fulton.
Samuel Lander, Livingston.
James M. Lasater, Hamilton.
William Laughlin, Adams.

George B. Lemen, DeWitt.
Isaac Linley, Fulton.
Samuel Drake Lockwood, Morgan.
Stephen Trigg Logan, Sangamon.
John Tinen Loudon, Williamson.
Andrew McCallen, Hardin.
John McCulley, St. Clair.
Wm. McClure, Will.
Alex. McHatton, Schuyler.
Uri Manly, Clark.
David Markley, Fulton.
Franklin S. D. Marshall, Mason.
Thos. A. Marshall, Coles.
John West Mason, Kendall.
James H. Matheny, Sangamon.
John Mieure, Lawrence.
Robert Miller, Hancock.
Richard G. Morris, Crawford.
Jacob M. Nichols, Adams.
Benj. F. Northcott, Menard.
Jesse O. Norton, Will.
John Oliver, Johnson.
Wm. A. Minshall, Schuyler.
Garner Moffett, Carroll.
William S. Moore, Hancock.
Geo. W. Pace, Marion.
Henry D. Palmer, Marshall.
John McAuley Palmer, Macoupin.
Onslow Peters, Peoria.
Daniel J. Pinckney, Ogle.
Wm. B. Powers, Adams.
O. C. Pratt, Jo Daviess.
George W. Rives, Edgar.
Ezekiel Wright Robbins, Randolph.
Benaiah Robinson, Madison.
Wm. W. Roman, St. Clair.
Hiram Rountree Montgomery.
Walter Bennett Scates, Jefferson.
Richard B. Servant, Randolph.
Thos. C. Sharpe, Hancock.
Francis Cornwall Sherman, Cook.
William Shields, Edgar.
Dorice Dwight Shumway, Christian.
John Sibley, McHenry.
Wm. Sim, Pope.
Lewis J. Simpson, Highland (Adams).
Jas. W. Singleton, Brown.
Edward O. Smith, Macon.

Jacob Smith, Gallatin.
John W. Spencer, Rock Island.
Wm. Stadden, LaSalle.
Hurlburt Swan, Lake.
Wm. Thomas, Morgan.
Wm. W. Thompson, Peoria.
Anthony Thornton, Shelby.
Thomas B. Trower, Coles.
Gilbert Turnbull, Henderson.
Oaks Turner, Putnam.
Wm. Tutt, Clark.
James Tuttle, Logan.
John W. Vance, Vermilion.
Zenas H. Varnor, Washington.
Hezekiah M. Wead, Fulton.
Thompson R. Webber, Champaign.
Edw. M. West, Madison.
Archibald Williams, Adams.
Franklin Witt, Greene.
John Davis Whiteside, Monroe.
Daniel Hilton Whitney, Boone.
David Meade Woodson, Greene.
Linus E. Worcester, Greene.
Attest, Henry W. Moore, Gallatin, secretary.
Harman G. Reynolds, Rock Island, assistant secretary.

Men of Prominence

The following members of the convention were prominent at that time or came to be men of distinction in after years.

John M. Palmer, lawyer, soldier, United States Senator, and governor of Illinois. Served in the capacity of probate judge, state senator, and as member of the Constitutional Convention of 1847. He was an anti-Nebraska democrat. Was president of the first Republican State Convention in Bloomington in 1856. He was one of the organizers of the republican party in Illinois. Entered the Civil war as colonel of the Fourteenth Regiment, Illinois Volunteers, was promoted to brigadier-general and later to a major-generalship. Commanded the Fourteenth Army Corps. Was elected governor of Illinois in 1868, United States Senator in 1891. Was candidate for the presidency on a "Sound Money" platform in 1896. Wrote a sketch of his own life which afterwards put in book form with the title, "The Story of An Earnest Life." Died in Springfield, September 25, 1900.

Zadoc Casey, prominent man of Southern Illinois; lived at Mount Vernon, which he helped to found as early as 1817. Was a member of the General Assembly. Was elected lieutenant-governor in 1830. Took an active part in the Black Hawk war. Served in Congress, and in the Constitutional Convention of

Courtesy of Illinois State Historical Library.

GOVERNOR JOHN M. PALMER

1847. Was a public spirited citizen and a man of considerable wealth for those days.

Alexander M. Jenkins was another prominent man of Southern Illinois of the early days. He was a member of the General Assembly, served as captain in the Black Hawk war, was lieutenant-governor, and was greatly interested in the internal improvement plans. Served in the Constitutional Convention of 1847. He is often spoken of as the father of the Illinois Central Railroad. He was an uncle of John A. Logan.

Walter B. Scates was a lawyer of considerable prominence and was a judge of both the circuit and the Supreme Court. Was a member of the Constitutional Convention from Jefferson County. He later served on the Supreme bench. Was a major in the Civil war, and held important offices under appointment by the President.

David Davis is a household word among Illinois citizens. He came to Bloomington in 1836. He was a lawyer of marked ability, served in the Legislature and in the Constitutional Convention. He was an intimate friend of Mr. Lincoln who nominated him to the Supreme bench where he served till 1877. In that year he was elected to the United States Senate, succeeding John A. Logan. His name was prominently mentioned as a candidate for the presidency. Had he not resigned from the Supreme bench in 1877 he would have been a member of the Electoral Commission of that year. Hon. Adlai E. Stevenson in "Something of Men I have Known," says in an address at the Bloomington home-coming in 1907, "It is our pride that our townsman, David Davis, was among the ablest of the great court (the United States Supreme Court), by whose adjudication renewed vigor was given to the constitution, and enduring safeguards established for national life and individual liberty."

John Dement won great honor in the Black Hawk war. He was a member of the General Assembly and was one of the younger set of "Indian fighters." He held many important offices by election or by appointment of the Legislature of Illinois or the President. He served not only in the Constitutional Convention of 1847, but in the one of 1862 and in the one of 1870. He lived in the northwestern part of Illinois where he served his state so well in the Black Hawk war.

Anthony Thornton was a lawyer, a member of the General Assembly, and of the convention of 1847. He was a Virginian, but tarried in Kentucky, Ohio, and Missouri before coming to Illinois about 1840. He served in the General Assembly and was a member of Congress for one term. He was a member of the Supreme Court of Illinois. He also served in the Constitutional Convention of 1862. He was the last survivor of the convention.

Samuel D. Lockwood was a very prominent man in Illinois

from the days of the admission of Illinois into the Union till his death in 1874. He was a lawyer, served as attorney-general of Illinois, but is best known as a member of the Supreme Court. He was a friend of Edward Coles in the convention fight of 1823-4. He was interested in the internal improvement scheme. He is recorded from Morgan County in the convention of 1847. He was a public spirited citizen and was especially interested in Illinois College.

Stephen A. Hurlburt won great distinction as a general in the Civil war. He was a lawyer and a member of the convention. He served in the General Assembly. He entered the Civil war as a brigade commander. He was a division commander at the battle of Shiloh, and was made a major-general before the end of 1862. He served in the diplomatic service and in Congress. He was a republican but in no sense partisan.

James W. Singleton was a citizen of Brown County at the time he was elected to the Constitutional Convention. He was a lawyer but seems to have been more interested in business matters and in politics. He was especially interested in railroad construction and in railroad management. He was president of two roads of the southwestern part of the state. He was proprietor of a very fine stock farm near Quincy in later years.

Stephen T. Logan was probably not regarded as a great man in his day but he was one whose name was known far and wide. He was a gentleman of the old school, born in Kentucky in 1800, he was admitted to practice law before he was of age, was a judge in the Springfield circuit by the time he was thirty-five, served in the General Assembly, member of the Constitutional Convention, took Lincoln in as a law partner in 1841. "He was assiduous in study and tireless in search of legal principles —Logan's example had a good effect on Lincoln."

Economy

The convention of 1848 was held at a time of "serious financial depression." The debt of the state was about $6,000,000. The nightmare which had been before the people of Illinois from 1837 up to 1847 was supposed to be the creature of the Constitution of 1818—that is, there were no safeguards in the first constitution against unbridled extravagance by the Legislature. The debt at one time reached the appalling sum of $15,000,000 and many good, honest, well-meaning citizens did not see how the debt could ever be paid, and the skeleton, repudiation, stalked about the state not failing to visit some men in high official position. It is even now not easy to understand how this enormous debt had been reduced more than half in less than ten years. It is not strange, therefore, that there was a very general feeling that there should be some limitations set upon the expenditure of money by the state's law-making body. The number of days in which the work of the Assembly must be done was fixed at forty-two while the compensation was fixed at $2 per day for the limited number of days, and if the session continued longer only $1 per day for the days beyond the forty-two was allowed.

The salary of the governor under the Constitution of 1818 was $1,000 per year. This was raised to $1,500 in the new constitution. Salary of Supreme judges was raised from $1,000 to $1,200. Circuit judges were to receive $1,000 per year. Auditor of public accounts, $1,000; treasurer and secretary of state, $800 each. Stuve states that the General Assembly for the year 1845 cost the state $5,500, while the cost of the first session under the new constitution was less than $15,000. However the same writer states that the total cost of the last session of the General Assembly under the Constitution of 1848 was $206,181, exclusive of printing, paper and binding, making nearly $75,000 more. Four items of that session—newspapers, stationery, postage, and pocket-knives cost $54,322.

The men who held the state offices under the Constitution of 1848 could not make "both ends meet," and the Legislature began a system of supplementary appropriations which became disgraceful. While the governor's salary was only $1,500 the Legislature appropriated $2,500 to be expended, or not, by the governor, as he pleased, on the grounds. This increased his salary to $4,000 per year. In a similar way the Supreme judges were paid $4,000 per year. The circuit judges in addition to the $1,000 provided for in the constitution were given an additional $1,000 for revisions and suggestions as to the laws. But the climax was reached when the per diem compensation of members for the session of 1861 reached $8,800, which was supplemented by $8,892 for postage; $1,812 for newspapers; for pencils, $2,664. Thus the members instead of getting $2 per day really got $8. One honorable member handed in a bill for traveling expenses to the capital of 1,200 miles, the same distance for returning. Thus the changed conditions which good crops and general prosperity brought to the people brought with it a lowering of public morals.

Other Changes

The Bill of Rights in the Constitution of 1818 contains twenty-three sections, while in that of 1848 there are twenty-six sections. Section 6 in the new Bill of Rights extends the right of trial by jury to all cases at law, whatever may be the amount in controversy. Section 8 in the new constitution omits the guarantees to villages to whom grants of lands had been made. Section 16 in the Constitution of 1848 declares: "There shall be neither slavery nor involuntary servitude in this state except as a punishment for crime whereof the party shall have been duly convicted." Section 20 is new in the new constitution. It says: "The military shall be in strict subordination to the civil power." Section 22 is also new: "No soldier shall in time of peace be quartered in any house without the consent of the owner; nor in time of war except in manner prescribed by law." Section 25 states the penalties for dueling or for taking any part in a duel. Section 26 prescribes an oath to be taken, by elective officers before entering on the duties of their respective offices. The oath prohibits anyone from serving as an officer who has in any way taken part in a duel since the adoption of the new constitution. The two Bills of Rights are almost alike, word for word, excepting the five sections pointed out.

The powers of the General Assembly under the new constitution were restricted as follows: Divorces shall be granted only for causes stated in the general law and not directly by the Legislature. No extra compensation shall be granted to any public officer after the contract has been entered into or the services rendered. No lotteries shall be granted for any purpose. No charter formerly granted to any bank shall ever be revived by the Legislature. The state was forbidden to contract any indebtedness exceeding $50,000 and for no purpose except "to meet casual deficits or failures in revenue." Neither was the credit of the state "in any manner to be given to, nor in aid of, any individual, association or corporation."

Section 30 of article 3 (legislative) says: "Every person who shall be chosen or appointed to any office of trust or profit shall, before entering upon the duties thereof, take an oath to support the Constitution of the United States, and of this state, and also an oath of office."

There was no subject which caused more genuine hard work than the disposition of the question as to whether Illinois was ever to have any more banks. Section 3, Article X (Corporations): "No state bank shall hereafter be created, nor shall the state own or be liable for any stock in any corporation or joint-stock association for banking purposes, to be hereafter created." Section 4 provides that stockholders in banks shall be personally liable for the redemption of any kind of paper credits that circulate as money. Section 5 is as follows: "No act of the General Assembly, authorizing corporations or associations with banking powers, shall go into effect, or in any manner be in force, unless the same shall be submittted to the people at the general election next succeeding the passage of the same, and be approved by a majority of all the votes cast at such election for or against such law." It would seem from these sections on banking that the convention wished to make it very difficult for any one to engage in the banking business in Illinois.

The slavery question in Illinois was definitely settled by the sixteenth section of the Declaration of Rights—"There shall be neither slavery nor involuntary servitude in this state except as a punishment for crime, whereof the party shall have been duly convicted." This settled the question of slavery, but the free black people were more objectionable than the slave black people. At the time of the making of the Constitution of 1848 there were slaves, indentured servants, and free black people in Illinois. The slaves were legally freed by the above sixteenth article; the indentured servants were gradually disappearing, but the free blacks were liable to increase; and so it was necessary to protect the state against the coming of more blacks. Article XIV provides—"The General Assembly shall, at its first session under the amended Constitution, pass such laws as will effectually prohibit free persons of color from immigrating to and settling in this state; and to effectually prevent the owners of slaves from bringing them into this state for the purpose of setting them free." This radical stand against the immigration of free blacks is said to have been the result of an agitation to grant civil rights to negroes. It appears the Legislature did not enact the law excluding free blacks till 1853. In this year it was made a crime for any one to bring in a colored person, and any negro who appeared in the state and remained ten days was liable to be arrested and fined $50. In case he was not able to pay his fine he could be sold to any one who would pay the costs of the arrest and sale.

A feature of the Constitution wholly divorced from political prejudice, and one that was full of wisdom and foresight, was Article XV which provided for a two mill tax. "There shall be annually assessed and collected, in the same manner as other state revenue may be assessed and collected, a tax of two mills upon each dollar's worth of taxable property, in addition to all other taxes, to be applied as follows, to wit: The fund so created shall be kept separate, and shall annually, on the first day of January, be apportioned and paid over pro rata upon all such state indebtedness, other than the canal and school indebtedness, as may, for that purpose, be presented by the holders of the same, to be entered as credits upon, and, to that interest, in extinguishment of the principal of said indebtedness."

This article was a blow to those statesmen if any were left who would have repudiated the state's indebtedness on account of the internal improvement system. This article also shows with what grace a people can bear self imposed burdens.

The Constitution of 1818 fixed the date for the general election, at which the governor and members of the General Assembly were to be elected, on the first Monday in August. The election for members of the General Assembly coming in

HISTORY OF ILLINOIS

August of each even year, the election of the governor each alternate even year, beginning August, 1818. This arrangement required the election of the members of the General Assembly, and the governor, in August, while the election for congressman and electors occurred on the first Tuesday after the first Monday in November of years divisible by four.

In the new Constitution the date for the general election was fixed to correspond with the congressional elections—first Tuesday after the first Monday in November of the even year, while the governor's election occurred on the same date in years divisible by four.

RATIFICATION

The convention fixed the date for the vote on the ratification of the new Constitution as the first Monday in March, 1848, and if ratified it should become the law of the land April 1st, 1848. Two separate articles were to be submitted at the same time; one, Article XIV on the proposition to prohibit the immigration into the state of persons of color, and the other, Article XV, was the proposition to provide for a two mill tax.

There was a general feeling that the new Constitution should be ratified. It has been said that all the papers in the state were for ratification except six. The result of the vote on ratification was as follows:

	For	Against
Constitution	59,887	15,859
Article XIV	49,060	20,883
Two-mill tax	41,017	30,586

On April 1st, 1848, therefore, the new Constitution went into effect. There were three other elections held in the year 1848. The second one was held in August to elect members of the General Assembly. A third one in September to elect the judges, and one in November to elect presidential electors and Congressmen. The Constitution also provided that the first election for governor under the new arrangement should take place on the first Tuesday after the first Monday in November, 1848. It was further provided that the governor, elected in November, should be inaugurated on the second Monday in January, 1849. From that date to this the general state elections, except for judges, corresponds in date with the congressional elections.

GOVERNOR FRENCH

In the campaign of 1846 the whigs made a poor showing. They hesitated about naming some one for governor, but finally brought out Thomas M. Kilpatrick, of Scott County, for governor, and Nathaniel G. Wilcox for lieutenant-governor. The democrats nominated Augustus C. French for governor, and Joseph B. Wells. The Mexican war was just beginning and the

GOVERNOR AUGUSTUS C. FRENCH

whigs generally were opposed to it, for they said it was a democratic war for the benefit of the slave interests. Wars as a rule are popular in democracies and any political party which opposes a war is usually a minority party. French was charged by the whigs of being entangled in the internal improvement schemes. while the democratic orators charged the whigs with being opposed to the Mexican war. The vote stood, French 58,700, Kilpatrick 36,775. Governor French was a man of unusually wide experiences in life. His father and mother died while he was still under twenty. Their deaths left him four younger brothers to care for. This he did in a very parental way. He was a lawyer of high rank, served in the Legislature, was receiver of public moneys at the Land Office at Palestine. He enjoyed the friendship of Stephen A Douglas, which in political life in Illinois was a large amount of capital.

It was seen that Governor French would be legislated out of office by the new Constitution, as his term would not expire till December, 1850. But the new Constitution provided that the governor should be elected in November, 1848, and be inaugurated in January, 1849. The democrats therefore nominated Mr. French for the first governor under the new Constitution. There was really no organized opposition and he was elected by a vote of 67,453.

Governor French had in the first part of his term proven that he was a good business administrator as well as a good politician. From the time of the collapse of the internal improvement scheme till 1845, no steps had been taken to pay any part of the debt, interest or principal. The interest on the outstanding bonds was at first in the neighborhood of three-quarters of a million a year. The debt had been decreased by Governor Ford by the exchange of bank stock for state bonds and by the transfer of the canal property in trust to the bondholders. This left the state still owing many millions and an accumulation of four years' interest, which probably was considerably more than a million dollars.

In 1845 the Legislature enacted a law which authorized the collection of a tax of $1\frac{1}{4}$ mills on the dollar's worth of property, to be used in paying the interest on the public debt. The annual income from this source was $125,000 in 1846, but this was not nearly enough to pay the annual interest, to say nothing of the amount already accumulated. But it was a start and made bondholders feel that the state was at least trying to do the right thing.

Now the 2-mill tax authorized by the new Constitution of 1848 provided a fund which should be applied on the principal of the improvement debt. In 1849 the amount collected from this source was $165,788.71. This of course would not go far toward decreasing the debt, but in a short time the assessed valuation would be greater and then the amount gathered from this source would materially lessen the debt from year to year.

Governor French showed his wisdom and his deep interest in the state when he recommended a system of funding the state's debt. It was believed that there was more or less counterfeiting of the state's securities. Then the bonds were of different dates and were not recorded, as it appears. Governor French suggested to the Legislature that all of the evidences of the state's indebtedness be called in and that in their place new bonds serially numbered and registered should be issued. It was further proposed that bonds be issued covering all the interest due at that time. The governor stated in 1850 that the indebtedness was $16,627,509. He said at this time that most of this sum had been funded.

CHAPTER XVIII

UNDER THE NEW CONSTITUTION

TOWNSHIP ORGANIZATION—HOMESTEAD EXEMPTION—CONTROVERSY WITH ST. LOUIS—STATE POLICY—TRIBUTE

The new Constitution provided that the first governor under the new order should be inaugurated the second Monday in January, 1849. The Legislature had been elected the preceding August and had been in session in December under the old Constitution. It has been stated that there was an absence of interest and of hangers-on, since the Legislature does not elect the judges of the supreme and of the circuit courts. Nor do they elect any state officers. They are now merely law makers. The Legislature was made up of twenty-five senators and seventy-five members of the Lower House. The democrats carried the state for Cass against Taylor for President by 56,300 to 53,047. Out of seven congressional districts, the whigs carried but one, Col. E. D. Baker, of the Galena district.

There were some strong men in the Legislature—Joseph Gillespie, John T. Stuart, Joel A. Matteson, Norman B. Judd, Richard Yates, Usher F. Linder, and a number of others who later came into prominence. The Legislature's first duty was to elect a United States senator to succeed Judge Sidney Breese. A contest arose. Judge Breese was a candidate for reelection, and John A. McClernand and James Shields were also in the race for the democratic caucus. Shields was finally chosen by the caucus and elected, but was declared ineligible on account of a questional citizenship. At a special session of the Legislature, Shields' ineligibility having been removed, he was nominated a second time over Breese and McClernand, and later elected by the joint ballot of the Legislature.

MORE REVENUE

The revenues of the state were in Governor French's term enough to meet the current expenses of the state. This had been brought about by several wise steps taken in earlier years. When Illinois was admitted into the Union, the enabling act, the fourth clause of section 6, provided that public lands sold in Illinois after the 1st day of January, 1819, should be free from any form of state taxation for a period of five years from the date of sale. This had been a great loss of income to the state at a time when the taxes were greatly needed.

The state made an earnest appeal to the Congress to remove this restriction and to allow Illinois to tax all lands from the time they came into private ownership. Senator Breese was untiring in presenting the needs of the state. After more than one unsuccessful request on the part of the state, the Congress repealed that part of the enabling act and allowed the state to tax all lands as soon as they became private property. The Legislature passed a law in conformity with this action by Congress and thenceforth the revenues were greatly increased. This was in 1847, and as soon as the Mexican war was over and the soldiers returned, the distribution of land warrants to the soldiers as bounties greatly increased the lands in Illinois subject to taxation. Another source of increased taxes was the lands belonging to the old salt reservation. These had been given to the state about 1827 or 1828 and had not all been disposed of till Governor French's term. Not only were these lands taxable after sold, but the income from the sale helped to meet the demands upon the public treasury.

Other incomes—the 1¼-mill tax and the 2-mill tax—also helped to swell the income; and the wonderful growth of all forms of industrial activity as well as the increased value of lands gave an annual income equal to the current expenses in 1850. This was the first time since 1839 that there had not been a part of the annual expenses of the state government remaining unpaid at the end of the fiscal year. The taxable property of the state in 1850 was more than $100,000,000.

Township Organization

There grew up in the old thirteen colonies, that afterward came to be states, two distinct forms of county government. One in the Southern colonies known as the commissioners' form of government, and the other in the North known as the township form of county government. The first savors of aristocratic government, the second of democracy. In the first all the affairs of the county were managed by a board of three men usually appointed by the court. These three men attended not only to the fiscal affairs of the county, but performed the duties of justices of the peace. In the counties of the Northern colonies the business of the county was attended to by a board of supervisors, one from each town. A writer has suggested that the town life of New England grew up around the church, while in the Northwestern states it centered about the township as a school unit.

The northern counties of Illinois were settled chiefly by people from the states north of the Mason and Dixon line, where town government prevailed, while the counties of the south half of the state were in the main from the Southern states, where the county form of government prevailed. Of course in 1818, when

SIDNEY BREESE

the first Constitution was made, there were very few settlers north of the middle part of the state. The Constitution was therefore modeled after the Southern states so far as county organization was concerned. When the immigrants began to settle the north half of the state there was general dissatisfaction with the commissioners form of county government. When, therefore, the opportunity came in the constitutional convention of 1847, the champions of township government were insistent that their plan of county government should at least have an equal chance with the old commissioners plan.

The friends of township government first asked for a committee with instructions to report the advisability of incorporating the several townships for municipal and other purposes. The convention was opposed. Other steps were taken by the friends of the township plan to get their proposition before the convention, and a committee of twenty-four was finally appointed to study the plan of better county administration. On July 16 the committee reported, but the report was laid on the table. On August 16 another section was suggested, and out of these the general committee on revision and adjustment reported the following, which became section 6 of Article VII. It reads as follows:

"The General Assembly shall provide, by a general law, for a township organization, under which any county may organize whenever a majority of the voters of such county, at any general election, shall so determine; and whenever any county shall adopt a township organization, so much of this Constitution as provides for the management of the fiscal concerns of the said county by the county court may be dispensed with and the affairs of said county may be transacted in such manner as the General Assembly may provide."

In pursuance of the provision of this section 6 of Article VII, of the new Constitution, the Legislature passed "An act to provide for township and county organization, under which any county may organize whenever a majority of voters of such county, at any general election, shall so determine." This act was approved February 12, 1849, and was in force April 16, 1849.

The law was modeled after the laws of the New England states and after that of New York. But owing to the fact that there had to be some compromises, the law was not well adapted to the needs of the people. However, as time has passed the original law has been modified and amended so that today it is a complete and somewhat complicated statute. Its details are so well known to the general reader that it is not needful to give them here.

Homestead Exemption

This law is based upon a recognized principle in sociology that the demands of society at large are paramount to the demands of an individual. This principle was section 20 of Magna Charta. The law is therefore very old. It was declared in Magna Charta that in case of amercement, the punishment shall not extend to the deprivation of the debtor of his necessary means of making a living, that is, the drayman by occupation must not be deprived of his horse and dray, for then he and his family would become a public charge. The gardener must not be deprived of his hoe, his rake, his spade and his wheelbarrow, for then he would be deprived of the only means he could make use of to support himself and his family. They would therefore become dependent upon the state or upon charity, but if he be allowed to retain these, even though he does owe a well-to-do man as much as his tools are worth, it is better upon the whole that the well-to-do man be obliged to cancel the debt than that the poor man be reduced to the state of a pauper.

When our English ancestors came to the new world they brought along many principles of civil life, and among them was this one of exemptions. Stuve says: "This subject had been brought before the Legislature repeatedly by Governor French in his messages. The principles of this beneficent law was not a new or untried one. Its practical effects upon the social relations of communities had been fully and successfully tested in different states. The claims of society in maintaining the integrity of the family relation, which is the foundation of all society, it was argued, were superior to those of the individual." The fact that some men might be dishonest and thus evade the payment of their debts did not argue that such a law in the interests of a higher duty from man to man should not operate to "shield the widows and orphans, the aged and decrepit, from the cruel demands of the Shylocks of the world."

The law of exemption applied only to personal property to the value of $60 until the passage of this law in the administration of Governor French; then the scope of the application of the principle was enlarged and included real estate. The law of 1851 provided that the homestead of a debtor if a householder should be exempt from sale on executions up to the value of $1,000; and in addition that personal property to the value of $400 should also be exempt. The Constitution of 1870 appears to have been written in a very generous spirit as to exemptions. Article IV of section 32 reads: "The General Assembly shall pass liberal homestead and exemption laws." The Legislatures have always given a very liberal interpretation to this mandate from the Constitution of our state.

Controversy With St. Louis

Prior to 1848, the people of St. Louis discovered an approaching danger to their water front. Sand bars were forming in the Mississippi on the west side just at the southern limits of the city. These obstructions had a tendency to deflect the current away from the St. Louis side and push it to the Illinois side. Some nearer the Illinois side, but above the main part of the City of St. Louis, lay Bloody Island. The City Council of St. Louis passed an ordinance in February, 1848, providing for the construction of a dyke from the island to the Illinois mainland, thus closing the channel on that side of the island and forcing the stream to the west, hoping it would clear the sand bars which were forming on the St. Louis side of the river. The enabling act which provided for the admission of Illinois into the Union fixed the western boundary along the middle of the Mississippi River. The action of the St. Louis authorities in presuming to construct an obstruction of the flow of the stream to the east of Bloody Island was considered nothing less than an encroachment upon the sovereignty of the State of Illinois. No permission from the State of Illinois was asked or granted. The City of St. Louis insisted that it had secured the permission from the owners of the island and from the owners of the land opposite the island on the Illinois side.

There had been for the past dozen years or more a very marked jealousy on the part of Alton and Quincy toward St. Louis. The Missouri city was growing rapidly in both population and in commercial interests. Alton and Quincy were loud in their complaints of the action of St. Louis in attempting to appropriate the advantages of the Mississippi to the use of that city. The theory was set up that it would seriously interfere with the navigation of the Mississippi above the Missouri city. The people of St. Clair County were also interested in the matter and secured an injunction against the contractors who were building the dyke. It appears that the work proceeded in spite of the injunction. The governor sent the secretary of state to the Village of Illinoistown to investigate the complaints that the contractors were proceeding with the building in spite of the injunction. He found that 200 to 300 tons of rock from the quarries on the Missouri side were unloaded every night, that the dyke was already twelve feet high, and that in four weeks the wall would be done. The governor's commissioner, the secretary of state, reported to the governor that there was little interest in the whole matter except that which the contractors had in getting pay for their work, and that which the Wiggins Ferry Company had in protecting its interests in the island, most of which the company owned. The legal steps taken to prohibit the work were delayed, but in September, 1848, the injunction suits came before Judge Koerner, of the Supreme

Court, at Belleville. The injunction suits were sustained as to part of the cases, while others were appealed. The wall was now as high as was really needed, and the case had no further interest, except as to the right of the Wiggins Ferry Company to build the wall twelve feet higher. In the meeting of the Legislature in 1849, a proposition was made by which the City of St. Louis was to give bond guaranteeing the free use of the dyke as a highway to the people of Illinois. A committee was appointed to visit the dyke and report the feasibility of its use as a highway to the island. The committee reported that the dyke was a stone wall forty feet deep, thirty-six feet wide and the top only three feet below the front street along the shore of the Village of Illinoistown. They also called attention to the fact that the distance from the west side of Bloody Island to the St. Louis shore was only 800 yards. This whole affair was a tempest in a teapot. The east passage, which was only a slough, soon filled, and the island and the mainland were joined, and today is the site of flourishing business places and busy thoroughfares.

State Policy

Article X, section 6, of the Constitution of 1848, provided that "The General Assembly shall encourage internal improvements, by passing liberal general laws of incorporation for that purpose." This section of the Constitution is a gentle reminder to the world that internal improvements will never again be undertaken by the state. At a special session of the Legislature called for October 23, 1849, for the purpose of electing a senator to fill the vacancy caused by the rejection of James Shields, elected in January to succeed Sidney Breese, among eleven objects to be considered, besides electing a senator, one was to enact a general railroad incorporation law. At this time the state had two lines of railroads—one running from Meredosia by way of Jacksonville, Springfield and on to Danville. This was the Old Northern Cross of internal improvement days. The other railroad was a road reaching from Chicago to Elgin.

A wonderful story is told of the growth and development of Illinois between 1834, when the second great banking scheme was authorized, and 1853, when the state had entered upon its most important period prior to the Civil war. The state had grown from 157,000 in 1830 to 851,000 in 1850, and it has been estimated that the state had 1,000,000 population in 1853. The counties numbered sixty in 1834. In 1851 there were 100, the increase in counties marking the great flow of immigrants from New York and New England into the northern half of the state. Chicago had grown from a village of not more than 1,000 in 1830 to 30,000 in 1850. In this period a great enterprise had been fostered by the state. The Illinois and Michigan Canal had been finished and was the source of an income to the state of $125,000 per year. True, the internal improvement scheme had miserably failed and left the state in debt to the staggering amount of $16,000,000. State bonds had passed current at from 10 to 20 per cent on the dollar, while auditor's warrants were selling for 50 cents on the dollar. There was an annual deficit in the running expenses of $30,000. By 1850 the income was sufficient to pay the annual cost of conducting the business of the state. In spite of these depressing facts, the state received a grant of land of more than 4,000 square miles with which to build a railroad from Cairo to Galena and from some point on this line to Chicago. In addition the state was given thousands of acres of "swamp lands." The one thing the state needed above all else was a well planned system of railroads.

OLD SUPREME COURT BUILDING IN MT. VERNON
Now used by the Appellate Court

The passage of a law for incorporating railroads was discussed in the Legislature, both in the regular session beginning in January and at the special session of October 23, 1849. A question arose over the right of the state to determine the terminus of a road entering Illinois from another state. The Indiana Legislature presented a petition to the special session in the fall of 1849, asking that body to incorporate a company for the building of the Ohio & Mississippi Railroad, running from Cincinnati, Ohio, through Ohio, Indiana, and Illinois, and terminating at the Mississippi River opposite St. Louis. There arose a division in the Legislature which reached out to the people and the towns. The majority in the Legislature was opposed to granting a company the right to cross the state with a railroad unless the company would submit to the determination of its western terminus by the state. This doctrine that the state ought to have the right to determine the western termini of roads crossing the state from east to west was known as state policy. The secret to the whole question of state policy was the jealousy of people interested in Alton, Quincy and other towns along the western side of the state towards St. Louis. It was pointed out that if a company wished to construct a road that would run parallel and have a terminus at the western end of the Illinois and Michigan Canal, then the state policy was that this injury to a public work of the state should not be permitted. Likewise a railroad coming into the state from Indiana and terminating at a point opposite St. Louis would greatly damage the City of Alton. Again it was argued that if roads were allowed to cross the state in any direction, that there would soon be roads running parallel to one another and thus a ruinous competition would result. There was a very general agreement that railroads were necessary to the development of the resources of the state, but it was so generally held, at least by the majority of the members of the Legislature, that all railroad building should be under the control of the state, and this doctrine was called the state policy, and it held sway from 1849 to 1853.

As soon as the Legislature adjourned in March, 1849, the people of the territory which would greatly profit by east and west roads across the south end of the state began seriously to consider how they could counteract what appeared to be a well-established theory in the state. There were twenty or more members of the General Assembly who represented th south end of the state who felt that a great injustice had been done the people of that section. They therefore called a convention to be held at Salem, in Marion County, in June, 1849, to take into consideration their grievances and to devise if possible what measures they might take to redress their wrongs. The convention was called a railroad convention and was attended by as many as 4,000 men.

Governor Zadoc Casey presided, and the principal address was made by Mr. Wait, of Bond County. The burden of Mr. Wait's address was the injustice that the state policy had done the people of the counties through which the Ohio & Mississippi Railroad would pass from Indiana to the Mississippi opposite St. Louis. The people attending the convention at Salem were urged to organize against a policy that would so manifestly deprive them of an opportunity to develop their part of the state.

A counter-meeting was held at Hillsboro, attended by those who wished to uphold the state policy. It was a part of the plan to outdo the Salem meeting. They claimed 10,000 or 12,000 people in attendance. It turned out that most of the leaders of the state policy were men who were interested directly or otherwise in Alton.

TRIBUTE

The Missouri Legislature, at its session preceding this agitation in Illinois, passed a law imposing a tax of 4½ mills on every dollar's worth of goods sold in Missouri which had been produced in any other state. This had a tendency to strengthen the friends of state policy. It was calculated at that time that this 4½-mill tax would yield Missouri the magnificent sum of $150,000 annually. This law was eventually declared unconstitutional by the Supreme Court of Missouri. When the Illinois Legislature again convened it still refused to grant ρ charter to the Vincennes & St. Louis Railroad.

This state policy was known far and near. Newspapers and public men of the states to the east of Illinois began to attack the attitude of Illinois toward such a public enterprise as a railroad from Cincinnati to St. Louis. They denounced such an attitude as narrow, selfish, and unreasonable, even as far as the development of Illinois herself was concerned. They told the story of Illinois' attempts to do something for herself along internal improvement lines, and how she had miserably failed, and now, like the story of the dog in the manger, she was not willing to allow others to do good things for her.

A new Legislature assembled in January, 1851. It probably represented public sentiment as to the state policy and the people of the south end of the state got a concession which was the entering wedge in splitting asunder the state policy. This was a charter to the Ohio and Mississippi Railroad Company to construct a road from Vincennes to Illinoistown passing through the same counties and towns as was afterwards the route of the Baltimore and Ohio Southwestern Railroad. Senator Douglas and other members of Congress from Illinois used their influence in securing a more liberal consideration of the problem of internal improvements.

An interesting picture is presented by an account of the beginning of the construction of this road. The friends of Belleville had been induced to vote for the charter for this road with the understanding that the road would pass through Belleville which at that day was a flourishing young city. The friends of the city contended that the City of Belleville should be named in the charter as one of the points through which the road should pass. Those who were managing the bill for the company, asked that the name Belleville should be omitted from the charter, for if it were included they would have trouble with other towns along the route. The friends of Belleville yielded and when the survey was made the road ran six or seven miles north of the city. Fifty thousand dollars were offered to the company if they would turn from a straight course and pass through Belleville. The company was determined to make an air line road. When the day came to throw the first shovel full of dirt at Illinoistown (East St. Louis), the Belleville and St. Clair people generally refrained from participating and there was the queer spectacle of people from Cincinnati, Vincennes, and St. Louis beginning on Illinois soil a great internal improvement enterprise.

Col. John Brough, a leading citizen of Indiana, desired a charter for a road called the Atlantic and Mississippi which would enter the state from Terre Haute and make a bee line for St. Louis. There was already a road under construction from Terre Haute to Alton, and the state policy people contended that the "Brough" road would be a boost for St. Louis to the detriment of Alton and it was more than two years before the Legislature yielded. A charter was granted the Atlantic and Mississippi railroad and the power of the state policy was crushed and Illinois awoke to a period of great progress and prosperity.

CHAPTER XIX

A NEW BANKING SYSTEM

MORE POPULATION—CHICAGO A BUSINESS CENTER—ART. X, SEC. 5—THE LAW OF '51—WILDCATS—ORGANIZING A BANK

There is a close connection between banks and banking systems and the industrial life of a people. Banks deal with the medium of exchange which a people make use of to carry on the simple as well as the more complicated business relationships. No people has ever arisen above the crudest stages of development in any of the forms of their institutional life if they were dependent upon barter as a system of exchange. Banks, which in some measure are the creators of the medium of exchange, are also the agencies for an equitable distribution of the medium in whatever form it may be. Banks are therefore means to an end—the stimulation of industrial and business transactions.

MORE POPULATION

The increase in population between 1840 and 1850 was nearly 400,000, a gain of 80 per cent. There were six counties out of the 102 which lost in population in this decade. There were three chief reasons for this incoming of so large a population. First, there was a very great increase in the agricultural interests in Illinois within this period. The rich prairie lands of the central part of the state were yet awaiting the plows, harrows, the cultivators, the reapers, mowers, and threshers of the farmers. The agricultural resources of the state were just beginning to be developed. We were just learning that the possibilities of the soil and climate could be seen in hundreds of thousands of bushels of wheat, corn, oats, rye, barley, potatoes, and apples. And in other thousands of bushels of other grains, fruits, and vegetables. In the line of hay and forage there were timothy, clover, prairie grasses, and other fodder. Berries lined the roadsides and the wild meadows, while the cultivated fruits though not extensively grown were an index of what might be produced. The raising of live stock as a phase of general farming had already assumed an important part of the progressive farmer's program, while already many of the "big" farmers had their herds of blooded cattle, and their flocks of the finest sheep, and their droves of imported horses. From these examples the common farmers began to improve their stock. The state agricultural society which was organized back in the days of Governor Coles and Morris Birkbeck came forward to encourage these improved conditions. In addition there were county agricultural societies in many of the counties which gave an added force to the already prevailing tendency toward more scientific farming.

The second explanation for an increased immigration to Illinois in the decade under consideration was the great amount of work which the improvement plans presented. Millions of dollars were being spent for day labor. The man whose only capital was his strong arms, hands, and back could earn from $2 to $2.50 per day. True, the work on the railroads ceased about 1842, but the canal furnished work for thousands of laborers till 1848. Out of the mania for public construction, came many private enterprises which carried over toward the middle of the century.

A third cause of an increase in population was the general impression in the East that there were many opportunities for business investments in Illinois between 1840 and 1850. Wheat must be ground into flour, farm machinery must be manufactured and repaired. There must be millwrights, brick-makers, quarry men, harness makers, blacksmiths, carpenters, doctors, architects, coopers, boot and shoe makers, foundrymen, wagon makers, engineers, tanners, sheet-metal workers, plasterers, teachers, preachers, bankers, lawyers, capitalists, and promoters. These various laborers, skilled mechanics, and professional men were creating desirable articles from the raw material. The products must be distributed, they must reach the people who want and need them. This would require capital or money, and money was not native to Illinois—that is all the money in Illinois at this time was the product of neighboring and other states. It was therefore desirable that Illinois should produce her own medium of exchange.

Chicago a Business Center

Very naturally in an early day the commerce of the state moved toward St. Louis and New Orleans. But after the work was begun on the canal the products of the central and northern part of the state began to find a market in Chicago. The Mississippi and the Illinois assisted some in the way of transportation, but the main dependence was by overland transportation. But in 1848 when the canal was finished a highway from the central and western parts of Illinois was opened and there was an ever increasing flow of agricultural products, as well as many manufactured goods, into Chicago. Pork packing was an important industry at Alton prior to the Civil war, but in an early day this industry began to move up the Illinois River and many small river towns were the centers of pork packing in a small way. But as time went on the industry reached Chicago via the canal. But in the mean time all lines of industry and enterprises of all kinds centered in Chicago. Its population grew at a most rapid rate. In 1840 the population of the city was 4,479. In 1850 it was 29,963, and in 1860 there were 109,026 people in Chicago. Chicago now had after 1848 in addition to the canal which made a continuous line of communication with the Mississippi, the Chicago and Northwestern road which came in 1848; the Michigan Central in 1853; Lakeshore and Michigan Southern in 1852; and the Chicago, Rock Island and Pacific in 1852. Chicago now became the chief business center in Illinois. At this time there were seventeen banks in Chicago, and scores of factories, wholesale and forwarding firms.

EARLY BANKING

Illinois had up to the Civil war a varied experience in the banking business. In 1816 banks were chartered by the territorial Legislature. In 1821 the state ventured into the banking business with a capital stock of $500,000. The state was responsible for the management of the bank and for the redemption of the bank's issue. The board of directors was made up of one politician from each county. The charter ran for ten years. At the end of that period the bank was short $100,000 and the state had to borrow that amount to meet the indebtedness. In 1834 the Legislature created two new banks. One the State Bank, the other the Bank of Illinois. The state was not responsible for the redemption of the bills issued from these banks though it was a stockholder in both of them. They both went into liquidation in 1842. There were no banks of issue in Illinois from 1842 till 1851.

ARTICLE X, SECTION 5

In the Constitutional Convention of 1848, there were steps taken to prevent the Legislature from involving the state in the banking business. There was plenty of money, but it was the money of other states. There was really a bit of sentiment among the people which caused them to feel a little ashamed that Illinois could not furnish her own people with a circulating medium. The money that business men were handling every day was from banks in the several states of the Union. But the men who made the Constitution of 1848, said that the people must authorize the next banking system in Illinois. Article X, Section 5 of the new Constitution says: "No act of the General Assembly, authorizing corporations or associations with banking powers, shall go into effect or in any manner be enforced, unless the same shall be submitted to the people at the general election next succeeding the passage of the same, and be approved by a majority of all the votes cast at such election for and against such law."

Section 3 of Article X says: "No state bank shall hereafter be created nor shall the state own or be liable for any stock in any corporation or joint-stock association for banking purposes, to be hereafter created." Section four also provided that stockholders in banking corporations shall be held liable to the amount of their respective shares for all debts or liabilities of every kind. These three sections aimed to protect the honest people who do not always take the trouble to protect themselves. But money was necessary for the transaction of business and as intimated above people took great pride in the fact that they were handling home-made money. Stuve says the state democratic platforms for several years prior to 1851 had condemned banks and banking. At this time the Legislature was democratic and so was the governor. The whigs shortly after the adoption

THE PIONEER, THE FIRST RAILROAD ENGINE IN CHICAGO

of the new Constitution, worked out a scheme for the organization of banks, not altogether different from our present National Banking system. The democrats and the democratic press were loud in their condemnation of a scheme to fasten upon the people a system destined to ruin the state and the people. But two years later the democratic party brought forward a system which originated in New York and which had been adopted in other states. Its general plan was also like the present National Banking system. It was now a question of adopting some system of banking or continuing to use many millions of issue from the banks of other states.

The eagerness of the people to furnish their own money was shown in the issue of currency by unincorporated organizations or private banks. It was believed that the state was suffering the loss of half a million dollars tribute money to foreign banking establishments.

The Law of '51

The Legislature met in January, 1851. It was seen that the big fight of the session was the passage of a banking law which would, before it could go into effect, have to be referred to the voters at a general election and receive a majority of the votes cast, before it could become the basis of a banking system. The law was in the main as follows:

The law required that before a company could be authorized to open a bank, the said company must deposit with the Auditor of Public Accounts $50,000 in bonds of, 1. The United States. 2. Bonds of any other state. 3. Illinois bonds which must be listed at 20 per cent discount below their regular market value. When the auditor had satisfied himself of the value of the deposit, he would issue to the company $50,000 worth of notes similar to those now issued to National banks. This was practically the capital of the bank. The law further provided that at any time the holder of a bill wished, the bank must pay gold or silver for the bill. This was called redeeming the issue. If the bank failed to redeem its issue, there was a penalty provided. In case the bank failed entirely, the business of the bank would be wound up by the auditor. He would proceed to offer the bonds, which the company had deposited in his office as security against loss to the bill holders, for sale; and with the proceeds he redeemed the outstanding bills that had been issued by the bank. In case the bonds on deposit in the auditor's office brought less than the amount of the indebtedness of the bank, the stockholders were personally liable for the balance.

A bank organized under this law could charge but 7 per cent on loans. The bank was prohibited from dealing in real estate, other than to sell real property which came into the possession of the bank in the foreclosing of mortgages. As a precaution a board of three bank commissioners was created who acted as a sort of examining board with authority to examine books and resources. The officers of the bank were obliged to make quarterly reports under oath to the Auditor of Public Accounts.

It would appear on the face of the proposition that bill-holders were guaranteed against loss. But when the law was passed it was vetoed by the governor, but it was passed over his veto by the Legislature. And now the law must go before the people in a referendum according to the provision in the Constitution.

Those who favored the law and hoped to have it ratified by the people brought forward arguments in support of the measure. They said the state is already flooded with paper money issued by similar banks in other states. The people in Illinois know nothing of the value of these bills, in fact did not know that they were not counterfeit. In allowing other states to furnish us our circulating medium we were yielding our state pride. It was also affirmed that in the use of this money from other states we were in a measure paying tribute to those who furnished it. It would be very much better to issue our own currency, then we could know something of the basis of the issue. Again if one wished to present bills for redemption the place of redemption was at most not far away. If the state issued its own money it would be an easy matter to adjust the amount of the circulating medium to the needs of the people.

Those who opposed the law said that the amount of the circulating medium could in no way be limited, and if the people endorsed the bill there would be a flood of money thrown into circulation; this would bewilder, and entice the people into all manner of speculation which would bankrupt the state. With a great abundance of money property of all kinds would rise in price and investments would be unwisely made, and when there came a contraction, property would sink and ruin would stalk about the land. Then the sheriff, and the mortgagee, and the money lender would all be busy and unsatisfied judgments would hang like a nightmare over many a home.

Again the securities being those of states, would fluctuate greatly in value and necessarily the money based on a fluctuating security would itself fluctuate. Suppose a bank fails to redeem its bills when presented, it would be a long tedious process to get relief through the courts or through the auditor's office. In such a case the unfortunate bill-holder would be willing to cash his bill for fifty or seventy-five cents on the dollar. There would then spring up the business of the shaver or discounter who would be about the only one to flourish. Finally the people were warned that according to the sixth section of the bank bill there were two kinds of banks in contemplation. One was a bank that must deposit $50,000 worth of bonds with the auditor and receive from him the circulating notes as described in the foregoing paragraphs, and another which was not hedged about by so much red tape. This sixth section says "to establish offices of discount, deposit, and circulation," with capital of not less than $50,000. This was interpreted to mean that by this law banks could be organized "under the supervision of the auditor, and issue non-secured notes." That is they were banks of issue and circulation. But the people wanted plenty of money and at an election in November, 1851, the referendum was taken and carried by a vote of 37,626 to 31,405.

WILDCATS.

It is reliably stated that a number of banks were promptly organized in the northern part of the state and that large quantities of paper money were put into circulation, and further that by the middle of the summer of 1852 there had been but two banks organized under the plan of depositing the $50,000 of securities with the auditor. "So that secured bank notes furnished but a small part of the circulating currency." So disappointing was the practical side of the law to those who favored an honest currency that there was a very general belief that the legislature, which would meet in January, 1853, would repeal the law. In order to save the law from repeal, as many as twenty-seven banks made application to organize under the law providing for the depositing of bonds with the auditor for the purpose of securing the redemption of the issue.

In 1854 the bank commissioners reported only twenty-nine banks operating under the note-secured plan. Ten of these were located in Chicago, two in Springfield, two in Naperville, with others one in a city. The number of banking institutions in Chicago as reported in 1855 was seventeen so seven of them must have been of the Wildcat order. There were still millions of money from other states in circulation in Illinois. Mr. Cole, author of Volume 3 of the Centennial History of Illinois, says that the twenty-nine banks operating under the law in 1854 had a capital of $17,000,000 and resources of more than $6,000,000. A million dollars of secured notes were issued in the first year of the banking act, but they were only a fraction of the entire amount of money circulating in Illinois. "Illegal issues by both private banks and certain newly authorized banking associations together with the notes of foreign banks comprised the vast bulk."

Organizing a Bank

Stuve's history gives an interesting procedure as to organizing a bank under the law of 1851. The scheme briefly told was as follows: A few schemers would get a small amount of money together to meet the expense of organization. They would then notify the auditor of public accounts that they wished to organize the bank of "Wildcat" in the town of "Podunk," "Brush" County, Illinois, with a capital stock of $200,000. By hook or crook, they secure $50,000 worth of, say, Missouri State bonds which they present to the auditor who delivers to the company the $200,000 in nice new crisp bills. A trusty one of the stock holders takes the bills and goes to Georgia where he exchanges them for new Georgia bills. The Georgia money is brought to "Podunk" and the bank is opened. Fifty thousand dollars of the Georgia money is paid over to the owners of the Missouri bonds or perhaps invested in pork or beef which is shipped east, the bill of lading turned over to the broker who collects and pays for the bonds and afterwards turns over the balance to the bankers.

In the meantime the bank of "Wildcat" was opened each day for any business which might come that way. The bankers had something like $150,000 of Georgia money and they were drawing 6 per cent interest on the $50,000 worth of Missouri bonds.

Now if this $150,000 of Georgia money can be loaned and good notes taken, and if the "Wildcat" money which was taken down to Georgia never gets back to "Podunk," the bankers will eventually make money. Again the scheme works better when the money taken to Georgia if it can be scattered quite generally over the state, and if the money brought back from Georgia is the issue of several different Georgia banks. One of the advantages of the system to the bankers came from the possibility that their issue would get so far from home that it would never find its way back to the bank of issue.

It may be that the foregoing outline never had its counterpart in a real situation, but there were real cases with some, if not all, of the elements in the above case presented.

In 1859 the Grayville bank sought to restrain the auditor from ordering it into liquidation on the ground that only one bill at a time could be presented for redemption. And when this view was sustained, the banker, began a slow process of redemption in order to wear out the bill holder, but the courts held that no obstacles should be put in the way of the redemption of the bills.

After all the bad features of this system have been enumerated, it still must be said that the system furnished the best circulating medium since the close of the United States Bank period.

In 1854 when there were panicky conditions in the financial world, the state bonds began to fall in value and general alarm seized the bill-holders. The panic reached Chicago in the fall of that year and runs on the banks began. Large quantities of currency were presented for redemption and several banks were forced to close their doors for lack of specie with which to redeem their bills. The storm soon blew over and normal conditions prevailed by the middle of the winter. However three banks did not open their doors and later others were forced into liquidation.

In 1857 the Legislature strengthened the law in several particulars which tended to encourage legitimate banking among which was one raising the interest rate from seven to eight. It appeared that a very large part of the securities deposited with the auditor of public accounts consisted of Missouri bonds which, by reason of internal improvement scheme in that state, were depreciating very rapidly. Everything looked like a final collapse. But strong men came to the rescue. Jesse K. Dubois, auditor, called for additional securities of nearly all the banks, the Chicago bankers agreed to receive the bills of the down state banks at par and the danger was averted.

This experiment in banking demonstrated the fact that the question of immediate redemption of bills of issue was the most troublesome question which had arisen. This was illustrated many times when bill holders presented currency for redemption. The bankers felt that the more troublesome they could make it for the bill holder to get specie for his bill, the less demand there would be for redemption.

By 1860 the banks had increased to 110 with a circulation of $12,320,964 which included most of the currency in circulation. In all of the fourteen banks which had withdrawn from the banking business since 1851, there was but one whose securities were not sufficient to redeem all outstanding notes.

In the winter of 1860-61 when the southern states were passing ordinances of secession, the securities of the southern states which were on deposit with the auditor fell so rapidly that the circulating bills of the banks which had southern securities were listed by the money brokers and the banks were forced out of business. By 1863 all except seventeen of the banks under the law of 1851 were in process of liquidation, and the total circulation fell to half million. By 1865 the circulation had dwindled to $132,436. The National Banking law had come to stay, and the federal law which taxed state bank issue two per cent, either drove the state banks out of business or forced their owners to convert them into national banks.

CHAPTER XX

THE RISE OF THE REPUBLICAN PARTY

SLAVE HISTORY—COMPROMISE OF 1850—REPEAL—A PLATFORM—SENATOR DOUGLAS—AT RIPON—IN ILLINOIS—STATE MASS CONVENTION—REPUBLICAN CONVENTION—THE DEBATE—THE OUTCOME—POLITICAL CLASS—PAUL SELBY—THE CALL—THE BLOOMINGTON CONVENTION—DELEGATE LINCOLN—IN MAJOR'S HALL—THE LOST SPEECH—RESOLUTIONS—DEMOCRATS IN 1856—BISSELL ELECTED

If a new political party is to be organized there must be found a basis of organization which is not found in any existing political party. The basis of an organization of the republican party which came into existence in the decade preceding the Civil war was "Opposition to the spread of slavery in the United States." African slavery began in the United States as early as 1619. The story of its introduction is a familiar one to the school children of this country. It was a disturbing element in the whole life of the American people. It divided the churches of the country; it disarranged the economic life of the people; it acted as a millstone tied to the educational ambitions of the people where slavery was permitted; it broke asunder, for four long years, the highest type of government the world had ever seen; and it dragged the social standards of the cavalier life of the South to the lowest levels by producing a race of half-breeds begotten out of wedlock. It was to protest against the spread of an institution that could work havoc that the republican party was organized.

SLAVE HISTORY

Let us briefly mention the occasions when this awful scourge demanded the attention of the master minds of the country. In the Constitutional Convention of 1787, the friends of slavery had to be placated. They said if we cannot count our slaves in determining the population of our states, we may as well return to our homes and abandon the effort to make a "more perfect union." Out of this determination of the statesmen from the slave holding states, that the slave should be counted in determining the population of the slave holding states, came what we know as the second great compromise. And, again it was feared that if Congress were given the power to regulate commerce, it would put such limitations and burdens upon the importation of slaves that the slave trade would be ruined. Out of this came a portion of the third compromise, that part forbidding Congress from interfering with the importation of slaves prior to 1808.

When the constitution was adopted and the government was organized it was found that there were seven free states and six slave states. The first state admitted after the thirteen was Vermont which of course was a free state. This gave considerable advantage to the free states in legislation relative to slavery. The next two states were Kentucky and Tennessee, both slave states. In the Senate there were now sixteen senators from slave states and sixteen from free states. From now to the admission of Maine and Missouri there was a regular alternation of free and slave states. Prior to the admission of Missouri there were eleven free states in the union and eleven slave states.

The application of the territory of Missouri to come into the Union as a slave state at once caused the greatest alarm among all people who had hoped that the Mississippi River would check or permanently stop the westward spread of slavery. Out of this application of Missouri to come into the Union as a slave state came the Missouri compromise with which the general reader is very familiar.

The long bitter fight in Illinois to make the state slave territory has also been discussed at much length. The next occasion for fear of the spread of slavery was the annexation of Texas. This was eventually a settled fact and the Mexican war was the result.

When the Mexican war was in its first stages, a bill was presented in Congress which set aside $2,000,000 with which the president was to prosecute a treaty with Mexico looking to the acquisition of territory which might be acquired of that country. A Mr. Wilmot, a congressman from Pennsylvania, introduced a proviso or amendment to the bill appropriating the $2,000,000 which would, if it had become a law, shut slavery out of all territory which might be gotten from the war with Mexico. This proviso said "Slavery, or involuntary servitude, except as a punishment for crime, shall be forever prohibited in any territory which may be acquired from Mexico." When this amendment or proviso came up in the house of representatives it was carried by a majority of six. Only four votes from non-slaveholding states were cast against this proviso and they were from Illinois—Douglas, Feklin, Hoge, and McClernand.

A vote taken in the State Legislature of 1849 shows that the Legislature of Illinois at that time, though largely democratic, had not yet entirely surrendered to the demands of the slave holders of the South. The action was a joint resolution instructing the representatives and senators in Congress "to procure the enactment of such laws for the government of the territories of the United States, acquired by the treaty of peace with Mexico as should contain the express declaration that 'there shall be neither slavery nor involuntary servitude otherwise than in punishment for crime whereof the party shall have been duly convicted.' It is pointed out that the Wilmot proviso said 'shall be forever' prohibited, while the Illinois resolution would, if adopted by Congress, prohibit slavery only as long as the region remained as territories of the United States."

Already there was growing up in Illinois two diverse views as to the powers of Congress to control the destiny of the public domain. An important group of Illinois democrats held that

THE FIRST MACON COUNTY COURT HOUSE
Lincoln attended court here

Congress had no constitutional right either to establish, prohibit, or in any wise interfere with slavery in the territories. Another group of public men in Illinois headed by Lincoln held to the doctrine that Congress has full power over the territory to prevent slavery in any or all parts of it. The vote on the resolution of instruction to the state's representatives in Congress show how there was this early a cleavage between those would eventually constitute the republican party and those would be definitely opposed. In the house the vote was, for the resolutions, 24 whigs and 14 democrats; against the instruction and resolution 34, all democrats. In the senate the vote stood for the instructions and resolutions 7 whigs and 7 democrats—14; against the instruction and resolution 11, all democrats. It is not to be inferred that all the men who voted for the instruction and resolution will eventually be found in the ranks of the republican party but some of them will be found there.

COMPROMISE OF 1850

Not only did Illinois ask Congress to exclude slavery from all territory acquired from Mexico, but all of the northern states except one made the same request. This expression of public sentiment in the North greatly angered the southern leaders, and Toombs of Georgia declared if Congress should attempt such a thing that he would vow before God that he would take his stand for disunion. Taylor, before his death, had advised California to ask for admission into the Union. The Californians did this, the convention making application voted unanimously to come in as a free state. But Taylor died in July, 1850. Now everything was confusion; the South saw it had lost California, which was the most valuable part of the Mexican acquisition. Clay now came forward with what we know as the Compromises of 1850. This compromise was intended to modify and soften the extreme views which were at that time held by both the northerners and the southerners. Clay saw that the north was organizing about the doctrine of opposition to the spread of slave territory, and so he plead for a "union of hearts" between the North and South through mutual concessions. The new president, Millard Fillmore, heartily supported the "Omnibus" compromise.

The measures provided for: 1. The admission of California as a free state; 2. The organization of New Mexico and Utah on the principle of "Squatter Sovereignty"; 3. The prohibition of the slave trade in the District of Columbia; and 4. The enactment of a more effective fugitive slave law. The first law was a great gain for those who opposed the further extension of slave territory, and was certainly a great loss to those who already saw the decline of political supremacy of the slave interests in the National Congress. The second law was a draw as to advantage. The day of decision was deferred indefinitely. The third law was without doubt a gain to anti-slavery advocates. There was great gain to the people who had been greatly humiliated by the buying and selling of human beings in the capital of "the land of the free and the home of the brave." But the fourth law was a great gain in sentiment for the slave holders. It was no great gain in a material way. It alienated many half hearted supporters of slavery. Dr. Channing says: "The passage of the Fugitive Slave Act was one of the worst blunders in the long series of errors which led to the perpetuation of slavery in the South. Every day that slavery existed, the South grew weaker morally, materially, and politically." It has been shown "that only one-thirtieth of one per cent of the slaves escaped in any one year." There seems therefore that there was no real need of the fugitive slave law as enacted in the compromise measures.

Daniel Webster who had opposed the annexation of Texas and the Mexican war, was willing to lend his aid to the adoption of the compromise. He went so far as to lay down the doctrine that slave labor could never flourish in the territory which had been acquired from Mexico and hence the opponents of the spread of slavery need have no fears as to slavery in New Mexico. It was not necessary to exclude slavery by law, since the laws of nature had decreed against the presence of slavery in the aforesaid territory. The old defenders and opponents of the spread of slavery were passing off of the stage of active life, Webster, Clay, Calhoun, and others. A new group of anti-slavery champions were coming upon the scene. The leader was Wm. H. Seward, who plead for the operation of the "higher law."

Repeal

In the session of the Legislature elected in 1850, the socalled Illinois Wilmot proviso was repealed. In other words the resolution passed in 1849 asking the congressmen and senators from Illinois to use all honorable means in their power to procure such laws as would prohibit the spread of slavery into the territory acquired from Mexico. In this action of 1851 the vote stood in the House 49 for repeal and 11 against. In the Senate 22 for repeal and 2 against. Party lines were deserted and there seemed to be a "union of hearts" for the time being.

It was under the spell of the Compromise of 1850 and the action of the Legislature of 1851, that Illinois entered the national campaign of 1852. The democrats had broken all precedents and had nominated Mr. Franklin Pierce of New Hampshire, while the whigs named Gen. Winfield Scott, the conqueror of Mexico. Both political parties agreed that the compromise of 1850 should remain inviolable.

In Illinois in 1852 the democrats were so well organized and so popular that the whigs felt that there was no use, except for the sake of holding their organization together, to put out candidates for state offices.

A Platform

In the quiet of a political calm in Ohio in the summer and fall of 1853, all of the opposing elements of the party in power began to discuss the feasibility of fusing their forces for a contest of the intrenched hosts. In a rather formal way those opposed to the democratic party put forth a platform upon which the dissatisfied could stand. It included the following principles: 1. Opposition to the fugitive slave law. 2. Opposition to the further extension of slavery. 3. Equal taxation and the suppression of intemperance.

Opposition to the democratic party was difficult to crystallize. The various elements which had been turned loose by the decaying whig party were drifting about hither, thither.

Senator Douglas

Senator Douglas had said of the Missouri Compromise line: "It is canonized in the hearts of the American people, and no ruthless hand will ever dare to disturb it." Not only did he feel that way about this boundary line between slavery and freedom, but following the acquisition of the territory from Mexico, Mr. Douglas introduced a bill to establish the line of 36° and 30′ from the crest of the Rocky Mountains to the Pacific Ocean. But in the period of calm between the passage of the Compromise of 1850 and 1854 Mr. Douglas developed a new theory. It was simply to take the control of the whole question of slavery in the territories out of the hands of Congress and put it into the hands of the people who must shortly organize this territory and present it to the Congress and ask for its admission as states. He was the chairman of the Committee on Territories. In December, 1853, the Thirty-third Congress convened. Douglas had come into the Senate in 1847, succeeding Gen. James Semple. He had served one term and had been chosen as his own successor. He had been honored with the chairmanship of the committee on territories. He had no doubt thought intensely on the matter of opening the great Northwest to settlement, so in the session of beginning December, 1853, he introduced a bill to provide for the organization of the territory west of Iowa and Missouri into two territories— Kansas and Nebraska. Almost at the same time a southern senator, Archibald Dixon from Kentucky, introduced a bill for the repeal of the Missouri Compromise. The two bills were combined and Senator Douglas became the champion of the amended bill.

From the opening of the session of Congress in 1853 to the passage of Kansas-Nebraska bill May 30, 1854, there was bitter denunciation of Douglas for his attitude toward the Missouri Compromise.

At Ripon

Among the many gatherings of the people of the North to consider what was wise in these troublous times, a meeting at Ripon, Wisconsin, has for us at this time a special interest. Ripon is some fifteen miles north of west of Fon du lac, and was in 1854 an unimportant village. Two months before the passage of the Kansas-Nebraska Act, a few whigs, free soilers, and democrats met in a school house in Ripon, Wisconsin, to discuss the political situation in the United States as to slavery. The conferences were held from day to day and on the 30th of March, 1854, a resolution was suggested that a new party be organized to be called the "republican party." It was also resolved that the object of the new party should be to secure the confinement of slavery within its present limits.

Vice President Henry Wilson in his great book, "The Rise and Fall of the Slave Power," says that the night following the passage of the Kansas-Nebraska Act, a meeting of all the senators and representatives that had opposed the bill in its passage through the two houses, about thirty in number was held and a party organized which had for its purpose the prevention of the further encroachment of slavery upon the national territory. It was proposed in the discussions that the party be known as the "republican party."

In Illinois

The Kankas-Nebraska bill was passed May 29, 1854. Immediately the whole country was up in arms against the action taken by Congress. The general feeling in Illinois was shown by protests from all kinds of local organizations. Twenty-six ministers in Chicago addressed a protest to Senator Douglas. Meetings were held in several counties, and newspapers were loud in condemnation. Congress adjourned and the representatives and one-third of the senators returned to their homes to carry on the campaign for reelection. Mr. Douglas was due in Chicago about the first of September. His friends were bold in their defense of his part in the repeal of the Missouri Compromise. His political enemies were bitter in their denunciation of his alliance with the slave interests. He was warned that he would better not attempt publicly to defend his part in the passage of the Kansas-Nebraska bill. But Douglas was as determined as they and he insisted that he would explain and defend his action in the passage of the bill.

Douglas caused announcement to be made that he would address his "fellow citizens" on the evening of Saturday, September 1st. As the time of the speaking approached, the air was rife with threats of personal violence. Douglas received threatening letters. On the afternoon of September 1st flags were displayed at half-mast, and the bells of the city were tolled for more than an hour.

At the time for the speaking to begin the streets about the North Market Hall were jammed. Delegations both for and against were present from other cities and even from other states. Senator Douglas appeared upon a balcony and after preliminaries began upon his main theme. At this point pandemonium broke loose; men hissed, yelled, groaned and gave vent to their anger in all manner of outrageous noises. Mr. Douglas was ready for such a demonstration. He ceased speaking and folding his arms deliberately surveyed the angry multitude. When the angry crowd would quiet down Mr. Douglas would begin to speak, but they were determined that he should not speak, and so for four long hours the mob howled and the speaker waited. Mr. Douglas seeing that what he might say would be heard by no one, and knowing he could not win in so unequal a combat, closed his speech and retired.

In many of the counties in Illinois there were held mass-meetings through the fall months of 1854 at which much anti-Nebraska sentiment was created. A state convention was called for Springfield for October 5, 1854, for the purpose of crystallizing anti-Nebraska sentiment. In some of the county meetings they took the name republican. In some they appointed delegates to attend the state convention that had been called for October 5th. In many of these meetings the whigs, democrats, know-nothings and anti-Nebraska men all met, forgot any previous differences in political matters, and united on a one plank platform—opposition to the extension of slave territory. In fact it is stated by Stuve that in many of these meetings the democrats took a leading part. A mass convention was held in Kane county on August 19, 1854, in which the people, opposed to the extension of slavery, expressed themselves as follows:

"We, the people of Kane County, in mass convention assembled, irrespective of party, in view of the long-continued encroachments of the slave power, culminating at last in the repeal of the law of freedom in all the hitherto unorganized territories of the union, will cooperate with the friends of freedom throughout the state in an effort to bring the Government back to just principles; to restore Kansas and Nebraska to the position of free territories; to repeal the fugitive slave law; to restrict slavery to the states in which it exists; to prohibit the admission of any more slave states into the Union; to exclude slavery from all territories over which the general Government has exclusive jurisdiction; resist the acquirement of any new slave territory, and the repeal of the inhuman and barbarous black laws of this state."

The following call for a state convention was published in the Free West, a newspaper of Chicago, September 7, 1854.

STATE MASS CONVENTION

"The convention of all the citizens of the State of Illinois opposed to repeal of the Missouri Compromise and to the further extension and consolidation of the slave power, and in favor of the overthrow of the existing state and national administrations which are pledged to the support of slavery, will be held on the 5th day of October, A. D. 1854, at 2 o'clock, at Springfield, for the organization of a party which shall put the Government upon a republican tack, and secure to the non-slaveholders throughout the Union their just and constitutional weight and influence in the councils of the Nation.

Papers throughout the state please copy."

The Free West, as its name implies, was an anti-slavery paper printed in Chicago and edited by Zebina Eastman. This paper in an editorial comment a few days later referred to this proposed mass convention as "the Republican State Convention."

REPUBLICAN CONVENTION

On Tuesday, October 3, 1854, the delegates to the first general convention, whose purpose was opposition to the extension of slave territory, met in Springfield. The delegates numbered 26 and included Owen Lovejoy, Ichabod Codding, Erastus Wright, Tuthill King, A. G. Throop, C. C. Flint, N. C. Greer, Joseph T. Morse, Dr. H. K Jones, Bronson Murray, S. M. Coe, T. B. Hurlbut, William Butler, Jesse Penrose, Dr. Henry Wing, John F. Farnsworth.

The state fair was in session in Springfield and it was considered a good time to make the first move for a state republican organization. When the call was issued earlier in the fall, the place designated was the state house. When the delegates began to arrive in Springfield, they discovered that the friends to the movement in that city had not secured before hand the promise of a room in the capitol building, nor was it very generally known in Springfield that the convention was to be held in that city. The friends who came as delegates were somewhat embarrassed at the situation but not entirely discouraged. However, they secured a place for the meeting and held the first session. No business was transacted and it was decided to adjourn till the morrow. It was decided to have printed a few hundred hand bills for distribution over the city notifying the public of the presence in the city of the delegates to the proposed convention, and inviting those interested to attend the sessions of the convention.

When those in charge approached the newspaper offices to get the bills printed they found that the papers had given no notice of the convention and were adverse to the printing of the handbills. Different newspaper offices were visited, and all refused to have anything to do with the convention. Finally one of the delegates found a job printing office that was generous enough to allow him to set up the type for his hand-bill and to print the required number.

On the morrow the delegates met for organization. The handbills had done some good as there was an increased attendance and interest. Tuthill King called the meeting to order and Mr. A. G. Throop was elected chairman and Mr. C. C. Flint was made secretary. A committee was selected to draft resolutions and suggest the name of a candidate for state treasurer, the only state officer to be elected at the November election. The committee was as follows: N. C. Greer, of Lake County; Joseph T. Morse, of Woodford County; Erastus Wright, of Sangamon County; Dr. H. K. Jones, of Morgan County; Bronson Murray, of LaSalle County; T. B. Hurlbut, of Madison County; William Butler, of Lee County; Jesse Penrose, of Whiteside County; Dr. Henry Wing, of Madison County.

While the committee was deliberating on a platform, Lovejoy and others discussed the issues then before the general public. One of the speakers said: "This convention is not large—owing to the unfavorable circumstances already mentioned and the persevering efforts of our opponents to prevent us from obtaining a place of meeting: but it is the little stone cut out of the mountain without hands, and it will fill the whole earth. Let us trust in God and in God's truth. He is for us; who can be against us? His truth is what we are contending for, and victory will crown our efforts." A Mr. Brown, of Alton, also made a short talk in which he said: "I can consent to no compromise with anything so abhorent as slavery. I am for no compromise with slavery in any shape." These two sentences are to be interpreted to mean that this anti-Nebraska movement was not getting the help it ought to have from the whig in Illinois.

The convention then adjourned to listen to Mr. Lincoln who was to make an address at that time as a reply to a speech which Mr. Douglas had previously delivered. Upon reassembling the convention listened to the report of the committee on resolutions. One of the resolutions was—"Resolved, that, as freedom is national and slavery sectional and local, the absence of all law upon the subject of slavery presumes the existence of a state of freedom alone." The convention named John E. McClun of McLean County as their candidate for state treasurer. The convention appointed a state central committee and adjourned. The committee was as follows: David J. Baker, of Madison; Major N. D. Coy, of Knox; N. C. Geer, of Lake; A. G. Throop, of Cook; Judge E. S. Leland, of La Salle; M. L. Dunlap, of Cook; Hon. Abraham Lincoln, of Sangamon; H. M. Sheets, of Stephenson; L. Eastman, of Cook; John F. Farnsworth, of Kane; J. B. Fairbanks, of Morgan; Ichabod Codding, of Chicago.

A writer who was present and set the type and printed the hand-bills has this to say of the convention:

"Such was the birth of the republican party in Illinois. Such were the men who set the ball in motion which is now rolling forward with irresistible force. Almost without exception they are men who loved liberty for itself and not for office. They

WHERE LINCOLN CLERKED, OLD NEW SALEM

were the founders, and they have been the pioneers and fighting men of the party. They have fought its battles, won its victories, and have brought it to the threshold of a great triumph. And now when they demand that principle shall not be sacrificed to a mistaken expediency—when they insist that the doctrines that gave life and strength to the republican party in its infancy shall be maintained inviolate—they are denounced, and abused and stigmatized by the hangers-on of the organization, as insane radicals, and as men wanting to hurt the party." This paragraph was written in 1860 and is a defense of the men who are not willing to compromise.

The Debate

The convention which has just been considered was held in Springfield at the time of the state fair. Another important gathering was also held in Springfield the week of the state fair. This was an informal debate between Lincoln and Douglas. The congressional campaign was carried on between Richard Yates, whig, and Major Harris, the democratic candidate. Douglas and General Singleton were assisting Major Harris. It had been noised about that Trumbull and Judge Breese, anti-Nebraska democrats, would be present to speak. Both Trumbull and Breese were candidates for the United States Senate. Mr. Lincoln also was casting glances toward the senatorship. The probability that these public men would speak drew politicians from far and near.

Other speakers not appearing, Mr. Lincoln and Mr. Douglas agreed to divide the time and discuss the questions of the day. This was the first time that these two great debaters had ever appeared before the public at the same time and place. Mr. Lincoln was the first speaker. He was among his friends and was willing to state frankly and plainly his position. He insisted that he was national in his views; that he was opposed to disturbing slavery where it legally existed; that he was in favor of an efficient fugitive slave law because the right to the return of the slave was guaranteed in the constitution; he believed that Congress had the power and should exercise it, to prohibit slavery in any territory belonging to the United States. He pointed out that the Ordinance of 1787 had forbidden slavery in the Northwest Territory and that the ordinance, though enacted by the Continental Congress under the Articles of Confederation, the ordinance had been reenacted at the first session in 1789. Mr. Lincoln further stated that according to the principles laid down in the Declaration of Independence the white man had no right to impose laws upon the black man without the black man's consent. He then paid his respects to his rival personally by calling the attention of his hearers to the position taken by Mr. Douglas in 1849 when he spoke of the Missouri

Compromise as having "an origin akin to that of the Constitution" and as having become "canonized in the hearts of the American people as a sacred thing which no ruthless hand would ever be reckless enough to disturb." Mr. Lincoln spoke with great power and earnestness and his audience hung upon his words in wrapt attention. This is the speech which the convention, then in session in Springfield, adjourned to hear.

It was now Mr. Douglas' time to address the assembled throng. His speech opened with an affirmation that in principle the Compromise of 1850, as to the public domain, Utah and New Mexico, was identical with the principles governing the matter of slavery in the territory affected by the repeal of the Missouri Compromise. He argued that the clause which opened the Kansas-Nebraska Territory to slavery was fathered by a southern whig. He said that the Compromise of 1850 opened all the United States Territory to settlement under the squatter sovereignty principle. He met each other argument of his opponent with a convincing array of defensive facts. Mr. Douglas was warmly supported by vast numbers of people attending the debate. He seemed to carry conviction to his hearers, and their enthusiasm expressed itself in rounds of applause.

Judge Breese and Lyman Trumbull arrived later, probably on the fifth, and spoke after Douglas was gone. The latter had left John Calhoun to answer the two former, which he did. A very fine audience gathered at night to hear Judge Trumbull, who took for his theme the one topic of the repeal of the Missouri Compromise. Many democrats like Trumbull were in full accord with democratic doctrine, but were anti-Nebraska, and claimed that the support of the Kansas-Nebraska act should not be made a test of loyalty to the democratic party.

The Outcome

The state fair had produced the occasion for a week's discussion which started the new party well on its way toward success. The convention and the debate both tended to call attention to the unwisdom of the repeal of the Missouri Compromise. The newly organized republican party received help from Ohio in the presence in the campaign of two great speakers, Salmon P. Chase and Joshua R. Giddings. These two men reenforced the work of the local men of the new party, and when the smoke of battle had cleared away five out of the nine congressmen were found to be anti-Nebraska men—Elihu B. Washburn, Galena, First District; James H. Woodworth, Chicago, Second District; Jesse O. Norton, Joliet, Third District; James Knox, Knoxville, Fourth District; and Lyman Trumbull, Belleville, Eighth District. Washburne, Knox, and Norton were put down as republicans, but Trumbull and Woodworth were classed as democrats, though as anti-Nebraska democrats.

LYMAN TRUMBULL

The anti-Nebraska party lost the organization of the House of Representatives in the Legislature, and also of the Senate, and of course lost the treasureship of the state. But the leaders were to be congratulated. They had made a valiant fight and were greatly encouraged.

During the year 1855 there was no great political activity, but everywhere the doctrines of the new party were taking deep root. The democrats were not unaware of the growing strength of the anti-Nebraska party. Late in the year 1855 the chairman of the democratic state central committee, Hon. J. A. McClernand, issued a stirring appeal directed to the committeemen and to the people generally preparatory to the selection of delegates to the State Democratic Convention to be held in Springfield May 1st, 1856. This address was directed chiefly against the know-nothings—"The malcontents, the intolerants, and the religious bigots of the country, have determined upon making a desperate effort to seize the reins of government. Their only hope is to excite popular passion and upon it ride into office and power. They have raised their black flag, with 'Abolition' on the one side and 'Disunion' on the other, surmounted with the know-nothing death's head and cross bones, and with hideous outcries are rallying their motly forces for the coming struggle. They pretend to be the peculiar friend of the negro. While they would make slaves of white men; they pretend to be the friends of freedom, yet murder men for exercising a plain constitutional right; they pretend to love liberty while they denounce the constitution as a league with hell.—Devoid of political principle themselves, they are for fusion with men of every shade of political principle."

Political Class

The Anti-Nebraska Convention held in Springfield in October, 1854, and the election which followed kept before the people the one idea which was the basic thing in the organization of the republican party. The fact that five out of the nine congressmen who were elected in the congressional election of November, 1854, were anti-Nebraska men, and that some of these men were democrats and had never been identified with the whig party, put the democratic managers in Illinois on the defensive, for there was danger that their ranks would be greatly depleted by more desertions. The whole situation was also an incentive to the anti-Nebraska people to redouble their efforts not only to hold what they had gained but to make further inroads in both the whig and the democratic party. A writer has said that— The condition of political affairs existing throughout the nation between 1854 and 1856 was one of practical chaos. Parties were disintegrating and their mutually repellent elements were seeking new associations. Anti-slavery democrats and anti-slavery whigs were drifting in a similar manner towards a common center. By anti-slavery was not meant abolitionists, but those who opposed the repeal of the Missouri Compromise. In nearly every section of the state, except in the south third, there were groups of men who were accustomed to meet together and to discuss the questions of the hour. In these groups were abolitionists, free-soilers, whigs, know-nothings and democrats. They were finding a common basis for action. In Jacksonville, which was a college town, the discussions were pitched upon a high plane of reasoning. Among those who were active in keeping the danger of the spread of slavery before the people were Prof. Jonathan B. Turner, President Julian M. Sturtevant, Dr. Samuel Adams, Elihu Wolcott, Richard Yates, Dr. David Prince, Dr. Hiram K. Jones, John Mathers, J. W. King, J. O. King, J. H. Bancroft, J. W. Lathrop, Peter Melendy, Anderson Foreman, and Paul Selby. These men were teachers, lawyers, doctors, editors, and business men.

PAUL SELBY

No man in Illinois is deserving of more honor in the work of creating sentiment against the repeal of the Missouri Compromise than Paul Selby, editor of the Morgan (County) Journal, printed in Jacksonville. This paper was originally a whig publication, but when Mr. Selby took charge of it in 1852, he made an independent paper of it. In 1854 when the Kansas-Nebraska bill was before Congress, Mr. Selby immediately took up the cause of the anti-Nebraska people.

In December, 1855, the Journal issued a call for a convention of anti-Nebraska editors. A fire in the office of the Journal destroyed the issue containing the "call" and it can not be reproduced, but the Chicago Tribune a short time before the meeting of the editors was held in Decatur February 22, 1856, had this to say: "It was moved by the Morgan Journal and seconded by the Winchester Chronicle that there be held a convention of free state editors at Decatur, February 22, 1856. The question had met the approval of the Pike County Free Press, Decatur Chronicle and other papers. The Morgan Journal called on the Alton Courier, The Democrat, Democratic Press, Tribune, Journal, and Staats Zeitung, all of Chicago; the Springfield Journal, and the Belleville Advocate, and the anti-Nebraska press generally, from one end of the state to the other, to express their sentiments on the propriety of the proposed convention." The Chicago Tribune heartily endorsed the call and promised to send a delegate to the convention. It urged the editors of the state to respond to the call of the Morgan Journal. The Winchester Chronicle was the first paper to endorse the call after it appeared in the Morgan Journal. Judge John Moses, who afterwards wrote a history of Illinois, was the editor of the Winchester Chronicle.

PAUL SELBY

The Call

The call for the convention as published in several of the anti-Nebraska papers was as follows:

"All editors in Illinois opposed to the Nebraska bill are requested to meet in convention at Decatur, Illinois, on the 22d of February next for the purpose of making arrangements for the organization of the anti-Nebraska forces in this state for the coming contest. All editors favoring the movement will please forward a copy of their paper containing their approval to the office of The Illinois State Chronicle, Decatur."

Twenty-five of the papers of the state endorsed the call for an editors' convention; this was 100 per cent of the anti-Nebraska papers in Illinois. The list is as follows:

The Morgan Journal, Jacksonville.
The Chronicle, Winchester.
The Illinois State Chronicle, Decatur.
The Quincy Whig, Quincy.
The Pike County Free Press, Pittsfield.
The Gazette, Lacon.
The Tribune, Chicago.
The Staats Zeitung, Chicago.
The Republican, Oquawka.
The Republican, Peoria.
The Prairie State, Danville.
The Advertiser, Rock Island.
The Fultonian, Vermont.
The Journal (German), Quincy.
The Beacon, Freeport.
The Pantagraph, Bloomington.
The True Democrat, Joliet.
The Telegraph, Lockport.
The Gazette, Kankakee.
The Guardian, Aurora.
The Gazette, Waukegan.
The Chronicle, Peru.
The Advocate, Belleville.
The Journal, Chicago.
The Journal, Sparta.

The convention met at the appointed time and place indicated in the call. The old Cassell House, afterwards the Oglesby House, and later the St. Nicholas Hotel, offered its spacious parlor for the sessions of the convention. On the day set for the meeting a dozen editors put in an appearance; a few came later. A severe snow storm over the state kept hundreds from coming. The names of the twelve editors who reported the first day are as follows: Dr. Charles H. Ray, of the Chicago Tribune; George Schneider, of the Staats Zeitung, Chicago; V. Y. Ralston, of the Quincy Whig; O. P. Wharton, of the Rock Island Advertiser;

T. J. Pickett, of the Peoria Republican; E. C. Daugherty, of the Register, Rockford; E. W. Blaidsell, of the Republican, Rockford; Charles Faxon, of the Princeton Post; A. N. Ford, of the Lacon Gazette; B. F. Shaw, of the Dixon Telegraph; W. J. Usrey, of the Decatur Chronicle; and Paul Selby, of the Morgan Journal, Jacksonville. Mr. Selby was made chairman, and Mr. Usrey was chosen secretary. A committee on resolutions was appointed consisting of Doctor Ray, Schneider, Ralston, Wharton, Daugherty, and Pickett.

Mr. Lincoln, who would not serve on the state central committee of the convention of 1852, was not willing at least to confer with the editors in convention in Decatur. He attended the convention and was in conference with the committee on resolutions. These resolutions constituted a sort of platform. It provided as follows:

The convention disavows any intention of interfering with the internal affairs of any state in reference to slavery.

It protests against the introduction of slavery into the territory already free.

It demands the restoration of the Missouri compromise.

The convention declared in favor of the widest toleration in matters of religion, and in favor of the protection of the common school system.

It also demanded "reform in the state government."

These principles were found in the platforms of state and national conventions for the succeeding years.

A separate resolution was probably the most important action taken by the convention. It issued a call for a state convention to be held in May. It is as follows:

"Resolved, That this convention recommend a state delegate convention to be held on Thursday, the 29th day of May, next, in the City of Bloomington, and that the state central committee be requested to fix the ratio of representation for that convention, and take such steps as may seem desirable to bring about a full representation from the whole state."

A state central committee had been appointed prior to the passage of the foregoing resolution. The committee was as follows:

First Congressional District, S. M. Church, Rockford.
Second Congressional District, W. B. Ogden, Chicago.
Third Congressional District, G. D. A. Parks, Joliet
Fourth Congressional District, T. J. Pickett, Peoria.
Fifth Congressional District, Edward A. Dudley, Quincy.
Sixth Congressional District, W. H. Herndon, Springfield.
Seventh Congressional District, R. J. Oglesby, Decatur.
Eighth Congressional District, Joseph Gillespie, Edwardsville.
Ninth Congressional District, D. L. Phillips, Jonesboro.

At large, Gustavus Koerner, Belleville, and Ira O. Wilkinson, Rock Island.

The convention closed its labors with a banquet given by the friends in Decatur. At the banquet short addresses were made, but the principal address was made by Mr. Lincoln who had remained in the city for that purpose. During the evening one of the editors proposed that Mr. Lincoln become the candidate for governor on the republican ticket. Mr. Lincoln in answer pointed out that he was an old time whig, but that it would be the part of wisdom for the new party to nominate an anti-Nebraska democrat, and he put in nomination his friend, Col. William H. Bissell. The suggestion was approved by the editors present and it turned out that Bissell was nominated at the Bloomington convention and was elected in November.

The state central committee appointed at the editorial convention issued a call for a "State Convention of the Anti-Nebraska party of Illinois," to be held in Bloomington on the 29th of May, 1856. Thus this little band of editors was the means by which the republican party was brought into being in Illinois. This band of editors was not only creating public sentiment but was interpreting to the world the sentiment which was rapidly growing in Illinois. On the same day that the editors met in Decatur, February 22, 1856, a similar meeting was held in Pittsburgh, Pennsylvania. The Pittsburgh meeting was made up of delegates of several of the states, and its purpose was to set in motion a movement that would produce a national party. Owen Lovejoy and J. C. Vaughan were delates from Illinois. This Pittsburgh meeting brought about the call of a national republican party, to meet in Philadelphia, June 17, 1856.

The Bloomington Convention

The state central committee, appointed at the Decatur editorial convention, issued a call for a state convention of the anti-Nebraska party to be held in Bloomington on the 29th day of May, 1856. The call asked for a delegate convention of 226 members, but so deeply were people interested in the new party that the convention was made up of 270 members. Something like thirty counties in the south end of the state did not send a single delegate. Lee County sent twenty-five and Morgan sent twenty delegates. The delegates came from the several counties with deep interest. There were men who sat in that convention who were destined to hold the attention of the people of the United States as great generals, great orators, and as great diplomats. A few of the great names may be mentioned: O. H. Browning, George Schneider, John Wentworth, C. H. Ray, I. N. Arnold, N. B. Judd, W. P. Kellogg, Burton C. Cook, John M. Palmer, Dr. John Logan, Richard Yates, I. L. Morrison, John G. Nicolay, T. Worthington, O. M. Hatch, Abraham Lin-

GUSTAVUS KOERNER

coln, William H. Herndon, J. C. Conklin, N. M. Knapp, John Moses, T. J. Henderson, and Ichabod Codding. In addition to these who were recorded as delegates, there were scores of visitors among whom were many great men.

Delegate Lincoln

The author remembers well the recital of an incident in connection with the Bloomington convention. Judge J. O. Cunningham of Champaign in his life-time was an active member of the State Historical Society. In 1905 Judge Cunningham read a paper before the society on the Bloomington convention of 1856. As several members of the society sat about waiting for the beginning of the work of the session, Judge Cunningham told a story of Mr. Lincoln's coming to Decatur on his way to the convention. Mr. Lincoln had been attending court in Vermilion and Champaign counties during the week prior to the date set for the Bloomington convention. In his work as a lawyer at the bar, he had some spare time which he used in stirring up sentiment in favor of the approaching convention. He had made some headway in creating interest in the convention, and on the 28th of May, the day before the convention, a number of delegates and visitors came from Champaign to Decatur among whom were Mr. Lincoln and Judge Cunningham.

They reached Decatur about noon and as there was no train north on the Illinois Central till the next morning, there was nothing to do but to wait till the next morning. In the afternoon a few friends with Mr. Lincoln walked into the woods near the Sangamon River and all sat down on the same log which lay near. Here Mr. Lincoln unburdened his heart to Judge Cunningham and others as to his fears for the success of the convention which would meet on the morrow. He seemed to be greatly anxious that the whigs from the south end of the state might be at the convention. His friends present, lawyers, editors, and laymen assured him that the prospects were very bright for a harmonious and reasonable procedure.

After talking of the political situation, there was a lull in the convention. The silence was broken by Mr. Lincoln who called the attention of his friends to the fact that twenty-five years previously he had come with his father, Thomas Lincoln, to this village and had assisted his father in opening up a small farm near. He pointed out the place in the village where he halted the ox team he was driving, and gave vivid pictures of the incidents of those early days. At the time that Judge Cunningham told his hearers this story it was not known that it would be incorporated in the paper which he later read.

On the morning of the 29th of May, 1856, Mr. Lincoln and his friends proceeded to Bloomington where hundreds of enthusiastic anti-Nebraska supporters were assembling. On the train

Mr. Lincoln found Jesse K. Dubois, an old-time whig who was on his way to the convention.

It was soon discovered that the convention would be a sort of melting pot for whigs, democrats, free soilers, and know-nothings. Lovejoy, Wentworth, Browning, Palmer, Cook, Judd and Koerner were mingling with the great crowds and talking with all their might for the anti-Nebraska cause. Governor Reeder the territorial governor of Kansas had been obliged to make his escape from that territory and had reached Bloomington the evening of the 28th. He had already made a speech in which he was able to show the wonderful advantages coming from the repeal of the Missouri compromise.

In Major's Hall

The convention assembled in Major's Hall which was soon filled. After the temporary organization was effected an enthusiastic delegate, Leander Hunsell from Edgar County got the attention of the convention and nominated Col. William H. Bissell for governor. The convention was on its feet in an instant and in this informal way Colonel Bissell, the choice of Mr. Lincoln for governor, was nominated. In much the same way Mr. Francis A. Hoffman was chosen for lieutenant-governor. The convention then settled down to work of permanent organization.

The Hon. John M. Palmer was made permanent chairman. "A man of heroic figure, less than forty years of age, at the meridian of his physical strength, florid of complexion, and with energy enough to well equip a platoon of ordinary men, his presence and bearing were such as to inspire even a stranger with the conviction that the right man had been chosen to direct the forces of the convention." His address was brief but vigorous and left no doubt of his attitude toward the repeal of the Missouri compromise. He and Douglas were personal friends and it must have taken no little effort on the part of Mr. Palmer to break with his friend, the little giant.

Mr. Palmer was followed by O. H. Browning, Owen Lovejoy, and James S. Emory an editor whose press had been thrown into the raging Kaw by the invaders of Kansas.

The Lost Speech

The last address was delivered by Mr. Lincoln. The great audience had just been fired with indignation by Mr. Emory as he described the awful wrongs that were being perpetrated on the free people of Kansas. Mr. Lincoln's speech was given without notes or manuscript and the reporters were so carried away that they failed to get the speech in shorthand. Several men who heard Mr. Lincoln have tried to describe the line of argument as well as to tell something of the wonderful power which the speaker seemed to possss. From the best description that can be obtained the speech began in a mild vein with some humor but merged into an argumentative style, changing to an appeal to his southern brethren and ending with the expression, "We won't go out of the Union, and you sha'nt!"

Resolutions

The most abiding work of the convention was the report of the committee on resolutions. This document was the product of a committee of nine, one from each congressional district, as follows:

First District, G. Walbrecht.
Second District, N. B. Judd.
Third District, O. Lovejoy.
Fourth District, A. C. Harding.
Fifth District, O. H. Browning.
Sixth District, Wickliff Kitchell.
Seventh District, S. C. Parks.
Ninth District, D. L. Phillips.

While the above gentlemen constituted the committee, their sittings were visited by several of the more prominent members of the convention. Mr. Lincoln conferred with the committee and evidently exerted some influence in the make-up of the report. The report contains two whereases and seven resolves. The third resolve was the one which determined the direction of the aggressive campaign which was waged in the summer and fall of 1856. It is as follows:

"Resolved, That the repeal of the Missouri compromise was unwise, unjust, and injurious; an open and aggravated violation of the plighted faith of the states, and that the attempt of the present administration to force slavery into Kansas against the known wishes of the legal voters of that territory is an arbitrary and tyrannous violation of the rights of the people to govern themselves, and that we will strive by all constitutional means, to secure to Kansas and Nebraska the legal guarantee against slavery of which they were deprived at the cost of the violation of the plighted faith of the nation."

Before the convention adjourned it named a central committee which should have general charge of the campaign; the committee was as follows:

James C. Conklin, Sangamon County.
Asahel Gridley, McLean County.
B. C. Cook, La Salle County.
Charles H. Ray, Cook County.
N. B. Judd, Cook County.

Delegates were also selected to a national anti-Nebraska convention to be held in Philadelphia.

Some of the more noted Illinoisans who were delegates were:

HISTORY OF ILLINOIS

George Schneider, N. B. Judd, Owen Lovejoy, I. J. Henderson, John M. Palmer, A. Lincoln and N. M. Knapp.

The campaign was carried on vigorously and resulted in the election of the anti-Nebraska ticket by majorities ranging from 2,000 to 20,000, but the democratic candidate for president, Mr. Buchanan, beat the anti-Nebraska or republican candidate, John C. Freemont, by more than 9,000.

The Democrats in 1856

We have followed the fortunes of the republican party from its inception in 1854 to the close of the campaign in the year 1856. But the democrat party was also very active. As early as December, 1855, the chairman of the democratic state central committee issued a call for the appointment of delegates of the state convention which was to meet in Springfield May 1, 1858. This was a month before the meeting of the anti-Nebraska convention in Bloomington. The democratic state convention was held in the capital city on May 1. They nominated for governor Col. William A. Richardson of Quincy; for lieutenant-governor, Richard J. Hamilton of Chicago; for secretary of state, William H. Snyder of St. Clair; for auditor of public accounts, Samuel K. Casey of Franklin; for treasurer, John Moore of McLean County; and J. H. St. Mathew of Tazewell, for superintendent of public instruction.

The ticket was considered a strong one and it was geographically well distributed. Colonel Richardson had served in both branches of the state Legislature, had been a presidential elector, served as major in the Mexican war, won great distinction at the battle of Buena Vista, had served in Congress and was a personal friend of Stephen A. Douglas.

The campaign of 1856 in Illinois was warmly contested. James Buchanan was the democratic candidate for the presidency, while John C. Fremont was the republican candidate for that high office. For the governorship, General Bissell and Colonel Richardson led the forces for the republican and democratic forces, respectively. General Bissell was so badly crippled up in an accident that he was unable to make a very active canvass. The result of the vote in the southern counties is an interesting study. The vote was as follows in the counties named: In Franklin, Fremont received only 5 votes, in Hamilton, 9; in Hardin, 4; in Johnson, 2; in Massac, 5; in Pope, 11; in Saline, 4; and in Williamson, 10. Without doubt the campaign produced a "rough house" in many localities. Moses tells a story about John M. Palmer that helps us to understand why he made a good soldier in the Civil war. The story briefly is as follows:

There was some ill-feeling between John M. Palmer and Thomas L. Harris both of the Sixth Congressional District. Harris was running for Congress and in his speeches was very abusive of the anti-Nebraska people who were now called "black abolitionists," "black republicans," and other bad names. Harris wrote a letter somewhat abusive of the anti-Nebraska people which was read at a democratic meeting which Palmer was attending. When the letter was read Palmer arose and said the writer would not make such charges in the face of an honest man. Harris heard of what Palmer had said and stated that he would resent Palmer's remarks at the first opportunity. Palmer attended one of Harris' meetings when Harris broke forth in very abusive language and pointing his finger at Palmer said, "I mean you, sir." Palmer said, "if you mean that language for me, you are a dastardly liar!" And drawing a pistol made his way to the speaker's stand. Harris modified his attacks and when he closed, Palmer took the platform and laying his cocked pistol on the table in front of him proceeded to show up the democratic party for its action in the repeal of the Missouri compromise.

Bissell Elected

Although the state cast its electoral vote for James Buchanan, and though the Legislature was democratic in both branches, the republicans elected their candidate for governor and other state officers. It is stated that there was a majority of some 20,000 votes against the democratic state ticket. Governor Matteson retired on January 12, and was succeeded by Governor Bissell. It is said that Governor Bissell's inaugural address was very complimentary to the administration of Governor Matteson. In reference, however, to the repeal of the Missouri compromise, the incoming governor was positive but not bitter. The democrats, however, were in no humor to be reminded of their action in the Kansas-Nebraska matter, and so very bitter attacks were made upon the governor. John A. Logan, then a young lawyer from Southern Illinois, was especially bitter in his denunciation of Governor Bissell. After a short sharp contest of words, the two parties quieted down and took up the business of the session. One of the most troublesome problems the General Assembly had to contend with was passage of a state apportionment bill. A law was enacted establishing a normal university and another providing for a second penitentiary. The Legislature was in session only till the 19th of February. The public mind was absorbed in national questions, and local matters were allowed to remain in the background.

CHAPTER XXI

THE LINCOLN-DOUGLAS DEBATE

THE MISSOURI COMPROMISE—STEPHEN A. DOUGLAS—A NEW PARTY—THE DREAD SCOTT DECISION—LECOMPTON CONSTITUTION—NOMINATIONS—DOUGLAS IN CHICAGO—OFF FOR SPRINGFIELD—THE CHALLENGE—THE NEWSPAPERS—PREPARATIONS—THE REPORTS—THE OTTAWA DEBATE—THE FREEPORT DEBATE—THE JONESBORO DEBATE—THE CHARLESTON DEBATE—THE GALESBURG DEBATE—THE QUINCY DEBATE—THE ALTON DEBATE—OTHER ESTIMATES.

The most profound and far reaching event in Illinois history was at the same time the culmination of a growing difference between two fundamentally opposing views in a time-honored political party in American history. Since the days of Thomas Jefferson's first inauguration as President in 1801 to the Civil war, a period of more than half a century, the democratic party had, with two very brief periods, controlled the national policies of the American Government. Slavery as an economic institution had been a disturbing factor in the political life not only of the democratic party but of the whole people regardless of politics. The shrewd policy of balancing the slavery and anti-slavery power in the United States Senate from the admission of the first state, Vermont, till the application of Missouri to enter the Union, could not continue. The slave interest had, by 1820, exhausted the territory out of which to make additional slave states, while the free state interests had vast areas which might be made into non-slave holding states.

THE MISSOURI COMPROMISE

The Missouri Compromise has been considered in the preceding pages, and it is not needful to consider it further than to show its connection with the Lincoln and Douglas debate. The slave interests were willing, in order to secure the admission of Missouri as a slave state, to forego the hope of ever making another slave state out of the territory of the Louisiana purchase north of the southern boundary of Missouri. This is shown by the fact that all the efforts of the slave power for the extension of slave territory, between the admission of Missouri in 1820 and the repeal of the Missouri Compromise in 1854, were directed elsewhere—never to that part of Louisiana territory north of the southern boundary of Missouri. In this interim noted above, from 1820 to 1854, we find the Government, which in those days practically meant the slave power, directed its attention to the acquisition of Cuba, the annexation of Texas, and the Mexican war. Longing eyes had been cast toward Cuba by the slave interests since the earliest days. All sorts of schemes had been set on foot to acquire that fertile island. The hopes of the slave power that some day Cuba might be annexed to the United States and made into at least two sovereign slave states never waned. Toward the middle of the nineteenth century, filibustering expeditions fitted out in the southern parts of the United States, evaded the watchful eye of the Government and landed on the coasts of Cuba. This illegal interference with the control of the possession of a friendly nation, kept the Cuban people in a constant state of turmoil and was the cause of serious international relations with Spain. In 1854 while the Kansas-Nebraska bill was before Congress, the United States ministers to the governments of Great Britain, France, and Spain met at Ostend, Belgium, and put forth a declaration which announced that Spain should forthwith cede Cuba to the United States. And further that if Spain would not willingly do this that he United States should proceed to annex the island by force. This again was an international insult to a declining power. The manifesto was not very generally countenanced in the United States and was strongly condemned in Europe. The demand for the reannexation of Texas following the treaty of 1819 in which the United States ceded Texas to Spain and at the same time acquired Florida, never ceased. Public men interested in extending slave territory assisted in the revolt of Texas against Mexico in 1836. Prior to this, Americans had colonized in different parts of Texas and it is said that in 1828 there were 12,000 Americans and only 3,000 Mexicans in the limits of that territory. The Mexican war is now generally explained in terms of the desire of the slave holders to extend slave territory. The several incidents in our history would seem to support the contention that the slave holders had given up the hope of ever extending slavery into the north part of the Louisiana Purchase.

Uncle Tom's Cabin had appeared in 1852 and added fuel to fires that were already burning. The Compromise of 1850 was spoken of as a "finality." Many people tried to make themselves believe that the storm was over, but one writer has said: "But the country was now a ship in a storm, and it was of no use for the passengers to meet in the cabin and resolve that it was fair weather." William Lloyd Garrison, Wendell Phillips, and others were among the irreconcilables and the country was ready for a political eruption.

STEPHEN A. DOUGLAS

For several years prior to 1854, Mr. Douglas had given some attention to the territory included in what is now Kansas, Ne-

STEPHEN A. DOUGLAS

BIRTHPLACE OF STEPHEN A. DOUGLAS

braska, the two Dakotas, Montana, and parts of Wyoming and Colorado. There was no form of government for this area and it had gotten the name of "no-man's-land." Minnesota, Iowa, and Missouri occupied the eastern part of the purchase, and "no-man's-land" was what was left of the purchase north of 36-30. Several subjects pertaining to this territory had occupied the public attention—Indian titles, land grants, railroads, and other matters. It has been said that one reason Congress was slow about taking up the matter of establishing a government over this "no-man's-land" was the determined opposition of certain statesmen to any congressional action which might appear favorable to the eventual making of free states of this territory. Investigation has shown that the movement for the repeal of the Missouri Compromise had its origin in the political situation in the State of Missouri. Thomas H. Benton, for thirty years a United States senator from Missouri, was constantly urging the settlement of the territory west of Missouri and Iowa by white settlers even though they went in as adventurers and trespassers upon the supposed rights of the Indians who occupied restricted areas of the vast territory. Senator Benton had a political opponent who eventually succeeded in winning the affections of the Missouri people away from Benton. This opponent was David R. Atchinson. Mr. Atchinson was a bitter foe of the Missouri Compromise. From time to time in public addresses he notified the people of Missouri that he would never agree to the organization of "Nebraska" into a territorial government unless at the same time the Missouri Compromise was repealed. Iowa was interested in a territorial government in "Nebraska." Senator A. C. Dodge of that state introduced a bill in the United States Senate on December 14, 1853, providing for the organization of the "Nebraska" territorial government. The bill was referred to the committee on territories of which Stephen A. Douglas was chairman. A similar bill was introduced into the House of Representatives by Mr. Miller of Missouri. This bill was referred to the committee on territories in the House of which the Hon. W. A. Richardson of Illinois was chairman.

Mr. Douglas had spent the summer of 1853 in Europe and returned to Washington only four weeks before the opening of the Congress on December 5, 1853. On November 11, 1853, Senator Douglas wrote a personal letter to the editors of the Illinois State Register, Springfield, giving among other things, the matters which he thought would come before the approaching session of Congress. In this letter he names five things which he thinks will absorb the attention of Congress, but the organization of the Nebraska territory is not one of them, nor is the repeal of the Missouri Compromise one of them. If either of these things had been resting heavily on his mind he certainly would have spoken of it to the editors of the Register, as the latter was a sort of review and preview of public questions.

Mr. Douglas, as chairman of the committee on territories, reported Senator Dodge's bill for the organization of the Nebraska territory. The bill contained some amendments, or changes, which provided for the control of the slavery question by the settlers—a sort of squatter-sovereignty idea. In the report of the committee accompanying the bill was a statement that the compromise of 1850 had superseded previous legislation and that there was no longer any barrier to the introduction of slavery into this territory. Senator Dixon of Kentucky, a whig, introduced an amendment to the Dodge bill which said the restriction of slavery as laid down in the Missouri Compromise should not apply to the territory under consideration in the Dodge bill.

Later, in January, 1854, Mr. Douglas introduced a new bill which in specific terms repealed the Missouri Compromise. Without doubt this action of Douglas was forced on him by Senator Dixon of Kentucky. At least in a speech in Springfield, October 3, 1854, Mr. Douglas, in explanation of the part he took in the repeal of the Missouri Compromise and the passage of the Kansas-Nebraska Act, said: "I have been chairman of the committee on territories for the past ten years, and it was my duty to act in this matter and bring forward the bill. I was no volunteer in this matter. It devolved upon me as a duty."

It has been suggested that the doctrine of "repeal of supersedure" was not originated by Senator Douglas, but was a bit of propaganda put forth "by at least three democratic newspapers." These were the Richmond (Va.) Inquirer of December, 1853; The Mississippian, December 30, 1853; The Albany Argus, December 10, 1853. All these papers argued that the compromise of 1850 had repealed the Missouri Compromise which excluded slavery from the Louisiana Purchase.

When Mr. Douglas made his speech in Springfield on October 3, 1854, one of his auditors was Mr. Lincoln who, on the next day, October 4th, answered Mr. Douglas in an extended address. This speech by Douglas before the state fair and Lincoln's answer the next day laid the foundation for the great debate which came four years later.

A New Party

There was in session in Springfield a convention of early republicans at the time Douglas spoke at the state fair on October 3, 1854. On the 4th, when Lincoln made a four-hour reply to Mr. Douglas, the members of the republican convention adjourned their session to hear the reply. At this time Lincoln was speaking as an anti-Nebraskan, not as a republican. The republican convention had only twenty-six men in their convention and it was too radical for Mr. Lincoln and he would not allow himself to be counted as a republican, but regarded himself as an anti-Nebraska whig. Lincoln was placed on the republican central committee by this convention, but Mr. Lincoln would not serve in that capacity.

The opposition to the repeal of the Missouri Compromise grew from month to month. The summer of 1856 witnessed the organization of the republican party. It was made up of whigs, democrats, know-nothings and others who had not previously allied themselves with any particular political group. This new party was able to elect a republican governor of Illinois and otherwise to show great strength. The democrats elected the president in November, 1856, but their leaders were thoroughly alarmed at the growth of the new party.

The year 1857, being an off year, no one anticipated much political activity. But like a thunder bolt driven from a clear sky, the Dred Scott Decision was handed down in the spring of 1857. Mr. Buchanan was inaugurated on March 4, 1857. Since the repeal of the Compromise in 1854, slavery as an abstract principle had continually grown weaker, and practically it was on the eve of losing the political and moral backing of thousands of its former ardent supporters north of the Mason and Dixon line and of the Ohio River. Charles Sumner of Massachusetts said the passage of the Kansas-Nebraska act marked the end of compromises on slavery. It was the beginning of a death struggle between the enemies and friends of slavery. Horace Greely said that Pierce and Douglas had made more abolitionists than Garrison and Phillips could have made in a century. The presidential election of 1856 had resulted in the election of James Buchanan an accomplice of the radical slave power of the south. The young republican party had made a vigorous campaign with John C. Fremont as their leader, but had failed to elect him. One of the great issues was "bleeding Kansas," shall it come into the Union as a free or a slave state? The republicans presented a fundamental doctrine as the foundation of their contentions—Congress has the legal and moral right—to prohibit slavery in the territories of the United States. Seward said in the campaign of the contention between the friends of slavery and the friends of freedom—"It is an irrepressible conflict between opposing and enduring forces, and it means that the United States must and will, sooner or later, become either entirely a slave holding nation or entirely a free labor nation. I know and you know that revolution has begun. I know and all the world knows that revolutions never go backward."

Governor Wise of Virginia said in the campaign of 1856, "The Southern States will not submit to a sectional election of a free-soiler or a black republican." But there was little danger of such a result as the slave states voted solidly for Buchanan and the northern states were supporting two candidates—Freemont, the republican candidate, and Fillmore, the candidate of the Native-American or know-nothing party. In the election in November, 1856, Buchanan won 174 electoral votes; Freemont, 114. But the popular vote stood, 1,838,000 for Buchanan, 1,342,000 for Freemont, and 874,000 for Fillmore. So after the result was known, the republicans consoled themselves that there were more votes against Buchanan than there were for him, and Mr. Lincoln, in a speech at a republican banquet in Chicago, encouraged and counseled the republicans by saying: "All of us who did not vote for Mr. Buchanan, taken together, are a majority of 400,000. But in the late contest we were divided between Freemont and Fillmore. Can we not come together for the future? Thus let bygones be bygones; let past differences as nothing be; and with new steady eye on the real issue let us reinaugurate the good old 'central idea' of the republic. We can do it. The human heart is with us; God is with us. We shall again be able not to declare that all states as states are equal, nor yet that all citizens as citizens are equal, but to renew the broader, better declaration, including both of these and much more, that all men are created equal."

Dred Scott Decision

Two days after Buchanan had taken the oath of office as President of the United States, the Supreme Court handed down a decision in the Dred Scott case. In his inaugural Mr. Buchanan, in speaking of the intense feeling about slavery which had characterized the preceding year's campaign, said: "This is happily a matter of but little practical importance. Besides, it is a judicial decision which legitimately belongs to the Supreme Court of the United States, before whom it is now pending, and will, it is understood, be speedily and finally settled." Just how the Prsident knew that the Supreme Court would shortly issue a decision which would speedily and finally settle this unimportant question may be easily answered by the reader.

Dred Scott, as we all know, was a negro slave held in Missouri. He was taken by his master into Illinois where he resided a short time. The Ordinance of 1787 as well as the constitution of Illinois prohibited slavery in Illinois. Dred Scott was later removed to Minnesota which was non-slave territory by the compromise of 1820. He was then returned to Missouri. He now sued for his freedom on the ground that his residence in Illinois and Minnesota had given him his freedom. The case was begun in the lower courts but finally reached the Supreme Court, and it was this decision that was rendered by that court on the 6th of March, 1857. The decision was that

Dred Scott, being a negro and the descendant of slave parents, could not be a citizen of the United States, and therefore could not come into the court of the United States. Since Scott had no standing in court the case was dismissed.

If the court had stopped with the dismissal of the case, there would have been general acquiescence in the decision. But the radical southern slave interests had too good an opportunity to lay down the principles which would "speedily and finally settle this unimportant matter." The court answered a question which had often been asked, "Did Congress have the constitutional authority to pass the Missouri Compromise? The court answered this query in the negative. The corollary was that Congress could not restrict or in any way prevent slavery in any United States territory. Therefor the Missouri Compromise, although repealed, was never constitutional. This decision as to the power of Congress to prevent the extension of slavery was directly opposite to a doctrine which the republicans had preached namely that Congress could legally prevent the extension of slavery in the United States territory. In other words the Ordinance of 1787 which prohibited slavery in the Northwest territory conformed wholly with the spirit and the letter of the constitution and was therefore constitutional. Not only was the decision of the Supreme Court directly opposed to the republican doctrine of the power of Congress, but was as directly opposed to the "squatter sovereignty" idea which had been the chief plank in the democratic platform in 1848, and was an important part in the compromise.

No one knew better than Douglas that the Dred Scott decision would disrupt the democratic party. He saw that the decision was antagonistic to his pet theory of squatter sovereignty. But Mr. Douglas must not allow the Southern people to feel that he is not loyal to the decisions of the Supreme Court. He was even then looking forward to the presidency of 1860. Mr. Douglas therefore began to proclaim the sacredness of the decision of the Supreme Court. Public men in the North talked of rebelling against the decision. "What," Douglas said, "oppose the Supreme Court. Is it not sacred? To resist is anarchy." As early as June, 1857, Mr. Lincoln, in a speech in Springfield, said: "We believe as much as Judge Douglas (perhaps more) in obedience to and respect for the judicial department of the government. But we think the Dred Scott decision is erroneous. We know the court that made it has often overruled its own decisions, and we shall do what we can to have it overrule this."

Lecompton Constitution

When the Missouri Compromise was repealed in the early part of 1854, and a form of government was provided under the Kansas-Nebraska act, the restless throngs who had been lingering along the western border of Missouri rushed across to take possession of the land. There were free state people and slave state people. The free state people had in most cases come as permanent settlers to obtain the advantages of the rich lands lying along the river valleys. The slave state people were probably in most cases not permanent settlers. If they were, they did not bring their slaves with them. Slave holders were averse to bringing their slaves with them into Kansas for they fully realized the possibility that Kansas might come into the Union as a free state if the principle of squatter sovereignty were honestly applied. It has been estimated that at no time were there more than three or four hundred slaves in Kansas. Slave defenders came, however, and left their slaves behind.

By the summer of 1857 the slave state people called a constitutional convention at the town of Lecompton on the Kansas River a few miles from the present City of Topeka. It was made up of slave state delegates. They made a constitution which recognized slavery. By a political trick the constitution was ratified, the free state people refusing to vote on ratification since they did not participate in its making. It was supposed at this time that the free state permanent settlers greatly outnumbered the slave state permanent settlers. When Douglas became aware of the utter lack of common decency which the slave men exhibited in this Lecompton constitution matter, he determined to oppose its acceptance when it came before Congress for ratification. He therefore went to the opening of Congress in December, 1857, determined to oppose the ratification of the Lecompton constitution.

In February President Buchanan sent a message to Congress recommending the acceptance of the Lecompton constitution and the admission of Kansas as a slave state. Powerful leaders and molders of public opinion steadfastly opposed the admission of Kansas as a slave state. Mr. Douglas in the Senate was almost violent in denunciation of the conduct of the slave interests in the Lecompton matter. The administration left no stone unturned to secure the ratification of the Lecompton constitution. Offices were distributed and threats made but all to no avail. The bill passed the Senate finally but failed in the House. Out of the hard battle which was fought in Congress, the Lecompton constitution failed, and Kansas was left to the unsatisfactory form of territorial government in the hands of the slave interests. Out of the struggle also came Douglas with the condemnation of the Buchanan administration resting on him. He was moreover under the necessity of making a canvass for his return to the Senate as his term would expire March 4, 1859, and the Legislature which was to make the choice of his successor was to be elected at the state election to be held in November, 1858.

Mr. Douglas' stand against fraud in the Lecompton matter, and his boldness to oppose the impatriotic conduct of Buchanan, won for him many friends in the North. In fact it was thought at one time that it would be best for the republicans not to put out a candidate, and all support Douglas. The Buchanan administration took a decided stand against Douglas and did everything in its power to defeat him for reelection for United States senator. So bold had been Douglas' stand against political wrongs in Kansas, that Horace Greeley was completely won over to Douglas' side. It looked as if the East would all favor Douglas in the campaign for reelection. Mr. Lincoln became alarmed and sent Mr. Herndon East to sound out such men as Seward, Greeley, Sumner, Phillips, Garrison, Beecher and Theodore Parker. Herndon brought back only fairly good reports of the attitude of the public men towards Lincoln's candidacy against Douglas for the senatorship.

Locally in Illinois the Democrats were divided into two hostile camps, known as the Douglasites and the Buchananites. All of Douglas' patronage was taken from him in Illinois. Postmasters who secured their appointments through Douglas were plainly told unless they should vote for Buchanan they must make way for men who would do so. Newspapers were also divided into the Douglas group and the Buchanan group.

Nominations

There had been no doubt anywhere that Douglas would be the choice to succeed himself as senator from Illinois. However, as has been said, the administration was bending all its energies to defeat Douglas not only for the nomination, but hoped if he succeeded in getting the endorsement of the party in Illinois, it might by hook or crook defeat him in the Legislature. The only state officers to be elected in 1858 were a state treasurer and a superintendent of public instruction. But the legislative elections in the several senatorial districts were important as the Legislature would chose the successor to Mr. Douglas. The date set for the state convention of the democratic party was April 21, 1858. That body was to meet in Springfield. The work of selecting delegates to this convention in the several counties was begun early. There was no trouble in most of the counties. In 97 of the 101 counties resolutions indorsing the action of Douglas and other Illinois congressmen who opposed the Lecompton constitution had been passed; and these resolutions really represented the public sentiment of the great mass of democratic voters in the state. But the administration's forces were busy everywhere. In every county where they could get a few Buchanan supporters together they would go through the form of electing delegates to a state convention.

On the day set for the state convention two district bodies

met in Springfield, one supporting Douglas and one supporting Buchanan. The administration men called themselves "nationals." Twenty-four counties sent delegates. John Dougherty of Union County presided. Speeches were made and some interest manifested but no ticket was named. They adjourned to the 9th of June when Dougherty was named as the candidate for state treasurer, and the candidate for state treasurer and Ex-Gov. John Reynolds as a candidate for the office of state superintendent of public instruction. Stuve says the republicans encouraged the nationals, hoping thereby to weaken the Douglas forces. In return for the kindly interest of the republicans the nationals resolved in their platform: "We deem the principles and the policy of the black republicans as utterly opposed to the spirit in which the Union was formed, and the success of that party would be disastrous to its prosperity."

The regular or Douglas democrats held an enthusiastic convention. The state candidates were W. B. Fondey for treasurer and Ex-Governor French for superintendent of public instruction. On the question of nominating Douglas for the party's candidate for United States senator, the convention ducked. The main thought was to heal the breach in the democratic ranks. It was conceded that Douglas would be the standard bearer in the campaign and so he was. Other ambitious aspirants quietly withdrew their names and before the canvass was well under way Douglas was recognized as the only candidate for those democrats who opposed the tactics of the national administration.

The Republican State Convention met in Springfield on June 16, 1858. It was composed of delegates from eighty-seven counties. James Miller was named as the candidate for treasurer and Newton Bateman for superintendent of public instruction. In a statement of principles the convention for the republican party disclaimed all intention of attempting, either directly or indirectly, to assail or abridge the rights of any of the members of the confederacy guaranteed by the constitution, or in any way to interfere with the institution of slavery in the states where it exists. The platform as it might be called condemned the democratic national government; showed up the Dred Scott decision; declared that Congress has the power to prohibit slavery in the territory of the United States; praised a recent decision of the Supreme Court of Illinois that property in persons was repugnant to the constitution of Illinois.

A resolution offered "That Abraham Lincoln is the first and only choice of the republicans of Illinois, for the United States Senate, as the successor of Stephen A. Douglas." The Cook County delegation had brought a banner with them which they displayed conspicuously which read "Cook County for Abraham Lincoln." In a lull in the proceedings, a delegate arose and

STATE CAPITOL, SPRINGFIELD, 1857

moved to amend the banner by substituting "Illinois" for "Cook County." Cook County accepted the amendment and amid the greatest enthusiasm, the banner was made to read "Illinois for Abraham Lincoln."

Mr. Lincoln was not unaware of the unanimity with which his candidacy for the senatorship had been received throughout the state. True, in many of the southern counties, there were few Lincoln supporters, but in more than three-fourths of the counties Mr. Lincoln had been designated by resolution or otherwise as the choice of the mass of the people as Douglas' successor. Mr. Lincoln knew that his friends would expect him to respond to their enthusiastic nomination of himself for the Senate. He accordingly prepared a speech which has been regarded by many as one of his most powerful arraignments of the persons and interests back of the efforts to extend slavery over the whole United States. The speech was delivered from manuscript, and Horace White says Mr. Lincoln was very anxious that it should be printed just as he had written it.

Dr. Edwin Earl Sparks, who compiled Vol. 3 of the "Illinois Historical Collections," has commented on this speech as follows: "The speech in which Lincoln acknowledged the courtesy of the convention was thought out in advance and every sentence carefully weighed. It marked the new lines upon which Lincoln proposed to argue the situation and which ultimately won success. Boldly casting aside the long-prevalent idea that the Union could be saved by compromise and by repressing agitation, Lincoln voiced the new opinion in a slightly altered Scriptural quotation, 'A house divided against itself can not stand.' He declared that the Government could not endure permanently half slave and half free; it must become all one thing or all the other. Whether Lincoln foresaw that the astute Douglas would construe this statement into a desire to dissolve the Union is a matter of doubt, as is also the question whether he appreciated the danger that his criticism of the Dred Scott decision would be twisted by Douglas into a revolutionary attack on the Supreme Court." A few paragraphs are given to show the line of Mr. Lincoln's thought in this convention address.

"If we could first know where we are, and whither we are tending, we could then better judge what to do, and how to do it.

"We are now far into the fifth year since a policy was initiated with the avowed object, and confident promise, of putting an end to slavery agitation.

"Under the operation of that policy, that agitation has not only not ceased, but constantly augmented.

"In my opinion it will not cease until a crisis shall have been reached and passed—'a house divided against itself cannot stand.'

"I believe this Government can not endure permanently half slave and half free. I do not expect the Union to be dissolved—I do not expect the house to fall—but I do expect it will cease to be divided. It will become all one thing, or all the other. Either the opponents of slavery will arrest the further spread of it, and place it where the public mind shall rest in the belief that it is in the course of ultimate extinction; or, its advocates will put it forward, till it shall become alike lawful in all the states, old as well as new—North as well as South."

This is known as the house-divided-against-itself speech. It preceded Mr. Seward's "irrepressible conflict" which brought down on that statesman's head the bitter shafts of his political opponents. Mr. Douglas called Mr. Lincoln's speech "sectionalism," and "abolitionism."

Douglas in Chicago

Congress adjourned early in July and the statesmen rushed to their homes to look after their political fences. Mr. Douglas was anxious to reach Illinois. On learning that Mr. Lincoln would be his opponent said: "I shall have my hands full. He is the strong man of his party—full of wit, facts, dates, and the best stump-speaker, with his droll ways and dry jokes of the West. He is as honest as he is shrewd; and if I beat him, my victory will be hardly won."

Mr. Douglas reached Chicago on July 9th. The city was attired in her best. Flags and banners fluttered from every available point. Cannons boomed, and thousands—probably forty or fifty —of voices proclaimed a thrice hearty welcome. Mr. Douglas spoke at night from the balcony of the Tremont House. Mr. Douglas knew that Mr. Lincoln was an attentive listener in a nearby room of the hotel, and he threw all his energies into his initial address of a long campaign. He praised the doctrine of popular sovereignty, acquiesced in the Dred Scott decision, and attacked with great power the house-divided-against-itself speech. At the close of Mr. Douglas' speech, loud calls were made for Mr. Lincoln, who appeared, but refused to speak but made an appointment to speak from the same balcony on the following evening.

On the following evening, July 10, Mr. Lincoln appeared on the balcony and after a very great demonstration proceeded to reply to Senator Douglas. Mr. Lincoln reminded Mr. Douglas that the doctrine of squatter sovereignty was as old as the Declaration of Independence, that governments always derive their just powers from the consent of the governed. But he showed the incompatibility of Mr. Douglas' doctrine of squatter sovereignty in regard to slavery and the Dred Scott decision, which Mr. Douglas said he was ready to stand by. Mr. Lincoln reiterated his former statement that Congress had the right to prohibit slavery in any territory owned and controlled by the United States.

OFF FOR SPRINGFIELD

Douglas rested after his Tremont House address for a week. On the morning of June 16th he left for Springfield. The train was elaborately decorated. Mottoes—"Champion of the people," "popular sovereignty," etc., were freely displayed. This was the regularly scheduled train, and Mr. Lincoln was also a passenger. Mr. Douglas was received by enthusiastic admirers all along the route. At Joliet a flat car was attached to the rear of the train upon which was a cannon which boomed his approach to the smaller towns along the way. A great reception was planned for Douglas at Bloomington. The day was rainy and the roads were muddy but the friends turned out in large numbers. At the close of Mr. Douglas' masterly effort, Mr. Lincoln was called for. He appeared on the platform, but refused to talk as he said, because the meeting was called in the interest of Mr. Douglas and it would be improper for him to speak at that time.

Really to us it seems a pitiful feature for Mr. Lincoln to be traveling along a railroad where his rival is lionized at every stop and he not permitted by the courtesies to present himself to the view of his friends. But Lincoln was not humiliated. He is listening to Mr. Douglas. He is gathering munitions of war which he will use in the great debate which was to follow. On reaching Springfield Judge Douglas spoke in the Edwards' grove near the northern limits of the city. It was a rainy day, and yet as many as five or six thousand people assembled to hear the man of the hour. Delegations were present from Madison, Macoupin, Jersey, Greene, Montgomery, St. Clair, Monroe and other nearby counties. Mr. Douglas lost none of his popularity in this Springfield speech.

Mr. Lincoln did not attend the Douglas rally in the Edwards' grove, but announced his purpose to speak in the city that night. In this address Mr. Lincoln defended himself against three charges which Judge Douglas had lodged against him. These were the charges: That Mr. Lincoln had preached dis-union in his house-divided speech; that he had favored a forcible opposition to the Dred Scott decision; and that Mr. Lincoln favored negro equality. Mr. Lincoln further charged that the Dred Scott decision was a conspiracy to which Douglas was a party.

Following the speech by Douglas in Edwards' grove and the one by Lincoln in Springfield that night, the two aspirants each went his way. Judge Douglas, after conferring with the state central committee of his party, announced his speaking dates throughout the state covering the months of July and August. Mr. Lincoln's friends also announced a speaking tour for their candidate.

It is stated by Dr. Sparks that Senator Trumbull, Judge Douglas' political foe, was throwing hot shot into Judge Douglas' canvass and was indeed occupying a good deal of public attention, especially in the East. Mr. Lincoln saw that there might be the possibility that Douglas and Trumbull would, as the summer wore along, attract to themselves the public attention in Illinois and his own canvass lag. He therefore in conference with his advisors decided to approach Douglas with a proposition for a series of joint discussions.

THE CHALLENGE

Lincoln returned to Chicago after his speech in Springfield and from there sent the following letter to Judge Douglas:

"Chicago, Illinois, July 24, 1858.
"Hon. S. A. Douglas.
"My Dear Sir: Will it be agreeable to you to make an arrangement for you and myself to divide time, and address the same audiences the present canvass? Mr. Judd, who will hand you this, is authorized to receive your answer; and, if agreeable to you, to enter into the terms of such agreement.

"Your obedient servant,
"A. Lincoln."

Mr. Douglas's reply was of considerable length and it will suffice if we make an abstract of its contents.

First, Mr. Douglas points out that the purpose of his visit to Springfield was to hold a conference with the state committee as to his speaking dates. These had all been fixed and it would be impossible to rearrange them.

Second, Mr. Douglas stated the fear he had that a third candidate (the Buchanan candidate for the Senate) might claim the right to appear on the same platform and address the same audiences. In that case Mr. Lincoln and the third candidate would both oppose Mr. Douglas.

Third, Mr. Douglas finds fault with Mr. Lincoln for not broaching the matter when they were together on the train from Chicago to Springfield, as his dates were not set at that time.

Fourth, M. Douglas took the liberty of accepting the challenge and naming seven points, one in each of the seven remaining congressional districts (both speakers having appeared in Chicago, the Second, and Springfield, the Sixth District), and where he proposed to meet Mr. Lincoln in joint debate. The seven places and the dates were as follows:

Ottawa, LaSalle County _____Aug. 21, 1858
Freeport, Stephenson County _____Aug. 27, 1858
Jonesboro, Union County _____Sept. 15, 1858
Charleston, Coles County _____Sept. 18, 1858
Galesburg, Knox County _____Oct. 7, 1858

Quincy, Adams County ----------Oct. 13, 1858
Alton, Madison County ----------Oct. 15, 1858

Following the challenge and this answer by Douglas other letters were passed between Mr. Lincoln and Mr. Douglas in which the details were worked out. Some of these matters were —that the one who opened the discussion at any point should have an hour for opening while the other who followed should have an hour and a half, and the one who closed should have a half hour. This would give each one the same time at any place. It was also agreed that Douglas should open at Ottawa and Lincoln at Freeport, and so on. This would give Douglas four opening addresses while Lincoln would have but three. The terms, dates, places, and minor matters were all agreed to and the contestants went about the state filling their own appointments.

THE NEWSPAPERS

A careful study of the expressions found in the newspapers as news items or as editorials reveals a very unreasonable and bitter attitude on the part of the papers toward the two candidates for the senatorship. A few extracts will be given:

Chicago Daily Journal, July 9, 1858.

"The senator's more active worshippers—have been begging and scraping together all the spare dollars, shillings, dimes, and six pences that could be obtained—and have expended large sums in hiring men and boys to make up a big procession and make a big noise." This was on the occasion of Douglas' return from Washington.

The Same Paper, July 10, 1858

"He (Douglas) spoke for an hour and a half, in his usual style—dispensing "soft soap" freely, setting himself forth as a hero of no common order, and indulging even more than ordinarily in that inexorable habit of misrepresentation and prevarication which appears in political matters to have become a sort of second nature to him."

The Chicago Union, July 11, 1858

"Yesterday placards appeared on the streets; a band went round in a wagon to announce to the republicans that Hon. Abraham Lincoln would reply to Hon. S. A. Douglas from the Tremont House balcony—the speaker attempted a reply to democratic principles, amidst applause and some spicy interruptions. We left when Deacon Bross announced that the seventh ward are coming. Band played, 'Hocklets Fizzled and We Mizzled.' "

Illinois Journal, July 12, 1858

"In sound, manly argument, Lincoln is too much for him. While the farmer (Douglas) shakes his black locks vain-gloriously and explodes in mere funstian of sound and smoke."

New York Herald, July 27, 1858

"Mr. Lincoln, though not so well calculated for a leader as Senator Douglas, is a remarkably able man. In addition to his talents as a lawyer, he has many personal qualities which have endeared him to the people of Illinois, and will be beyond all question the strongest opponent that could be found in the state to oppose Mr. Douglas."

New York Post, August, 1858

"Mr. Lincoln was regarded as the man for the place. A native of Kentucky where he belonged to the class of poor of "poor whites," he came early to Illinois. Poor, unfriended, uneducated, a day-laborer, he has distanced all these disadvantages, and in the profession of the law he has risen steadily to a competence, and to the position of an intelligent, shrewd and well balanced man."

Philadelphia North American, August 25, 1858

"The republicans, generally speaking, have not a particle of faith in Mr. Douglas' professions. He has not their confidence and is plainly unable to win them to his support. Mr. Lincoln, the republican candidate, follows him wherever he addresses the people, and has the best of the argument."

Quincy Whig, June 23, 1858

"Judge Douglas has left the democratic party, or the party has left him. He opposed the administration in its darling measures to enslave Kansas—and there is no forgiveness for him. He sees that his fate is sealed, but he is determined to die hard."

Quincy Daily Herald, July 20, 1858

"His (Lincoln) campaign through this state will pretty effectually destroy the hopes of the republican party; and Abe Lincoln, who compared himself to a 'living-dog' and Douglas to a 'dead lion,' will rapidly discover that instead of 'living' he is one of the smallest of defunct puppies—it is very much like a puppy-dog fighting a lion."

Chicago Times, July 30, 1858

"But we venture to say that never before was there heard of in any political canvass in Illinois, of a candidate unable to obtain an audience to hear him! But such is the case. Abe Lincoln, the candidate of all the republicans wants an audience—

he came to Chicago and declared it impossible for him to get the people to turn out to hear him, and then it was resolved to try and get him a chance to speak to the crowds drawn out to meet and welcome Douglas.—He went yesterday to Monticello in Douglas' train; poor, desperate creature, he wants an audience; poor unhappy mortal, the people won't turn out to hear him, and he must do something, even if that something is mean, sneaking and disreputable."

Illinois State Register, September 25, 1858

"The fact is, Mr. Lincoln can't draw large crowds—the sympathy of the people is not with him—consequently he resorts to this highly disreputable course (following Douglas) to make a show."

Chicago Times, July 28, 1858

"After Senator Douglas had concluded and the cheers which greeted him ceased, green goggles rose and proposed three cheers for Lincoln, which were given by about ten men who stood immediately around him. Mr. Lincoln then gradually lengthened out his long, lank proportions until he stood upon his feet—and stood washing his hands with invisible soap in unperceptible water, until his friends, seeing that his mind was wandering, took charge of him and bundled him off the ground."

Chicago Daily Journal, July 27, 1858

"The friends of Senator Douglas claim that Mr. Lincoln is no match for him before the people.—In courteous demeanor, as well as in honorable conduct of an argument before the people Mr. Douglas will find, as in many campaigns, he has heretofore found, Mr. Lincoln to be at least his equal."

Preparations

It will be noticed that Mr. Lincoln sent his challenge to Mr. Douglas on July 24, 1858, and on July 31, the arrangement was closed. The first joint debate was set for Ottawa on August 21. This gave only three weeks for the two parties to get ready for the joint meetings.

The democratic state central committee arranged Mr. Douglas' speaking dates so as not to interfere with the dates set for the joint debates. The republicans did the same for Mr. Lincoln. The St. Louis Republican, a great admirer of Mr. Douglas, selected one of its best reporters, Mr. Henry Binmore, to attend the homecoming of Senator Douglas in Chicago, July 9, and make a full report. His services were so highly appreciated that the Chicago Times, also a staunch supporter of Mr. Douglas, secured the services of Mr. Binmore to attend and report the joint debates. Mr. Binmore was assisted in this task by a short hand reporter, Mr. James B. Sheridan, who was sent into Illinois by the Philadelphia Press. These two men not only reported the speeches verbatim but sent out news items to scores of democratic papers in the eastern states.

The republicans were equally fortunate in securing the services of Mr. Horace White and Mr. Robert R. Hitt to look after the interest of their party. Mr. White was an editorial writer on the Chicago Press and Tribune in the spring of 1858. Mr. White was a very talented newspaper man and had held some very important positions in the newspaper world. The Tribune was very much interested in Mr. Lincoln's political fortunes and designated Mr. White to accompany Mr. Lincoln on his campaign and especially to attend the joint debates and to report them to the Tribune. Mr. White was not a short hand reporter and would have been obliged to make a long hand report from notes which he might have taken at the time of the discussions. But fortunately a young man appeared on the scene which greatly relieved Mr. White's embarrassment and greatly enhanced the value of the reports to the Tribune. The young man was Robert P. Hitt. Mr. Hitt was a graduate of Rock River Seminary and of Asbury (now DePauw) University He was an expert short hand writer. He opened an office in Chicago in 1856 and by 1858 had gained a wide-spread reputation as a court reporter and newspaper man. He was at that time the only short hand reporter in Chicago at this early date. He attracted the attention of Mr. Lincoln and other campaign orators and was kept busy in this then novel line of work. Mr. White tells of a "scoop" which Mr. Hitt made upon Messrs. Binmore and Sheridan. On the night of July 9th when Mr. Douglas made his initial address in his campaign in Chicago, the address was taken down by Mr. Hitt for the Tribune, and by Messrs. Binmore and Sheridan for the Times. Mr. Hitt put his short hand notes of the speech into long hand and turned it over to the Tribune that night, and it was set and printed and on the streets early the next morning. The two Times reporters had taken the speech but not suspecting that any one else could do such a thing, had delayed handing in the long hand report so the speech did not appear in the Times that day.

The Reports

It is easy for us at this date to understand the bitter partisan feeling which prevailed during this campaign. Immediately after the publication of the speeches made at Ottawa, the first joint debate, the press began to print unjustifiable attacks upon the speeches as reported. "The republican press claimed that Lincoln was not given a fair report, and the democratic editors replied that Lincoln was by nature ungrammatical and uncouth in his utterances." The Chicago Times, the democratic paper of Chicago, in speaking of Lincoln's speech at Ottawa, said: "We did not attempt, much, to 'fix up' the bungling effort: that was not our business. Lincoln should have learned, before this, to 'rake after' himself—or rather to supersede the necessity of 'raking after' by taking heed to his own thoughts and expressions—But it seems the republicans have a candidate for the Senate of whose bad rhetoric and horrible jargon they are ashamed, upon which, before they would publish it, they called a council of 'literary' men to discuss, reconstruct, and rewrite; they dare not allow Lincoln to go into print in his own dress, and abuse us, the Times, for reporting him literally—There is no orator in America more correct in rhetoric, more clear in ideas, more direct in purpose, in all his public addresses, than Stephen A. Douglas."

The Galesburg Democrat accused the Chicago Times and its two reporters of "outrageous frauds" in reporting Mr. Lincoln's speeches. The Galesburg Democrat says: "There is scarcely a correctly reported paragraph in the whole speech. Many sentences are dropped out which were absolutely necessary for the sense; many are transposed so as to read wrong end first; many are made to read exactly opposite of the orator's intention, and the whole aim has been to blunt the keen edge of Mr. Lincoln's wit, to mar the beauty of his most eloquent passages, and make him talk like a booby, a half-witted numbskull.— We have taken the pains to go over the reports of the speeches carefully and note the material alterations—and find that they number one hundred and eighty. We believe that an action for libel would hold against these villians, and they richly deserve the prosecution."

The Ottawa Debate, August 21, 1858

The first joint debate occurred at Ottawa August 18, 1858. There were two weekly papers published in Ottawa. One, the Free Trader, was a democratic publication, while the other, The Republican, was republican in politics. These and the nearby local papers took pains to urge a big attendance of the people upon the debate. Special trains were run. A train left Chicago at 8 A. M. and reached Ottawa at 11:45. It returned leaving Ottawa at 6 P. M., reaching Chicago at 9:45. The train from Chicago over the Rock Island brought fourteen passenger coaches loaded to the guards. A train from Peru and La Salle brought eleven coaches full. It was estimated at the time that 20,000 people were on the grounds, but more conservative estimates placed the number at 12,000.

The following newspapers gave accounts of the debate more or less colored in favor of Mr. Douglas:

The Philadelphia Press.
The Baltimore Sun.

St. Louis Morning Herald.
The Missouri Republican.
Illinois State Register.
The Chicago Times.
Louisville (Ky.) Democrat.

The following papers gave reports more or less favorable to Mr. Lincoln:
The Chicago Press and Tribune.
The Peoria Transcript.
The Chicago Journal.
The Quincy Whig.

These papers gave correct accounts with little coloring:
The New York Evening Post.
The Boston Daily Advertiser.

The Freeport Debate, August 27, 1858

Freeport in Stephenson County is in the extreme northwestern corner of the state. The attendance was estimated at 15,000. Special trains were run to accommodate the people from the distant parts of the territory. Considerable effort was made to send a good delegation from Chicago. In order to reach Freeport in time for the debate in the afternoon, it was necessary for Chicago people to leave that city at 10 o'clock the night before. The Galena special brought over a thousand people. The day opened with prospects of rain. The wind was chilly and clouds and sunshine alternated throughout the day. The town of 7,000 was taxed to feed and care for the great throng. A correspondent to the New York Evening Post said: "They have a wretched way in Illinois of leaving the platform unguarded and exposed to the forcible entry of the mob, who seize upon it an hour or so before the notabilities arrive and turn a deaf ear to all urgent appeals to evacuation."

It had been barely a week since the joint debate at Ottawa. Mr. Douglas and Mr. Lincoln had both been engaged in filling individual appointments, and there had not been much time for rest. But they were both eager for the second engagement. Mr. Lincoln had spoken at Augusta, Hancock County, and had come to Freeport by way of Dixon, and was accompanied by delegations from Ogle, Lee, and Whiteside Counties. Mr. Douglas had been speaking in Jo Daviess County and reached Freeport from Galena on the night of Thursday 26. He was received by a great concourse of people amid the strains of music and the booming of cannon. Mr. Lincoln arrived in Freeport at ten o'clock on the day of the debate and he too was acclaimed the champion of the rights of the people.

Both orators were quartered in the Brewster House, an elegant and spacious four story building centrally located, corner of Stephenson and Mechanic Streets. The hotel had just been completed in the summer of 1858. At the hotel there were receptions, speeches, and conferences. The public men of both parties were mingling freely with the people. Banners were flying and mottoes upon all available space proclaimed the slogans of the two parties. Some of them read: "Old Abe Lincoln," "Douglas and Popular Sovereignty," "The Little Giant," "Honest Abe," "Carroll County for Lincoln."

The great crowd hurried to the grove, not far from the hotel, where the speaking was to occur. There was much confusion—some real disorder. There seemed a lack of real good management. It appears from the reports that orators, reception committees, invited guests, and newspaper reporters all engaged in a hand-to-hand conflict for seats and in some cases for standing room. This joint discussion in some ways was considered the most important of the series.

The interest manifested by the newspapers following the Freeport debate had not abated from what it was at the time of the Ottawa discussion. There was a more sober tone to both the reports and the editorials. The eastern newspapers were taking a different attitude toward the debates. They saw that the participants were discussing national questions instead of personal differences. The report sent to the New York Evening Post was an unbiased description of the matters of general interest.

Gen. Smith D. Atkins, a resident of Freeport, wrote his recollections of the debate and told the following interesting story: Mr. Douglas was entertained in the home of Mr. F. W. S. Brawley, the postmaster. Mr. Brawley secured a very fine carriage and a beautiful team to take Mr. Douglas from the hotel to the place of speaking. When the republicans found that Mr. Douglas was to be driven to the speaker's stand in the finest outfit in Freeport, they went out into the country and got Uncle John Long's Conestoga wagon, which was just from Pennsylvania, and his six big horses and drew them up in front of the hotel. Lincoln refused at first to ride in the Conestoga, but was persuaded finally to do so. When Douglas saw what the republicans were doing, he refused to ride in the fine carriage and walked with friends to the grounds.

The Jonesboro Debate, September 15, 1858

The third of the joint discussions was held in Jonesboro, the county seat of Union County. This town was within about forty miles of Cairo, the extreme south end of the state.

Mr. Horace White, who accompanied Mr. Lincoln on all his trips, reports that from Freeport Mr. Lincoln went to Carlinville, thence to Clinton, Bloomington, Monticello, Paris, Hillsboro, Greenville, and to Edwardsville. Here Judge Gillespie had arranged for and presided over a very enthusiastic meeting at which Mr. Lincoln spoke. From Edwardsville Mr. Lincoln and

UNVEILING OF MARKER AT SITE OF JONESBORO DEBATE AT FIFTIETH ANNIVERSARY

Mr. White went to Decatur whence they left on the Illinois Central for Anna, the station opposite Jonesboro.

The setting for the Jonesboro debate was so very different from what it was at the other six places that some local coloring will be of general interest. Mr. A. J. Phillips was a lad of eleven years. His father was D. L. Phillips, about the only prominent republican in Union County. Mr. A. Phillips now seventy-seven years of age says he remembers Lincoln's visit very well. He says Mr. Lincoln stayed over night in his father's home on the street leading from Anna to Jonesboro. Mr. Horrace White wrote the author that he remembered two things distinctly about the Jonesboro debate. He says he and Lincoln and some friends sat in front of the old hotel in Jonesboro the evening of the 14th and looked at Donati's comet, and talked about what meaning should be put into its appearance at this time. Mr. White further says that the next day when people began to arrive "the country people came into the little town with ox-teams mostly, and a very stunted breed of oxen too. Their wagons were old fashioned and looked as they they were ready to fall to pieces." Mr. White says that Jonesboro was the only place where he saw people coming to the debates with ox-teams.

On the morning of the 15th, Dr. McVane, a next door neighbor to Mr. Phillips, who owned a very fine team and carriage, took Mr. Lincoln, Mr. Phillips and the younger Phillips for a drive into the country. On their return Mr. Lincoln called to see Mrs. Dr. Hacker, the daughter-in-law of Colonel John Hacker. Mrs. Hacker told the writer that Mr. Lincoln and Mr. Douglas both came to see her that day. The Hackers were friends of Douglas.

The whereabouts of Mr. Douglas have not been traced immediately following the Freeport debate. On September 11, he was in Belleville. A special train of twelve coaches brought Mr. and Mrs. Douglas from St. Louis to Belleville, where Mr. Douglas spoke to the people. Mr. Douglas and his wife had spent a day or two in St. Louis prior to the 11th. The St. Louis Daily Morning Herald says of Mrs. Douglas: "Of the beauty and grace of this lady much has been said: and all who saw her yesterday are quite ready to testify, with entire truth." From Belleville Mr. Douglas went to Waterloo. On Sunday, the 12th, he visited either in Waterloo or Chester. On Monday, September 13th, he was in Chester and spoke. That night he took the steamer, James H. Lucas. On Tuesday morning, the 14th, he was in Cairo where there were dinners, receptions, speeches, bands, and a fashionable ball. Here he was met by Uriah Linder, Judge Marshall, and John A. Logan, Wm. A. Hacker, C. G. Simmons, H. Watson Webb and others. A band of sixteen pieces had been sent from Jonesboro to Cairo under the leadership of Professor Terpinitz. This was the only music at this debate.

DUGLAS HAS KUM.

Immense Gathering!

THE MASSES IN COUNCIL!!

DUGLAS RECEIVED BY THE COMMITTEE!!!

THE COMMITTEE!

The Reception.

ICE WATER!

MUCH ENTHUSIASM.

Twelve Men Give Cheers!

DUG APPEARS AT THE WINDOW AND SMILES!!!

SEVEN CHEERS FOR MARSHALL, BY THE IMMORTAL TWELVE!

Ye Refrigerating Committee!

ITS DOINS!

YE SHORT AND YE TALL MAKE CONNEXIONS!

THE RUGGED ROAD UP THE LEVEE WITH NARY CHEER!!

ENTHUSIASM!!

CHEERS.

DOUGLAS, A LONG MAN AND A SHORT MAN!!!

FOUR BANNERS!

A FLAG!

Yesterday morning about 9 o'clock the James H. Lucas, with the lilliputian giant, on board, announced her coming by the report of a cannon, whereupon the committee appointed for the purpose hoisted their collars, straightened their hair and mustaches, wiped the last "licker" off their lips with their coat sleeves, and made tracks for the wharf boat. As soon as the boat landed, a cannon brought from Mound City for the purpose (the brass piece here is a Buchanan cannon, and would certainly have bursted on such an occasion) commenced belching. The committee then went to the Lucas. Judge Duglas was visible and the chairman said "How d'ye do Mr. D?" as natural as possible. Mr. D. replied "I am tolerable!" The rest of the committee were then introduced to the circus giant, and a procession was formed.

PROCESSION.

In the lead was Mr Douglas! adorned on one side by Mr. S. S. Taylor, six feet two or seven inches high, and on the other by Mr. S. S. Brooks, five feet four inches high. Mr. Douglas had on a white hat, and a coat. The balance of the procession consisted of fifteen or twenty persons who marched up to the top of the levee, where they were met by four banners, one flag, and ten or fifteen more people, who joined them promiscuously. The imposing spectacle then moved, led on by the immortal twelve, up to Whites corner, thence down to Bailey Harrell's and thence down commercial avenue to the Tailor House. Here was the grand display. Little Mr. Douglas and his large white hat went into the Taylor House parlor, followed by several of the committee. About a dozen of the faithful had collected at the corner, and one of them proposed three cheers for Mr. Douglas. An attempt was made to give them, but barring the aforesaid dozen or two it was an ignominious failure. Three cheers were then proposed for Sam Marshall which were given by about eight persons in the very weakest kind of style. When Mr. Douglas was cheered, he appeared at the parlor window, and smiled very benignly upon the crowd. One of the committee then appeared at the window, called the attention of the crowd, and stated that Mr. Douglas' time was too much occupied with speaking and he could not speak more than once a day, speaking would therefore be commenced at 2 o'clock. The crowd quietly dispersed without a word, save from one man, who exclaimed, "Well, let him rip, then!" The band then played one more tune, and everything was soon quiet as if Mr. Douglas was not in town. From the time of his arrival on the Lucas till he reached the Taylor House, there was not the least enthusiasm among the crowd— not even a cheer was proposed, and the march through the hot sun was gloomy indeed. Altogether, it was the flattest, dryest and most insipid reception we ever saw.

LATER.

At 1 o'clock Mr. D. assembled himself upon a platform which had been erected for his benefit in front of the Taylor House, and delivered his stereotyped speech. The remainder of the day was spent in various amusements until evening, when the ball commenced. Politics having been confined to the kitchen, the ball went off very pleasantly. Judge Douglas' enthusiastic (?) reception, will long be remembered by our citizens. Verily there was ice mixed with it.

FROM ISSUE OF "CAIRO WEEKLY TIMES AND DELTA," AN ANTI-DOUGLAS PAPER, SEPTEMBER 15, 1858

On the morning of the 15th, a special train left Cairo for the State Fair then being held in Centralia (or better Central City). Mr. Douglas came to Anna on this train. A flat car upon which a small brass cannon was mounted was the rear car. This little cannon was fired along the way as the train passed the stations. Douglas reached Anna about twelve and was driven to Jonesboro one mile west. The band, cannon and friends formed a creditable procession.

The debate occurred about one-half mile, or less, north of the courthouse, on the grounds of the Union County Fair Association. The little cannon was placed at the foot of an incline and boomed for Douglas at proper intervals.

Mr. Douglas as well as Mr. Lincoln had uphill work in Jonesboro. The vote that fall showed that Mr. A. J. Kuykendall of Vienna, the Douglas candidate for state senator in the 25th senatorial district received 4,425 votes. Wm. A. Hacker the Douglas candidate for representative to the general assembly received in Union County 566 votes; while John S. Hunsaker the Buchanan candidate, received in Union County 620 votes. It has been surmised that Douglas knew that the administration was strong in Union County, and he hoped to win some of his opponents over at the debate in Jonesboro. It may also be concluded that Lincoln had a warm friend—at least for that day—in every "Danite" as Douglas had called Buchanan's friends in Illinois.

Personal interviews with more than a score of men who saw Douglas in Cairo revealed that there was little enthusiasm for him in that town. The vote in Alexander County for Kuykendall, the Douglas candidate for state senator, was 307; and for Stout, the "Danite" candidate, the vote was 225. It is seen that the democratic party was pretty badly divided. Horace White wrote the author his recollection of the debate in Jonesboro and said: "My impression was that the audience at Jonesboro was rather stolid, and took little interest in the questions discussed, but it was composed of honest, well meaning, old fashioned country folks. I do not think Lincoln made any converts at Jonesboro. I doubt if Douglas made any or even held his own."

The Chicago Press and Tribune estimated the crowd at Jonesboro at fourteen hundred. Interviews with old citizens of Union County revealed the fact as stated by the reporters that the people of the county gave very little heed to the debate.

THE CHARLESTON DEBATE, SEPTEMBER 18, 1858

The Charleston debate was set for Friday, September 18. Mr. Douglas left Anna on the morning of the 16th and went to Benton, the home of John A. Logan. Here he spoke to a fair sized crowd of friends, and was presented with a flag made by the ladies of the town. From here he went on to Centralia where the state fair was in session. Here he mingled with the people and made a short address. Mr. Lincoln also spent some time on the fair grounds at Centralia and also made an address. On the morning of the 18th, both Lincoln and Douglas were in Mattoon ready to go to Charleston, some ten miles east for the fourth joint discussion. Mr. Douglas' friends led out of Mattoon about 9 o'clock. Thirty-two young ladies on horse back representing the states of the union led the way. Hundreds of people in carriages and on horseback accompanied Mr. Douglas' carriage. On arriving at Charleston, Mr. Douglas was entertained at the Union Hotel. Here the Hon. O. B. Ficklin welcomed Douglas in an eloquent address.

HOME OF JOHN A. LOGAN IN BENTON

Mr. Lincoln left Mattoon about 10 o'clock accompanied by a band of music and a great procession. A great car bearing the names of Lincoln, Oglesby, Marshall, and Craddock carrying also thirty-two young ladies left Charleston to meet the republicans a short distance from the county seat. Mr. Lincoln was welcomed to Charleston by Hon. H. P. H. Bromwell in front of the Capitol House where Lincoln was entertained.

It is interesting for the reader to recall that Mr. Lincoln's parents lived not far from Charleston. Lincoln was represented on the banners as a backwoods farmer in Coles County thirty years previous.

The Charleston crowd is reported to have been from fifteen to twenty thousand. There were delegations present from Coles, Edgar, Cumberland, Clark, Champaign, and Vermilion Counties. The speaking was held at the fair grounds. The reporters gave very favorable accounts of the arrangements for the joint discussion, and of the kindly treatment by the people of the young city of their visitors.

The Galesburg Debate, October 7, 1858

The Galesburg debate was set for October 7. This would give the two debaters about three weeks between the joint discussion at Charleston and the one at Galesburg. The whereabouts of the two orators can not now be stated during this interim. Each had appointments which were fulfilled. Mr. Lincoln and Mr. Trumbull were evidently canvassing Central and Northern Illinois during the better part of the time between the Charleston meeting and the one at Galesburg. These two men were in Pekin in a meeting on October 5th. Trumbull spoke in Peoria on the 6th. Mr. Douglas came to Galesburg from Monmouth. Mr. Douglas and Mr. Lincoln were both received with much enthusiasm. Everything done in the way of receptions was in a very fine spirit. Nothing crude or out of taste was seen. Mr. Douglas was presented with a beautiful satin banner by the students of Lombard University. He gave a reception to everybody at the Bonney House. Mr. Lincoln was also presented with a beautiful banner by the republican ladies of Galesburg. He was entertained at the home of Mr. Henry R. Sanderson.

The weather had been very fair for several days prior to the debate, but on the night before the day of the debate the rain, winds, and cold combined to present a very disagreeable day for the debate. The joint discussion was held on the campus of Knox College. The platform was placed close to the east end of the college, and stretched across the college just over the stand a broad streamer bearing the inscription, *"Knox College for Lincoln."* The two speakers came to the grounds in carriages driven side by side, which exhibited a different spirit from that exhibited at other joint discussions. The crowd was estimated from 18,000 to 20,000. Complaints were entered by the reporters of the utter lack of conveniences afforded them by the committees of arrangements of the towns where previous joint debates had been held. Better arrangements were obtained at Galesburg.

The Quincy Debate, October 13, 1858

Quincy is on the Mississippi River on the extreme west side of the state. It would seem therefore that the attendance could come only from the north, the east and the south. But there were hundreds of people from west of the Mississippi River. A correspondent to the Quincy Herald from Lineus, Missouri, a town in Linn County, said: "The people of Northern Missouri are taking a lively interest in the canvass in Illinois between

Judge Douglas and Mr. Lincoln, and the democrats are wishing success to the "Little Giant." It is a long way to travel (120 miles) to hear a man speak, where we have to stage it nearly half the way, but such is the enthusiasm of the people, and their curiosity to hear the exponent of popular sovereignty, that from 5,000 to 10,000 from Missouri will be there on the occasion." Many republicans came to the Quincy meeting from Southeastern Iowa.

The meeting at Quincy was given much publicity. The Quincy Whig and the Quincy Herald kept the meeting before the people. They appealed to the people to make the Quincy meeting one of the biggest of the series. Handbills were used by the thousands by both democrats and republicans. Special excursions were provided by many Mississippi River steamers. The crowd was estimated at from 12,000 to 15,000.

Douglas reached Quincy on Tuesday evening late and was a guest of the Quincy House the most pretentious hotel in the town. Mr. Lincoln was the guest of his friend, Hon. O. H. Browning. One feature of the Quincy meeting was the interest taken in processions. Both sides organized extensive parades, with bands, banners, young ladies in costume and most important of all a marshal, who was decked out with sash, and caparisoned charger. The local processions would go out to meet incoming organizations. The river boats, chartered to carry republican or democratic delegations were important factors in the general display features of the day. Dr. I. T. Wilson was the marshal for the Douglas side, while Mr. E. K. Stone served in that capacity for the republicans.

The speaking took place in Washington Square; the weather was favorable to an outdoor gathering, and the crowd was attentive and well ordered. After the speaking was over, hundreds lingered in the town to take part in the program provided for the evening. Senator Douglas had reached Quincy the evening before the day of the speaking and his friends had received him with bands and a big torch light procession. The republicans provided their torchlight parade for the evening following the debate. The Hon. Carl Schurz was secured as a speaker for a night meeting at the courthouse where he championed the republican cause. He spoke in German. The building was crowded to its utmost capacity. Mr. Schurz wrote for the McClure Magazine a very impartial and dignified account of the Quincy meeting.

The Alton Debate, October 15, 1858

Only two days intervened between the Quincy meeting and the final meeting of the series at Alton, October 15. Alton was so easy of access from St. Louis, that the papers of the latter city urged a large attendance from the Missouri metropolis.

Boats were advertised to leave St. Louis in the forenoon of the day of the debate. The Baltimore and the White Cloud were two large river steamers which carried the partisans of the two orators. Special trains came into Alton over the Chicago and Alton railroad. A military band and a cadet corps came from Springfield over the Chicago and Alton.

The debate was held at the southern side of the city hall which still stands in a barren open space overlooking the river. The crowd filled the space between the city hall and the Presbyterian Church to the south. No banners were allowed on the stands —only the stars and stripes. But all about were cartoons and banners inscribed with such expressions as: "Popular Sovereignty," "Illinois Born a Free State Under the Ordinance of 1787," "Lincoln Not Yet Trotted Out," "Old Madison for Lincoln," "S. A. Douglas, the People's Choice," "Too Late for the Milking." There was evidence that the democratic party was pretty badly divided in the territory about Old Madison between Douglas' cause and that of the administration. Many Buchanan democrats were present and there was some tendency to heckle Mr. Douglas by these "Danites."

Mr. Douglas and Mr. Lincoln both came from the Quincy debate on the same river steamer, the City of Louisiana. It is reported that there was a lack of interest in the debate at Alton. This is accounted for from the fact that the people who cared to do so had already familiarized themselves with the general line of argument pursued by the two orators. It was getting late in the campaign and people were anxiously awaiting an opportunity to test their strength at the polls. Few reports put the crowd that listened to this last debate at more than five or six thousand, though many more people were in the town.

Thus closed the memorable debate. It has been charged that the plan of a joint debate upon political issues was crude, "western," and undignified. The Cincinnati Gazette speaking editorially said: "We do not quite agree with those who hold that the stump is the best way by which to judge candidates and their principles." The Mississippian wished that Lincoln and Douglas would give each other a drubbing, "and then, by way of making honors easy and ridding the country entirely of a pair of depraved, blustering, mischievous, low down, demagogues, we would have them make a kilkenny cat of it, and eat each other up. We have no choice to express between them."

OTHER ESTIMATES

In attempting to get at the estimate placed upon the character of the debates and of the debaters, we must distinguish between the accounts sent to the various papers by hired reporters and the editorials which appeared from time to time as the joint discussions proceeded. The local papers were rarely temperate in their reports and editorials, but as the debates were held from time to time, the eastern papers took a very serious view of the character of the line of thought presented by the two debaters. In order that we may judge of this matter a few quotations are presented.

New York Evening Post: "They (the debates) have been next in importance and interest to some of the great senatorial debates when the whole nation has stood still to listen to the voice of its greatest men."

Boston Daily Courier: "The contest for the senatorship between these two gentlemen is one of very great interest to the country at large, since by its issue will be substantially determined the political character of their state at the next Presidential election * * * The contest has begun with every commendable exhibition of courtesy between the rivals."

The New York Daily Tribune: "A mode of discussing political questions which might well be more generally adopted * * * It is not merely a passage at arms between two eminent masters of the art of intellectual attack and defense that this discussion is worthy of study. It touches some of the most vital principles of our political system."

Cincinnati Commercial: "Both champions upon this occasion exhibited extraordinary power and candor. In the whole history of the American stump we do not recollect that there is a record of a discussion so searching and comprehensive, so thorough in its analysis of issue, so absorbing in its scope, as this at freeport."

Mr. Douglas had nine appointments to fill between the Alton debate and the election on November 2, while Mr. Lincoln was to speak at eleven or twelve places. The election results were quickly known, and both sides easily adjusted themselves to the decision of the people. Mr. Douglas had a clear majority of the joint assembly, the vote standing fifty-four for Douglas and forty-six for Lincoln. The vote for state treasurer was for Miller, the republican candidate, 125,430; for Fondey, the democratic candidate, 121,609. Mr. Dougherty, the Buchanan candidate for treasurer, receiver 5,071 votes.

CHAPTER XXII

THE FREEPORT DEBATE

NOTE: Although books containing the joint debates were published and freely distributed following the campaign of 1858, it is only in our larger libraries, or in the libraries of a limited number of our private citizens, that copies of the debate can be found. It has therefore been thought advisable to insert at this point at least one of the joint discussions, and the one given at Freeport has been selected as it was in this discussion that Mr. Douglas was forced to take a stand which admittedly won him the senatorship, but lost him the presidency.

MR. LINCOLN'S SPEECH

Ladies and Gentlemen: On Saturday last, Judge Douglas and myself first met in public discussion. He spoke an hour, I an hour and a half, and he replied for half an hour. The order is now reversed. I am to speak an hour, he an hour and a half, and then I am to reply for half an hour. I propose to devote myself during the first hour to the scope of what was brought within the range of his half-hour speech at Ottawa. Of course there was brought within the scope of that half-hour's speech something of is own opening speech.

In the course of that opening argument Judge Douglas proposed to me seven distinct interrogatories. In my speech of an hour and a half, I attended to some other parts of his speech, and incidentally, as I thought, answered one of the interrogatories then. I then distinctly intimated to him that I would answer the rest of his interrogatories. He made no intimation at the time of the proposition, nor did he in his reply allude at all to that suggestion of mine. I do him no injustice in saying that he occupied at least half of his reply in dealing with me as though I had refused to answer his interrogatories. I now propose that I will answer any of the interrogatories upon condition that he will answer questions from me not exceeding the same number. I give him an opportunity to respond. The judge remains silent. I now say that I will answer his interrogatories, whether he answers mine or not; and after that I have done so, I shall propound mine to him.

I have supposed myself, since the organization of the republican party at Bloomington, in May, 1856, bound as a party man by the platforms of the party, then and since. If in any interrogatories which I shall answer I go beyond the scope of what is within these platforms, it will be perceived that no one is responsible but myself.

Having said thus much, I will take up the judge's interrogatories as I find them printed in the Chicago Times, and answer them seriatim. In order that there may be no mistake about it, I have copied the interrogatories in writing, and also my answers to them. The first one of these interrogatories is in these words:

Question 1. "I desire to know whether Lincoln today stands as he did in 1854, in favor of the unconditional repeal of the Fugitive Slave law?"

Answer. I do not now, nor ever did, stand in favor of the unconditional repeal of the Fugitive Slave law.

Q. 2. "I desire him to answer whether he stands pledged today, as he did in 1854, against the admission of any more slave states into the Union, even if the people want them?"

A. I do not now, nor ever did, stand pledged against the admission of any more slave states into the Union.

Q. 3. "I want to know whether he stands pledged against the admission of a new state into the Union with such a Constitution as the people of that state may see fit to make?"

A. I do not stand pledged against the admission of a new state into the Union, with such a constitution as the people of that state may see fit to make.

Q. 4. "I want to know whether he stands today pledged to the abolition of slavery in the District of Columbia?"

A. I do not stand today pledged to the abolition of slavery in the District of Columbia.

Q. 5. "I desire him to answer whether he stands pledged to the prohibition of the slave trade between the different states?"

A. I do not stand pledged to the prohibition of the slave trade between the different states.

Q. 6. "I desire to know whether he stands pledged to prohibit slavery in all the territories of the United States, north as well as south of the Missouri Compromise line?"

A. I am impliedly, if not expressly, pledged to a belief in the right and duty of Congress to prohibit slavery in all the United States territories.

Q. 7. "I desire him to answer whether he is opposed to the acquisition of any new territory unless slavery is first prohibited therein?"

A. I am not generally opposed to honest acquisition of territory; and, in any given case, I would or would not oppose such acquisition, accordingly as I might think such acquisition would or would not aggravate the slavery question among ourselves.

Now, my friends, it will be perceived, upon an examination of these questions and answers, that so far I have only answered that I was not pledged to this, that, or the other. The judge has not framed his interrogatories to ask me anything more than this, and I have answered in strict accordance with the interrogatories, and have answered truly, that I am not pledged at all upon any of the points to which I have answered. But I am not disposed to hang upon the exact form of his interrogatory. I am rather disposed to take up at least some of these questions, and state what I really think upon them.

As to the first one, in regard to the Fugitive-Slave law, I have never hesitated to say, and I do not now hesitate to say, that I think, under the Constitution of the United States, the people of the Southern States are entitled to a congressional fugitive-slave law. Having said that, I have had nothing to say in regard to the existing Fugitive-Slave law further than that I think it should have been framed so as to be free from some of the objections that pertain to it, without lessening its efficiency. And inasmuch as we are not now in an agitation in regard to an alteration or modification of that law, I would not be the man to introduce it as a new subject of agitation upon the general question of slavery.

In regard to the other question, of whether I am pledged to the admission of any more slave states into the Union, I state to you very frankly that I would be exceedingly sorry ever to be put in a position of having to pass upon that question. I should be exceedingly glad to know that there would never be another slave state admitted into the Union. But I must add that if slavery shall be kept out of the territories during the territorial existence of any one given territory, and then the people shall, having a fair chance and a clear field, when they come to adopt the constitution, uninfluenced by the actual presence of the institution among them, I see no alternative, if we own the country, but to admit them into the Union.

The third interrogatory is answered by the answer to the second, it being, as I conceive, the same as the second.

The fourth one is in regard to the abolition of slavery in the District of Columbia. In relation to that, I have my mind very distinctly made up. I should be exceedingly glad to see slavery abolished in the District of Columbia. I believe that Congress possesses the constitutional power to abolish it. Yet as a member of Congress, I should not, with my present views, be in favor of endeavoring to abolish slavery in the District of Columbia, unless it would be upon these conditions: First, that the abolition should be gradual; second, that it should be on a vote of the majority of qualified voters in the District; and third, that compensation should be made to unwilling owners. With these three conditions, I confess I would be exceedingly glad to see Congress abolish slavery in the District of Columbia, and, in the language of Henry Clay, "sweep from our capital that foul blot upon our nation."

In regard to the fifth interrogatory, I must say here, that as to the question of the abolition of the slave trade between the different states, I can truly answer, as I have, that I am pledged to nothing about it. It is a subject to which I have not given that mature consideration that would make me feel authorized to state a position so as to hold myself entirely bound by it. In other words, that question has never been preeminently enough before me to induce me to investigate whether we really have the constitutional power to do it. I could investigate it if I had sufficient time to bring myself to a conclusion upon that subject; but I have not done so, and I say so frankly to you here, and to Judge Douglas. I must say, however, that if I should be of opinion that Congress does possess the constitutional power to abolish the slave-trade among the different states, I should still not be in favor of the exercise of that power unless upon some conservative principle as I conceive it, akin to what I have said in relation to the abolition of slavery in the District of Columbia.

My answer as to whether I desire that slavery should be prohibited in all the territories of the United States, is full and explicit within itself, and can not be made clearer by any comments of mine. So I suppose in regard to the question whether I am opposed to the acquisition of any more territory unless slavery is first prohibited therein, my answer is such that I could add nothing by way of illustration or making myself better understood, than the answer which I have placed in writing.

Now in all this the judge has me, and he has me on the record. I suppose he had flattered himself that I was really entertaining one set of opinions for one place, and another set for another place; that I was afraid to say at one place what I uttered at another. What I am saying here I suppose I say to a vast audience as strongly tending to abolitionism as any audience in the State of Illinois, and I believe I am saying that which, if it would be offensive to any person and render them enemies to myself, would be offensive to persons in this audience.

I now proceed to propound to the judge the interrogatories, so far as I have framed them. I will bring forward a new installment when I get them ready. I will bring them forward now, only reaching to number four.

The first one is:

Question 1. If the people of Kansas shall, by means entirely unobjectionable in all other respects, adopt a state constitution, and ask admission into the Union under it, before they have the requisite number of inhabitants according to the English bill—some 93,000—will you vote to admit them?

Q. 2. Can the people of a United States territory, in any lawful way, against the wish of any citizen of the United States, exclude slavery from its limits prior to the formation of a state constitution?

Q. 3. If the Supreme Court of the United States shall decree that states can not exclude slavery from their limits, are you in favor of acquiescing in, adopting, and following such decision as a rule of political action?

Q. 4. Are you in favor of acquiring additional territory, in disregard of how such acquisition may affect the nation on the slavery question?

As introductory to these interrogatories which Judge Douglas propounded to me at Ottawa, he read a set of resolutions which he said Judge Trumbull and myself had participated in adopting, in the first republican state convention, held at Springfield in October, 1854. He insisted that I and Judge Trumbull, and perhaps the entire republican party, were responsible for the doctrines contained in the set of resolutions which he read, and I understand that it was from that set of resolutions that he deducted the interrogatories which he propounded to me, using these resolutions as a sort of authority for propounding those questions to me. Now, I say here today that I do not answer his interrogatories because of their springing at all from that set of resolutions which he read. I answered them because Judge Douglas thought fit to ask them. I do not now, nor never did, recognize any responsibility upon myself in that set of resolutions. When I replied to him on that occasion, I assured him that I never in any possible form had anything to do with that set of resolutions.

It turns out, I believe, that those resolutions were never passed in any convention held in Springfield. It turns out that they were never passed at any convention or any public meeting that I had any part in. I believe it turns out, in addition to all this, that there was not, in the fall of 1854, any convention holding a session in Springfield, calling itself a republican state convention; yet it is true there was a convention, or assemblage of men calling themselves a convention, at Springfield, that did pass some resolutions. But so little did I really know of the proceedings of that convention, or what set of resolutions they had passed, I really did not know but they had been the resolutions, pass then and there. I did not question that they were the resolutions adopted. For I could not bring myself to suppose that Judge Douglas could say what he did upon this subject without knowing that it was true. I contended myself, on that occasion, with denying, as I truly could, all connection with them, not denying or affirming whether they were passed at Springfield. Now, it turns out that he had got hold of some resolutions passed at some convention or public meeting in Kane County. I wish to say here, that I don't conceive that in any fair and just mind this discovery relieves me at all. I had just as much to do with the convention in Kane County as that at Springfield. I am just as much responsible for the resolutions at Kane County as those at Springfield—the amount of the responsibility being exactly nothing in either case; no more than there would be in regard to a set of resolutions passed in the moon.

I allude to this extraordinary matter in this canvass for some further purpose than anything yet advanced. Judge Douglas did not make his statement upon that occasion as matters that he believed to be true, but he stated them roundly as being true, in such form as to pledge his veracity for their truth. When the whole matter turns out as it does, and when we consider who Judge Douglas is—that he is a distinguished senator of the United States; that he has served nearly twelve years as such; that his character is not at all limited as an ordinary senator of the United States, but that his name has become of world-wide renown—it is most extraordinary that he should so far forget all the suggestions of justice to an adversary, or of prudence to himself, as to venture upon the assertion of that which the slightest investigation would have shown him to be wholly false. I can only account for his having done so upon the supposition that that evil genius which has attended him through his life, giving to him an apparent astonishing prosperity, such as to lead very many good men to doubt there being any advantage in virtue over vice—I say I can only account for it on the supposition that that evil genius has at last made up his mind to forsake him.

And I may add that another extraordinary feature of the judge's conduct in this canvass—made more extraordinary by this incident—is, that he is in the habit, in almost all the speeches he makes, of charging falsehood upon his adversaries, myself and others. I now ask whether he is able to find anything that Judge Trumbull, for instance, has said, or in anything that I have said, a justification at all compared with what we have, in this instance, for that sort of vulgarity.

I have been in the habit of charging as a matter of belief on my part that, in the introduction of the Nebraska bill into Congress, there was a conspiracy to make slavery perpetual and national. I have arranged from time to time the evidence which establishes and proves the truth of this charge. I recurred to this charge at Ottawa. I shall not now have time to dwell upon it at very great length; but inasmuch as Judge Douglas, in his reply of half an hour, made some points upon me in relation to it, I propose noticing a few of them.

The judge insists that, in the first speech I made, in which I very distinctly made that charge, he thought for a good while I was in fun; that I was playful; that I was not sincere about it; and that he only grew angry and somewhat excited when he found that I insisted upon it as a matter of earnestness. He says he characterized it as a falsehood as far as I implicated his moral character in that transaction. Well, I did not know, till he presented that view, that I had implicated his moral character. He is very much in the habit, when he argues me up into a position I never thought of occupying, of very cosily saying he has no doubt Lincoln is "conscientious" in saying so. He should remember that I did not know but what he was altogether "conscientious" in that matter. I can conceive it was possible for men to conspire to do a good thing, and I really find nothing in Judge Douglas's course or arguments that is contrary to, or inconsistent with, his belief of a conspiracy to nationalize and spread slavery as being a good and blessed thing; and so I hope he will understand that I do not at all question but that in all this matter he is entirely "conscientious."

But to draw your attention to one of the points I made in this case, beginning at the beginning. When the Nebraska bill was introduced, or a short time afterward, by an amendment, I believe, it was provided that it must be considered "the true intent and meaning of this act not to legislate slavery into any state or territory, or to exclude it therefore, but to leave the people thereof perfectly free to form and regulate their own domestic institutions in their own way, subject only to the constitution of the United States." I have called his attention to the fact that when he and some others began arguing that they were giving an increased degree of liberty to the people in the territories over and above what they formerly had on the question of slavery, a question was raised whether the law was enacted to give such unconditional liberty to the people; and to test the sincerity of this mode of argument, Mr. Chase, of Ohio, introduced an amendment, in which he made the law—if the amendment were adopted—expressly declare that the people of the territory should have the power to exclude slavery if they saw fit.

I have asked attention also to the fact that Judge Douglas and those who acted with him voted that amendment down, notwithstanding it expressed exactly the thing they said was the true intent and meaning of the law. I have called attention to the fact that in subsequent times a decision of the Supreme Court has been made, in which it has been declared that a Territorial Legislature has no constitutional right to exclude slavery. And I have argued and said that for men who did intend that the people of the territory should have the right to exclude slavery absolutely and unconditionally, the voting down of Chase's amendment is wholly inexplicable. It is a puzzle, a riddle. But I have said that with men who did look forward to such a decision, or who had it in contemplation that such a decision of the Supreme Court would or might be made, the voting down of that amendment would be perfectly rational and intelligible. It would keep Congress from coming in collision with the decision when it was made.

Anybody can conceive that if there was an intention of expectation that such a decision was to follow, it would not be a very desirable party attitude to get into, for the Supreme Court—all or nearly all its members belonging to the same party—to decide one way, when the party in Congress had decided the other way. Hence it would be very rational for men expecting such a decision to keep the niche in that law clear for it. After pointing this out, I tell Judge Douglas that it looks to me as though here was the reason why Chase's amendment was voted down. I tell him that, as he did it, and knows why he did it, if it was done for a reason different from this, he knows what that reason was, and can tell us what it was. I tell him, also, it will be vastly more satisfactory to the country for him to give some other plausible, intelligible, reason why it was voted down than to stand upon his dignity and call people liars.

Well, on Saturday he did make his answer; and what do you think it was? He says if I had only taken upon myself to tell the whole truth about that amendment of Chase's no explanation would have been necessary on his part—or words to that effect. Now, I say here that I am quite unconscious of having suppressed anything material to the case, and I am very frank to admit if there is any sound reason other than that which appeared to me material, it is quite fair for him to present it. What reason does he propose? That when Chase came forward with his amendment expressly authorizing the people to exclude slavery from the limits of every territory, General Cass proposed to Chase, if he (Chase) would add to his amendment that the people should have the power to introduce or exclude, they would let it go. (This is substantially all of his reply.) And because Chase would not do that, they voted his amendment down. Well, it turn out, I believe, upon examination, that General Cass took some part in the little running debate upon that amendment, and then ran away and did not vote on it at all. Is not that the fact? So confident, as I think, was General Cass that there was a snake somewhere about, he chose to run away from the whole thing. This is an inference I draw from the fact that, though he took part in the debate, his name does not appear in the ayes and noes. But does Judge Douglas's reply amount to a satisfactory answer? There is some little difference of opinion here.

But I ask attention to a few more views bearing on the question of whether it amounts to a satisfactory answer. The men who were determined that that amendment should not get into the bill and spoil the place where the Dred Scott decision was to come in, sought an excuse to get rid of it somewhere. One of these ways—one of these excuses—was to ask Chase to add to his proposed amendment a provision that the people might introduce slavery if they wanted to. They very well know Chase would do no such thing, that Mr. Chase was one of the men differing from them on the broad principle of his insisting that freedom was better than slavery—a man who would not consent to enact a law, penned with his own hand, by which he was made to recognize slavery on the one hand, and liberty on the other, as precisely equal; and when they insisted on his doing this, they very well knew they insisted on that which he would not for a moment think of doing, and that they were only bluffing. I believe (I have not, since he made his answer, had a chance to examine the journals or Congressional Globe and therefore speak from memory)—I believe the state of the bill at that time, according to parliamentary rules, was such that no member could propose an additional amendment to Chase's amendment. I rather think this is the truth—the Judge shakes his head. Very well. I would like to know, then, if they wanted Chase's amendment fixed over, why somebody else could not have offered to do it? If they wanted it amended, why did they not offer the amendment? Why did they stand there taunting and quibbling at Chase? Why did they not put it in themselves?

But to put it on the other ground: Suppose that there was such an amendment offered, and Chase's was an amendment to an amendment; until one is disposed of, by parliamentary law you cannot pile another on. Then all these gentlemen had to do was to vote Chase's on, and then, in the amended form in which the whole stood, add their own amendment to it, if they wanted to put it in that shape. This was all they were obliged to do, and the ayes and noes show that there were thirty-six who voted it down, against ten who voted in favor of it. The thirty-six held entire sway and control. They could in some form or other have put that bill in the exact shape they wanted. If there was a rule preventing their amending it at the time, they could pass that, and then, Chase's amendment being merged, put it in the shape they wanted. They did not choose to do so, but they went into a quibble with Chase to get him to add what they knew he would not add, and because he would not, they stand upon that flimsy pretext for voting down what they argued was the meaning and intent of their own bill. They left room thereby for this Dred Scott decision, which goes very far to make slavery national throughout the United States.

I pass one or two points I have, because my time will very soon expire; but I must be allowed to say that Judge Douglas recurs again, as he did upon one or two other occasions, to the enormity of Lincoln,—as insignificant individuals like Lincoln,—upon his ipse dixit charging a conspiracy upon a large number of members of Congress, the Supreme Court, and two Presidents, to nationalize slavery. I want to say that, in the first place, I have made no charge of this sort upon my ipse dixit. I have only arrayed the evidence tending to prove it, and presented it to the understanding of others, saying what I think it proves, but giving you the means of judging whether it proves it or not. This is precisely what I have done. I have not placed it upon my ipse dixit at all.

On this occasion, I wish to recall his attention to a piece of evidence which I brought forward at Ottawa on Saturday, showing that he had made substantially the same charge against substantially the same persons, excluding his dear self from the category. I ask him to give some attention to the evidence which I brought forward that he himself had discovered a "fatal blow being struck" against the right of the people to exclude slavery from their limits, which fatal blow he assumed as in evidence in an article in the Washington Union, published "by authority." I ask by whose authority? He discovers a similar or identical provision in the Lecompton constitution. Made by whom? The framers of that constitution. Advocated by whom? By all the members of the party in the Nation, who advocated the introduction of Kansas into the Union under the Lecompton constitution.

I have asked his attention to the evidence that he arrayed to prove that such a fatal blow was being struck and to the facts which he brought forward in support of that charge,—being identical with the one which he thinks so villianous in me. He pointed it, not at a newspaper editor merely, but at the President and his Cabinet and the members of Congress advocating the Lecompton Constitution and those framing that instrument. I must again be permitted to remind him that although my ipse dixit may not be as great as his, yet it somewhat reduces the force of his calling my attention to the enormity of making a like charge against him.

Go on, Judge Douglas.

Ladies and Gentlemen: The silence with which you have listened to Mr. Lincoln during his hour is creditable to this vast audience, composed of men of various political parties. Nothing is more honorable to any large mass of people assembled for the purpose of a fair discussion than that kind and respectful attention that is yielded, not only to your political friends, but to those who are opposed to you in politics.

I am glad that at last I have brought Mr. Lincoln to the conclusion that he had better define his position on certain political questions to which I called his attention at Ottawa. He there showed no disposition, no inclination, to answer them. I did not present idle questions for him to answer, merely for my gratification. I laid the foundation for those interrogatories. by showing that they constituted the platform of the party whose nominee he is for the Senate. I did not presume that I had the right to catechise him as I saw proper, unless I showed that his party, or a majority of it, stood upon the platform and were in favor of the propositions, upon which my questions were based. I desired simply to know, inasmuch as he had been nominated as the first, last, and only choice of his party, whether he concurred in the platform which that party had adopted for its government. In a few moments I will proceed to review the answers which he has given to these interrogatories; but, in order to relieve his anxiety, I will first respond to these which he has presented to me. Mark you, he has not presented interrogatories which have ever received the sanction the party with which I am acting, and hence he has no other foundation for them than his own curiosity.

First, he desires to know if the people of Kansas shall form a constitution by means entirely proper and unobjectionable, and ask admission into the Union as a State, before they have the requisite population for a member of Congress, whether I will vote for that admission. Well, now, I regret exceedingly that he did not answer that interrogatory himself before he put it to me, in order that we might understand, and not be left to infer, on which side he is. Mr. Trumbull, during the last session of Congress, voted from the beginning to the end against the admission of Oregon, although a free state, because she had not the requisite population for a member of Congress. Mr. Trumbull would not consent, under any circumstances, to let a state, free or slave, come into the Union until it had the requisite population. As Mr. Trumbull is in the field, fighting for Mr. Lincoln, I would like to have Mr. Lincoln answer his own question and tell me whether he is fighting Trumbull on that issue or not.

But I will answer his question. In reference to Kansas, it is my opinion that as she has population enough to constitute a slave state, she has people enough for a free state. I will not make Kansas an exceptional case to the other states of the Union. I hold it to be a sound rule, of universal application to require a territory to contain the requisite population for a member of Congress before it is admitted as a state into the Union. I made that proposition in the Senate in 1856, and I renewed it during the last session, in a bill providing that no territory of the United States should form a constitution and apply for admission until it had the requisite population. On another occasion I proposed that neither Kansas nor any other territory should be admitted until it had the requisite population. Congress did not adopt any of my propositions containing this general rule, but did make an exception of Kansas. I will stand by that exception. Either Kansas must come in as a free state, with whatever population she may have, or the rule must be applied to all the other territories alike. I therefore answer at once, that it having been decided that Kansas has people enough for a slave state, I hold that she has enough for a free state.

I hope Mr. Lincoln is satisfied with my answer; and now I would like to get his answer to his own interrogatory—whether or not he will vote to admit Kansas before she has the requisite population. I want to know whether he will vote to admit Oregon before that territory has the requisite population. Mr. Trumbull will not, and the same reason that commits Mr. Trumbull against the admission of Oregon, commits him against Kansas, even if she should apply for admission as a free state. If there is any sincerity, any truth in the argument of Mr. Trumbull in the Senate, against the admission of Oregon because she had not 93,420 people, although her population was larger than that of Kansas, he stands pledged against the admission of both Oregon and Kansas until they have 93,420 inhabitants. I would like Mr. Lincoln to answer this question. I would like him to take his own medicine. If he differs with Mr. Trumbull, let him answer his argument against the admission of Oregon, instead of poking questions at me.

The next question propounded to me by Mr. Lincoln is, Can the people of a territory in any lawful way, against the wishes of any citizen of the United States, exclude slavery from their limits prior to the formation of a state constitution? I answer emphatically, as Mr. Lincoln has heard me answer a hundred times from every stump in Illinois, that in my opinion the people of a territory can, by lawful means, exclude slavery from their limits prior to the formation of a state constitution. Mr. Lincoln knew that I had answered that question over and over again. He heard me argue the Nebraska bill on that principle all over the state in 1854, in 1855, and in 1856, and he has no excuse for pretending to be in doubt as to my position on that question. It matters not what way the Supreme Court may hereafter decide as to the abstract question whether slavery may or may not go into a territory under the constitution, the people have the lawful means to introduce it or exclude it as they please, for the reason that slavery cannot exist a day or an hour anywhere, unless it is supported by local police regulations. Those police regulations can only be established by the local legislature; and if the people are opposed to slavery, they will elect representatives to that body who will by unfriendly legislation effectually prevent the introduction of it into their midst. If, on the contrary, they are for it, their legislation will favor its extension. Hence, no matter what the decision of the Supreme Court may be on that abstract question, still the right of the people to make a slave territory or a free territory is perfect and complete under the Nebraska bill. I hope Mr. Lincoln deems my answer satisfactory on that point.

In this connection, I will notice the charge which he has introduced in relation to Mr. Chase's amendment. I thought that I had chased that amendment out of Mr. Lincoln's brain at Ottawa; but it seems that it still haunts his imagination, and he is not yet satisfied. I had supposed that he would be ashamed to press that question further. He is a lawyer, and has been a member of Congress, and has occupied his time and amused you by telling you about parliamentary proceedings. He ought to have known better than to try to palm off his miserable impositions upon this intelligent audience. The Nebraska bill provided that the legislative power and authority of the said territory should extend to all rightful subjects of legislation consistent with the organic act and the Constitution of the United States. It did not make any exception as to slavery, but gave all the power that it was possible for Congress to give, without violating the Constitution, to the Territorial Legislature, with no exception or limitation on the subject of slavery at all. The language of that bill which I have quoted, gave the full power and the full authority over the subject of; slavery, affirmatively and negatively, to introduce it or exclude it, so far as the Constitution of the United States would permit. What more could Mr. Chase give by his amendment? Nothing. He offered his amendment for the identical purpose for which Mr. Lincoln is using it—to enable demagogues in the country to try and deceive the people.

His amendment was to this effect. It provided that the Legislature should have the power to exclude slavery; and General Cass suggested, "Why not give the power to introduce as well as exclude?" The answer was, They have the power already in the bill to do both. Chase was afraid his amendment would be adopted if he put the alternative proposition, and so make it fair both ways, but would not yield. He offered it for the purpose of having it rejected. He offered it, as he has himself avowed over and over again, simply to make capital out of it for the stump. He expected that it would be capital for small politicians in the country, and that they would make an effort to deceive the people with it; and he was not mistaken, for Lincoln is carrying out the plan admirably. Lincoln knows that the Nebraska bill, without Chase's amendment, gave all the power which the Constitution would permit. Could Congress confer any more? Could Congress go beyond the Constitution of the country? We gave all—a full grant, with no exception in regard to slavery one way or the other. We left that question as we left all others, to be decided by the people for themselves, just as they please. I will not occupy my time on this question. I have argued it before, all over Illinois. I have argued it in this beautiful City of Freeport; I have argued it in the North, the South, the East, and the West, avowing the same sentiments and the same principles. I have not been afraid to avow my sentiments up here for fear I would be trotted down into Egypt.

The third question which Mr. Lincoln presented is, "If the Supreme Court of the United States shall decide that a state of this Union cannot exclude slavery from its own limits will I submit to it? I am amazed that Lincoln should ask such a question. ("A schoolboy knows better.") Yes, a schoolboy does know better. Mr. Lincoln's object is to cast an imputation upon the Supreme Court. He knows that there never was but one man in America claiming any degree of intelligence or decency, who ever for a moment pretended such a thing. It is true that the Washington Union, in an article published on the 17th of last December, did put forth that doctrine, and I denounce the article on the floor of the Senate, in a speech which Mr. Lincoln now pretends was against the President. The Union had claimed that slavery had a right to go into the free states, and that any provision in the Constitution or laws of the free states to the contrary were null and void. I denounced it in the Senate, as I said before, and I was the first man who did. Lincoln's friends, Trumbull, and Seward, and Hale, and Wilson, and the whole black republican side of the Senate, were silent. They left it to me to denounce.

And what was the reply made to me on that occasion? Mr. Tooms, of Georgia, got up and undertook to lecture me on the ground that I ought not to have deemed the article worthy of notice, and ought not to have replied to it; that there was not one man, woman, or child south of the Potomac, in any slave state, who did not repudiate any such pretension. Mr. Lincoln knows that reply was made on the spot, and yet now he asks this question. He might as well ask me, Suppose Mr. Lincoln should steal a horse, would I sanction it, and would be as genteel in me to ask him, in the event he stole a horse, what ought to be done with him. He casts an imputation upon the Supreme Court of the United States, by supposing that they would violate the Constitution of the United States. I tell him that such a thing is not possible. It would be an act of moral treason that no man on the bench could ever descend to. Mr. Lincoln himself would never in his partisan feelings so far forget what was right as to be guilty of such an act.

The fourth question of Mr. Lincoln is, Are you in favor of acquiring additional territory, in disregard as to how such acquisition may affect the Union on the slavery question? This question is very ingeniously and cunningly put.

The black republican creed lays it down expressly that under no circumstances shall we acquire any more territory, unless slavery is first prohibited in the country. I ask Mr. Lincoln whether he is in favor of that proposition. Are you (addressing Mr. Lincoln) opposed to the acquisition of any more territory, under any circumstances, unless slavery is prohibited in it? That he does not like to answer. When I ask him whether he stands up to that article in the platform of his party, he turns, Yankee fashion, and without answering it, asks me whether I am in favor of acquiring territory without regard to how it may affect the Union on the slavery question.

I answer that whenever it becomes necessary, in our growth and progress, to acquire more territory, that I am in favor of it, without reference to the question of slavery; and when we have acquired it, I will leave the people free to do as they please, either to make it slave or free territory as they prefer. It is idle to tell me or you that we have territory enough. Our fathers supposed that we had enough when our territory extended to the Mississippi River; but a few years' growth and expansion satisfied them that we needed more; and the Louisiana Territory, from the west branch of the Mississippi to the British possessions, was acquired. Then we acquired Oregon, then California and New Mexico. We have enough now for the present; but this is a young and a growing nation. It swarms as often as a hive of bees; and as new swarms are turned out each year, there must be hives in which they can gather and make their honey.

In less than fifteen years if the same progress that has distinguished this country for the last fifteen years continues, every foot of vacant land between this and the Pacific Coast, owned by the United States, will be occupied. Will you not continue to increase at the end of fifteen years as well as now? I tell you, increase, and multiply, and expand, is the law of this nation's existence. You cannot limit this great Republic by mere boundary lines, saying, "Thus far shalt thou go, and no further." Any one of you gentlemen might as well say to a son twelve years old that he is big enough, and must not grow any larger; and in order to prevent his growth, put a hoop around him to keep him to his present size. What would be the result? Either the hoop must burst and be rent asunder, or the child must die. So it would be with this great nation. With our natural increase, growing with a rapidity unknown in any other part of the globe, with the tide of emigration that is fleeing from despotism in the old world to seek refuge in our own, there is a constant torrent pouring into this country that requires more land, more territory upon which to settle; and just as fast as our interest and our destiny require additional territory in the North, in the South, or in the islands of the ocean, I am for it; and when we acquire it, will leave the people, according to the Nebraska bill, free to do as they please on the subject of slavery and every other question.

I trust now that Mr. Lincoln will deem himself answered on his four points. He racked his brain so much in devising these four questions that he exhausted himself, and had not strength enough to invent the others. As soon as he is able to hold a council with his advisers, Lovejoy, Farnsworth, and Fred Douglass, he will frame and propound others. You black republicans who say good, I have no doubt think that they are all good men.

I have reason to recollect that some people in this country think that Fred Douglass is a very good man. The last time I came here to make a speech, while talking from the stand to you, people of Freeport, as I am doing today, I saw a carriage—and a magnificent one it was,—drive up and take a position on the outside of the crowd; a beautiful young lady was sitting on the box-seat, whilst Fred Douglass and her mother reclined inside, and the owner of the carriage acted as driver. I saw this in your own town. All I have to say of it is this, that if you, black republicans, think that the negro ought to be on a social equality with your wives and daughters, and ride in a carriage with your wife, whilst you drive the team, you have a perfect right to do so.

I am told that one of Fred Douglass's kinsman, another rich black negro, is now traveling in this part of the state, making speeches for his friend Lincoln as the champion of black men. All I have to say on that subject is, that those of you who believe that the negro is your equal and ought to be on an equality with you socially, politically, and legally, have a right to entertain those opinions, and of course will vote for Mr. Lincoln.

I have a word to say on Mr. Lincoln's answer to the interrogatories contained in my speech at Ottawa, and which he has pretended to reply to here today. Mr. Lincoln makes a great parade of the fact that I quoted a platform as having been adopted by the black republican party at Springfield in 1854, which, it turns out, was adopted at another place. Mr. Lincoln loses sight of the thing itself in his ecstasies over the mistake I made in stating the place where it was done. He think that that platform was not adopted on the right "spot."

When I put the direct questions to Mr. Lincoln to ascertain whether he now stands pledged to that creed,—to the unconditional repeal of the Fugitive-Slave law, a refusal to admit any more slave states into the Union, even if the people want them, a determination to apply the Wilmot proviso, not only to all the territory, we now have, but all that we may hereafter acquire,— he refused to answer; and his followers say, in excuse, that the resolutions upon which I based my interrogatories were not adopted at the "right spot." Lincoln and his political friends are great on "spots." In Congress, as a representative of this state, he declared the Mexican war to be unjust and infamous, and would not support it, or acknowledge his own country to be right in the contest, because he said that American blood was not shed on American soil in the "right spot." And now he cannot answer the questions I put to him at Ottawa because the resolutions I read were not adopted at the "right spot." It may be possible that I was led into an error as to the spot on which the resolutions I then read were proclaimed, but I was not, and am not, in error as to the fact of their forming the basis of the creed of the republican party when that party was first organized.

I will state to you the evidence I had, and upon which I relied for my statement that the resolutions in question were adopted at Springfield on the 5th of October, 1854. Although I was aware that such resolutions had been passed in this district, and nearly all the Northern Congressional districts and County Conventions, I had not noticed whether or not they had been adopted by any state convention. In 1856, a debate arose in Congress between Major Thomas L. Harris, of the Springfield district, and Mr. Norton, of the Joliet district, on political matters connected with our state, in the course of which, Major Harris quoted those resolutions as having been passed by the first Republican State Convention that ever assembled in Illinois. I knew that Major Harris was remarkable for his accuracy, that he was a very conscientious and sincere man, and I also noticed that Norton did not question the accuracy of this statement. I therefore took it for granted that it was so; and the other day when I concluded to use the resolutions at Ottawa, I wrote to Charles L. Lanphier, editor of the State Register at Springfield, calling his attention to them, telling him that I had been informed that Major Harris was lying sick at Springfield, and desiring him to call upon him and ascertain all the facts concerning the resolutions, the time and the place where they were adopted. In reply. Mr. Lanphier sent me two copies of his paper, which I have here. The first is a copy of the State Register, published at Springfield, Mr. Lincoln's own town, on the 16th of October, 1854, only eleven days after the adjournment of the convention, from which I desire to read the following:

"During late discussions in this city, Lincoln made a speech, to which Judge Douglas replied. In Lincoln's speech he took the broad ground that, according to the Declaration of Independence, the whites and blacks are equal. From this he drew the conclusion, which he several times repeated, that the white man had no right to pass laws for the government of the black man without the nigger's consent. This speech of Lincoln's was heard and applauded by all the Abolitionists assembled in Springfield. So soon as Mr. Lincoln was done speaking, Mr. Codding arose, and requested all the delegates to the Black Republican

Convention to withdraw into the Senate chamber. They did so; and after long deliberation, they laid down the following abolition platform as the platform on which they stood. We call the particular attention of all our readers to it."

Then follows the identical platform, word for word, which I read at Ottawa. Now, that was published in Mr. Lincoln's own town, eleven days after the convention was held, and it has remained on record up to this day never contradicted.

When I quoted the resolutions at Ottawa and questioned Mr. Lincoln in relation to them, he said that his name was on the committee that reported them, but he did not serve, nor did he think he served, because he was, or thought he was, in Tazewell County at the time the convention was in session. He did not deny that the resolutions were passed by the Springfield convention. He did not know better, and evidently thought that they were; but afterward his friends declared that they had discovered that they varied in some respects from the resolutions passed by that convention. I have shown you that I had good evidence for believing that the resolutions had been passed at Springfield. Mr. Lincoln ought to have known better; but not a word is said about his ignorance on the subject, whilst I, notwithstanding the circumstances, am accused of forgery.

Now, I will show you that if I made a mistake as to the place where these resolutions were adopted,—and when I get down to Springfield I will investigate the matter, and see whether or not I have,—that the principles they anunciate were adopted as the Black Republican platform, in the various counties and Congressional Districts throughout the north end of the state in 1854. This platform was adopted in nearly every county that gave a Black Republican majority for the Legislature in that year, and here is a man who knows as well as any living man that it was the creed of the Black Republican party at that time. I would be willing to call Denio as a witness, or any other honest man belonging to that party. I will now read the resolutions adopted at the Rockford convention on the 30th of August, 1854, which nominated Washburne for Congress. You elected him on the following platform:

"Resolved, That the continued and increasing aggressions of slavery in our country are destructive of the best rights of a free people, and that such aggressions cannot be successfully resisted without the united political action of all good men.

"Resolved, That the citizens of the United States hold in their hands peaceful, constitutional, and efficient remedy against the encroachments of the slave power,—the ballot-box; and if that remedy against the encroachments of the slave power is boldly applied,—liberty and eternal justice will be established.

"Resolved, That we accept this issue forced upon us by the

slave power, and, in defense of freedom, will co-operate and be known as republicans, pledged to the accomplishment of the following purposes:

"To bring the administration of the Government back to the control of first principles; to restore Kansas and Nebraska to the position of free territories; to repeal and entirely abrogate the Fugitive-Slave law; to restrict slavery to those states in which it exists; to prohibit the admission of any more slave states into the Union; to exclude slavery from all the Territories over which the General Government has exclusive jurisdiction; and to resist the acquisition of any more territories, unless the introduction of slavery therein forever shall have been prohibited.

"Resolved, That in furtherance of these principles we will use such constitutional and lawful means as shall seem best adapted to their accomplishment, and that we will support no man for office under the general or state Government who is not positively committed to the support of these principles, and whose personal character and conduct is not a guarantee that he is reliable, and shall abjure all party allegiance and ties.

"Resolved, That we cordially invite persons of all former political parties whatever, in favor of the object expressed in the above resolutions, to unite with us in carrying them into effect."

Well, you think that is a very good platform, do you not? If you do, if you approve it now, and think it is all right, you will not join with those men who say that I libel you by calling these your principles, will you? Now, Mr. Lincoln complains; Mr. Lincoln charges that I did you and him injustice by saying that this was the platform of your party. I am told that Washburne made a speech at Galena last night, in which he abused me awfully for bringing to light this platform, on which he was elected to Congress. He thought that you had forgotten it, as he and Mr. Lincoln desires to. He did not deny but that you had adopted it, and that he had subscribed to and was pledged by it, but he did not think it was fair to call it up and remind the people that it was their platform.

But I am glad to find that you are more honest in your abolitionism than your leaders, by avowing that it is your platform, and right in your opinion.

In the adoption of that platform, you not only declared that you would resist the admission of any more slave states, and work for the repeal of the Fugitive-Slave law, but you pledged yourselves not to vote for any man for state or federal offices who was not committed to these principles. You were thus committed. Similar resolutions to those were adopted in your county convention here, and now with your admissions that they are your platform and embody your sentiments now as they did then, what do you think of Mr. Lincoln, your candidate for the

United States Senate, who is attempting to dodge the responsibility of this platform, because it was not adopted in the right spot. I thought that was adopted in Springfield; but it turns out it was not, that it was adopted at Rockford, and in the various counties which comprise this Congressional District. When I get into the next district, I will show that the same platform responsibility of it upon the back of the Black Republican party throughout the state.

A Voice.—Couldn't you modify, and call it brown?

Mr. Douglas.—Not a bit. I thought that you were becoming a little brown when your members in Congress voted for the Crittenden-Montgomery bill; but since you have backed out from that position and gone back to abolitionism you are black, and not brown.

Gentlemen, I have shown you what your platform was in 1854. You still adhere to it. The same platform was adopted by nearly all the counties where the Black Republican party had a majority in 1854. I wish now to call your attention to the action of your representatives in the Legislature when they assembled together at Springfield. In the first place, you must remember that this was the organization of a new party. It is so declared in the resolutions themselves, which say that you are going to dissolve all old party ties and call the new party republican. The old whig party was to have its throat cut from ear to ear, and the democratic party was to be annihilated and blotted out of existence, whilst in lieu of these parties the Black Republican party was to be organized on this abolition platform. You know who the chief leaders were in breaking up and destroying these two great parties. Lincoln on the one hand, and Trumbull on the other, being disappointed politicians, and having retired or been driven to obscurity by an outraged constituency because of their political sins, formed a scheme to abolitionize the two parties, and lead the old line whigs and old line democrats captive, bound hand and foot, into the abolition camp. Giddings, Chase, Fred Douglass, and Lovejoy were here to christen them whenever they were brought in. Lincoln went to work to dissolve the old line whig party. Clay was dead; and although the sod was not yet green on his grave, this man undertook to bring into disrepute those great compromise measures of 1850, with which Clay and Webster were identified.

Up to 1854 the old whig party and the democratic party had stood on a common platform so far as this slavery question was concerned. You whigs and we democrats differed about the bank, the tariff, distribution, the specie circular, and the sub-treasury, but we agreed on this slavery question, and the true mode of preserving the peace and harmony of the Union. The compromise measures of 1850 were introduced by Clay, were defended by Webster, and supported by Cass, and were approved by Fillmore, and sanctioned by the national men of both parties. They constituted a common plank upon which both whigs and democrats stood. In 1852 the whig party, in its last National Convention at Baltimore, indorsed and approved these measures of Clay, and so did the National Convention of the democratic party held that same year. Thus the old line whigs and the old line democrats stood pledged to the great principle of self-government, which guarantees to the people of each territory the right to decide the slavery question for themselves. In 1854, after the death of Clay and Webster, Mr. Lincoln, on the part of the whigs, understook to abolitionize the whig party, by dissolving it, transferring the members into the abolition camp, and making them train under Giddings, Fred Douglass, Lovejoy, Chase, Farnsworth, and other abolition leaders. Trumbull undertook to dissolve the democratic party by taking old democrats into the abolition camp. Mr. Lincoln was aided in his efforts by many leading whigs throughout the state, your members of Congress, Mr. Washburne, being one of the most active. Trumbull was aided by many renegades from the democratic party, among whom were John Wentworth, Tom Turner, and others, with whom you are familiar.

When the bargain between Lincoln and Trumbull was completed for abolitionizing the whig and democratic parties, they "spread" over the state, Lincoln still pretending to be an old line whig, in order to "rope in" the whigs, and Trumbull pretending to be as good a democrat as he ever was, in order to coax the democrats over into the abolition ranks. They played the part that "decoy ducks" play down on the Potomac River. In that part of the country they make artificial ducks, and put them on the water in places where the wild ducks are to be found, for the purpose of decoying them. Well, Lincoln and Trumbull played the part of these "decoy ducks," and deceived enough old line whigs and old line democrats to elect a black republican Legislature. When that Legislature met, the first thing it did was to elect as Speaker of the House the very man who is now boasting that he wrote the abolition platform on which Lincoln will not stand.

It has been published to the world and satisfactorily proven that there was, at the time the alliance was made between Trumbull and Lincoln to abolitionize the two parties, an agreement that Lincoln should take Shield's place in the United States Senate, and Trumbull should have mine so soon as they could conveniently get rid of me. When Lincoln was beaten for Shield's place, in a manner I will refer to in a few minutes, he felt very sore and restive; his friends grumbled, and some of them came out and charged that the most infamous treachery had been practiced against him; that the bargain was that Lincoln was to have had Shields' place, and Trumbull was to have waited for mine, but that Trumbull, having the control of a few abolitionized democrats, he prevented them from voting for Lincoln, thus keeping him within a few votes of an election until he succeeded in forcing the party to drop him and elect Trumbull. Well, Trumbull having cheated Lincoln, his friends made a fuss, and in order to keep them and Lincoln quiet, the party was obliged to come forward, in advance, at the last state election, and make a pledge that they would go for Lincoln and nobody else. Lincoln could not be silenced in any other way.

Now, there are a great many black republicans of you who do not know this thing was done. I wish to remind you that while Mr. Lincoln was speaking there was not a democrat vulgar enough to interrupt him. But I know that the shoe is pinching you. I am clinching Lincoln now, and you are scared to death for the result. I have seen this thing before. I have seen men make appointments for joint discussions, and the moment their man has been heard, try to interrupt and prevent a fair hearing of the other side. I have seen your mobs before, and defy your wrath. My friends, do not cheer, for I need my whole time. The object of the opposition is to occupy my attention in order to prevent me from giving the whole evidence and nailing this double dealing on the black republican party.

As I have before said, Lovejoy demanded a declaration of principles on the part of the black republicans of the Legislature before going into an election for United States Senator. He offered the following preamble and resolutions which I hold in my hand:

"Whereas, Human slavery is a violation of the principles of natural and revealed rights; and whereas the fathers of the Revolution, fully imbued with the spirit of the principles, declared freedom to be the inalienable birthright of all men; and whereas the preamble to the Constitution of the United States avers that that instrument was ordained to establish justice and secure the blessings of liberty to ourselves and our posterity; and whereas, in furtherance of the above principles, slavery was forever prohibited in the old Northwest Territory, and more recently in all that territory lying west and north of the State of Missouri, by the Act of the Federal Government; and whereas, the repeal of the prohibition last referred to was contrary to the wishes of the people of Illinois, a violation of an implied compact long deemed sacred by the citizens of the United States, and a wide departure from the uniform action of the General Government in relation to the extension of slavery, therefore,

"Resolved, by the House of Representatives, the Senate concurring therein, That our Senators in Congress be instructed, and our Representatives requested, to introduce, if not otherwise introduced, and to vote for, a bill to restore such prohibition to the aforesaid territories, and also to extend a similar prohibition to all territory which now belongs to the United States, or which may hereafter come under their jurisdiction.

"Resolved, That our Senators in Congress be instructed, and our Representatives requested, to vote against the admission of any state into the Union, the Constitution of which does not prohibit slavery, whether territory out of which such state may have been formed shall have been acquired by conquest, treaty, purchase, or from original territory of the United States.

"Resolved, That our Senators in Congress be instructed, and our Representatives requested, to introduce and vote for, a bill to repeal an act entitled 'an Act respecting fugitives from justice and persons escaping from the service of their masters,' and, failing in that, for such a modification of it as shall secure the right of habeas corpus and trial by jury before the regularly constituted authorities of the state, to all persons claimed as owing service or labor."

Those resolutions were introduced by Mr. Lovejoy immediately preceding the election of Senator. They declared, first, that the Wilmot Proviso must be applied to all territory north of 36° 30'. Secondly, that it must be applied to all territory south of 36° 30'. Thirdly, that it must be applied to all the territory now owned by the United States; and finally, that it must be applied to all territory hereafter to be acquired by the United States. The next resolution declares that no more slave states shall be admitted into this Union under any circumstances whatever, no matter whether they are formed out of territory now owned by us or that we may hereafter acquire, by treaty, by Congress, or in any manner whatever. The next resolution demands the unconditional repeal of the fugitive-slave law, although its unconditional repeal would leave no provision for carrying out that clause of the Constitution of the United States which guarantees the surrender of fugitives. If they could not get an unconditional repeal, they demanded that that law should be so modified as to make it as nearly useless as possible.

Now, I want to show you who voted for these resolutions. When the vote was taken on the first resolution it was decided in the affirmative—yeas, 41, nays, 32. You will find that this is a strict party vote, between the democrats on the one hand and the black republicans on the other. The point I wish to call your attention to is this: that these resolutions were adopted on the 7th day of February, and that on the 8th they went into an election for a United States Senator, and that day every man who voted for these resolutions, with but two exceptions, voted for Lincoln for the United States Senate.

On the next resolution the vote stood—yeas, 33, nays 40; and on the third resolution—yeas, 35, nays 47. I wish to impress it upon you that every man who voted for those resolutions, with but two exceptions, voted on the next day for Lincoln for United States Senator. Bear in mind that the members who thus voted for Lincoln were elected to the Legislature pledged to vote for no man for office under the state or Federal Government who was not committed to this black republican platform. They were all so pledged. Mr. Turner, who stands by me, and who then represented you, and who says that he wrote those resolutions, voted for Lincoln, when he was pledged not to do so unless Lincoln was in favor of those resolutions. I now ask Mr. Turner, did you violate your pledge in voting for Mr. Lincoln, or did he commit himself to your platform before you cast your vote for him?

I could go through the whole list of names here and show you that all the black republicans in the Legislature who voted for Mr. Lincoln had voted on the day previous for these resolutions. For instance, here are the names of Sargent and Little, of Jo Daviess and Carroll; Thomas J. Turner, of Stephenson; Lawrence, of Boone and McHenry; Swan, of Lake; Pinckney, of Ogle County; and Lyman, of Winnebago. Thus you see every member from your congressional district voted for Mr. Lincoln, and they were pledged not to vote for him unless he was committed to the doctrine of no more slave states, the prohibition of slavery in the territories, and the repeal of the fugitive-slave law. Mr. Lincoln tells you today that he is not pledged to any such doctrine. Either Mr. Lincoln was then committed to these propositions, or Mr. Turner violated his pledges to you when he voted for him. Either Lincoln was pledged to each one of those propositions, or else every black republican Representative from this congressional district violated his pledge of honor to his constituents by voting for him.

I ask you which horn of the dilemma will you take? Will you hold Lincoln up to the platform of his party, or will you accuse every Representative you had in the Legislature of violating his pledge of honor to his constituents? There is no escape for you. Either Mr. Lincoln was committed to those propositions or your members violated their faith. Take either horn of the dilemma you choose. There is no dodging the question; I want Lincoln's answer. He says he was not pledged to repeal the fugitive-slave law, that he does not quite like to do it; he will not introduce a law to repeal it, but thinks there ought to be some law; he does not tell what it ought to be; upon the whole he is altogether undecided, and don't know what to think or do. That is the substance of his answer upon the repeal of the fugitive-slave law. I put the question to him distinctly, whether he indorsed that part of the black republican platform which calls for the entire abrogation and repeal of the fugitive-slave law. He answers, No that he does not indorse that; but he does not tell what he is for, or what he will vote for. His answer is, in fact, no answer at all. Why cannot he speak out, and say what he is for, and what he will do?

In regard to there being no more slave states, he is not pledged to that. He would not like, he says, to be put in a position where he would have to vote one way or another upon that question. I pray you, do not put him in a position that would embarrass him so much. Gentlemen, if he goes to the Senate, he may be put in that position, and then which way will be vote?

A Voice.—How will you vote?

Mr. Douglas.—I will vote for the admission of just such a state as by the form of their constitution the people show they want; if they want slavery, they shall have it; if they prohibit slavery, it shall be prohibited. They can form their institutions to please themselves, subject only to the Constitution; and I, for one, stand ready to receive them into the Union. Why cannot your black republican candidates talk out as plain as that when they are questioned?

I do not want to cheat any man out of his vote. No man is deceived in regard to my principles if I have the power to express myself in terms explicit enough to convey my ideas.

Mr. Lincoln made a speech when he was nominated for the United States Senate which covers all these abolition platforms. He there lays down a proposition so broad in its abolitionism as to cover the whole ground.

"In my opinion it (the slavery agitation) will not cease until a crisis shall have been reached and passed. 'A house divided against itself cannot stand.' I believe this Government cannot endure permanently, half slave and half free. I do not expect the House to fall, but I do expect it will cease to be divided. It will become all one thing or all the other. Either the opponents of slavery will arrest the further spread of it, and place it where the public mind shall rest in the belief that it is in the course of ultimate extinction, or its advocates will push it forward till it shall become alike lawful in all the states—old as well as new, North as well as South."

There you find that Mr. Lincoln lays down the doctrine that this Union cannot endure divided as our fathers made it, with free and slave states. He says they must all become one thing, or all the other; that they must all be free or all slave, or else the Union cannot continue to exist; it being his opinion that to admit any more slave states, to continue to divide the Union into free and slave states will dissolve it. I want to know of Mr. Lincoln whether he will vote for the admission of another slave state.

He tells you the Union cannot exist unless the states are all free or all slave; he tells you that he is opposed to making them all slave and hence he is for making them all free, in order that the Union may exist; and yet he will not vote against another slave state, knowing that the Union must be dissolved if he votes for it. I ask you if that is fair dealing? The true intent and inevitable conclusion to be drawn from his first Springfield speech is, that he is opposed to the admission of any more slave states under any circumstances. If he is so opposed, why not say so? If he believes this union cannot endure divided into free and slave states, that they must all become free in order to save the Union, he is bound as an honest man to vote against any more slave states. If he believes it, he is bound to do it. Show me that it is my duty, in order to save the Union, to do a particular act and I will do it if the Constitution does not prohibit it. I am not for the dissolution of the Union under any circumstances. I will pursue no course of conduct that will give just cause for the dissolution of the Union. The hope of the friends of freedom throughout the world rests upon the perpetuity of this Union. The down-trodden and oppressed people who are suffering under European despotism all look with hope and anxiety to the American Union as the only resting place and permanent home of freedom and self-government.

Mr. Lincoln says that he believes that this Union cannot continue to endure with slave states in it, and yet he will not tell you distinctly whether he will vote for or against the admission of any more slave states, but says he would not like to be put to the test. I do not think that the people of Illinois desire a man to represent them who would not like to be put to the test on the performance of a high constitutional duty. I will retire in shame from the Senate of the United States when I am not willing to be put to the test in the performance of my duty. I have been put to severe tests. I have stood by my principles in fair weather and in foul, in sunshine and in the rain. I have defended the great principles of self-government here among you when northern sentiment ran in a torrent against me and I have defended that same great principle when southern sentiment came down like an avalanche upon me. I was not afraid of any test they put to me. I knew I was right; I knew my principles were sound; I knew that the people would see in the end that I had done right, and I knew that the God of heaven would smile upon me if I was faithful in the performance of my duty.

Mr. Lincoln makes a charge of corruption against the Supreme Court of the United States, and two Presidents of the United States, and attempts to bolster it up by saying that I did the same against the Washington Union. Suppose I did make that charge of corruption against the Washington Union, when it was true, does that justify him in making a false charge against me and others? That is the question I would put. He says that at the time the Nebraska bill was introduced, and before it was passed, there was a conspiracy between the judges of the Supreme Court, President Pierce, President Buchanan, and myself, by that bill and the decision of the court, to break down the barrier and establish slavery all over the Union.

Does he not know that that charge is historically false as against President Buchanan? He knows that Mr. Buchanan was at that time in England, representing this country with distinguished ability at the Court of St. James; that he was there for a long time before, and did not return for a year or more after. He knows that to be true, and that fact proves his charge to be false as against Mr. Buchanan. Then, again, I wish to call his attention to the fact that at the time the Nebraska bill was passed the Dred Scott case was not before the Supreme Court at all; it was not upon the docket of the Supreme Court; it had not been brought there; and the judges in all probability knew nothing of it. Thus the history of the country proves the charge to be false as against them.

As to President Pierce, his high character as a man of integrity and honor is enough to vindicate him from such a charge; and as to myself, I pronounce the charge an infamous lie, whenever and wherever made, and by whomsoever made. I am willing that Mr. Lincoln should go and rake up every public act of mine, every measure I have introduced, report I have made, speech delivered, and criticise them; but when he charges upon me a corrupt conspiracy for the purpose of perverting the institutions of the country, I brand it as it deserves. I say the history of the country proves it to be false; and that it could not have been possible at the time.

But now he tries to protect himself in this charge, because I made a charge against the Washington Union. My speech in the Senate against the Washington Union was made because it advocated a revolutionary doctrine; by declaring that the free states had not the right to prohibit slavery within their own limits. Because I made that charge against the Washington Union, Mr. Lincoln says it was a charge against Mr. Buchanan. Suppose it was: is Mr. Lincoln the peculiar defender of Mr. Buchanan?

Is he so interested in the Federal administration and so bound to it that he must jump to the rescue and defend it from every attack that I may make against it? I understand the whole thing. The Washington Union, under that most corrupt of all men, Cornelius Wendell, is advocating Mr. Lincoln's claim to the Senate. Wendell was the printer of the last black republican House of Representatives; he was a candidate before the present democratic House, but was ignominiously kicked out; and then he took the money which he had made out of the public printing by means of the black republicans, bought the Washington Union, and is now publishing it in the name of the democratic party, and advocating Mr. Lincoln's election to the Senate. Mr. Lincoln therefore considers an attack upon Wendell and his corrupt gang as a personal attack upon him. This only proves what I have charged,—that there is an alliance between Lincoln and his supporters, and the Federal office-holders of this state, and presidential aspirants out of it, to break me down at home.

Mr. Lincoln feels bound to come in to the rescue of the Washington Union. In that speech which I delivered in answer to the Washington Union, I made it distinctly against the Union, and against the Union alone. I did not choose to go beyond that. If I have occasion to attack the President's conduct, I will do it in language that will not be misunderstood. When I differed with the President, I spoke out so that you all heard me. That question passed away; it resulted in the triumph of my principle, by allowing the people to do as they please; and there is an end of the controversy. Whenever the great principle of self-government,—the right of the people to make their own Constitution, and come into the Union with slavery or without it, as they see proper,—shall again arise, you will find me standing firm in the defense of that principle, and fighting whoever fights it. If Buchanan stands, as I doubt not he will, by the recommendation contained in his message, that hereafter all state constitutions ought to be submitted to the people before the admission of the state into the Union, he will find me standing by him firmly, shoulder to shoulder, in carrying it out. I know Mr. Lincoln's object: he wants to divide the democratic party, in order that he may defeat me and get to the Senate.

Mr. Douglas' time here expired, and he stopped on the moment.

Mr. Lincoln's Rejoinder

As Mr. Lincoln arose he was greeted with vociferous cheers. He said:

My Friends—It will readily occur to you that I cannot, in half an hour, notice all the things that so able a man as Judge Douglas can say in an hour and a half, and I hope, therefore, if there be anything that he has said upon which you would like to hear something from me, but which I omit to comment upon, you will bear in mind that it would be expecting an impossibility for me to go over his whole ground. I can but take up some of the points that he has dwelt upon and employ my half hour specially on them.

The first thing I have to say to you is a word in regard to Judge Douglas' declaration about the "vulgarity and blackguardism" in the audience—that no such things, as he says, was shown by any democrat while I was speaking. Now, I only wish, by way of reply on this subject, to say that while I was speaking, I used no "vulgarity or blackguardism" toward any democrat.

Now, my friends, I come to all this long portion of the judge's speech—perhaps half of it—which he has devoted to the various resolutions and platforms that have been adopted in the different counties in the different congressional districts, and in the Illinois Legislature, which he supposes are at variance with the positions I have assumed before you today. It is true that many of these resolutions are at variance with the positions I have here assumed. All I have to ask is that we talk reasonably and rationally about it. I happen to know the judge's opinion to the contrary notwithstanding, that I have never tried to conceal my opinions, nor tried to deceive any one in reference to them. He may go and examine all the members who voted for me for United States Senator in 1855, after the election of 1854. They were pledged to certain things here at home, and were determined to have pledges from me; and if he will find any of these persons who will tell him anything inconsistent with what I say now, I will resign, or rather retire from the race, and give him no more trouble.

The plain truth is this: At the introduction of the Nebraska policy, we believed there was a new era being introduced in the history of the Republic, which tended to the spread and perpetuation of slavery. But in our opposition to that measure we did not agree with one another in everything. The people in the north end of the state were for stronger measures of opposition than we of the central and southern portions of the state, but we were all opposed to the Nebraska doctrine. We had that one feeling and that one sentiment in common. You at the north end met in your convention and passed your resolutions. We in the middle of the state and further south did not hold such conventions and pass the same resolutions, although we had in general a common view and a common sentiment. So that these meetings which the judge has alluded to, and the resolutions he has read from, were local, and did not spread over the whole state. We at last met together in 1856, from all parts of the state, and we agreed upon a common platform. You who held more extreme notions, either yielded those notions or, if not wholly yielding them, agreed to yield them practically, for the sake of embodying the opposition to the measures which the opposite party were pushing forward at that time. We met you then and if there was anything yielded, it was for practical purposes. We agreed then upon a platform for the party throughout the entire State of Illinois, and now we are all bound, as a party, to that platform. And I say here to you, if any one expects of me—in the case of my election—that I will do anything not signified by our republican platform and my answers here today, I tell you very frankly that person will be deceived.

I do not ask for the vote of any one who supposes that I have secret purposes or pledges that I dare not speak out. Cannot the judge be satisfied? If he fears, in the unfortunate case of my election, that my going to Washington will enable me to advocate sentiments contrary to those which I expressed when you voted for and elected me, I assure him that his fears are wholly needless and groundless. Is the judge really afraid of any such thing? I'll tell you what he is afraid of. He is afraid we'll all pull together. This is what alarms him more than anything else. For my part, I do hope that all of us, entertaining a common sentiment in opposition to what appears to us a design to nationalize and perpetuate slavery, will waive minor differences on questions which either belong to the dead past or the distant future, and all pull together in this struggle. What are your sentiments? If it be true on the ground which I occupy,—

JOHN HAY
Joint Author with Nicolai of the Life of Abraham Lincoln

ground which I occupy as frankly and boldly as Judge Douglas does his—my views, though partly coinciding with yours, are not as perfectly in accordance with your feelings as his are, I do say to you in all candor, go for him and not for me. I hope to deal in all things fairly with Judge Douglas, and with the people of the state, in this contest. And if I should never be elected to any office, I trust I may go down with no stain of falsehood upon my reputation, notwithstanding the hard opinions Judge Douglas chooses to entertain for me.

The judge has again addressed himself to the abolition tendencies of a speech of mine made at Springfield in June last. I have so often tried to answer what he is always saying on that melancholy theme that I almost turn with disgust from the discussion—from the repetition of an answer to it. I trust that nearly all of this intelligent audience have read that speech. If you have, I may venture to leave it to you to inspect it closely and see whether it contains any of those "bugaboos" which frighten Judge Douglas.

The judge complains that I did not fully answer his questions. If I have the sense to comprehend and answer those questions, I have done so fairly. If it can be pointed out to me how I can more fully and fairly answer him, I will do it, but I aver I have not the sense to see how it is to be done. He says I do not declare I would in any event vote for the admission of a slave state into the Union. If I have been fairly reported, he will see that I did give an explicit answer to his interrogatories; I did not merely say that I would dislike to be put to the test, but I said clearly, if I were put to the test, and a territory from which slavery had been excluded should present herself with a state constitution sanctioning slavery—a most extraordinary thing, and wholly unlikely to happen—I did not see how I could avoid voting for her admission. But he refuses to understand that I said so and he wants this audience to understand that I did not say so. Yet it will be so reported in the printed speech that he cannot help seeing it.

He says if I should vote for the admission of a slave state I would be voting for a dissolution of the Union, because I hold that the Union cannot permanently exist half slave and half free. I repeat that I do not believe this Government can endure permanently half slave and half free; yet I do not admit, nor does it at all follow, that the admission of a single slave state will permanently fix the character and establish this as a universal slave nation. The judge is very happy indeed at working up these quibbles. Before leaving the subject of answering questions, I aver as my confident belief, when you come to see our speeches in print, that you will find every question which he has asked me more fairly and boldly and fully answered than he has answered those which I put to him. Is not that so? The two speeches may be placed side by side, and I will venture to leave it to impartial judges whether his questions have not been more directly and circumstantially answered than mine.

Judge Douglas says he made a charge upon the editor of the Washington Union, alone, of entertaining a purpose to rob the states of their power to exclude slavery from their limits. I undertake to say, and I make the direct issue, that he did not make his charge against the editor of the Union alone. I will undertake to prove by the record here that he made that charge against more and higher dignitaries than the editor of the Washington Union. I am quite aware that he was shirking and dodging around the form in which he put it, but I can make it manifest that he levelled his "fatal blow" against more persons than this Washington editor. Will he dodge it now by alleging that

I am trying to defend Mr. Buchanan against the charge? Not at all. Am I not making the same charge myself? I am trying to show that you, Judge Douglas, are a witness on my side. I am not defending Buchanan, and I will tell Judge Douglas that in my opinion, when he made that charge, he had an eye farther north than he has today. He was then fighting against people who called him a black republican and an abolitionist. It is mixed all through his speech, and it is tolerably manifest that his eye was a great deal farther north than it is today. The judge says that though he made his charge, Toombs got up and declared there was not a man in the United States, except the editor of the Union, who was in favor of the doctrines put forth in that article. And thereupon I understand that the judge withdrew the charge. Although he had taken extracts from the newspaper, and then from the Lecompton Constitution, to show the existence of a conspiracy to bring about a "fatal blow," by which the states were to be deprived of the right of excluding slavery, it all went to pot as soon as Toombs got up and told him it was not true.

It reminds me of the story that John Phoenix, the California railroad surveyor, tells. He says they started out from the Plaza to the Mission of Dolores. They had two ways of determining distances. One was by a chain and pins taken over the ground. The other was by a "goit-ometer,"—an invention of his own,—a three legged instrument with which he computed a series of triangles between the points. At night he turned to the chainman to ascertain what distance they had come, and found that by some mistake he had merely dragged the chain over the ground without keeping any record. By the "goit-ometer" he found he had made ten miles. Being skeptical about this, he asked a drayman who was passing how far it was to the Plaza. The drayman replied it was just half a mile, and the surveyor put it down in his book—just as Judge Douglas says, after he had made his calculations and computations, he took Toomb's statement. I have no doubt that after Judge Douglas had made his charge, he was as easily satisfied about its truth as the surveyor was of the drayman's statement of the distance to the Plaza. Yet it is a fact that the man who put forth all that matter which Douglas deemed a "fatal blow" at state sovereignty, was elected by the democrats as public printer.

Now, gentlemen, you may take Judge Douglas' speech of March 22d, 1858, beginning about the middle of page 21, and reading to the bottom of page 24, and you will find the evidence on which I say that he did not make his charge against the editor of the Union alone. I cannot stop to read it, but I will give it to the reporters. Judge Douglas said:—

"Mr. President, you here find several distinct propositions advanced by the Washington Union editorially, and apparently authoritatively, and every man who questions any of them is denounced as an abolitionist, a free-soiler, a fanatic. The propositions are, first, that the primary object of all government at its original institution is the protection of persons and property; second, that the Constitution of the United States declares that the citizens of each state shall be entitled to all the privileges and immunities of citizens in the several states; and that, therefore, thirdly, all state laws, whether organic or otherwise, which prohibit the citizens of one state from settling in another with their slave property, and especially declaring it forfeited, are direct violations of the original intention of the Government and Constitution of the United States; and, fourth, that the emancipation of the slaves of the northern states was a gross outrage on the rights of property, inasmuch as it was involuntarily done on the part of the owner.

"Remember that this article was published in the Union on the 17th of November, and on the eighteenth appeared the first article, giving the adhesion of the Union to the Lecompton constitution. It was in these words:—

"'Kansas and Her Constitution.—The vexed question is settled. The problem is solved. The dead point of danger is passed. All serious trouble to Kansas affairs is over and gone—'

"And a column, nearly, of the same sort. Then, when you come to look into the Lecompton constitution, you find the same doctrine incorporated in it which was put forth editorially in the Union. What is it?

"'Article 7, Section 1. The right of property is before and higher than any constitutional sanction; and the right of the owner of a slave to such slave and its increase is the same and as invariable as the right of the owner of any property whatever.'

"Then in the schedule is a provision that the Constitution may be amended after 1864 by a two-thirds vote.

"'But no alteration shall be made to affect the right of property in the ownership of slaves.'

"It will be seen by these clauses in the Lecompton constitution that they are identical in spirit with this authoritative article in the Washington Union of the day previous to its indorsement of this constitution.

"When I say that article in the Union of the 17th of November, followed by the glorification of the Lecompton constitution on the 18th of November and this clause in the constitution asserting the doctrine that a state has no right to prohibit slavery within its limits, I saw that there was a fatal blow being struck at the sovereignty of the states of the Union."

Here, he says, "Mr. President, you here find several distinct propositions advanced boldly, and apparently authoritatively."

By whose authority, Judge Douglas? Again, he says in another place, "It will be seen by these clauses in the Lecompton constitution that they are identical in spirit with this authoritative article." Who do you mean to say authorized the publication of these articles? He knows that the Washington Union is considered the organ of the administration. I demand of Judge Douglas by whose authority he meant to say those articles were published, if not by the authority of the President of the United States and his cabinet? I defy him to show whom he referred to, if not to these high functionaries in the Federal Government. More than this, he says the articles in that paper and the provisions of the Lecompton constitution are "identical," and, being identical, he argues that the authors are co-operating and conspiring together. He does not use the word "conspiring," but what other construction can you put upon it? He winds up with this:—

"When I saw that article in the Union of the 17th of November, followed by the glorification of the Lecompton constitution on the 18th of November, and this clause in the constitution asserting the doctrine that a state has no right to prohibit slavery within its limits, I saw that there was a fatal blow being struck at the sovereignty of the states of this Union."

I ask him if all this fuss was made over the editor of this newspaper. It would be a terribly "fatal blow" indeed which a single man could strike, when no President, no cabinet officer, no member of Congress, was giving strength and efficiency to the movement. Out of respect to Judge Douglas's good sense I must believe he did not manufacture his idea of the "fatal" character of that blow out of such a miserable scapegrace as he represents that editor to be. But the Judge's eye is farther south now. Then, it was very peculiarly and decidedly north. His hope rested on the idea of enlisting the great "black republican" party, and making it the tail of his new kite. He knows he was then expecting from day to day to turn republican, and place himself at the head of our organization. He has found that these despised "black republicans" estimate him by a standard which he was taught them only too well. Hence he is crawling back into his old camp, and you will find him eventually installed in full fellowship among those whom he was then battling, and with whom he now pretends to be at such fearful variance.

CHAPTER XXIII

THE ILLINOIS CENTRAL RAILROAD

CANAL OR RAILROAD—WHOSE HONOR—THE FIRST CHARTER—THE SECOND CHARTER—THE THIRD CHARTER—THE FOURTH CHARTER—A CONTENTION—FINAL PASSAGE—THE GIFT—THE MEMORIAL—THE FIFTH CHARTER—WORK BEGUN—FOREIGN OWNERSHIP—COST OF ROAD—THE CHARTER—THE INCOME—A CONTENTION.

The first railroads in the United States were of the tramway type. They were constructed for the transportation of heavy freight or in construction work. One of the first was a road for the removal of earth in the digging of the Delaware and Chesapeake Canal, near Philadelphia. The Mohawk and Hudson River road was chartered in 1826. A road was constructed in Massachusetts to haul granite from the quarry to the Neponset River as early as 1826. It was operated by horse power. As many as a dozen or more roads were begun and some completed in the East between 1825 and 1835.

CANAL OR RAILROAD

The earliest reference to railroads to be found upon the statute books of Illinois is an act passed by the Legislature on January 28, 1831, for the survey of a canal or a railroad in St. Clair County. The proposed road was to extend from the bluffs, along the east side of the American Bottom, to the Mississippi River opposite St. Louis. The purpose of the road was to transport coal from the bluffs across the bottom lands to the river. A commission was appointed to look into the feasibility of a road or canal at this place. Nothing immediate came out of this movement, but five years later John Reynolds, who was later governor, built a road from the bluffs to the river, a distance of some six or seven miles. This road was run by mule power.

On January 19, 1825, the general assembly created the "Illinois and Michigan Canal Association" with a capital stock of $1,000,000. The company was to build a canal from the lake to the headwaters of the Illinois River, and was to receive any land donations which the general Government should make for the building of such canal. The Hon. Daniel P. Cook, Illinois representative in Congress, raised serious objections to the act giving any grants of land which Congress might make to a private corporation. It so happened that just at this time Mr. Cook had a good chance of securing a liberal grant of land for the canal with the understanding that the state would construct and own the same. Mr. Cook put forth an address to the people of Illinois in which he showed them how difficult it would be to obtain the grant if Congress should know that it would be given over to a private corporation. No stock was ever subscribed to the $1,000,000 capital and the charter was repealed by consent of those in whose favor it was granted. The state now assumed the responsibility for the building of the canal. A memorial was addressed to Congress pointing out the wonderful advantages which would come to the whole people as well as to the people of Illinois from a canal reaching from the lake to the navigable waters of the Illinois. This memorial, together with heroic work done by Mr. Cook in the House and the good work done by Senators Kane and Thomas, won Congress over to the cause of the Illinois and Michigan Canal. Congress by act of March 2, 1827, granted to the State of Illinois, "for the purpose of aiding her in opening a canal to connect the waters of the Illinois River with those of Lake Michigan," the alternate sections of the public lands on each side of the canal for a distance of five miles and extending the entire length of the canal when constructed. The grant of the land was specifically for the building of a canal and could not be used for any other purpose. The grant contained 224,322 acres of land and was subject to the disposal for the purpose of constructing the canal.

In 1829 the Legislature organized a new board of canal commissioners and authorized them to examine into the route, cost, etc., of the canal. Because of "hard times" there was not much done and there grew up a sentiment in favor of changing the plan of building a canal to that of building a railroad. An amendatory act to that of 1829 passed in 1831, February 15, authorized the board to lay out the towns of Ottawa and Chicago and to sell town lots in those two young cities and with the money to proceed with the work of the canal. The income from the sale of the lots in Ottawa and Chicago amounted to $18,924.83. A new engineer, Mr. James M. Bucklin, was employed and he proceeded to make new estimates of the cost of the canal. The estimate ran into millions instead of into hundreds of thousands, as was formerly reported. In 1833 the new board reported to the Legislature that Mr. Bucklin's estimate for the cost of the canal was $4,043,386.50 and that a railroad could be constructed for $1,052,488.19. The cost of making the two surveys and estimates by Mr. Bucklin was $16,974.83. The report was unsatisfactory and very discouraging and by an act of March 1, 1833, the board of commissioners was abolished and all records and property was transferred to the treasurer of the State of Illinois.

The report by Mr. Bucklin revealed the fact that a high level canal could not be supplied with water in the dry season without an expense beyond the ability of the state to meet in construction. All minds then turned to the construction of a railroad instead of the canal. Now, however, arose new trouble. The grant of land could not be used for a railroad, so a memorial was presented to Congress asking that the state might have the option of using the grant for the construction of the railroad or canal as the Legislature might direct. But no actual steps were taken to build the railroad and public sentiment now shifted to the canal which was eventually constructed.

Thus the state's first venture in railroad building came to naught. From this time till the great improvement schemes were launched in 1837 there was little done in the matter of railroad building in Illinois. In 1832 the Legislature chartered the "Springfield and Alton Turnpike Road Company." The road was to extend from Springfield to Alton and thence to Illinoistown, and was authorized to "transport, take, and carry property and persons upon the same by the power and force of steam, of animals or of any mechanical or other power, or of any combination of them which the said corporation may choose to employ.

Whose Honor

Alexander M. Jenkins, a representative in the lower branch of the Legislature, in 1832-4, was speaker of that body. While serving this term he suggested that a survey be made of a central railroad from Cairo to Peru. There is no record of any favorable action upon the suggestion. On October 16, 1835, Judge Sidney Breese addressed a letter to John Y. Sawyer, Esq., a judge on the bench of the first judicial circuit, in which he outlines a plan for a central railroad from Cairo north to the western terminus of the Illinois and Michigan Canal. Judge Breese says the plan was suggested to him by Mr. William Smith Waite, an intelligent and enthusiastic advocate of railroads in Illinois.

The plan was to build a railroad from the western terminus of the Illinois and Michigan canal directly south along the third principal meridian to the junction of the Ohio with the Mississippi. Let the credit of the state be pledged for the completion of both the canal and the railroad. Judge Breese, in the letter, suggested that the general government might be induced to give liberal portions of the unappropriated land along the contemplated road as it had for the canal. The writer was of the opinion that "Posterity will have no cause of complaint if we do leave them a debt to pay, when at the same time we leave them the most ample means for discharging it." At that time the work on the canal had been begun and so he says—"Let the expenditures on both works commence at the same time and be prosecuted with equal energy." It was not then known just where the western terminus of the Illinois and Michigan canal would be, it was suggested in this letter that the counties to be passed through might be, beginning at the south, Alexander, Union, Jackson, Perry, Washington, Clinton, Bond, Fayette, Shelby, Macon, McLean, and LaSalle. The towns on the line would be Jonesboro, Brownsville, Pinckneyville, Nashville, Carlyle, Vandalia, Decatur, Bloomington and on to Ottawa, or La Salle, or Peru. Taking the estimated cost of the Alton and Springfield road as data, which is on an average a fraction over $7,000 per mile, the cost of the road would be not to exceed $2,500,000."—they who shall be instrumental in its commencement and completion will have erected for themselves a monument more durable than marble and throughout all future time will receive, as they well deserve, the grateful thanks of a generous people."

The First Charter

Judge Breese's letter was published and soon meetings were being held for the purpose of creating sentiment. The Legislature was called in extra session December 7, 1835, for the purpose of redistricting the state as the census of 1835 showed an increase in population. On January 18, 1836, the Legislature passed an act incorporating an "Illinois Central Railroad Company." There were fifty-eight incorporators and among these was Sidney Breese. The charter authorized the incorporators to build a railroad from near the mouth of the Ohio River to the Illinois River near the termination of the Illinois and Michigan. The evident purpose of this company was eventually to establish a rail communication between the lakes and the gulf. The charter provided that no other railroad should be authorized within ten miles of this central road for a period of fifty years. Alexander M. Jenkins, who probably was the one who first conceived a central railroad, resigned the office of lieutenant-governor of Illinois to accept the presidency of the first Illinois Central Railroad Company. Some money was expended on this road but the whole enterprise was swallowed up in the great internal improvement schemes of 1837.

The Second Charter

The great Internal Improvement Convention which met in Vandalia in the fall of 1836 to urge the Legislature to undertake the building of canals, railroads, and the improvement of rivers has been described in a previous chapter. The work of the Legislative session of 1836-7 has also been considered. In this legislation there were six roads and their branches provided for. Of these, the road from Cairo to the Illinois River and thence to Galena was the most important. For the building of this road

$3,500,000 was appropriated. The road was 300.99 miles from Cairo to LaSalle, and from LaSalle to Galena 146.73 miles. The estimated cost of $3,500,000 would allow about $7,600 per mile. Mr. Ackerman, the president of the Illinois Central in 1884, says that the 700 miles of the Illinois Central including the branch from Centralia to Chicago, cost $25,000,000. This would make the cost per mile a little in excess of $35,000.

The story of the collapse of the improvement schemes has been told. Enormous quantities of money had been spent on the dozen or more objects of expenditure. The Central road received its share.

The internal improvement system was abandoned by acts of the Legislature in February, 1840. Considerable amount of work in the way of excavations and embankments had been done on all the roads but these were in detached places along the line.

The Third Charter

The charter granted in the spring of 1836 to the Illinois Central Railroad Company and noted above as the first charter, was surrendered by the incorporators when the internal improvement work began. Now that the improvement plans had failed, the Cairo City and Canal Company, a company organized in the spring of 1837, desired to fall heir to the abandoned Illinois Central Railroad. A Mr. Darius B. Holbrook who was concerned in getting the first charter was now very active in getting the state to regrant a charter to himself and others for the completion of the abandoned Illinois Central. The Legislature was disposed to listen to Mr. Holbrook who seemed to be a man of great resources and experience. In 1843, March 6, the Central railroad as it was when it was abandoned in 1840 was restored to the Holbrook interests under a charter called the "Great Western Railway Company." The company was authorized to construct the road through the towns through which the state proposed to pass. The charter was very complete and liberal in all its parts.

The company made no effort to push the work of building the road. In March 1845, the act of March 6, 1843 was repealed and the state again came into possession of the Illinois Central Railroad.

The Fourth Chapter

On February 10, 1849, the General Assembly authorized the Great Western Railroad Company, the Holbrook interest, to build the Central railroad. The governor of the state by the terms of the charter was authorized to hold in trust for the company whatever lands the general government might donate to the state for the completion of the Central or Great Western Railway. At that time a bill was before Congress granting

3,000,000 acres to the state for the completion of the Central railroad.

Senator Douglas was very busy urging Congress to make this donation to the state, but he argued that the Holbrook interests must yield up to the state all claims which they had to any interests in the proposed Central railway. Mr. Holbrook as president of the Great Western Company executed two releases, the first of which Douglas thought was not valid. He then executed a second one which was satisfactory to Mr. Douglas who urged Congress to make the gift of land which it had been considering.

A Contention

A very unpleasant controversy sprang up between Judge Breese and Senator Douglas relative to the part each took in securing the grant of land from Congress. It will be remembered that Judge Breese as early as 1835 in his letter to John Y. Sawyer, outlined a plan by which a central railroad might be constructed from Cairo to the western end of the proposed Illinois and Michigan canal. In that letter he said, "The general government also would grant some of the unappropriated land on the contemplated road throughout its whole extent in aid of the undertaking." Now in the charter granted in the spring of 1836 to a corporation of fifty-eight persons for the building of a central railroad. Among these incorporators was Darius B. Holbrook, Sidney Breese, Alexander M. Jenkins, and fifty-five others. This company taking its cue from the letter of Breese to Sawyer, made application to Congress for aid by a pre-emption right. That is, the company wished the right to purchase from the Government at $1.25 per acre within a certain length of time all the unsold land along the route. No grant was made and the following year the charter was canceled.

From that date to 1850 Judge Breese's name was linked with the efforts of the Holbrook interests. The controversy between Douglas and Breese took place in 1850 and 1851 and reviews the relations of these two men to the question of government aid in the building of the Central railroad. In the year 1843 Judge Breese entered the United States Senate and Mr. Douglas entered the lower branch of Congress. On the 27th of December Judge Breese introduced a bill in the Senate to grant the Holbrook interest the right of pre-emption to the public lands through which the proposed central railroad should run. The bill was favorably reported from the committee on public lands. When Mr. Breese approached Douglas and other representatives from Illinois in the House of Representatives and asked their support of the bill, they refused on the ground that any grants of Illinois lands for the construction of any railroads should be made to the State of Illinois and not to a private corporation. This was the same position as that taken by Congressman Cook back in 1826-7 relative to grants of land for the aid of the Illinois and Michigan canal. Mr. Douglas stated that another reason why he opposed Senator Breese's bill was that he had no faith in Holbrook and his schemes. Mr. Douglas thought that the Holbrook interests would, if a grant were made, proceed to sell their charter and its belongings in the east or in Europe and put the money in their pockets. Douglas also thought that a pre-emption right would stop the sale of lands in Illinois and check the progress of the people's interests. The bill did not become a law.

In the short session beginning in December, 1844, Mr. Breese introduced a bill providing for a pre-emption in favor of the state but the bill was not warmly supported and was not passed. In January, 1846, Senator Breese introduced another bill in the Senate granting alternate sections of the public lands to "aid in the construction of the Northern Cross and the Central railroads in the said state." The bill was referred to the committee on public lands of which Senator Breese was chairman. The bill was reported favorably but for some cause or other the bill was never taken up. On December 17, 1846, Senator Breese introduced a bill for the right of way and pre-emption rights for a central railroad through Illinois, but this also "died a bornin."

This seems to be the story up to December, 1847, when Mr. Douglas entered the Senate. Mr. Breese had two more years to serve; so, for two years Breese and Douglas worked side by side, Mr. Breese all that time seeming to champion the Holbrook interests and a grant of pre-emption rights, while Mr. Douglas favored the grant of lands to the state of alternate sections. Mr. Douglas says that in the summer of 1847 he traveled over the state to get the sentiment of the people. Everywhere he went he explained the advantages of a donation to the state over a pre-emption right or donation to a private corporation. Mr. Douglas also told the people that in order to get a grant of land, it would be necessary to show the representatives and senators from Pennsylvania, New York, and New England that this central railroad would stimulate commerce through the lakes to the east. For that reason the road when built must have a terminus at Chicago. A road with the north end at Galena and the south end at Cairo would draw the trade toward New Orleans and this would be disadvantageous to the lake commerce.

As Douglas and Breese sat in the Senate they disagreed as to the policy to be pursued, Breese insisting on pre-emption rights and Douglas on donations from the Government to the state. Their disagreements came to a test on the 20th of

January, 1848. On that day, since the two senators could not come to an agreement, they each introduced a bill. Mr. Douglas' bill provided for a grant of land to the state and for making Chicago one of the northern termini of the road. Mr. Breese's bill provided for pre-emption rights. Douglas' bill was favorably reported and passed, and was sent to the House of Representatives. Mr. Breese's bill languished as most of his previous bills had done.

In the House at this time were the following members of the Illinois delegation: First district, Robert Smith, Alton; second district, John A. McClernand, Shawneetown; third district, Orlando B. Ficklin, Charleston; fourth district, John Wentworth, Chicago; fifth district, Wm. A. Richardson, Rushville; sixth district, Thomas J. Turner, Freeport; seventh district, Abraham Lincoln, Springfield. When Mr. Douglas' bill came up in the House it was laid on the table greatly to the disappointment of everyone of the Illinois delegation. Usually when bills are laid on the table it is their finish as it takes a two-thirds vote to take the bill from the table and place it on the calendar. So Mr. Douglas thought the fate of his bill was sealed. Accordingly in December, 1848, Mr. Douglas introduced another bill in the Senate and it was making some headway when he learned that his friends in the House had succeeded in taking the bill from the table and had placed it on the calendar. Mr. Douglas says that Mr. Breese appealed to him to allow his pre-emption bill to pass the Senate for the sake of a bit of honor as his time was up March 4th and he would be succeeded by Gen. James Shields. Mr. Douglas agreed that Mr. Breese's bill might pass the Senate with the distinct understanding that it could not pass the House. Mr. Breese's bill accordingly passed the Senate but never came before the House. Mr. Breese retired from the Senate on March 4th.

Final Passage

On the reassembling of Congress in December, 1849, Mr. Douglas says he called a conference of the two senators and the representatives in the House and they all agreed to a definite line of action, which was to support a bill providing for a grant of land by the general Government. It was agreed by all the Illinois delegation that identical bills should be introduced into the House and Senate at an early date. Accordingly Senator Douglas and Representative McClernand drew up the bills. Mr. Douglas introduced his bill into the Senate in January, 1850. It was referred to the committee on public lands of which General Shields was a member. It was reported back with some amendments, discussed in the Senate and passed. It was sent to the House where after a hard fight it passed and was signed by the President, and became a law.

THE GIFT

The law which granted to Illinois a large quantity of land to aid in the construction of a central railroad may be stated very simply. The Government granted the state the right of way through the unsold lands of Illinois 200 feet wide. The road should extend from Cairo north to the Illinois River, and thence to Galena and the state line. A branch from this line should extend to Chicago. Congress granted to Illinois the even numbered sections for a distance of six miles on each side of the right of way, equivalent to a strip of land 705.5 miles long and six miles wide. The road must be built within a period of ten years. If any even numbered section falling inside the six-mile strip on either side of the right of way had already been purchased or was a school section, then the state was to have the right to select any even numbered section on either side of the road to a distance of fifteen miles. The total land granted was 2,707,200 acres. At the same time that the state was given this grant of land, the Government withdrew from sale the odd numbered sections in this twelve-mile strip through which the road was run.

As soon as the bill passed and the people were aware of the grant there began to be discussed the question as to what method of building the road should be adopted. There were those who thought the state ought to build the road on money borrowed on the land grant as security. Others thought that the land grant ought to be given to some company that would build the road for the land.

THE MEMORIAL

The Legislature assembled in January, 1851, and on the 15th of that month the governor transmitted to the House of Representatives a memorial as follows:

To the Honorable Senators and Representatives of the people of the State of Illinois in the General Assembly convened:

The memorial of Robert Schuyler, George Griswold, Governeur Morris, Jonathan Sturges, Thomas W. Ludlow, and John F. Sanford of the City of New York; and of David A. Neal, Franklin Haven, and Robert Rantoul, Jr., of the City of Boston and vicinity, respectfully represents:

That, having examined and considered an act of Congress of the United States, whereby land is donated by the United States for the purpose of insuring the construction of a railroad from Cairo, at the mouth of the Ohio River, to Galena and the northwestern angle of the State of Illinois, with a branch extending to Chicago on Lake Michigan, on certain conditions, therein expressed; and having also examined the resources of the tract of country through which it is proposed that the said railroad shall pass, and the amount of cost, and the space of time necessary for constructing the same, the subscribers propose to form a company, with such others as they may associate with them, including among their number persons of large experience in the construction of several of the principal railroads of the United States, and of means and credit sufficient to place beyond doubt their ability to perform what they hereinafter propose, make the following offer to the State of Illinois for their consideration:

"The company so formed by the subscribers will, under the authority and direction of the State of Illinois, fully and faithfully perform the several conditions, and execute the trusts, in the said act of Congress contained. And will build a railroad with branches between the termini set forth in the said act, with a single track, and complete the same, ready for the transportation of merchandise and passengers, on or before the fourth day of July which will be in the year of our Lord, eighteen hundred and fifty-four. And the said railroad shall be in all respects, as well and thoroughly built as the railroad running from Boston to Albany, with such improvements thereon as exerience has shown to be desirable and expedient, and shall be equipped in a manner suitable to the business to be accommodated thereby. And the said company, from and after the completion of the said road, will pay to the State of Illinois annually —— per cent of the gross earnings of the said railroad, without deduction or charge for expenses, or for any other matter or cause; provided, that the State of Illinois will grant to the subscribers a charter of incorporation, with terms mutually advantageous with powers and limitations, as they, in their wisdom, may think fit, as shall be accepted by said company, and as will sufficiently remunerate the subscribers for their care, labor, and expenditure in that behalf incurred, and will enable them to avail themselves of the lands donated by the said act to raise the funds, or some portion of the funds, necessary for the construction and equipment of the said railroad.

Robert Schuyler,
George Griswold,
Governeur Morris,
    of Morrisinia,
Franklin Haven,
David A. Neal,
Robert Rantoul, Jr.,
Jona. Sturges,
Thomas W. Ludlow,
John F. A. Sanford.

December 28, 1850.

The memorial was laid on the table and ordered printed. Mr. Rantoul, one of the above memorialists, was present in Springfield and gave personal attention to every detail. He was a man of high repute in Massachusetts. He succeeded Daniel Webster as United States senator, and was a lawyer and financier of prominence. He was entirely frank about every question that came up and succeeded in establishing the greatest confidence of the Legislature in the value of the proposition which the company proposed.

There was a lack of unity in judgment among the legislators as well as among the leaders of thought of the state as to the best way of proceeding with the gift and with the land. There were those who believed the nearly 3,000,000 acres of land was sufficient to build the road and to have enough left to pay the debt which the state still owed. But when seriously minded men recalled the experiences of the state in attempting to build railroads, there was much doubt as to the wisdom in the state's undertaking the construction of the new Illinois Central. It has been pointed out that at least 75 per cent of the land in this grant was of unsurpassed fertility, but it had laid out in the central part of the state for twenty-five years waiting for buyers at $1.25 per acre. But it was confidently believed that this valuable land would rise to $10 to $20 an acre as soon as the road was completed and the markets of the North, East and South were brought to the door of the settlers. The very short time within which the company proposed to complete the road was a strong argument in favor of accepting the company's proposition.

THE FIFTH CHARTER

As early as January 14, 1851, a bill was introduced granting a charter to the Illinois Central Railroad Company by Senator Asahel Gridley from McLean County. Other bills were introduced, but one presented by Senator James L. D. Morrison of St. Clair County was eventually made into the now famous Illinois Central Railroad charter. It is as follows:

Mr. Robert Rantoul, on behalf of the company, accepted the terms of the charter and the Illinois Central Railroad Company came into being. On March 22, 1851, Mr. Roswell B. Mason of Bridgeport, Connecticut, was appointed the chief engineer. He left the East May 14th and reached Chicago in five days. Mr. Mason organized his forces without delay. The following engineers were placed over the several sections of the road as indicated: N. B. Porter from Chicago to Rantoul; L. W. Ashley, from Rantoul to Mattoon; C. Floyd Jones, from Mattoon to Central City, and all the main line between Ramsey's Creek and Richview; Arthur S. Ormsby, from Richview to Cairo; H. B. Plant, from Ramsey's Creek to Bloomington; Timothy B. Blackstone, from Bloomington to Eldena; R. B. Provost, from Eldena to Dunleith; B. G. Roots had charge of surveying parties between Big Muddy and the Ohio and Mississippi Railroad.

WORK BEGUN

The first contract let was for the construction of the road from Chicago to Calumet, near Calumet Lake, a distance of fourteen miles. This was completed in order that the Michigan Central could get into Chicago. By the action of the common council of Chicago the Illinois Central was allowed to come into the city along the lake front. From the vicinity of Calumet the road veered to the southwest and was soon lost in the wild prairies of Kankakee, Iroquois, and Champaign counties. Mr. Ackerman, who was later president of the road, said that in 1853 he rode for twenty miles on this branch of the road without seeing a sign of human life. In 1851 an engineering party came in sight of a herd of thirty deer at Maroa a few miles north of Decatur. Mr. Ackerman says that when the road was built there were not more than a dozen towns through which the road ran that could be found put down a good map of Illinois.

From Big Muddy River, some four miles north of Carbondale to Chicago, the land presented no problems for the engineers, but from that stream south toward Cairo there were some real engineering problems.

The work was pushed with all dispatch. The line from Cairo to La Salle, 300.99 miles, was completed January 8, 1855. The branch from La Salle to Galena, 146.73 miles, was finished June 12, 1855. The Chicago branch from Chicago to Central City, 249.78 miles, was finished September 26, 1856. On Saturday, September 27, 1856, Col. R. B. Mason, engineer-in-chief, sent a telegram to the board of directors in New York that the last rail was laid on the Illinois Central and its branches.

In the gift by the Government to the State of Illinois there were a few strings attached. The Government reserved the right to the free use of the road for the transportation of United States troops and of any form of Government property, including munitions of war, etc. Again the road must be completed in ten years. The land granted must not be used for any other purpose.

Foreign Ownership

In the early days of the history of the road there was the charge that this road had been built by foreign capital, that it was owned by foreigners and that the road would never develop the state as well as if it had been built with home capital and home people. But it should be remembered that nearly if not all the money that ever developed any new state came into it from older states. The fact is that Illinois people were too near to the enterprise to really appreciate the wonderful possibilities which were bound up in this grant of land and in the value of the road when constructed. It takes distance sometimes to reveal the true worth of a thing. This seemed to be the case in this instance. Men in New York and Boston were far enough away calmly to judge of the merits of the enterprise. But the facts are that the management of the Illinois Central Railroad has always been kindly disposed toward the progress of the state and of the interests of the general government. In 1861 when the Civil war was beginning, the Illinois Central freely offered its services to the War Governor, Richard Yates, the use of the road for the transportation of troops and munitions was a right with the Government, but the road went further and offered free transportation to the sick and the wounded, and in many other ways showed its loyalty not only to the general government but also to the State of Illinois. Mr. Ackerman has pointed out that many of the most prominent men in the military service in the Civil war were former employees of the Illinois Central Railroad. Major-General George B. McClelland was a civil engineer on the Illinois Central before the war. Also Major-Generals Ambrose E. Burnside, and Nathaniel P. Banks. Brigadier-Generals Freeman E. G. Ransom, John B. Turchin, William Robinson, Mason Prayman, and Colonels John B. Wyman, David Stuart, Lieutenant William DeWolf, and the celebrated army scout, Charles W. Everett Carson, were all employes of the Illinois Central before the outbreak of the war.

Cost of Road

There have been some very positive statements made by those who were out of humor with the gift of the land to the company to build the road. It was said the state had the land and afterwards the land and the road both belonged to the company. Mr. Ackerman says the bare fact remains that the cost of the road to the shareholders has been in round numbers, $40,000,000, and that the total proceeds from the sales of its lands during the construction of the road only realized a sufficient sum to pay the interest on the debt before any dividends were paid on the shares, and that portion of the line which the state engineers in 1837 had estimated the cost $3,500,000 actually cost in round numbers $25,000,000 in paid-up capital. And within five years after the construction of the road was begun the incorporations found themselves embarrassed by a debt of over $23,000,000 while the income from the road was scarcely sufficient to pay its running expenses. He further says that from 1857 to 1859 were dark days in the history of the road and that it was only saved by the heroic work of Richard Cobden, the great British statesman, who had nearly his entire fortune invested in the enterprise. He visited this country and helped the board of directors to put the road on a sound and permanent basis.

The Charter

The charter granted to the Illinois Central Railroad Company conveyed to that corporation all the lands which Congress had so generously given to the state by act of September 20, 1850. The provisions of the charter, pertaining to the returns which the company should make to the state for the gift of the lands, were the result of much discussion and several compromises. The memorial addressed to the Legislature by the nine gentlemen who proposed to form the Illinois Central Railroad Company, contained near the close this clause: "And the said company, from and after the completion of the said road, will pay to the State of Illinois, annually _____ per cent of the gross earnings of the said railroad, without deduction or charge for expenses or for any other matter or cause." After a thorough discussion of all the interests involved, the charter as given above was drawn up.

Section 18 of the charter reads: "In consideration of the grants, privileges, and franchises herein conferred upon said company for the purposes aforesaid, the said company shall, on the first Mondays of December and June in each year, pay into the treasury of the State of Illinois 5 per centum on the gross or total proceeds, receipts, or incomes derived from said road and its branches, for the six months then next preceding." The same section then provides for the keeping of accurate and detailed records of such income, and for reports, etc., to the governor of the state.

The charter provides that all the lands which are included in the grant to the company shall be exempt from taxation until sold by the company. The stock also shall be exempt from taxation for six years.

Section 22 is as follows: After the expiration of six years, the stock, property, and assets, belonging to said company, shall be listed by the president, secretary or other officer, with the auditor of state, and an annual tax for state purposes shall be assessed by the auditor upon all the property and assets of every name, kind and description belonging to said corporation. Whenever the taxes levied for state purposes shall exceed three-fourths of 1 per centum per annum, such excess shall be deducted from the gross proceeds or income herein required to be paid by said corporation to the state, and the said corporation is hereby exempted from all taxation of every kind, except as herein provided for. The revenue or income arising from said taxation and the said 5 per cent of gross or total proceeds, receipts or income aforesaid, shall be paid into the state treasury in money, and applied to the payment of the interest-paying state indebtedness until the extinction thereof: Provided in case the 5 per cent, provided to be paid into the state treasury and the state taxes to be paid by the corporation, do not amount to 7 per cent of the gross or total proceeds, receipts, or income, then the said company shall pay into the state treasury the difference so as to make the whole amount paid equal, at least, to 7 per cent of the gross receipts of said corporation.

The Income

The first four semi-annual payments from the Illinois Central Railroad into the treasury of the state were calculated at 5 per cent of the gross earnings. After the fourth payment the amount has been based on 7 per cent of the gross earnings. The first payment was $29,751.59. The income since the road was put in operation will be considered in Volume III.

The Contention

As the records show the company has never paid more than 7 per cent of the gross earnings into the state treasury for any one year. The road has contended that this amount meets the requirements of the twenty-section section of the charter. A former attorney-general, Hon. W. H. Stead, has furnished to the audits of public accounts an opinion upon the subject of taxation of the Illinois Central Railroad Company, which briefly stated is as follows:

1. As provided in the eighteenth section of the charter, the company must pay to the state treasury semi-annually on the first Mondays in December and June, 5 per cent of the gross earnings for the preceding six years.

2. Section 22 of the charter makes it the duty of the said company to list the stock, property, and assets belonging to the said company with the auditor of public accounts for the purpose of taxation.

3. It is the duty of the auditor of public accounts to levy upon said property as listed, an annual state tax which shall be paid as are other state taxes.

4. This tax so levied and collected must be paid into the state treasury; and if this tax, together with the 5 per cent of the gross earnings, shall not equal 7 per cent of the gross earnings then the company is bound by the charter to make good such deficiency.

5. If the tax levied by the auditor of public accounts together with the 5 per cent of the gross earnings shall exceed 7 per cent of the gross earnings the said tax must nevertheless be paid in full.

6. The provisions of the charter apply to the Illinois Central Railroad from Cairo to La Salle, a distance of 400.99 miles; from La Salle to Dunleith via Galena, a distance of 146.73 miles; and from Central City to Chicago, 249.79 miles; total 697.5 miles. The provisions of the charter do not apply to any roads leased, purchased, or built by the company other than the 697.5 miles referred to above.

CHAPTER XXIV

ON THE EVE OF A GREAT CONFLICT

Douglas in the South—Southern Sentiment—Lincoln Active—Cooper Union Speech—The Charleston Convention—Douglas Nominated—Presidential Candidates—The Campaign—The Rivals—Lincoln in Springfield—Douglas in the Campaign—Threats of Secession—Secession Begins — Compromise — Lincoln Silent — The Cabinet—Inaugural Address—Visits His Mother—Farewell to Springfield—Illinois' War Governor—Lincoln in Washington—Courtesies.

For the time being, Mr. Lincoln went back to his law office following the election of November, 1858. Mr. Douglas returned shortly after the election to attend the short session of the National Congress and to receive the congratulations of his friends and the bitter denunciation of his enemies in his own political party. Mr. Douglas knew as well, if not better, than anyone else, that he had greatly offended the slave holders in his "Freeport Doctrine." He knew that this doctrine, squatter sovereignty, and especially the practical application of it as he explained at Freeport, was diametrically opposed to the Dred Scott decision, which the South saw would enable the slave holder to take his slaves into any United States territory. Something therefore must be done to hold the statesmen in the South to his cause, at least till after the presidential campaign of 1860.

Douglas in the South

Mr. Douglas had rather extensive business interests in the South. It was therefore with some justification that he announced soon after the election in November, 1858, that he was going into the South for a short business trip and for a short rest prior to the opening of the "short session" of Congress which would open in Washington in December, 1858. Naturally, Mr. Douglas was received in the South as a prominent statesman and in many places the people were anxious to hear the man who had won for the slave owner's cause the repeal of the Missouri Compromise. He spoke in many of the larger cities of the South, taking pains to urge loyalty to the decisions of the Supreme Court, our highest judicial tribunal. He restated in the presence of his audiences his willingness to bring about the annexation of Cuba, and referred to his previous loyalty to the interests of the people among whom he was temporarily sojourning. There was at this time growing in the South a desire for a renewal of the slave trade. To this Mr. Douglas offered objections and in many ways alienated the radical leaders in the South.

It appears Mr. Douglas arrived at Washington a short time after the opening of the session of Congress. At least the democratic caucus under the whip of Buchanan had formally deposed Mr. Douglas from the chairmanship of the committee on territories which he had held for eleven years. Mr. Douglas had been bold in his opposition to the policy of President Buchanan. The "Danites," as Mr. Douglas had called President Buchanan's friends in Illinois, had left nothing undone in this state to embarrass Mr. Douglas in his canvass for the senatorship. The unkindly, not to say bitter, feeling was mutual. While the canvass was proceeding and especially while the joint debates were in progress there were rumblings in the South. The Cincinnati Commercial of July 13, in giving an account of Douglas' trip through Ohio on his way home to begin his canvass, and regretting the possibility of a split in the democratic party, said: "The original Buchanan man, and those whose interests it is still to appear to cling to the presidential faction, could not, of course, have anything to do with him, 'Douglas.'" The Commonwealth of Frankfort, Kentucky, September 7, said: "The position of Mr. Douglas upon the question of slavery in the territories is, if possible, more objectionable than that of Mr. Lincoln." The Wilmington, North Carolina, Journal said in commenting on Douglas' answer to Lincoln's question at Freeport: "This is at variance with the principles laid down by the Supreme Court in the Dred Scott case, with those avowed by the President in his annual message, with those entertained by the whole southern democracy. It is, in our opinion, radically unsound. It won't begin to do for our use."

The loss of the chairmanship of the committee on territories was a great blow to Mr. Douglas. But he had taken a decided stand against the Lecompton constitution, and had championed the state sovereignty doctrine and both of these positions were against the pet notions of Buchanan, and so Douglas must suffer. "The administration had come to dominate the Senate; and that august body, by an act of injustice and outrage unprecedented, summarily removed Senator Douglas from the position he had long held and honored, the chairmanship of the committee on territories. Scarcely anything could be more mortifying, but it did not humiliate the great statesman. He was still great and proud and strong, every day demonstrating his superiority to those who sought to overwhelm him."

Senator Douglas had friends in Congress who were loyal to him and with their advice he prepared a public statement of his defense against the attack of his southern enemies. This exposition was offered to Harper's Magazine, which was glad to publish a contribution from so prominent a personage as Senator Stephen A. Douglas. It appears that this article was not so much an effort to convince the South, and win the leaders to his cause, as it was to secure the allegiance of the people of the North.

The "short session" ended March 4, 1859. The presidential canvass had already begun. It was admitted in all parts of the North that Mr. Douglas was the only logical candidate for the democratic nomination for presidency in the campaign which would be waged in the summer of 1860. The Little Giant was

OLD HOTEL IN JONESBORO
Where Douglas and Lincoln Held Public Receptions on the Occasion of Their Visit in 1858

therefore occupied, together with his friends, in preparing for the great convention in which the democratic standard bearer would be named.

Following the adjournment of Congress in March, 1859, Mr. Douglas was very active in making public addresses east and west. He was invited into Ohio to assist the democrats in their state canvass. Here he made a number of telling addresses; at least the leaders of the republican organization of that state felt it was necessary to call for Mr. Lincoln, the only man in their estimation who could counteract Douglas' work in that state.

SOUTHERN SENTIMENT

In the United States Senate, May 28, 1860, Senator Judah P. Benjamin, of Louisiana, in reviewing the fitness of Mr. Douglas for the position of standard bearer of the democratic party, made it clear that the candidacy of Mr. Douglas could not be supported by the people for whom Senator Benjamin was speaking. An extract from that speech will show the attitude of the friends of the Dred Scott decision toward Mr. Douglas:

"Up to the years 1857 and 1858, no man in this nation had a higher or more exalted opinion of the character, the services, and the political integrity of the senator from Illinois (Douglas) than I had * * * Sir * * * I have been obliged to pluck down my idol from his place on high, and to refuse him any more support or confidence as a member of the party. * * *"

The causes that have operated on me have operated on the democratic party of the United States, and have operated an effect which the whole future life of the senator will be utterly unable to obliterate. It is impossible that confidence lost can be restored. * * *

We accuse him for this, to wit: That having bargained with us upon a point upon which we were an issue, that it should be a judicial point; that he would abide the decision; that he would act under the decision, and consider it a doctrine of the party; that having said that to us here in the senate, he went home, and under the stress of a local election, his knees gave way; his whole person trembled. His adversary stood upon principle and was beaten; and lo! he is the candidate of a mighty party for the presidency of the United States. The senator from Illinois faltered. He got the prize for which he faltered; but, lo! the grand prize of his ambition today slips from his grasp because of his faltering in his former contest, and his success in the canvass for the senate, purchased for an ignoble price, has cost him the loss of the presidency of the United States.

Lincoln Active

The wonderfully clear manner in which Mr. Lincoln built up the doctrines which must be incorporated in the republican national platform of 1860 was perceived by the unprejudiced leaders of that party. Day after day in the joint discussions, Mr. Lincoln was looking forward two years to a greater contest than the one which was engaging his present thought. It is true that the eastern republicans were slow to recognize the logic which must force them to yield to the inevitable nomination of Mr. Lincoln as the republican standard bearer.

"One of the first men to conceive that idea was Jesse W. Fell, a local politician of Bloomington, Illinois." While the debates were in progress Mr. Fell was traveling through the middle and easern states. The leading papers of the East were printing reports of the debates and in many instances giving characteristic extracts of the discussions. Mr. Fell found that the debate, though held in low esteem in the East as a form of logical and oratorical contest, was attracting considerable attention from the most important newspapers of those sections.

On one occasion, following the debates, three young journalists, Scripps, Hitt, and Medill, were holding a conference in the office of the Chicago Tribune on the merits of Mr. Lincoln's line of argument in the debates, when one of them produced a letter he had just received from an eastern statesman in which was the following: "Who is this man who is replying to Douglas in your state? Do you realize that no greater speeches have been made on public questions in the history of our country; that his knowledge of the subject is profound, his logic unanswerable, his style inimitable?" The New York Evening Post, in commenting on the rapid rise of Lincoln during the joint debate said: "No man of this generation has grown more rapidly before the country than Lincoln in this canvass." Just shortly after the election of Mr. Douglas to the senatorship in the spring of 1859 Mr. Lincoln said: "I am glad I made the late race. It gave me a hearing on the great and durable question of the age which I would have had in no other way; and though I now sink out of view and shall be forgotten, I believe I have made some marks which will tell for the cause of civil liberty long after I am gone." Mr. Lincoln was anxious to conserve what the republicans had gained. "We have some 120,000 clear republican votes. That pile is worth keeping together. * * * The cause of civil liberty must not be surrendered at the end of one or even one hundred defeats."

In the summer of 1859, Mr. Lincoln received scores of invitations to deliver addresses in various parts of his own state as well as in many of the neighboring states. As has been noticed in a previous paragraph, the republican central committee of Ohio sent an urgent invitation to Mr. Lincoln to come to that state to assist in the canvass for governor. In response, Mr. Lincoln delivered two masterful speeches, one at Columbus, September 16, and another at Cincinnati on the 17th. In his Columbus speech he took for his text Mr. Douglas's article in Harper's Magazine. In this article Mr. Douglas had announced this doctrine: "Under our complex system of government it is the first duty of American statesmen to mark distinctly the dividing line between Federal and local authority." The burden of the article was the doctrine of "popular sovereignty." In Mr. Lincoln's Columbus speech he said: "What is Judge Douglas's popular sovereignty? It is, as a principle, no other than that if one man chooses to make a slave of another man, neither that other man nor anybody else has a right to object." Again he says that Mr. Douglas's popular sovereignty doctrine of unfriendly legislation by the local territorial Legislature means that "a thing (slavery) may be lawfully driven away from where it has a lawful right to be." But for powerful effect nothing surpasses these words in the Columbus speech:

"I suppose the institution of slavery really looks small to him (Douglas). He is so put up by nature that a lash upon his back would hurt him, but a lash upon anybody else's back does not hurt him. That is the build of the man, and consequently he looks upon the matter of slavery in this unimportant light.

"Judge Douglas ought to remember, when he is endeavoring to force this policy upon the American people, that while he is put up in that way, a good many are not. He ought to remember that there was once in this country a man by the name of Thomas Jefferson, supposed to be a democrat—a man whose principles and policy are not very prevalent amongst democrats today, it is true; but that man did not take exactly this view of the insignificance of the element of slavery which our friend, Judge Douglas does. In contemplation of this thing, we all know he was led to exclaim, 'I tremble for my country when I remember that God is just.' We know how he looked upon it when he thus expressed himself. There was danger of the avenging justice of God, in that little unimportant popular-sovereignty question of Judge Douglas. Jefferson supposed there was a question of God's eternal justice wrapped up in the enslaving of any race of men, or any man, and that those who did so braved the arm of Jehovah—that when a nation thus dared the Almighty, every friend of that nation had cause to dread His wrath. Choose ye between Jefferson and Douglas as to what is the true view of this element among us."

In Cincinnati on the 17th of September, 1859, Mr. Lincoln delivered another powerful address. The republicans of that state published this speech with the title, "Douglas an enemy to the North. Reasons why the North should oppose Judge Douglas. His duplicity exposed." It is said this speech was circulated in the South by Douglas's friends to show the people there that Douglas was a better friend of the people in that section than they were accustomed to think he was.

Cooper Union Speech

Without doubt the performance which gave Mr. Lincoln standing among the best thinkers of the whole country was his Cooper Union speech of February 27, 1860. In the fall of 1859 while he was busy with political addresses, he received an invitation to deliver a lecture in Plymouth Church, Brooklyn. This invitation was a great surprise to Mr. Lincoln, for it invited him into a new field of activity. This was an invitation to deliver a lecture, not to make a speech. After conferring with his friends, he agreed to accept the invitation provided his Plymouth Church friends would accept a political discourse in case he could not find time to prepare a lecture on some general subject. His eastern friends were quite willing to give him a wide latitude in the selection of a subject. When the time came for fulfilling his Plymouth engagement, he started East. On arriving in New York City, he found that his friends had provided for the address to be given in New York instead of in Brooklyn. The place selected for the meeting was Cooper Union or Cooper Institute, a spacious structure recently completed and designed in part for such occasions. Mr. Lincoln reached New York on the 25th of February, and learning that the place of meeting had been changed from Brooklyn to New York, and further that the audience would be a very distinguished one, he used the two or three days intervening to revise and polish up the matter he expected to constitute his address.

The audience was indeed a notable one. William Cullen Bryant presided. Horace Greeley and David Dudley Field were present to drink in the new doctrine of the West. All of Mr. Lincoln's eastern friends looked upon the Cooper Union venture as a sort of crisis. If he succeeded, it would be easy going in the future; if his speech was a disappointment, his cause would receive a set-back in the middle and eastern states. But those present were not long in suspense as to the ability of this western rail-splitter to hold the attention and to instruct the most cultured and thoughtful audience New York could gather in Cooper Union. It was feared that Mr. Lincoln would by his queer manner and quaint expressions fail to do more than amuse and interest his hearers. Some feared his logic would not be appreciated in the presence of his long gaunt form, his homely face, his awkward gestures, and his crude illustrations. But from the beginning his audience forgot all except the seriousness of the speaker, his dignity, and his mastery of the power of expression. "His manner was, to a New York audience, a very strange one, but it was captivating. He held the vast meeting spellbound and as one by one his oddly expressed but trenchant and convincing arguments confirmed the soundness of his political conclusions, the house broke out in wild and prolonged enthusiasm. I think I never saw an audience more thoroughly carried away by an orator."

From New York Mr. Lincoln went to New Hampshire, where his son Robert was a student in Phillips Exeter Academy. Here he spoke, also at other points in New Hampshire. From here to Connecticut, where he spoke in four of their chief cities. The eastern papers commented in the most flattering terms upon his addresses in New England.

Mr. Lincoln had now, in the spring of 1860, become a national character. He had contested the senatorial election with Judge Douglas in Illinois, had made two great speeches in Ohio, had taken part in the Kansas fight by delivering several speeches in that territory, had delivered the Cooper Union address, and had made less pretentious efforts in New Hampshire and Connecticut.

The Charleston Convention

During the summer and fall of 1859, and in the winter following, Mr. Douglas and his friends were working like beavers to secure friendly delegates to the Charleston, South Carolina, national convention which was to meet April 23, 1860. As early as January 4, 1860, the Illinois State Democratic Convention met and took steps to establish its identity by reaffirming the Cincinnati Democratic Convention of 1856. The convention also pledged itself and the democracy of Illinois to support the nominees of the Charleston convention. The delegation was, of course, a unit for Mr. Douglas. Col. Wm. A. Richardson was the chairman of the Illinois delegation. He was a leader with great powers of organization and execution. He was authorized to take complete charge of Senator Douglas' interests. Colonel Richardson was fresh from Washington, where Senator Douglas and the five democratic Congressmen had framed the platform which Mr. Douglas and his friends were willing to present to the rank and file of the national democracy. It contained every concession which the Illinois leaders were willing to make.

On January 10, 1860, the Buchanan democrats of Illinois met in state convention and appointed the delegates who should present themselves at Charleston and asked to be seated as the representatives of true democracy in Illinois. The "Danites" formulated a platform in which they affirmed the doctrines of Calhoun as to the nullifying power of a state, upheld the Supreme Court in the case of the Dred Scott decision, endorsed the Buchanan administration but bitterly denounced the Freeport Doctrine.

When the convention assembled, the Douglas party secured some advantages by reason of technical decisions. Colonel Richardson was an astute manipulator, and captured the organization of the convention. The "Danites" delegation was not admitted from Illinois. The real fight was upon the platform. The committee presented a majority and a minority report. The majority report was favorable to the southern doctrine. One plank read as follows: "Neither Congress nor a territorial Legislature, whether by direct legislation or legislation of an indirect or unfriendly character, possesses the power to annul or impair the constitutional right of any citizen of the United States to take his slave property into the common territories and there hold and enjoy the same while the territorial conditions remain." The minority report corresponded in the main with the platform formulated by Senator Douglas and the democratic Congressmen in Washington. When the test came the convention rejected the majority report and adopted the report of the northern wing of the party. When the convention had adopted the Douglas platform, forty-five delegates from the states of Alabama, Mississippi, South Carolina, Louisiana, Florida, Texas, Arkansas, and three-fourths of those from Georgia seceded. The convention originally contained 303 delegates. When the 45 seceded, there remained 258. The balloting then began. Mr. Douglas received at one time 151½ votes. The other 107½ votes were scattered among five candidates. There was an old rule in force in the Democratic National Conventions which required that two-thirds of the entire membership of the convention to nominate. This would require that the successful candidate should receive 202 votes. Mr. Douglas had a majority of the 303 but not a two-thirds vote. After voting fifty-seven times, the convention adjourned to meet at Baltimore June 7. Those who withdrew formed an organization and adjourned to meet at Richmond.

Douglas Nominated

The convention reassembled in Baltimore on June 7, and spent some time in an attempt to secure harmony between the northern and southern factions. But nothing could be done. More of the delegates who sympathized with the southern wing withdrew. Their places were filled, however, by new delegates from some of the southern states. When the convention finally settled down to business there were fewer than 200 delegates present. Mr. Douglas was nominated with 181½ votes while a dozen or more were cast for other candidates. The southern faction nominated John C. Breckinridge of Kentucky and adopted a platform which declared: 1. That Congress had no right to abolish slavery in the territories. 2. That a territorial Legislature had no right to abolish slavery in a territory. Alexander H. Stephens of Georgia said: "Men will be cutting one another's throats in a little while. In less than twelve months we shall be in war."

Presidential Candidates

When Jesse W. Fell returned from the East, he reported to Lincoln the interest the eastern people were taking in his public speeches. Mr. Fell suggested to Mr. Lincoln that there was already some talk of running him for the presidency. Mr. Lincoln said why should the republicans be talking of him for the presidency when there were such men as Seward, and Cameron, and Chase who had long been known as leaders of the party. But Lincoln's timidity and his deference to others were some qualities his friends saw in him which the better fitted him for the great office they were dangling before his eyes. John

Wentworth, editor of the Chicago Democrat, gave a column to the praise of Mr. Lincoln's qualities of heart and mind and urged the republican party to present his name to the next republican state convention for the nomination for the governorship of Illinois. He also suggested that the party in Illinois should present his name for the presidency and if not successful here to offer it for the vice-presidency. There was a silent but powerful influence at work in the state building up public sentiment in favor of Mr. Lincoln as the republican candidate for the presidency. Some of the men who were behind this movement were David Davis, Leonard Swett, Stephen T. Logan, John M. Palmer, Joseph Medill, Norman B. Judd, Richard J. Oglesby, Jesse W. Fell, Wm. H. Herndon, Orville H. Browning, Richard Yates, Jesse K. DuBois and Gustavus Koerner. A paper, the Central Illinois Gazette, Mr. W. O. Stoddard, editor, as early as May 4, 1859, nominated Mr. Lincoln for President. By a bit of good campaign work on the part of the Chicago Tribune, there appeared a sort of spontaneous demand for the candidacy of Mr. Lincoln. As early as April, 1859, an editor asked Mr. Lincoln for permission to use his name as a candidate for the republican nomination, and Mr. Lincoln answered by saying: "I must in all candor say I do not think myself fitted for the presidency."

By the spring of 1860 Mr. Lincoln had persuaded himself that the only thing he could do was to allow his friends to urge his candidacy with his consent. He wrote to Norman B. Judd: "I am not in a position where it would hurt much for me to not be nominated on the national ticket, but I am where it would hurt some for me to not get the Illinois delegates. * * * Can you help me a little in your end of the vineyard?" Correspondents from Washington wrote to those papers that favored Lincoln saying that public sentiment was changing in Washington, and that Mr. Lincoln was growing in popular favor.

Norman B. Judd is given credit for securing the meeting of the National Republican Convention in Chicago. No one, or few at least, saw at first the value to Mr. Lincoln of the meeting of the convention in Chicago. As the spring of 1860 passed the county conventions for the selection of local candidates were held very early. It was soon demonstrated that Mr. Lincoln was a very popular candidate for the presidency. Many counties resolved in favor of "Honest Abe." The Republican State Convention met in Decatur May 9. It was full of interest. Mr. Lincoln had been invited to be present. When he came into the session of the convention there was a boisterous reception. He was seated on the platform with the officials and notables. At an opportune time an old citizen of Macon County entered the hall and marched up its aisles bearing aloft two rails on which a banner said Abraham Lincoln had made on his father's

Courtesy of Illinois State Historical Library

THE WIGWAM WHERE LINCOLN WAS NOMINATED IN 1860

farm back in 1830. Another banner proclaimed Lincoln the candidate of Illinois for President. Great enthusiasm prevailed. Mr. Lincoln, when called on, said he was not certain that he made those rails, but that he had made many just as good. Mr. Lincoln's speech was very favorably received. In a short time John M. Palmer introduced a resolution instructing the Illinois delegation to vote in the Chicago convention as a unit for Abraham Lincoln.

An interesting thing occurred in New York in the close of the year 1859. A list of "prominent candidates for the presidency in 1860" containing twenty-one names does not mention Mr. Lincoln. Another list of "our living representative men" containing thirty-four names does not contain Mr. Lincoln's name. The first eastern paper to recognize Mr. Lincoln as a prominent candidate was Harper's Weekly. It printed May 12, 1860, the pictures of eleven prominent candidates for nomination at Chicago with a brief sketch of each man. The shortest biographical sketch was of Mr. Lincoln.

Chicago in 1860 was a city of 112,000 people. A new grade for the city streets had recently been established and in many places this grade was from 12 to 15 feet above the level upon which the city had been started. A few of the streets had been filled, but many unpretentious homes along the streets had not yet been raised and pedestrians along the streets looked into the second story windows of the dwellings alongside. The enterprising citizens erected a temporary structure to house the convention. It was built at the corner of Market and Lake street. It was constructed wholly of wood 180 feet long and 100 feet wide, and had a seating capacity of 10,000. The eastern delegates were almost dumbfounded when the reached a city on stilts, streets unpaved, hotels with slight capacity, and wooden sidewalks. They soon found that what the city lacked in these particulars was more than made good by the generous welcome, the western hospitality, and the native superiority of the westerners in initiative. As the delegations began to arrive, it was found that many of them were accompanied by thousands of shouters. It was estimated that Seward's friends from New York State alone numbered 2,000. Pennsylvania sent 1,500. New England sent Gilmore's celebrated band and trains of excursionists. There were fully one-half of the members of Congress in Chicago.

When the friends of Lincoln saw what the East was doing, they got busy, sent out an S. O. S. call and before the convention opened on May 16, there were 10,000 Lincoln shouters in Chicago. Special trains were brought into requisition and the prairies of Indiana, Illinois, and Iowa soon filled the streets with shouters. Delegations vied with each other in making the best showing in the streets of the western city. On the

LINCOLN TELEGRAM, "YOU ARE NOMINATED"

morning of the 16th while the eastern shouters were marching and counter-marching, the friends of Lincoln—the Illinois managers—were filling the wigwam with men and women who would shout for Lincoln.

The work of the Chicago convention was not different from similar gatherings of the present time, that of winning delegations from those states that did not have a favorite son. The Illinois delegation commenced in real earnest three days before the convention opened. In those three days the Indiana delegation was won for Lincoln. Nothing but preliminary work was done on Wednesday and Thursday forenoon. By noon on Thursday it looked as if Seward would be the nominee. At the afternoon session of Thursday the delegations from Illinois, Indiana, and Pennsylvania, secured an adjournment till Friday. All Thursday night the friends of Seward and Lincoln were working like beavers. The nomination speeches were made Friday morning. Norman B. Judd nominated Mr. Lincoln. The nomination was seconded by Caleb B. Smith of Indiana. Wm. H. Evarts presented the name of Wm. H. Seward. When the balloting began Lincoln started with 102 votes; Seward had 173½ votes; Chase, 49; Blair, 48; Cameron, 50½; with 32 votes scattering. On the second ballot Mr. Lincoln had 181 and Seward 184½. On the third ballot Lincoln had 231½—two and a half votes short of nomination. As soon as the result was known, Ohio changed 4 votes from Chase to Lincoln. This gave Mr. Lincoln the nomination. "Honest Abe" received the news announcing his choice amid the shouts of his neighbors. Men cried, shouted, laughed, threw hats and canes in the air. Lincoln tried to be calm, but his best friends saw that the trial was too great for him and he repaired to his home where Mrs. Lincoln awaited him with the good news.

The Campaign

The committee on notification visited Mr. Lincoln a few days following the adjournment of the convention. The letter of acceptance was written, the real contest was on. There were 303 electoral votes in the thirty-three states of the Union. A majority of these was 152 votes. Twenty-four states had sent delegates to the Chicago convention. These twenty-four states would cast 234 electoral votes. Eleven of these had cast 114 votes for Fremont in 1856. If Lincoln could carry these eleven states he would need only thirty-eight additional votes. Illinois and Pennsylvania would give forty additional which would give 154, two votes to spare. But Lincoln and his friends hoped to carry also New Jersey. This would give Mr. Lincoln 169 electoral votes. But it was now certain that Mr. Douglas would not carry all of the slave states. In fact the opposition to Mr.

HISTORY OF ILLINOIS 483

Lincoln must be divided among Douglas, Bell, and Breckenridge.

Although Mr. Lincoln had served one term in Congress, had held a debate with Mr. Douglas, had made speeches in Ohio, New York, and in some of the New England States, there were people who did not know anything about him or if they did know, they had no faith in him. It was thought necessary for some of the people of the East to send special reporters and investigators to Illinois to find out what standing the nominee had in the social and political world. It had been reported that Lincoln was uncouth, coarse, clumsy, could not speak good grammar, could not quote Latin or Greek, had never traveled and had no pedigree. The New York Herald had said that he would be a nullity. The Chicago Tribune said that a man who could raise himself from a penniless, uneducated flat boat man to the position now occupied by Mr. Lincoln was surely not a nullity. And William Cullen Bryant said of Lincoln that he was "a real representative man." The reporters sent word back East that he lived in good style; his home was an elegant two-story building; that he wore a suit of broadcloth every day; that Mrs. Lincoln was a cultured lady who spoke French fluently; that the oldest son in the family was a graduate of Phillips Exeter and was then a student in Harvard College; that the Lincolns of Illinois were related to the Lincolns of Massachusetts; and that the Lincolns wherever found were people of "good blood." All of this stir about the nominee was good advertising propaganda, but Mr. Lincoln was awaiting more substantial news from the East.

His Rivals

What Mr. Lincoln wanted to know was what was the attitude of the men whom he had defeated in the Chicago convention. He was not long to remain in darkness about the course his rivals for the nomination would pursue. A prominent eastern republican complained to Mr. Seward in Auburn, New York, that there was no one in the town who would venture to go on record as endorsing the nominee. He said the Daily Advertiser would like to say something for the nominee but had failed to find any one who would venture to say a good word for Mr. Lincoln. Whereupon Mr. Seward took pencil and paper and wrote for the daily advertiser the following in reference to the platform and Mr. Lincoln:

"No truer exposition of the republican creed could be given, than the platform, adopted by the convention, contains. No truer or firmer defenders of the republican faith could have been found in the Union, than the distinguished and esteemed citizens on whom the honors of the nomination have fallen. Their election, we trust by a decisive majority, will restore the

Government of the United States to its constitutional and ancient course. Let the watchword of the republican party be Union and Liberty, and onward to Victory." All the prominent men whose names were voted on in the Chicago convention wrote Mr. Lincoln without delay pledging him their loyal support.

In the arrangements for the campaign, speakers of national prominence were engaged. Among these may be mentioned Wm. H. Seward, Salmon P. Chase, Cassius M. Clay, Horace Greeley, and Thaddeus Stephens. One of the most powerful of the western statesmen was Carl Schurz. He spoke in German and in English and was untiring in his devotion to Mr. Lincoln. One of his most powerful addresses was on the subject—"The Doom of Slavery." Newspapers, magazines and even books played their part in the work of the campaign. As the campaign proceeded many devices came into vogue. One was the marching clubs. These clubs often carried torches and wore capes of glazed cambric to protect their clothing. From this idea a sort of uniform was developed and the Wide Awake Clubs attracted much attention in the campaign. The writer remembers seeing one such club mounted on white horses. It was a great sight for a small boy. Great political rallies were a feature of the summer of 1860. Perhaps the greatest of these in Illinois was held in Springfield August 8. It was estimated that 75,000 people assembled in the capital city on that day.

Lincoln in Springfield

The republican convention was held in the middle of May and the election came early in November. During this five and one-half months Mr. Lincoln remained in Springfield. It was not customary in campaigning in those days for the presidential candidate to take a very active part—at least Mr. Lincoln was not an active participant in the canvass. He had an office or reception room in the statehouse and here he received individuals and delegations. He is said to have lived the simple life that summer. He could be approached by the humblest citizen, and he greatly delighted to meet his old-time acquaintance. He came to the "office" about eight each morning, stopping at the stores along the way and talking to the people as he had formerly been accustomed to do. He often went to the postoffice for his mail and returned to his "office" with arms full of letters and papers. He had no hours for receiving delegations—they were received when they reached the capitol. It is recorded that many people sent or brought gifts to Lincoln during that summer. An old lady came one day holding a bundle carefully, and when Mr. Lincoln shook hands and inquired how the "folks" were, she untied the package and handed Abe a pair of coarse wool socks. She said, "I wanted to give you somethin,' Mr.

Linkin, to take to Washington, and that's all I had. I spun that yarn and knit them socks myself." Mr. Lincoln held one in each hand and turning to a group of prominent visitors, said, "That lady got my latitude and longitude about right, didn't she, gentlemen?"

It is stated that Lincoln made no speeches, wrote few letters, and gave no interviews. His justification was that all of his political philosophy might be found in the speeches that he had previously made. And thus passed the long summer days between the nomination and the election.

Douglas in the Campaign

The Baltimore convention met June 18, 1860, and after two or three days spent in confusion, and the withdrawal of the southern delegates, Mr. Douglas was nominated. Congress adjourned some weeks later and Douglas was free to enter heartily into his own campaign. When the news of Lincoln's nomination reached Washington, some republican friends gathered about Douglas to learn his opinion of the work of the Chicago convention. Mr. Douglas said: "Gentlemen, you have nominated a very able and a very honest man."

Douglas decided to break a long established custom which required presidential candidates to refrain from taking an active part in his own behalf. Douglas was wise enough to see that his only chance was to unite the southern democrats and the northern democrats. This he had some hope of doing—at least he worked to that end. But we can see now that his work was without return. He may have had some thought that the choice of a president might be thrown into the House as was the case in 1825. As Mr. Douglas visited the southern states in his canvass he became more and more impressed with the danger to the Union if Mr. Lincoln were elected. He continually urged upon the South the duty of submitting to the result of a constitutional election, whatever the result might be. In Norfolk, Virginia, he was asked whether, in the event of the election of Mr. Lincoln, the South would be justified in seceding from the Union, Mr. Douglas said very frankly: "I answer emphatically, no! The election of a man to the presidency—in conformity with the Constitution—would not justify any attempt at dissolving this glorious confederacy." He further said that if Mr. Lincoln were elected president that he (Douglas) would aid him to the full extent of his powers.

As the canvass progressed, Mr. Douglas saw the growing strength of Mr. Lincoln. The logic of Mr. Lincoln's speeches in the campaigns of 1856 and 1858 began now to bear fruit. Mr. Douglas's course was against the current, and in addition there was a powerful eddy which was threatening his safety. It is scarcely possible for the people of this day to fully appreciate the difficulties under which Mr. Douglas carried on his campaign. He was conscious of the fact that he had been nominated by a very great majority of the democratic party. But he was pursued by an administration which he had done more than any other individual to place in power. "Yet, with all the bitterness and malice of revenge, the President and the whole administration pursued him with malignant hatred from the opening of the campaign to its close."

Every possible inducement which the Buchanan administration could hold out to democrats to desert Douglas was offered. Officers of all kinds, collectorships, postmasterships, marshalships, were offered prominent democrats if they would desert the Douglas ship. Not only were inducements held out, but threats were freely made against ambitious men. They were told they could have no appointments of any kind if they supported Douglas. In the face of all this Mr. Douglas kept on with his canvass. He knew there would be no electoral votes for him in the slave states. He also knew that Mr. Lincoln would carry most of the free states. The following table will show the vote:

	Popular Vote	Electoral Vote
Lincoln	1,866,452	180
Douglas	1,376,957	12
Breckenridge	847,514	72
Bell	587,830	39
	4,678,853	303

Threats of Secession

As indicated in the preceding paragraphs, Mr. Douglas found the South threatening secession in case Mr. Lincoln was elected. Mr. Crawford of Georgia said at one time: "We will never submit to the inauguration of a black republican President." Lincoln himself was fully advised of the spreading movement toward secession. He conferred with many people from the South prior to the election. These were heart to heart talks and from these Mr. Lincoln kept abreast of the growth of the secession doctrine. Without doubt the doctrine of secession had from year to year grown stronger. The admission of Texas was in 1845. It was the last slave state to be admitted. Between 1845 and 1860 the states of Iowa, Wisconsin, California, Minnesota, and Oregon—all free states—had been admitted. The Senate was largely a free state body, also the House. If the free state people would hold together no legislation favorable to slavery could be passed. This situation was full of danger to the slavery interests. The failure of the democratic party to indorse the Lecompton constitution was also an intimation that the northern democrats might not always do the bidding of the slavery interests. The John Brown raid on Harper's Ferry showed what might happen on a larger scale in any slave state. The split in the Charleston convention also brought vividly before the South the comparative strength of the northern and southern democrats. All through the summer of 1860, the southern mind was rapidly approaching the point of secession. It was indeed generally understood in the South that if Mr. Lincoln should be elected that secession would be certain.

Secession Begins

South Carolina was the only state which in 1860, had not yet turned over to the people the right of naming the presidential electors. Every other state at that time elected its electors by popular vote. The Legislature of this state met in session on November 6th to name the state's electors. After selecting electors pledged to the support of the Breckenridge ticket, the Legislature remained in session to await the news as to the presidential election. The election of Mr. Lincoln was known within a day or so. On the 10th of November the Legislature appropriated money for the purchase of arms, and also called a state convention to act on the question of seceding from the Union. The state convention met on December 17th, and on the 20th unanimously passed an ordinance of secession repealing the act of ratification of the Constitution of the United States passed by the ratifying convention in 1788. The ordinance of secession said that "the State of South Carolina has resumed her place among the nations of the world." By February 1st, 1861, six states, South Carolina, Georgia, Florida, Alabama, Mississippi, Louisiana, and Texas, had passed ordinances of secession.

It must not be thought that all the public men in the South were favorable to secession. Alexander H. Stephens, one of Georgia's great leaders, was not favorable to secession. He said: "The election of no man, constitutionally chosen to the presidency, is sufficient cause for any state to separate from the Union. Let the fanatics of the North break the constitution —let not the South; let not us be the ones to commit the aggression."

On Monday, December 8, Congress convened and listened to the last annual message of President Buchanan. In this message the President took the ground that secession was partly justified by reason of the constant agitation of the slavery question by the North. In like manner the "personal liberty laws" also justified secession. He did not believe secession was legally right, but felt that there was no constitutional power conferred by the Constitution which would enable the general government to coerce a state. But Mr. Buchanan was not alone in his idea that the case was hopeless. Many northern papers and some public men expressed their belief in secession, or at least were unwilling to use force to require the southern states to remain in the Union.

Compromise

While the southern states were seceding and setting up a Confederate Government, the national Congress was drifting, groping, temporizing. Mr. Douglas was determined to use his best efforts to save the Union. He felt that war was inevitable, unless an immediate solution could be found. To the task of finding that solution he devoted his great talents and his powerful influence. He had already frankly told the people of the South that if Lincoln were elected he should consider himself bound to support him in the constitutional discharge of his duties.

Two committees were made up, one a committee of thirteen in the Senate, and one of thirty-three in the House. It was the purpose in organizing these committees to strike upon some plan of compromise. The committee of thirteen Senators was, after mature deliberation, unable to reach any general agreement. Mr. Douglas was a member of this committee and worked incessantly to reach common ground upon which the opposing forces could stand. He appealed to both the republicans and the democrats to recede from their extreme positions. He offered to surrender his doctrine of popular sovereignty if that would aid in satisfying the contending parties. The committee of thirty-three, one from each state, from the House of Representatives, was able to present a recommendation consisting of several resolutions which for a while looked like the basis of a permanent compromise. But Mr. Lincoln would not agree to any compromise that necessitated the setting aside of the fundamental principles for which the republican party had contended in the campaign. In a letter to Mr. Kellogg, the Illinois member of the committee of thirty-three, Mr. Lincoln said: "Entertain no proposition for a compromise in regard to the extension of slavery. The instant you do they have us under again; all our labor is lost, and sooner or later must all be done over. Have none of it. The tug has come, and better now than later."

One more effort at compromise was the famous Crittenden compromise. Senator Crittenden of Kentucky proposed a compromise amendment to the Constitution which if it had been adopted would have deprived the slaveholder of his rights under the Dred Scott decision, at least as to new states north of the Missouri Compromise line, but would have quarantined his rights south of that line.

LINCOLN SILENT

Immediately after it was known that Mr. Lincoln was elected, scores of letters were received by him in which he was importuned to make some public statement which would allay the excited mind of the people both North and South. In addition many public men came to Springfield to hold personal conversation with him. In answer to the pleadings of one visitor, Mr. Lincoln said: "I know the justness of my intentions, and the utter groundlessness of the pretended fears of the men who are filling the country with their clamor. If I go into the presidency they will find me as I am on record, nothing less and nothing more. My declarations have been made to the world without reservation. They have been often repeated, and now self-respect demands of me and of the party which has elected me that, when threatened, I should be silent." Mr. Lincoln's notion was that since 1854, he had been busy stating plainly his position to the world. The fact was there was only one point upon which the South wanted anything from Mr. Lincoln: that was some giving in on the slavery question. Mr. Lincoln was very wise in his position. In one case he was appealed to by a group of commercial people of the East. They asked him to make some public statement that would restore confidence in the business world. Mr. Lincoln wrote: "I am not insensible to any commercial or financial depression that may exist, but nothing is to be gained by fawning around the 'respectable scoundrels' who got it up. Let them go to work and repair the mischief of their own making, and then perhaps they will be less greedy to do the like again." To the New York Times, in answer to an appeal to say something to set the public mind at rest as to his purposes when he should take up the reins of government, he showed that the papers of the East were using Senator Trumbull's statements as to the principles which would actuate the incoming administration for different purposes. One paper was shouting the purposes of the new administration to abandon the republican ground upon which the party stood in the presidential canvass, and another paper used the same speech to show the South that it meant an unrelenting war upon the people of that section. Mr. Lincoln very shrewdly observes: "This is just as I expected, and just what would happen with any declaration I could make. These political fiends are not half sick enough yet. Party malice, and not public good, possesses them entirely. 'They seek a sign, and no sign shall be given them.' At least such is my present feeling and purpose." When Mr. Kellogg from the committee of thirty-three from the House of Representatives, wrote Mr. Lincoln asking for some direction, he said to Mr. Kellogg: "Entertain no proposition for a compromise in regard to the extension of slavery." Again: "They (the Southerners) now have the Constitution under which we have lived over seventy years, and acts of Congress of their own framing, with no prospects of their being changed; and they can never have a more shallow pretext for breaking up the Government, or extorting a compromise, than now."

When his supposed friends found they could not get anything from Mr. Lincoln on the subject of "compromise," they turned to the subject of "coercion." What was to be done about secession? Did Mr. Lincoln agree with President Buchanan as to the right of the Federal Government to use force to bring a seceded state back into the Union, or to prevent a state from taking steps of secession? Will Mr. Lincoln use force to regain possession of the forts, arsenals and other United States property? Will he seize the custom houses and the postoffices within the territory of the seceded states? Mr. Lincoln had heard so much of this sort of twaddle that he often answered his inquirers in a somewhat humorous manner. On one occasion he said: "My opinion is that no state can in any way lawfully get out of the Union without the consent of the others; and that it is the duty of the President and other Government functionaries to run the machine as it is."

The Cabinet

Mr. Lincoln had a real, positive and constructive line of work to do in the time between the November election and his inauguration. Two of these tasks were the selection of a Cabinet and the writing of his inaugural address. Without doubt, Mr. Lincoln, at odd times while the canvass was continuing, marshaled before his mind the great men of his party who were suited by nature and by training to assume the direction of the various executive departments of the Government. There are evidences that Mr. Lincoln would under certain conditions be quite willing to invite into his Cabinet not only his rivals in the republican party, but that he was at least willing to consider the fitness of certain political opponents for the exercise of executive duties.

Mr. Lincoln had too fine a sense of the Proprieties to say anything about Cabinet building to any one prior to the November election, but a statement by Nicolay and Hay in their "Life of Lincoln," together with a quotation from Lincoln himself certainly make it safe for us to conclude that Cabinet making was often the subject of serious consideration with him prior even to the election in November.

The day of the election, Tuesday, November 6, 1860, Mr. Lincoln passed in the usual routine. He received callers, talked with friends, opened his mail, voted in the afternoon, and retired to his home in the early evening. The citizens of the city had arranged for the receipt of the election returns in the Representative hall of the statehouse. But of course the candidate for the presidency could not afford to go to what promised to be a very demonstrative gathering. However, following a short stay at his home and partaking of the evening meal, he returned to the state house where he mingled with the "boys" as the earlier reports came in. But at 9 o'clock he accepted the invitation of the superintendent of telegraph in Springfield and repaired to a room where that official had three or four operators. Here, in company with only a friend or two, Mr. Lincoln received the news till a late hour. Here he heard from the eastern states, and received the congratulations from many prominent men throughout the country. When the first excitement of large majorities had quieted down, Mr. Lincoln gave a few minutes to the names of his future Cabinet and he said to a friend in the summer of 1861, "Before I left the telegraph office that night I had substantially completed the framework of my Cabinet as it now exists."

One of the first men to be notified of his choice as a member of the new Cabinet was William H. Seward. During the weeks following the election a large number of the great men of the nation visited Mr. Lincoln at Springfield. Most of these came upon invitation, and were not seeking anything for themselves. They were high-minded, patriotic citizens who had as their chief thought the best interests of the country. Mr. Lincoln conferred with these visitors as to the making of his Cabinet, without doubt. On December 8, 1860, Mr. Lincoln invited Mr. Seward to become his secretary of state. Shortly after this he offered the position of attorney-general to Edwin B. Bates of Missouri. And so as time went on the different members were decided upon, as follows:

William H. Seward, New York, secretary of state.
Salmon P. Chase, Ohio, secretary of treasury.
Simon Cameron, Pennsylvania, secretary of war.
Gideon Welles, Connecticut, secretary of navy.
Caleb B. Smith, Indiana, secretary of interior.
Edw. Bates, Missouri, attorney-general.
Montgomery Blair, Maryland, postmaster-general.

Inaugural Address

In addition to the task of selecting his Cabinet, the President-elect must prepare his inaugural address. This was begun about the midde of January, 1861. Secession had made considerable headway, and the whole country was desperate and apparently helpless. Mr. Lincoln had his office on the north side of the square and here he retired for several hours each day to assemble the matter which had already taken rather definite form in his mind. He was not swerved from his determination to hold to the faith in the principles upon which the campaign had been won. Miss Tarbell says that he had for his sources as he composed his inaugural address the Constitution, Henry Clay's speech of 1850, Jackson's Proclamation against Nullification, and Webster's Reply to Haynes. And it has been shown by Nicolay and Hay that the speech as delivered by the President on March 4th differed from the original in only one or two paragraphs, though there were several minor changes. When he had finished his manuscript copy, he called to his office the manager of the State Journal, Major W. H. Bailhache, with whom he made arrangements to put it in printed form. This friend of the President-elect says that the type was set in a room of the Journal establishment behind locked doors by a sworn typesetter. Mr. Lincoln did not read the proof, but found the printed form agreed perfectly with the manuscript which had been very carefully prepared. Twenty printed copies were made one of which was returned to Major Bailhache for a keep-sake.

Visits His Mother

The time for the inauguration was coming on apace. The President-elect was being urged to go on to Washington a week or so earlier than it was at first arranged. Mr. Lincoln was shown that he might get a much better grasp of the problems at Washington than at Springfield. There were also ugly rumors that there were designs upon the life of the President-elect and an early journey to the capital would frustrate any such plans.

But Mr. Lincoln had one duty yet to perform before he left for the nation's capital. His step-mother, Sarah Bush Lincoln, lived a short distance from Charleston, Coles County, where the family lived, having moved there from near Decatur. He must visit his aged mother and receive her blessing upon his life which she felt would be a very perilous one. Mr. Lincoln loved his step-mother very tenderly, and his parting visit to the one who had so much to do in shaping his boyhood and early manhood life, must have been a very touching parting. Mr. Lincoln spent a full day at the homestead. In company with his mother he visited the grave of his father for a final sad farewell, and at the close of the day he bade adieu to his mother, now seventy-two years old, who expressed the fear that she would never see her son again.

Mr. Herndon has given a very touching account of Mr. Lincoln's last visit to the law office where they had been partners in the business of practicing attorneys.

Farewell to Springfield

The 11th of February had been set as the date for leaving Springfield. On that morning, a Monday, he and a small party of friends who were to accompany him to Washington, sat in the dingy waiting room of a small depot. At five minutes to 8 o'clock he was summoned to board the special train then ready to start. From its rear car he addressed a large concourse of his neighbors and friends. There was no effort to suppress the sobbing or to check the flow of tears as he lifted his hand for silence as he attempted to say good-by. He was visibly affected Mr. DuBois of Springfield, who as a young man of fourteen, heard the farewell address and gazed upon the kindly face tinged with sadness, said in after years that he could repeat the speech almost word for word. The State Journal said: "We have heard him speak upon a hundred different occasions; but we never saw him so profoundly affected, nor did he ever utter an address which seemed to us so full of simple and touching eloquence so exactly adapted to the occasion, so worthy of the man and the hour—when he said with the earnestness of a sudden inspiration of feeling, that with God's help he should not fail, there was an uncontrollable burst of applause. The following is the good-by as given in Nicolay and Hay's History:

"My friends, no one, not in my situation, can appreciate my feeling of sadness at this parting. To this place, and the kindness of these people, I owe everything. Here I have lived a quarter of a century, and have passed from a young to an old man. Here my children have been born and one is buried. I now leave, not knowing when or whether ever I may return, with a task before me greater than that which rested upon Washington. Without the assistance of that Divine Being who ever attended him, I can not succeed. With that assistance, I can not fail. Trusting in Him who can go with me, and remain with you, and be everywhere for good, let us confidently hope that all will yet be well. To His care commending you, as I hope in your prayers you will commend me, I bid you an affectionate farewell."

ILLINOIS' WAR GOVERNOR

It must not be thought that because the national campaign of 1860 was so far reaching in its interests and so profound in its consequences, that the state's political interests were flagging or unimportant. Never was the interest in a state campaign greater than in the summer of 1860. The republicans had elected the gallant Colonel Bissell as governor in 1856, and the state's interests had been in the keeping of that party for the past four years. As the spring and summer of 1860 opened up, the political pot began to boil. The republican organization began activities first and met in state convention in Decatur in a wigwam built for that purpose. Every county in the state sent delegates except Pulaski. The convention was large, enthusiastic, and determined. There was present either as visitors or as delegates—Lincoln, Logan, Browning, Wentworth, Palmer, Hurlbut, Oglesby, Peck, and Gillespie. The last named was made president of the convention. There were three prominent names before the convention as candidates for governor —Richard Yates of Morgan County; Norman B. Judd of Cook County; and Leonard Swett of McLean County. On the fourth ballot Richard Yates was nominated. Francis A. Hoffman of Cook was named for the position of lieutenant-governor.

The democratic state convention met in Springfield on June 13, and on the second ballot, Judge James C. Allen of Crawford County was named as the candidate for governor. The other positions were filled by prominent men in the party. The Buchanan party in Illinois put up I. M. Hope for governor, and the Union party (the Bell-Everett party) named John T. Stuart for governor. The canvass was of necessity closely interwoven with the national campaign. Mr. Yates and Judge Allen were both fine speakers, popular with their respective parties and full of enthusiasm. They were in no sense enemies—friendly rivals. They had served in Congress together and their canvass was free from any discourtesies.

The election returns showed that Mr. Yates had received 172,196 votes; Judge Allen, 159,253; I. M. Hope, 2,049; and John T. Stuart, 1,626.

Richard Yates, the governor-elect, was a native of Kentucky. He had come to Illinois at the age of sixteen. He was one of the two graduates who were given diplomas from Illinois College in 1835, the first graduating class. He studied law with Col. John J. Hardin in Jacksonville. He took an active part in the campaign of 1840 as a whig supporter of "Tippecanoe and Tyler too." In 1842 he was elected to the Legislature where he served three terms. In 1850 he defeated the gallant Maj. Thomas L. Harris for Congress. Here he served two terms. He was not prominent in politics till 1860.

Governor Yates was inaugurated January 14th, 1861. His inaugural address is said to have been the most scholarly state paper that had ever been presented to the people of Illinois up to that time. It was devoted largely to the discussion of secession and to the necessity of preserving the Union. From the fact that Governor Yates served during the period of the war, and from the fact of his devotion to the Union and to President Lincoln was one of unquestioned loyalty, he was called "Illinois' War Governor."

LINCOLN IN WASHINGTON

The train which bore Mr. Lincoln from Springfield on the morning of February 11th reached Indianapolis before nightfall. Here he was received by the governor, and delivered two short addresses. From here to Columbus, Ohio, and thence on to New York and through New Jersey and on to Philadelphia. Lincoln was very careful in all his addresses not to reveal any specific policies of his administration. In Philadelphia the reception, speeches, and the setting were all historical. In Harrisburg he paid a compliment to the loyalty and power of Pennsylvania in case of an emergency.

Much has been written of Mr. Lincoln's secret ride from Philadelphia to Washington by way of Baltimore. But the facts are very simple and entirely justifiable. On the evening of February 21st, Mr. Lincoln and one or two friends in a conference in the City of Philadelphia, agreed to a change in the time table from the latter city to Washington. Mr. Lincoln was due to raise the flag over Independence Hall at 6 o'clock Friday morning, February 22, and then to proceed to Harrisburg where he was to be received by the governor and the assembled Legislature. It had been the plan that he should leave Philadelphia for Washington in the forenoon of Saturday, the 23d, passing through Baltimore about 11 o'clock. There were no invitations to Mr. Lincoln to speak or to attend a reception from any person or group in Maryland. There was therefore no arrangements for a stop in that state. But from two sources, the Pinkerton detective agency and from the work of the secret agents of the Army under General Scott, there was thought to be great danger of mob violence in the City of Baltimore if Mr. Lincoln should pass through that city on Saturday, the 23d. It was therefore planned that following the ceremonies in Harrisburg Mr. Lincoln should be entertained at the hotel in a very public way till 6 o'clock, when he was quietly to depart and take a special train for Philadelphia. Here he was to take the regular night train for Washington via Baltimore. The train left Philadelphia at 11 o'clock Friday night and passed through Baltimore considerably after midnight, and lo! Saturday morning, February 23, found Mr. Lincoln safely domiciled in the spacious parlors of the Willard Hotel.

Courtesies

The President-elect had now ten days to get ready for the inauguration. In the week following his arrival he called first on President Buchanan and the members of his Cabinet. The President received Mr. Lincoln with every mark of politeness; the Cabinet likewise extended every courtesy. Congress, the Supreme Court, and public men generally were very cordial. In return the President and the Cabinet officially returned the calls, the Supreme Court, the Peace Conference with Ex-President Tyler at its head called to pay their respects. His old friend and rival, Senator Stephen A. Douglas, was kindly greeted by Mr. Lincoln. Mr. Breckenridge also paid his respects. In fact there was little time for any other matter than the necessary preliminaries to his induction into office. His political advisers secured some of his time and cabinet-making was the order of the day. However, Mr. Lincoln had his Cabinet selected and though much advice was given by good-intentioned friends, Mr. Lincoln's mind was unchanged.

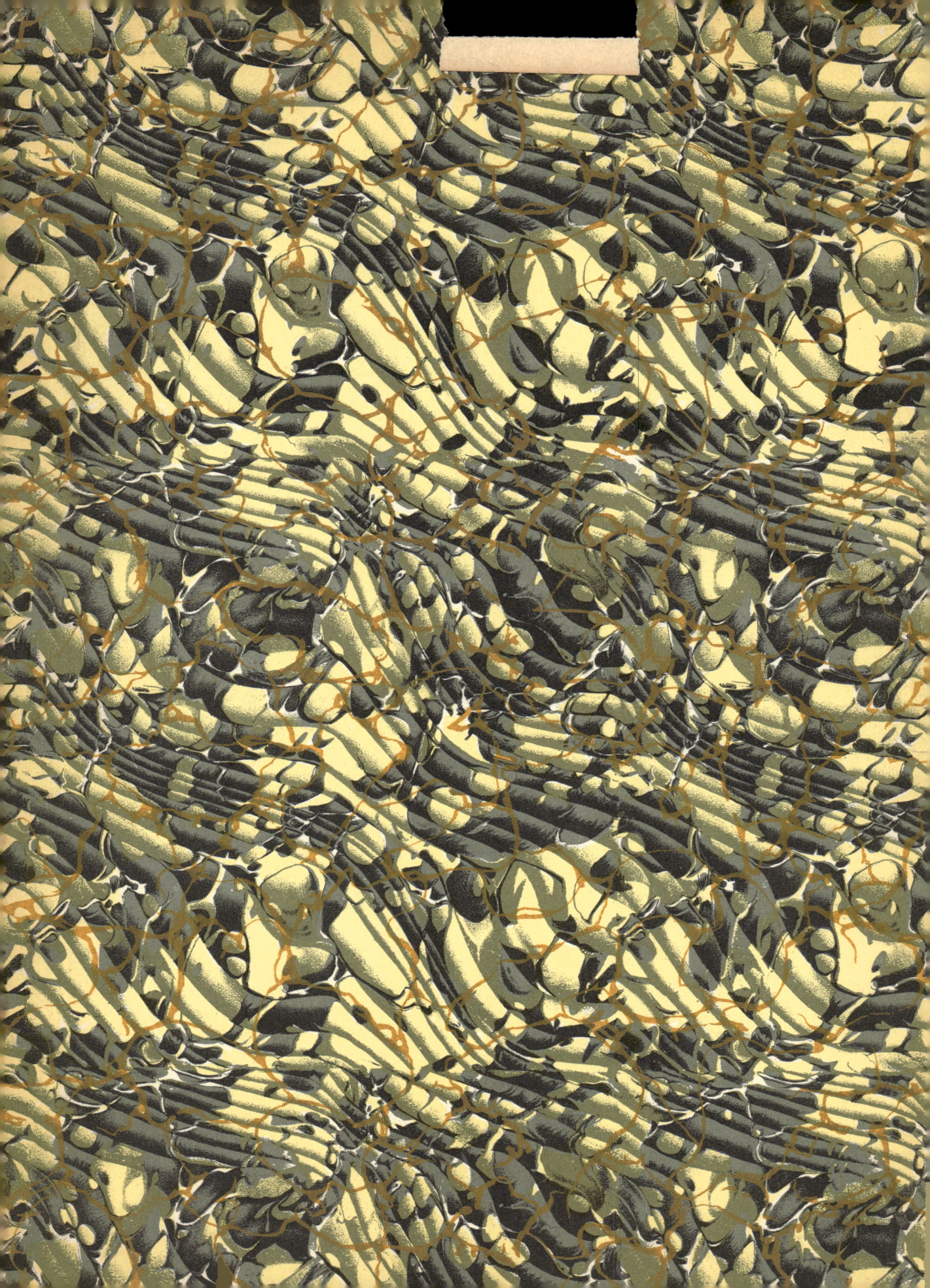